MARCHING
THROUGH
GEORGIA

THE STORY OF SOLDIERS
AND CIVILIANS
DURING
SHERMAN'S CAMPAIGN

LEE KENNETT

D0104508

Perennial

An Imprint of HarperCollinsPublishers

To the people of Georgia, who made me welcome
in their state for thirty years.

Contents

CONTENTS

Maps and illustrations follow page 178.

Acknowledgments

It would have been impossible for me to write this book without drawing on the riches of half a hundred repositories, and in each I encountered people who were cordial and helpful. A number went to considerable lengths to be of assistance: Franklin Garrett and Ted Ryan at the Atlanta History Center; Elliot S. Meadows, New-York Historical Society; Steven Engerrand and Peter Schinkel at the Georgia Department of Archives and History; Pat Webb, Perkins Library, Duke University; Alan Aimone and Judith A. Sibley, U.S. Military Academy, West Point; John Sellars, Manuscript Division, Library of Congress; Carrie Keylor of the Columbiana and Fairfield Township Historical Society, Columbiana, Ohio; Mary Ellen Brooks and Linda Aaron, University of Georgia Libraries; Alexandra S. Gressitt, Indiana Historical Society; Peer Edwin Ravnan, Middle Georgia Regional Library, Macon, Georgia; Richard Sommers and John Slonaker, U.S. Army Military History Institute; Nancy Bray, Ina Russell Dillard Library, Georgia College; E. Cheryl Schnirring, Illinois State Historical Library; Fred Edmiston, Ralph Draughon Library, Auburn University; Sue Husband, Regional History Collections, Western Michigan University; Polly Boggess, Crown Gardens and Archives, Dalton, Georgia; Pamela A. Wasmer, Indiana State Library; Raymond A. Schott, State Museum of Pennsylvania; Stacy B. Gould, Michigan State University; Mary Jo Madison, Alabama Department of Archives and History; Gary J. Arnold, Ohio Historical Society; Michael Musick and Tim Connelly, National Archives; Pamela Wasmer, Indiana State Library; and John Hoffman, Illinois Historical Survey, University of Illinois Library; and Adrienne Cannon, Alderman Library, University of Virginia. I am also indebted to Jennifer L. Martinez, the

Huntington Library, San Marino, California; in addition the Huntington graciously gave permission to quote from the Lyman Augustus Brewer Papers (HM 53153) and the William Frazier True Papers (HM 38331).

A number of other people generously provided advice or assistance in the course of my research, among them John Barrett, Andrew Ainslie, Charles S. Harris, Suzanne McDaniel, Lawrence J. Adams, Rod Paschall, Jonathan Sarris, Charles Paine, and Keith Bohannon. James Ingram, Cartographical Laboratory, University of Georgia, saw to the execution of the maps included in this volume. Several historians read all or part of the manuscript and offered very useful comments and suggestions: Kenneth Coleman, Richard McMurry, Steven Davis, Archer Jones, Nash Boney, and David Evans; several friends agreed to serve as "lay" readers: Richard Fields, Mary Ellen Briley, Alleene Nall, and Phil Pearce. Allison Kennett helped her father master the intricacies of the word processor, while Bonnie Cary and Gretchen Stripe assisted in the preparation of the final manuscript. And from beginning to end, my editor, Cynthia Barrett, displayed the two qualities an author most appreciates in an editor: patience and tact.

To the Reader

Written in its classical form, campaign history places its readers at the general's elbow, then allows them to follow his orders from conception to execution. They are also privy to the opposing general's thoughts and actions; what is more, they have a privileged view of move and counter-move on what General Sherman called "the chessboard of war." The exposition is orderly and the game intelligible; readers will put the book down with the conviction that they understand the campaign.

They understand it, and yet they do not know it. To the soldiers who fought it, the campaign was no game. To those whose homes and lands lay in the path of the armies, it was a catastrophe akin to a natural disaster. To almost all, the war was a vivid, aberrant period in their lives that would mark them for the rest of their days. The present work attempts to recapture a collective experience of this kind, that of soldiers and civilians caught up in one of the Civil War's most celebrated campaigns. There are no battle diagrams and little treatment of strategy and tactics. The reader will rarely be at the general's elbow, but will spend considerable time with captains and privates and civilians with obscure names and destinies. Why? Because at their level we come closest to the war's quintessence—wrenching human experience whose components are suffering and destitution, despair and death; but also humanity and generosity, courage and endurance.

PART ONE

◆

INVASION

1

◆

Mise-en-Scène

On Saturday, April 30, 1864, President Lincoln spent part of his day with his correspondence. He drafted several orders and directives and wrote three letters that we know of. Two of the letters are insignificant from the historian's point of view; the third, though brief, is remarkable. Lincoln addressed it to Ulysses S. Grant, whom he had recently appointed lieutenant general and general in chief of all the Union forces. The letter was both an expression of confidence in the man and a carte blanche for his proposed campaign, to be set in motion within the week, for Lincoln knew the plan of campaign only in broad outline: "The particulars of your plan I neither know nor seek to know. You are vigilant and self reliant; and pleased with this, I wish not to obtrude any constraints or restraints upon you." The president did have one concern. If there were to be reverses, he preferred them to be small ones that would not shake the people's resolve or ruin his party's chances in an election year: "I am very anxious that any great disaster, or the capture of our men in great numbers, shall be avoided." Having deftly inserted this word of caution, Lincoln wished his general in chief Godspeed: "And now with a brave Army, and a just cause, may God sustain you."

This expression of confidence was remarkable considering the doubts and disappointments the president had known with commanders he had previously sent into the field. But in Lincoln's eyes Grant had the qualities now needed for command: He could be counted on to push the campaign along relentlessly and grind away at the enemy as long as the South continued to resist. It was a costly and uninspired way of winning a war, but it seemed to be working—albeit slowly—where nothing had worked before. A certain momentum had been built up that Grant would sustain. The Rebel invasion of Pennsylvania had been handsomely beaten back at Gettysburg; Grant's own victory at Vicksburg had sundered the Confederacy along the line of the Mississippi; then too, Tennessee, Kentucky, the western part of Virginia—now called West Virginia—and portions of other rebellious states had fallen to the Union army. But if the scale had clearly tipped in the North's favor, after three years of war the core of the South had not been pierced, and large Rebel armies were still intact; there was much work to be done.

A hundred miles to the south in Richmond another president sat in another executive mansion on that same Saturday, and his mind too was on the coming campaign, for Jefferson Davis had to prepare a message for the opening of the Second Confederate Congress, set for the following Monday, and there he would have to lay out the prospects for the coming campaign. His work was interrupted that afternoon by tragedy; his five-year-old son, Joseph, fell to his death while playing on the balcony of the Confederate White House. For a time Davis was as if stunned, unable to write and barely able to speak. But drawing on an inner strength, the stricken president finished the drafting of his message and delivered it as scheduled.

It was a somber document. On the diplomatic front the president could find no encouraging news, no hint that either Britain or France had moved closer to recognition of the Confederacy, much less intervention on its behalf, and he confessed that he saw "no prospect of an early change." In the recent fighting there had been some minor successes in North Carolina and Florida; the Federal forces seemed completely balked in their effort against Charleston. Confederate forces in the trans-Mississippi Davis scarcely mentioned. Speaking of the two great armies the Confederacy still maintained east of the river he said: "The armies in northern Georgia and in northern Virginia still oppose with unshaken valor a formidable barrier to the progress of the invader." Davis thus cast the two armies in the role of shields, essentially defensive. Some of the lawmakers may have shaken their heads as they recalled the situation just a year ago, when the Army of Northern Virginia was winning a dazzling victory at Chancellorsville and opening the door to invasion of the North. If Lincoln's watchword was perseverance on the exhausting road to victory, Davis seemed to be saying that as long as they endured they had a basis for hope. Perhaps the "Second American Revolution," as some called the Southern cause, could be won the same way the first one had been: Their opponents, for all their superior resources, would finally decide the game wasn't worth the candle.

It would not have been possible for Davis to draft the kind of letter Lincoln sent to Grant; it accorded neither with his conception of the office he held nor with his appreciation of his own abilities. And in a sense Davis was far more qualified for the supreme direction of war than Lincoln was: The Confederate president had commanded a regiment in the Mexican War and had served with distinction as secretary of war in the Pierce administration, while Lincoln's previous contact with the military was as a militia captain in the Blackhawk War. So though there was talk of creating a Southern general in chief, the president was cold to the idea; he himself had largely assumed that role—with indifferent results, due in large part to his own flaws in character and judgment. Recently Davis had had a particularly frustrating exchange with General Joseph E. Johnston, commanding the Army of Tennessee. Davis believed that Johnston had the resources and the opportunity to launch an offensive against the Federal forces in Tennessee and tried to prod the general forward; Johnston resisted, saying he did not have the means. The exchange was not a frank and open one on either side. Davis relied on other, confidential sources of information about the state of Johnston's army, notably General John Bell Hood, a close friend of the president and one of Johnston's corps commanders. Johnston was a man of prickly sensibilities (he once returned an important letter from the secretary of war because the secretary had inadvertently failed to attach his signature); resenting what he considered an intrusion on his authority, he put up one argument, then another, or simply failed to respond. Thus the Confederacy's western army, like the one in Virginia, entered the month of May waiting for the enemy's initiative. Neither army would have long to wait.

General Grant had hastily put together a plan of campaign after his appointment as lieutenant general and commander of all the Union armies on March 9; he conferred first with General George Meade, who would continue to command the Army of the Potomac; then, after a brief stop in Washington to speak with Lincoln, Grant headed west to see General William T. Sherman, who would direct the Union effort in the vast Military Division of the Mississippi. The two friends had both made their reputations in the West, and they spent considerable time discussing what should be done there. Since Grant would be returning soon to the East where he could be at Meade's elbow, he and Sherman would have contact only by mail or telegraph, so they tried to cover all the problems and opportunities that might arise in the West. Their deliberations stretched over three days, ending with a long session in a map-strewn Cincinnati hotel room.

The plan they agreed upon was a simple one. Grant believed that earlier campaigns had often come to grief because the eastern and western armies had not established a harmony in their efforts; in Grant's phrase they had been "like a balky team." The Confederates had profited from this discordance by shifting troops to one theater, then to another, as need arose or opportunity presented itself. Now both Union armies would begin operations simultaneously (Grant later fixed the date as May 5), and thereafter maintain a strong and unrelenting pressure for as long as it took to topple the Confederacy. There were no timetables or deadlines, no complex schemes for combined operations. Each of the two Union hosts would have an opposing army to defeat and, they hoped, to destroy, and a city to take. Grant would drive for Richmond—he had already pledged to Lincoln he would take it if given enough men—and Sherman would push toward Atlanta.

While high strategy and the generals who formulated and executed it are for the most part peripheral to the subject at hand, an exception must be made in the case of the general commanding the Military Division of the Mississippi. In the spring of 1864 William Tecumseh Sherman was forty-four years old. The most momentous year in his life was before him, and it probably caught him at the peak of his intellectual powers. In 1861 his West Point years lay a quarter-century behind him, and in the 1850s he had left the service for a succession of positions in civilian life. He had returned to the army after the attack on Fort Sumter, but his wartime career had a shaky start. Given a command in Kentucky in the fall of 1861, he grossly exaggerated the Confederate forces in the area and bombarded his superiors with demands for reinforcements; his panicky behavior led to his replacement and newspaper stories that he was insane; the following April he redeemed himself with his performance at Shiloh. While he would still know fleeting periods of self-doubt and depression, and those who met him in 1864 would sometimes note his voluble, almost manic conversation and other quirks, his biographers agree that in thought and action the William Tecumseh Sherman of 1864 was clearly within the parameters marked "normal." If in his final campaigns his soldiers sometimes referred to him as "Crazy William," the term was one of affection.

Still, Sherman's habits of mind, his "way of looking at things," are of some interest in the present study, for they can help explain just what happened in Georgia in 1864 and why. If the general's mind was essentially sound, and quick and fertile as well, it nevertheless ran in its own fashion. While his correspondence reveals that when time permitted, his interest covered a remarkable range of problems and concerns, he dedicated the great bulk of his time and thought to war in the narrow sense: marches and engagements, energetic and relentless effort against the enemy army. He felt military needs should override all other considerations; if it benefited the operations of his army, he might seize railway cars, put journalists in irons, refuse to feed starving civilians, stop the movement of evangelists and the shipment of religious tracts to his army, or forcibly displace populations that got in his way. Yet on the back shelf of his mind Sherman carried a range of problems and solutions on matters that did not bear directly on military operations in the narrow sense; for example, he came to Georgia armed with a considerable mass of data on the state's economy and resources; he was also interested in the challenges the state's topography would pose, and he brought with him a crack team of topographical engineers. He had picked up a great deal of information about how to run railroads and also how to wreck them. He was also interested in the social and psychological dimensions of the struggle, to which he had given some thought. When problems surfaced in any of these spheres, the general would rummage in that back shelf, pull out a field order or other directive, sometimes a draconian one and occasionally a bizarre one, and then return to the war at hand.

If he ranked his concerns in this manner, his mind also tended to label matters in rather emphatic fashion—a policy was good or bad, an argument or a decision right or wrong: On most subjects the general was a man of strong opinions. This tendency was linked to another: He also sought to reduce things to what seemed to him their essentials—to the point of seeing problems as simpler than most of his contemporaries found them. He knew exactly what the war was about: "The government of the United States is the issue. Shall it stand or fall?" Slavery he regarded as a "minor question," and so apparently were the economic antagonisms between North and South. As the issue was clear and simple, so was its resolution. The Rebels had only to admit their error and lay down their arms and they would be welcomed back into the Union—a scenario most students of the war would find highly improbable. And very often to simplify is to exaggerate, to brush aside all qualification and nuance and think in absolutes. Thus if we define peace as essentially the total absence of violence, then the essence of war would be total violence—a proposition that could open many doors. At the very least the general believed with Clausewitz that war tended naturally toward absolute violence; occasionally he said that trying to stop the war's momentum was like trying to stop a hurricane or other natural calamity.

Then too, Sherman brought to the war a number of well-matured prejudices that would color his policies and actions. At the beginning of the war he had a negative view of the volunteer soldiers he commanded, which he shared with virtually every officer who had soldiered with "regulars." He complained notably about the volunteers' lack of discipline and the depredations they committed. But he was not a strict disciplinarian and was primarily concerned over the soldiers' availability for and comportment in battle. By 1864 he occasionally noted that his troops plundered or pillaged, but the tone of reprobation was largely gone. At the end of that year he would pronounce his volunteers good soldiers. In civil society Sherman disliked people of certain callings: journalists, politicians, religious activists and zealots; oddly enough, he had very little good to say about Southern Unionists; judging by conversations he had with them at various times, he felt they should have opposed secession more energetically. There is no evidence of any contempt for civilians in general—Sherman had after all made his way in their world for a number of years.

Many of the general's political and social views would today be labeled both fascist and racist. He was a strong friend of order; indeed his most recent biographer sees this as Sherman's most significant trait. He felt blacks were inferior, and he had no use for abolitionists who would improve their lot. Before the outbreak of war he had expressed his opinion that Southern whites and blacks would have to continue a master-servant relationship, for if equality reigned between the two races the result would be "amalgamation," which he associated with decline; he saw proof of this very danger in the chaotic state of Mexico, whose misfortunes he traced to the intermarriage of Spaniards with the indigenous population. He did not think freed slaves would make good soldiers and stated his views to all who would listen; when Confederate troops under the command of General Nathan Bedford Forrest shot down black Union soldiers rather than accept their surrender—what came to be known as the Fort Pillow Massacre—Sherman was neither shocked nor surprised. "Of course Forrest and all Southerners will kill them and their white officers," he wrote his brother, U.S. Senator John Sherman, "we all knew that." A year after the Emancipation Proclamation he did not think the welfare of three million blacks should get in the way of an honorable peace: "When a people submit, I would not bother with little local prejudices & opinions."

Sherman's views in these and other matters would have made him feel at home in the Confederate high command, had he not seen secession as the crime that precipitated the war. As it was, that summer he wrote his wife, Ellen, from deep in Georgia: "I have been more kindly disposed to the people of the South than any general officer in the whole army." From time to time in the course of 1864 he corresponded across the battle line, sending cordial messages to Confederate General William J. Hardee and writing well-turned letters to Southern women he had known twenty years before.

In truth, for Sherman the march into Georgia would be something of a return; he had spent considerable time in the state on army assignments in the 1840s. Then he had visited places he would soon see again—Marietta, Allatoona, the area around Cartersville, where he had stayed with a hospitable planter named Tumlin; indeed, he and Colonel Tumlin had corresponded for some years thereafter. But the extreme northwest corner of the state Sherman knew chiefly from maps, so on April 30, the same day Lincoln wrote his note to General Grant, Sherman rode out of Chattanooga, ascended nearby Lookout Mountain, and looked southward at the land his armies would invade within the week. Here he could see that the Southern Appalachians formed themselves into several lines of ridges and peaks with a general north-south alignment, though as they ran south they angled to the west into Alabama. They made an impressive ensemble: When one of Sherman's soldiers from Illinois—the second flattest state in the Union—first beheld them he said: "I think God Almighty might have made the world in four days if he had not ruffed it up so"; another, with an eye to the coming campaign, allowed that nature had created the area for General Joe Johnston's "special benefit."

Clearly, North Georgia would be rough country for Sherman's infantry. Here and there one found bare, perpendicular surfaces, such as Rocky Face Ridge, where there would be severe fighting; though generally the mountains' flanks were more sloping, they tended to be densely wooded and could have considerable undergrowth as well. Wheeled traffic—artillery, supply wagons, ambulances, and the like—could move only through passes and gaps; they would be roadbound in a region where roads were few. It was something of an undeveloped country, a frontier. People called the northern third of the state "Cherokee Georgia" with good reason, for only thirty years before it had been Indian country. The Cherokees were hardly savages; by the 1830s they had a newspaper, an alphabet of their own creation, and an enlightened form of government. But when they were packed off to Oklahoma with the Creeks, Choctaws, and others, they left behind only a few thin settlements; the

Georgians who took their place had not had much time to add improvements or even move very far beyond subsistence farming. The general knew he was also looking at a largely uncharted area; he had ordered new maps of the region, incorporating everything his cartographers could learn about it. In Chattanooga his mapmakers were putting the final touches on a "base map" of North Georgia that should help his troops find their way through the fastness before them.

Why was he obliged to invade Georgia across this particularly rough and inhospitable landscape? The answer lay below him—a thin, sinuous line of iron that ran from Chattanooga all the way to Atlanta: the Western and Atlantic Railroad. It was not strategy that dictated the general's route, but logistics, for by 1864 the war had demonstrated that a rail line was virtually as good as a navigable waterway in supplying an army far from its base; where waterways were lacking, it was the only means to sustain an army in a deep penetration of enemy territory. Since Sherman's base was Nashville and secondarily Chattanooga, and Atlanta was his goal, only the Western and Atlantic would take him there. General Johnston understood this quite as well as Sherman. He had his Army of Tennessee in position athwart the railroad some thirty miles to the south.

If driven south, the Confederates probably would leave behind them nothing but the roadbed, but Sherman knew his men could replace ties and rails quickly and had taken measures to provide them with a plentiful supply of both; putting bridges and trestles back would take a little longer. The single most important feature in the line, the one that gave him the most worry, lay beyond the range of his view that day: the twenty-five-hundred-foot-long tunnel that had been cut through the granite mass of Tunnel Hill, close to the town of Dalton (it would fall into Sherman's hands intact). The line meandered quite a bit, especially as it approached Chattanooga. Because of the low tractive power of locomotives of the day, the grade had to be held to thirty feet per mile. The builders were obliged to bypass the important town of Cassville and put in more than a score of major bridges as well as innumerable cuts and fills. Engineers had to hold their speed down on such a road; the "fast passenger train" that ran between Dalton and Atlanta in the 1850s averaged fourteen miles an hour. Then too, the railroad had been built by the state of Georgia; the designers, mindful of the taxpayers' feelings, made it a single-track affair for its entire length. Later, when it had become his army's lifeline, Sherman would give serious thought to double-tracking it.

The general knew that as his army moved south the way would be easier, and he would find more maneuvering room; the landscape would become less tortured, mountains would change to hills—he called the region below the Etowah "sub-mountainous"—and finally, in the vicinity of Atlanta, they would find rolling country with occasional prominences like Kennesaw Mountain. The streams, the Etowah, Oostenaula, and Chattahoochee, posed no great obstacle unless swollen by heavy rains. But the thick carpet of timber that clothed every ridge and valley within the general's view would not disappear as his army moved southward; right to the gates of Atlanta, cleared ground would be the exception. Finally, under all the vegetation was a soil that was usually a distinctive red clay, "the reddest I ever saw," wrote one Union soldier. In dry weather a much-traveled road made of such soil would produce dust particles of extreme fineness; they would billow up about the traveler in choking clouds, then drift off to give a reddish hue to trees, houses, and even animals. With sufficient rain the clay would take on the consistency of butter. Footing would become treacherous, wheeled traffic would cut hub-deep ruts, and an entire army could mire down.

Beyond Atlanta lay the rest of Georgia, indeed most of it. Georgia was then and is today the largest of the eastern states, with some fifty-nine thousand square miles of territory; a Northern officer, translating those fifty-nine thousand square miles to forty million acres to be subjugated, concluded that the Union army had its work cut out for it. An invader coming from Chattanooga to Atlanta would have traveled over a hundred miles without penetrating a third of the state. Sherman himself would say at the outset: "When we reach Atlanta the campaign will be but just begun." Georgia's other important cities—they were the same then as they are now—lay at some distance. To reach Macon the general would have had to go another 80 miles in roughly the same direction he had been following; to reach Augusta, whose arsenal Sherman had inspected back in 1844, he would need to turn east and march 150 miles; to reach the Atlantic he would have to strike out to the southeast over roads ranging from indifferent to bad, through red clay and sandy soil, through pine forest and swamp and marsh, and 250 miles later he would come to the Atlantic at Savannah.

This then was the land over which the general was to take his army, with the obstacles it could set before him; add to it an enemy army ably led and strongly fortified only a few miles south of Chattanooga, and almost any general would find he had all the challenges he could deal with. Not so Sherman. Like Grant and other more thoughtful leaders on the Union side, he sought to come to grips not only with the Confederate military challenge in the field, but with the baffling phenomenon of a whole population standing behind the Southern army and the Southern cause through thick and thin. As the war entered its fourth year the steadfastness and the perseverance of the Southern people clearly intrigued the general. Judging from his correspondence it was a matter he increasingly pulled from the back shelf. In a letter of March 12, 1864, he shared his fascination with his wife, Ellen:

> The devils seem to have a determination that cannot but be admired. No amount of poverty or adversity seems to shake their faith—niggers gone—wealth and luxury gone, money worthless, starvation in view within a period of two or three years, are causes enough to make the bravest tremble, yet I see no sign of let up—some few deserters—plenty tired of war, but the masses determined to fight it out.

This is the sort of conundrum few of his fellow generals spent much time with, and it is a clear indication of the keen, roving intellect ascribed to him by all who have studied his life.

But General Sherman was not content simply to identify and examine this ultimate line of resistance, he was also interested in the means of overcoming it; if the real enemy was the mindset of the Southern people, then perhaps there was a way to make them change their minds. One could thus say that Sherman was an early student of human motivation and the psychology of the masses—but one could not say that he was a particularly accomplished student. For one thing, he could devote relatively little time to this "other enemy"—in his day-to-day correspondence the subject appears only occasionally—then too, his own bent of mind hampered him. The general seems to have had an underdeveloped empathetic sense, a difficulty in grasping how others would react to words or actions, more specifically his own words and actions. What was the simplest way to make men change their minds? Demonstrate to them the errors in their thinking, Sherman believed, and they would think differently. It was simply a matter of making clear to others what was abundantly clear to him.

In January 1864, when he was to address the leading citizens of the conquered city of Memphis, he took his task very seriously, and he mused in a letter to Ellen: "I yet may realize my dream that I may be a positive instrument in adjusting this fearful family quarrel." Sherman had told Ellen his speech would be "short and strong," but judging from what he wrote her afterward, it must have been a somewhat rambling discourse. He told his listeners they should have accepted the results of the election of 1860; he demonstrated to them that the seizure of the Federal arsenal at Baton Rouge three years before was "a breach of soldierly honor," as was sniping at Federal steamboats from behind the cottonwood trees along the Mississippi—a practice that particularly irked the general. One can imagine the audience listening to such things with all the polite attention a conquered population would pay to a major general with a hundred thousand bayonets at his disposal. Sherman seems to have been pleased with the effect; he wrote Ellen that while his remarks were "gall and wormwood to some, they made others think." A bit later he drafted a letter of instructions to be circulated to the inhabitants of Huntsville, Alabama, also occupied by his troops. The general reported to his brother John that the letter contained some home truths that "had a powerful effect on the people of Huntsville." He was willing to let it be printed up for wider distribution, but Senator Sherman did not think it advisable "just now." And in the course of 1864 the diaries of Sherman's aides offer occasional glimpses of the general in conversation with Georgians he encountered along the roads or beside their plundered homes; sometimes in those conversations the general could be heard explaining why Confederate General Joseph Wheeler was causing them to lose their corn and pigs to Yankee foragers, and how Georgia had brought such catastrophe upon itself.

There is little doubt that at the beginning of 1864, when Sherman made his speech in Memphis, he had at least a fleeting vision of himself as peacemaker, and even afterward he held out some hope of a reasoned solution to the conflict. Later in the year he would take it into his head that he could negotiate Georgia out of the Confederacy and back into the Union. But increasingly he saw the need to somehow force the other side to come to its reason. The way to do this was through a kind of shock therapy; if words weren't forceful enough, then there were actions that could be taken. He spoke at various times about the need to "impress" or "astound" the foe. Late in 1863 he wrote General John A. Logan and Admiral David Porter that he had an idea for "one or two quick blows" that would "astonish the natives of the South" and bring an end to all Rebel resistance along the Mississippi. But other matters claimed his attention, and he never carried out the punitive expedition he contemplated. That was just as well, for the expedition was based on the premise that Southerners along the Mississippi would quit shooting at Federal steamboats when they learned their actions were causing other

Southerners a hundred miles away to come under bombardment by the Union navy.

Then the general realized that there might be other Southerners, individuals and perhaps whole classes, who would be irreconcilable, who could never be brought to reason. He had given this matter some thought, and as he packed his modest baggage for the Georgia campaign, he also brought along some ideas about dealing with these people.

2

Joe Brown's Georgia

Among the more striking documents printed in that vast compilation known to Civil War scholars as the *Official Records* is a letter General Sherman wrote in his camp at Big Black, Mississippi, on September 17, 1863. The letter was in reply to a query by General Henry W. Halleck, President Lincoln's military alter ego: Now that the Union army had control of considerable territory along the lower Mississippi, what were Sherman's thoughts about the type of government that should be set up there? Sherman must have spent considerable time on his reply. It runs to some six pages in print and contains an elaborate portrait of the people the general was trying to conquer.

Before prescribing a government for these people, he told Halleck, one had to understand the four classes "into which they naturally divided themselves." There were first of all the large planters, who held a virtual monopoly of political power, and who could possibly be allowed to retain that power once the full significance of their defeat was brought home to them. There was the pro-Union segment of the population, which Sherman held to be of little account. There were the "smaller farmers, mechanics, merchants and laborers," who made up about three-fourths of the white population, a docile, pliable mass who looked to the planters for leadership. Then finally there was a fourth class that Sherman labeled the "young bloods."

The "young bloods" were the flaming youth of the Confederacy, the hard-riding, quick-shooting young men of good family who followed leaders like Jeb Stuart and Nathan Bedford Forrest and gave the Southern army a cavalry that Sherman frankly admired. Other Union generals also admired the Southern horsemen but did not see them as a class; this was an idea unique to Sherman. These men he regarded as "dangerous subjects in every sense." If no way could be found to harness and redirect their violent, disruptive inclinations, then "this class of men must all be killed."

Halleck had probably sought Sherman's counsel because among Union generals he passed for something of an authority on the South. Sherman's inclusion of the great mass of "yeomanry" and plain people in his analysis of Southern society does put him well ahead of most of his contemporaries, who tended to think of white Southerners as either planters or "poor white trash." But these common people did not blindly follow the lead of the planters in political matters, as Sherman claimed, for they had begun to find able leaders among themselves. Perhaps half the governors of the various Confederate states were these "new men," commoners in origin and in identity. This was emphatically the case with Georgia's wartime governor, Joseph Emerson Brown.

Joe Brown—and that seems to be what his contemporaries generally called him—was born in upland South Carolina in 1821. While he was still a youth his father moved the family to Cherokee County, in North Georgia. The elder Brown was a farmer of very limited means. His few acres were described as "a scrap of hillside"; it was said that for want of oxen he for a time plowed his fields with a bull. Joe Brown joined his father in the fields at the age of eight, yet somehow he found a way to get himself an education. With rigid economy and a little borrowed money he attended a small South Carolina academy and then went on to Yale, where he studied law. Despite the Yale degree Brown remained unsophisticated in manner or bearing. He always pronounced words such as "department" the country way, with stress on all three syllables. Eliza Frances "Fanny" Andrews, a young Georgian with a quick pen, described Brown at the end of the war as "a regular barebones," gaunt and angular in ill-fitting clothes.

Brown tried teaching, had a law practice, then got into politics and found his vocation. Colonel I. W. Avery, an acquaintance and a historian with a gift for well-turned prose, gave this explanation for Joe Brown's rise to wealth and power: "There was nothing brilliant about him. He made the progress ever achieved by hard and continuous work. . . . He never went backwards. He made no blunders. His investments were all safe and judicious." The colonel might have added that Brown was guided by a very clear vision of what was right and what was advantageous and held in his course by a will of iron.

But there was something else: Great masses of Georgians of modest station saw Joe Brown as one of them and gave him their complete trust and allegiance; Avery claimed Brown had a "homely, direct power" to reach the hearts of these people. This is the sort of power we associate with a demagogue, but Joe Brown was not one of these. Power never corrupted him or tainted him with scandal. There was no flamboyance to the man, and indeed no discernible emotion (none of his biographers has much to say about a sense of humor). A Baptist and a Son of Temperance from his youth, he never used alcohol or tobacco. A close associate said he had never known Brown to "use a profane oath or relate an obscene or vulgar anecdote." And the great mass of Georgians, who had done some or all of these things, revered their governor all the more. Small wonder that Colonel Avery wrote that "his clutch of the popular heart was a miracle of personal achievement."

Brown's election as governor in 1857 was something of an accident. The Democratic party's leaders were not accustomed to choosing gubernatorial candidates from the sparsely settled counties of North Georgia, but they had been unable to agree on a candidate from among the more obvious choices, so they settled on "the Cherokee Cow Driver" as a way out of the impasse. Since the state's electoral system gave the vote to all white males and chose governors by popular election, the people of Georgia did the rest. If Brown's election was not a revolution, it was a clear change of course; according to Avery it reversed "a drift of things to a stately and aristocratic regime." The change was obvious as soon as the homespun Brown replaced the patrician Herschel V. Johnson in the governor's mansion. It had been the custom for the new governor to host a "levee" in the mansion to which any and all Georgians were invited, and the "plebeians," as Colonel Avery called them, made the most of this unique opportunity to move in circles of prominence and power. The press was enormous, large quantities of food and spirits were consumed, and large quantities of crockery were broken. Then, when the mansion was in shambles, everyone was content to go home, leaving the government in the hands of "the better sort of people."

Governor-elect Brown announced that there would be no levee. Later, when the mansion was opened to guests, the receptions were sedate affairs without alcohol or tobacco. And very quickly it became apparent that government was not being run by and for "the better sort of people." The new governor went to war against the state's bankers, who had suspended specie payments. He said banks would have to honor their obligations the same way private citizens did. He tightened up the state administration and increased the revenues of the Western and Atlantic. By the time the war broke out the railroad was producing almost enough revenue to run the state government; Brown was thus able to reduce property taxes. At the outbreak of the war they were a minuscule six and a half cents per hundred-dollar valuation.

Brown provided strong leadership in the crisis over secession, a step that he personally favored. The war that ensued revealed the governor's surprising taste for military matters. The Constitution of 1861 gave him the title of "Commander in Chief of the Army and Navy of this State and the Militia thereof," and he felt quite comfortable with that title. He sometimes dated his letters from "Headquarters" and issued "General Orders." He began buying arms long before Georgia seceded, and in the course of the war he commanded five separate bodies of state troops, only to see most of them absorbed into the Confederate army. At the beginning of the war he had more soldiers than rifles, so he devised a substitute armament: a "Georgia pike," six feet long, and a "side knife" with an eighteen-inch blade. He assured dubious legislators that Spanish mountaineers had used such weapons against Napoleon's soldiers "with terrible effect." In his conception of tactics (he had clearly been doing some reading on the subject) the pikemen would come onto the field after conventionally armed units had exhausted themselves. His men would "move in double quick time and rush with terrible impetuosity into the lines of the enemy," who would throw down their rifles and flee. Then Brown's men would cast aside their pikes to "keep close at their heels with the knife, till each man has hewed down at least one of his adversaries." By September 1862 he had seven thousand pikes and five thousand "side knives" stored in the state arsenal at Milledgeville.

While Brown proved a vigorous war governor there were signs quite early that he would be a jealous guardian of the "sovereignty" of the State of Georgia and a devotee of state's rights even to the point of jeopardizing the common cause. In January 1861, when the standoff in Charleston harbor seemed to be at the flash point, some officers in Macon telegraphed the governor to know if he would give his approval for Georgia volunteers to go to the aid of South Carolina. He answered: "I will not. Your first duty is to Georgia." Such was the man who led Georgia into the storm.

The Federal Census of 1860 offers us a good statistical portrait of the people who lived in Joe Brown's Georgia. The total population was 1,023,801, with the number of white inhabitants 576,719. The 447,002 blacks made up forty-four percent of the total. The black Georgian was invariably a slave; the number of "free persons of color" was infinitesimally small: 1,225. At the other extreme of the social scale there were very few planters who counted their acres by the hundreds and their slaves by the score. Only a few grandees in South Georgia had what we call today "old money" and a well-developed capacity for spending it in genteel ways. The vast majority of slave owners had fewer than twenty slaves and were no strangers to hard work themselves. And a sizable majority of white Georgians owned no slaves at all. With the total number of inhabitants six and a half times smaller than now, population density was only sixteen persons per square mile—about the same as the State of Utah today. The pattern of settlement in the state had its curious side. Georgia had expanded its frontiers chiefly through cessions of Indian territory, which the state government was anxious to have settled as soon as possible. Much of the land was distributed by lottery, carved up into farm-sized pieces; towns were launched by choosing a spot where the courthouse would be, then marking off the city limits around it; the result was a land of square farms and round towns.

The vast majority of Georgians lived in countryside or village, with no high urban concentrations. Only one of Georgia's 136 counties had over thirty thousand inhabitants, and only one other had over twenty thousand. The state's residents had been there for some time, with the heavy waves of immigration long past; black Georgians were by now third or fourth generation, and the only noticeable immigration in recent years could be found in Savannah's Irish Catholic colony. It was a young population, fueled by early marriages and large families. Village and countryside abounded with youths in their late teens and early twenties who were accustomed to physical labor and at home in field and forest—the ideal raw material for infantry.

There were certain antagonisms between sections and classes. Since black slaves were counted according to the three-fifths rule used in Federal apportionment, the areas of the state with large slave populations had greater political power. Some tension existed between white and slave artisans; in January 1861 the Atlanta City Council moved to bar slave mechanics sent into town to work by their masters, since it was "very injurious" to the interests of "citizen mechanics." But one of the offending parties was the wealthy Ephraim Ponder, who lived in the north end of the town; he let his slave artisans contract for their own work, and Mrs. Ponder flouted state law by teaching her slaves to read. For wealth had its privileges in antebellum Georgia, and among whites the rich and poor did not live in complete harmony; the war would increase their antagonisms. The word "cracker" was used by Georgians to describe other Georgians whom they regarded as socially and culturally beneath them. Thus a man might say that half of his home guard company was made up of men of culture and sophistication (like himself), and the other half composed of "wild swamp crackers"—though they all got along tolerably well. Curiously, in this period the term "cracker" was rarely used by other Southerners to describe Georgians; instead they used the term "goobergrabbers."

Georgia's demographic and economic statistics mesh in a curious way in the census of 1860. The forty-four percent of its people who were black also constituted forty-five percent of its wealth. The value of slaves, a little over three hundred million dollars, made them the state's most valuable property, worth twice as much as the land they tilled. Other figures testify to the preponderance of rural over urban Georgia: taxable land was valued at $161,764,955 and city property at only $35,139,415. The economic data in the census confirms that cotton was king in antebellum Georgia, but his throne was not a secure one. While the value of the 1860 cotton crop was more than twenty-five million dollars, it barely exceeded in value the state's corn crop of thirty million bushels. Within a few months corn would become the most important crop in Confederate Georgia; by 1865 it was almost the only thing standing between its people and starvation.

But in 1861 Georgians could not conceive of such things. The first months of that year were a heady time, exciting but hardly menacing. For the few weeks between Georgia's secession and its adherence to the Confederacy, its people had the novel experience of being an independent country. They devised a flag for the occasion, a red star on a white field; Georgia's newly founded army and navy rendered it the appropriate honors. Governor Brown in person presided over the state's first military operation, which was bloodless and successful. He went to the arsenal in Augusta and demanded and obtained the surrender of the small Federal detachment there. He told the commandant that the presence of "foreign troops" on Georgia's soil without its consent was an act of hostility. At the time there was a spirited rush to arms, and even in villages and countryside it was often accompanied by expressions of high resolve. The historian of Evans County records that ten young men of the Antioch and Long Branch sections before they marched off took a vow not to shave until the war was won. She also records that all ten returned four years later and "wore long beards until their deaths."

The first impact of the war was psychological. It brought stirring times to quicken the pulse of life in even the most complacent. Mobilization, particularly, had its emotional dimension. Drums rolled in country villages from one end of the state to the other as companies formed and drilled. Then the boys had to be seen off, with brass bands and oratory, and then they had to be written to and their exploits followed in the press. And then there was work to be done on the home front, and this work mobilized the energies of Georgia's women. There were the benefits and the hospital and the aid societies, food to be collected and socks to be knitted. In Columbus the local foundry got the women to collect scrap metal for the casting of cannon, promising that the guns would "bear the names of those ladies most zealous in the matter." Occasionally people could be mobilized en masse. At one critical juncture, when Lee's army was about to run out of cartridges, the director of the Augusta arsenal appealed to Dr. Joseph R. Wilson, pastor of the Presbyterian church. Dr. Wilson called on his congregation and directed a small army of women and children in the rolling of cartridges. They worked all day and into the evening. When the deadline of 9 P.M. arrived they had filled an entire boxcar with cartridges, and the train rolled off to Virginia. Among the boys enlisted for the work was the pastor's eight-year-old son, future President Woodrow Wilson.

The war seemed to have a tonic, bracing effect on Georgia's economic life. Being far removed from the fighting certainly helped. A traveler passing from Atlanta to Augusta noted: "This part of the Confederacy has as yet suffered but little from the war. At some of the stations provisions for the soldiers were brought into the cars by ladies, and distributed gratis." Another traveler coming from Virginia at the beginning of 1864 found Georgia an oasis: Augusta had a busy, prosperous look, and a visitor would think there was no war going on—until he went into a store and tried to buy something. But when "Yankee" goods first began to disappear from the stores, many people saw it as an opportunity—they could be replaced by goods made in Georgia. Local entrepreneurs rushed to fill the void, launching their businesses with a barrage of publicity. An item in the Macon newspaper fairly shouted, "Hurrah for the Macon Envelope Factory." Atlantans were assured that they were no longer dependent on the outside world for shoe blacking, while the Griffin Match Company proclaimed the quality of its products: "Try them. They are as good as any Yankee matches."

More important—and usually more successful—were the undertakings that sprang up to supply the war effort, invariably swelling the populations of the towns in which they appeared. Atlanta was soon without rival in the quantity and variety of war matériel it produced. Atlanta's population grew accordingly; in 1860 it was about three thousand; by 1864 it had increased almost tenfold.

The Confederate government was attracted to Georgia as a site for its own armaments plants, drawn by the state's rail net and relative remoteness from areas of military operations. Augusta already had an arsenal, whose capacity could be expanded; soon it was supplying the Southern army with everything from gun carriages to hand grenades. At the beginning of the war the Richmond authorities decided that a single powder plant of large capacity would supply the needs of all its armies; after considerable study they decided that it too should be built at Augusta. The Confederate States Powder Works went into operation in April 1862, and from then until the end of the war it turned out nearly fourteen hundred tons of powder. Technologically it was a triumph, an ultramodern facility that stirred the admiration of foreign visitors and produced ample supplies of high-quality powder (Northern soldiers complained from time to time the Rebel powder was "stronger" than their own, but tests by Federal ordnance officers failed to detect any difference).

Macon was selected as the site of another ultramodern facility, the Confederate States Ordnance Laboratories, charged with testing and developing new munitions and weapons. Its superintendent, John W. Mallet, was to oversee a vast complex of half a hundred buildings on a 150-acre tract. President Jefferson Davis intended for Macon to be the Confederacy's great armory long after independence was won. The Confederate navy also contributed modestly to armaments development in Georgia. Savannah was one of its bases, though the most impressive vessel stationed there, the huge ram *Georgia*, had been commissioned by the Ladies' Gunboat Association. The city of Columbus, located on the Chattahoochee where it flows between Georgia and Alabama, was a logical place for another naval yard. It too maintained a flotilla, including the *Muscogee*, a 140-foot-long behemoth plated over with two inches of iron. By 1864 a large naval ironworks was under construction, the contract having been let to a free black engineer named Horace King.

As the Confederacy's frontiers shrank, various enterprises relocated in Georgia. The firm of Cook and Brother, manufacturers of rifles, had begun operations in New Orleans, but when the city was threatened by the Federals in the spring of 1862, the Cook brothers crated up their machinery and moved it to Vicksburg, Mississippi, to Selma, Alabama, and finally to Athens, Georgia, where they went back into business at the end of the year.

Of all the sections of Georgia the southwest was considered the most secure from enemy attack, and rightly so. There refugees could settle in with some assurance they would not be evicted by an enemy army; indeed most of the population did not see a blue uniform until after Appomattox. There the farmer's work was not disrupted, so that the area eventually became the granary of the Confederacy, or more properly its corncrib. Its huge crops of 1863 and 1864 became the surest source of supply for the Confederate army in Virginia. It is not surprising then that late in 1863 the Confederate government chose the area for a new prisoner of war camp. A few miles north of Americus the government's agents found what they were looking for, a wooded tract watered by a branch of Sweetwater Creek. The first prisoners arrived in February and pronounced the camp an improvement on what they had known in Virginia. The new facility was named Camp Sumter, but everyone took to calling it by the name of a nearby village: Andersonville.

As the war ground on, Georgia's luck continued to hold: Its frontiers remained essentially inviolate. The most serious loss was on the coast, where in the spring of 1862 Federal forces attacked Fort Pulaski, fifteen miles downstream from Savannah. Confederate authorities felt the old fort, which was made of brick, would not be able to resist a bombardment with modern rifled cannon, and that proved to be the case. The old ramparts dissolved "in puffs of yellow dust." The fort's surrender sparked a brief panic in Savannah, but the Yankees showed no immediate disposition to expand their lodgement, and things soon returned to normal in the port city. Two years later the situation had scarcely changed.

The spring of 1863 brought two brief descents. In early May Union Colonel Abel Streight came across Alabama leading a large cavalry force, with Confederate General Nathan Bedford Forrest in pursuit. Streight hoped to cross into Georgia at Rome, burn the bridge behind him, and gain a respite. But a Confederate postman named John Wisdom played the role of Paul Revere, warning the Romans and giving them time to put up defenses. With his route blocked, Streight surrendered to Forrest, unaware that the Rebel force was vastly inferior in numbers to his own. Hardly had Georgians gotten over the excitement of Streight's raid when a second Federal assault came at the other end of the state. On June 11 a seaborne force attacked the little town of Darien, not far from Savannah. A major purpose of the raid was to sack and burn. In the words of its commander, Colonel James Montgomery: "Southerners must be made to feel that this was a real war and that they were to be swept away by the hand of God like the Jews of old."

But these were only pinpricks; after nearly two years of war a Georgia girl could write in her diary: "so far Georgia has been free from the polluting tread of the Vandals." To Southerners from other states that had been largely overrun by Union forces Georgia seemed a safe haven; from 1862 on they settled in the state in increasing numbers. Often their newspapers followed them—the *Chattanooga Rebel* began to appear in

Griffin, Georgia—and sometimes other institutions moved as well: Early
in 1864 the treasury of the State of Tennessee with its half-million dollars
in specie was located in Atlanta. The migration of the refugees was
something like that of seabirds, for in their movement and destination
they were guided by deeply imprinted notions. Such was their attach-
ment to their native state that they were loath to leave it as long as there
was a scrap of it under Southern control where they could find shelter.
Once driven out of the state, they stopped and settled as soon as possible, so as to be closer to home when the fortunes of war changed; thus
Rome and Columbus attracted people fleeing from neighboring
Alabama. Of course if the limits of the Confederacy shrank further, then
the refugees were soon in harm's way again. This is what generally happened, so that the exiles were often birds of passage, driven from one
shelter to the next as the storm approached.

Once settled in, they made contact with one another, formed social
groups, and tried to reconstitute in miniature the world they had left.
Among people from Louisiana, those from New Orleans were a distinct
group—there were some sixty New Orleans families concentrated in the
small town of La Grange, for example. People from Tennessee divided
themselves—as they still do—into East Tennesseans, West Tennesseans,
and Middle Tennesseans. A refugee from East Tennessee wrote a friend:
"We East Tennesseans get together some times and we make the folks
here think E. Tenn. is a *fair heaven* of a place. We don't think or talk about
much else when we get together." The refugees also turned to one
another in time of adversity. Mary Elizabeth Humphrey Howes of Kentucky, temporary resident of Macon, left a diary that shows she spent
much of her time helping others from her home state; this including taking in a woman from Louisville who was addicted to morphine (she also
treated her "neuralgia" by rubbing her forehead with a mixture of lard
and chloroform). This woman was a houseguest for over three months.

While some refugees, those we know the least about, were virtually
destitute, squatting in abandoned houses and living hand-to-mouth, a
good many were fairly well-off and able to live in some style (Mrs. Irby
Morgan, from Tennessee, carried with her fourteen thousand dollars in
specie). These people mingled easily with the locals and stimulated the
social life of the towns and villages in which they settled. In Athens the
pulse of life quickened with the presence of "crowds of charming
refugees." In Washington (called Washington-Wilkes to distinguish it
from the city on the Potomac) "life frequently went on at a merry pace"
thanks to the leavening added by the newcomers. Fanny Andrews, who
spent her youth in Washington, wrote years after the war: "never was

social life in the Old South more full of charm than when tottering to its fall."

Governor Brown called upon his fellow Georgians to accept the exiles graciously: "Having as a class made sacrifices for Southern independence to which we are yet strangers, they are entitled to our highest respect and most profound sympathy, and we should welcome them with warm hearts, divide with them as long as we have bread . . ." But the refugees had their special problems that the warmest hospitality could not resolve. Homesickness was chronic among them; the lack of news from their homes and the loss of contact were sore trials. One expatriate wrote a friend from Eatonton: "I am so anxious to arrive at some place where I can rest & be stationary long enough to get a *few letters*. Plague the Yankees, they have got more than one letter of mine." (Oddly enough they also got this letter; it was brought back by a Northern officer and is in his papers at Cornell University.) They sometimes complained about the lack of hospitality on the part of the Georgians, and sometimes the Georgians did lose patience with their visitors, particularly when they descended on a place in large numbers. By 1863, with mounting shortages and inflation, the economy was beginning to fray badly; it was natural to blame the succeeding waves of refugees for hard times.

At first the war economy had seemed to augur good times, with full employment and easy money. Young Joel Chandler Harris, still ignorant of the phenomenon of inflation, was astounded and delighted that he could now have "folding money." He had never seen money more plentiful: "Everybody seemed to have some, and yet nobody had enough." That was not the case with a young man named William Frederick Penneman, who found himself with forty thousand dollars in his hands after a transaction with the Confederate Engineers Department. Since he was going to pay a visit to his sweetheart, he had a Savannah tailor make him a new suit for eighteen hundred dollars and complemented it with a nine-hundred-dollar pair of shoes. But as is generally the case, Georgians found prices rising faster than their incomes, so that while there were some cases of affluence, there were many more of hardship and misery. Probably the lowest rung on the employment ladder, the one just above begging in the streets, was reserved for women and was called "taking in sewing." In 1864, when a pound of sugar sold for seven dollars, women sewing uniforms for the Confederate Quartermaster Department received a dollar for each pair of pants and fifty cents for a shirt. In Savannah their average earnings were seventy-five cents a day.

Before long even those who had the money to buy could not find the products they sought. By 1862 there was a serious shortage of kerosene; the next year the Episcopal bishop of Savannah had to write his counterpart in Charleston to ask his help in finding some olive oil for the Holy Thursday ceremony. Letters and diaries for the period contain endless complaints about the lack of shoes. A young Georgian confided to his diary: "I ride regularly on horseback to save shoe leather." A New Orleans woman who spent part of the war years in Georgia recalled that while her shoe size was two and a half, she bought and wore anything she could find up to size five, packing the toes of the shoes with cotton. It has been said that of all the sacrifices people make in wartime, what seems to hurt them most and what they remember longest is the deprivation of the everyday things. This was certainly the case with an old man who tried to explain to an interviewer in 1887 what it had been like to do without coffee a quarter-century before:

> My old 'oman had the headache for three years, I know, just for want of coffee, and she tried everything in the Southern Confederacy— parched corn, wheat, meal, okra seed, sweet potatoes and every 'tarnal thing she could think of, and she made it and we called it coffee, and we drank it, but it warn't no use, the headache would come.

Food was the most basic commodity, and one might suppose that in an overwhelmingly agricultural society it would have been the one most easily supplied. But by 1864 the farmers of Georgia were having their problems. Some had found it difficult to switch from cotton culture to foodstuffs, though cotton growing was now limited by law. The conscription laws eventually had an adverse effect on farming, since the farmer's wife and children were obliged to take his place in the fields, where they generally labored to less effect. Overseers too went into the army and were difficult or impossible to replace. Blacksmiths were in uniform in sizable numbers, though their services were as vital to the agriculture of that era as those of the mechanic are today. Then too, the pool of draft animals was insufficient, even though no foreign army had yet come to decimate it. Georgia's supply at the beginning of the war was already low relative to what other states possessed, and the impressment of horses and mules by Confederate authorities did not help matters. By 1864 impressment officers and Georgians who owned horses were playing a cat-and-mouse game, the owners trying to keep their animals out of sight and the officers trying to find them. Officers impressing in and around Atlanta found horses stabled in the most unlikely places, including upstairs bedrooms.

The Confederate Commissary Department took to contracting for a farmer's crop while it was still in the field, so while there might be an abundance of corn or potatoes grown in a county, little or none would be available for local consumers. Dr. Thomas Green, superintendent of the State Lunatic Asylum, ran into this problem early in 1864. He had the necessary funds to buy food for the inmates, and the farmers had the extra corn, but they were under government bond and afraid to sell to him. He appealed to the Confederate secretary of war, telling him that in his desperation he had even considered closing the institution and sending the inmates home, only to discover that in many cases there was no male family member at home who could take responsibility for them.

By 1864 people in many North Georgia communities had taken to pooling their orders and buying corn from the other end of the state, but once they did their problems were not over; they had to figure out a way to get it delivered at a time when the transportation system was already overburdened. That food shortages were real and widespread in 1864 there seems no doubt. The situation was complicated by the fact that in the upper Piedmont and mountains, where an essentially rural population customarily grew its own needs in food, the country stores stocked little more than coffee, sugar, molasses, and a few other items. Thus there was no commercial food distribution system; when a man lost his stock of food he had to ask a neighbor for help; failing that, it was steal or starve. If there are no documented cases of outright starvation among Georgia's people, there is abundant testimony that they were malnourished and undernourished; food or lack of it was a constant topic in home-front correspondence, while thefts from pantries, smokehouses, and corncribs multiplied. Beekeepers reported the theft of entire hives—honey, bees, and all.

We can get some idea of the difficulties in the industrial sector of the state's economy from correspondence between the Confederate War Department and the managers of several Georgia textile firms in the latter half of 1864. The most immediate crisis was in labor. The Augusta Factory had lost so many male operatives—called up for either state or Confederate service—that it had ceased making cloth deliveries to the Confederate Quartermaster Department; the Eagle Factory had suffered a drop in production for the same reason. Though the plants had a mixed labor force of men, women, children, and slaves, their managers felt the force of male employees was critical, so Confederate quartermaster officers proposed supplying them with prisoners of war. The idea was not well-received. One plant manager feared sabotage; another was alarmed that the Yankee prisoners would be in contact with the women workers, a state of affairs he felt would be "very disagreeable." The manager of the Graniteville plant was more explicit: The appearance of a single Yankee soldier in the plant, he said, "would cause a rebellion among my female operatives."

W. E. Jackson, president of the Augusta Factory, took advantage of his correspondence with the government to unburden himself of a whole series of grievances. His plant was paying the staggering sum of $196,000 in taxes for 1864. It had made a gift of cloth worth a quarter-million dollars for distribution to the needy families of soldiers. And with all of that, he was obliged to sell textiles to the government at a special price well below what could be had in the open market—and the government used only part of the cloth, marketing the rest in its bartering operations, thus competing in a sense with its own supplier. In these letters and others like them that passed between the Confederate War Department and Georgia entrepreneurs there are hints of other difficulties that could only grow worse in time: Accounts receivable are settled with great delay, and no debtor is more tardy than the Confederate government. The highly skilled workers of previous years have been replaced by others who are not up to the job. Raw materials do not reach the plant, and outgoing shipments of finished goods remain on the loading dock because the rail lines are clogged. Machinery is wearing out and replacements must come from England; there is a shipment of vital parts at Nassau, but if it cannot be run in through the blockade soon the plant must shut down.

One cannot read documents such as these without concluding that like the power looms in the Graniteville Factory, the economy of Confederate Georgia was badly worn and overstrained, running erratically and headed for a breakdown. One could probably find in the debris of Confederate records enough figures for car loadings, production reports, and the like to add some statistical detail to this grim picture. But to gauge the disintegration in human terms, to measure the misery in Georgia, one needs to read the letters that streamed into Governor Brown's office from one end of the state to the other. They are eloquent proof of Brown's "clutch on the popular heart," as Colonel Avery called it, and clear evidence that great masses of people saw him as their best hope in grim and tragic times. To most of the correspondents writing did not come easily, and their letters show it. Sometimes the crudely scrawled plea was on a ragged scrap of paper and contained a word of apology: "Paper is very scarce with us [in] Catoosa County." People would write about personal predicaments that had nothing to do with the war, situations that seemed serious enough to them, but from a perspective of over a century come close to being hilarious. There was the minister of the Gospel in Box Spring, Georgia, who had left his wife because of "extreme incompatibility of temperaments." He had just learned that in his absence she had sold off all his property and pocketed the proceeds; were this not enough, her brother was looking for the minister and had stated his intention of killing him if he did not return to his wife.

But in most of the letters there is little to make a reader smile. Sometimes the tone is one of anger or indignation. Is it right, asks a correspondent in Dawson County, for a deserter's family to receive a ration of corn from the state when the deserter has been "lying out" not far from his home for over a year? There are moving appeals, as in an anonymous note: "Do for God's sake put an end to this unrighteous war . . . You are the representative of the Yeomanry of the land, who are now helpless." There are petitions from a score or more of "heads of families," half of them women, asking that a blacksmith be released from the militia because there is no other smith within twenty miles. And there are appeals on behalf of people in the most varied predicaments: a militiaman who needs a thirty-day furlough to move his family from the path of the advancing enemy, a deaf-mute man who has been robbed of all he owned.

A goodly proportion of the letters written to Brown in 1864 were from people who were hungry or felt they soon would be. Here too there is sometimes anger or despair. A woman with three small children put this question to her governor: "Would you not think it very hard to set down to a meal of drie bread 3 times a day for 3 mon[ths] at a time?" And Mrs. Elizabeth Fields of Colquitt County, also mother of three, began her letter: "I write with tears in my eyes." But often the women's letters—for almost all the appeals for food were from women—had a more stoic cast. One suspects they were not complete strangers to hard times; given a little help they would cope and survive. Such was the message of Mrs. Samantha J. Adams, who wrote in from Meriwether County on May 23, 1864. The letter must have been a chore for her. She did not wield the pen easily and her spelling was approximate, but her message was clear. She said that she had four children under the age of twelve and a "brave and esalent husban" who was fighting in the field; she had not seen him since 1862. "If I cood feed my famley untel I can mak a crop," she wrote, "I can get a long som way."

Most people who turned to Joe Brown knew their man, but one woman who wrote ended with this appeal: "Mr. Brown, answer this letter if you please as some people says you would not condescend to write to me." She had no cause to worry: notations on these letters indicate they were answered without fail and without delay; sometimes the routing and attendant notations tell us what disposition was made, though unfortunately the governor does not seem to have kept copies of his responses to letters of this type. But what is clear is that he dedicated a considerable portion of his time and energies to softening the impact that war was having on the masses. In doing so he and the state legislature significantly transformed the scope and function of government.

In the Georgia of 1860 the rule still held that in matters of government least was best. The capital city, Milledgeville, was a visible expression of this idea. It was not a city, but in fact a very modest town containing an equally modest governmental structure. The governor had his mansion and the legislature convened in the capitol, but there were no structures for the bureaucracy of the various executive departments—because there were no departments. The state had virtually no role in education, welfare, health, or police and regulatory functions. The governor had no cabinet worthy of the name and very little by way of administrative hierarchy; his essential link with the counties was the judges of Inferior Court, whom he could order to do this or that, but whom he could not compel to obey him. This minimalist approach to government was inexpensive and accorded well with the fiscal conservatism then in vogue, but it could not meet the demands of war.

A succession of crises, more than anything else, served to extend the sway of government in general and more specifically to expand the functions and responsibilities of Governor Brown, who accepted every new task with alacrity. At first came interventions in the state's economic life, beginning with a measure that must have given the governor considerable personal satisfaction. His proclamation of February 1862 prohibited the distillation of spirits in Georgia, ostensibly to conserve grain for other uses (the governor was shortly obliged to make an exception for Georgia distillers working under contract for the Confederate authorities; they supplied the army with a million gallons of whiskey in 1863). Shortly after this the state was obliged to take action in the matter of salt. A serious shortage was developing, attended by speculation, hoarding, skyrocketing prices, and complaints from the "plebeians" who were the governor's chief constituents. Brown's intervention was forceful. He confiscated the salt in the market, or all he could get of it, prohibited its transport out of Georgia, and took control of its distribution. He put the state into the salt mining business, acquiring a concession at Saltville, Virginia. In 1863 he transferred the concession to a corporation that undertook to produce twenty-five thousand pounds a day, "Sabbaths excluded." But Brown still kept his hand in the operation, supplying a locomotive and cars, among other things.

In its December 1862 session the legislature began to appropriate money on an unprecedented scale. There were five hundred thousand dollars for the supply of salt, one hundred thousand dollars for the purchase of cotton cards (comblike implements used to prepare the fiber for spinning) and one and a half million dollars for soldiers' clothing; in addition there was a five-hundred-thousand-dollar subvention for the Georgia Relief and Hospital Association. The most important item of new expenditure was two and a half million dollars for the relief of "indigent widows and soldiers' families." In addition there was a special appropriation to help move indigent noncombatants from portions of the state that might be threatened by invasion. The budget for 1863 in fact contained a whole "package" of benefits that were in a sense class legislation, destined for members of the class that was at once most loyal to Brown and most vulnerable to the wrenching economic changes the state was undergoing. They were the recipients not only of the "indigent" appropriations, but also of the cotton cards and of salt at special low prices. According to Colonel Avery, in the course of 1863 the indigent funds were distributed to some eighty-four thousand Georgians.

When the legislature convened again at the end of 1863 it took a revolutionary step and introduced an income tax in an effort to increase its revenue; it was a thoroughly modern measure, with a sliding scale of rates up to twenty-five percent. But the fiscal Rubicon had already been crossed: The state had taken a debt on its shoulders and had little choice but to increase it; the sinking value of the Confederate dollar obliged Georgia's political leaders to deal in sums that would have boggled the mind a year or two before. The legislature gave the governor a special "military fund" for contingencies that might arise and authorized him to purchase blockade runners in the state's name. And it increased the appropriation for indigent widows and soldiers' families to six million dollars. By then Brown saw that simply giving money to destitute people would not do them much good, since they would still lose out in the competition for foodstuffs; hence the state undertook a massive buying program, particularly of corn, with the judges of Inferior Court supervising purchase and distribution in each county. In 1864 that corn would be the means of survival for a fair proportion of Georgia's people; in Carroll County, a heavily foraged area west of Atlanta, twenty percent of the inhabitants figured on the distribution lists; in other areas the percentage was no doubt greater. The judges of Inferior Court of Dawson County spoke for a great many people when they wrote the governor in September 1864: "We have looked to you as the 'Joseph' of our 'Egypt.'"

By 1864 Governor Brown was devoting more time to political problems than to economic ones, for he had become embroiled in a running battle with the Confederate government in Richmond—a battle that has assured Joe Brown an enduring place in Civil War history books. He concluded that the Confederate Conscription Act of 1862 was unconstitutional and wrote a letter to Jefferson Davis telling him so. Davis, characteristically, prepared a lengthy response in which he pointed out all the governor's errors in legal reasoning. Had he known Brown as courtroom opponents knew him, he would have saved himself the trouble. As it was, back came a twenty-six-page letter in which the governor of Georgia returned to the charge more vigorously than ever. The quarrel gradually expanded from constitutional issues to the allocation of manpower, fiscal matters, the distribution of resources, military operations—Brown offered Davis a scathing critique of Confederate strategy—and even foreign affairs: The governor sent a "commissioner" abroad to represent Georgia to the governments of a dozen European powers from Portugal to Russia.

Brown's rigid defense of state's rights in the midst of a life-and-death struggle troubled a number of the state's leading political figures, particularly among the "patricians" who had earlier run the state, and they were vocal in their criticisms. Brown's public utterances, in turn, seemed calculated to stoke the anger that many of his constituents already felt toward the privileged few. In a message to the legislature in 1863 he said that while the enormous majority of the Confederate army were poor men and non-slaveholders, "a large proportion of the wealthy class of people have avoided the fevers of the camp and the dangers of the battlefield, and have remained at home in comparative ease and comfort with their families." Brown's relations deteriorated rapidly with General Howell Cobb, a prominent member of the class Brown was denouncing and commander of the Confederate Reserve force in Georgia. In the spring of 1864, when the two men would have done well to put their heads together over the dangers threatening their state, they were exchanging insults. In May Cobb ended a letter to Brown with these words: "I shall leave you . . . to the full enjoyment of all the pleasure which a low and grovelling mind derives from the repetition of stale and malicious slanders."

While the public followed these broils with interest—Brown published his exchanges with Jefferson Davis and others in the newspapers—now its more immediate preoccupation was with its own security.

The towns were turbulent, and to many the countryside seemed increasingly unsafe. Citizens reported coming across suspicious men, and sometimes whole groups of them, in out-of-the-way places. Joel Chandler Harris, out tramping the woods one day, came across an old cabin that was being shared by deserters from the Southern army and slaves who had left their plantations; a similarly constituted band was found outside Atlanta at the beginning of 1864. In truth the state had acquired a floating population that was both sizable and suspect. To the customary vagrants and transients of a rural society were now added penniless refugees, deserters, large numbers of runaway slaves, young men trying to stay ahead of the conscript officer, and soldiers with furloughs and no particular place to go; there were also some few Northern spies and scouts, whose numbers and importance the public tended to magnify. The legislature struck out particularly at deserters. Though the military authorities punished them when caught, the state added a law making it a crime to aid and abet in desertion. The legislature also voted to give a woman grounds for "total divorce" if her husband deserted to the enemy (Governor Brown, who had very conservative views on marriage, opposed the measure, but it passed anyway).

The legislature amended the penal code to provide death for anyone guilty of communicating with the enemy or abetting such act; this measure was no doubt a stern reminder to the pro-Union element in Georgia's population. There is no way to know how large this element was, even in 1861, when it was still possible to express such views. While there was no referendum on secession, the votes received by the various candidates for the Secession Convention lead us to think that between a third and a half of Georgia's people were either completely opposed to secession or wanted to put it off and see what might emerge by way of compromise. Once that step was taken the fate of those who had opposed it varied considerably. Some, especially those who had recently come from the North, simply liquidated their holdings and left the state for good, but those whose roots were deep tended to stay on, come what may. Unionists who were prominent political and social leaders suffered least from being on the losing side. They kept their prominence and their possessions—and without renouncing their views or even trimming their sails. Augustus Wright of Rome, always called Judge Wright, and Joshua Hill of Madison were two men who enjoyed this sort of immunity (it is true that Hill was burned in effigy in Talbot County in 1861, but the very act was a kind of distinction). Even more remarkable, Hill ran against Brown in the gubernatorial election of 1863 and made a respectable showing. How was this possible? Senator Ben Hill, one of

Georgia's shrewder politicians, said the most prominent Unionists were left alone because "everybody knew from their character that they would not be treacherous; that is, they would not subject themselves to criminal prosecution for infidelity to the Confederate Government."

But life was not necessarily easy for Unionists of this privileged class. Their own children could become enemies. Thus Joshua Hill's son Legare joined the Confederate army over his father's objections and would fight in the spring campaign in North Georgia; Judge Garnett Andrews's Unionist views were not embraced by his daughter Fanny. A strong-minded, redheaded woman then in her twenties, Fanny sewed together the first Confederate flag to be raised over the Wilkes County courthouse. In later life she acknowledged that her rebelliousness "had brought on scenes that were not conducive to the peace of the family."

A man with pro-Union views could not count on much toleration if he were on the other end of the social scale. He could expect to be hounded by the authorities and threatened by his neighbors. If a mob gathered it was not to burn his effigy, but his barn or his house, and he might have cause to fear for his life. Sometimes he found a solution by "lying out," going into concealment, more often than not near his home, and trusting that his family would be less harshly treated with him out of sight. From time to time in 1864 Northern troops would encounter one of these "hideouts" and find themselves greeted as liberators. Where pro-Unionists were numerous among the "little people," as they were in parts of North Georgia, they did not submit tamely to the harassment, but gave as good as they got; then a kind of brush war would develop, with sniping from ambush, sudden descents, and firebrands in the night.

In between these extremes, known Unionists of respectable but not distinguished station might undergo a certain amount of surveillance by the authorities and a degree of ostracism by neighbors and acquaintances. Such was the case of Miss Abby, for so she styled herself in a remarkable diary that she began in January 1864 and abandoned abruptly seven months later. Her real name, only recently discovered, was Cyrena Bailey Stone, and she was a thirty-four-year-old Atlanta schoolteacher. She and her husband were originally from Maine and had come south in 1850. Mr. Stone decided to return North in the middle of the war, but Miss Abby stayed behind and took to confiding to her diary the hopes and fears she could no longer share with her spouse.

Miss Abby visited the military hospitals around Atlanta, where she made a specialty of befriending the Union prisoners she found there. At her home she kept a pet turkey named George McClellan and a small American flag that she would occasionally bring out from its hiding place and display to selected visitors. These activities hardly seem seditious, but there was more: In the spring and summer of 1864 she concealed a number of runaway slaves in her cotton house, and on at least one occasion she altered the date on a soldier's leave papers so that he could remain home longer. She thus had some grounds for worry when she heard that her name was on a list kept in the office of the provost marshal of Atlanta. But at the same time Miss Abby found reason to take heart—old acquaintances who had earlier shown a certain coolness toward her were now increasingly cordial. And she was thrilled beyond measure when she first heard that faint rumble of cannon to the north that announced the coming of Sherman's army. These things were surely signs that a new day was coming.

To Georgia's leaders and to the bulk of her people Miss Abby and others of her persuasion were only a minor worry; people were far more preoccupied over the state's 440,000 black bondsmen. These were at once a resource and a menace. The danger they constituted was still only a potential one, while the manpower resource they offered was being tapped increasingly. Black labor was now contributing directly to the military effort, with perhaps as many as ten thousand slaves toiling to build fortifications in the state, including the vast complex that girdled Atlanta. Early in 1864 the Confederate Congress went a step further, sanctioning the use of blacks as army teamsters, hospital attendants, and the like; they would replace white soldiers who had been "detailed" for these purposes. Applied systematically, the measure could swell the ranks of the army's combat components by hundreds and even thousands—by Africanizing its rear echelons. Already there was guarded talk of an even more radical step, arming and training slaves and putting regiments of them in the battle line. At the beginning of 1864 a correspondent of the *Chattanooga Rebel* who styled himself "Aristides" even proposed introducing them into existing regiments, pairing each slave with a white soldier.

The menace that the great mass of blacks posed to the white population of Georgia and other Southern states was the old, nightmarish one of insurrection, now made even more frightening because it would break out in a society whose coercive force had all been mobilized and directed at an outside enemy. At the beginning of 1864 Confederate authorities estimated they had mobilized 106,000 Georgians, some seventeen percent of her white population. That summer about ten thousand more would be called up for militia duty. With those customary symbols of authority, masters and overseers, increasingly absent, with the countryside largely stripped of white men of military age, once the spark was struck and the conflagration began to spread it could sweep unhindered from one end of the state to the other. All white Georgians saw this specter, but those who lived scattered in the countryside saw it in all its frightfulness—the people of rural Putnam County, for example, where Joel Chandler Harris lived: "The whites who were left at home knew it was in the power of the negroes to rise and in one night sweep the strength and substance of the Confederacy from the face of the earth. Some of the more ignorant whites lived in constant terror."

So white Georgians watched black Georgians, looking for the first signs. They looked for insolence in the tone of a laundress and for conspiracy in a group of field hands gathered around a well—and they tended to see the signs, whether they were there or not. But what was really running through the minds of the black people of Georgia in 1864? Here there are no diaries to guide us, and precious little else by way of direct testimony. Most seem to have known that something momentous was happening to the society they knew and that their bondage might be ended by it. Sometimes they revealed a knowledge of affairs that surprised their owners: One of Miss Abby's servants told her mistress that she knew about schemes to arm the blacks to help defend the Confederacy—and she added that the whites would be ill-advised to do it, since they could not be sure which way a black soldier might shoot. Most Georgia blacks chose to go about their daily tasks, waiting with varying degrees of hope and apprehension for what the future would bring. The young and the impatient, caught up in the vision of a new day, often chose to act; when they did it was not insurrection that attracted them but flight. The Union army—or sometimes the navy—was often the magnet that drew the runaways. It has been estimated that perhaps as many as two thousand reached the Union forces operating on Georgia's coast; as many or more failed in the attempt and sometimes paid with their lives. A compilation in 1866 showed that during the conflict thirty-five thousand Georgia blacks served with the Union forces.

Beginning late in 1863 the area along the Tennessee border began to be more attractive to blacks fleeing bondage in Georgia. There the Union army was established in force, and there black regiments were being formed. One of these units was the Forty-fourth U.S. Colored Infantry, Colonel Lewis Young commanding, which was authorized to begin recruiting fugitive slaves from Georgia and Tennessee on March 2, 1864. Those who came to sign up appear in the records as names and nothing more—all except one, Private Hubbard Pryor of Company A. He was one of the first to enlist, just five days after recruiting began in Chattanooga. He said that he came from Polk County, Georgia; he gave his age as twenty-two and his profession as "farmer." Someone thought to photograph him "before" and "after," wearing the rags of slavery and in the uniform of the United States Army. Colonel R. D. Mussey, in charge of recruiting black troops, included the two photographs in his report, and so they were preserved in the National Archives.

A young officer named Morris Stuart Hall was attracted by the challenge the new black regiments offered, so he joined the Forty-fourth early in the year and plunged into training the men. The new soldiers were ignorant of even the most basic functions of the military calling; of eighty-six mustered in Company C, all but nine were illiterate. But they were eager to learn (all who remained with the regiment learned to read), and Captain Hall found he enjoyed his work. Within a short time he was referring to his men with the term any officer used when his rapport with those under him was close and informal: "the boys." The Forty-fourth USCI would have a rare distinction among the black regiments in Sherman's army, for it would play an active role in the war in Georgia.

In that spring of 1864 the thoughts of all Georgians were on that border with Tennessee, for there the Union army was massing in unprecedented numbers, and no one doubted that the state would be tested as it had never been before. There were any number of calls to arms addressed to the population, appeals for all to make a maximum effort now that Georgia was faced with invasion. A correspondent of the *Augusta Daily Chronicle and Sentinel* had just returned from a visit to the border area; he felt it his duty to warn the paper's readers of what would be in store for them if the Confederate forces there could not best the enemy: "An army of invasion will come down upon us, formidable [in] numbers and ferocious in its purposes of plunder and destruction. No man, woman or child will escape. One universal ruin awaits us all."

Perhaps such apocalyptic visions were necessary to prepare a people who, despite the stories the refugees brought, had no clear idea what they were in for. They had not seen for themselves the full face of war. Joel Chandler Harris was trying to imagine that face. Writing long after and referring to himself in the third person as "Joe Maxwell," Harris recalled his first glimpse of its frightfulness. He was present when his employer told a woman that her husband had been killed in battle:

> Her screams when the editor told her of it, and the cries of her little daughter, haunted Joe Maxwell for many a long day. Sometimes he lay awake at night thinking about it, and out of the darkness it seemed to him that he could build a grim mirage of war, vanishing and reappearing like an ominous shadow, and devouring the people.

3

◈

The Hosts

The census of 1860 put the population of Whitfield County, Georgia, at 10,047, and that of Catoosa County, its neighbor to the west, at 5,082; but in the first half of May 1864 the two counties contained well in excess of a hundred thousand persons. The newcomers were everywhere: Their wagons jammed the streets of the two county seats, Dalton and Ringgold, and their columns filled the country roads leading from neighboring counties. Farther away, in Alabama and Tennessee, other columns were on the roads, all moving toward the northwest corner of Georgia. The Confederate Army of Tennessee had been the first to arrive, having been driven out of Tennessee after its defeat at Missionary Ridge in November 1863. The Rebels settled in at Dalton and began fortifying the hills that hedge around it. In the spring the army's commander, General Joseph E. Johnston, had in and around Dalton a force of about sixty thousand.

Union forces had followed the retreating Confederates as far as Ringgold, which they garrisoned through the winter as a base of observation and future operations, but the bulk of the Union soldiers in North Georgia that May were more recent arrivals. They had begun the slow and complicated process of concentration a few weeks before, so that by late April thousands of them were on the roads in a vast arc stretching from Knoxville, Tennessee, to Huntsville, Alabama. The force that General Sherman brought together that spring was an impressive one by any standard. Properly speaking it could not be called Sherman's army, since he had three, each of them named for a river: the armies of the Cumberland, the Ohio, and the Tennessee—the last of which is all too easy to confuse with the Confederate Army of Tennessee. These armies were made up of seven corps, over four hundred infantry regiments, twelve thousand cavalry, and 254 guns, nearly twice the number of artillery pieces General Johnston had. Sherman's host was so large that its order of battle fills twenty-five pages of the *Official Records*; in all he would have a hundred thousand men, several thousand more than General Meade had at Gettysburg the year before.

In its structure, in its operational routine, the gray army was essentially a copy of the blue one, understandable enough considering that it had been hastily created three years before by men whose military expertise had been acquired in the service of the United States. As a consequence a soldier passing from one army to the other would feel at home with the layout of the camps, with the bugle calls that regulated a soldier's day on both sides of the line. A Federal staff officer trying to establish the enemy's order of battle knew the building blocks were the same: regiment, brigade, division, corps. Through and between these constituent bodies of both armies moved that same river of paper—requisition forms, reports, and the like—that were the lifeblood of military administration; if a company clerk in the Southern army needed to prepare his roster and was out of Form 642b, in a pinch he could use Union army Form 358b. But the two armies were similar, rather than identical. There were differences in organizational detail, for example; the Confederate cavalry company was not the same size as the Union troop, and the word "effectives" on Southern muster rolls did not have the same meaning as in Union service. The most notable disparity to us would be in the matériel of the two opposing armies, in the riches of the Northern one and the poverty of the Southern one; this was a problem the Confederates had faced from the beginning, and it was not getting any better. In North Georgia there were occasions when one could actually look at the two armies and see the disparity for oneself. Confederate General Samuel French climbed to a mountaintop late that spring and found the two armies spread out before him in what he called "a vast panorama." What struck him most were the signs of a difference that went far beyond numbers of men:

> There are new, large trains to the left of Lost Mountain and at Big Shanty, and the wagons are moving to and fro everywhere. Encampments of hospitals, quartermasters, commissaries, cavalry, and infantry whiten the plain here and there as far as the eye can reach. Look at our side of the battle line! It is narrow, poor and quiet, save at

the front where the men are, and contrasts, with here and there some spots of canvas amid the foliage, strangely with that of the enemy.

A good many of the tents General French saw belonged to the Union army's medical service. General Thomas's army had an entire hundred-tent mobile hospital and was probably the best equipped army to take the field in the entire war. "He had the best supply trains," wrote an authority on the medical matériel in Thomas's army, "the best engineer equipment, the best ambulance arrangements, the best railway and hospital trains." A number of the tents General French saw would have been packed with pharmaceutical supplies, for the army's medical director would write after the campaign was over that supplies had always been ample, even over a precarious and often broken supply line. As for Dr. Samuel Stout, medical director of the Army of Tennessee, that spring he and his staff entered "the most difficult period of their hospital service. From this point on the shortage of supplies would become more and more acute. . . ." Imported medicines such as quinine were disappearing from the pharmacopoeia of the Confederate medical service, to be replaced by "indigenous" remedies; hospital directors sometimes sent convalescents out to search the woods for blackberry root, slippery elm bark, and the like. Chloroform was never plentiful and brought a handsome price on the black market; late in the war fifteen bottles from a Confederate hospital in Oxford, Georgia, were bootlegged in Augusta for three thousand dollars. While Southern surgeons generally did not like to cut until the patient was "limber," there must have been chilling scenes like that in the film Gone With the Wind, in which a soldier faced the amputation of his leg without anesthesia. Fannie Beers, who served as a nurse in Confederate military hospitals in Georgia in 1864, said chloroform and ether were so scarce that "in all minor, and in some severe operations, the surgeon relied on the manly fortitude of the patient."

While the Northern army had lived through the winter on monotonous rations, the Southerners had made it on short rations—with little possibility of supplementing the meager commissary issue. The Confederate private's pay of eleven dollars a month did not go far in a period of relentless inflation: "Eggs are $3.00 per doz," a Virginia soldier wrote home from Dalton, "Sweet potatoes 75cts per b. peas of all kinds 1.00 per quart molasses 24.00 per gall and that is about all we can buy. Gingercakes it aint worth while to talk about. I can get satisfied on about 5.00 worth." And the Confederates had spent the winter cold as well as hungry; so short had they been of blankets that patriotic hotelkeepers in several Georgia towns had taken up their carpets, cut them into blanket-sized squares, and sent them to the boys at the front; the Georgia legislature voted to do the same thing.

There was a significant and ever-widening discrepancy between the Northern and Southern armies in the matter of armament. That spring a number of Sherman's infantry and cavalry regiments were receiving new weapons—Spencer rifles and carbines, modern cartridge arms that could be fired seven times without reloading; other units went into the field armed with Henry repeating rifles, better known in the ranks as "sixteen-shooters." Confederate ordnance could not match this quantum leap in firepower; indeed, it had its hands full just meeting the demand for conventional weaponry. There was a growing shortage of copper in the Confederacy; Southern arsenals now made cannon barrels out of iron rather than bronze, which was an alloy requiring much copper. The iron barrels left little to be desired ballistically, but they were several hundred pounds heavier and consequently less mobile; it was sometimes necessary to "double team" them to get them over the hills of North Georgia, a slow and tedious process. Confederate artillery units had battered and much repaired carriages, caissons, and forges, and endlessly patched harness. A Federal artilleryman who looked over the Rebel battery taken at Resaca said the equipment looked as if it had been used "either before or during the Revolution." In one aspect of armament the Rebels had superiority: the Whitworth sharpshooter's rifle they used was said to be the most accurate in the world, effective at up to fifteen hundred yards; but the Whitworths came from England and were scarce; the story ran among the soldiers that they cost the Confederacy one thousand dollars apiece, and there were probably not more than a score or so in the entire Army of Tennessee. General French had five in his division, where the habit was to send out two men with each rifle; if something happened to one man, the other could bring back the Whitworth (the rarity of these weapons is reflected in the price a Whitworth bullet from one of the Georgia battlefields will bring among collectors of Civil War artifacts—over two hundred dollars).

Being armed with inferior weapons would have a profound impact on the morale of a modern army, but in truth these technological and material differences are more significant to us than they were to the men who fought this last of the pretechnical wars. The need for new weaponry is rarely evoked in the soldiers' letters and diaries. If one Union regiment received sixteen-shooters, the other regiments in the brigade did not set up a clamor for them. Nor did the introduction of new armament in the Union army provoke any discernible agitation or slump in morale on the Confederate side. The Southerners would admit Northern superiority in armament, and would probably have conceded that they were behind the Yankees in other technical aspects of warfare as well: in transport, in signals and telegraphy, in cartography—all matters in which the Northerners' acknowledged "mechanical skill" could be brought to bear. But that all seems to have mattered very little to the rank and file of the Southern army, for theirs was an age that still subscribed to the Napoleonic maxim: "In war the moral is to the physical as three is to one"—an army's psychological makeup, its élan, tenacity, and qualities of heart were far more important than numbers or matériel.

The Southerners suffered from another, more subtle disadvantage. The Union army was the outgrowth—admittedly a gigantic one—of a preexisting force. The Confederate army had been cut from whole cloth. The military establishment, from the highest echelons of the War Department on down, was brand-new in 1861 and had no "break-in" period; from its creation it had been occupied with war. What it lacked was the long honing of tradition and routine, the habit of doing things the "army way," whether it was parking a wagon train or digging a latrine—just the sort of things that are best done the army way, and can be picked up from the "regulars." To anyone who had a chance to compare the two armies in their everyday workings, this difference could be seen everywhere. A good scout, coming upon the tracks of a body of horsemen, could usually tell whether they were Northern or Southern by the way the horses were shod. Yankee farriers put on shoes the regulation way, and by 1864 the shoes themselves were "keg" shoes, uniformly stamped out by machine; the tracks of a Southern cavalry horse bespoke the individuality, sometimes the whimsy, of the farrier. A Tennessean civilian named H. V. Redfield frequently visited both of the "western" armies and considered himself an unprejudiced observer (he had been plundered by both armies). Whether it was how the supply wagons were maintained or how the camp was laid out or how the blockhouse was built, he could see "strength, conformity, system and durability" in what the Federals did; the Southern approach to doing things was haphazard and improvised, and the result was often "slipshod."

Comparing the armies requires us to look at the kinds of men who made them up; here the orders of battle are a good place to start, for they reveal among other things that each army had a distinct sectional cast. Sherman's army was not so much northern as it was midwestern, or as the soldiers in it would have said, western. The three states of Indiana, Illinois, and Ohio supplied half of his infantry, and it has been estimated that one soldier out of four was from Ohio. There were enough men from the Central Atlantic states to make their presence known among the Westerners—New York supplied sixteen infantry regiments and Pennsylvania eleven—but New England had only token representation, two Connecticut regiments and two from Massachusetts.

The Confederate Army of Tennessee also had a clear geographic base. The heaviest contributors were the states of the Lower South, particularly Georgia, Alabama, and Mississippi; by contrast North and South Carolina supplied only four infantry regiments each. There were only two regiments of Virginians. The divided allegiance of the border states is also reflected in the orders of battle: Northern and Southern armies each had a First Missouri Infantry and a Second Kentucky Cavalry. In sum, the manpower of both armies was essentially young men in their late teens and early twenties, drawn from farms and country villages in that broad band of states stretching from the Great Lakes down to the Gulf of Mexico. That the men in both armies were country-bred is obvious from their letters and diaries. They had an eye for the land, commenting on the way the crops looked, noting that the corn was about to tassel. Their agricultural background would stand them in good stead in the 1864 campaign with its escalating use of field fortification: They were accustomed to wielding shovel, pick, and axe, so digging trenches and clearing zones of fire came more easily.

If they were rural in background, they also had something of the bucolic, the provincial, that always attaches to the hinterlander. The Westerners had never eaten an oyster, had never seen the ocean; some of them would examine with awe the railroad tunnel near Dalton, for there was nothing like that in Illinois. The Texans, Arkansans, and Missourians in Johnston's army found themselves a world away from their homes, and even a lieutenant from Alabama found South Georgia an exotic place: "The whites and negroes both do not talk like us, and I have seen some intelligent and aristocratic ladies whom I could scarcely understand." And just a hint of frontier rudeness clung to them. When the Southerners picked up their pens they revealed that they came from a region where the public school was still not firmly implanted. When the Westerners spoke, their direct and matter-of-fact parlance ignored some of the subtleties inherent in human relationships—those a soldier should be aware of when he spoke with his colonel, for example.

Tempting as it is to characterize masses of men in this fashion, a closer look at the orders of battle reveals the perils of generalization. Among Sherman's cavalry units we find the First Alabama, raised back in 1862 from the Unionist population of North Alabama; to heighten the paradox, its I Company served as Sherman's mounted escort for part of the 1864 campaign. In the old Eleventh Corps, which had been merged with the Twelfth to form General Hooker's Twentieth Corps, there were a number of foreigners, notably Germans. The Confederate Tenth Tennessee Infantry was composed chiefly of Irishmen, including its Catholic chaplain. (Over half a million foreign-born served in the Civil War armies; in addition, Federal authorities recruited heavily abroad, particularly among the Irish and Germans.) Within the regiments there were other anomalies and curiosities. The Twenty-first Wisconsin had a contingent of Winnebago Indians, while the Thirty-ninth North Carolina had a company of Cherokees. The Eleventh Wisconsin had in its ranks a Filipino named Felix Balderry. Company E, First Louisiana Infantry had on its rolls a man from Indiana named Lutz; he had rushed south immediately after Lincoln's election because "if we despised anything, it was the idea of free niggers."

There were sizable numbers of blacks with both armies, where generally they were the hewers of wood and drawers of water. Many Northern units had taken on "contrabands" as cooks under vague contractual arrangements. Southern units had large numbers of slaves as servants, while others came and went as couriers of sorts, carrying messages and parcels between soldiers and their families. But blacks could also work for wages in the Southern regiments, contracting to cook for a group of soldiers, for example. Sherman had a number of recently created black regiments in his Military Division of the Mississippi, but they had been formed over his objections; he had grave doubts about their value in combat and he brought none of them to the battlefront. Still, blacks in limited numbers fought on both sides that summer. In the Twentieth Connecticut there was a black body servant named William Manning who often joined in the fighting; he was wounded in a charge in one of the first engagements that spring. Isaac, the black body servant of Colonel John Nisbet of the Sixty-sixth Georgia, joined his master in the breastworks from time to time to try his hand at shooting Yankees. Amos Rucker was technically a body servant in another Georgia regiment, but it was "well known that he was in the fights around Atlanta on several occasions." When Rucker died many years later, his former comrades-in-arms saw to it that he was laid to rest in the uniform of the Confederate States Army.

There were also women in the armies—very likely hundreds of them. There were first of all those who worked in hospitals as staff members or simply volunteers. Among these the best known to Sherman's soldiers was Mary Ann Ball Bickerdyke, called Mother Bickerdyke with some reason, for her maternal instincts seem to have embraced all of Sherman's armies. When the war came she was a widow with two sons living in Galesburg, Illinois, where she practiced the trade of a "botanic physician." She soon gave up her practice to nurse soldiers in the western campaigns; men recalled seeing her moving about the battlefield the evening after Shiloh, a lantern in one hand and a canteen of brandy in the other. Other women openly attached themselves to fighting units. In one of the Kentucky infantry regiments in Federal service the color-bearer had apparently brought along his wife. Union soldiers in another regiment saw the Kentuckians pass on their way into battle, the woman marching along beside the colors: "She was plainly dressed and looked like she had been with the regiment for some time." A few minutes later they saw the regiment stream back off the field; one of the men was being carried on a stretcher and the woman was walking beside him crying.

An unknown but probably appreciable number of women on both sides cut their hair short, put on uniforms, and fought in the ranks. General Joseph Wheeler, commanding the cavalry in the Army of Tennessee, acknowledged after the war that he knew of one woman who served in his command. Colonel Arthur Fremantle, a British officer traveling from Chattanooga to Atlanta in 1863, had pointed out to him a "goodish looking woman" in the same railway car; several men told him they had served with her in a Louisiana regiment: "They said she had been turned out a short time since for her bad and unmoral conduct. They told me that her sex was notorious to all the regiment, but no notice had been taken of it as long as she had conducted herself properly." Women in soldiers' uniforms were caught from time to time by the provost guard in rear areas behind Sherman's army. In August the provost marshal's men in Nashville picked up a woman named Louisa Hoffman; she had just enlisted as an artilleryman, and investigation revealed that she had served earlier with cavalry and infantry units. Two months later, on a train headed to the front, the provost guard seized a woman in male attire who claimed to be in the Twelfth Indiana Cavalry. Inquiries established that she was in fact the wife and assistant of the regiment's surgeon; they released her and she went on her way.

Women soldiers were also discovered after a battle when they were taken prisoner or encountered among the wounded or the dead; surgeons sometimes mentioned treating them after major battles. They were obviously curiosities to their captors. One Union soldier wrote his wife that after the Battle of Peachtree Creek they had found "a female dressed in men's clothes & a cartridge box on her side." She had been shot in the chest, and when they found her she was "still alive & as gritty as any reb

I ever saw"—and by "gritty" he meant full of pluck.

In dress and appearance, in the first impression they made on observers who visited their camps, the men of Sherman's army probably contrasted as much with their comrades in arms in the Army of the Potomac as with their adversaries in the Army of Tennessee. To someone coming from the front in Virginia the impression was one of slackness, even slovenliness, and a glaring lack of smartness and bearing. The troops in the Twentieth Corps who had come from the East the year before made a better impression. These soldiers had not yet abandoned their regulation caps for hats; they still rolled their blankets on top of their knapsacks in the prescribed manner, and they kept their places better in the line of march. "It is no use to deny," wrote one midwestern officer, "that they are better soldiers than Western men, so far as discipline, order and neatness are concerned." Some army commanders had tried to make the western soldier change his ways; Generals Burnside and Rosecrans, for example, insisted that the soldiers carry the complete regulation kit and accoutrements, whether they felt they were superfluous or not. But Sherman had no interest in such matters. As a consequence the men felt free to shed knapsacks, overcoats, and other items. Then too, in his person Sherman set a certain fashion in shabbiness. He conducted the 1864 campaign in rumpled uniform and a shapeless, unadorned wool hat that was the despair of his aides. Officers who encountered him alluded to a certain "carelessness in dress," but an Ohio soldier was more forthright: "His shirt is generally bordering on the dirty & he is not the kind of man to put on style. We all like him for that."

The Southern army had its own style in clothing and equipment. Here too there was a general tendency to shed superfluous items like the bayonet, and the same inclination to lighten the soldier's burden, though by the end of 1864 the Southern soldier carried a new item of his own invention—a corn grater made from a canteen half. In the Southern ranks the word "uniform" had less and less meaning. Already in 1863 Colonel Fremantle noted that the men of an Arkansas brigade he visited were "well clothed but without any attempt at uniformity in color or cut." Fremantle discovered that their unmilitary appearance was not simply the fault of Confederate quartermasters:

> I was told that even if a regiment was clothed in proper uniform by the Government, it would become particolored again within a week, as the soldiers preferred wearing the coarse home spun jackets and trousers made by their mothers and sisters at home. The Generals

very wisely allow them to please themselves in this respect, and insisted only upon their arms and accoutrements being kept in proper order.

Letters that Southern soldiers wrote home tend to corroborate this view, for they frequently contain orders for jackets, trousers, and the like. The habit was so ingrained that when Georgia authorities raised troops for state service they didn't even try to give the men uniforms, but offered instead a clothing allowance they could send home to their wives or mothers along with their orders for "country jeans." Even when uniforms were worn—by officers, for example—shabbiness was in style in the Southern army. The rips and stains were so many badges of honor, while a pristine uniform bespoke a man who was a stranger to battle. The same notion prevailed among civilians. One night late in the war an officer in Confederate uniform appeared at the home of Fanny Andrews seeking directions. The night was stormy, the officer young and handsome; Fanny and her sister thought of inviting him to spend the night. In the end they didn't. Said Fanny: "his uniform was too fresh and new anyway to be very heroic."

Though the men of the two armies looked and dressed so much alike that there were frequent cases of mistaken identity, there is some suggestion of a difference in physique, with the Southern men smaller and more slender. One Union officer was struck by the "thin, catlike men of the South," compared to the big-limbed men of the Union forces. Another described the Army of Tennessee as composed of the "bone and gristle" of the Confederacy (curiously, something of the same regional variation was noticed among army inductees in the Second World War). Sherman's units may have had more than their share of taller men. The Twenty-seventh Indiana was noted for them, claiming to have the tallest officer in the Union army: Captain David Buskirk, who stood six feet, eleven and a half inches in his stocking feet. Yet even in the Midwest men of six feet and over do not seem to have been all that common: Captain Buskirk wanted to recruit an entire company of them but had to abandon the idea as "impracticable." In the Georgia Militia there was a man seven feet, two inches in height, weighing three hundred and twenty pounds, but significantly he was called "the Georgia Giant."

A visitor to the camps of either army would be struck by the number of handicapped and infirm; when the army was on campaign many of the more lightly wounded preferred to recuperate "at home," that is, with their company and regiment; others returned from the hospital long before they should have. Still others were entitled to a discharge for disability, but they too stayed on, held by a kind of "social glue"—men like Liberty Stevens Duncan, a Confederate soldier from Tennessee who suffered the amputation of one leg in North Georgia, rejoined his regiment, and went through six more battles on crutches. So numerous were these men in the Army of Tennessee that in August 1864 its commander issued a directive for all men with only one arm or hand to "come out of the regiments" and replace able-bodied men who had been detailed to stock driving and other tasks.

We know not only how the western soldier appeared to others, but also how he saw himself. He thought of himself in comparative terms— not so much by comparison with the Southern soldier who faced him, but with what he called "Potomac men," and by this term he meant both the Easterners in Sherman's legions and those serving in the Army of the Potomac. This comparison was generated by frequent contact with the Easterners in the Twentieth Corps, contact that was very often accompanied by friction. According to one officer with General McPherson's Army of the Tennessee, "the 11th and 12th Corps Potomac men and ours never meet without some very hard talk." It was the Westerners who usually initiated these confrontations by asking the Potomac men if it wasn't time they stopped to black their shoes or if they had seen "P.J." (for "Pugnacious Joe," the Westerners' name for "Fighting Joe" Hooker). A western officer acknowledged that "the Potomac men are better bred than our men and do not retort to the same extent." But the Easterners' very forbearance could imply a disdainful superiority that provoked the Westerners all the more. The disdain was often real enough. "We cannot stand being put on a half-ration of letters," a New England officer pleaded with a female correspondent: "We shall get entirely uncivilized in this howling wilderness of Hoosiers, Buckeyes, Suckers, and Wolverines, unless you give us occasional glimpses of our eastern home. . . ."

The western soldier saw himself as frank, and indeed plainspoken, even with his superiors. His discourse, which "Potomac" officers found overfamiliar and sometimes insolent, was grounded in the view that "if a fellow is willing to stand up and be shot at, he is entitled to a little freedom of speech." Andrew Hickenlooper, an officer on General McPherson's staff, claimed that the western soldier had more "independence and contrariness" than "Potomac men," so that leading him was more of a challenge. At the same time he saw a solid loyalty and dependability in the Westerners, and there is some statistical evidence those qualities were indeed there. The western soldier's desertion rate was distinctly lower than that of the Union army generally.

Finally, the western soldier held himself to be superior in the rough and bloody business of the battlefield: "We are better fighters." The statement was made categorically and buttressed with references to the western army's past victories—and the eastern army's lack of them. The notion that the Army of the Potomac could not take Richmond because it wouldn't fight was more or less prevalent in the western army. As for Sherman's men, they gave every evidence of facing the coming campaign with confidence. Some felt the Rebels would not last the year, others felt peace was further away—but sooner or later they would win.

Extracting a self-portrait of the rank and file of the Army of Tennessee from their letters and diaries is a more daunting task. They did not have the same stimulus to comparison because they had relatively little interchange with the Army of Northern Virginia, their eastern counterpart. There are only scattered allusions to the fact the Easterners appeared to be "bandbox soldiers," which meant their uniforms came closer to regulation dress. Then too, the soldiers of the Army of Tennessee were not accustomed to thinking in terms of belonging to one region of the South or the other; to them the line of demarcation was the state line. One of the striking things the orders of battle of the opposing armies reveal is the difference in the composition of brigades. Union commanders brigaded regiments from three or four states together, with a brigade composed of troops from one state a rarity. In the Confederate army the one-state brigade was the rule. One of General Johnston's first acts as a commander was to cater to this localist tendency, shuffling brigades around so that the army had an entire division of Tennessee troops. "Hurrah, all Tennesseans again," wrote a soldier in one of the brigades. General Winfield Scott Featherston, a brigade commander from Mississippi, was offered promotion to the command of a division. "I declined," he recorded in his memoirs, "because it was not a division of Mississippi troops." In the Army of Tennessee, then, to the greatest degree possible men had the privilege of fighting alongside others from their state. If they were wounded, there was a good chance they would be sorted out and hospitalized by state. And if they died and the authorities could manage it, they would be buried the same way, Georgians here and Mississippians there.

This particularism of the Southern soldier, more deeply ingrained than that of his opponent, had adverse effects on the cohesion of the Army of Tennessee, and on that sense of identity that all armies tend to develop. The Kentucky and Tennessee regiments had already become essentially exiles—the Army's Orphan Brigade was aptly named. Kentuckians wanted to transfer to the command of John Hunt Morgan, whose raids took him into their state. Tennessee troops wanted for the same reason to join the forces of General Nathan Bedford Forrest. If they could not get transfers they would often go anyway. Several times in early 1864 officers from Tennessee regiments went to bring them back, but a surgeon in one of the Tennessee units predicted: "very few of them will stick." Texans and Arkansans were unhappy at being on the wrong side of the Mississippi. One day in January 1864 twenty Texans deserted in broad daylight; at one point that winter a massive departure by troops of the two states was imminent, and was only headed off by a strong appeal from General Patrick Cleburne. And of course Virginians and North Carolinians felt their proper place was with the Army of Northern Virginia and dreamed of transfer. "We North Carolinians and Virginians feel lost here," lamented one North Carolina soldier.

In sum, large numbers of men in the Army of Tennessee felt they were in the wrong army and too far from their home states. In the inactivity of winter quarters they tended to brood about the tribulations of their far-distant families. "Times are dull here," an Alabama soldier wrote in March 1864. "The men are so badly disheartened that a good many are leaving here of a night. Some call it deserting. Those that leave call it going to protect their families, which I think is a man's duty." The pattern of desertions that spring was sufficiently disturbing for General Johnston to make a severe example. Just before the campaign opened he had fourteen North Carolinians executed as deserters. They were shot, sitting blindfolded on their coffins, while several thousand of their comrades watched.

If to these sources of discontent within the Army of Tennessee we add a harsh winter passed in privation and the memory of a disastrous defeat that ended the previous campaign—a defeat at the hands of a foe who would be returning to the field more formidable than before—we can only ask what must have been the state of the Southern army's morale as it began the campaign of 1864. There is good reason to believe that it was as reported to an Alabama newspaper by a soldier-correspondent: "The army is dirty, but well fed, saucy, jolly, full of fight, with a sublime and unwavering faith in Joe Johnston." The rank and file of the Army of Tennessee embarked on the 1864 campaign with high hopes and good morale; on this point their letters and diaries leave little doubt. Their actions too reveal a surprisingly buoyant, exuberant youth in that third year of the war. The campaign was not a week old when a Tennessee soldier recorded in his diary: "During the fight our skirmishers were hollowing, neighing, crowing, barking, gobbling and cheering for the benefit of the Yanks."

One of the best antidotes to low morale had been to take the troops out of winter quarters and lead them into the field. Army physicians knew that in periods of inactivity soldiers tended to develop a kind of depression; they called it "nostalgia" and thought of it as a disease characterized by a morbid preoccupation with the soldier's home and induced by the monotony of winter camps. Army doctors also noted that "even the rumor of an intended movement generally sufficed to ruffle the mental surface . . . and arouse the men to their wonted activities and energies." So in the spring of 1864 the orders to leave winter quarters came as a tonic to both armies. When it was rumored that a Wisconsin unit would leave Huntsville, Alabama, for the front, the soldiers in it could not contain themselves. One of them wrote in his diary: "once the excitement gets up, there is a general impatience to be on the way"; Huntsville was by then jammed with troops, and "broils and squabbles" between impatient soldiers were becoming frequent; finally the order came, and they marched off to the war in Georgia like schoolboys on an outing.

If it's not too hard, then, to understand the enthusiasm that came with the return of active campaigning, there are other reasons why those spirits did not flag after that particularly grueling campaign got under way. Part of the explanation may lie in the optimism and the resilience of youth, but it also rests on a sustained delusion, a substructure of myth that made things look better than they were in both armies. Objectively speaking, there was little to be cheery about with a return to the blood-letting, particularly in the Southern camp, but the soldier's view of the war was anything but objective. He was uninformed, but more than that he was misinformed. Military officialdom was in part responsible. Just as the 1864 campaign was getting under way General Sherman had read to all commands a dispatch from Virginia that said in effect that Grant had whipped Lee at Spotsylvania. Feeling expansive at the news, one soldier went out to share it with others. But as he noted in his diary, he "learned from 2 Reb prisoners that they had similar news—that is that Lee had whipped Grant and was within three miles of Washington." The newspapers also felt it their duty to highlight victories and minimize reverses, and the soldiers in both armies read the newspapers, which were sometimes hawked in the very trenches.

But the troops themselves were selective about the news items they tended to dwell on and pass on to others—and these tended to be positive in content and tone. In the Southern army the loss of the *Alabama* and the death of General Jeb Stuart were not events the men lingered over or commented on in their letters and diaries—though they got extensive commentary in the trenches opposite. Then too, both armies were constantly swept by rumors, some of them elaborate distortions surrounding a kernel of truth, others completely groundless. These were more often than not "good news" items as well; at least it is the good rumors that find echo in what the men wrote. Thus it was usually the enemy general who was reported killed or captured, the enemy's capital that was in imminent peril.

A Northern officer noted this tendency in the workings of the rumor mill and suggested that it was a reflection of the Northern army's supreme self-confidence, that it rarely generated bad news about itself. But things were no different in the Southern army: reinforcements were always on the way to them, not to the army opposite, etc. It seems likely the wish was father to the rumor, that good news, real or imaginary, was prevalent in both camps simply because the men were inclined to savor such things and share them with others; the soldiery of both armies was thus wrapped in a cocoon of half-truth and hearsay largely of their own making. Men new to the army and its ways railed over the way they were kept in ignorance: "We still do not know what is to be done with us," "We have been told nothing"; the veterans seem to have been more satisfied with army rumor, with "grapevine," which they analyzed, refined, and passed on at their leisure.

For the veterans had acquired their own way of looking at things, their own "mindset." They had kept their youth and buoyant spirits but had lost a certain innocence. They had "seen the elephant," to use the then-current expression, and in the process many of them had acquired an armor of coarseness and cynicism. Having seen more suffering and death than most men would in a lifetime, they accepted these things in their day-to-day existence; thus a lieutenant from Illinois was not being dramatic when he wrote in his diary: "in eight days I'll be twenty-two years old, if alive." Sometimes the men's letters home must have struck the recipients as blasé, even callous. "I was very sorry to hear of bro. Sam's great misfortune in losing his leg," an Alabama soldier wrote his sister, "but better a leg than life."

Death seems to have touched the men emotionally only if it struck a brother or a comrade beside them. It would interest them as a curiosity only if it came in some bizarre way or form. The men in the Fifty-third Ohio told of one of their number struck in the head and killed instantly, the ball making a noise on impact that was heard in three different companies. "It sounded as if someone had been struck in the face with an open hand." There were stories of dead men found in bizarre positions and places, like the Rebel soldier who had been discovered on his knees behind a stump at Shiloh. He had been struck while in the act of loading his rifle; he still had his bullet clenched in his teeth and his cartridge in his hand: "We couldn't straighten him out so we buried him just so." Then there was the coarsening effect of life on campaign, sleeping without a bed, and eating crouched in a ditch, living in an extemporized warrior society cruder than the milieu most of them had left.

Nominally the regiment was the soldier's home, it was his address, the smallest easily distinguishable unit to which he belonged—but the company was a smaller, more intimate home, and its members were his family; it was here that the social glue was strongest of all. The company usually had a closeness and homogeneity from the start, for the men were often from the same village or township and already knew one another. Nominally a company was composed of a hundred men, but by 1864 a sixty-man company was a "big" company. Not all the losses had come from casualties in the strict sense of the word. There had been many departures for other reasons: "The thin-skinned man, who could not take a joke, wore himself out with homesickness and was discharged, and the quarrelsome camp-bully deserted long ago."

The cohesion, the "oneness" of this little society was achieved at some cost: In their common language and behavior, in their shared attitudes about what to admire and what to ridicule, they took the lowest common denominator; some had their pretensions ground away, others developed calluses over their sensibilities. But the half-hundred comrades who emerged from the crucible had forged the strongest and most lasting of bonds. State officials in Tennessee learned just how durable those bonds could be when they circulated questionnaires to Civil War veterans about the time of the First World War. After half a century the old soldiers had difficulties with the questions; their recollections were often hazy and garbled. But when asked to name the members of their company, they brightened up and reeled off names with remarkable facility.

So strong were the bonds that many of the veterans who got leave and returned home in the first months of 1864 soon found themselves thinking about the "boys"; the younger, single men particularly were not sorry to start back to what had become their other home. If both armies had a constant stream of stragglers and deserters headed away, there was always a stream of men hurrying back to their units, partly from obligation and loyalty, but also because they just wanted to get back to "the boys." Just before the campaign opened, one such man returned to General Johnston's army after an absence of several months: He had been wounded and captured at Missionary Ridge, but had managed to slip out of a Union army hospital in Chattanooga. Traveling only at night, he had made the seventy-mile trip to Dalton on crutches.

The company and the regiment constituted a coign of vantage from which the "boys" looked at the military world about them and the civilian world beyond. As experienced practitioners of the art of war, the men were quick to judge the military competence of others. They were quick to ridicule the recruits and conscripts who arrived that spring, greeting them with the cry "fresh fish." Union veterans went by the hundreds to take a look at the Seventy-first Ohio, which had spent all its time on garrison and outpost duty and was new to the battlefront. In the Seventy-first a corporal was obeyed with an alacrity an officer could not expect in a veteran regiment. No swearing was allowed in the Seventy-first, and the soldiers stood "all day with their knapsacks and cartridge belts on." The judgment of the old soldiers: They were "green, greener than hundred-day men." The men of the Army of Tennessee had essentially the same way of looking at the Georgia Militia, which joined them in the field. The militia never appeared without provoking jest and ridicule, despite the fact that overall its performance was good.

The infantrymen, who were the combat soldiers par excellence, had only contempt for those in the army who did little or no fighting, and they generally included the cavalry in this group as well as quartermasters, provost guards, and the like. And as front-line troops they had very little patience with the rear echelon: A Union veteran recalled that when the men reached Louisville on their way home for furlough, they were told they could not take their "contraband" cooks and servants with them across the Ohio River. They faced down the provost guard: "When we were marched to the ferry-boat, a cordon of guns surrounded each darkey, and the provost, seeing the determined looks of the men, overlooked the contrabands and they were soon free men on Indiana soil."

And the men did not hesitate to pass judgment on those who led them. In both armies the qualities the men looked for in the commanding general were essentially cerebral ones; they wanted him to have intelligence, foresight, a gift for divining the enemy's intentions, and the mysterious coup d'oeil, the ability to read the terrain and use it to greatest profit. Such a general would send them into battle when they had the greatest chance of winning—and surviving. In Generals Sherman and Johnston both armies had leaders who seemed to possess these qualities—"my men think I know everything," Sherman said to a Southern clergyman. Once this belief was solidly planted, the confidence in the leader could become blind and unswerving; about General Johnston there emerged a myth of omniscience that has never been completely dispelled. "Although we can't understand General Johnston's movements," wrote a Tennessee officer, "yet our confidence in him is not impaired one particle." And so as Johnston executed one retrograde movement after the other that spring—because he could not do anything else—his troops marveled at the sagacity with which "Old Joe" drew Sherman forward to his doom.

Sherman's men admired in him that same sagacity, though they did not accord to him the sort of veneration Johnston enjoyed. A Union officer named Albion Tourgee wrote of his commander: "He seemed to forget nothing, to neglect nothing, to foresee everything . . . An infinitude of detail, instead of wearying him, seemed to stimulate him to new activity." The army knew in a vague way that Sherman had taught in a military academy; this prewar experience in Louisiana was transformed and magnified. Soon the rumor ran that he had taught at the Georgia Military Institute in Marietta, where among his students were some of the Confederate generals now opposing him. And now he was about to give them another lesson.

Sherman inspired confidence in those he led, but apparently no wild enthusiasm. An officer with the 103rd Illinois noted at the opening of the campaign: "The men think more of Sherman than of any general who ever commanded them; but they did not cheer him." An officer-journalist named David Conyngham noted the same thing. While Sherman was in fact cheered by his men from time to time, he did not get the wildly effusive reception other generals sometimes received. Conyngham thought Sherman was not saluted in this way because he was too cold and austere, but there is any amount of evidence to the contrary. He was eminently approachable; soldiers coming from the rear often asked him where they could find their units. Oddly enough, there is good reason to believe that it was his appearance that deprived him of the more enthusiastic ovations. A comment of the chaplain of the Fifty-eighth Indiana is highly indicative. He saw the general pass and was not impressed: "He had new clothing and looked neater than he had ever appeared to me before, but at his best there were no signs of outward greatness. He is a very ordinary man."

Who in Sherman's army possessed the appearance, the outward trappings of greatness? "Fighting Joe" Hooker, for one, with his "fine martial bearing," as Conyngham described it. One day a rumor circulated in the Twentieth Corps that Hooker had been badly wounded, but the next morning he and his glittering retinue came by "riding the lines," to be greeted by a tremendous ovation. A New York soldier who was there wrote: "Such chering and yeling i never hird." Another who enjoyed such acclamation was General John A. Logan with his dark, flowing mane, and still another was General Lovell Rousseau: "His fine physique, noble bearing, his thoroughbred horse and gorgeous trappings caught their eyes and roused their enthusiasm."

Western soldiers also liked to see in their leaders a democratic streak. They liked General McPherson because he never obliged a column of infantry to abandon the road to him and his staff; he always skirted the road himself. They liked General Stanley because once within his hearing a soldier had wondered what time it was and Stanley had taken out his watch and told him, thus demonstrating that he was "not too high up to notice any soldier." A lieutenant in the Fifty-ninth Illinois boasted that in Sherman's army it was possible to see "real, live major generals . . . talking cheerily and interestingly with privates in the rear ranks."

The senior leaders in Sherman's army seem to have understood the importance of cultivating the men under them. "Political" generals with the savoir faire of John M. Palmer or John A. Logan were old hands at playing to the crowd. And among the "regulars" we find Hooker "continually among the troops," where he has "a friendly nod for the men and a kind word for the officers." And Sherman himself did not hesitate to make flattering remarks to his troops that they could be counted on to repeat. He told a group of artillerymen whose battery he visited: "I would rather be a gunner of this battery than to be a Major General of the Rebel Army." Sherman's opposite, Joe Johnston, though a somewhat formal and distant man, seems to have taken much the same tack; he told Governor Brown, where he was sure to be overheard, that with the quality of the troops he had, he would not need much by way of defensive fortifications.

In the Confederate service the various corps, divisions, and brigades carried the names of their commanders, thus Hardee's Corps, Cantey's Brigade, etc. The practice has a vaguely feudal ring to it, and in a way the custom was a fitting one. With the more popular commanders at least, one has the impression that the Southern soldier felt his loyalty and obedience were personal and direct—a kind of fealty. With leaders like Frank Cheatham and Patrick Cleburne, for example, it was emphatically not the stars on their collars that commanded obedience, but the charisma of their persons. If such a leader were to leave the army, on the eve of his departure his men would come by the hundreds and stand awkwardly around his tent to bid him farewell. If he returned after a month's absence recuperating from a wound—a fairly common occurrence—his reception would be tumultuous; the men would swarm about him noisily, trying to touch him, even embracing his horse. This sort of effusiveness seems to have been peculiar to the Southern soldier. What quality was it in the leader that inspired such devotion? More than anything else it seems to have been the most basic quality of the soldier—raw courage.

If sagacity was the characteristic that the men looked for in their supreme commander, the man who sent them into battle, then they wanted to see bravery in those subordinate commanders who led them into the field. This was true of the men in both armies, but if we may believe Colonel St. Leger Grenfell, a British officer serving in Johnston's army, the Southern soldier was particularly demanding in this regard. Colonel Fremantle, who talked with Grenfell at length, recorded his views as follows:

> Colonel Grenfell told me that the only way in which an officer could acquire influence over Confederate soldiers was by his personal conduct under fire. They hold a man in great esteem who in action sets them an example of contempt for danger; but they think nothing of an officer who is not in the habit of leading them; in fact, such a man could not possibly retain his position. Colonel Grenfell's expression was "every atom of authority has to be purchased by a drop of your blood."

The general officers of the Army of Tennessee seem to have made a particularly heavy payment in blood. At least a score of them would be killed in 1864; among them there was an impressive contingent of the permanently disabled and disfigured: John Bell Hood, with a leg gone and a near-useless arm; W. W. Loring, with an arm missing; William B. Bate, on crutches since his hips were shattered at Shiloh; Thomas C. Hindman, limping along with one leg shorter than the other; W. H. T. Walker, hobbling and pain-wracked from a variety of wounds, some of them going all the way back to the Seminole War—"literally shot to pieces" in the words of Colonel Avery; Pat Cleburne, disfigured by a singular wound received at Richmond, Kentucky: As he was shouting a command a bullet entered his open mouth and exited through his left cheek, knocking five teeth out of his lower jaw. To this list could be added those whose scars and infirmities were less obvious, plus those temporarily disabled and recuperating on leave, or limping about like General E. C. Walthall, who had received a ball in the foot at Missionary Ridge.

From tactical considerations these men sometimes had no choice but to expose themselves to enemy fire, but some of them also felt a moral compunction, an obligation to set the right example for others. Colonel T. B. Roy, who was General Hardee's adjutant general and son-in-law, said

Hardee felt he should always be at the point of greatest danger to his command. General A. P. Stewart wrote a friend after a bitter contest at New Hope Church: "I am vain enough to believe that my own example inspired my men. So at least it is said." Many felt the obligation to remain mounted during an action, a practice that made them more likely targets for enemy fire. Such was the case with General Hood, who often invited his staff to dismount and take cover but did not join them (it took the efforts of two or three men to remove the crippled general from his horse).

Bravery was also at a premium in the blue army, and those who led it probably paid about the same blood price as their Southern counterparts: In the course of the campaign Sherman's regimental, brigade, division, and corps commands—something over five hundred commands— had an average of eight changes a day, with 165 officers killed, wounded or captured and 56 others sent to the rear for illness or mustering out.

The risks were understood and accepted by leaders in both armies. Sherman warned his wife: "I daily pass death in the most familiar shape and you should base your calculations on that event." Hardee, on the other hand, tried to reassure his wife that with General Leonidas Polk's death his own chances of survival actually increased, though his logic is not easy to follow. However they figured their chances, the stress on leaders must have been considerable and the ways of easing it limited. Alcohol was a relief for many and a problem for more than a few. Colonel Grenfell told Colonel Fremantle that several Southern generals were "somewhat addicted to alcohol." General Cheatham was one of this number, for his men occasionally noted in their diaries that he had been drinking. The men who served under Union General William Ward sometimes called him "Old Shaky," but the term was used affectionately.

Both Northern and Southern soldiers were suspicious of leaders who were West Point graduates or veterans of the regular army. An Illinois soldier named Levi Ross explained why the men did not like their division commander, Jefferson C. Davis: "He is a regular army officer and therefore unpopular with volunteers. He has the reputation of being unsympathetic, overbearing and tyrannical." (General John Geary, though of civilian background, was known and disliked among the western soldiers for the same reasons.) In the Army of Tennessee General W. H. T. Walker had something of the same bad reputation. The man who served as his orderly in 1864 said when he took the job he had already heard "a good deal about the General's quick temper and stern ways"; an officer on his staff recalled Walker made far too frequent use of courts-martial.

In both armies the men disliked rigid disciplinarians. They could virtually be counted upon to react violently when their superiors—of whatever rank—applied cruel and humiliating punishments such as "bucking and gagging," in which the offending soldier was trussed up like a fowl and left on display for hours. Sherman's men felt such punishments might be suitable for "regulars," but for volunteers they were intolerable. One day in December 1863 the captain of I Company, Seventy-ninth Ohio, ordered a man tied up by his thumbs for two hours. A corporal who was there related the outcome: "This so enraged the whole company, or the greater portion of it, that they went and cut him down." The Southern soldier's attitude toward such things as stringing a man up by his thumbs was similar: "To see a white man, a volunteer serving the Confederacy, subjected to a punishment that public opinion would have considered brutal even on a negro slave . . . went to our hearts." No less a figure than General Johnston stirred the soldier's anger that spring when he authorized the placing of men in stocks as punishment. It was apparently inflicted mainly on deserters, and certainly preferable to execution. But the men didn't see it that way; time after time they would liberate the prisoners and destroy or carry off the stocks.

If the antagonism between the men and some superior reached sufficient intensity, there could be violence of another form: In the heat of battle, or whenever there was enough confusion and random firing to mask their action, they would try to kill him. At least two soldiers admitted after the war that they had shot at General Geary—and missed. General Jefferson C. Davis also passed for a hard taskmaster; some who served under him spoke hopefully of his "meeting with an accident." An Ohio major wrote his wife in July 1864 that as he came back to his breastworks after leading an assault "some miserable traitor with murder stamped upon his countenance deliberately shot at me." And two decades after Appomattox a Confederate veteran recounted a murder conspiracy involving his entire company. Their intended victim, their lieutenant, had ridden a popular sergeant unmercifully. The men urged the sergeant to kill the lieutenant in cold blood, but instead he challenged him to a duel—and got the guardhouse for his pains. The hapless sergeant subsequently deserted, and the men heard that he had been killed by the provost guard as he was burying his daughter. They then resolved to kill the lieutenant themselves as soon as they found an opportunity. But before they could act a Yankee shell landed in their midst, killing the lieutenant without harming any of the score of men about him. This they saw as "divine retribution," God settling their accounts for them.

With volunteer armies composed of men such as these, the giving of an order did not automatically lead to its prompt and faithful execution, particularly if it went against the grain. This is clear in an account of a minor cavalry action just before the beginning of the campaign: "Col. Murry tried to get them [the Third Kentucky Cavalry] to make a sabre charge but they thought the rebs were two strong and would not go. He then told the 92nd to draw their sabers and charge. Some of the boys told him we had no sabers. he said charge any how and awy we went or the most of us. some few did not go." Men due to be mustered out soon did not think they should have to do heavy fighting in their final days of service; if given the order to assault the enemy works they would refuse (several Union companies and regiments did just that in the Atlanta campaign). Or the men could negate the effects of an order they did not like: If, toward the end of a long, hard march, the regiment was about to pass through a town and the colonel ordered the men to put on their coats and straighten their ranks so as to impress the locals, the men would resent the order and let their resentment show. They would clown about, marching with exaggerated awkwardness until the colonel was "almost ready to burst." Or they could interpret an order in their own fashion, often simplifying it and at the same time altering its scope and effect; much of the indiscriminate pillaging done by both sides during the Georgia campaign had its origin in orders for foraging. As General Sherman said when the campaign was over, "these men are of no common sort, for they think for themselves. . . ."

In fine, these amateur soldiers would not give blind obedience—that was for "hireling" soldiers (the Union volunteers had even more contempt for "regulars" in their midst than they had for rear echelon troops). In these attitudes and in their way of looking at things generally the soldiers had perhaps most in common with those they faced across the skirmish line. At the same time they had the least in common with the civilian world from which they had come. The visit of civilians in camp and bivouac was noted, but with no pleasure; the visitors seemed so many intruders. Should a civilian appear on the battlefield, somehow he seemed shockingly out of place. When the soldiers ventured into the civilian world, they frequently behaved as if they were out of place. Their appearance there was often a raucous, rowdy eruption, with occasional free-for-alls and broken furniture; there had been any number of complaints when Northern units returned home on furlough in the first months of 1864. It was not simply that the soldiers had forgotten how to behave; they seemed almost to be spoiling for a fight (this phenomenon occurred only when the soldiers were in groups; when they appeared singly among civilians there was never any problem).

It has been suggested that this conduct betrays a kind of resentment of men who were in a sense outcasts from civil society; or it may simply reflect the resentment of that hapless minority that has put on the uniform to do the fighting and dying for all the others. For whatever reason, the estrangement could have serious consequences for civilians, whether the soldiers they encountered were nominally friend or enemy. For the soldier had developed a certain detachment, a certain lack of concern and empathy regarding them and their problems. Beyond that, he had developed a certain predatory instinct. The population of Tennessee had discovered this in the course of the preceding campaign; now the people of Georgia would learn it in their turn.

4

From Dalton to the Chattahoochee

Whoever would follow in detail the operational history of the Atlanta campaign would find it a story with an infinity of twists and turns. In the literal sense this is certainly true: A postwar calculation by the U.S. Engineers revealed that though the distance from Dalton to Atlanta is one hundred miles, the various Union army corps, with their "average distance traversed in maneuvering," marched 178 miles in getting from the one place to the other. The combat history of the campaign is an unusually intricate one. The editors of the *Official Records* identified in the period May 1–July 17 one battle (Resaca), one engagement, one affair, three demonstrations, three sets of operations, six actions, twenty-four combats, and thirty-three skirmishes, plus other combats and skirmishes not identified as to number or place. All of this would fill a very large book, and such a book is Albert Castel's scrupulous and exhaustive *Decision in the West*, the vade mecum for those who want to follow the marches and battles in all their details.

What struck those who fought in the campaign, and what concerns us here, was not its complexities—most were not aware of them—but its relentless continuity; all the engagements and skirmishes seemed to merge into one, for if the soldiers had a basic impression of the war in North Georgia it was of one endless, unrelieved struggle, rather than of distinct clashes separated by periods of relative inactivity—though in fact there were brief respites, as when Sherman let his army rest from May 20 to May 23. Seven weeks into the campaign Sherman himself described it to a correspondent as "one grand skirmish," while in the ranks they sometimes spoke of fighting a never-ending "battle of Georgia." In their letters home the men would speak with only slight overstatement of "a hundred continuous days under fire" (others went a bit further, claiming that they had grown so accustomed to the din of musketry and cannon that if it stopped in the middle of the night they would wake up instantly). This unending battle was all the more remarkable to them for the contrast it offered with their experience of earlier campaigns. Chesley Mosman, an observant young officer in the Fifty-ninth Illinois Infantry, found the new campaign very different from the previous two and a half years of campaigning: "Then we would move out and fight and after the battle wait for three or six months, recuperating and pluming ourselves on our valiant fight or great victory before starting out again." The medical director of the Army of the Cumberland, who was well-placed to see the extraordinary demands the campaign placed on the men's health and stamina, said that in this respect it had "no parallel" in previous operations. He could provide figures to back up his argument: Of the seventy-one thousand men in General George Thomas's Army of the Cumberland, forty-three thousand were sufficiently sick to require hospitalization during the campaign.

Then there was continuity of another sort. The impulsion, the initiative, always seemed to come from the Northern side, and when the battle lines shifted the new positions always seemed to be a little closer to Atlanta. Albion Tourgee of the 105th Ohio was struck by this phenomenon: "In all this hundred miles from Dalton to Atlanta, there was never any backward movement on the part of the Union Army. Every day, almost every hour, it gained a little." And what was one advance after another by the Federals was an uninterrupted succession of retreats by the Southern army that ultimately eroded its morale.

Finally participants noticed a certain cyclical quality; they kept doing the same sequence of things over and over again, each time in a different place. There was the sequence of marching, entrenching, and fighting that seemed to be the soldier's daily fare. So regular was this cycle that some compared the operations in North Georgia to the repetitive steps in a siege. Then the campaign incorporated the flanking operations that became its hallmark. In effect, there was a series of major flanking movements beginning with General McPherson's march to the south of General Johnston's forces concentrated at Dalton (May 7–12), which compelled Johnston to withdraw to Resaca; the second occurred when Sherman passed to the west of the impregnable Confederate position astride the Western and Atlantic at Allatoona, compelling the Confederates to shift in turn to cover Atlanta—a maneuver that led to the particularly hard fighting in the Dallas–Mount Hope Church region and ultimately brought the Federals back to the railroad at Acworth (May 23–June 12); the third occasion was the threats Sherman presented to Johnston's left and right flanks successively (July 3–17), compelling him to take his forces south of the Chattahoochee and bringing the Union army to the gates of Atlanta. The soldiers in both armies understood these maneuvers; by the end of the campaign the word "flank" was a stock word in their vocabularies. The population of North Georgia had learned the term too, though their grasp of it was not always firm. An old mountain woman once told a group of bluecoats their army did not fight fair because it used a "flanking machine," which when put in place shot Southern soldiers "endwise."

Yet few imagined that there was anything immutable about the campaign, or that a flow of events was carrying them all inexorably to Atlanta, a mile at a time. There were at least two occasions when the pattern came close to being broken in a spectacular way. Had General McPherson been more aggressive in his march on Resaca, had he wrecked the railroad that was both the supply line and the avenue of retreat for the Confederate army, that army might have received a mortal blow at the very outset. And the whole rank and file of the Southern army was witness to General Johnston's electrifying decision to stand and fight at Cassville on May 19. He had a proclamation read to his soldiers that morning saying that the series of retreats before the enemy was over: "You will now turn and march to meet his advancing columns." Then Johnston changed his mind and resumed his retreat. Both of these episodes were much discussed at the time and have continued to intrigue historians attracted by the "what if" questions. The soldiers in both armies and their leaders as well continued to expect a "great battle" that would decide the campaign in a single day of fearful carnage.

A decision General Sherman made before the campaign opened virtually guaranteed that it would be a hard one for his troops. He resolved to take into Georgia the largest possible force that his logistical system could support, his goal being to have two soldiers for every one in the Southern army. Sherman was taking a hundred thousand men into the field, supplying them over a long and tenuous lifeline: over three hundred miles of single-track railway passing through guerrilla-infested territory. The army's needs would have to be reduced to the essential and the force stripped of "impedimenta," as Sherman called it. Even then there would be little margin for error, and here the general did considerable figuring with car loadings, consumption rates for rations, munitions, and the like. Some of his contemporaries were dubious; General Halleck estimated that no more than sixty thousand or seventy thousand troops could be supplied on a single-track rail line; after that "the difficulty of supply is great." The authors of a later monograph on Sherman's logistics concluded the whole operation was "without precedent in military history." Though Sherman has sometimes been charged with strategic oversights and with fiddling about when with more decisiveness he might have ended his campaign sooner, one can only admire his boldness and resolution in letting a huge army's survival hang by such a slender thread—and one can appreciate the jealousy with which he guarded that fragile and indispensable rail line stretching behind him.

Sherman's General Order No. 6, dated April 6, 1864, essentially reserved the railroad for military use (President Lincoln asked him to make an exception and transport food for Unionist inhabitants of Tennessee but Sherman refused). As a rule the cars were reserved for the army's supplies, with priority given to the heavily laden "down cars." Soldiers returning from furlough found they had to rejoin their regiments in Georgia by foot—and in a further economy measure the returning soldiers were turned into cattle guards for herds of steers being driven south—or if they were allowed on the train it was generally on top of the cars rather than in them, what was called "deck passage." Sitting on the roof the men were treated to what someone called "the full benefits of sun, rain and cinders"; they also had a prospect of asphyxiation when their wood-burning steam locomotive pulled them through a long tunnel. No passenger cars were allowed south of Nashville, though the Army of the Cumberland had specially designed hospital cars for transporting the wounded. Sherman's two other armies and the Confederates used boxcars whose floors were covered with straw; since it was not possible for the attending surgeon to pass from one of these boxcars to the next while the train was in motion, he had to make hurried rounds whenever there was a stop. Nor did Sherman intend for the railway to be encumbered by the transportation of the dead; the shipment of bodies north for reinterment was prohibited before October 31.

Since the transportation of fodder was particularly onerous (Sherman calculated a horse consumed fifteen pounds per day), cavalrymen, artillerymen, and mule skinners received limited rations for their animals and instructions to look for forage locally, an arrangement that opened the door to marauding and pillage. Army rations for the men consisted chiefly of food that was easily transportable or would transport itself, such as herds of cattle. The rations shipped by rail were compact and imperishable—hardtack, preserved meat, coffee, and sugar—a virtual recipe for scurvy. The Southern soldier's ration of corn bread and pork was no better in this regard, so both armies suffered from this malady. Antiscorbutics such as apples and fresh vegetables were carried on the Federal commissary's inventory, but seem to have made their way to the front only rarely. A Union soldier from Missouri found it worth noting in his diary that on July 5: "Each soldier in our brigade received a pickle." Sherman was probably not exaggerating when he claimed he had seen his men fight pitched battles for control of a blackberry patch. Southern troops, more acquainted with the region's plants, varied their diet with pokeweed, potato tops, maypop vines, and other plants found locally. Scurvy disappeared from the armies only when Georgia's green corn crop came in.

In his memoirs written a decade later Sherman said that he doubted if there was any occasion when another army "went forth to battle with fewer impedimenta; and where the regular and necessary supplies of food, ammunition, and clothing were issued, as called for, so regularly, and so well"; but shortly after the campaign ended he confessed to Colonel Horace Porter: "We did get a little short of rations at times on the march down here." In the regiments the shortages were also noted. The campaign was not forty-eight hours old when an officer in the 105th Illinois recorded: "they have cut us down to three-quarter rations of bread and one-fourth rations of meat." Similar entries appeared intermittently in soldiers' letters and diaries through June, along with notations that "the boys are grumbling," "the men don't like it," etc. It is quite possible that in the first weeks of the campaign the Confederate army was the better supplied of the two; at least there was less grumbling among the Rebels.

The effect of short rations on the horses in Sherman's army was telling, especially in the opening weeks, when the campaigning was in a region that supplied little forage (once the army got south of the Etowah, where the country was more settled and cultivated, the forage problem eased). In the Seventh Pennsylvania Cavalry the horses were going without food for four and five days running, at the end of which time they "peeled bark from the trees. They ate dry leaves. They chewed at the bridle reins and the picket lines." By June 1 the brigade to which the Seventh was attached had had fifty horses fall in the road from inanition. At that same time an artilleryman with an Illinois battery recalled: "our horses were beginning to eat up the carriage wheels whenever they could get to them."

The Union soldier left on campaign equipped with little more than what he carried, and it proved insufficient. The medical department claimed the men were not supplied with enough cooking gear to prepare their meals properly, hence higher rates of illness. Clothing wore out rapidly during the campaign, and more was not forthcoming from the quartermaster. Union soldiers took to doing what Southern soldiers did, writing home for clothing to be sent to them. Among Sherman's railway regulations was one limiting to one car per day the space allocated for sutler's goods. This was not adequate to supply the soldier's needs in writing paper, envelopes, playing cards, and other items—so the men wrote home for these as well. The sutler was also the chief source of tobacco. Union soldiers who indulged swore there was not a single sutler to be found south of Chattanooga. In their desperation those who chewed tried the bark and roots of various plants; those who smoked tried filling their pipes with ground coffee. The smokers and chewers wrote home too, and must have waited for the mails with a special impatience. But they could have a long wait, for Sherman had another regulation limiting the shipment of parcels and packages to officers and men to one carload per day. Everyone on the Union side knew there was plenty of tobacco among the troops opposing them, so the impulsion to make informal truces and do some trading with the Rebels was strong.

The terrain of North Georgia initially posed a good many problems for the infantry of both armies. Little had been done to prepare the men for heavy campaigning beyond exercises on the drill ground and practice on the firing ranges, and particularly there had been no extensive road marches to harden the men for what lay ahead. In addition starchy rations and sedentary camp life had made many soldiers put on pounds; in their letters home they confessed they were "stouter" than usual. So the first days on the roads of North Georgia were exhausting; in both armies men fell out along the roadsides and came straggling into their regiments well into the evening. The track of the Union forces in particular was marked by overcoats and other gear discarded along the roadside. For William J. Norrell, a forty-one-year-old merchant who had recently joined the Sixty-third Georgia, every hill was a Calvary. On May 25 he confided to his diary that on the previous day's march he "completely broke down and had to fall out and rest several times." Three days later he was doing no better: "Climbing the hills would almost break my legs and take my breath." But the men soon grew accustomed to marches of twenty miles, and as the battlefront shifted south the terrain was less of a challenge; but by then a new challenge had appeared—the heat. There were complaints even in early May, but when a prolonged rainy spell ended late in June the sun reappeared as a redoubtable enemy. A regiment might depart six hundred strong, but when it arrived at its destination there would be fewer than a hundred with the colors, the rest strung out behind, felled by the heat. But the hospitals treated very few cases of sunstroke or heat exhaustion:

> Your old soldier, when in this condition, drops out of the column, throws aside his gun, and stretches himself at full length in the shade of some tree, where he lies alternately fanning himself and sipping his stock of water. By the time he has finished his canteen he is quite recovered, and as he has no desire to be challenged by the division provost guard, he immediately returns to the road, rejoining his command most likely at its next resting place.

In the first days of the campaign there was considerable marching and countermarching by Union columns, with the men cursing their officers under their breath and their officers trying to figure out if they had taken the right road in the right direction. Competent and trustworthy guides were next to impossible to find; blacks, who were regarded as most reliable, were a very small part of the local population. Maps of the region were often misleading. Federal mapmakers had drawn a wide, direct road leading from Snake Creek Gap to Resaca when no such road existed. "Our maps are all wrong," an angry Sherman wrote at one point, "the quicker we get our surveys up the better" (General Thomas's well-equipped cartographers revised their maps steadily, turning out new editions by the hundreds, using a photocopying process). General Johnston was also a victim of inaccurate maps at least once. He planned to make a stand near Adairsville where the terrain appeared to favor him but found when he examined it that he had been misled.

Strangely enough many natural features in North Georgia—hills, creeks, fords, and the like—still had no names, or at least that is what the locals said. A small abandoned settlement just inside the Georgia line fell into that category, so Federal mule skinners who stopped there gave it the name "Desolation." Those places that bore names did not always show up on Northern maps, so that generals and their staffs had to puzzle over the discrepancies. Most soldiers had even less idea where they were, and some contented themselves with dating their letters from "Wilderness of Georgia," "In the woods as usual," etc. Any number of the place names had a bizarre, primitive ring: Jug Tavern, Shakerag, Dogdip, Possum Snout, Trickum. A Southern soldier wrote an acquaintance in June that it looked like the great battle everyone was expecting would occur soon "in the vicinity of Big Shanty," adding, "What a name for a victory!" Would place names in the West enter into song and story as had those in the East? A Southern soldier-poet who signed himself "Squash" offered reassurance on this point:

All quiet along the Potomac tonight
Was touching and filled the heart with delight;
But glory of glories, how pale grows the cheek,
As all is serene on Pumpkinvine Creek.

While we have sketched out the salient features of the war in North Georgia, we have yet to place the soldier in what he himself would have acknowledged was his true habitat and setting. If asked where he spent the spring and summer of 1864 he would have answered unhesitatingly, "In the ditches." It was not just that he lived there, but that these field fortifications—his and those of his enemy a few hundred yards in front of him—were his chief preoccupation as a soldier: If his were strong enough, if the enemy's were not too strong, the chances were he and his buddies would survive.

Such fortifications had figured in military manuals since Roman times. The Continental army had got its first extensive experience with them at Yorktown, and more recently, in the Crimean War, they had figured prominently in the struggle over the great fortress of Sebastopol. But Yorktown and Sebastopol were sieges; the Americans now used fortifications in the open field, a practice General Sherman claimed was "peculiar to America." He also described the rather impromptu way they were erected:

Troops, halting for the night or for battle, faced the enemy; moved forward to ground with a good outlook to the front; stacked arms; gathered logs, stumps, fence rails, anything which could stop a bullet; piled these to their front, and, digging a ditch behind, threw the dirt forward, and made a parapet which covered their persons as perfectly as a granite wall.

Traditionally an army in the field was found in one of three "modes": If it was in movement it would be in columns of march; if it was at rest it would be encamped and surrounded by a chain of pickets, or it would be deployed in order of battle, usually behind a screen of skirmishers. The system of field fortifications that emerged during the war had the effect of merging these two latter modes, so that an army could be constantly ready for battle, yet so disposed that it could subsist and the soldiers could "live" after a fashion for an indefinite period. Many of the soldiers in the western armies had learned this way of warfare during the Vicksburg campaign, but there were regiments newly created or new to the front that had never seen a rifle pit. The system was in a state of constant evolution; thus the single line described above by Sherman was by the summer of 1864 two lines and sometimes three; the line of pickets or skirmishers was itself in the process of becoming a fortified line, with the men sheltered in rifle pits or "gopher holes" and shielded with small earthworks or piles of fence rails. To man these elaborate emplacements properly required the commitment of about five thousand soldiers per mile. As time went on more work and more specialized labor—that of pioneer units—added further refinements: "head logs," mounted so as to leave the defenders vulnerable only through their narrow firing slit, emplacements for cannon, cleared fields of fire, and sharpened stakes and other obstacles to impede the enemy in his approach. Sometimes the occupants of the trenches devised novel defenses of their own to put outside their works under cover of night: grapevines and telegraph wire strung to trip up the enemy, or in the case of the Thirtieth Ohio, a ditch five feet wide and four feet deep that the Rebels would tumble into when they charged.

Virtually all the improvements brought to the trench system enhanced its defensive capacity rather than its suitability as a place to live. Life in the ditches did have certain advantages over the camp routine: There were no dress parades or guard mountings and the atmosphere was generally more relaxed, with officers and men thrown together within the confines of the works. But trench life required constant vigil; reveille at three A.M. is often mentioned, though the men had to be instantly ready at any hour, hence obliged to sleep fully clothed; the colonel of the Eighty-ninth Ohio noted in his diary for July 11 that the previous night he had slept out of his uniform for the first time since the opening of the campaign. Food had to be prepared in the trenches, though on occasion no fires were permitted; likewise the men had to sleep within their works. Rarely were those works high enough so that a man could move around erect. The men went about in a half-crouch that became a habitual stoop (even after the two armies severed contact and moved back into regular camps that September, men would sometimes forget and walk about bent over, to the hilarity of their comrades). Bathing was impossible, though after a hard shower the trenches would be ankle-deep in red mud. Since in the daytime it was worth a man's life to try to go to the rear, he could not retire to the latrines, although diarrhea—also known in the trenches as the "Georgia shits"—was the most common malady in both armies. A Mississippi soldier tells us how the men coped with this dilemma: "Some use spades or shovels, some use haversacks, one poor fellow in an adjoining company made a thunder mug of his breeches." All in all, said another young soldier, it was "a most tedious and vexatious way of fighting."

When the Union army stood outside Meridian, Mississippi, two years before, the distance between Northern and Southern pickets was so great that soldiers went out beyond the picket lines to hang up their wash. Now the opposing pickets were often no more than a hundred yards apart; near Kennesaw they were so close they could amuse themselves throwing rocks at each other; at other places the opposing works were separated by such a narrow strip of terrain that no pickets could be set out. When a line of pickets was posted, it had to be done before dawn, and the men would have to wait until dark to be relieved. They lived in fear of being suddenly overrun or "gobbled" by an enemy rush—and their comrades back in the breastworks knew they might have to beat off an enemy assault at any moment. The armies were in such close contact that firing along the picket line would crackle and sputter throughout the day. From time to time the fire would intensify at some point on the line, and soldiers near that point would grab their muskets and hurry to their firing positions, only to discover there was no enemy in sight. Curiously, a rain shower had the effect of stopping this fusillade completely; when the rain stopped the gunfire recommenced.

Whether it was the light rattle of musketry along the picket line or the thunderous discharges of pitched battle, much of the firing was high, so that bullets and shells fell far to the rear. Couriers who moved back and forth behind the lines chose their route through woods or followed the bottom of valleys and ravines; when they had to cross open ground they went at a gallop. The breastworks on the second line were not just there for contingency, men lived, ate, and slept behind them as well— and occasionally fell to bullets that seemed to come from nowhere. When this happened an enemy sharpshooter was usually blamed, and occasionally these marksmen did send death far behind the lines: On a quiet Sunday, June 26, 1864, Captain W. D. Neal was chatting with a Lieutenant Stewart near the headquarters of General M. D. Leggett, about a mile behind the Union front line; Lieutenant Stewart was on horseback, Captain Neal standing beside the horse's withers. Suddenly Captain Neal fell lifeless to the ground; at the same time the horse staggered, then went down in its turn. Investigation showed that the same missile had passed through Captain Neal and entered the horse, nearly going through it too. Lodged in the animal's shoulder blade was the long hexagonal slug of a Whitworth rifle.

Those heavy and exceptional engagements that occurred when one side attempted major assaults on the positions of the other can best be treated later as part of the more general phenomenon of combat, but it would be well here to note the unusually high degree of night fighting that went on during the Georgia campaign, especially in the first month. Night operations were after all exceptional in that era of warfare, and limited to reconnaissances and coups de main carried out by specially prepared troops; anything more ambitious usually ended in confusion and failure. Yet night after night the hills of North Georgia reverberated with musketry and cannonade. The *Official Records* contain many reports of night attacks beaten off, but corresponding reports of night attacks initiated are hard to find. Occasionally limited battles did occur at night, as on the evening of June 20, when the Thirty-fifth Indiana called in its pickets at dusk and departed the works before the arrival of its relief, the Forty-ninth Ohio. Rebel troops took advantage of the interval to occupy the works, and driving them back out took a good part of the night.

When General Johnston read General Sherman's memoirs some years after the war he was surprised by descriptions of night assaults made on the Union lines: "Night attacks," Johnston said, "were *never* made by our troops." The origin of these fierce nocturnal exchanges can no doubt be traced to a certain edginess on both sides, quite understandable in light of the proximity of the two opposing lines and their consequent vulnerability to assault under cover of night. By day the firing of nervous pickets rarely led to prolonged alarms because the enemy never came into sight, but at night the other senses and the imagination took over. Anything could start one of these phantom engagements: the accidental discharge of a musket, pickets making a racket as they went out to relieve others, and in at least one case fireflies, whose flashes of light were like those of small arms being discharged. But once begun, the firing fed on itself: "Night attacks, after opening at one point, often extended until a long line had participated. Frequently one would begin far away, to the right or left, and, like a thunder shower, would approach nearer and nearer, with increasing clatter and roar." Casualties in the usual sense were not heavy in these night "battles," but as frequently as they occurred, they left a legacy of exhaustion and strain.

An even greater burden was placed upon both armies by the frequent movements they made, for hardly had the soldiers fixed their works to their satisfaction than they had to abandon them, move a distance southward, and then construct others. As the campaign advanced men kept a tally of sorts: An Alabama soldier wrote his wife that in the space of thirty days his regiment had thrown up ten sets of works; at the end of the campaign the lieutenant colonel of the Fifty-eighth Illinois recorded that his regiment had constructed 2,885 yards of breastworks. For in the course of the first two weeks Sherman's army moved south at an average of about three miles a day. The progress is uneven, with several miles gained one day with a significant flanking movement, and a few hundred feet the next when the Confederates were levered out of one line of entrenchments and fell back to their second line. But the pressure of the Northern forces was rarely relaxed. Both armies were in fact being prodded and driven by Sherman, who seems to have been everywhere. "I must see everything," he wrote his wife that summer. So one moment he visits a signal station, looks down over the country with his glass, and checks what he sees against his map; then he appears in the fortified position of an artillery battery, studies the terrain through the embrasures, and chats briefly with the men. On the picket line he suddenly looms up in front of an Illinois private who comes close to shooting him; or he accompanies the picket line as it moves forward, picking blackberries and asking the soldier advancing beside him if the men are comfortable and dry.

But Sherman was not an idle spectator; he probed, he prodded, and where feasible, he pushed. He apparently stayed up and active much of the night: At two-thirty A.M., May 13, the headquarters diary of the Fourth Corps recorded receipt of a message from the commanding general to "feel" the enemy's line immediately with infantry and cavalry and report their findings, and at three A.M. a reply was sent that the enemy still held his position in force; at midnight, May 14, Sherman sent word to General Thomas to have Jefferson C. Davis's division turned out to take the road on receipt of his order, so that the movement he wanted them to make could be completed by dawn. And subordinates often indicate in their own orders the impulsion, the drive that came from Sherman; thus on May 17 General Palmer sent notes to the brigade commanders in his division saying: "I have just seen General Sherman, who says we must get to Adairsville tonight." In the ranks the more observant sensed the campaign's new tempo and impetus almost immediately: "We are crowding the Rebel Army," wrote one soldier; another wrote home to tell his mother, "we are going to war in earnest this time. Gen. Sherman is no trifler."

To the night battles were thus added night marches, for this was the best time to disengage and slip away without the other side knowing of your movement. The Federals often initiated their flanking movement then. The Confederates executed their withdrawals at night, usually following a kind of pattern: After dark the infantry would quietly turn its positions over to General Wheeler's cavalry; they would keep up picket firing if called for, tend a number of campfires, chop wood as though they were getting timber to strengthen their works, and generally give the impression the line was solidly held. Then in the dead of night they would withdraw quietly to where their horses were kept and follow the rest of the army south. Johnston's rear guard was mounted cavalry, which was charged with rounding up stragglers and seeing that nothing of value was left to fall in the enemy's hands. Sooner or later the Union pickets would report that the works opposing them were empty, and Sherman's advance units, which were also cavalry, would start in pursuit. If overtaken the Rebel troopers would find a good spot to fortify, dismount and throw up temporary works by piling up fence rails, and stand at bay. This usually obliged the Northern cavalry to draw back until infantry could come up to drive the Rebels back to their horses, then the pursuit would start again.

The night marches were by all accounts punishing. The men were usually tired to begin with, the roads rough and tortuous, and the darkness sometimes almost total—"dark as a stack of black cats" was the saying. Sergeant Levi Ross of the Eighty-sixth Illinois had an imperishable memory of a march through one rainy night that May: "Many times during that long, tedious night did I think that if the enemy could be overcome by cursing and swearing, the rebellion would be speedily stamped out." Bizarre things could happen on these marches. A soldier in the Eighty-first Indiana recorded: "Some of our boys were affected with a disease of a strange nature called by some 'moonblindness.' As soon as the sun went down they became perfectly blind. During the night's march they had to be led by the hand, as they were perfectly helpless." And from time to time a whole column of troops would be seized by a strange panic: It usually started when a loud noise of some kind startled a half-sleeping soldier and he concluded that cavalry or artillery was coming up behind them at a fast clip. This seems to have been every soldier's nightmare on such marches, so the men would scramble out of the way of the oncoming horses, creating a commotion that in turn panicked others ahead of them and produced pandemonium in the entire column. In their blind flight the men collided with others, fell headlong into ditches, or crashed into trees. The confusion eventually subsided and the column re-formed, the men groping for lost equipment, feeling their bruises and scrapes, and cursing.

Had these nocturnal movements been occasional things with a

chance for the troops to rest up afterward, they would have been little more than irksome to the hardy youth that made up the bulk of both armies. But they were frequent, and when the soldiers were not on the roads by night, they were crouched in their works, waiting for an enemy assault or firing into the blackness at phantom attackers. If kept up long enough, this pattern of activity could reduce an army to exhaustion. Occasionally this exhaustion shows up in diary entries. "Have not slept an hour in three days," an Alabama soldier wrote on May 27, "am almost overpowered with sleep. Have dozed three times since I commenced this note." A Confederate soldier named Clark could not forget the terrible march that brought his regiment to the vicinity of Kennesaw Mountain on the night of June 19–20; normally the men would put up works of some sort wherever they stopped, but this night they didn't feel they had it in them. Their captain told them they could entrench or not, but they would have to hold that line the following morning, breastworks or no breastworks. "Only one man remained awake to fortify," Clark recalled, "and he dug his trench in the wrong direction."

Armies that moved by night and spent their days behind ramparts were mostly invisible to their foe, and even when one of the two armies advanced against the other its movement was largely masked by forest and undergrowth. Sherman said well into the campaign he had only seen a few hundred of the enemy altogether; T. E. Smith, an Ohio officer new to the front, had brought with him storybook images of serried ranks of men advancing across field and plain; he could not get over what he found. After a month and a half of campaigning he wrote his brother: "You may be astonished when I tell you that to the best of my knowledge and belief I have not seen plainly more than 100 of the enemy altogether and that from 500 to 1,000 yards off. I have often seen where they were thick but concealed in their works and bushes." For most soldiers the enemy's presence was almost spectral—the glint of a gun barrel, a hint of movement behind a wall of raw earth on a distant hillside. Hence, in the words of an Indiana soldier, "a constant curiosity" to know more about the other side:

> This curiosity, if not gratified, grew with each passing day. The air of mystery that an army always presents for its adversary was probably the cause of this. The men of each army know that the other army exists, perhaps that it is in the near vicinity, and that it is a tremendous engine of death, requiring the utmost watchfulness. But beyond these facts they know very little.

The men in some units were more than just curious. They were anxious to meet the enemy because they had a score to settle with him. This sort of grudge was most common among mounted units and was probably traceable to the kind of warfare they waged. On April 23 Confederate cavalry overran or "gobbled" a picket post at Nickajack Trace; the sixty-odd men they took prisoner were a detachment from the Ninety-second Illinois Volunteers, a mounted infantry regiment. Accounts of the affair are garbled and contradictory, but the version the men of the Ninety-second believed was that the Rebels headed back to their own lines with their dismounted prisoners in tow, and when these couldn't or wouldn't move fast enough, the Rebels began to shoot them. The men of the Ninety-second knew or thought they knew the unit responsible; some said most of the killing had been done by a Lieutenant Pointer. And Northern cavalrymen were also looking for at least an explanation from the Third Texas Cavalry, for stories circulated that the Third Texas carried a black flag, symbolizing no quarter. Some of the Confederate units started the campaign with similar scores to settle.

With the infantry there is less evidence of this urge to seek reprisal or revenge, and when it is found it is directed at the enemy more generally, rather than at a specific unit. To be sure, among Southern soldiers there was considerable evidence of a special grudge against black troops and white officers who commanded them, but the dearth of black combat units in Sherman's forces meant they had little chance to vent their anger. At the beginning of the campaign there was still much talk in the Northern press of the Fort Pillow Massacre. John Brobst, a soldier of the Twenty-fifth Wisconsin, wrote his sweetheart Mary that this affair was on the minds of a Minnesota regiment when they attacked and took some Rebel rifle pits on May 20: "twenty-three of the rebs surrendered but the boys asked them if they remembered Fort Pillow and killed them all." In the same letter Brobst confided to Mary: "When there is no officer with us, we take no prisoners. We want revenge and we are bound to have it one way or another. They must pay for those deeds of cruelty."

But unless there were fresh provocations this sort of animus could soon fade. Brobst himself could testify to that, for in August he wrote Mary that he had had "guests" for dinner—two Confederate soldiers who had slipped through the lines: "They stayed about two hours and then went back. They were real smart fellows both of them." Nor was this all. Later in the year, while encamped in Tennessee, Brobst had as his houseguest a Rebel soldier who had deserted the Southern army and was passing discreetly through the Northern one on his way home. Brobst was still grieving over the loss of a photograph of Mary, which

had been in a knapsack he'd had to abandon on one of the Georgia battlefields. His guest said that he on the other hand had picked up a few
pictures here and there; he spread out his collection, and there among
the photographs was the picture of Mary.

Contacts of a reasonably amicable sort developed between Northern
and Southern soldiers when the two armies were still around Dalton.
Somewhere near Rocky Face a corporal in Company I, Sixtieth Illinois
called over to the Confederate position nearby and asked if they would
like to hear "Old Abe's Amnesty Proclamation," and the Rebels replied,
"Yes, Yes, give us the ape's proclamation." But at a certain moment they
didn't like what they were hearing and signaled their displeasure with a
volley of stones. Conversations between pickets were a well-established
habit by the end of May, and occasionally they met to exchange newspapers, Yankee coffee for Southern tobacco, and the like.

But trading wares was not the real purpose of most of these meetings; this much we can see in the letter of a young Northern soldier
named Drake:

> I done something yesterday that i never thought of before. When we
> went out on the skirmish line some of the boys hollered over to the
> rebbels and told them we would meet them half way and leave our
> guns at this post and so we did. We came together and shuck hands
> and had a general talk together. Now you might think that strange
> but I cant help but be just friendly to one of them as I would to one of
> my own country. I traded canteens and carterages with them and not
> only that, we agreed not to fire at one another while we were on sen-
> try unless one party or the other advanced.

While army commanders sometimes authorized a "flag of truce" to
pass through the lines civilians and army noncombatants (physicians
and chaplains) who had been taken prisoner, they took a dim view of the
frontline parleys the soldiers arranged on their own. By June there were
sufficient cases of brief, informal truces to attract official condemnation,
as in Special Field Order No. 47, issued in the Second Division, Seventeenth Corps on June 13: "It appearing that the skirmishers and pickets
of this division have on two or three occasions established an armistice
with those of the enemy, it is ordered that every officer be particularly
vigilant to prevent a recurrence of the same." But these truces continued
to be arranged, often with the tacit consent of regimental and brigade
commanders.

There was one occasion when soldiers of the opposing sides saw a good bit of each other, and that was when a party of prisoners was sent back from the front under military escort. Invariably a kind of friendship, almost a bonding, developed between the two groups, prisoners and guards. George Washington Morris helped escort a party of Rebel prisoners to Kingston, Georgia, and particularly recalled the farewells: "Before leaving some of them expressed a wish that we were going all the way through with them. Some of us wished so too." There were similar scenes when Federal prisoners and their escorts parted company at the gates of Andersonville prison.

As the movements of the armies took them closer and closer to Atlanta, the story spread through both that General Sherman intended to take his Fourth of July dinner in the conquered city; indeed one version of the story had Sherman dining in Atlanta and Grant in Richmond. The same tale was picked up by Georgia newspapers and broadcast throughout the state, and virtually everyone waited for the fateful date to arrive—save perhaps Sherman, who had made no specific plans. By the beginning of the month, when it became obvious the general would not be able to keep the date, still another story started through the Confederate ranks that on the morning of the Fourth the entire Union army would launch an assault of unprecedented proportions (a prospect not even considered by the Confederate high command); but then the morning of the Fourth came and there was little forthcoming from the Federal lines beyond patriotic music. That day a nameless Confederate soldier sent a letter addressed to "Mr. Sherman"; just how he sent the letter is not clear, but it did reach its destination, since it is in the general's papers:

> July 4, 1864
> Mr. Sherman—
> Come on!
> Yours with anxiety,
> Rebel
> P.S. We intend to give you a whipping.

Documents like this inevitably raise questions about morale in the two armies and how it had evolved in the two months of marching and skirmishing from Rocky Face to the banks of the Chattahoochee. There is no doubt that Sherman's men were disappointed when the torrential rains of June and then the formidable defenses they encountered as they approached Atlanta slowed the pace of their army's advance. While their hopes of an early end to the campaign and a long furlough thus faded, there was no doubt among them of the campaign's ultimate success. With the Southerners the picture is full of nuances. General Johnston seems to have held the confidence of his soldiers rather generally, though there was concern after his refusal to fight at Cassville. A Tennessee surgeon noted: "for the first time the men begin to grumble and grow dispirited." Many soldiers—and Georgia civilians as well—believed or hoped that the succession of withdrawals would stop at the Chattahoochee, though the stream would be a very difficult line to hold. There were also misgivings in the Confederate leadership. General Hardee wrote his wife on June 18: "My convictions are, and have been for some time, that we are drifting to the Chattahoochee and that we shall cross that stream in a week or ten days." At the same time an army correspondent in the *Mobile Daily Advertiser and Register* described Johnston's conduct as "timorous, mincing, irresolute," and there were jokes about the general preparing his pontoons to retire on Cuba. For Johnston's public image the Chattahoochee would be a Rubicon of sorts.

But there are other ways to gauge the climate of opinion in the Army of Tennessee. The desertion rate, for example, is generally a good barometer of morale; there is a good deal of truth in Lenin's remark that "an army votes for peace with its legs." Northern officers and soldiers wrote home that desertion in the Rebel army had become massive, a near-fatal hemorrhage, while stories ran through Sherman's regiments of whole companies or regiments of Rebels who had given themselves up—always in another section of the line. Fortunately there are some statistics, and these indicate that desertions were not massive. In the six months ending May 1, 1864, the Army of the Cumberland recorded 3,371 Confederate deserters received, about 600 per month. The figures for May and June 1864 are close to that average; for example, while the army took 1,827 prisoners in May, the number of deserters for that month was 580.

While we think of desertion as a one-way street in this late period of the war, Northern soldiers did cross the line from time to time. In one case two Union soldiers accidentally walked into the Confederate picket line. Since it was an understandable error, the pickets generously gave the two men the option of going back where they came from. One did, while the other decided to stay on the Southern side. There he might simply go where he pleased as a civilian or join a "foreign" unit in Confederate service (these were mostly former Northern prisoners recruited out of Andersonville and other prisons with the understanding that they would not be ordered to fight their former comrades). On the Union side the distinction between deserters and prisoners of war was also an important one: A man taken prisoner went to a prison in the North for the duration of the war. A man who deserted to Union forces—and volition was the litmus test—had only to reside north of the Ohio River until the end of the conflict; with luck he might be able to get his family passed through the lines to join him there (a steady trickle of women and children left Georgia for this purpose, usually by way of a flag of truce boat out of Savannah). And there was always the hope that one could desert one army and slip through the other without being detected and simply go home to Missouri or Kentucky. In September Sherman wrote his Confederate counterpart: "We hold a good many of your men, styled 'Deserters,' who were really stragglers"; but he added he was going to give them the benefit of a doubt and let them go north of the Ohio.

There were enough risks in desertion to make a man think twice. A Northern officer recounted the experience of one deserter who came into his regiment on the night of July 4:

He was a Mississippi boy about 18 or 19 years old. He was dreadfully alarmed. Was afraid he would be discovered by the Rebels and shot. Afraid we would shoot him before he could let us know he was deserting and afraid we would shoot him *any how*, as his officers had told him we would shoot all deserters, but he "didn't hardly believe it, at any rate he had determined to try it." He was wringing wet with sweat, had crawled on his belly 300 yds. and had been two hours making the trip.

The most spectacular case of mass desertion among Southern troops that summer occurred on the night of June 12–13 in General Carter L. Stevenson's division. At two-thirty A.M., June 13, Colonel Robert C. Trigg, brigade commander, was awakened to receive a note from General Stevenson that must have given him quite a shock: A captain, a lieutenant, and twenty men of the Fifty-fourth Virginia—the regiment Trigg commanded—had deserted to the enemy while on picket, leaving a dangerous gap in his line that would have to be filled immediately. Apparently it was another case of troops posted so far from home that they could not endure the "exile" any longer. But a new and disturbing pattern manifested itself as the campaign progressed: the defection of men from North Georgia regiments who found it impossible to retreat past their own homes. The record of Company A, Fortieth Georgia Infantry has been painstakingly reconstructed by local historian Dorothy Herring. That record was virtually unblemished at the beginning of the campaign, with a single desertion recorded at Resaca. But Company A had been raised in Paulding County, in which lay Dallas and New Hope Church. The Fortieth Georgia fought there, then moved on, but five men of Company A stayed behind. Other accounts indicate the first Northern troops to pass through often missed the Rebel soldiers, who successfully concealed themselves, only to be taken by Federal forces following behind. Those who eluded the advancing Yankees generally headed first for home, and if it was not safe to stay there, they became "hideouts" nearby.

The deserters generally came in with accounts of hardship and despair in the army they had left, accounts that were often colored—either to justify their own defection or to tell the Yankees what they wanted to hear. Officers experienced in talking with them knew to discount much that they said. Prisoners taken in the field were more of a mixed bag; sometimes they showed passive acceptance of their situation, and sometimes even relief that it was all over. But quite often they displayed a confidence, even a cockiness, that must occasionally have disconcerted their interrogators. One Confederate soldier, brought in to be questioned by General Jacob Cox, had a question of his own to ask. Since the Northern army was surrounded, did General Cox intend to surrender or to cut his way out? The general, who accepted the question in good spirit, said he thought he would cut his way out.

General Sherman detected this same confidence, not by questioning prisoners but by reading Southern soldiers' letters in mails his cavalry intercepted. "It is wonderful," he wrote his wife, "to see how the soldiers talk of driving me back to the Ohio and then returning to their loving families in Tennessee and Kentucky." While he admired such determination, he thought it would be hard to sustain through the coming campaign: "All that has gone before is skirmishing. The war now begins. . . ."

5

The District of the Etowah

The war that came to North Georgia in 1864 was a calamity without parallel, but it struck a part of the state that already had more than its share of difficulties. In its geography, in its economy, and even in its culture, Cherokee Georgia stood apart from the rest of the state. It was still thinly settled; most of its inhabitants worked hardscrabble farms where slavery had no place and often felt they and their interests were neglected by those in power. Viewed by Georgians who lived farther to the south, it seemed somewhat remote and backward. "There were whole settlements in which practically no-one could read or write," wrote a local historian, ". . . some families did not get a letter for years, and when a letter did come, it usually meant that some relative who had moved to Arkansas or Texas had died." Living in isolation, with few teachers, newspapers, or books, they knew little about the rest of their state and virtually nothing about the world beyond—this much we may infer from an encounter a Federal soldier related. He wrote his wife that he and his comrades had talked with some of the local girls, to whom they bragged about Indiana. One of the young women asked them what part of Tennessee it was in. "Another said her father had considered moving to Indiana but did not like living in a city. So you can see how sharp the fare secks of Georgia is."

The region had no significant role in determining the state's political course until Joe Brown appeared, and even then the governor's policies were not always well-received in North Georgia's hills and mountain coves. There the people were at best lukewarm about defending slavery and less than enthusiastic about secession. In Pickens County a clear majority of the population was opposed to leaving the Union; in the county seat of Jasper the Stars and Stripes continued to fly over the court-house for several months after secession. Hotheads in the capital at Milledgeville urged Governor Brown to send an expedition to take the flag down by force, but Brown knew better; Colonel Avery says he diplo-matically "let it float" until eventually the locals took it down themselves.

The reasons for the region's disaffections were various, with attach-ment for the Union not always the most important. Many of the hard-scrabble farmers had no use for slavery, or for blacks, for that matter, and resented the domination of the richer and more populous sections of Georgia to the south. In part they became disaffected simply because their isolation was violated and the tempo of their existence disturbed by "outsiders." They resented the Confederacy's tax collectors and impressment officers; and beyond that they resented its conscription officers. As their opposition mounted, Governor Brown had to parade state troops through North Georgia in a show of authority.

Hostility toward the Confederate and state governments continued to grow in Cherokee Georgia. In the gubernatorial election of 1863 Brown was reelected with a solid majority, but in the northern counties support for the Unionist Joshua Hill was disturbingly high; Hill even carried the governor's home county of Cherokee. Among themselves the mountain people tended to quick anger and a long memory for injuries received; now political differences, perhaps grafted onto preexisting antagonisms, produced a feuding that threatened to grow into full-blown partisan war. The presence of two opposing armies in North Georgia from late 1863 on could only add fuel to this smoldering mass.

Were this not enough, the economic sacrifices the war called for were more painful in North Georgia than in any other part of the state. To begin with it had less in wealth and resources. The presence of two armies in the region put a considerable strain on the supply of food-stuffs, and to complicate this problem North Georgia's farmers had a very poor crop in 1863, their fields being struck first by a summer drought, then an early frost; the grain crop in the northeastern counties was an almost total loss. In the strip of territory the Union army held around Ringgold the authorities began distributing food to families in need and continued the practice until Sherman had it stopped in April. In Dalton the situation was so critical by the beginning of 1864 that Colonel M. H. Cofer, post commandant, took the unusual step of appeal-ing to Governor Brown on behalf of the civilian population: "Many wives and mothers with their helpless children are suffering both for food and for clothing." Colonel Cofer had already appealed to General Johnston, but Johnston said the army itself was on short rations and refused to allow army stocks to be issued to "even the most destitute." On Governor Brown's order the state's quartermaster general directed a considerable quantity of supplies to the northern counties, including ten thousand bushels of corn sent to Dalton and Whitfield County. To help the northern counties further Governor Brown exempted a number of them from militia call-ups, so that the men could remain in the fields. In a curious irony state officials reported the 1864 crops were coming along very well and the fall would bring a bountiful harvest.

As the storm clouds approached in 1863 any number of people in North Georgia read the signs, particularly the affluent and the politically well-connected. The directors of the two colleges in Cassville closed their institutions with the end of the fall term; the students went home, never to return. Confederate Congressman Warren Akin moved his family out of Cassville at the beginning of 1864 and found accommodations farther south; the authorities generously made three boxcars available for that purpose. After the Confederate defeat at Missionary Ridge and the Union advance to Ringgold a first wave of refugees started south; they and others who followed headed toward Atlanta, which became a principal place of refuge. A probing expedition of Federal troops against Dalton in February and obvious preparations for a new campaign in March and April convinced still others to leave. In April General Johnston ordered away a number of civilians who had come to visit relatives in the army. Thus when fighting began in May a number of houses already stood empty in North Georgia's villages and towns, a fact travelers commented on.

People who stayed agonized over whether they too should leave. The most harrowing tales of refugees from other states made the rounds, and newspapers carried stories of rapes and other atrocities committed by the invaders in unusually graphic terms; yet the attitude of the press and of officialdom as well was one of unrelenting optimism: Sherman would soon be stopped, Johnston was about to spring his trap, etc. All too often people clung to hope until the last moment, then fled with few possessions, abandoning the accumulations and treasures of a lifetime, and in many cases never recovering them. A Federal officer named Oliver Lyman Spaulding reflected on this error in his memoirs: "It was a mistake for people to abandon their houses on the approach of our army. If they remained in them there was more than an even chance that they would be respected to some extent—that the family would not have been turned out of doors and the house burned." For there was a rule in the Union soldier's logic that any abandoned house was the property of someone so deeply compromised in the rebellion that he dare not stay and defend his possessions; thus the soldiers arriving in an area felt justified in taking anything they wanted and even consigning the rest to the flames, and no doubt a good many houses in North Georgia were burned under this "rule." Unfortunately no one explained this to the distracted population of North Georgia. While there is no clear indication what proportion of the population took flight, those in the countryside tended to stay in their homes more often than those in the towns, perhaps because so much of what they had of value, their farms, crops, and livestock, was not transportable—even there one has the impression that more families left than remained.

Slaves were valuable property and thus most of them were taken farther south. In this connection an Alabama private named Joseph Cannon found himself in an unusual predicament. His father had a number of slaves on a farm near Cartersville. Cannon could not leave his regiment to evacuate them, but he did make a quick trip to see them. He told them the Northern army would soon be in the vicinity. As to what they should do, "I could give no advice more than to tell them to take care of themselves the best they could." One of the slaves, a young man named Henry, told Cannon he did not want to stay there and wait for the Yankees. Cannon told him what regiment and brigade he was in, and said Henry could join him if he wanted to. Some time later Henry turned up and Cannon got him a job with the Confederate commissary. But other blacks were eager to reach the Union army and be of service to it. When Jefferson C. Davis's troops marched on Rome they had at least two guides who were former slaves from the area. When they reached the outskirts of the town another black man swam the river to bring them information.

For those who stayed on, the first tangible evidence of the coming storm was the faint rumble of cannon off to the north—this was enough to set some to packing trunks and loading wagons; then there was the visit of Wheeler's cavalry, which had been ordered to drive off stock so the Yankees would not get it. Those who lost horses and cattle or other possessions in this way were furious; they wrote Governor Brown, who extracted from General Johnston the admission that Wheeler's men might have committed "some excesses" in their work—this was the first of many charges that Georgians would levy against the Confederate cavalry in the course of the year. Those who lived near the Western and Atlantic got another sobering reminder of what was coming when the Confederates began tearing up the track.

Then the army itself withdrew. If it was abandoning a town, it was sometimes hard to keep the Southern soldiers from breaking ranks and plundering shops and stores as they filed through. Once again, in their logic—and it was also the logic of the men in the Northern army—better that merchandise should be carried off by them than benefit the enemy, who would surely take it if they did not. This was what happened, for example, when the Confederates abandoned Rome on May 19; the inhabitants, who felt there would be desperate fighting before the city was given up, were taken by surprise and preoccupied with crowding themselves and their possessions in the departing railway cars; in this scene of wild confusion the soldiers helped themselves. In Dalton too those civilians who remained thought they would have more time. They packed frantically on the morning of May 13 and streamed south along with the army, hindering its movement. An army correspondent for the *Mobile Daily Advertiser and Register* has left us a sharply drawn portrait of those hapless travelers on the roads of North Georgia:

> For the most part they are irresolute and uninformed, the women in tears and the men in dreadful perplexity. You may see them on the highway, jogging along in a hopeless sort of manner, in search of a hiding place, or at the little stations along the railroad, huddled together in boxcars, negroes, dogs and household goods indiscriminate. Here a handsome mirror, there a pot or kettle, a coop of chickens, a cat on an ottoman. . . .

Because they had no idea quite what to expect, some people imagined that if they could just get out of the way while the two armies fought through their neighborhood, then once the battlefront had moved on south they could somehow resume their lives. The essential thing was to avoid what one old mountain woman called the "streak of fight" that would pass through. The solution was to take bedding and provisions and head for a remote or secluded spot for a few days; others, not knowing what else to do, simply took to the woods. Northern officers and soldiers on reconnaissance and scouting missions reported from time to time finding such "hideouts." Captain David Conyngham, who traveled about the country quite a bit, wrote that more than once he came upon "groups of affrighted, starving women and children huddled together in the woods."

Then there were those who simply stayed and watched the columns of their army file by southward. Early one morning those columns passed by the Charles Howard home, not far from Adairsville. The

Howard daughters went down to the road to watch them go by; it was a very foggy morning, and though at first they could not see the soldiers, they could hear their voices reverberating loudly in the damp air. Years later Frances Howard recalled that scene as the veterans of the Army of Tennessee filed by in the mist: "They laughed and joked with each other as they passed, and occasionally they gave us the cheering assurance that they were 'going to whip Sherman and be back next week.'" One soldier left ranks long enough to ask Jane Howard to take his Bible, for he couldn't carry it anymore and yet he couldn't throw it away. She took it and found that everywhere there was a space he had laboriously written "levi Bartlett his Booke." The regiments passed all morning and on into the afternoon; eventually the Sixty-third Georgia came along, and the girls got to visit briefly with their brother and their father, who were officers in one of the companies. Then in the late afternoon cavalry replaced foot soldiers as the army's rear guard began to pass. Some Mississippians set up a battery of artillery on the other side of the road, not two hundred yards from the Howard home. "We were wild to see the fight," Frances Howard remembered, "and ran to the brow of the hill, though the soldiers tried to make us go back." But there was to be no fighting there, for the battery limbered up and went down the road in its turn. Then the Howards waited for the first appearance of the bluecoats.

A few days later the same retreating columns passed through Cartersville. For three days they streamed by the home of Mrs. Rebecca Hood, and she too kept watch because she had two sons in the First Georgia Cavalry. Early one morning her son William came in and said his brother was behind him, but he did not know how far back. "About noon of the same day," Mrs. Hood wrote later:

> I looked up the dusty road and saw my son John coming, riding a black horse, looking as if he could barely sit up, his clothes all covered with dust. I knew at a glance something was the matter with him, and as quick as I could get to him and put my arms around him, I said, "My son, what ails you?" He said, "I am sick," and he was very sick with pneumonia.

She put him to bed immediately, but she and her husband knew they could not keep him, for at best he would end up in a Northern prison, and they even feared that if Yankee soldiers found him they might shoot him on the spot. His brother made arrangements for one of the wagons to pick him up, and when it arrived early in the morning they got him up and wakened his two little sisters so they could say goodbye; then they helped him into the army wagon and watched it carry him away. They had no word of him for the next nine months. Then one night in February 1865 the Hoods heard footsteps on their porch, and as the steps approached their door they could hear the jingle of spurs such as cavalrymen wore. There was a knock: "Father said 'who are you?' The answer was 'I am John.' That was enough for me to know. I sprang from my resting place and embraced my long lost boy. . . ."

In the most fortunate scenario the Southern army retired quietly to the south and Sherman's forces came down the same road a little later, so that the transition to Federal occupation was at least a peaceful process. But often it was attended by violence, with civilians and their possessions caught in the middle. When troops began throwing up works they incorporated into it anything they could find. Occasionally the men dismantled whole houses and fitted the boards and beams into their defenses; there is some evidence that Confederate troops tore down New Hope Church for this purpose. Then too, any structure could become a field hospital or dressing station if it occupied a sheltered position not far from the fighting; thus on May 10 Federal surgeons set up shop in the house of James Johnson, who lived in Dug Gap, not far from Dalton. There they treated their wounded, and if a patient died they called in a burial detail. When Mr. Johnson reclaimed his residence it resembled a slaughterhouse; the yard around it had been turned into a cemetery.

Just south of Adairsville was an unfinished house, a large mansion of octagon form, so striking that a number of soldiers spoke of it in their letters and diaries. It stood by the roadside at a spot where the Confederates decided to mount a rear guard action. The Fifty-first Tennessee was thrown around the house as skirmishers and the rest of the brigade posted a thousand yards farther down the road. Quite a warm action developed, with both sides bringing up artillery. A gunner with Battery M, First Illinois Light Artillery, recalled that after silencing the Confederate guns the men in his battery trained their guns on the octagon house, "for we knew that the rebels always sought such places." Before long the mansion was "so well perforated with shell holes as to make it quite airy during the approaching hot weather." But the infantrymen claimed they had been so harassed by fire coming from it that they insisted on putting it to the torch. It made a memorable blaze, burning most of the night. The next day other troops commented on the impressive ruin they passed. The artilleryman with Battery M also recalled another instance in which they had fired a round into a house behind which some Confederate sharpshooters had taken refuge: "Upon reaching the house we found two women in it. One of them had become a mother about an hour before." The artilleryman's projectile had passed over the new mother's bed at a height of five feet.

Occasionally a man would stand and defend his own home. South of Resaca a Union soldier named George Cadman witnessed a scene that he said "would make an angel weep." They were following the retreating Rebels when at a plantation they came upon the enemy's rear guard, making a stand to slow their pursuit.

> The owner of the plantation was in the rebel army, fighting at his own doorstep, while his wife was encouraging the rebels by waving a rebel flag from the windows. One of our batteries, a mile away, seeing the rebels make a stand there, threw a few shells into the group, killing the husband and two children, and breaking the woman's leg.

Many of the towns fell into Union hands fairly peacefully, and this seems to have been the case with Dalton. The historian of Battery M recorded a little incredulously: "Many of its inhabitants cheered us as though they were really glad of our being there." As everywhere, the soldiers were looking for tobacco and were famished for anything edible that was not army rations; in Dalton they found peanuts, and soon every artillery caisson was carrying a bag of them. The shops and stores drew the men inexorably. A Kentucky cavalryman recorded that on the morning of May 13 "a number of infantrymen, unrestrained by their officers, were bursting open stores and rifling them of their scanty contents." At some point the soldiers seem to have rummaged extensively through public buildings and empty houses, for a correspondent passing through some ten days later noted: "a harvest of rags strew the streets and depots, mingled with a resurrection of mercantile and law office documents, and the debris of correspondence." Curiously, everywhere the soldiers were attracted to documents and letters, not just to throw about—though there was a good bit of that—but also for interesting things to read. At Cassville they pored over "sweet little notes" found at the girls' college; at Burnt Hickory and other places where they took post offices they would open the letters and sometimes read them aloud. A soldier passing through the little town of Calhoun recalled that the main street was "full of papers of every sort," but contained not a single inhabitant.

This was generally the pattern: No town official appeared to arrange the surrender of the town, and its population had vanished. Cartersville was a ghost town, though occupied early in the morning; the soldiers went into the abandoned houses looking for something for breakfast. At Kingston only one family remained. At Rome a small crowd of blacks watched the Northern troops march in, along with a solitary white youth. One of the soldiers said: "Thank the Lord, there is one white Union man that has come out to welcome us." "No, damn it," the boy spoke out, "I am a reb." At Cassville, which General Johnston had ordered evacuated in preparation for a battle, a Union officer named Brant led a frantic predawn search through the empty town looking for anyone who could give him information on the Confederate troops that had passed through. "In one house we found a full coffee pot and only part of the cups filled, some plates filled and others empty, a few chairs overturned and the door open, showing how the horrors of war had come like an earthquake shock." Union forces found other towns populated chiefly by Confederate wounded. At Resaca four hundred were discovered laid out in rows alongside the railroad; at Dallas they filled most of the town's houses.

Most of the plundering in the towns was done in the first hours of occupation, before a provost guard could be set. While all unattended homes and businesses were fair game, the soldiers frequently pushed their way into occupied houses as well, initially seeking food, but often taking other things as well. The situation was essentially the same in the countryside, save that there was no provost guard, and unless a sentry or "safeguard" was detailed to protect the property, succeeding waves of soldiers could descend upon it. Mr. and Mrs. Hood had the first descent just a few hours after they saw their son off. There was skirmishing near the house and wounded bluecoats were brought in by their attendants, who seemed to Mrs. Hood to be "Christian gentlemen." The use of their house as a hospital saved it from being ransacked, but infantry camped in their yard for three days and left their mark: "They tore down the fencing, burnt rails, and took everything they could get their hands on, and left us without a chicken to crow or a dog to bark. They even shot the dog." Mrs. Minerva McClatchey, who lived at Marietta, found the grounds of her home engulfed in a sea of blue. But virtually the first man in a blue uniform to enter her house was General Hooker, who shook her hand and greeted her "as cordially as an old friend." He told her he was glad to see a citizen at home, and he left a couple of officers in the house who did nothing worse than play her piano and dance. They stopped when she told them she did not permit such things on the Sabbath. The Howard family had a more difficult time of it. They had put most of their valuables in an upstairs room, locked the house, and posted themselves on the verandah. But soon their property was inundated with Yankee soldiers, some of whom found their way into the house. A swarm of men led by a sergeant began a general ransacking, but Frances Howard ran out and found two lieutenants who agreed to come to her assistance. After some difficulties the two officers were able to push the swarm of men back out of the house (they recognized their own major in the crowd). The Howards also received a distinguished visitor on their verandah in those first hours—General O. O. Howard, commander of the Fourth Corps. The general had a map with him and asked Frances some questions about roads and so forth, which she undertook to answer "evasively." Then the conversation took another tack:

HE: "Did you say the whole of Johnston's Army passed on this
      road yesterday?"
SHE: "I did not say so."
HE: "Ah no, it was the Corps to which your father belongs."
SHE: No answer.
HE: "To what Corps did you say your father belonged?"
SHE: "I did not say he belonged to any Corps."
HE: "If he is in the army he must belong to some corps."
SHE: "It would seem probable."

At this point Frances noticed that the general's face had become very red. He drew himself up, said to her, "Madam, when you meet a gentleman treat him as such," and took his leave.

The Howards had in the meantime learned something about surviving in Union-held Georgia. They invited General Thomas Sweeny to make their home his headquarters; he accepted, and for a time his presence gave them protection. When he left they took other measures, such as nailing up windows. They knew that their horses were now their most precious possessions, so they began to stable them in a sturdily built smokehouse. Across the door they laced a heavy chain attached to a cowbell, making a burglar alarm of sorts. Later, for even greater security, they moved the horses into their kitchen, sealing off its outer door and bringing the animals in every evening through the parlor.

Like the Hoods and the Howards, thousands of other Georgians had their first encounters with the Yankees, and very often their view of the invaders would jell around that initial encounter. It is not easy to generalize about these first contacts, for the impressions they created seem to have varied greatly. Sarah Pinkard, a widow who lived west of Dallas, would remember Federal soldiers taking apart her fence and using the palings to dig up all the potatoes in her garden. When they left her place they had stripped it of everything edible. To feed her family she was obliged to gather watercress along the creek bank and scavenge the grains of hard corn that had dropped on the ground where the soldiers fed their horses—these grains she converted to grits by crushing them with a rock. Not far away lived her daughter-in-law, Lucy Pinkard, likewise widowed, who found a detachment of Yankees camped in her yard. The first morning they were there, and every morning until they left, a soldier brought a steaming cup of coffee to her door, probably the first she had had in many months; that evening a Union officer sat with her, holding her two-year-old daughter, and his eyes filled with tears as he told her that he had a daughter just the same age.

In general terms the movement of the armies through any particular locality was a process that took perhaps a week or two, during which the area was saturated with troops and suffered depredation accordingly—and in this connection we must include the Southern army as well as the Northern one. "They talk about the ravages of the enemy in their marches through the country," a Southern soldier wrote in his diary on May 21,

> but I do not think that the Yankees are any worse than our own army. This morning when the train was passing the house of a farmer a lady gave the men all the milk, butter and butter-milk she had. They were not satisfied with this. They took all the chickens she had, robbed all the nests they could find, went to the stables and took all the fodder. . . . I am sorry to say this has been the case all along the road by our army.

Observers who traveled through the country after the passage of the armies speak of a swath of destruction between five and ten miles in width, bounded on each side by an additional strip of countryside that had been very heavily foraged by the cavalry covering the armies' flanks. The most visible scar on the land was the succession of fortified lines. They ran across field and through forest, but were sometimes erected inside towns and could be thrown up in such unlikely places as cemeteries, with tombstones incorporated into the breastworks. In Cobb County alone it has been estimated that there were some two hundred miles of trenches and rifle pits.

Then throughout the countryside the fencing had been torn down and carried off. The rails by the thousands were incorporated into the breastworks or stacked up to protect rifle pits; the habit of using rails in this way became so ingrained that when soldiers heard firing ahead of them they would often pick up rails as they advanced, knowing they would soon have to build works. Other thousands of rails were consumed in campfires, for the soldiers had neither the axes nor the time to chop wood; good water and plenty of rails were thus the essential criteria for any campground. The pioneers in both armies felled large numbers of trees for incorporation into breastworks; the sound of chopping could often be heard throughout the night. Here and there the land would be virtually cleared, on top of Pine Mountain, for example, where the lack of cover cost Confederate General Leonidas Polk his life when Sherman noticed his party and had an Indiana battery throw some shells in their direction.

In a region as heavily forested as North Georgia the trees were no great loss; the rails, on the other hand, were vital to a farmer's livelihood. Georgia had what was known as the "open stock" system of agriculture, with the cultivated fields fenced and hogs and cattle allowed to roam free; under state law, unless a farmer kept his fences mended and maintained at a height of five feet, he had no legal recourse if other people's stock invaded his corn or wheat fields. Now the farmer was condemned to hundreds of hours of labor in the slow and tedious process of felling trees and splitting them up for rails.

Given the difficulties of supplying fodder in the field, both Northern and Southern cavalry and artillery units took what grain they could from granaries and corncribs, but their most common practice was simply to turn their famished animals into a field of young wheat or corn and let them graze. In this way the grain crop of 1864 was consumed before it was even harvested. Large "official" forages, those in which scores or hundreds of wagons were sent out under military escort in what was virtually a military operation, were relatively few in North Georgia, partly because the limited areas under cultivation did not make them worthwhile, but also because the troops and transport could not be spared from the front. This left the smaller expeditions by mounted units in search of fodder and "irregular" foraging and pillaging expeditions by infantrymen. These latter were done on the initiative of the men themselves and often with the approval of their company officers, ostensibly for the purpose of getting something to eat, or at least something more palatable than hardtack. These too were sent out less frequently later in the campaign, chiefly because the almost constant fighting kept men confined to the ditches. An Illinois soldier complained: "There is so much confounded fighting to be attended to that we can't forage any."

These parties never roamed far from the body of the army, which itself was operating on a fairly narrow front.

The official attitude toward foraging was in the process of changing. While it was permitted by the laws of war, as long as the proper forms were observed, commanders at the beginning of the conflict tended to rely on their own supply systems; they were a surer source, while taking provisions from the civilian population was attended by excesses and indiscipline; besides that, many commanders had moral reservations about it; a few, on the other hand, felt it was perfectly all right to punish the enemy population this way. But "eating off the locals" was feasible, particularly when the army was moving through rich country. Sherman had already proved this on his Meridian expedition. Seizing food along the line of march could also extend an army's logistical reach. Then too, there were other dividends not mentioned in treatises on the laws of war: Reducing the food supply of a hostile population and carrying off its livestock meant that thereafter the inhabitants would have that much less to share with guerrillas and bushwhackers; what is more, it was the kind of exaction that could bring the war home to an enemy population as nothing else could. For all these reasons those who planned the 1864 campaign of the Northern armies favored this policy of consuming the resources of civilians in hostile areas. The new policy found official expression in an untitled "Instruction" issued by the adjutant general's office on April 30, 1864. It stressed the advantages of drawing the army's needs in "animals and provisions" from the territory in which operations were being conducted. "Special care will be taken to remove horses, mules, live-stock, and all means of transportation from hostile districts infested by guerilla bands of rebels." The document was unusual in several respects: it was addressed to all senior commanders, including General Sherman and the heads of his three armies, with instructions to acknowledge receipt; moreover the instruction was not to be printed. Who inspired this circular is unclear; what is clear is that it was already being put into effect. Its spirit was in Sherman's General Order No. 6, issued at the beginning of April. As for General Grant, that same month he had incorporated the idea into his plans for opening the campaign. He wrote General Halleck on April 29 that he was issuing fifteen days' rations to his troops, but thought they would have enough for twenty to twenty-five days by adding in what could be taken from the countryside: "All the country affords will be gathered as we go along."

As for irregular foraging by Sherman's men that summer, the order books of subordinate commanders contain frequent denunciations and prohibitions of the practice. Sherman, for his part, seems to have cared

little what the men did in their idle hours, as long as it did not interfere
with their availability for battle. During the campaign through North
Georgia his only pronouncement regarding the men's conduct—couched
in language unusually violent even for him—concerned men who were
skulking and prowling in the army's rear when there was fighting for
them to do at the front: "The only proper fate of such miscreants is that
they be shot as common enemies to their profession and country, and all
officers and patrols sent to arrest them will shoot them without mercy
on the slightest impudence or resistance." Once arrested, the stragglers
and skulkers were to be set to the roughest and most menial work. Officers who avoided battle were promised exactly the same treatment,
"instant death or the harshest labor." The measure seems to have had no
implementation or practical effect. Though Sherman made no reference
to depredations committed by such men, in his constant roaming about
he could not have failed to see such things. He was aware, for example,
that the estate of his old friend Colonel Tumlin had not been spared, for
he wrote in an early draft of his memoirs: "I know that my armies swept
over his place with terrible destruction." At some point the sentence was
stricken, for it does not appear in the published memoirs.

If the depredations were limited, it was for lack of opportunity, not
for lack of inclination. The soldiers on both sides—not all, but many and
probably most—were prone to roam about, "see what they could find,"
and in the process forage and pick up things—"capture" was their
euphemism. Sometimes they were genuinely hungry, nearly always they
were looking for a change from the monotony of army rations, and
sometimes they were looking for excitement or adventure. H. V. Redfield, in his article on the "characteristics" of the western armies, indicates that by 1863 these habits were well-developed in the soldiers of
both, with the Federals being the more rapacious and more inclined to
take from their own kind. It was not simply something that those
recently arrived in the regiment eventually picked up from the old, cyni-
cal veterans; too many of the new soldiers were trying their hand at
"jayhonking" even before they reached the front—or learned to spell the
term. One is tempted to say that just putting on a uniform produced a
sea change in a man, or at least in his perception of property rights.
Sometimes old soldiers talking about their war experiences hinted as
much: "We had been brought up not to steal and lie," wrote Elisha
Stockwell, "and I despise a thief or a liar now. When we foraged,
though, we thought of it as a part of war and punishment of the enemy."
Others deplored the conduct of those around them, and still other soldiers deplored their own conduct—or seemed to: "Oh, I am of the lowest

grade of men," the Ohio soldier John Brobst wrote his Mary, "I go right in a man's yard, steal a sheep, hog, or chicken, cow or anything that I can find, take off a corpse before the eyes of the owner, and if [he] says anything tell him to dry up or he will get his wind shut off for a year or two."

But the inhabitants soon noticed that descents of this sort were becoming less frequent, for the hordes of bluecoats were thinning out. The combat units packed up and moved on south; before long their support facilities, hospitals, trains of wagons, and the like, also departed. Yet the invader's presence remained in the form of garrisons in the various towns, blockhouses here and there along the railway, and patrols that the locals encountered on country roads. The war had passed them now, and left a new allegiance in its wake. They were no longer inhabitants of Joe Brown's Georgia, but of a new military circumscription called the District of the Etowah. Sherman, who already had districts of Kentucky and Tennessee, added the new circumscription on June 10 and confided it to Major General James B. Steedman. The initial order gave Steedman control of the country from Bridgeport, Alabama, to Allatoona, "including Cleveland, Rome, and the country east as far as controlled by our troops."

Steedman set up his headquarters at Chattanooga and began organizing his command. To maintain his authority he took over or created garrisons in the chief towns: Rome got four regiments of infantry and one of cavalry, Kingston got a thousand men, etc.; other detachments were posted in blockhouses and fortified camps to guard bridges and other important points. These various posts were linked by telegraph, but also by patrols that covered the region, concentrating on the rail line. As Sherman advanced, as the rail link increased in length, General Steedman's domain grew. In July the boundary of the district was moved south to the line of Marietta and Kennesaw Mountain, making Steedman the nominal ruler of about a third of the state. By the end of August Sherman had about seventy-two thousand men at the front and another sixty-eight thousand guarding his rear. General Steedman's portion of the long supply line had the heaviest concentration of troops— 233 men per mile.

A "War Democrat" and former editor of the *Toledo Times*, General Steedman proved a competent administrator, though as Sherman's proconsul he was charged not so much with the administration of the region as with the security of the railway that ran through it. This in itself was a daunting task, for the Western and Atlantic had the distinction of being more frequently attacked by guerrillas, saboteurs, and the like than any other rail link running through occupied portions of the South. But that was not all; the line was in bad shape when Sherman inherited it and in need of constant repairs, yet so intense was the traffic that these were difficult to effect. It was no ordinary railroad: For security reasons night operations were limited; trains often ran in convoys or "gangs" of five or more; then too, they usually did not run on a fixed schedule, but according to advice they received by telegraph on the condition and availability of the road ahead. Their running speed was generally ten miles per hour, but numerous delays made that average meaningless.

An Ohio soldier named John Wesley Marshall has left a record of his trip on the W&A that is highly revealing: He left Chattanooga for Kingston at nine-thirty on the morning of May 19, seated on the roof of a boxcar loaded with munitions; after a reasonably uneventful run of eighteen miles they arrived at Ringgold at eleven A.M. But once there they had to wait for an "up" train that did not arrive until four-thirty P.M., having suffered a derailment down the line. Marshall's train was approaching Tunnel Hill when it was discovered the engine was low on water. The engineer left the cars sitting on the track while he ran the locomotive ahead for water, then returned for the cars, so the entire train finally pulled into Dalton at nine P.M. Here there was a layover until the next morning. Scheduled to leave at seven A.M., they got off a half-hour late after taking on a last-minute order of medical supplies. En route it was discovered that one of the ammunition cars was afire, so the train stopped again, the passengers jumping off in some haste. Eventually they succeeded in putting the fire out, and the train finally pulled into Kingston at four P.M.—having covered a distance of eighty-six miles in thirty hours.

Though Marshall had no encounters with bands of Confederate partisans, they were a constant plague. They frequently cut telegraph wires, halting Sherman's communications and partially disabling the railroad, since the movement of trains was often regulated by that means. So frequently was telegraphic communication interrupted that in August Sherman told his signal officers to resurrect the visual signal system that had been used as the army came south. As for the railroad itself, it was all too vulnerable. Steedman had to guard bridges and trestles, but also water towers, mountains of wood along the right of way that served as fuel, and even parties of woodchoppers. Eventually he formed "train guards" for the trains themselves. Train crews had to be on their guard against intentionally loosened rails and "torpedoes" (we would say mines) and metal devices the Confederates sometimes attached to the rails to cause derailments. Rebel scouts occasionally bored holes in the ends of logs in the railroad's woodpiles and filled the cavities with gunpowder, hoping by this means to blow up a locomotive's firebox. If they could find nothing more harmful to do, the partisans simply fired into the cars as they went by (they were somewhat hesitant to fire into "up" trains, which often contained Confederate prisoners). In the middle of June, as Steedman was taking over, the attacks were frequent. On June 11 guerrillas planted a torpedo under an "up" train and derailed it; on the 18th they provoked a derailment and then plundered and burned sixteen cars. On the 19th they clashed with a patrol that came upon them removing a rail, and in the ensuing fight two Federal soldiers were killed.

These particular episodes were hardly more than pinpricks, but added to many others occurring in Kentucky, Tennessee, Alabama, and other parts of Sherman's Military Division of the Mississippi—notably a raid by Confederate cavalry leader John Hunt Morgan—they caught Sherman's attention. Earlier he had wrestled with the way to get a more loyal, tractable population in the areas his army occupied by diluting it through "repeopling," with wholesale transfer of houses and property to the newcomers. He wrote his brother John just before the campaign opened: "The whole population of Iowa & Wisconsin should be transferred at once to West Kentucky, Tennessee and Mississippi. . . ." At first glance the idea is at the very least extraordinary, confirming the eccentricity of Sherman's thought. In 1864 it would have seemed less bizarre; the massive displacement of populations had already occurred in North Georgia, with the Cherokees moving out and white Georgians replacing them—and it seemed to have solved the problem. That Sherman was inspired by this episode is obvious; in the same letter he described the Rebel population as being even more recalcitrant than the Indians.

Now, in June, the general decided to attack the problem from a different angle: culling out the chief troublemakers and irreconcilables in his domains. At the beginning of the year he had mentioned the idea of "banishment," and now he took it up again. The aid and comfort bushwhackers and saboteurs received was proof the local population refused to accept the fact that they were conquered. The impress his forces made on regions they took over he compared to the movement of a ship through the sea: "Our armies traverse the land and the waves of disaffection, sedition and crime close in behind and our track disappears."

This frustration can clearly be read in the letters Sherman wrote to General Stephen Burbridge, commander of the District of Kentucky, and to Secretary of War Edwin M. Stanton. These letters were written on

June 21, the day after Sherman issued the special field order creating the District of the Etowah; there is no doubt that all three sprang from a common preoccupation. In the letter to Burbridge there was anger but also a hint of agitation, for the letter lacked the coherence Sherman's missives usually had. He made an opening reference to guerrilla activity, denouncing it as "nothing but simple murder, horse stealing, arson and other well defined crimes, which do not sound so well under their real name"; then he instructed Burbridge to tell his subordinates that guerrillas were not soldiers, but "wild beasts, unknown to the usages of war," and were to be treated accordingly. He argued that in the end societies must protect themselves, and if civil authority couldn't bring itself to act, then "we the military must do it." He went on: "Everybody can be made to 'stay at home and mind his or her business,' and if they won't do that, can be sent away." In this case being sent away meant not just banishment north of the Ohio River but deportation as well. Burbridge was to have his officers and agents arrest "all males and females who have encouraged or harbored Guerillas and Robbers," and have them collected at Louisville. When there were three or four hundred—a good shipload—Sherman would have them transported down the Mississippi and put aboard a vessel headed abroad.

The letter to Stanton outlined what he wanted to do and acknowledged that Lincoln would probably not approve of his deportation scheme. But one thing was certain: "there is a class of people who must be killed or banished, men, women and children, before you can hope for peace and order even as far south as Tennessee." Sherman wanted Stanton's help in finding a place to send the deportees, and he mentioned some places he thought might be suitable: Santo Domingo, Honduras, the Guyanas, possibly Baja California and Madagascar. Why Sherman should have undertaken this démarche at this particular time in mid-campaign is not easy to say; perhaps he simply found time for it since the campaign and the fighting had come to a virtual stop. The armies were immobilized for much of the month of June by torrential rains and seas of red mud—and possibly Sherman in his frustration shifted his restless energies to this other problem. In any event, on June 22 the rains stopped, the sun came out again, and the war soon resumed, absorbing Sherman's attention. But his creation of the District of the Etowah and his orders to General Burbridge would have their effect: A number of Georgians would find themselves taken from their homes and banished to distant places from which some of them never returned.

Copies of the letter to Burbridge were disseminated to the more important territorial commands, for Sherman intended its provisions should apply to all regions held by his armies. General Steedman got his copy of the letter via General Thomas, with the instructions to make it known to the people of his district "for their information." Steedman incorporated these new powers into his plan for protecting the vital rail line. On June 28 he published his General Order No. 2, whose essential provision was as follows:

> All citizens except government employees found within three miles of the Railroad from Bridgeport to the Federal Army in Georgia, outside of any post or station of troops after the 7th day of July, 1864, will be arrested and forwarded to these headquarters to be tried before a military commission as spies "found lurking" within the lines of the United States.

Patrols would sweep the prohibited zone daily, inspecting culverts, bridges, and tracks and looking for "lurking" people. For those Georgians who would be forced to leave their homes within the zone, there was possibility of exemption from the order if they were citizens of "undoubted loyalty"—and could prove it.

The applicants for exemptions were numerous if we may believe a Kentucky soldier who helped process them; he recalled over two hundred showing up one hot day in July. They came trudging in on foot (they were prohibited from riding the train) and were ready to take the loyalty oath and present attestations regarding their political reliability. A register of exempted families survives in the National Archives; it contains 291 "authorized" households—not a very large number for a zone embracing six hundred square miles. Perhaps this was because Steedman's order said: "none need apply who is not unqualifiedly loyal to the Federal Government and will aid by all means the success of its armies." In effect, those who got authorization were expected to give ongoing proof of their loyalty by reporting suspicious activity and the like. As Sherman put it, "men who manifest loyalty by oaths, and nothing more, are entitled to live, but not to ask favors of a government that demands acts and personal sacrifices."

Steedman's regime had a veritable power of life and death over the citizens of North Georgia—demonstrated graphically in Dalton one day in July when a man named Edwards was hanged as a spy. But the penalty most often inflicted by the military commissions was banishment north of the Ohio River until the end of the war. People picked up in the three-mile zone in violation of General Order No. 2 often got this punishment unless aggravating circumstances called for a more severe penalty. Banishment also awaited anyone whom the commissions found to be a "notorious rebel" or "suspicious character." In such cases the transportation order indicated the deportation was "according to General Sherman's Letter to General Burbridge."

Beginning in July there was a steady trickle of people expelled from Georgia, transported by the United States government to points north of the Ohio. The stream of exiles swelled as they joined those banished from other portions of the Military Division of the Mississippi. Some were simply unloaded at the pier in Cairo, Illinois (people there later claimed twenty thousand had come in the course of the year). Others were put ashore on the Indiana side of the river, in most cases without money or provisions; the town of Jeffersonville was inundated with them. A good many passed through Louisville, where a local refugee relief agency did what it could to help them. A reporter from the *Indianapolis Daily Journal* visited a group of women and children, including some from the Cassville area, who had taken shelter in the local railway depot; though it was December "the little children were barefooted, bare headed, bare-armed, and . . . without a change of even such poor garments as they wore."

Not all of the Georgians moving north were deportees under the provisions of the Burbridge letter. Those convicted of more serious offenses traveled under armed guard and were headed to Northern prisons. Most of these people are unknown, nothing but names on a list. But there is one about whom we know a bit more, chiefly because she was an acquaintance of Frances Howard, who speaks of her, and because she also figures in the diaries of two Northern soldiers. Though Frances Howard did not give her real name, other sources indicate her family name was Murchison; her first name was probably Sallie, though she was referred to as "Julia." She was about twenty years old and lived with her parents and sisters near the banks of the Etowah, not far from Kingston—a region that gave Federal authorities a good bit of trouble. The Murchisons were suspected of helping the guerrillas; the authorities had been told that the daughters made clothes and carried letters for them. "Julia" was in fact a thoroughgoing and uninhibited partisan of the Cause. She kept her hair cut short and sometimes wore a gray jacket with a Confederate captain's bars and regulation buttons, a sword belt with straps, and a pistol holster.

On Tuesday, July 19, while wearing this costume, she had a confrontation with either Union pickets or a Union officer—here the accounts vary. This encounter apparently was her undoing, for two days later an Iowa soldier noted in his diary: "this afternoon three of Murchison's daughters were sent north, being considered dangerous characters; the rest of the family will 'follow suit' if they don't carry themselves very straight." But the Murchison daughters were not just ordered north of the Ohio; they were arrested and sent to the Female Military Prison in Louisville, where "Julia" fell ill. She seems to have been released from prison at some point and tried to make her way home; her body was found along a roadside in Tennessee. The other sisters were apparently released in April 1865. One of them told Frances Howard: "We were never tried nor were we ever told the cause of our arrest."

There were others who went north voluntarily, because they had relatives there or simply because they felt the chances of survival were better than in the District of the Etowah. In July Sherman dispatched from Marietta several hundred women taken when his forces seized and destroyed the textile mills where they worked. The women who worked at the mills in Roswell, along with their children, Sherman seems to have shipped north *manu militare*, while those who worked at the Sweetwater factory were given a choice: Go north and work there, or go south after signing a pledge not to work for the Confederacy. Most chose to go north. One of the employees at the Sweetwater factory was William Causey, then seventeen years old; when interviewed in 1932 he related that his mother, who also worked there, decided to head north because as a widow with small children she had her best chance there. Just before they left, Mrs. Causey revealed to the Federal officers that she had an older son, home on sick leave from the Confederate army, who was hiding not far away; they agreed to let him come as well: "The Federals faithfully carried out their part of the agreement," said William Causey, "and treated us kindly as long as we were in their charge. None of the women was molested and everyone had plenty of food."

General Steedman appears in his official correspondence and actions as levelheaded and under the circumstances quite fair-minded. He had the final word on criminal matters, and here he showed a certain leniency. He released a citizen who faced prison on a rather flimsy charge of trying to poison a Union soldier and let another go who was accused of "advising to hang a Union man." When a citizen shot and killed a Union sergeant who was entering his house, Steedman reduced the charge from murder to manslaughter since the sergeant "had assumed a menacing attitude." He seems to have kept expulsions to a modest number (unfortunately we have no figures here), though Sherman from time to time encouraged him to do more of this: "Whenever the people get in the way ship them to a new country, north or west." And from time to time Sherman got in touch with him and with other subordinates about sending troublesome people overseas. In July, when a man named Polk came to the attention of the authorities, the general sent word: "Imprison Mr. Polk and tell him to convert his personal property into money & prepare to be sent to South America via New Orleans in a sailing vessel." But a month later he relented: "If you think he can behave himself," he wrote General Webster, "you may let his friends and neighbors execute heavy bonds, say $50,000 for his good behavior." In August the case of the "McConnel women" came to Sherman's attention. These four women turned up in the Nashville prison, where they had supposedly been sent on Steedman's orders, though the "papers" on them had been lost. They had been there for six weeks, and nobody knew what to do with them. Sherman settled the case: He wrote General Webster that they were to "go to foreign parts. Ask General Burbridge if he cannot make up a shipload." The general had given more thought to destinations for the exiles; now he favored Jamaica and Pernambuco, Brazil. What became of the McConnel women is not known.

In truth Sherman's scheme of moving populations in and out of conquered areas amounted to very little in North Georgia; a few hundred exiles at very most. Nor is there much indication that those forcibly removed belonged to that elite group of two or three hundred thousand Southerners that Sherman said would have to be dealt with in some fashion if the region would know true pacification. Nor do they look like ringleaders or provocateurs. Most of the deportees seem to have been of modest station at best; the names on General Steedman's lists are often those of women and children. In a way Sherman himself ensured that the policy of "banishment" would not get far. He was opposed to getting heavily involved with the local population—setting up governmental systems and the like—while military operations were under way; he had indicated as much in his letter to General Halleck on the future government of the South. But the idea continued to linger in Sherman's mind after the war was over, especially the scheme for an invigorating transfusion of Westerners. Had the general returned to Georgia immediately after Appomattox, armed with the sweeping powers of a proconsul, present-day Georgians might have had even greater cause to remember him.

As it was, General Steedman had his hands full trying to bring a modicum of peace and order to the District of the Etowah; had he exercised his powers of coercion and repression to the fullest, it is doubtful he would have had any greater success. His chief problem—one no amount of expulsions would resolve—was the very large "clandestine" population hidden in the woods of North Georgia. First of all there were, by estimate of the Confederate military, between three thousand and five thousand men who owed military service either to the Confederacy or to the state; there were Confederate cavalrymen who were detached in company-sized units to secrete themselves among the population and harass the railway, sometimes for three months at a time. There were Rebel scouts gathering information and more than a few Southern cavalrymen who had come into Steedman's domain to "recruit" a horse while on thirty days' leave. Then there were the locals, pro-Union and pro-Southern, who were carrying on their own war in the shadows, which became enmeshed with the larger conflict; finally, to this mass one could add the not negligible number of deserters and skulkers from the Union forces. All these groups needed food and shelter, and they often took it from others by force.

Steedman's troops—and others he occasionally borrowed—were unable to keep the railroad secure; at best they could try to intervene quickly once the Rebels attacked the line, and thus limit the damage. In the end it was the ability of repair crews to fix the breaks quickly that kept Sherman's supplies flowing. Then too, these "forces of order" were themselves frequently at the root of disorders. All too often their forays into the countryside turned into irregular forages and provoked bloody collisions with the local population. Frustrated in their efforts to come to grips with guerrilla leaders such as the fearsome John T. Gatewood and his band, they did not scruple at reprisal, hostage-taking, and torture. The garrison of Rome at one time included the First Alabama Cavalry, which had a special reputation for rough behavior, and the Forty-fourth U.S. Colored Infantry, whom we last saw being organized early in the year. The arrival of a black unit must have been a shock to the Romans and its stay a provocation, but strangely the presence of the black troops seems to have been forgotten in histories of the locality. But memory of the First Alabama Cavalry must have lingered for some time. The troopers reached the town with a terrible craving for tobacco—to the point that they surrounded male pedestrians and took any they had. One Roman who took to his heels they shot. In truth, the regiment was a law unto itself. When one of their men was killed outside Rome where he had gone to visit a girl, his comrades settled accounts by burning down five houses near the scene of the crime.

In Resaca General Steedman had a miscreant of another stripe. His name was James E. Graham, a twenty-two-year-old lieutenant in the Eightieth Ohio Infantry. Though he was provost marshal of the town his chief activity was having a good time, as he indicates in a remarkable diary. Sometimes he complains about the paperwork, occasionally he wonders how he would comport himself if he were in combat, for he has never seen the elephant—but mostly he writes about women. His position brought him in contact with the local inhabitants, whom he did not hesitate to call on if they had pretty daughters; and since his position was one of considerable power, he could count on being well-received. He spent a surprisingly large amount of time with young women, much of it in playing parlor games and petting. On July 20 he and Julia played "hunker-munker," and a little later he recorded a game of "muggins" with Miss Mollie and Miss Emma Buckner. On August 3 he "had a splendid time hugging and kissing" Julia; two days later he "kissed Mollie about ten or twelve times after supper." But other entries indicate that in sexual matters Lieutenant Graham had seen the elephant, and that his dalliance had a dark side. After all, it was often desperate and therefore vulnerable women who came to see him, to importune him for a pass, an exemption, or some other paper absolutely vital to them—and who would therefore agree to go with him into the back room of his office. After he received one female visitor he made this entry in his diary: "Before she left could well and truly say *I knew her.*"

The District of the Etowah must have been filled with desperate people that summer, but we know all too little about them, and what we do know comes largely from the diaries and letters of their conquerors. Most of these describe plain country people, for example the gaunt women, children in tow, who came to the Union camps to trade garden produce or wild berries for coffee, sugar, meat, and salt. Occasionally we are offered other glimpses: In Rome a Union army surgeon got into a heated argument over slavery with an old man who insisted there was a passage in the Bible that said: "his har shall be kinky, his skin black, and a sarvant of sarvants shall he be all the days of his life"; an Illinois soldier saw a woman, "a regular secesh," sitting on the front porch of her freshly plundered house in Dallas, rocking back and forth and repeating, "Oh Lord save us, we shall surely starve! Oh, have mercy on me and my child!"

In the right setting the encounter could be a mutually pleasurable one, as it often was when young soldiers met young women. On a road east of Snake Creek Gap a column of bluecoats was halted. Alongside the road was a log cabin, and sitting on a crude bench by the door was, in the words of one of the soldiers, "a very good looking young woman of the southern 'cracker' type." The men in the road stood staring at the woman; the woman sat staring out into space, fully aware that she was being admired by an entire army. Before long the men started up a conversation with her. As the narrator remembered it, with his rendition of her southern accent, it went something like this:

> "Are you married?"
> "Yaas."
> "Where is your husband?"
> "Oh, he's down yander. You'ens gwine down whar he is."
> "Aren't you afraid we'll kill him?"
> "Dunno. Maybe he'll kill you'ens."
> "How many Rebs are there down yonder?"
> "Dunno, a heap on'em. We'ens got a might smart crowd."
> "What will you do if the Yanks kill your husband?"
> "Dunno."

"Then," says the narrator, "a smile seemed to creep over her face which deepened into a grin, then hitching along on the bench she said: 'Dunno, I 'spect I'd hab to marry one ob you'ens.'" That provoked an outburst of laughter from the men, then a bugle sounded, there were shouted commands, and the column moved on.

There was one question these people asked their conquerors over and over again, for the soldiers often recorded it in their diaries, trying to imitate the country accents in which it was posed. It was, in essence, "Why did you come down here to fight us?" One suspects it was often asked by people who were genuinely mystified, but some were not afraid to ask it in a tone of anger and reproach. Near Roswell an Illinois soldier named James Snell encountered a distracted woman who had been stripped of everything, including food for her baby. She burst out at him: "All we want's to be lef' alone by o'rselves, without [you] coming down here to kill us all. What do you do it for? We didn't pester you any." Then, holding up her sickly, fretful baby, she said: "Its blood will be on your hands."

To the south, other Georgians were hearing disquieting stories of what was happening in the District of the Etowah. Sherman's letter to General Burbridge, as well as the edicts of General Steedman, had been printed in Georgia newspapers; refugees freshly arrived from the area brought their own accounts. Persistent stories circulated of depredations carried out with a refined cruelty: At each farm and plantation the Yankees were destroying all farming tools and implements except one hoe.

As for the Yankees' commanding general, he "says he will not treat them as civilized nations do—that the families of rebels have no right to anything to eat, drink, wear or life—the latter he gives them for the moment." Previously Sherman had had no greater claim to a Georgian's detestation than any other Union general, but now he was making a name for himself.

PART TWO

◆

ATLANTA

6

◆

The Citadel

The Union soldiers who occupied Marietta on July 3, 1864, were completely charmed by the town. Some found in it the picturesque charm of New England, others said it would do honor to Ohio or Indiana—though these sentiments did not save the town from a plundering. And Marietta was only the gateway to another Georgia, more peopled and more prosperous; though the region was still heavily wooded, there were enough broad fields and enough impressive homes to reassure those Union soldiers who were beginning to believe that the plantation South was a "humbug." The countryside now appeared "magnificent and well improved"; after the grim fastness around Dallas–New Hope Church the contrast was striking. General Howard said the arrival of his corps at Marietta "was, in fact, coming out of the woods and desert places into the brightness of civilization."

And as Sherman's army fought and maneuvered its way to the Chattahoochee, his soldiers by the hundreds got their first glimpse of Atlanta. Captain Orlando Poe set up a large telescope belonging to the engineers on top of Kennesaw Mountain and studied both the city and the 150,000 fighting men visible in and about it. "It was a grand picture, such as one does not behold more than once in a lifetime." Other men climbed trees for a quick look at it or sought out hills for a more leisurely view. When they recorded their experience in letters home the words they chose suggest they considered it significant: They spoke of having seen "the promised land," "the Mecca of our pilgrimage"; Colonel Thomas Taylor was moved to write his wife: "It is a glorious scene and most forcibly reminded me of Christ beholding Jerusalem." Among the spectators was General John Geary, who was above all mystified by the city—he could not for the life of him understand why it had been built where it was. He wondered if it weren't "the result of some accidental start," as if one surveyor stuck his rod in the ground while he tied his shoe and another immediately made it the point of reference for laying off the city limits.

In point of fact the city's location had been carefully chosen by the surveyors for the Western and Atlantic Railroad a quarter-century before. Since the state railroad was to connect with other lines the surveyors looked for a terminus on ground with good elevation, accessible from several directions without encountering prohibitively steep grades, and they found it six miles south of the Chattahoochee. Atlanta's first name was therefore the uninspired one of "Terminus," and it was probably little more than a country village by 1844. Briefly the burgeoning settlement called itself "Marthasville," then in 1847, about the time it took its charter, it took the name "Atlanta." It was one of Georgia's "round towns," its limits being marked off by a circle a little over six miles in circumference; within that circle the Atlanta of 1860 fitted very comfortably, with room to spare for woods and fields (modern-day Greater Atlanta is still bounded by a circle of sorts, Interstate 285; though it is sixty-five miles around, the city and its satellites spill over in several directions).

While many of Georgia's antebellum towns took as their center the courthouse or central square, Atlanta considered its the central train depot; its city seal bore neither an eagle nor a Greek goddess, but a locomotive, a fitting symbol for a city that owed both its birth and its growth to the Iron Horse. By 1860 Atlanta was at the center of a spiderweb of rail lines, some twelve hundred miles of them, that tied the state together and would soon hold the Confederacy together with bonds of iron. The Western and Atlantic approached the city from the northwest; a second line, the Georgia Railway, connected Atlanta with Augusta, and through it the Carolinas and Virginia; the Macon and Western came from the south, and from East Point on into the city it shared the roadbed with the Atlanta and West Point, the key link to states to the west. But the city was not just a roundhouse and a place where people changed trains; it was the site of numerous shops and plants that serviced the railroads and kept the trains running. These establishments and the workers who thronged to them fostered the creation of other enterprises, so Atlanta grew rapidly. One of its historians has described it in the 1840s as "a lively and picturesque frontier town." The charge of disorderly conduct appeared frequently on its court dockets, and there is a persistent story of miscreants liberated from jail by friends who lifted the wooden structure so they could crawl out from under it. Some reminders of the turbulent frontier town lingered in the place names of Confederate Atlanta and its environs: Lick Skillet, Snake Nation, Tight Squeeze, and Rough and Ready, a stop on the Macon line that would play a tragic role in the lives of a number of Atlantans.

By the 1850s, with further growth and prosperity, Atlanta acquired gaslights and mansions and a certain propriety, but it never lost the bustling, forward-looking ways that marked it apart; it took to calling itself "the Gate City" in the best chamber-of-commerce tradition of a town going somewhere. Seen from Augusta or Macon it was a fast-growing younger sister; from Savannah, the grande dame of Georgia's towns, it probably appeared a presumptuous parvenu. These impressions were confirmed in 1861 when the young city sent five representatives to lobby the first Confederate Congress at Montgomery in hopes the representatives would select Atlanta as the permanent seat of the new government. The lobbyists argued the advantages of their city's central location and the ease of communication in a town with forty-four trains a day. While the city's prosperity rested on solid economic foundations—fifteen manufacturing firms—its eighteen newspapers and periodicals proclaimed it a place of culture and enlightenment. Finally, in nearby Stone Mountain there was enough granite to construct the public buildings for "a thousand Confederacies."

Despite its material interest in the changes that were sweeping the South, Atlanta was caught up in the excitement of those first, heady days of secession. Drums rolled in its streets and men in new uniforms practiced drill and the manual of arms. As in every other town in Georgia, the young men organized themselves into companies with martial and patriotic names: the Gate City Guards, the Atlanta Grays, the Safe Guards, the Free Trade Rifles. There were enough German-Americans in town to form a company called the Steuben Jaegers, and no shortage of older men of martial temperament to fill the ranks of the Silver Grays. Subsequently men who were exempted from military service because of their work or calling created home guard units such as the Ordnance Guards and the Atlanta Press Guards.

The metalworking capacities of the railroad shops virtually ensured that the city would be a major producer of military hardware. Its rolling mill, the only one south of Richmond capable of rolling iron rails, also produced armor for Southern ironclads, as did Winship's Foundry and Machine Shop. Industrial plants evacuated from Nashville and other towns threatened by the Northern armies were welcome, as was a pistol factory opened by the Richmond firm of Spiller and Burr. The Confederate quartermaster's Atlanta facility employed over two thousand women to sew uniforms. Other firms made bits, spurs, artillery projectiles, and hand grenades. There is an oft-told story that the city first came to General Sherman's notice when he remarked the name "Atlanta" on so much of the ordnance used against his forces. Because of its central location and rail facilities the city became an important administrative center and entrepot, notably for quartermaster, commissary and medical departments; these and other government agencies had bureaus and offices paralleling those in Richmond. As it turned out Atlanta's pretensions at the beginning of the conflict proved well-founded: By 1864 it was the second city of the Confederacy.

This new stature was acquired at some cost. The city grew too fast and in disorderly fashion. The population, 9,554 in 1860, had jumped thirty percent by the end of 1861; at its peak early in 1864 Confederate Atlanta may have tripled its 1860 population, though many were transients and others had no formal address; the hotels and boardinghouses could not accommodate the newcomers, so individuals and sometimes whole families lived in tents, lean-tos, packing crates, and empty boxcars. In 1862 there were already problems with privies. The streets could not handle the traffic, though in 1863 the city fathers put up street signs for the benefit of newcomers. As early as 1862 military authorities decided martial law was the only way to impose order on this roiling mass. People continued to complain of gangs of mischievous boys and any number of idle blacks up to no good. Newcomers were victims of price gouging and other shady practices; a visiting Tennessean pronounced Atlanta "the swindling hole of the South." Arts and letters thrived in Confederate Atlanta. There were four local newspapers and a refugee press as well. Among new periodicals was *The Soldier's Friend*. Its chief service to its readers, said a reviewer, was "to prepare them, if possible, for the greatest of emergencies, *Death*." At least one novel was published in the city in 1864, and theater lovers could see dramas such as *The Plains of Manassas* and *King Linkum the First*.

Atlanta's mayor, a good and patient man named James Calhoun, touched on all these problems in his remarks to the city council in January 1864. These have been preserved in the minutes of the council, though in the hand of a clerk with an original approach to orthography. Mayor Calhoun began by saying that despite many vexing problems he and members of the city council faced, they had worked together harmoniously, with "no scisoms or clicks or feelings of anger, disappointment or mortification." The times, he said, were "peculiarly exciting," which made the task of keeping good order more difficult. Then, turning to the problems before them, mayor and council decided to impose a "dray license" to bring order to the traffic in the streets; they discussed a plan to set up free schools in the city, Mayor Calhoun feeling that for a thousand dollars a year they could hire "computent teachers." In the course of the meeting the mayor cited some figures that revealed that whatever impressions visitors might have formed, Atlanta was not a hard-hearted city: Of the $166,000 disbursed by the city fathers in 1863, a fourth had been spent on aid for the poor and the needs of wounded soldiers.

The city's churches did their part in relief work and welcomed refugees to their services, setting aside pews that were labeled "Tennessee," "Alabama," and so forth. There is considerable evidence that the people of Atlanta supplemented the meager resources of their government and charitable institutions with their own efforts in an impressive show of voluntarism. There were the raffles and benefits and collections, but Atlantans made heavy investments of time in other ways. For some time the Soldiers' Executive Aid Association for the Relief of the Army of Tennessee had maintained a sort of welcome center at the passenger depot, where women served refreshments to soldiers passing through the town. Then when trainloads of wounded began arriving from battlefields in Tennessee and later North Georgia, some citizens began sending their carriages to the depot to help transport them, while others volunteered to assist with unloading the trains. When there were large numbers of wounded to be handled, stores and businesses in the vicinity of the depot would close temporarily to free their employees for this kind of work. A preacher and storekeeper named Lewis Lawshe noted in his diary for May 29, 1864: "Sunday morning, seven o'clock: Took my turn again for twenty-four hours at the car shed." That morning one of the wounded he encountered was an old acquaintance, Captain Charles Daniel: "I once made him very angry by dunning him for an account," Lawshe noted, "and this was the first chance I had to put him in good humor." He fed the captain, who had a bad wound in his arm, and helped change his bandage in a nearby saloon that served as a dressing station. That spring medical authorities relaxed the rules to make it easier for patients to be cared for in private homes, and Atlantans opened their doors to numbers of them. This same hospitality manifested itself in Georgia's other "hospital towns"; when fire destroyed a large military hospital in downtown Americus, the local residents somehow made room for over two thousand patients.

For if armaments plants had earlier been the hallmark of Confederate

Atlanta, in the first months of 1864 the most obvious feature of the city was its hospitals, which were set up all over town, usually in hotels and public buildings. The receiving hospital was at the fairgrounds and the hospital for contagious diseases isolated on a 195-acre tract. The women of Atlanta worked in them in sizable numbers, supplementing the nursing staff. Something is known of what went on in these hospitals, thanks to the reminiscences of Dr. R. J. Massey, who ran Brown Hospital, named for Governor Brown. The job, Dr. Massey asserts, was no sinecure. He was not only the director, therefore saddled with the administrative burdens, but also the sole surgeon for a facility with four hundred beds, all of them occupied. Brown Hospital was unusual in that it had been created by Governor Brown, who appointed the staff—all Georgians—and intended it for Georgia troops only. Later the Confederate government took it over, but Governor Brown continued to have his say in the way it was run and insisted on receiving duplicates of all hospital correspondence, which imposed an onerous burden on Dr. Massey. Were that not enough, Confederate military authorities pressed to have the patients discharged and returned to duty as soon as possible, while Governor Brown intervened to get longer convalescences. The hospital was also noted for its sexton, charged with removing the bodies of patients who died and seeing to their burial. A blunt, no-nonsense man, he made his daily rounds, calling into each ward: "Anybody dead here? Anybody about to die?"

The hospitals often contained wounded Union soldiers undergoing treatment before their transfer to Andersonville, and women doing volunteer work there sometimes had a less than charitable view of the Yankee patients, at least initially. One woman wrote: "It is as much as I can do not to abuse them even when they are sick in the hospital. Unless they are very ill I never look at them." Such attitudes rarely persisted; a Confederate nurse named Fannie Beers remembered that when she first went into the prisoners' ward she took a certain hostility with her: "I had been five minutes in the low, brick ward where lay the most dangerously wounded Federals, when all animosity vanished and my woman's heart melted within me." Miss Abby, the staunch Unionist from New England, visited the prisoners in the Atlanta hospitals quite often. She recorded in her diary: "I have heard of strange, beautiful stories—of captives now & then catching glimpses of some sweet, pitying face—of vows being exchanged in mysterious ways, and promises given of returns and welcomes after the war." Miss Abby is also the source for an improbable story that somehow has a ring of truth: A Northern prisoner became fast friends with one of the soldiers guarding him in the hospital; when the Yankee became sufficiently ambulatory his friend brought him a Confederate uniform and they went out on the town together.

Until the spring of 1864 Atlanta's tribulations were scarcely different from those of any other city in the Confederacy. To be sure there were the fearful, who found the Yankees at Ringgold entirely too close and departed the city for a refuge farther south, and the prudent, who took steps to liquidate their holdings in the city. Dr. Henry Huntington, the transplanted Vermonter practicing dentistry in the city, learned that he was soon to be drafted, though he was in his forties and theoretically exempted from conscription by his profession; he decided to leave, but to go north rather than south. On May 7, just as the campaign was opening, he left with a guide whom he paid a hundred dollars a day to get him through the lines to Chattanooga. He left behind a wife with two small sons and a three-week-old baby; the guide was to come back for her and the children in a few days, but Mrs. Huntington did not get out of the city for another three months. At that time people leaving Atlanta were still a small minority. Most believed the Great Battle would take place somewhere to the north that spring, and they would make their plans according to its outcome; in the meantime they were assured by the massive fortifications going up around the city. Construction of the city's defenses had begun a year before, and now they were being compared to the celebrated fortifications of Sebastopol, the great Russian naval base besieged in the Crimean War a few years before. The Confederate authorities had contracted for thousands of slaves, providing them with food, shelter, and medical care and paying their masters a dollar a day for their labor (a special government agency was set up to compensate their owners if they were killed or injured on the job or if they ran off to the enemy). The blacks had moved immense quantities of earth, constructed elaborate works, and cleared the ground in front of them so as to create unobstructed fields of fire. At the same time army engineers had sophisticated obstacles made to impede the enemy's advance—abbatis and chevaux-de-frise—these being in some cases attached to the ground with wire, so the enemy could not push them aside. These were fortifications to make those the Confederates were throwing up in North Georgia look like the work of children. To Atlantans who went out to look at them, the city's defenses were extremely impressive. They would also impress General Sherman, who later pronounced them the strongest fortifications he had ever seen.

But in May the menace to the city became more clearly defined as Sherman's army moved down the Western and Atlantic at the rate of about a mile a day; in that month the city began to live the most perilous period in its history. On the 18th Governor Brown issued a proclamation calling out the state militia, and on the 23rd Mayor Calhoun issued a proclamation of his own calling on all able-bodied men in the city to appear before the town hall so that they could be organized into companies for the defense of the city. The mayor also had some words for those who didn't intend to heed his call: "All male citizens who are not ready to defend their homes and families are requested to leave the city at their earliest convenience, as their presence embarrasses the authorities and tends to the demoralization of others." One of the Atlantans called up for duty was Samuel Richards, who confided to his diary: "I trust we may never be called into action, I hate the sight of a musket."

The mayor's proclamation had an immediate effect. Miss Abby recorded in her diary: "May 24th. This has been a day of wild excitement. From early morning until now—engines have screamed—trains thundered along; wagons laden with government stores, refugees, negroes and household stuff have rattled out of town. Every possible conveyance is bought, borrowed, begged or stolen." A military correspondent called "Shadow" who wrote for the *Mobile Daily Advertiser and Register* witnessed the same chaotic exodus; he had been out of town for two weeks and was amazed by the way things had changed. He told his readers with unusual frankness: "I observe my own feeling on the subject and I think Atlanta will fall." The commotion following the mayor's proclamation had not completely subsided when May 27 brought a harbinger to stir the most complacent: That day it was possible for the first time to hear the faint thunder of cannon to the north. Almost everyone listened to it with a sense of grim foreboding, but that day Miss Abby exulted in her diary: "O that music!—the first notes of our redemption anthem."

On June 1 the Atlanta city council called on the people to invoke the Almighty on their town's behalf, "to give us strength to resist the vandal hordes"; June 10 was to be a day of fasting and prayer. The city council met again on the 10th, and that day all was not harmony. Someone offered a resolution condemning the depredations and "outrages" that stragglers from Johnston's army were committing against citizens and their property; in the end the council decided not to adopt the resolution. There was clearly some antagonism between the town and the troops defending it; late in July soldiers pillaged several stores and a lieutenant wrote his mother: "If Soddom deserved the fate that befell it Atlanta will not be unjustly punished."

The second half of June brought bad news from the front, then good news. On the 16th the town's leading citizens assisted at a funeral service for General Leonidas Polk, who was also a bishop in the Episcopal church. Polk had been struck by a Federal artillery shell while on Pine Mountain looking at the Union positions; though somewhat out of touch with military matters—he was in his late fifties and had been away from the army for decades—he was immensely popular and his loss was much felt. But on June 27 this loss was counterbalanced. On that day General Sherman launched assaults against the Confederate defenses at Kennesaw Mountain; the Confederates hurled them back with heavy losses to the assailants. Though it was a Confederate victory of sorts, Mayor Calhoun took the precaution of sending his family to South Georgia (he did not send the thirty slaves he owned; they would eventually find their way north to freedom).

But July began with further bad news. On the 3rd Sherman's forces occupied Marietta, just a few minutes' ride up the Western and Atlantic. On the following day Miss Abby was invited to a picnic. It was a somber affair, and she tactfully kept a tight rein on her own soaring spirits; when the day was over she made the usual entry in her diary, but this time she ended it with a flourish: "I feel quite assured that this is the last picnic I shall attend in the *Southern Confederacy*." As if to bear out her prediction, General Johnston began withdrawing his troops across the Chattahoochee, with the Federals following and watching for opportunities to get bridgeheads across the stream—opportunities they soon found and exploited. Briefly the populace clung to a bit of incredibly good news that went the rounds on the 7th and 8th: Sherman had been captured! Unfortunately the man in question was Colonel Frank Sherman, an officer on the staff of General Howard. Colonel Sherman, who passed through the city on July 8 on his way to the officers' prison at Macon, had time to look around and record in his diary: "the citizens are leaving." Two days later Samuel Richards wrote in his: "the city has been in a complete swarm all day and for several days." For the news from the Chattahoochee had sparked another panic and another cycle of departures. But Richards had made up his mind not to join the exodus: "Sallie and I have decided to stay at home, Yankees or no Yankees. We hear and read terrible things about them, but I don't think they are as bad as they are said to be."

Now it was not just people who were packing up and leaving, but institutions as well. Some businessmen had long since decided their concerns would do better elsewhere; early in March the Spiller and Burr firm packed up its machinery and moved to the greater security of Macon. Large government facilities had to be more careful, lest their departure have a serious impact on public opinion. Colonel M. H. Wright, who ran the Atlanta arsenal, began shipping surplus machinery and stores to Macon and Augusta toward the end of May, "in view of the proximity of the enemy to this place." He wrote Colonel G. W. Rains, head of the Augusta works: "I propose to make these shipments at intervals as facilities may offer and with a view not to create any uneasiness with the people here." Colonel Wright said General Johnston had assured him he could hold the city, so he regarded the shipments as simple precaution: "I consider Atlanta perfectly safe." The colonel's efforts to make his shipments without attracting attention were not very successful; in a city where hearsay increasingly supplemented the news, one of the stories that circulated concerned secret shipments of government stores.

On July 6 orders went out to begin evacuating the hospitals. This was a delicate and complicated operation accomplished for the most part in the first half of July. As a first step the hospitals reduced the number of patients by granting convalescent furloughs to as many as possible. At the expiration of their leaves the soldiers were to rejoin their units, but it didn't always work like that. A soldier named S. H. Clayton got sixty days' leave after being treated for a jaw wound. A half-century later he confessed to an interviewer: "As I had not been at home in three years I made my way home to Tennessee, stayed at home two weeks, got me a horse, come out with Gen. Forest."

When a hospital packed up, of necessity it deprived its patients of normal access to care and medication, so the move needed to be completed as quickly as possible. For that reason the movement of hospitals had priority over the shipment of ordnance stores, for example—a rule that caused considerable problems for Colonel Wright in his efforts to reduce the stocks in the Atlanta arsenal. Given the overworked rail system and its dilapidated condition, priority status did not ensure rapid movement. Dr. Massey got orders for moving the Brown Hospital on July 8 but the staff and patients did not board the train until the 13th; their original destination was Macon, but was changed to Milledgeville, where they arrived on the 15th. For the sick and wounded, being moved in such conditions was traumatic; it is small wonder that Dr. Massey said his patients arrived "in fair condition." Some patients died during evacuation, including several killed in a train wreck on July 19. One patient simply vanished: Private William V. Taylor of the Thirteenth Tennessee Infantry. Family and friends later searched hospitals as far away as Macon, but in vain. A month later they were reduced to appealing for information in the newspapers; they believed he had died on a train and been buried at some stop and were hoping someone could tell them where. A Mississippi soldier who was involved in moving patients out of Atlanta wrote his wife he could not tell her how bad it was: "The battle field is a mear Trifal compared to it."

In the first days of July there was an unusual amount of activity in newspaper offices and print shops. Though the correspondent of the *Augusta Daily Chronicle and Sentinel* reported on July 4 that the city was facing the future "with remarkable hopefulness, nerve, and composure," and though the *Atlanta Daily Intelligencer* proclaimed on the 5th, "our advice to all is to *stand firm*," the newspapers too were preparing to evacuate the town. The last newspaper, the *Memphis Appeal*, left July 22. The city fathers were taking measures as well. On July 11 the city council authorized the removal of the city's mules, "provided such emergency for their safety should arrive," and gave the mayor authority to evacuate the city records whenever he thought it necessary. On July 15 the council met but did not have a quorum; on the 18th it decided that the city's two best fire engines should be sent out to some sure place "in case of Atlanta's being occupied for a time by the enemy." Then the mayor and council adjourned their meeting; the record does not indicate when they planned to assemble again.

Atlanta was now to suffer the fate North Georgia had previously met. At a certain point in the final crisis leaders fell silent and authority entered a kind of eclipse—perhaps because crisis management of this sort was beyond the ken of government as it was then understood. Governor Brown came to the city briefly, but offered it only the moral support of his fleeting presence. Mayor Calhoun and the city council would not assemble again for six months, though the mayor and several councilmen would play a role in the final agony of Confederate Atlanta. The mayor's court did not meet after July 1 and neither did the county superior court. Firemen would stay at their posts until overwhelmed, but municipal police powers seem to have been less and less exercised. Soon the only symbol of order remaining in the city was the military. The departure of nearly all the newspapers by the middle of July cut the city's dwindling population off from the outside world more effectively than the "semi-siege" the Union army was beginning to impose.

The city was now like a ship adrift in dangerous waters, its passengers and crew abandoning it as whim or panic took them. The harrowing tales of refugees could provoke stampedes: Mrs. Irby Morgan listened to the testimony of a family whose home had been sacked by the Yankees: "After hearing of the treatment they had received, we were terribly frightened and begged to be taken farther south." Her party headed for Augusta. "By this time," she recalled, "pandemonium reigned in the streets—soldiers' wagons, artillery wagons, drivers shouting and hurrying, and the 'tramp, tramp, tramp' was heard everywhere." As had been the case in North Georgia, it was the poor, ignorant, and gullible who most often bolted in blind and headlong flight. Miss Abby watched them streaming through the streets of Atlanta: "Poor families—who can barely live where they are—frightened at the reported doings of the terrible foe—fleeing with the rest—sometimes only taking half of their little all in their flight. No home to go to—no money to procure one—but the Yankees are coming, & they must go somewhere."

Others, with the time and the means, were more methodical in their evacuation. Lewis Lawshe had a place of refuge south of Atlanta, outside the town of McDonough. He wrote in his diary for Saturday, July 9: "Loaded up the wagon and at 9 o'clock started for Butler County with a one-horse wagon, three negroes, a cow, a calf, a yearling, a dog and the most valuable stuff I could pack in my wagon." He reached McDonough the next morning at eight, then started back to Atlanta the morning of the 11th, for he had two more wagonloads to move. Lawshe was fortunate to still have his horse and wagon, for the army had impressed heavily in Atlanta. Many who fled the city that month could take only what they could carry. People departing made various dispositions of the property they were forced to leave behind. Merchants tried to liquidate their stocks with sales at sacrifice prices; Confederate soldiers wrote home that they had plenty of food, for the local inhabitants were selling it to them for a pittance or simply making a present of it. A man whose house was near the lines of the Twenty-seventh Alabama passed by with his slaves, headed south. He told the soldiers, "Boys, I want you to take everything I leave, for I know the Yankees will get it, and I don't want them to eat or drink anything that belongs to me."

The value of things changed rapidly under these conditions. In Atlanta a ramshackle cart would bring a thousand dollars, a horse perhaps three times that sum. While food was being given away outside the city, prices continued to rise in town; on July 14 cabbage was quoted at from three to four dollars a head. While food was climbing in price each day, the price of real estate was dropping fast. Some homeowners, after advertising their houses in vain, simply locked the doors and left, hoping somehow their homes would be there when they returned. Mrs. Henry Huntington, wife of the dentist who had fled to Chattanooga, found a buyer for their house early in June. He agreed to pay in gold and Bank of England notes, but would give her only a tenth of what the property was worth. She accepted his offer, and wisely so; the house was later destroyed in the fighting. Mrs. Huntington also sold her husband's professional library, dental tools, and office furniture. They were insured for $2,000, but she accepted an offer of $125.

While the minds of most people were now on leaving Atlanta, others were still coming into the city. One of these was Episcopal Bishop Henry C. Lay, who had come to help supply the spiritual needs of the Army of Tennessee and was destined to come and go throughout the city's agony. He first arrived in the middle of the hubbub over General Johnston's move across the Chattahoochee; in the house where he was staying there was a stir before daylight, sparked by the story the city was to be evacuated. Though he had scarcely unpacked, the bishop went to the depot and managed to get on a train to Augusta. He came back on July 16, and on the 19th he tried to hold confirmations in Clayton's Division, but was hindered because the army was in movement. On the 20th affairs began to "look very serious" in Atlanta, and he again joined the exodus, this time taking a train for Macon. Sick and wounded were still being evacuated; at the depot scores of them lay waiting on the platform with "every ghastly wound, limbs amputated a few hours before." The bishop was shaken by what he saw. He wrote his wife from Macon: "Oh! it is an awful sight, and suggests a terrible reckoning when God shall make requisition for blood." In Macon Bishop Lay sat at the deathbed of a young lieutenant, and after his death he accompanied the coffin and the lieutenant's widow to Savannah; once again the train was jammed and there were no seats; the widow, overcome by grief and exhaustion, stretched out on her husband's coffin. But by early August Bishop Lay was back in Atlanta, where he carried out a number of confirmations, including that of General John Bell Hood.

Sometime in the middle of July a young man in the uniform of a Confederate sergeant arrived in Atlanta on the train from Macon. His name was S. H. M. Byers and he was in reality an adjutant in the Fifth Iowa Infantry, recently confined in the Confederate military prison in Macon. He had procured the uniform from a prison guard, put it on at the opportune moment, and walked out of the prison with a detail of Confederate soldiers. At the Macon train station he had talked the conductor into giving him free passage to Atlanta, for his intention was to gain the Union lines. For the moment he needed a place to stay, and by mid-July this was no longer a problem in Atlanta. He soon found and settled down in a house whose owner had departed. Byers generously agreed to share it with a refugee family, who in turn invited him to share their dinner. Adjutant Byers's chance presented itself on July 22, when the Confederate forces moved out to attack the enemy east of the city.

Byers's plan was to pose as an ordnance sergeant and stay behind the troops going into battle, in the anticipation that they would soon be coming out again, with the Federal army at their heels. As the Confederates passed by he would fall to the ground as though shot, then get up again and present himself to the troops in blue. The troops he was following went into battle, and he posted himself where he could watch for their return. He waited a considerable length of time as the battle thundered in front, then lost patience, struck out toward what he hoped were the Union lines, and got himself picked up by a Confederate provost patrol; after an interview with Colonel B. J. Hill, provost marshal of the Army of Tennessee, he found himself on his way back to Macon.

Then there were those who stayed in their residences with no thought of leaving, for like Adjutant Byers, they would consider the appearance of Union forces as the moment of their liberation. Miss Abby, who lived on the edge of the town, noted the signs as the tide of battle moved toward her hill. First a Confederate field hospital pitched its tents nearby, then packed up and left, to be replaced by a battery of Louisiana artillery that came thundering up and unlimbered in her yard. An officer told her politely that she would not be safe in her house and should move. The artillerymen helped her pack, and on July 22 she wrote that she had found refuge with a Mrs. Frank. When she saw her first blue uniforms we do not know, for that was the last entry in her diary.

Farther out from the city was another loyalist, William King. He waited for the liberators in his country house near the Sandtown Road. He saw something of the same procession of forces, beginning with great numbers of wagons and artillery rolling south. On July 2 a Confederate captain named Lee stopped to tell him he should be making preparations to depart and was probably taken aback when Mr. King told him he was planning to stay at home. That evening friends stopped by for tea, having spent the day sending off horses, servants, and wagonloads of possessions. Mr. King wrote a letter to his wife, then retired, where his anxious and depressed state kept him from getting much sleep; Hardee's Corps was now passing his house, and he was disturbed by the noise the soldiers made trying to catch his chickens. Confederate infantry passed most of the next day, then cavalry; an artillery battery took up post near the house and sparred for a time with the advancing Federals, then headed south in turn. After a brief lull a party of Union cavalry came down the road. Soon Mr. King was talking with a Lieutenant Harvey of the 115th Illinois Infantry, then with a major, a colonel, and finally with Brigadier General Washington Elliott. That evening, his first back under the "old flag," Mr. King wrote in his diary that it had all been "very gentlemanly."

Inside Atlanta the citizens who remained in the second half of July were kept constantly on the qui vive by a series of occurrences that had direct bearing on their chances of survival: On the 18th President Davis removed Joseph E. Johnston from command of the Army of Tennessee, for reasons communicated by the Confederate adjutant general: "You have failed to arrest the advance of the enemy to the vicinity of Atlanta, far in the interior of Georgia, and express no confidence that you can defeat or repel him." Hardly was his successor General Hood in place before he took the offensive in not one but three major engagements fought outside the city: the battles of Peachtree Creek (July 20), Atlanta (July 22), and Ezra Church (July 28).

Most important, the city itself became a battleground. On July 22 the Confederates had withdrawn to lines closer to the city; in fact the large white mansion of Ephraim Ponder stood like a blockhouse overlooking the trenches and chevaux-de-frise of the Confederate line. On July 20 General McPherson ordered De Gress battery to fire a few shells into Atlanta "to let them know that we are coming and are in reach of them." The artillerymen unlimbered a twenty-pound Parrott, dug a hole so as to sink the trail and raise the trajectory, and fired several rounds into the city. One of the shells struck at the intersection of Ivy and Ellis streets, killing a small girl. As the bombardment intensified, so did the effectiveness of the Federal fire. The shelling caused several fires. Bishop Lay expressed his opinion that Sherman was using Greek fire; what the Union artillerymen were doing was heating projectiles in a furnace before firing them (they fired about 150 rounds before abandoning the experiment as producing "no perceptible results"). One battery created an observer's post high in a pine tree:

A man stationed in this tree would tell us whether we fired too high, too low, too far to the right or too far to the left, until we could hit any house we chose that stood within range. By our reckoning we were just one and 7/8 miles from the round house that stood near the middle of the city as to north and south. Our fire was directed mostly at this point.

The infantrymen occasionally joined in the bombardment, holding their muskets at about thirty degrees in the belief that would make the balls carry all the way into the city; according to a participant this was "rare sport."

Initially the bombardment drove hordes of people to the depot or to the roads leading south, largely emptying the city. The shelling continued, sometimes heavy and sometimes light, through July and well into August. Those citizens who stayed counted themselves lucky if they had a basement, those who did not constructed dugout shelters in their yards; those who lived near tall smokestacks and church steeples did so with a certain uneasiness. Lieutenant William J. Neal, whose position in the defenses was about a hundred yards from the Ponder mansion, could also check on what was happening to the family home nearby. "I see two balls have gone into our house," he wrote in a letter of August 4, "one in Bud James' room and one in the parlor." (Lieutenant Neal was killed six days later.) Now few civilians entered the city; when Fannie Beers came in on August 4 she was the only woman aboard a train full of soldiers. Shells were falling on the town, and she was astounded to see the soldiers pile off and go about their business. She could find no hotel room, so she moved into the first floor of an abandoned house whose upper story had been wrecked by a shell.

The town appeared to be largely deserted, but there was one center of movement and animation—the passenger depot. Charles H. Smith, who would acquire a considerable reputation as a humorist under the pen name Bill Arp, had recently refugeed from Rome, but in early August he was trying to get his family back out of the city. He spent most of the day at the depot, waiting and watching the scene about him: "train after train of goods and chattels moved down the road, leaving hundreds of anxious faces waiting their return." But the afternoon was not without its humorous moments as Bill Arp helped load a baggage car:

"Won't you let these boxes go as baggage?"

"No, madam, it is impossible!" Just then someone's trunk as big as a nitre bureau was shoved in and the poor woman got desperate.

"All I've got ain't as heavy as that," said she. "I am a poor widow and my husband was killed in the Army. I've got five children and three of them cutting teeth, and my things have to go!"

We took up her boxes and shoved them in. Another good woman asked very anxiously for the Macon train. "There it is, Madam," said I. She shook her head mournfully and remarked, "You are mistaken, sir. Don't you see the engine is headed right up the State road, towards the Yankees? I shan't take any train with the engine on the wrong end of it. No sir, that ain't the Macon train."

About sundown Arp and his family managed to get aboard a train, though they had no idea where it would stop. They left behind them a city living a curious twilight existence. Within it rumors circulated of appalling deaths but also of miraculous survivals. A shell passed through a hotel room where Confederate telegraph operators were sleeping; it clipped the legs from their cots and dumped them on the floor before passing on without exploding. The Reverend Charles Quintard reported that a large shell had entered St. Luke's Episcopal Church, smashing a prayer desk. A Bible fell on the live shell "so as apparently to smother it and prevent its exploding." Then there was the projectile that passed harmlessly through the bedroom of a woman who had just given birth, prompting her to exclaim: "That baby's name is Sherman." Then on August 25 the shelling stopped. Soon the news of another miracle filtered through the city. The enemy was gone! Those who went to see for themselves came back describing great stretches of breastworks filled with discarded clothing, cracker boxes, newspapers, and flies, but empty of Yankees. At that point there were perhaps four thousand people left in the battered town, beginning to hope again that somehow their city might yet be saved. When the calm held the next day they began to venture out and breathe freely again. A wild, exhilarating rumor ran through the town and through the Confederate forces defending it: Sherman was retreating, he had already recrossed the Chattahoochee! A reporter for the Milledgeville paper wrote: "Cellars gave up their occupants, basement stories were evacuated; holes in the Rail Road cuts were suddenly left alone in their glory, and Atlanta was herself once more." But the enemy army that had vanished would soon reappear, and within a week the Stars and Stripes would fly over the Gate City.

7

◆

The Raids

As chief engineer and a member of General Sherman's staff, Orlando Poe was well-placed to comment on the bombardment of Atlanta. His opinion was that the shelling did not advance the city's fall by a single second. It was of course Sherman's opinion that counted, and that opinion seems to have changed as the campaign advanced. As he was preparing to cross the Chattahoochee early in July he wrote General Halleck: "Instead of attacking Atlanta direct, or any of its forts, I propose to make a circuit, destroying all its railroads." This policy he believed would force the Confederate army to offer battle or to evacuate the city. Sherman already held one of the four rail lines, and by July 18 his army had begun the destruction of a second, the line running east to Augusta; at this juncture Sherman briefly believed that Johnston might abandon the city, and he was also tantalized by the idea that the town itself was so lightly defended that it might be seized in a coup de main before the bulk of the Confederate forces in the outer works could intervene, but by the 21st he felt the chance of taking it by "a quick move" was past; moreover the cards had been further scrambled by General Hood's assumption of command and—temporarily—of the initiative.

By the 21st Sherman had worked his army sufficiently close to the city to get a good idea of the inner perimeter of defenses. He wrote General Halleck that he was now in position to try a new tack:

The city seems to have a line all round it, at an average distance from the center of the city of a mile and a half, but our shot passing over this line will destroy the town, and I doubt if General Hood will stand a bombardment; still he has fought hard at all points all day. I will open on the town from the east and northeast tomorrow. . . .

When he wrote again two weeks later it was evident that the new policy had not yet produced very encouraging results. In virtually identical telegrams to Halleck and Grant, Sherman reported: "We keep hammering away here all the time, and there is no peace inside or outside of Atlanta." He had at the same time been moving his forces farther to the west of the city, but was now going to turn up the heat on Atlanta itself:

I do not deem it prudent to extend more to the right, but will push forward daily by parallels, and make the inside of Atlanta too hot to be endured. I have sent to Chattanooga for two 30-pounder Parrotts, with which we can pick out almost any house in the town. I am too impatient for a siege, but I do not know but here is as good a place to fight it out as farther inland. One thing is certain, whether we get inside Atlanta or not, it will be a used-up community by the time we are done with it.

To Grant he appended a more informal message, and further rationale for a policy that had yet to pay any dividends: It was important "to give those southern fellows all the fighting they want," he told Grant, "we must manifest the character of dogged courage and perseverance of our race."

At the same time Sherman had been experimenting with still another way to make Atlanta fall into his hands, although this involved using a part of his forces that had thus far remained in the background—the cavalry. We have not said much about this arm in the Georgia campaign, chiefly because its role in the first two months of fighting had been a modest one. By 1864 it was not feasible to commit mounted troops directly to the battlefield because of the lethalness of the fire they would encounter; moreover the increasing use of field fortification put other obstacles—quite literally—in their way. Then too, in regions such as North Georgia the rugged and heavily wooded terrain was ill-suited to cavalry operations in the traditional sense. As a consequence in the North Georgia campaign cavalrymen often found themselves fighting on foot and manning the trenches; as one veteran of the Georgia campaign put it, they fitted Dr. Johnson's definition of the word "Dragoon," since they "fought indifferently on foot, or on horseback." Finally the

cavalrymen of Sherman's forces had a special obstacle to overcome—
their commander's often-expressed belief that they were inferior to their
Confederate counterparts and generally not up to their job.

In both Northern and Southern armies the cavalryman also had a
poor image among the infantry. Part of this animosity was the understandable resentment soldiers who travel on foot feel against soldiers
who ride; there was also a very practical reason that foot soldiers did not
like close association with mounted units, especially when encamped—
their horses drew flies. But the chief charge against the cavalrymen was
that they did little fighting and that poorly. Though casualty figures
seem to justify this prejudice, in fact many of the cavalryman's important duties for which he was uniquely fitted, guard and messenger and
escort work, scouting and reconnaissance—a chain of vedettes was an
army's early warning system—did not normally involve combat.

Many Georgia farmers and planters also had made the acquaintance
of the major Confederate cavalry commands operating in their state,
Iverson's, Dibrell's, and the like, and they had come to regard their
arrival in the locality as bad news. In truth the cavalrymen placed a
heavy burden on the rural population in areas where they operated.
Often detached and out of touch with the main army, they had to find
sustenance for themselves and their mounts; they took it where and how
they could, and it made little difference whether they were in friendly or
enemy territory. A planter named Joseph Printup, who lived in an area
frequently visited by Southern cavalry, wrote his brother early in 1864
that he had abandoned his acres and moved to another part of the state:
"I found it utterly impossible to stay so near our army & keep a suffi-
ciency to feed my family." One of General Forrest's foraging parties had
taken five hundred bushels of corn, a large quantity of fodder, and fifteen or twenty hogs "& refused to pay me one cent for it." Cavalrymen
helping themselves to the contents of a farmer's barn and smokehouse
might or might not offer the farmer a receipt and the possibility of even-
tual reimbursement. But if they did not, the farmer was in no position to
insist. A Wilkes County planter kept his own careful record of what it
cost him when he was visited by Companies A and B of the Thirtieth
Georgia Cavalry between ten-thirty A.M. and two P.M. on Friday, June 17,
1864: 135 pounds of flour, 62 pounds of bacon, 1,200 pounds of corn, and
135 bales of fodder. In addition several of the officers took dinner with
him, and after they left he discovered that while they were at table the
men had roamed about his place and stolen countless items.

Northern and Southern cavalry were both known for their forag-
ing/plundering habits, though in truth they outdistanced the infantry in

this regard mostly because the nature of their service gave them greater opportunities. The mounted services of both armies seem to have had a more casual attitude toward military procedure and discipline than either the infantry serving with them or cavalry in the eastern theater. In the Northern service the loose ways of the First Alabama have already been noted, but regiments raised in Kentucky and Tennessee also stood out. According to Stephen Starr, who wrote a book on the Union cavalry in the West, "the 1st Kentucky made itself a byword for indiscipline in every possible form"; to cite but one example, it began the 1864 campaign with all its officers technically under arrest. Among regiments in the Army of Tennessee the mounted units from the other side of the Mississippi had this same sort of reputation. A Tennessee cavalryman recalled them vividly: "They came out of the wilds of Arkansas and Texas and were the roughest lot of humanity I ever saw." The Texas regiments particularly seem to have engaged in a sort of blood feud with certain Northern units.

Then too, both services were imbued with "the Cavalry Spirit," which a British officer once described as "a disdain for all calculation." Arguably the cavalrymen did have a distinctive mindset, a dashing and impulsive nature; if not, at least they tried to cultivate one. Union General Lovell Rousseau came to the cavalry service late in his career, but adapted to it perfectly. His aide remembered that he "would not even study his maps, and often turned them over to me unopened"; yet "the men thought he knew it all." On the Southern side General Joseph Wheeler also had the cavalry spirit, according to a Texas trooper and war correspondent who served with him. He relates that Wheeler once led his men headlong into a rain-swollen river; several men were swept away in making the opposite shore. Then Wheeler's men discovered that they were on an island and had a second perilous crossing before them. The men who followed such leaders had a certain impulsive, devil-may-care spirit too: After this crossing or another equally difficult one, Georgia cavalryman Ford McWhorter recalled that several of the "boys" tried to get him to go back across the turbulent river with them, for they wanted to "have fun with the Yankees." He declined, but did contribute some dry cartridges to the venture, and the men took off. They were never seen again.

As the war continued the cavalry on both sides altered their tactics and made changes in their weaponry. In both services the firearm became increasingly important, the saber—"cold steel"—more infrequently carried and almost never used. The Southern horsemen seem to have made this change more rapidly than their opponents, who tended to retain the more traditional "regulation" armament. An inspection of Wheeler's cavalry at the end of the Georgia campaign revealed that among 7,670 officers and men there were 6,607 firearms, mostly rifles and pistols. In Anderson's Brigade the inspectors found fifty or sixty sabers, but in the nine other brigades they found none; moreover most officers had no sabers either. By 1864 the matériel of the Confederate mounted units was very varied and often inferior; the weapons in Wheeler's Corps in the inspection mentioned above were of nine different calibers. In their appearance and appointments generally the Southern horsemen stood out: A party of Union soldiers who had escaped from Andersonville were close to the Union lines when they saw a body of cavalry go by. Even in the dim light they had no difficulty identifying them: "We saw at once, as they hurried by, that it was genuine sesesh, being mounted partly on mules and partly on horses, and being armed with carbines, shot guns and pistols. . . ."

These shortcomings seem to have counted for little, certainly in the estimation of General Sherman, who felt that initiative, aggressiveness, and activity were far more important, and in these qualities the Confederate cavalry far outshone his own horsemen. He complained to Grant and to others that his cavalry needed an infantry guard "and it is hard to get them within 10 miles of the front." Early in the year he wrote his wife: "Somehow our cavalry is not good. The secesh with poor mean horses make 40 & 50 miles a day, whereas our fat & costly horses won't average 10." Later in the year he decided that the basic problem was one of leadership: General Garrard lacked drive, General Kilpatrick was only good for "small scouting," etc. At the same time Sherman was trying to incite his cavalry leaders to greater exertion: "If our cavalry will make bold and handsome dashes," he wrote General Garrard, "I promise to make full and public acknowledgement of their services." Yet in July 1864 when Atlanta proved a hard nut to crack, Sherman turned to his cavalry. The reason was that this arm had a unique ability to penetrate enemy territory to considerable depth, carry out missions that could be rapidly performed, and make its way back into the lines without suffering great loss—this through the technique known as the raid. It was in fact an operation Civil War cavalry leaders had perfected, and one that impressed European observers sufficiently for them to introduce the word "raid" in cavalry manuals from Paris to Saint Petersburg. The two essential elements in such an operation were speed and surprise. There was only a short span of continuous front, that along the line of contact between the two armies (about a dozen miles in front of Atlanta), so on either wing bodies of fast-moving horsemen could pass, and even if they were detected they would not encounter anything more than screening forces in their passage. Once on the enemy's flank and rear they would burn bridges behind them to forestall pursuit and tear down telegraph wires so as to prevent news of their movements being relayed. They would thus sow confusion while accomplishing their main objective, usually the gathering of intelligence and the destruction of enemy stores, facilities, etc. If they kept on the move and kept the enemy confused about their movements, they had a good chance of riding through his territory unscathed. Such a raid would be hard on horses, but those that broke down could generally be replaced by others seized along the way. The operation was also very demanding on the men, especially in depriving them of sleep, though a good cavalryman was supposed to get his rest by dozing in the saddle.

If the Union cavalry could shake off what Sherman saw as its timidity and lethargy and send large raiding forces to strike at the railroads that were Confederate Atlanta's lifelines, and if those forces could make sufficiently serious breaks in those lines, the Rebels would either have to come out and fight for the city or give it up. The mounted troops could thus save Sherman the trouble of maneuvering the entire army about the city to accomplish the same task, a complicated and time-consuming operation, and one attended by some risk. Thus in July and August the Union general briefly changed his mind about his mounted arm, committing it to one of the largest and most ambitious cavalry operations of the war. A raid he had authorized into neighboring Alabama in June gave encouraging results: General Rousseau led twenty-three hundred horsemen out of Decatur, Alabama, to strike at rail lines in the vicinity of Opelika in the middle of July; by the 22nd Rousseau reached Atlanta, bringing in several hundred captured mules and the news that he had destroyed more than a dozen miles of rail line. He had ridden four hundred miles in twelve days and had suffered fewer than fifty casualties. Then on the night of July 20 General Kenner Garrard took his division east toward the town of Covington to put another hole in Atlanta's link to Augusta; to Sherman's delight he was back on the 24th, having burned vital bridges and trestles; he too returned with trophies in the form of prisoners and horses. Cavalry operations were paying off now; if they were intensified they might make Atlanta fall like a ripe apple. An enthusiastic Sherman threw himself into the preparation of what he called the "big raid," a large and complex operation that would involve an entire corps of cavalry, some ten thousand horsemen.

There is an old aphorism that in war only what is simple succeeds. Sherman's "big raid" offers sad proof of its validity, for the enterprise was a disaster. Of the three separate bodies of cavalry that left Atlanta on July 27, only the force under General Garrard returned essentially intact. He and General George Stoneman took their commands around east of Atlanta, then parted company, for Garrard was to occupy the attention of the Confederate cavalry while Stoneman and his men headed farther south; near Lovejoy's Station, Stoneman was to rendezvous with a third force under General Edward M. McCook, which would have swung around Atlanta to the west. There they were to accomplish the real purpose of the raid, a thorough job of destruction on the railways, particularly the vital Macon and Western, the least accessible of Atlanta's lifelines. Thereafter they would carry out a supplementary mission for which Stoneman had obtained Sherman's last-minute approval: the liberation of prisoners in an officers' prison in Macon and then of the thousands in Andersonville. Sherman was not very sanguine about the chances of this operation, but he was receiving nearly a hundred letters a day from relatives of the prisoners begging him to do something; if the rescue could be brought off it would be a spectacular coup.

The "big raid" was barely launched before it began to unravel. General McCook's progress was troubled by poor roads, by a slow moving pontoon train—those unforeseen little checks and impediments in war that Clausewitz called "friction"—and he began to fall behind schedule for his rendezvous at Lovejoy's Station. General Stoneman never made the rendezvous at all, heading instead toward Macon and Andersonville, where he planned to liberate the prisoners. Stoneman was checked before Macon and never got to Andersonville. McCook marked time at Lovejoy's Station; both expeditions lost steam, being composed now of overworked horses and exhausted men. The Confederates reacted quickly and vigorously. A Southern trooper recalled: "We entered into this chase like schoolboys in a game of baseball." With Rebel forces beginning to coalesce around him, McCook was forced to run a gauntlet back to the Chattahoochee, and soon he was losing men every foot of the way; Stoneman was brought to bay near the town of Clinton, where the general maintained a fighting stance with part of his command, while the rest escaped in various directions—"cut their way out," as the cavalrymen liked to put it. Stoneman himself surrendered with tears of mortification in his eyes. His captors were sympathetic; they let him send an explanatory telegram to his wife.

For several days Sherman was without hard news of his horsemen; what vague stories filtered in seemed to indicate things were going well. Then the tone changed; the reports were discouraging, then ominous, then disastrous. The colonel of the First Tennessee Cavalry came in barefoot, followed by a score of men—all that remained of his regiment. The rest, and most of General McCook's force and the general himself, were undoubtedly dead or prisoners (McCook and a large number of his men did make it out, though some were a month getting through the lines). The only good news the colonel brought was that the line to Macon had been so severely damaged that the Confederates would not be able to get trains running for fifteen days. The first hard news on the fate of Stoneman, even more grim, reached Sherman's headquarters from Richmond via Washington; the press in the Confederate capital was exulting over Stoneman's surrender on the battlefield at Sunshine Church.

General Sherman was undoubtedly shaken by the news. The day he got the details of McCook's debacle he found the story hard to believe; the day after he wrote General Howard that he was "quite unwell"; on August 6, when he still had the taste of the whole fiasco in his mouth, he wrote a somber letter to his wife, Ellen, in which he hinted that he and Grant might soon be replaced by "other favorites," in which case the Sherman family "might escape to California or some other distant land." But his depression, if such it was, did not last long. The failure of the raids had been a check, but not a major one; the campaign continued with advantage. A telegram from Grant on August 7 no doubt helped Sherman's spirits: "Your progress, instead of appearing slow, has received the universal commendation of all loyal citizens, as well as of the President. . . ." As for Sherman's own letters and directives of that date, they crackle with energy and purpose. He was even willing to authorize still another cavalry raid against Atlanta's jugular, the Macon road. General Judson Kilpatrick, who led this new effort, was told: "There is good reason to hope that you might be able to accomplish what the whole army would otherwise have to do at great risk, by a long and difficult movement." (The expedition started out on August 18, did only moderate damage to the rail line, and returned intact four days later.)

The fundamental failure of the "big raid" only became apparent gradually, as intelligence filtered in from the Confederate side of the line: Despite the large number of troops in the expedition and the length of time they spent in Middle Georgia, they had barely put a dent in the rail traffic to and from Atlanta; instead of being shut down for fifteen days, the Macon line was open again in a third of that time. Yet to the Northern soldiers engaged in it, the destruction of a railroad was a relatively simple affair. A body of troops would line up on one side of the track, one or two men to each tie; on command they would lift their end of the ties and the rails with them, then simply push the tracks on over; with enough men one could flip as much as a mile of track at a time. Once this was done it was usually possible to separate the ties from the rails, even without tools. Bonfires were made of the ties, the rails placed across them; if the iron was sufficiently heated the rails would bend of their own weight, though the process could be hastened by weighting down each end of the rail. Sometimes the soldiers stayed there while the rails heated, roasting ears of corn over the fire if a cornfield was nearby. When the rails were hot enough they might also take them to the nearest tree, where they put a hairpin bend into them.

When the wreckers were through the road appeared to be totally demolished. Yet Herman Haupt, who directed the Federal army's rail system for the first part of the war, demonstrated that trackage so destroyed could generally be put back in no more time than it had taken to wreck it, provided the construction team had the expertise, the labor, and the proper equipment. Rails could be scavenged from less vital lines, or the bent ones straightened on the spot, often without heating. If a large proportion of the ties had been burned repair took a little longer, but there was never any shortage of wood for this purpose. If the troops demolishing the road went a step further, attacking the roadbed itself, excavating fills and filling in cuts, these could be restored with about the same amount of time and labor. Only bridges and trestlework took more time, and even here there was usually something to build on.

But by 1864 the destruction of railroads had become something of a science. If cuts were filled in and brush and tree branches added in the process, then they could not be excavated with the same speed—and if live shells were added, excavation would be slowed to snail's pace. Herman Haupt and his assistants had developed easily portable tools to make destruction faster and more thorough; of these the most important was the cant hook, which resembled the hook that timbermen use to roll logs. In its simplest form it was an iron claw with a loop through which a sturdy fence rail could be passed as a lever. If rails were heated and then twisted in corkscrew fashion with this device, then bent as well, Haupt insisted that "it is not possible that any attempt would ever be made to repair or use them." With the cant hook it was even possible to twist the rails without heating them; one simply left one end of the rail attached to the ties and applied the cant hook to the other. Using this technique a force of twenty-two hundred men could wreck a railroad at the rate of five miles per hour. Haupt had drawings and descriptive material about the device distributed throughout the army. Among the recipients was William Tecumseh Sherman. He had the hooks supplied to his forces—they are sometimes visible in old photographs—and he put out a special field order on the subject. In his instructions to General Rousseau and to others he was explicit: "If simply bent, the rails may be used, but if they are twisted or wrenched they cannot be used again."

These sophisticated procedures are of interest to us because they should have made shambles of the rail lines in Middle Georgia during the "big raid," but they did not—essentially because they were not used. Nor, for that matter, did the cavalry generally do this type of work effectively—a statement that is equally applicable to the Confederates (General Wheeler's big raid against the Western and Atlantic that August shut the line down for only two weeks). The "breaks" made in the lines were almost always superficial ones, quickly repaired. Even when the bulk of the Confederate army—cavalry and infantry—applied itself to the task, tearing thirty-five miles out of the Western and Atlantic in October 1864, the line was restored in about three weeks. To be sure, on this occasion the Northern railroad men could draw on a great wealth of matériel, including "duplicates" of bridge beams and timbers. But the general rule is no less valid: The restorers were good at their work, the demolishers were not.

It was a peculiar characteristic of the cavalry that it was the arm best qualified to attain such objectives as enemy railroads and at the same time the arm least suited to destroying them. The matter of numbers helps explain this phenomenon. A large body of cavalry did not mean a large workforce. When in the field one trooper in four would usually hold the horses of dismounted comrades. Then a considerable number of men would have to be posted as pickets and vedettes; others would be organized into parties to seek out gardens, smokehouses, and cornfields, for food and fodder were constant preoccupations for a force operating without a supply line. Herman Haupt calculated that of a force of five thousand cavalry attacking enemy railroads, no more than twenty-two hundred would be available for the work of destruction. Then there was the question of time, the necessity to keep moving, which ruled out such time-consuming activities as attacking the roadbed itself with pick and shovel, filling cuts, etc.

There is evidence that Sherman's precise directions for rendering the rails unusable were not passed on and were largely ignored by the cavalrymen even if they received them. Special field orders for General Garrard prepared in the headquarters of the Army of the Tennessee made no mention of cant hooks or twisting the rails, but rather of "tearing up the ties, piling them up, putting the iron rails on top, and setting the ties on fire." This was the method used by McCook's men to disable the Macon road. David Evans, the author of a meticulous and highly detailed study of McCook's expedition, said that if Sherman had seen McCook's men at work, "he would have cringed." For them railroad wrecking was a tough and dirty chore that had to be accomplished under a July sun in Middle Georgia, and so was best done as quickly as possible, without tending fires and waiting for the rails to become red hot; their officers no doubt agreed with them, and all moved on, leaving the rails to bend themselves. In truth, Southern horsemen were no less anxious to finish and be gone. As one of them put it, "such a mode of warfare was exceedingly distasteful to our feelings."

By the same token the cavalrymen seem to have paid little attention to the technical subtleties involved in destroying telegraph lines. These, as put forward by the Signal Corps, stressed the value of cutting the wire into small pieces, burying it, or throwing it into streams; there was also a clever technique in which the wire was cut and then put back in place, with the gap hidden by an insulator, so that the Rebel repair crews would be distracted trying to find the break in their lines. But for the cavalrymen, breaking the wire seemed sufficient. This nonchalance was no doubt that of a generation less interested than our own in technical details, but in it there was probably something of the cavalry spirit.

If the men were not excited about the hard and humdrum work of wrecking a railroad, they liked the idea of the raid itself as soon as they learned about it. It offered excitement and an escape from routine. Then too, the talk around the campfires was that their foray could open the gates of Atlanta. In some of the letters speaking of the coming operation there is more than a hint of self-importance: The campaign hinges on their success. For the first couple days of movement through enemy territory there was plenty of excitement, but as was almost always the case with raids, enthusiasm and energy were soon sapped by fatigue. When McCook's men turned back toward the Chattahoochee they had already gone without sleep for forty-eight hours, and those who escaped Stoneman's fiasco at Sunshine Church were not in much better shape. For those who fled back toward the Union lines what had begun as a great adventure became something of a nightmare.

The raids had profound repercussions throughout Georgia. In two places the news that the Yankees were coming was greeted with wild elation: in the vast prison pen at Andersonville and at Camp Oglethorpe, the prison for Federal officers at Macon. The men in Andersonville had been waiting for such news since Sherman opened his campaign; in their excitement they gave no more thought than General Stoneman had to how he might "cut his way" back to the Chattahoochee with thirty thousand weak and half-starved ex-prisoners in his columns; what they did worry about was the rumor that the Confederate garrison would open on them with artillery if rescuers came within seven miles of the prison. In Camp Oglethorpe excitement ran high; the officers had been hatching plans for some time; some wanted to stage an uprising, seize the prison, disarm the guards, and march out, either to join forces with their rescuers, or according to another scenario, take the city of Macon hostage. Then one day they heard the boom of cannon and saw the citizens of Macon taking to the rooftops to watch the battle that would bring deliverance. They waited all day for the appearance of General Stoneman. He arrived, under guard, not long afterward.

For the people of Georgia the raids were an installment in a continuing nightmare, heightening the mood of crisis that had already begun to spread over the land that summer. As Sherman's army approached Atlanta the city's fate increasingly occupied the public mind. Many people felt that unless the line of the Chattahoochee could be held Atlanta's days were numbered, so when Johnston abandoned the river the impact was profound. Julia Pope Stanley, an intelligent and observant young woman who lived in the university town of Athens, some sixty miles east of Atlanta, left letters that accurately mirror the change of mood in that town. On July 12 she wrote to her husband, who was in the Confederate army in Florida: "We think of but little else & talk of but little else but the Yankees since we heard they had crossed the Chattahoochee." The news had reached Athens the day before, and as she wrote neighbors were packing up and leaving and breastworks were going up around the town. She had no choice but to stay, since she had small children and a sick mother who could not be moved. She thought she should prepare her children, particularly her daughter Sallie:

> I woke her in the morning & told her to dress herself, that the Yankees were coming. She began to cry and was very much frightened, but I soon quieted her by telling her they might not come, but that it was best that she should dress anyway. I don't think Tom knew exactly what to think, he certainly has not been scared at all. . . .

As for herself, she told her husband: "I feel rather calm & cool considering our danger and our helplessness." Three days later she wrote that the "commotion" had subsided somewhat, though people were still packing and sending off their valuables.

On July 22 began a bizarre episode that sparked joyous celebration in the North, consternation in the South, and something bordering on panic in Georgia. On the night of July 21, following orders from General

Hood, the Confederate forces along part of the line in front of Atlanta
quietly left their works and withdrew to the inner defense perimeter at
the edge of town. Union pickets probing the Confederate position the
next morning found the enemy works empty and the town before them
in easy walking distance. Word spread that General Hood had abandoned Atlanta, and notice to that effect was circulated from the headquarters of the Army of the Cumberland; for a brief period of time even
Sherman believed it. So did several newspaper correspondents with the
army. J. B. Berry of the *Louisville Daily Journal* took a chance he would
long regret, rushing off a quick note saying the city had fallen, adding a
few flourishes about the Stars and Stripes floating over the town hall as
Union soldiers marched through the streets of Atlanta to the plaudits of
the populace. Y.S. of the *Cincinnati Gazette* succumbed to the same temptation, and possibly other army journalists as well. A number of newspapers across the country picked up the story and had to correct their error
in the next issue. Strangely, the "news" also swept through Georgia. In
Athens it struck like a thunderclap on the morning of the 23rd, but on
the 24th word came that Atlanta was still "free." Julia Stanley reported
some very panicky Athenians at the train station during the scare: a
woman with her dress unfastened, a man who came running up barefooted, and "Mary Franklin . . . with her corsets and three pairs of stock-
ings in her hand."

Into this charged atmosphere now came a succession of confused and
unsettling reports of "raiders," first in one place, then in another. Such
stories had circulated before; rumors of a Yankee raid had run through
several towns in mid-June: In Athens they were reported to be ten miles
from the town; the mayor of Augusta even issued a proclamation warning of the danger. Earlier in July someone brought false news of a raid to
Hillsboro, in Jasper County; the resulting stampede broke up a neighborhood barbecue. But now the raiders were real enough, of that there
was no doubt; what no one knew for sure was exactly where they were
and where they were heading. As a result the alarm bells rang frequently, and most often it was a false alarm. The raiders seemed to be
"all around," wrote a worried inhabitant of the town of West Point: "It is
the impression here that the dark cloud of invasion which has been so
long gathering around our homes is even now bursting forth in a tem-
pest of fire."

The major towns put themselves in the best posture of defense they
could. In Augusta the newspaper reported that all the citizens were
under arms; Columbus was reported in the same state: "nearly every
kind of business is suspended. . . . Every man and tall boy able to load a

gun and draw a trigger is under arms." Macon too was making preparations and not in vain, because Stoneman appeared before the town on
July 30, and Macon had its moment of truth. The local militia stood to
arms, reinforced by a considerable number of convalescent soldiers from
local hospitals (in the summer of 1864 Macon had some six thousand
sick and wounded soldiers, a number about equal to its own population). In addition the male citizens generally had turned out with whatever arms they had, stirred by a proclamation of Governor Brown. Leaders were not lacking: General Joe Johnston, who had just come from
Atlanta; Governor Brown, who was about to get his baptism of fire; and
General Howell Cobb, whose command post was a large armchair
placed under a chinaberry tree. There was some skirmishing; the Federals fired several shells, one of which hit a column on Mr. Asa Holt's
house on Mulberry Street, and then General Stoneman decided not to
persist. Bishop Henry Lay was there, and he believed that this success
for Southern arms was a manifestation of divine favor for the Cause. A
Macon native wrote in his diary that the affair proved "wonders will
never cease."

When the raiders did show up in a locality they often took the inhabitants completely by surprise, particularly in the first day or two of their
expedition. They thus had no opposition and rarely any problems with
the locals, though here and there they did encounter resistance. The chief
source of trouble were older men, "old citizens," as the soldiers generally called them, particularly temperamental old men easily moved to
violence, which Civil War Georgia seems to have had in considerable
numbers. Near the village of Hillsboro lived a man named McShot, a
"peculiar" man, according to the person who recorded his story. McShot
had told anyone who would listen that he intended to kill the first Yankee that touched any of his possessions. When Stoneman and his men
arrived in the village, Mr. McShot's wife and mother-in-law knew they
had to get him out of the house. They were in the process of cajoling him
out the back of his home when Yankee troopers entered at the front. The
women succeeded in getting him through the back door, but he managed to grab his shotgun in his passage. The Federal soldiers had seen
him and started after him, calling on him to halt. He did stop, but it was
to turn around and fire, striking one of the soldiers in the chest with a
load of birdshot. After a brief scuffle the other soldiers seized him, put
him on a spare horse, and told his wife to say goodbye to him forever. A
Federal officer who was standing nearby drinking a glass of Mrs.
McShot's buttermilk opined: "If I had my way with the damned rebel, I
would hang him to his own doorpost." But in their rush the Yankees

simply took him along, and when Stoneman surrendered, McShot came home wearing the mantle of a hero. The trooper he shot was too badly wounded to be moved, so he was cared for by someone in the community until well enough to be sent off to Andersonville.

Another affair of this kind ended more tragically during General Garrard's raid into the town of Covington. One inhabitant of the town, an old man named Jones, had sworn a similar oath—he would kill the first Yankee soldier he saw. It was said that "his hatred of everything blue had been inflamed by reports of outrages committed by Sherman's army." For whatever reason, he got his gun, went out to the street, and awaited his opportunity. When a Federal trooper came Jones raised his rifle; the soldier saw him do it and shouted: "Don't shoot!" but fell dead an instant later. Mr. Jones reloaded, shifted his position, and shot a second soldier, then fired into a party of Union cavalrymen, wounding two. The troopers captured him, put him up against a wall, and pumped several bullets into him, then "beat his brains out with the butts of their rifles." News of this episode spread rapidly. The version that circulated among the people in the locality did not mention Jones's firing first, making him an innocent victim of the bluecoats. Dolly Lunt Burge, who lived a few miles away, recorded in her diary: "They cruelly shot a George Daniel & a Mr. Jones of Covington." As for the soldiers, they were infuriated at this unexpected attack from a "citizen"; during their stay they killed one and possibly two other men in the town who made the mistake of appearing with guns in their hands.

Covington was a hospital town with no fewer than six army hospitals, most of them scattered about in abandoned stores and churches. There was just enough warning for the ambulatory patients to take off for the woods. "Grandma" Smith, a nurse in the Hill Hospital, watched them hobble off: "If ever I saw what is called pell-mell I saw it there and then. Everyone who could walk broke for the pine thicket." The remaining patients were not bothered by the Yankee troopers, though one trooper with a score to settle inquired for members of the Eighth Texas Cavalry. When General McCook and his men passed through towns they diligently collected as prisoners all Confederate soldiers they found in condition to travel, despite the fact that taking along these "trophies" would inevitably slow their march. A Georgia soldier named McBride was picked up in Fayetteville despite his insistence that he could not be moved. After an argument with a Federal officer he insisted on speaking to General McCook, who called in a surgeon to examine him; the surgeon concurred that travel would indeed endanger McBride's life, and McCook agreed to release him on parole.

Not many hours later McCook was obliged to release all his prisoners in his increasingly desperate flight; farther to the south Stoneman's command was meeting its Waterloo, with some of its men soon off to Andersonville, the rest fleeing for the safety of the Union lines. Those who took flight sometimes kept together as a military unit, while many preferred to travel in twos and threes, for now that they were fugitives in a hostile land, they were trying not to attract attention. But the alarm had been sounded; anyone traveling the roads or stopping at houses was the object of suspicion. A man living in Hancock County was suspicious of two men who stopped at his uncle's house. Asked if they were Yankees, they said they were not. But word of their presence spread through the locality; five armed citizens showed up to escort them to the authorities in the county seat of Sparta. Six survivors of Stoneman's expedition showed up at Dolly Burge's house one morning for breakfast. They inquired about Wheeler's cavalry and tried to pass themselves off as part of his command. According to Mrs. Burge the following exchange took place:

"Who are you," said I.
"We are a portion of Wheeler's men," said one.
"You look like Yankees," said I.
"Yes," said one, stepping up to me, "We are Yankees. Did you ever see one before?"
"Not for a long time, & none such as you," I replied.

She asked them how many she had to get breakfast for and they said: "twenty-six," for they had comrades concealed nearby. "They were in a great hurry," Mrs. Burge noticed, "& were so frightened that I became reassured." She prepared their breakfast, but she also managed to send word of their presence. Confederate troops picked them up shortly after and recovered three mules they had taken from Mrs. Burge's barn.

An Illinois trooper named Sanford belonged to a little band of stragglers from Stoneman's command that had some singular adventures. On a country road they encountered and "captured" a Confederate conscription officer who had a canteen half-full of brandy, and for a while they compelled him to hasten along with them: "After we had travelled four or five miles pretty lively, our prisoner sat down and said we might kill him or turn him loose, as he had heart disease and now had an attack, and could go no further. We gave him some of his brandy and took a little ourselves to prevent catching his disease." After some deliberation they simply turned him loose. As they drew nearer the Union

army's lines they encountered a woman who refused to believe their
story that they were some of Wheeler's men. They finally confessed that
they were Northern soldiers, whereupon she said she was also a loyal
supporter of the Union. She produced her husband, who had been hiding in a nearby cornfield, and the couple fed the fugitives and gave them
directions to another Unionist family near the lines; there they were also
taken in. The man of the house agreed to serve as their guide, and they
made it back to their lines.

For many of the bluecoats fleeing across Middle Georgia that August
their flight ended in capture or death. It was difficult to travel without
being challenged; and as one straggler put it, "every old Georgia farmer
with a gun was on the lookout for our men." A large party of Stoneman's men led by Colonel Horace Capron were perhaps forty miles from
Atlanta when on the evening of August 2 their scouts asked a local man
where a body of horsemen might spend the night undisturbed. The man,
Wiley Bush, was a Confederate soldier home on furlough. He led them
to a place called Cedar Hill, then alerted the Confederate troops in the
area. The Federals were so exhausted that they made no defensive
arrangements; the men had simply dropped down along the side of the
road and fallen asleep instantly. They were awakened at daylight by a
Confederate attack. A Northern officer who was there conceded the fight
was all one way: "Badly armed and out of ammunition, our men could
make but feeble resistance. They could only escape by dodging into
fields or into the woods. A weak bridge spanning the Mulberry river, as
our men were crossing, gave way and many were drowned." Colonel
Capron painted a less flattering picture: "Brave men as ever drew a
saber in battle ran past their officers in a confused, frenzied mass. . . ."
Capron himself gave serious thought to surrender, but he had his nineteen-year-old son with him and did not think the young man would survive "the sepulchre of Andersonville." Father and son both made it to
Union lines. Most of those who escaped did so in small parties, traveling
by night as best they could, subsisting on green corn, berries, and roots.
"They were hunted by rebel soldiers, bloodhounds, guerillas and citizens. Some were murdered on the spot, those captured taken to Andersonville and other prisons."

A Yankee trooper's chances of fair treatment were better if he was
taken by the Confederate military than if he fell into the hands of civilians. Their degree of anger toward the raiders was considerable and
manifested itself frequently in the aftermath of the raids, both in word
and in deed. One reason for this was the plethora of stories about Yankee
atrocities that circulated. A Macon man wrote his wife that he had been

watching prisoners brought in: "Sixty-eight were marched in this morning. I wish every mother's son of them had been 'lost,' in other words killed. Have you seen the accounts of atrocities committed by them?" Where prisoners were collected in public places, they were apt to receive some verbal abuse; women would call them "vandals" and old men would shake their fists at them. Most instances of physical violence against captured soldiers went unrecorded, occurring in remote places. But in one instance abuse of a prisoner prompted a strong reaction from the usually mild-mannered General Wheeler. An old farmer knocked a prisoner down, and the Confederate guard who was there then knocked the farmer down. The old man went to Wheeler and protested. Wheeler told him: "If you want to fight, go join a company and fight, but don't hit a prisoner."

At the same time Georgians were reminded of the protection their own troops represented. The Confederate cavalryman, particularly, was the hero of the hour. Even the rough, hardbitten regiments from Texas now got an enthusiastic reception wherever they went. An officer in Terry's Texas Rangers recorded the unaccustomed warmth of the greeting they got as they tracked the raiders: "The mothers and the maidens were upon the roadside with water for the thirsty. What a wondrous change does the presence of the foe work upon the patriotism of some folks! Ten days ago they would have looked upon us as intruders, and Gadarene-like in their hearts, wished us to depart from their plantations." Confederate nurse Fannie Beers was on duty in the hospital town of Newnan when the raiders came; Confederate forces were already there, so fighting occurred in the center of the town. The inhabitants fled, as did all patients who could get about. Most of the staff departed, the firing moved off, and Mrs. Beers found herself and her seriously ill patients in the middle of a completely empty town. Night came, and the stillness in the deserted streets was oppressive. Then suddenly she heard hoofbeats, and in an instant the streets were filled with shouted commands and the distinctive jingle and clatter of cavalry. With a pine knot for her light she went out to see who they were: "To my almost wild delight the torch-light revealed the dear old gray uniforms."

The raids again raised the question of just how reliable the black population would be in a time of crisis. People who owned slaves watched their servants. Julia Stanley noted that after the Federal raids into Athens did not materialize, "some of our negroes look disappointed." When Stoneman passed through Covington he picked up a number of blacks; they found horses and rode out of town with the Northern troopers, saying they were going off "to fight the white trash."

By the time Stoneman fought at Sunshine Church he probably had several hundred with him. William Sanford, who was with Stoneman at the time, recalled: "a lot of negroes who were with us were very strongly urged to escape while they could, as their fate would be severe if captured with us. Some did, but some stayed." And when the band led by Colonel Capron was attacked that morning at Cedar Hill, they had a large number of blacks with them as well. What fate they met with is not known, but it could not have been a pleasant one.

Immediately after the raids, and no doubt because of them, there was a great outcry that the countryside was unsafe, the blacks too insolent and restless. Citizens of Randolph and Clay counties petitioned for the release from militia duty of John W. Sealy, who owned and "managed" a pack of tracking dogs for catching runaways, and who possessed "great tact and skill in the management of unruly negroes." But the clamor was general, and in response the governor began releasing one man from militia service for every five hundred blacks in a county. In the first half of July he took this measure in one county; in the last half he acted on requests from a score of them.

Finally, the raids brought a deepening concern over the special danger threatening the women of Georgia. News of the rape and murder of a Miss Iverson was still circulating, and the affair was being talked about in hushed tones. "Have you read the horrible outrage on Miss Iverson," asked one correspondent. "Fanny King says she saw a private letter relating the circumstances & she is really dead." No incident of rape can be documented during the cycle of Federal raids, but stories about atrocities began to spread in the following days and weeks. Some men at the front had dashed off notes of warning to their wives: "I am in hopes if they should go through our county they will not abuse you. I don't think they will if you act firm & cool. . . ." A Georgia soldier had heard "that some of our men found some of their wives tied to stakes and dead from the cruel treatment that they received from their foul hands." Other Georgia soldiers at the front were anxious to hear from their wives. "Write soon and tell me all the particulars," wrote militiaman H. T. Howard, "where you were and if you were insulted by the enemy or not."

A Lieutenant Barringer received a letter from his sweetheart saying something had happened to her that would make his Southern blood "boil." An officer with the raiders had asked her why she was wearing two stars on her collar. When she said it was for her sweetheart in the Confederate army he told her to hand the stars over. "I put one hand over the stars and with the other held a piece of palm fan to my face and pretended to cry—I said 'you shant take my stars—my sweetheart gave them to me—and no Yankee shall have them.' " The officer let her keep the stars, but she told Lieutenant Barringer: "Think how we have been treated and fight with a double purpose." It is clear that "outrages" of a far more serious nature preoccupied many women. They were clearly on the mind of Julia Stanley that July: "Oh that I had more faith," she wrote. "But when I hear of how our women are insulted by the Yankees, my heart almost faints within me." The solution, she thought, was for the women to arm themselves: "Col. M. A. Cooper says every woman ought to be armed with a dagger to defend herself." Many women appear to have acquired arms that summer, for there are references to them in letters and diaries. There is the man in Macon who writes that his mother and sister feel "quite secure" out in the country since he has supplied them with a pistol and a long knife. There is the woman who lives on a remote plantation, and who in moments of fear restores her self-confidence by firing her pistol out the back door. One might be tempted to smile at such things if these people had not been so serious about them. For apparently they were deadly serious: One day late in the war when President Jefferson Davis and his wife were about to part for a time, he presented her with a pistol and showed her how to fire it. He said to her: "You can at least, if reduced to the last extremity, force your assailants to kill you."

8

◆

In the Ditches

The arrival of the Union army before Atlanta caused a further deterioration of Governor Brown's relations with the Confederate authorities in Richmond. President Davis addressed Brown rarely now; the Confederate secretary of war, James Seddon, usually had the chore of answering the governor's letters. As the Federal invasion of his state progressed, Brown became increasingly free with his advice on military matters. More of the Confederacy's military strength needed to be sent to the Georgia front, where the stakes were higher than anyone in Richmond seemed to realize. One way to do this, Brown wrote, would be to send onto the battle line the plethora of officers and soldiers the War Department had seen fit to post to various towns in Georgia and the other states, where they did little good and much mischief. As for the threat Sherman posed, it could best be countered by creating a great mass of cavalry—drawing some from the East—which would shut down the Western and Atlantic Railroad for good; then the Federal army in Georgia would have to withdraw or wither on the vine.

But Joe Brown also took action. Late in May he mobilized most of the troops at his disposal and began preparing them for use at the front. His proclamation of May 18 ordered the militiamen to report to "Camp Georgia" with a blanket or quilt; if they had it, they should bring along "a good double-barrel shot gun." He wound up his proclamation with a ringing appeal: "To arms and to the front, and the Vandal hordes will soon be driven back." On July 9 Brown called up his reserve militia, working into his proclamation a slap at President Davis. He was obliged to send the state's last reserves into the field, he said, because his correspondence with Davis had taught him that "Georgia is to be left to her own resources to supply the reinforcements to General Johnston's army." Brown succeeded in fielding a force of some ten thousand men, about half of whom were used for keeping order in the counties, with the other half destined for service with the Army of Tennessee under their commander, General Gustavus W. Smith. To raise such a force Brown had been obliged to take what the Confederate army had left, so "Joe Brown's Pets," as they were called, were mostly youths of sixteen and seventeen or old men from fifty to fifty-five years old. The governor also took into service an even younger contingent, the cadets of the Georgia Military Institute, among them Brown's own son.

So it was that in this crisis a mass of amateurs took their place in the ditches alongside the veterans of Johnston's army. In truth they were not as much alongside as behind; a militiaman explained to his wife: "the Confederate soldiers stay between us and the enemy the most of the time & when they get whipt we will have to go in." General Johnston was glad to have them, and indeed asked Brown for even more, for he hoped to use them to man part of the defenses of Atlanta. But officers on Johnston's staff wanted nothing to do with such amateurs; when General Hood took over he promised that he would not make any of his officers work with the militia, but Major Joseph B. Cumming reluctantly accepted a temporary assignment on the staff of General Smith, as did a Captain Troup. Some officers who saw the militia up close felt that despite their lack of experience the men would fight and fight well, if for no other reason than that their pride was involved. Major Cumming did not share this opinion. He believed that "with such troops we were threatened not only with disaster but also with disgrace."

Somewhat later Major Cumming felt his worst fears were realized when he had to lead a detachment of militia on a road march. At one point he called a halt to let the men rest. He too was resting some distance away, feeling "some anxiety" over his new command, when he noticed to his astonishment that his column was in movement again. He quickly mounted and returned to the road, where he ordered the men to halt. They paid him no attention but continued on, the stream of men parting around him and his horse. He left the road, and putting his horse to a gallop through the woods, emerged again just in front of his head of column; this took some time because the men were walking at their own pace and badly strung out. Placing his horse across the road and drawing his pistol, he threatened to shoot the men if they did not halt. "They stopped, but one old man began loading his gun, saying 'By

God, if there is going to be any shooting, I'll shoot too.'" Cumming considered dropping the man with a shot from his pistol but thought better of it. "I then . . . made the men a speech, the key-note of which was not honor or duty but self-preservation." He told them that unless they moved in compact formations the Yankee cavalry could make short work of them. They accepted his argument, and the march continued without incident.

The seasoned veterans of the Army of Tennessee also had serious doubts about the Georgia militiamen who began to appear in their midst. The newly arrived reinforcements were conspicuous for their homemade brown jeans, their white knapsacks, and "bed quilts and pillows and packs large enough for a mule." Soldiers who witnessed their arrival wrote home that the "new issue" sometimes reported for duty with umbrellas and walking sticks as well. Their behavior too provided a good deal of amusement to old soldiers. After a shell had burst nearby, they scrambled to collect the fragments for "souvenirs." A Texas trooper recorded that one man in his unit was killed by a stray ball as they were passing through the militia's lines; since the militiamen had never seen a man killed in battle before, the Texans were "very much amused" by their reaction. And of course it was "laughable . . . to see their awkward motions and blunders at the simple military evolutions." Their officers had been trained to give outlandish orders, such as "Cobb County aim! Cobb County fire!" Of course the old soldiers speculated on what the militia might be worth if it came to a battle, and the consensus was: "not worth a low-country cow tick."

Dr. Massey, who treated a number of militiamen at Brown Hospital, said that they were so "accustomed to the comforts and luxuries of home" that they did not stand life in the trenches very well. Fortunately for these new soldiers campaigning lost some of its rigors now that the opposing armies had Atlanta as their bone of contention. With rapid movements over considerable distances now a thing of the past, supply was easier and rations more plentiful. For the infantry soldier particularly, the war seemed to "settle down"; the headlong night marches over unknown roads were pretty much a thing of the past, though both armies shifted troops from one portion of their line to another under cover of night. If the men were on the road less, they were of necessity spending a greater proportion of their time within their entrenchments, "in the ditches," and they were spending time making them more comfortable: Thousands of chestnut trees around Atlanta were stripped of their outer bark to line the soldiers' beds; these had been made softer by "plucking a Georgia goose," which is to say stripping branches from a

pine tree. Other trees were stripped to construct leafy "arbors" that kept
the direct rays of the sun out of the trenches. Union troops in one part of
their line looted a furniture factory, equipping their trenches with high-
back chairs. Though the Federal offensive ground on, now each forward
movement was a "nibbling" operation, measured in yards rather than
miles. An Ohio soldier explained the process in a letter to his father: "We
are creeping up slowly towards Atlanta. We advanced a few hundred
yards two or three days ago. The skirmish line advances and digs holes
in the ground and in a night or two we have a line of works, then the
skirmish line creeps up a little further and the troops occupy the works
and so forth." The two opposing battle lines now stretched a dozen
miles and more, curving gradually around the beleaguered city. These
lines were very nearly continuous, though a ravine or creek bottom
might be guarded from higher ground nearby (men on both sides could
still lose their bearings and find themselves inside enemy lines; thus one
evening at suppertime a Union soldier carrying a coffeepot and a frying
pan wandered up to a Confederate campfire—and paid for his error
with his life a few months later at Andersonville). So widely extended
were the opposing lines that a fierce struggle could rage at one end of
the front and troops at the other end barely detect the noise of battle.

It is possible to gauge the continuing intensity of the fighting after a
fashion, thanks to the meticulous records of the Army of the Cumberland: In June its troops expended three and a half million rifle cartridges,
in July a little over two and a quarter million, and in August three million. Given such figures, one can understand why a Union officer had
"almost reached the conclusion that lead was a primary element in the
Georgia atmosphere." In the fighting around Atlanta the firing tended to
be concentrated in a relatively small area, with the space between the
two armies virtually saturated with bullets and shells. When General
French found the Federals had withdrawn from a section of the line
opposite his own he sent men out to collect the bullets they could find
lying about in an open field between the lines. One of his brigades
picked up two and a half tons of musket balls. French recalled: "the
ground was literally covered with them—oxidized white like hail-
stones."

Most of this lead was not fired in what could properly be termed a
battle, though in July there were three engagements of sufficient scope to
merit the name. The great bulk of the firing was in skirmishing. A veteran of the campaign later wrote: "The investment of Atlanta, from July
22d until late in August, was in the main a gigantic battle of skirmishers.
The picket firing never ceased, day or night. Sometimes it was lazy, scat-

tered, and weak, and again swelling into volleys like the beginning of a battle, and now and then being followed by the roar of artillery." The consumption of munitions of all sorts was prodigious; in the records of both armies there are warnings against "promiscuous" firing and pleas to conserve ammunition, though they tend to be more frequent and more urgent on the Southern side. On July 1 Colonel Wright, head of the Atlanta arsenal, wrote to his counterpart in Macon: "The question of supplying the army with ammunition is getting to be a serious one." He said the Army of Tennessee was expending "100,000 rounds daily, on an average, on nothing but skirmishing," while cartridge production in Atlanta had stopped in order to move the facility, and the daily output of the arsenals at Macon, Columbus, and Selma, Alabama, was only about forty thousand rounds per day. In artillery, where the Confederates were already outgunned, a serious shortage of artillery shells developed in the course of the summer, a predicament Colonel Wright also wrestled with. Northern troops sometimes received graphic proof of this dearth of munitions in the Southern batteries: The colonel of the Thirty-third Massachusetts wrote that on one occasion: "A rebel battery was literally throwing old junk at our men, old rusty spikes, nuts and hinges, old files and padlocks and pieces of old coffee mills were flying through the air in the most promiscuous manner"; on August 17 a correspondent of the *Louisville Daily Journal* reported his section of the line being bombarded from Atlanta with what appeared to be window weights.

This continuous firing produced an endless flow of casualties. A Confederate commissary officer named Edward Brown was often on the roads immediately behind the Confederate battle line and so saw the dead and the disabled being evacuated; he estimated that the Army of Tennessee lost on an average day about three hundred. General Sherman confided to his wife in August: "Our losses are 300 to 1000 a day." In the month of July, with its three battles, there were 5,421 cases of battle wounds sufficiently serious to be treated in the hospitals of Sherman's three armies. That same month Confederate medical personnel treated ten thousand for wounds, accidents, and injuries. It has been estimated that that summer about one Confederate soldier in six was wounded each month. In the Union army the battle wounds were scrupulously categorized: 5,331 of them were "gunshot wounds"; the "incised," "lacerated," and "punctured" wounds—those that could have been made by swords and bayonets—numbered 90. By no means all those who walked or were carried to the hospitals went there because of wounds; in fact only a minority were the victims of enemy action. In that same month of July 1864 some sixty-five hundred of Sherman's men entered the hospitals to be treated for "fevers," which were simply the most prominent symptoms of various underlying infections and disorders. Even more common were acute and chronic forms of dysentery and diarrhea, and if we add to them colic, constipation, and other complaints of the gastro-intestinal system, then this general category of illness put some ten thousand Union soldiers in the hospital in that same month of July (from scattered references on the Confederate side, it appears that the same types of illnesses prevailed there).

The number of Northern soldiers absent from the field that summer because of wounds or illness was regarded as excessive, and attributed to "the extreme rigors of the campaign." At any given time that summer between a third and a fourth of the Union force before Atlanta was hospitalized. On the Confederate side it appears that better than a third of the army was hospitalized at one time or another during July. It would seem that the Georgia Militia was particularly hard-hit. Dr. Massey, who was running Brown Hospital, found his wards "overflowing" with militia, and anywhere between two and eight dying each day.

Yet as a rule the maladies that brought the men to the hospitals were seldom fatal; neither "fever" nor the "Georgia shits" seem to have kept the men in the hospitals for very long. The latter malady can probably be attributed to the filthy conditions in which compact masses of men lived and to the bacteria that multiplied there—thriving all the more in an army that was totally unaware of their existence. For the ingrained notion shared by medical authorities and the army's rank and file alike was that much of the illness came from "miasmas" or noxious vapors and exhalations—thus fevers were classified as "miasmatic diseases." It was also known that disease could come from "bad water," though this last generation before Pasteur and Koch had no clear grasp of what made the water bad or how it could be purified. But all were agreed that the water in the Atlanta area was a likely villain: "With 150,000 men and 50,000 animals crowded into the space occupied by the two great armies in the siege operations around the city, all the flowing creeks became badly fouled."

Flies too were a source of contagion, though they were seen as a vexation rather than a danger. They were everywhere, but were particularly troublesome for mounted units; the First Wisconsin Cavalry was so harassed by them that it changed its campsite every few days, leaving behind the flies and the mounds of manure that attracted them. Not that the infantry was neglected: "But oh! the *flies*," a foot soldier from Illinois wrote his wife, "dog flies or ox flies or whatever they should be called. One needs three hands to eat with—or rather 2 to fight *flies* with & the

other one to steal what he eats away from them. But they go to roost
after dark, so we sleep well." And after the campaign was over another
Northern soldier concluded: "That Atlanta was finally taken was not the
fault of the flies and other pests of the region. Many did their full share
to defend it." If insects became a plague of sorts, the sun became a veritable scourge after the prolonged rainy spell ended in late June. The
Northern soldiers, who were especially affected, began to ransack their
vocabularies to tell their friends and relatives at home what a Georgia
summer was like: "I nearly smothered"; "excruciatingly warm"; "nearly
delirious from the effects of the sun"; "hot enough to roast Indians"; and
the like. The men on both sides of the line put up blankets over their
ditches as awnings or constructed "bowers" and "arbors." The Union
physicians said the temperature never got above ninety degrees in the
shade, but that was no consolation to men baking in a trench in the middle of a field of scrub pines. Now any exertion like a march would leave
half the men in a regiment strung out along the road. In combat extraordinary exertions were often called for, and the heat would have its effect
on the way the men performed in the July battles.

The men in both armies suffered from a variety of other ills, minor
for the most part, which they either treated themselves or simply
endured. Both armies were lousy, but in addition they had to contend
with chigger or "red bug" bites and the itching and infection that
attended them; some found the chiggers could be warded off by rubbing
the wrists and ankles with a bacon rind. Skin problems of all sorts
cropped up, and though they were often lumped under the designation
"army itch," they were traceable to a variety of causes, among them the
heat, lack of bathing, uniforms far too heavy for the climate, and contact
with certain poisonous plants. A soldier, particularly a Northern soldier,
may mention that his face has been "poisoned" by something in the
woods where he slept. There is only occasional mention of "poison oak,"
but many of the cases of "army itch" sound suspiciously like exposure to
poison ivy; this plant, like the sun and the chiggers, could be considered
a natural ally of the Confederacy.

The soldiers' diaries and letters reveal that the Civil War generation
had a strong belief in folk remedies and self-treatment. The hospitals
saw very few cases of scurvy, for the men knew how to treat this disease—hence the countless Northern soldiers who went out blackberry
picking in the midst of the campaign that summer, some of them getting
lost and ending up in Andersonville. In some cases they would make
their own diagnoses, attributing their indisposition to "sweet potato
consumption" and other afflictions unknown to the world of formal

medicine. They treated themselves with the remedies at hand, among them gunpowder, which had—in folklore at least—a tonic, bracing effect on the system. A self-reliant Indiana soldier wrote his wife that summer: "I want you to send me about four ounces of cloves and a half dozen of nutmegs. I'm going to make me some diahrorea medicine." Some men carried medicines into the field with them, for they mention dosing themselves with "blue pills," Rochelle Salts, Dover's Powders, and other remedies. A chaplain named John Hight seems to have had an extensive pharmacopoeia, none of which was doing him any good, if we may believe his diary entry for July 26, 1864: "I have taken blue mass, calomel, opium, sugar of lead, castor oil, quinine, whiskey, wine, and the rest of it. Opium made me sleep and the whiskey stimulated. I could observe no other results."

Those soldiers who kept diaries day in and day out were by nature persons of orderly and methodical bent; not only were the entries made faithfully each day, they frequently followed a set form. There were, for example, the meteorologically oriented who were careful to begin each entry with notations on atmospheric conditions, to which they clearly attached considerable importance. Others took as their leitmotiv not the state of the weather but the state of their health. Their diary entries began with "heavy, sluggish feeling and no life," "bowels running like a sluice," and so forth. One suspects that these youthful armies had their share of hypochondriacs who, though they lived in showers of lead projectiles, occupied much of their time with real or imaginary complaints. On the day that three thousand men were struck down in battle at Kennesaw Mountain a soldier noted in his diary: "Kennesaw battle. I am quite unwell today, slight diarrhea, pain in the bowels and side, also head."

But the diaries and letters reveal a good deal more than the state of the armies' health as the Georgia campaign reached its apogee; they are in fact the best source for understanding that bundle of perceptions and preoccupations that made up the ethos of the ditches. Perhaps the first thing one notices about a Civil War soldier's correspondence was how vital that correspondence was to him. However much military life might have changed a man's habits or viewpoints, it did not destroy his need to identify with the old, civilian world he had left, and letters were the indispensable link to that world.

Every ploy, every stratagem was used to make the soldier's correspondents take up their pens. A Northern soldier began a letter to his negligent sister with the announcement: "I am dead. I was interred last evening." He goes on to say that the marker on his grave reads: "Died of the blues, friends at home failing to keep up a correspondence with him." A New York officer named Arthur Fitch, having had no letter from Helen, sent her a message via mutual friends: "Tell her I am 'sparking' a young lady, a Southern girl who chews tobacco and dips snuff, in desperation of the moment engendered by not having heard from her. I shall ask the said girl for her photograph if I don't get a letter soon." Andrew Bush tried still another tack with his wife: "Do write or don't any more, but write me once more and tell me which you will do so that I will know what to expect."

Reid Mitchell has observed in his study of Civil War soldiers that they tended to lose their prewar identities. The letters from the men fighting in Georgia indicate some of them had detected this change in themselves; what is more they worried about it, since it would make their return to the civilian world all the more difficult. An Ohio soldier worried that "the absence of all the softening and restraining influences of religion, home and virtuous women" would demoralize the men and make them reckless. Many acknowledged the crudeness and the privations of military life. "I haint eat the first egg sense I left home," a young soldier wrote home to Illinois, "we don't see eggs down here, all we see is rebels." And a sergeant named Phinehas Hager shared his concern with his wife: "I have not slept between white sheets since I left home June 25, 1861. I feel as though I was getting perfectly wild." Young men who were single could not help worrying that by the time they got back home all the desirable girls would have married. A Confederate officer from Tennessee recorded in his diary that spring: "A meeting was called in the Regt. to express our indignation of the conduct of the young ladies of West Tenn. who are marrying forgetful of their promises to us." Copies of the soldiers' "Resolution" were sent through the lines for distribution in Henry County, which many of the men called home. Yet that spring any number of soldiers in Georgia were busy conducting courtships by mail. Samuel King Vann, a nineteen-year-old soldier from Alabama, arrived at an "understanding" with Miss Nancy Elizabeth Neel, having proposed to her by letter on January 2, 1864, four days before her fourteenth birthday: "Will you join with me in a matrimonial engagement at the close of this war provided we both live to see it end, which I pray God we may do?" (They survived and married, though Samuel Vann died from the kick of a mule in his twenty-fourth year.)

We do not know whether Corporal Rudolphe Rey of the 102nd New York Infantry was successful in his campaign to win the affections of Miss Lizzie DeVoe of 80 West 19th Street, New York City, but no one can read his letters to her without feeling that such a valiant effort deserved its reward. Rey had special difficulties with English, and some of the errors he made suggest his native language was German. But in those letters he tried his best to describe to Miss DeVoe a stirring, martial world in which he himself appeared in favorable light. He explained to her that he was one of an elite group, "Hooker's fighting men . . . the corps that wood never yeald." On the eve of the campaign he tells her he is waiting to hear "the Order of our commanding Generl to say 'Forward my men Onwerd to victory.' When that orders has come we are gon to see som hard times." For him the order cannot come soon enough: "i wate in vane," he tells Miss DeVoe. Throughout the campaign his letters ring with the clash of arms, the sound of the bugle "witch ses 'to armes to arms again my brave. Onwerd again to *Victory*.' " Yet at the same time Corporal Rey is a man who can see also himself as he is. He has written Miss DeVoe that he will send her a photograph of himself, but he has not done so and he explains why: "I looke at myselve in the looking glass and then look at the photographs, to see witch was the humblest. You know that i am pity bad looking but O it was nothing to wot the photographs was."

As for the men who had marched off leaving behind wives and children, their letters were understandably full of family concerns. Men who are on their first campaign reveal the most acute homesickness, writing at length of some trivial episode in a happier time. With the new soldiers of the Georgia Militia, some of whom had never been out of their home counties, the pain of separation is palpable: "I never knew how dearly I loved home before," wrote one; another wrote across the bottom of his letter in crude, laborious script the names of all his children; somehow that made him feel closer to them. A man's wife might write that there was an addition to their family; while he was invariably pleased, his response could tell a good bit about how the household was run. When Colonel Ephraim Holloway of the Forty-first Ohio learned he had a daughter he wrote his wife: "I will send you a name for her soon." Captain Henry Ankeny of the Fourth Iowa was already father of a girl named Josey, so when his wife wrote him she had given birth to another girl, he wound up his reply with the words: "A thousand kisses for Josey and 'What's-its-Name.' "

Some men sent their wives long, elaborate instructions about managing affairs, about working the farm; others seem to have felt the futility of such measures. If there is one counsel that is repeated endlessly in men's letters to their wives, whether North or South, it is the simple phrase: "Do the best you can." The wife thus assumed an authority to which she was not accustomed, and the soldiers' letters sometimes reflect this change and the altered relationships it implied. A surgeon with a Tennessee regiment in Confederate service observed to his wife who was managing their affairs in Union-occupied territory: "I can scarcely realize it when I recollect how timid you used to be."

Southern soldiers who were slave owners show a special preoccupation in their letters. They frequently included instructions concerning "the servants" or "the negroes" (never "the slaves") and messages to be transmitted to them. The wording of these messages suggests a certain ambivalence. The writer is clearly concerned about how they might behave but uncertain how to ensure good behavior. Sometimes he sends word that he is relying on them, sometimes he speaks vaguely of a reckoning with those who misbehave, and sometimes the message contains both promises and warnings. A Georgia militiaman named R. T. Wood had been mobilized in the May call, leaving his teenage son James to "keep the plows running" on his plantation; then he learned from his wife, Mary, that James had been called up with the reserve militia. "How I do hate it," he answered, "but Mary try to give him up cheerful." With James's departure a slave named Steave was the logical person to keep the plows running. Wood relayed a message to him via Mary: "I shal Look to him to cary on the busines under your dyrection & shal hold him responcable & should him or any of the rest disobey you . . . I will settle with them when I get home." In the same letter he instructed Mary to "tell all the negroes howdy for me." As a general rule, in these letters written in the final hours of American slavery the kind words appear to be more numerous than the threats.

John H. Marshall, on the other hand, filled his letters to his wife with all the dire things he planned to do to his body servant Rube if he ever got his hands on him. Marshall's troubles began in the fighting at Jonesboro, where many in his regiment, the Forty-first Mississippi, were captured. He wrote his wife immediately afterward: "Well, Jane, this leaves me well but naked. The Yankees captured Rube and all my cloths." But the Federals had no reason to hold Rube, and he apparently crossed the lines again to the Southern side, though he did not return to the regiment. Marshall was furious when he learned this and sent his wife instructions that if Rube showed up at home she was to sell him. Then word came to him that his body servant was still with the Army of Tennessee; other soldiers said they had seen him one place or another and he talked about coming back to the regiment but didn't say when. Marshall vented his anger in his letters to his wife. He would make Rube fear for his life; he would "make a Christian of him." On September 23 he wrote: "I will send him off south and sell him first or kill him. He shall not treat me any such a way and then stay at home. And me in the Army." But apparently Marshall didn't carry out his threats; other materials in Marshall's papers indicate that Rube did eventually return to the Marshall home, where apparently all was forgiven.

From time to time the letters reflect misunderstanding and discord between marriage partners. Edward Brown was in the habit of expressing himself frankly in his letters to his wife, and she was in the habit of quoting him to her neighbors, but since the men in his company came from the same small community in Alabama, Brown's comments, no doubt distorted and embroidered, were relayed to his comrades by their folks at home. Among other things Brown had written his wife that he had no use for slaves and would not give a hundred dollars for one. Now, because of her irresponsible chattering to the neighbors, word of his remark had spread through the regiment, where he was acquiring a reputation as "an unsound Southern man." For Judson Austin of the Nineteenth Michigan and his wife, Sarah, the marital problems were more serious. Austin had been receiving anonymous letters charging that his wife was taking advantage of his absence to have an affair with "Mr. B." Austin told his wife about the letters, and she apparently denied she was doing anything wrong (only his side of the correspondence survives in the archives). Austin accepted her word, but he was a much troubled man. A little later he wrote Sarah: "I hear of husband and wife dissolving partnership in almost every letter or every mail that comes."

Reid Mitchell has written about the "cultural inadmissibility" of the subject of sex in Civil War correspondence. In truth, judging from the lack of sensual overtones in the letters most soldiers exchanged with their wives, there was no sexual side to their marriage, or at least none worth mentioning. Occasionally one encounters letters with portions put in code or cipher, suggesting intimate or steamy passages reserved for the eyes of the marriage partner alone. But when the historian turns cryptanalyst and deciphers such messages they appear anything but racy. Thus when Wayne Morris of the Twenty-third Michigan Infantry wrote his wife in June 1864, referring to her as "the light & life of my own existence," then lapsed into a half-page of cipher text, his transports of passion carried him no further than this: "How I long to clasp that beautiful form & press it to my bosom & feel those loving arms around my neck, those rosy cheeks & ruby lips pressed against my own. . . ."

But in some situations sexual matters had to be admitted into the correspondence. This was the case when there was a possibility that the soldier could get leave and come home or the wife might be able to come where he was. In an age without effective contraceptives the husband's desire to have sex could collide with the wife's wish to avoid pregnancy; hence it was essential to deal with this matter in advance. Letters treating this subject were usually exercises in circumlocution. When Edward Brown thought he had a chance for a furlough he wrote a masterpiece in this genre:

> You sometime since hinted that I need not defer coming for fear of a 'Calamity.' I am about as much inclined to run the risk of the aforementioned 'Calamity' as I ever was in my life if I had the chance. And I am of the opinion that you would have cause to fear it if you are at all fearful, for I believe that I am stouter now than you ever knew me. You had better not want me to come.

It is unlikely that the correspondence of all couples was so decorous and circumspect, so "Victorian," regarding this aspect of their lives. When a soldier addresses his wife as "Sweetcake" and signs himself "Honeyboy," even though the rest of the letter is tame enough, one senses a couple whose rapport, sexual and otherwise, is on the same wavelength as our own. But most of these couples were probably plain country people for whom writing any kind of letter was painful, and who were not the sort to leave literary remains that would find their way into the archives. One of the exceptions is the letter that William Herrick wrote to his wife, Dot, on September 18, 1864. Herrick says only that he was doing cooking in Company D near Carrolton, Georgia, and most likely he was a member of the Georgia Militia. His letter is frankly and graphically erotic. Among other things he tells Dot about a dream he has had: "I dreamed I was with you Dot and we was on the bed. I had covered you two or three times and we joied ourself tarnal well." And he even ends the letter with an amatory flourish: "Well now Dot ise must stop, for thinking of you makes my old thing look me rite up in the eyes. . . ."

Occasionally soldiers corresponded back and forth, and letters of this type can also deal very graphically with sexual matters—and like William Herrick's letter they tell us there was a side to the Civil War soldier we rarely glimpse in his writings. Such is the case with letters of the Yoder brothers in the Manuscript Division of the Library of Congress. There are accounts of high times in various towns that soldiers on furlough passed through, with descriptions of brawls, drinking bouts, and anatomical discoveries made in the course of encounters with young women. And we may assume that the drift of the soldiers' correspondence with one another was no different from the tenor of their conversations when they were together. The camps and the ditches were thus the home of the barnyard joke and the four-letter word. We know this chiefly from the shock that new soldiers registered when they joined their regiments. John D. Vail, a pious, churchgoing man who was drafted from Belmont County, Ohio, in 1864, left a record of his impressions of army life that is eloquent in this regard. Even before he left to join his regiment in Georgia he complained about the "continued noise of profanaty & vulgarity" that assailed his ears morning and evening. By the time he reached Rome, Georgia, the atmosphere had become even worse: "Around me is the gibber of reckless men & I am compelled to Listen day and night to their profanaty, filthy talk and vulgar songs. I have some conception of how Lot felt in Sodom."

While Vail does not get more specific about the language used, we know from other sources that the words and expressions were earthy and for the most part in use today. Court-martial records are useful in this connection, because of their meticulous way of relating what was said and done. In the case of a Pennsylvania corporal named Harrison Adams the court-martial was the outcome of a long-smoldering feud between Adams and Allen Anchors, another soldier in his company. The offense for which Adams was tried was his posting in the company street of an obscene drawing that carried the inscription: "Allen Anchors Fucking a Cow."

The language employed to describe the opposite sex was rarely respectful. One of the less offensive terms the Union soldiers used to describe the women of North Georgia was "mountain ewes"; women of easy virtue were called "elmpeelers." But such habits were not confined to the Union soldiers of the western army. Women who had the occasion to eavesdrop on soldiers' conversations in other places were usually shocked by the language they heard applied to their sex. A woman named Loreta Janeta Velazquez, who liked to pass herself off as Lieutenant Harry T. Buford of the Confederate army, said many of the conversations about women she heard while in disguise were "thoroughly despicable." Another practice we hear mentioned in Sherman's regiments was teasing someone about his female relatives and acquaintances. An Iowa soldier tried to warn his younger brother about the "rude society" he would encounter when he joined the army. "When young men get to joking with each another they very often cast very deriding epithets at each other's sisters or relations. I like to see men respect each other's kin enough to keep the female portion out of their deriding jests."

One might be inclined to see something vicious or depraved in such practices if they did not so closely resemble the banter and raillery one could hear whenever adolescents are thrown together for any length of time. For life in the ditches was characterized by a good deal of juvenile behavior and animal spirits. The same sally, the same prank, would get laughs endlessly, no matter how many times repeated. In one company there was a simple but infinitely obliging youth who knew only one song—an obscene ditty about the copulative capacities of his grandfather's ram. The song was always in demand, chiefly because the singer had no idea that what he sang was obscene. "He sang daily and nightly for nearly four years, until, poor fellow, he was killed at Bentonville. In his innocence he never suspected that his comrades were 'guying' him when they asked him to sing."

If a man flinched too often or moved about the trench with unusual caution, he was teased about it unmercifully. His tormentors regarded what they were doing as therapeutic. "Some of our boys are yet a little chicken hearted," a Southern soldier confided to his wife, "but Dunwoody teases them until it soon wears off." There were endless practical jokes. Lieutenant Chesley Mosman was told that in a nearby regiment there was a 160-pound shell they were going to use on the Rebs. He went over to see and found "a man of that name and weight." Another source indicates that in a single day two hundred men came to see the "shell." When the opportunity presented itself the men indulged in other pranks. At night Northern pickets would sometimes make howling and hissing noises to set the dogs of Atlanta to barking. The troops that occupied and plundered Decatur found among other things a large quantity of "lances," probably some of Governor Brown's pikes. A soldier who was there recalled: "Scores of them were carried around by our boys, giving the troops the appearance as though we were still living in the middle ages."

It was difficult to contain the energies and exuberance of youth within the trenches. There were scuffles and horseplay, and men who dozed were pelted with clods by persons unknown. There were raucous disputes over the most trivial things. One day in a section of the Confederate line some Tennessee soldiers fell to arguing over whose shells were passing across their works, Yankee shells or their own. At one point a soldier named Andy Youngblood raised his arm, pointing with his index finger, and said, "I bet you $5.00 it is a Yankee battery." Hardly had he said this when a stray minie ball clipped off his finger. For despite the very real danger, the men were often negligent. Officers complained that it was difficult to make them stay under cover. Edward Brown, whose duties usually kept him in the rear, visited an Alabama unit in the ditches and found the place "really dangerous"; yet he discovered that "the men go in & out, and up and down the lines where they are firing just as though nothing was going on." Some who remarked this behavior blamed it on the confining nature of trench warfare. "They have become reckless and it is so tiresome for days behind works that they will face danger for the sake of exercise." But this is not the whole explanation.

Sometimes the men would deliberately expose themselves to enemy fire in what were essentially acts of bravado, with one man trying to outdo another. John H. Marshall, though married and a settled man, confessed to his wife that he had been caught up in the spirit of the thing and had risked his life in such stunts several times. Once he had even jumped up on the breastworks and shouted across to the Union lines, "Try me, Mr. Sherman." These episodes also took place in the Union lines. In Company E of the Eightieth Illinois a man named Sam Musgraves could do an excellent imitation of a rooster. One day while in a "gopher hole" on the picket line he bet the man who came to relieve him that he could jump up on the edge of the hole, flap his wings, and crow, and that the Rebels couldn't hit him. "Well, he jumped, flopped and crowed all right but the rebs brought him down with a bullet hole in the fleshy part of both thighs, and we would have laughed if they had killed the fool." Occasionally they did just that, as in the case of a daredevil in the 105th Illinois: "Elias Burns sang out 'The Rebel Bullet is not yet made, that is to kill me.' At that, he jumped up and fell down the same instant with a bullet in his brains." The narrator continues: "He fell across my lap—I was still sitting—and his brains and blood ran into my haversack, spoiling my rations. So I took his."

Occasionally there were feats of derring-do that were witnessed by both armies: At one place in the defenses of Atlanta a house stood behind the Confederate skirmish line but in front of their main works. At that point the Federal skirmish line was in a depression, so from the house Southern riflemen had the Federal skirmishers at their mercy. On July 27 the Federal soldiers in that sector made a surprise attack; a wave of troops dashed forward and "gobbled" the Confederate picket line. Following close behind was a special detachment of the Thirteenth New Jersey Infantry armed with matches and bundles of kindling; these men rushed into the house and set fires in various rooms, so that soon the entire structure was in flames. The attacking force and the house burners then returned to the Union lines, to the cheers of thousands on both sides of the line.

Then sometimes in the middle of the firing back and forth something hilarious would happen. One day some Federal infantrymen took shelter under a railway water tower. A Confederate battery managed to put a shell in the tower, sending down a deluge that nearly drowned the soldiers; those who witnessed it found it "rich." Another time shells fell behind the Union line just as commissary wagons were making the rounds. "I never heard such a racket," recalled a witness in the Southern trenches, "teams running, camp kettles and cooking utensiles rattling and drivers yelling 'Whoa!' 'Whoa!' 'Whoa!' Of course we enjoyed it, and the Yankees hearing us laughing over it said it was a blank shame to shoot right into their commissary wagons before they got their supper, and they would get even with us before the campaign was over."

Perhaps the most singular assault of the entire Atlanta campaign was recorded by a Union soldier who was a witness to it. The men in his section of the line were taking their ease when they suddenly heard yelling and cheering from the direction of the Confederate works several hundred yards opposite. Since this was often the first sign of an attack the men scrambled to their firing positions and watched for the appearance of the Rebel assault columns. Instead they saw a single Rebel soldier appear. He came on at a run, and since he was alone the men on the skirmish line assumed he was deserting and let him pass through. He ran straight on toward the main works:

He came rushing up the dirt bank and jumped over the rifle pitts, landing among us and ordered us to surrender. It was now seen that he was 'crazy drunk' and had a canteen of whiskey with him. After humoring him by pretending to surrender to him he became good humored and offered us all [a] round from his canteen. He said that he had told his people that if they were too cowardly to make a charge on us he would do it himself, and that he had done it. When he became sober and found himself a prisoner and was told how he had become such, he was much cast down.

On both sides the fascination with the enemy continued. In the two months spent before Atlanta the soldiers had numerous occasions to satisfy their curiosity about those facing them, for there were any number of truces, both formal and impromptu, that brought Northern and Southern soldiers together. Though there had been contacts for some time, the truce arranged on June 29 after the fighting at Kennesaw was a significant step in what we might call the "relations" between the two armies. Ostensibly the truce was for disposing of the dead who lay between the lines, with the space cordoned off so that none but burial parties could enter, but no one seems to have paid attention to such matters of form, and for several hours officers and men met and talked. William Parker of the Seventy-fifth Illinois was able to see his brother, who was in Frank Cheatham's division. A soldier from Michigan fell to talking with some Southern soldiers from Franklin, Tennessee. It was the Michigan soldier's "favorite" Southern town, where he had recently been on garrison duty. "They haven't had letters for most a year, so I told them all the news."

A number of "celebrities" appeared between the lines at Kennesaw. Officer-journalist David Conyngham was able to see in the flesh the Confederate generals whose names figured in his columns:

> There were Generals Cleburne, Cheatham, Hindman, and Maney, in busy converse with a group of Federal officers. Cheatham looked rugged and healthy, though seemingly sad and despondent. He wore his fatigue dress—a blue flannel shirt, black neck-tie, grey homespun pantaloons, and slouched black hat. . . . I saw Pat Cleburne with that tall, meagre frame, and that ugly scar across his lank, gloomy face, stand with a thoughtful air, looking on the work his division had done.

The Southern generals asked their Northern counterparts about old friends; a bottle appeared and made the rounds, and Conyngham heard someone say graciously, "You have better whiskey than we have got."

The Chattahoochee River provided the stage for another cycle of contact, for while the stream became for a time the no-man's-land between the armies, it was irresistible to men who had had all too little chance to bathe or wash their clothes; here there were frequent truces and a considerable amount of trading and conversation and even cavorting among men of both sides. That the lure of the river itself played a role in the increased fraternization there is no doubt. An observer noted: "the boys are more friendly with each other than they have been heretofore. Yesterday and today they have been swimming in the river." Once the lines moved south of the Chattahoochee the pattern of impromptu truces continued, and to the soldiers it had another benefit; it gave temporary relief from confinement in the ditches: Hardly had the agreement been made to cease firing along the picket line before "all the men on both sides were out in plain view, enjoying the sunshine and straightening out their limbs in perfect safety." There was another quite different impulsion for cease-fires along the picket line. In the soldier's logic there was an important distinction between the functions of picketing and skirmishing. Though the terms "picket" and "skirmisher" were used synonymously, two very different functions were involved. A picket was after all nothing but an essentially inoffensive watchman, on the lookout for any movement or activity by the opposing side—and it was a function virtually every soldier was called to fulfill. The shooting of a picket seemed to many men an act of "bushwhacking," "beneath the dignity of civilized warfare." Why? Because it was a life taken to no useful purpose. A Union officer explained: "The shooting of a few men on picket, as it cannot affect the ultimate result, amounts to little less than murder, especially as the chances are the losses will about ballance." If one or the other side intended an advance, then the line of pickets could well become a line of skirmishers, for such men were customarily the first wave of an attack, having as their purpose to distract and harass the defenders. To the soldiers, at least, the solution was simple: Picket fire and its attendant loss of life could be done away with by mutual consent; however when one side undertook an advance beyond a certain fixed point, the other could use its firepower freely.

These notions ran counter to the standing prohibition against communication with the enemy save on proper authority. Sherman did not pronounce himself on these truces, though he later boasted he had not availed himself of a flag of truce until the Atlanta campaign was over. General Hood, on the other hand, took a strong stand against any treating with the enemy, and his views seem to have been passed on to the rank and file, for after he took command some Southern units refused picket line cease-fire agreements, or sent word they would not fire but could not parley. Nor was Hood the only Southern general who took action. General French ordered fire directed at Federal and Confederate cavalrymen when they were swimming together in the Chattahoochee. His rationale: "Our men are not seeking fords; they are." And a Confederate officer recorded in his diary in mid-July that General Strahl was "calling all who have held communication with the Yankees to a strict account."

Most of the truces seem to have been oral, informal affairs arranged by brigades, regiments, and sometimes simply by the men on the firing lines, with their own officers not even informed. These truces figure so frequently in diaries and letters that it is easy to gain the impression they were widespread. But some units, the 112th Illinois, for example, never made any agreement with the Rebels to suspend picket firing; Texans and Kentuckians are particularly mentioned as rejecting overtures for cease-fires. At least once the Georgia Militia rebuffed an offer for a parley. The Northern troops they rebuffed concluded: "After they have seen more service they will be wiser." Artillerymen seem to have been largely strangers to these friendly contacts. Perhaps it was their location, which generally kept them at a distance from the enemy, and perhaps the technical nature of their work distanced them emotionally. According to a correspondent of the *Savannah Daily Republican* on one occasion opposing artillerymen did converse after a fashion: One day shells landed near a Confederate battery but failed to explode; examination of one of the shells revealed that instead of gunpowder it contained a message that said: "Your artillery isn't worth a damn." The truces, then, were the exception, not the rule; the armies were throwing too much lead at each other for it to have been otherwise.

When the soldiers did meet, it was in an atmosphere of mutual respect and even cordiality. To be sure, in the shouting back and forth across the picket lines one could easily taunt the enemy into opening fire. Thus when a Southern soldier bragged about plentiful rations a voice from the Union side called over: "If you have so much bacon why don't you grease your britches and slide back into the Union?" And this repartee was answered by a volley from the Southern lines. But when the soldiers met face to face by prearrangement, no instance has been found in which the meeting degenerated into mutual insults or violence. H. V. Redfield, the Tennessean who saw so much of both armies, was emphatic: "I never knew an instance of bad faith on either side."

Units that opposed each other in the battle line for any length of time got to know each other in a sense; thus Deas's Alabama Brigade made acquaintance with the Iowa troops opposite: "It was the custom to each day ascertain from each other what regiment was on duty in the pits." The Twenty-seventh Indiana and the Tenth Georgia got acquainted on the Chattahoochee. An Indiana soldier recalled the Georgians as "warm-hearted, full of fun, ready to give or take a joke, never harsh or ill-tempered in their language, in all except their uniforms they seemed one with ourselves." Then the Indiana troops were withdrawn briefly and did not return until after the Battle of Peachtree Creek:

After it was over we found the names of the Georgia lieutenant and several of his men on headboards marking the graves of those killed in front of our regiment. The thirty years and more which have gone over our heads since then have not entirely removed the pain we have always felt when recalling this episode of the war.

In August a Wisconsin volunteer wrote home: "If they would let the soldiers settle this thing it would not be long before we would be on terms of peace." Perhaps. But if we have seen these soldiers associate with such cordiality and amity, we must now see them meet in some of the most savage and desperately fought battles of the war.

9

❖

Battle

Traditionally the great battle has been the centerpiece of warfare. According to a notion that goes back at least to Jericho and Thermopylae the fate of nations and empires must hang upon its outcome. In the summer of 1864 soldiers and civilians alike waited for just such a battle in the vicinity of Atlanta, but they waited in vain, for none of the three battles that July involved more than a part of the forces concentrated around the Gate City; none of them could be called decisive or even did much to affect the course of the campaign. The "semi-siege" of Atlanta went on through August, then Sherman finally took the city the way he had said he would at the outset: by severing its rail lines.

Yet the battles—around Atlanta and elsewhere in the Georgia campaign—interest us because they were a crucial experience in the lives of the participants. Recreating that experience should be an easy task, for the literature on Civil War battles tends to be voluminous, and the battles in Georgia are no exception. But there are problems in reconstructing a Civil War battle, and apparently there always have been. Speaking of the Battle of Franklin, General Cheatham said: "I have never read a true story of this battle"; another veteran lamented: "No battle of the war has been accurately described." The historian is inclined to discount these complaints, for old soldiers tend to quarrel about their battles when they do not find in the accounts of others the same things they themselves saw and experienced, and part of the historian's work, after all, is to reconcile such conflicting testimonies.

Battle accounts, official and otherwise, present difficulties in part because they rely on sights and impressions registered in a period of distraction and stress. Even shortly after the event what remains in the memory of the eyewitness is often nothing more than a jumble of images and impressions. One soldier will say they beat back six attacks, and another will swear he counted seven. The combatant's sense of time can also be affected, so that it becomes difficult to figure out such a simple matter as the duration of an engagement. Then too, consciously or not, soldiers tend to color their accounts of combat, and the colors may change with the passage of time; they may fade but they may also become more vivid: On the day of the battle the enemy's fire is heavy; five years later it has become a storm of shot and shell. While the sources have their limitations, then, their very lack of objectivity has a certain value: To anyone trying to reconstruct battle as men experienced it, the way things seemed is in fact as important as the way they were. And the logical procedure for this reconstruction would be to begin with the preparatory phase of the encounter, passing on to the action, and finally reviewing the battle's impact—not on the campaign but on the combatants.

We tend to think that a battle begins as an idea in the general's head, an idea that he rarely communicates to the rank and file he will call upon to do the fighting. Still, most battles were preceded by rumors in the regiments, for if an engagement was being planned there were certain signs that veterans knew to look for. For example, when a battle was in the offing the surgeons would begin discharging patients from the hospitals wholesale in anticipation of battle casualties they would be receiving, and the return of convalescents to their regiments in large numbers was a clear signal. When an old soldier saw musicians moving to the rear he knew there was a good chance fighting was imminent, since the musicians' post in battle was with the hospitals, where they helped take care of the wounded. As a rule the warning or preparation time for most battles in the Georgia campaign was very short even for the generals, so the men had little chance to mull over the chances of an impending fight. General Hood, for instance, decided on the attacks of July 20 and July 22 only a few hours beforehand, and the Battle of Ezra Church was essentially an unplanned battle, being initiated by one of Hood's subordinates, General Stephen D. Lee. For the Union troops that Hood's army attacked, the battle often began with no warning at all. Some of the Northern soldiers who fought in the Battle of Atlanta got their first intimation of trouble when their own berrypickers came flying back toward the lines, followed by masses of gray infantry. There were occasions when battle seemed imminent—as at Cassville—and then the prospect faded away. "Sometimes," wrote Union artilleryman William

Wheeler, "when we are all cocked and primed, and have screwed our courage to the fighting point, we are balked of our little muss; this last produces a sensation similar to that of going up one stair too many in the dark, and is altogether disgusting."

The assault Sherman made on Kennesaw Mountain was distinctive in the length of time that elapsed between the general's Special Field Order No. 28 covering the assault, issued June 24, and its execution on June 27, and in fact some preparation was made even earlier. Already on June 23 unaccustomed numbers of general officers were seen riding the lines together, looking at the Confederate defenses around Kennesaw. One officer noted the passage of Generals Thomas, Howard, and Newton; when they stopped to reconnoiter his sector, he said the troops there "instinctively knew something was up." Lieutenant Chesley Mosman saw Sherman go by with Generals Howard, Thomas, and Stanley in tow; they stopped at a battery and the artillerymen claimed they overheard Sherman say: "flanking is played out." By that same evening rumors of an impending assault on Kennesaw began running through the lines, where one soldier recalled that they "disturbed the usual serenity of the men and excited their nerves to the highest tension." Over the next three days there were other signs of the coming action, and these too were sent along the "grapevine": inspection of cartridge boxes had been ordered; medical chests were being packed, and the surgeons were having their saws polished. There was unusual activity in various headquarters, where in fact officers were preparing orders and directives and regiments were being chosen for the assault and allotted their place in the skirmish lines or the assault columns.

On the evening of the 26th a party including General McPherson came to a section of the lines for a last look at the ground. When the soldiers bedded down that night a good many of them must have known they would be wakened for battle. While they slept lanterns burned through the night in many headquarters tents as orders and reminders went out. For the men were to be roused at three A.M. but no bugles were to be sounded; the troops were to have had their breakfasts and be ready to march by dawn. That morning an Ohio soldier wrote in his diary: "June 27th, 1864. six a.m. Our officers are all called up to Brigade Headquarters, some say to get their Bitters. We are ordered to pack our knapsacks and leave them at headquarters. This seems portentous. We must take nothing but haversacks, canteens and sixty rounds of cartridges." A thirty-four-year-old brigadier general named Walter Gresham penned a few hurried lines to his wife: "At 8 A.M. today we assault the enemy's works. I hope and believe I shall come out of the terrible struggle . . .

alive, but if Providence decrees otherwise you will receive this last token of love from your devoted husband. God bless you and take care of you and the children. . . ." The troops moved to their designated positions, and at eight o'clock a single cannon shot signaled the beginning of the Battle of Kennesaw Mountain.

How many of the men had spent a sleepless, agitated night waiting for dawn and the battle it would bring? Most likely very few, or at least none seems to have mentioned it when he wrote about the affair. When a correspondent asked William Wheeler if he had difficulty sleeping on the eve of battle, he replied that he had had no trouble: "It is not like a duel, you know, where a man centralizes and absorbs every feeling in himself, but here every man knows that it is his duty, and that he *must* do it, and the stronger his body is the better he can do that duty, and so he 'puts in a big ration of sleep.'" But waiting to go into battle in the morning calm was another matter altogether. Ambrose Bierce remembered waiting quietly in the ranks just before that attack on Pickett's Mill, when in the stillness they heard birds singing in the trees in front of them: "Some one said it was a pity to frighten them but there would necessarily be more or less noise. We laughed at that: men awaiting death on the battlefield laugh easily, though not infectiously."

One veteran of the war wrote that as long as an old soldier was not ordered into a battle he would be "the image of peaceful contentment, within hearing of a fierce engagement, apparently wholly indifferent as to the result." He might have appeared indifferent, but he was not. He would be listening to the sounds of the firing first of all, for its loudness and intensity could tell him something of how the battle was going. If he was a Union soldier and he heard the shrill, keening sound of the Rebel yell, he knew enemy was attacking; then he would wait to hear the deeper cheering of the Union troops once they had repelled the Rebel onrush. If that sound did not come and if the noise of battle seemed to grow louder, he would watch the field or the woods ahead with increasing anxiety. Above all, troops held in reserve watched for a single horseman galloping in their direction, for such a rider would bring orders for them to advance onto the field of battle. The wait might be a few minutes, it might be several hours. The tension worked on the soldiers, so that they frequently had to quit ranks and step behind a tree to empty their bladders; they seem to have always returned to their places. One soldier remembered that his brigade was kept in this state of suspense for the entire battle, the galloping staff officer never appearing. He said he knew more anguish that day than in any battle he had fought.

But more often than not the fateful rider did appear. He would rein in his lathered horse and present himself to the brigade commander; other officers would gather around briefly, then fan out toward their units; the men are already bestirring themselves. If the unit was being shelled as it waited, an experience one soldier described as "very trying to one's nerves," the order to advance could be received with relief: "I went forward with a will," said the soldier whose nerves were being tried, "certain we would do them up in a hurry and have this over with." But far more often the order provoked just the opposite response. "In General Harker's brigade," David Conyngham noted on the day of Kennesaw, "the men were under orders to advance when a sergeant retired to his tent and shot himself through the head. I have known several cases of this kind." As the troops moved forward, some men found they were hanging back in spite of themselves: "There were some with whom the sense of danger was so oppressive that they had to be literally pushed along as we advanced upon the enemy, being overcome by a dread of death, which to them was very humiliating; patriots they were nevertheless and often fought like tigers when the battle was fully joined."

Did anyone advance into battle serene and confident about how things would go for him? Precious few, apparently, could go into combat with the sort of equanimity that Wayne E. Morris of Company A, Twenty-third Michigan Infantry seemed to possess. He had quite probably had an intense religious experience not long before; he wrote his wife frequently of how Jesus protected him from the illnesses that were all around him, and he said he could relate to her specific instances in which through direct intervention the Lord had made enemy bullets turn to the right or left of him. James F. Sawyer, who was new to battle that summer, was also religiously oriented. After being in a fight at Calhoun Station in mid-May he wrote his wife that he had trusted in God and made it through the day; thereafter he intensified his reading of the Scriptures and it paid him dividends, though not quite the ones Wayne Morris enjoyed. After the Battle of Peachtree Creek Sawyer wrote his wife: "I poot my trust in God. I went into the charge with the boolets a flying around us without hardly enney fear. I was not excited at all hardley."

At the other extreme is the anguish of W. W. Gordon, a Georgia soldier who wrote his wife a despairing letter when battle seemed imminent and he didn't think he would survive it: "I can't be good, Nell, I have neglected it too long. I pray constantly and earnestly but it does no good. I cannot feel that God has given me his grace and I cannot amend without it." (Three days later, when the crisis had passed, he wrote again, asking his wife to pardon his "rather hysterical letter.") Hiram

Yerkes of the Sixty-third Indiana probably gave an accurate assessment of the prevailing attitude toward religion in both armies—in battle and out—when he wrote a friend that "most of the boys don't have the interest they should." But they all hoped for its solace in their hour of need and were impressed when they saw a man die "in the Grace," as one of them put it. A Confederate officer in a Tennessee regiment wrote some years after the war:

> Private A. D. Beckwith of our Co. (D), who had been a very wicked youth but had been converted during a revival in camp about a month before, was sitting against a small hickory tree and was struck in the body by a minnie ball. He dropped his rifle and commenced clapping his hands, dying in less than a minute. It gave me a higher conception of the power of religion to stay a dying man than anything I ever saw.

If anyone went into battle actually looking forward to the experience, no statement to that effect surfaced in the research done for this study. One cannot help but suspect that some of the generals found a certain exhilaration on the battlefield; Confederate General A. P. Stewart, for example, described some of the fighting at New Hope Church as "superb." That Southern Hotspur General W. H. T. Walker may well have been a war lover. His aide, Major Cumming, recalled that on the evening of July 21, after General Hood made plans for the Battle of Atlanta the following day, General Walker returned to his quarters "full of furious enthusiasm." The general remained "aglow with martial fire"; he would not sleep, he would not even lie down, on what proved to be his last night on earth. According to Cumming "his attenuated, tireless figure sat his horse, erect all through that weary night."

As for those who were not professional soldiers, we know from their letters and diaries that there were moments on the battlefield when they too were transfixed by the stern beauties of war. This was notably the case with a number of Federal officers and men who watched the Army of Tennessee appear before them in battle array on July 20 and 22. "A beautiful sight," said a New Jersey officer. As Colonel Thomas T. Taylor watched Confederate General T. C. Hindman's division deploy before him on July 20 he could not hide his admiration: "How well did they move, how perfectly and how grandly did their first line advance, with the beautiful battle flags waving in the breeze." And a Union soldier named C. H. Dickinson put in his diary this description of the Confederate army preparing to charge at Peachtree Creek:

Never before in the war had we been able to see so long a line of battle. . . . And now to see that whole plain covered with troops, each one standing out plain and distinct under that bright July sun, their burnished arms and gleaming bayonets flashing in the sunlight and when in motion seemed instilled with life. It was a magnificent sight. . . .

General John Geary continued to watch this same spectacle and noted with a cool professional eye how the great mass set itself in motion, heading straight toward him:

The appearance of the enemy as they charged upon our front across the cleared field was magnificent. Pouring out of the woods, they advanced in immense grey masses (not lines), with flags and banners, many of them new and beautiful, while the general and staff officers were in plain view, with drawn sabres flashing in the light, galloping here and there as they urged their troops on to the charge.

But by this time there were few to watch the spectacle; the Union soldiers were looking to their rifles and their cartridge boxes, settling into their firing positions. The firing itself had begun and the white smoke of battle was beginning to sift across the landscape. Now, as the enemy came on, as the battle was joined, the *vue en grand* dissolved, to be replaced by a confused succession of sights and scenes, very few of which would merit the adjective "magnificent." Few soldiers in the battles of 1864 tried to tell what it was like to be in the midst of one. It was by now familiar to most of them—no less frightful, but certainly no longer a novel experience. It was the new soldiers for the most part who tried to share their impressions in their letters or to sort them out as they made their diary entries. Most of them had little success. Some could only recount what had happened to themselves, perhaps too preoccupied with standing the test to pay much attention to others. One wrote his parents: "i thought that i should run but i mad out to stick to it." Another told his wife: "I never felt so worked up and queer in my life as I remember of." He also confessed that he and another man had been sent to the rear to fill canteens, and that they had stayed there until the worst was over. Some found it impossible even to describe their own emotions. "Oh mother," wrote a young soldier, "there was neve[r] no words ever printed that would express those feelings at that time."

Sergeant Levi Ross of Company K, Eighty-sixth Illinois, was a veteran by 1864. When he fought at Jonesboro on September 1 he was careful to note his own comportment for a special reason. His captain had become ill just before the battle, and with no other officers then present, it was Ross who led the company in the fighting. So he watched how he behaved with this new responsibility, and he was pleased with what he saw:

> I will modestly confess that I was surprised at my own feelings under the hottest fire and in the midst of the thickest flying missiles. . . . I think I was never cooler or more self possessed. . . . Several boys fell at my side. Two friends were mortally wounded and I stopped and placed their heads on their knapsacks.

Thomas E. Smith, who got his baptism of fire at Resaca, gave his wife a capsule impression: "It was *terrible* and *terrifying* beyond all description. I couldn't see how anyone could escape." But Smith was observant and articulate, and after reflecting he wrote his wife what he had noted about the fighting and his reaction at the time:

> It was so different from my expectations (that is the *character of the fight*) that I can form but little idea of what gallantry under such circumstances should be. We all got mixed up. Some officers left the field. Some lost their Cos. Everybody seemed to be acting on their own account. I did the best I could to bring some sort of order out of the confusion. And was assisted to some extent by other officers. But if I had it to do over again I should pursue an entirely different course. I should assume a great deal more authority. I *saw* but little manifestation of cowardice. And some heroic conduct by officers and men. But they were individual acts. There was a lack of *concert*. But on the whole I believe the charge did honor to the brigade.

Two months later Smith had learned that the confusion and lack of concert he found so deplorable in his regiment were in fact prevalent in the army in general, and nowhere more visible than on a day of battle. He wrote his sister on July 11:

> I think I begin to know about what a *battle* is (a thing so different from all my previous conceptions of it that I would have sooner taken it for a mixed-up mess of miserable and unheard of *blunders* than the most perfect management of trained and veteran armies, each handled with the most consummate skill by consummate masters of the Art of War).

What Smith had discovered old soldiers already knew, for there were occasions in battle when it was obvious even to the rank and file that their own leaders were floundering about, confused and unsure. This certainly would have been the case with the men of Confederate General Mark Lowrey's brigade as he attempted to lead them into battle on July 22. Lowrey recounted his brigade's tribulations a few days after the battle:

> I was ordered to follow Smith's brigade 500 yards in rear. The whole country through which we passed was one densely set thicket—so much so that it was found very difficult either to follow Smith's brigade or to keep the proper interval, as a line of battle could not be seen fifty yards. The advance line soon seemed to have had much difficulty in keeping the proper direction—soon moved to the right flank, then forward; then by the right flank again, then forward; then by the left flank. The difficulty of following their movements in such dense woods can scarcely be imagined, and to add to the difficulty a part of General Maney's command, which I had been informed was to remain 300 yards in my rear, soon passed through my line, creating great confusion, which required a considerable amount of time to repair. . . .

Oddly enough, when one came upon a battle from the rear, it was there that the impression of confusion and chaos was most marked—and as one moved toward the firing there seemed to be more purpose and more order in what was going on. This same observation was made in other wars as well. Old soldiers were familiar with the phenomenon; Sherman himself speaks in his memoirs of "the always sickening confusion as one approaches a fight from the rear." What signs there were of meaningful activity were not reassuring to troops moving up to the front: From a mile to a mile and a half from the front lines they would encounter field hospitals being set up, with men busy erecting tents and arbors to shelter the wounded, while surgeons laid out their instruments and prepared to operate through the night and into the next day. A keen observer like T. E. Smith recorded the excitement and apprehension as his regiment moved up toward the front: "We began passing musicians, surgeons, ambulances and the multitude of evidences that *Something* was ahead, the firing in front constantly increasing. We soon began to see wounded men. And some cannon balls began to crash through the trees about us." The rear was often awash with wild rumors about what was going on up front; stragglers and malingerers would invariably

paint a dark picture of what was happening, implying the rest of the
army would soon be following them to the rear. At Resaca a Northern
artilleryman watched a chaotic mass of cooks and servants hurrying by,
spurred by the rumor that the army was pulling back: "One man came
limping along, groaning at every step. As soon as he heard the word
'They're falling back,' he sprang toward the rear with great agility, being
cheered as long as he could be seen by the men who had seen him limping but an instant before."

Smith was concerned that the men in his regiment seemed to be
fighting individually, rather than in concert, but to seasoned soldiers this
seemed quite natural. Such a soldier was C. H. Dickinson, and he had
the time and the presence of mind to put into his diary a brief word portrait of his regiment as he saw it fighting behind breastworks in the
action at Kolb's Farm on June 22: "There was Lieutenant Colonel Blood-
good [the regimental commander], sitting on the bank with his feet in
the ditch, his lap full of cartridges, which he was biting off and handing
to a tall German soldier who had lost his front teeth." There was a cau-
tious soldier named Chris, who was crouched so low behind the breastworks that his head was well below the firing space under the headlog.
As a result he was aiming his rifle at a high angle and firing bullets
harmlessly into the trees overhead. On the other hand there was a new
recruit nicknamed "Yankee" who was standing on the bank fully
exposed to enemy fire, calmly shooting at Rebels concealed behind trees.
To Dickinson this tableau was perfectly natural: "Such incidents show
the different dispositions and temperaments of the men, some nervous
and excitable, others cool and quiet."

It would probably have been impossible for Dickinson to present a
tableau embracing anything more than the little scene he described, and
it was not just the battle smoke that made the *vue en grand* impossible.
On this point we have the testimony of Ambrose Bierce:

> It is seldom indeed that a subordinate officer knows anything about
> the disposition of the enemy's forces—except that it is unaimable—or
> precisely whom he is fighting. As to the rank and file, they can know
> nothing more of the matter than the arms they carry. They hardly
> know what troops are on their right or left the length of a regiment
> away. If it is a cloudy day they are ignorant even of the points of the
> compass. It may be said, generally, that a soldier's knowledge of
> what is going on is coterminous with his official relation to it and his
> personal connection with it; what is going on in front of him he does
> not know at all until he learns it afterward.

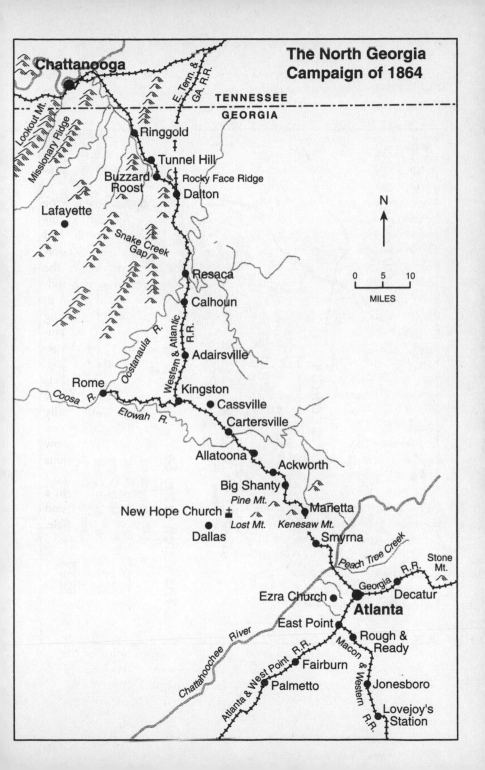

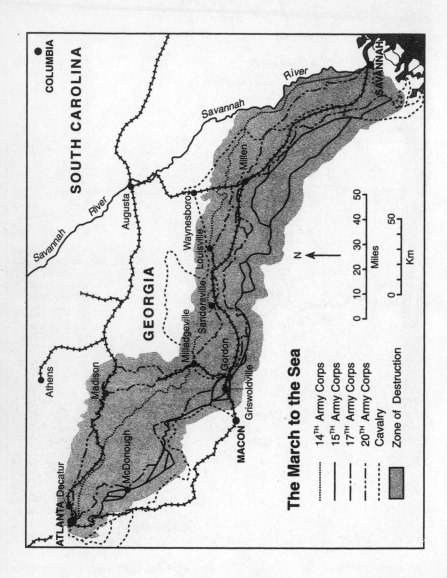

The March to the Sea

- 14TH Army Corps
- 15TH Army Corps
- 17TH Army Corps
- 20TH Army Corps
- Cavalry
- Zone of Destruction

COLUMBIA

SOUTH CAROLINA

Savannah River

Augusta

Savannah River

GEORGIA

Athens

Madison

McDonough

ATLANTA Decatur

Milledgeville

Sandersville

Gordon

Griswoldville

MACON

Louisville

Waynesboro

Millen

Savannah River

SAVANNAH

N

0 10 20 30 40 50
Miles

0   50
Km

"The most American looking man I ever saw." So a young Federal officer described William Tecumseh Sherman when he met him in December 1864. "Tall and lank," continued the description, "not very erect, with hair like thatch, which he rubs up with his hands, a rusty beard trimmed close, a wrinkled face, sharp, prominent red nose, small, bright eyes, coarse red hands." (Cumberland Gallery Collection)

Major and minor actors in the drama of 1864. UPPER LEFT: Joseph Emerson Brown was the only man elected governor of Georgia four times, serving from 1857 to 1865. (Atlanta Historical Society) UPPER RIGHT: Union General John A. Logan, an Illinois politician turned soldier, commanded the Fifteenth Corps in the Atlanta campaign. (U.S. Army Military History Institute) LOWER LEFT: Private S. J. Baldwin of the First Georgia State Line, mobilized in 1864 at the age of sixteen and wounded in the fighting near Atlanta. (Kennesaw Mountain Battlefield National Park) LOWER RIGHT: Orlando Poe, though holding only a captain's rank, served as chief engineer of Sherman's Military Division of the Mississippi; he designed the defenses of Federal Atlanta, then supervised the city's destruction. (Cumberland Gallery Collection)

Some of "the boys." Photographs of men in the opposing "western" armies often reveal a certain casualness in pose and in dress. ABOVE: A group of enlisted men from the Federal Fourth Corps. (Cumberland Gallery Collection) BELOW: Officers of Company H, Fifty-seventh Georgia Infantry. (Special Collections, Ina Dillard Russell Library, Georgia College, Milledgeville)

Scenes from the war in North Georgia. ABOVE: An abandoned house converted into a storage facility for Sherman's army; empty structures in North Georgia towns were often converted to this purpose. The chances are this home was later destroyed, since Sherman ordered the burning of all storage structures when the army evacuated North Georgia. (National Archives) BELOW: Refugees on the move, and more fortunate than many, since they had a wagon and a team. Such people could be encountered virtually anywhere military operations were under way. (Library of Congress)

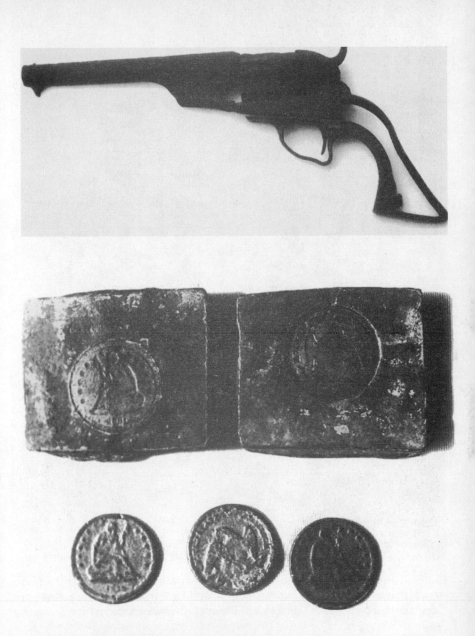

Artifacts from the North Georgia battlefields. ABOVE: The Colt revolver of a Federal soldier named C. Henry Schmidt, lost on Rocky Face Ridge and found a century later. (Charles S. Harris) BELOW: Mold for casting counterfeit quarter-dollars and three lead coins cast in it; found at a Confederate campsite near Tunnel Hill. (Charles S. Harris)

Hubbard Pryor, before and after. Pryor is shown in the garb in which he fled from a plantation in Polk County, Georgia, and in the uniform of a private in Company A, Forty-fourth U.S. Colored Infantry. (National Archives)

Four women caught up in the war: UPPER LEFT: Mary Ann Ball Bickerdyke, a nurse known to Sherman's men as "Mother Bickerdyke"; it was said that in emergencies she tore up her own garments for bandages. (U.S. Army Military History Institute) UPPER RIGHT: The Civil War diarist Eliza Frances "Fanny" Andrews; preferring a career to marriage, after the war she became a successful novelist and a noted botanist. (University of Georgia) LOWER LEFT: Emma Jane Kennon of Oxford, Georgia; when her fiancé, Willie Ross, was mortally wounded and captured, she received his last message through the kindness of a Union officer. (Courtesy of the Middle Georgia Archives, Washington Memorial Library, Macon) LOWER RIGHT: A house servant of the C. C. Jones family whose name is not known; if she was at the Jones plantation, Montevideo, in December 1864, the Yankees brought her freedom. (University of Georgia Libraries)

How to protect a railroad. This fortified bridge was at the upper end of Sherman's long supply line, on the Cumberland River near Nashville. In addition to the cupolas with firing slits, it is equipped with heavy wooden doors. (Cumberland Gallery Collection)

How to wreck a railroad. The first step was usually the heating of the rails over a fire made of crossties. The wreckers could leave the rails to bend themselves as they heated, or if they were more thorough, they would bend and twist them in ways that made their salvage more difficult. (National Archives)

The boy colonel. Arthur MacArthur Jr., father of Douglas MacArthur, served with the Twenty-fourth Wisconsin Infantry and won the Medal of Honor for his heroism at the Battle of Missionary Ridge in November 1863. He further distinguished himself at Kennesaw Mountain; by then, at the age of nineteen, he was commanding his regiment. (State Historical Society of Wisconsin)

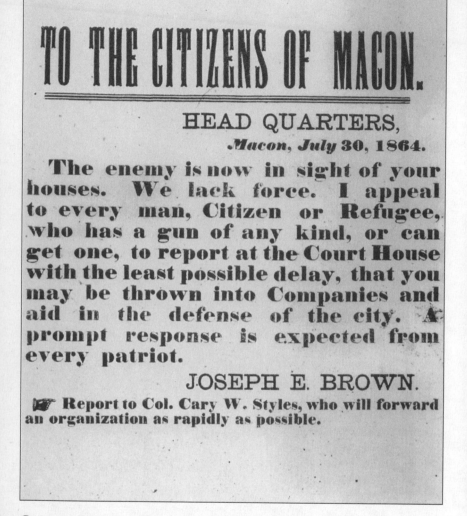

TO THE CITIZENS OF MACON.

HEAD QUARTERS,
Macon, July 30, 1864.

The enemy is now in sight of your houses. We lack force. I appeal to every man, Citizen or Refugee, who has a gun of any kind, or can get one, to report at the Court House with the least possible delay, that you may be thrown into Companies and aid in the defense of the city. A prompt response is expected from every patriot.

JOSEPH E. BROWN.

☞ Report to Col. Cary W. Styles, who will forward an organization as rapidly as possible.

Governor Brown's call to arms. One of many stirring appeals issued by the governor in 1864, this notice was posted throughout Macon when it was threatened by General Stoneman and his raiders; a large number of men answered the call. (Courtesy of the Middle Georgia Archives, Washington Memorial Library, Macon)

Scenes of "Fortress Atlanta." ABOVE: Picture taken by George Barnard, looking eastward from Fort Hood, a bastion at the northwest corner of the city's inner defensive perimeter. The elaborate defenses included abbatis, embedded stakes, and chevaux-de-frise. The frame structures have contributed their siding either to the defenses or to the soldiers' cooking fires, while the large white structure in the distance appears to be intact. (National Archives) BELOW: The structure was Ephraim Ponder's brick-and-stucco mansion, often erroneously identified as the "Potter House." It was the target of Federal artillery because its upper floor was said to harbor Confederate sharpshooters. One Union battery alone recorded firing 102 rounds at the house; subsequently more than a ton of shell fragments were removed from it. (National Archives)

Scenes in occupied Atlanta. ABOVE: The rulers of Federal Atlanta photographed before their headquarters; seated to the left of the table is Colonel William Cogswell of the Second Massachusetts Infantry, post commander, while seated opposite him is Lieutenant Colonel Charles F. Morse of the same regiment, Atlanta's provost marshal. They are surrounded by other officers of the Second Massachusetts. (Cumberland Gallery Collection) BELOW: Downtown Atlanta with the huts or "shebangs" of the Second Massachusetts Infantry filling the square; the Trout House in the background was a well-known hotel, reopened under "Northern" management. (U.S. Army Military History Institute)

Atlanta's roundhouse, before and after. The stone structure was knocked apart, using rails as battering rams. The operation took considerable time and attracted a large number of soldiers as onlookers. (National Archives; Library of Congress)

On the march. ABOVE: An artist's conception of Atlanta abandoned to the flames. (State Historical Society of Wisconsin) BELOW: Hoisting the Stars and Stripes over the state capitol in Milledgeville. According to the artist, the honor of raising the flag went to a Sergeant Holmes of the 107th New York Infantry. (State Historical Society of Wisconsin)

The prisons. ABOVE: The vast stockade at Camp Lawton, near Millen, Georgia. (State Historical Society of Wisconsin) BELOW: This postwar picture shows the stockade at Andersonville rotting away peacefully. (National Archives)

A living relic of a vanished army. Uncle Steve Eberhardt, born into slavery near Rome, Georgia, campaigned with the Confederate army in the capacity of body servant. This photograph was taken at a Confederate commemoration in Mobile, Alabama, in 1931, when Eberhardt was in his one hundredth year. (Special Collections Department, Robert W. Woodruff Library, Emory University)

But if we put together the episodes and occurrences that the soldiers witnessed and remembered on this or that tiny portion of a battlefield, these vignettes confirm the remarkable range of behavior in troops engaged in combat. Some men seemed to draw themselves in and became almost furtive in their movements, as if such unobtrusive comportment would make a passing bullet overlook them. Others seemed to throw caution to the winds, standing up on prominences to get a better shot. When James H. Goodnow's unit fought for the first time behind breastworks they were delighted with the arrangement. Yet he adds: "I could not for the life of me keep them from getting on top of the breast works and shooting, or none of them need have been hurt." Some men hummed as they fought, some sang. A Mississippi officer named Robert M. Gill confessed: "It is impossible for me to keep from cursing when I get under fire." This particular habit seems to have been fairly widespread; Levi Ross complained about "men swearing and blaspheming the name of God while cannon balls were screaming about one's head," and a Georgia soldier named Ford McWhorter recalled: "I have seen a lot of men curse in the heat of the fight, and I never did see one fail to call on God when the bullet struck him."

In the heat of battle a man's temperament could change: "I know one man in our company was a mighty bully," wrote McWhorter, "but when we went into battle you could curse him and call him anything you wanted, but as soon as it was over no man would dare cross him at all." If one man paid no heed to insults, another could forget how to perform the simplest task: A Northern soldier named Elliott McKeever recorded one such case:

> Our carbines were hinged at the breech so that by pressing a spring the barrel dropped for re-loading. A boy to my left was so excited after shooting his first load off he forgot how to "break" or drop the barrel for reloading. He tried twisting and bending over his knee and that failing he went to a stump and was just going to hit it on the stump when another boy stopped him.

Others, driven by haste and excitement, left out steps in the reloading of their rifles, so that the weapon would not fire. One Union soldier recalled how the Confederate troops opposite "snapped" their guns at him harmlessly, since they had forgotten to put on percussion caps; he attributed it to their being drunk, but the failure to load a gun properly was probably very widespread on Civil War battlefields. (After the Battle of Gettysburg all the small arms found on the field were collected and examined; a goodly proportion were loaded, with half containing multiple loads; one musket was found containing a score of rounds, filling the barrel entirely.)

One is led to believe that firing was thus an essentially compulsive act; as a Confederate veteran put it: "action under such circumstances becomes intuitive, mechanical." Yet the men retained a certain level of perception in their work, they did not fire blindly. The veteran just cited went on to say that at some point in the Kennesaw Mountain fighting a Union officer appeared on a white horse; the word came down the line: "Shoot the man on the white horse," and they fired at him until he rode off the field and out of range. Anything that stood out, that caught the eye, would be sure to draw fire, whether it be a flag being waved or a man on horseback.

Firing discipline was difficult to maintain despite frequent reminders; the men were tempted to open up long before the enemy was in effective range, and they tended to keep at it until there was either no target or no more ammunition (they also tended almost universally to fire high). Here probably lies the explanation for the enormous consumption of munitions: It was therapeutic for those doing the firing. Loading and firing kept them busy; it gave them something to do. Sometimes soldiers said as much; a Wisconsin rifleman wrote his cousin that during a recent battle a wounded Confederate soldier nearby kept up "a terrible mournful crying for a 1/2 hour." Under other circumstances it would have been a trying experience for him, "but I had no time to spare for reflection but to load & fire & this I done to my best ability." A Confederate soldier recently commissioned found at Resaca that without a rifle in his hands it was harder to keep his courage up: "Being only a subordinate, and only required to repeat commands, I had nothing to do but think of the danger, without the loading and firing to occupy my mind."

But a preoccupation with loading and firing does not completely explain how the soldier could be oblivious to things that should have been more than obvious to him. Once when the men of the Twenty-third Kentucky Infantry (U.S.) were making their way back to their own lines after an unsuccessful assault on the Confederate works at New Hope an officer on horseback appeared from nowhere, called on them to halt, and tried to rally them to make another assault. Perhaps the men were simply preoccupied with getting back safely to their own lines, but they not only refused to obey the officer, they ignored him; it did not even register on them that he was an officer very much in the wrong place, for he was a Confederate colonel in full uniform.

Certain actions on the battlefield were clearly made under the impress of fear. From time to time a man advancing into battle and already under fire would be seen to step behind a tree and shoot himself in the foot or blow one of his fingers off. Under these circumstances such self-maimings were perhaps more desperate than irrational, the action of a man who had at least figured the odds before he pulled the trigger. But fear in battle could provoke other actions that do appear irrational, notably stripping off one's clothes and running across the battlefield. This phenomenon was noted several times in the Atlanta campaign, and doubtless on other battlefields elsewhere. Those who observed it ruled it out as a ruse, for the naked runners headed toward the enemy lines as often as toward their own. It was perhaps the elemental fear response the battlefield could engender, the terrorized individual simply fleeing a place that had become intolerable. The uniform was shed perhaps because it seemed confining, or because by removing it a man ceased to belong to the world of battle.

Sometimes groups of men would undertake things that somehow made sense in the midst of battle, though they were in fact nonsensical and suicidal. On July 22, while the Seventy-eighth Ohio was desperately contesting possession of its breastworks with assailants so close they could reach out and touch them, Captain J. B. Mills saw an enemy flag being flaunted continuously some distance away. He went to his colonel and asked permission to take his company down there and capture the flag "or drive it away." The colonel acquiesced in this senseless proposal, and Captain Mills sprang to his feet, sword in hand, shouting, "Fall in, Company C." Only twelve of the company responded; the others either did not hear the call or decided not to heed it, "as it looked like it would be staring death in the face to make such an attempt." A soldier named Francis R. Baker, who recorded the episode, saw that the flag in question was protected by at least a brigade of Confederate infantry and cannon as well—yet he was one of the twelve who went with the captain. They did not get far before three of the little party were shot down; then, said Baker, "we scattered, every man for himself."

Then there were moments when the men were caught up in the elation of a rapid advance and outran their leaders and went beyond their objectives. On June 15 a Union brigade sent forward to "gobble" a Confederate picket line had taken the enemy positions handily when someone shouted: "Let's take the hill," and instantly the men abandoned their prisoners and stormed up a hill where the enemy's main works were and took them before the stunned defenders knew what was happening.

"One captain offered me his sword," recalled one participant in this headlong rush, "but I didn't have time to stop. We wanted that hill, then." In the Battle of Ezra Church, on July 28, Confederate troops were advancing to the line of a stream when they spotted a Union battery on a hillside beyond, a magnificent trophy that seemed theirs for the taking. They could not be held back; their élan carried them on and they went for the guns.

Another group response was panic, a term rarely used in the *Official Records,* though when a Federal division commander reported that at a certain point in the Battle of Atlanta his whole command "broke in confusion to the rear," one suspects that the word "panic" might just as well be used. Such flights were sometimes provoked by the loss of leadership at a critical time, the death or severe wounding of a commanding officer; by the same token there is no doubt that a steadying word from a respected officer nipped many stampedes in the bud. The most common cause for flight to the rear was the belief that the enemy had succeeded in flanking the unit in question or had even gotten to its rear, a notion that caused several regiments to carry out "spontaneous withdrawals" during the Battle of Atlanta. Two types of troops were particularly susceptible to a panic reaction when news of this sort spread. One was the Georgia Militia, whose members were strongly tempted to desertion or flight if they became convinced they were "cut off"—not from the rest of the army but from their homes, a penchant understandable in civilians recently put in uniform. Cavalry units fighting dismounted felt the same urge to rush to the rear if they believed the enemy was going to deprive them of their mounts; indeed one Confederate trooper recalled that in the confused fighting near Newnan during McCook's raid a report reached the Third Texas Cavalry that it was cut off from its horses, whereupon Lieutenant Colonel Giles Boggess shouted the bizarre command: "About Face, Charge!" Stoneman's debacle at Sunshine Church may have been precipitated when word spread among his dismounted command that the Confederates were getting to their horses.

Luther Bradley recalled that his regiment once stampeded for an unusual reason: In changing position they stirred up a mass of hornets. So wildly did the men scatter that they had to be taken to the rear to get them re-formed. But within an hour they were back in action and lost ninety-five men to enemy fire in the space of thirty minutes without flinching: "They didn't mind being shot but they couldn't stand being stung by hornets." No one was ever sure just what lay at the root of a stampede on the picket line of an Illinois regiment near Dallas:

About six in the evening, a panic seized our picket line commencing on Company B, who fled without firing a shot. Company D saw the line fall back and supposed it was a general order from proper authority. That outfit fell back too. Companies F and G did exactly the same, though not in any particular terror, but because the notion was those were our orders. Consequently Companies F and G fell back about a hundred yards before the true character of the order was ascertained. That being done, all the men returned to their respective posts somewhat wiser, and I think better men.

On the other hand we have a good idea what caused a Michigan regiment to bolt from the battle line. A soldier named W. F. True wrote his brother from Dallas "I have got the 'blues' the worst kind. Again the 4th Mich. has run!" True said it all started when a drunken scout told them they were facing four regiments of Rebel infantry, and he suspected some recently arrived conscripts of having precipitated the flight of his regiment: "You know how a few men running will start the best troops in the world." David Evans describes an episode during McCook's raid that he calls "a sort of mass hysteria," a phenomenon that might indeed happen to completely exhausted troops lost deep in enemy territory: "McCook and his men became convinced that they were surrounded by three divisions of cavalry and two brigades of infantry, perhaps as many as eight thousand Rebel soldiers." But for many of these episodes, the word "panic" may be misleading. A veteran of the campaign drew this distinction:

> Old soldiers when overpowered or taken at a disadvantage may yield ground; but they will keep together as if attracted to each other by a sort of moral gravitation, and will halt when beyond the missiles of the enemy. On the contrary, when raw troops become panic-stricken they cannot be rallied within the noise of battle. Not having acquired that cohesion which long association and discipline give, they will so disperse that much time and effort must be employed to collect them for further duty.

Under certain circumstances, then, the veteran troops of both armies would take to their heels, but their departure was calculated rather than chaotic, and they would not run far.

Here we find evidence of a distinction—a rather fine one, to be sure—drawn between the Federals and the Confederates. On this matter H. V. Redfield was categorical: The Rebels were more susceptible to panics (he claimed to have witnessed three), while the Federals tended to stay and fight in what seemed a perilous situation. Luther Bradley echoed this view. The Rebels tended to be "a little more fiery" on the battlefield, but if they had more élan, they had less steadiness and composure in tight situations: "If we beat them in battle we could keep them running if we pressed them hard. But if they beat us and drove us from the field we could keep our men in hand and reform them on the first good position, where they would fight as steadily as though they had never thought of defeat."

Flight from the battle line required some rationalization on the part of those who did it, for most of the men clung to simplistic notions of bravery and cowardice, judging their conduct—and more often the conduct of others—by fairly inflexible rules. Bravery in battle seems rarely to have been a topic of discussion, but then it rarely is among combat troops. The men of the western armies did sometimes refer to "grit," a term still in American dictionaries. Though it would seem to be an innate quality, it was sometimes said of demoralized troops that they had lost their grit. Cowardice the soldiers saw as a flaw of character that could not fail to manifest itself in time of danger. Cowards were held to be relatively rare, if we may judge by the soldiers' letters. When their companies were first formed or when they received fresh levies of men there seems to have been a discreet scrutiny of one's comrades to see if they had grit, and almost all seem to have passed muster. An Illinois soldier wrote home to his friends: "there is not a coward in our Co. I do not think." On the other hand Moses Yoder wrote his brother: "We have three or four cowardly pups in our co. Tom Stinchcomb the Idol of Mary Cook is the biggest of all." From time to time one encounters the case of the company officer incapable of leading his men in battle. The men tolerate his presence, perhaps because in combat he abdicates command. A Confederate sergeant named John Hagan had to deal with this sort of situation: "Lieutenant Tomlinson stays along but pretends to be so sick he cannot go in a fight but so long as I Keepe the right side up Co 'K' will be all right."

Even a good man could have a bad day on the battlefield; the men probably grasped this, and certainly their officers understood it. During the fighting at Cassville the Eighty-fifth Indiana's picket line was advancing over some particularly treacherous ground when Captain Frank Crawford encountered a soldier headed to the rear:

I met a man from my own regiment, whom I knew to be a good soldier, and a brave man, and whom I had seen active on the skirmish-line all day. He was coming back from the Front and shaking like a person with the ague. I called him by name and asked him, 'why, have you been hit?' He put his hand on the shoulder of my horse and looked up with tears in his eyes and said, 'no, but I'm just scared to death, can't I go back?' I gave him some message as an excuse to go back to the wagon-train. Next day he was in front and all right as ever.

What caused a man to "stick" in a fight, to stay in a position of extraordinary danger when all his senses told him he should leave? Grit or determination may be an element in the explanation, but *why*, to what end, does one determine to lay his life on the line? Modern studies of behavior in combat have weighed a number of factors. S. L. A. Marshall has written, for example, that for a man in battle the mental horizon is extremely circumscribed. The only things that matter—his friends and his enemies—are in a circle that extends around him for a distance of only a hundred feet or so. So while a man enlists for the sake of his country, he goes into battle and stays there for the sake of his buddies. We have already noted the bonding that took place among soldiers of the same "outfit," and it was on the battlefield that this unit cohesion, as it is called, could have its most remarkable effects. One old man confessed a half-century after the war that as his unit waited to go into action—in a state of anxiety one can imagine—he fashioned for himself a secure hiding place, a "hole," as he called it. The fateful order to advance came, and the men started forward to meet the Yankees without him. But he left the security of his hole and caught up with them. He had to "go with the boys."

But a man fought for his regiment, not just for its members. In battle the visible sign of the regimental presence was its colors; at the same time they were its vital center and nucleus (each Union regiment carried the Stars and Stripes and state or regimental colors as well; Confederate regiments carried the familiar battle flag with its Saint Andrew's cross). They were first of all guides or markers that the men could rally to and follow in the confusion of battle. They marked the van of the attack and were sometimes its spearhead in the literal sense; this was seen clearly the year before by observers who followed the Federal assault on Missionary Ridge from below. "As the Union line swept up the ridge, it became a series of 'regimental flying wedges, with their colors forming and leading the apex.'" The colors could also regulate the men's conduct when the battle went against them. "Abandoning the colors," "quitting his standard," such terms were synonymous with cowardice. The colonel of the Thirty-fifth Indiana issued this circular for his men's guidance: "It is an act of cowardice for an officer or man in retreat to get one step in advance of the Colors he is honor bound to defend. When the colors come to a halt for the purpose of a Rally, it is the duty of every officer and man to rally around them, and if necessary to die beneath its folds."

As the most visible symbol of the regiment and its fighting tradition the colors were powerful totems and the objects of a considerable cult. The men would fight with great ferocity to keep them from being captured (and the other side would fight equally hard to take them, for they were trophies as prized as enemy cannon). If the situation was hopeless and the men had the time, they would tear their colors to pieces or burn them, rather than let them fall into enemy hands. When most of the Seventy-third Pennsylvania was captured Captain John Kennedy managed to conceal the flag on his person, and even held on to it during his imprisonment, the precious banner being "studiously preserved from rebel eyes." In battle the colors were confided to the color-bearer and color guard, who held positions of distinction and trust but also of considerable risk. There seems never to have been any hesitation to take up the colors, despite the heavy mortality: At the Battle of Ezra Church the Forty-fourth Mississippi lost five color-bearers, and that was by no means a record. At Resaca, after the Thirty-eighth Alabama had three color-bearers hit in succession, the regimental commander, Colonel A. R. Lankford, took up the colors himself and carried them straight to the enemy line. The Northern soldiers watched him come on. They would not fire at him, "deeming him too brave to be shot." They let him come into their lines, where he was made prisoner.

Colonel Lankford's gesture was that of a regimental commander who took a most desperate step to bring his unit up to and over the enemy works, a feat that was by 1864 extremely difficult to accomplish. The assault on breastworks usually marked the zenith of the battle, and taking those works—and a second and perhaps a third line of works further on—had become the major tactical problem of the war. Time after time the scene would be repeated: Great masses of men would sweep toward the opposing line, those masses thinning and losing momentum as they advanced. Then the surge forward would stop, usually before it could wash up against the breastworks, and the mass or what was left of it would begin to recede. One or more waves might arrive to reinforce the first, and occasionally the surging mass would sweep over the barrier, and the line of works would fall. But the victors soon found themselves isolated and assailed on front and flanks, while before them lay a second line, equally formidable, and sometimes a third. Even when a charge against works was successful, the advantage was no more than temporary. It was all too easy to see the problem as a physical one, and to seek the solution in a new tactical formula, a different application of the laws of physics that would provide mass and momentum sufficient to overcome resistance. One might sustain momentum, for example, if the men in the assault wave did not stop to fire; thus on at least one occasion Union troops were sent forward with empty rifles.

The word "charge" usually evokes an image of masses or lines of men sweeping unhindered across a vast open field, but such an image could only occasionally be glimpsed in the major actions around Atlanta; most of the area was woodland, and what fields there were were often overgrown. In some places on the so-called battlefields there was heavy brush and undergrowth. Assault columns found they were also slowed by mires and creek bottoms; they had to detour around thickets and patches of brambles before they could even reach the felled trees the defenders had put in their path. The country itself constituted what one veteran called "an abbatis by nature." If the brush or foliage was thick enough, it could impose a psychological restraint as well as a physical one; the men would lose sight of one another and lose the moral support of "the touch of elbows." Another obstacle was the heat of a Georgia summer; on July 20 some of the Southern troops advanced at the double-quick for perhaps a half-mile, so that when they finally reached the Northern lines they were completely winded. A Northern soldier who was in a picket line watching them approach said: "they were so tired and it was so hot they could only walk."

As the attackers approached, some obstacles they encountered—a fallen tree, a ravine or streambed—slowed their movement for other reasons. Men dropped down behind the cover they afforded to take a drink from their canteens or to examine an arm or leg grazed by a bullet, others coming along needed no further inducement to follow their example. Once down, they found it hard to move forward again, though the call of an officer would usually bring them back into the open. So common was this habit that Sherman complained: "a fresh furrow in a plowed field will stop the whole column." A Confederate officer recalled his unit was making good progress when it encountered a fencerow only thirty or forty steps from the enemy's works: "Our line halted and it was fatal to them, for never did they advance again. . . ."

But the final and most lethal obstacle was now in view, a long rampart of earth and logs, usually wreathed in smoke through which winked the flash of muskets. Or the rampart might be ominously silent, which in a way was worse, for the assailants knew that when the enemy's volley did come, as it could any second, it would be all the more devastating. An officer recalled a dawn assault on Rebel works in which the attackers had removed anything that would clatter so they could get as near as possible before they were detected. The ramparts remained silent as they came on and even reached the enemy skirmishers' pits. "Our suspense was intense," the officer recalled, as they climbed the rampart—and found the trench empty. "We had wound ourselves up to the highest possible point of tension, and the sudden relief was like the snapping of a taut cable. We laughed and cried, or hugged one another in an uncontrolable hysteria of emotion."

But usually the assailants came under fire quite early. As they approached the works and the fire grew more deadly, the temptation to drop down behind any protection increased; it often proved irresistible by the time the attacking troops reached the enemy's abandoned picket line with its inviting holes and piles of fence rails. Confederate Colonel Bushrod Jones, commanding Holtzclaw's Brigade at Jonesboro on August 31, said his men started forward "with spirit and enthusiasm and in very good order"; nor did they lose their order or momentum when the remnants of an earlier wave of assailants passed back through them on their way to the rear. But just forty yards from the Federal works they came upon the rail piles of the Federal picket line: "The line halted without orders, and the men sought shelter behind these piles, throwing the line in disorder." For a half-hour Jones tried to get his men moving again, then had to give up and order them to retire. "The men seemed possessed of some great horror of charging breast-works, which no power, persuasion or example could dispel. . . ."

Sometimes little groups of assailants would spring up at one place or another and make a dash forward, only to be smothered by fire from the works, "shivering little efforts," one veteran called them, which "the next instant fell to pieces." Ambrose Bierce watched this phenomenon at Pickett's Mill: "Occasionally one of these groups, which had endured the storm of missiles for moments without perceptible reduction, would push forward, moved by a common despair, and wholly detach itself from the line. In a second every man would be down." Once stalled within close range of the defenders, the assaulting troops could hope for another attacking wave to come to their rescue, but eventually they would try to withdraw if ground and cover favored it (even if no order to withdraw was sent to them, the men would sometimes swear they heard one—as well they might have if one of their number issued it on his own initiative). Some would "crawfish" to the rear as unobtrusively as possible; others would watch for a favorable moment and bolt. An Indiana soldier named Parsons was pinned down in front of the Confederate trenches at Kennesaw when he heard the Rebels cheering: "Thinks I now or never. I jumped to my feet and started and made as good time as ever a hoosier did untill I got back to where our men were." But often it was as dangerous to go back as to go forward; then they stayed where they were and waited the coming of night; they might fight on, at great disadvantage, taking casualties quickly or slowly, depending on the degree of cover they had. They never had enough. A Rebel soldier who had been marooned thirty feet from the Federal works recalled: "O, I would have given the world for a hole in the ground four inches deep. I felt as big as a cow stretched out there."

Those who were stranded close to the enemy sometimes played dead to keep further fire from coming their way. Union Captain Joseph Major was within only a few feet of the Confederate line at Kennesaw when he was struck in the chest by a rock thrown by one of the defenders. Stunned, Major fell backward, then came to his senses lying amid the dead and dying, in clear view of the Confederates a few paces away. He decided to pretend he was in his death agony; his gasps and groans prompted a Rebel to venture out from the works, offer Major a drink from his canteen, and relieve him of his watch and other valuables. Major's groans and continued movements seemed to be attracting shots, so he decided to "die." As a consequence he was obliged to lie motionless from about nine o'clock in the morning until the coming of night. Unfortunately he had chosen to expire lying on his back; he was tormented by the blistering sun and swarms of insects. Finally dark came and he made it back to his lines.

Occasionally the wave of assailants would actually sweep up to the barrier of the breastworks, so that the combatants were separated by perhaps a yard or so; here the firing would tend to slacken as the men could not take the time to reload, fighting instead with bayonets or more often with clubbed muskets. Curiously, surgeons treating the wounded could tell when their brigade or division was fighting across breastworks, for the cracked skulls and puncture wounds were an infallible sign of combat at close quarters; if on the other hand the wounded received gunshot wounds in various parts of their bodies they were advancing on the enemy; wounds limited to the head and upper extremities meant they were fighting behind works. The wounds surgeons saw could also be an indication of the severity of the action and the determination with which an assault was made. Dr. W. Grinstead of the Union army's medical service was impressed by the fact that the Confederate wounded he examined after the Battle of Peachtree Creek often bore "from three to five wounds, a single wound being exceptional."

In postwar accounts men spoke of advancing against a storm of lead, a hail of bullets and shells—"breasting the cyclone," one of them called it. And those who took part in these assaults often gave the impression that they were advancing against an almost physical resistance; so a Union soldier at Resaca saw the Florida troops advancing toward his position at Dallas "with heads bowed down and their hats pulled over their eyes." But it was not the storm of shot that compelled the men to push and drive themselves on; the real resistance was within each advancing soldier, and he had to overcome it before he could hope to overcome the enemy. His leaders knew this, and they also knew ways to help him along his perilous way. Some of these ways are not treated in official correspondence and reports, and we know about them only by inference and by what individuals wrote. There is no doubt that on the Confederate side the soldiers could be incited by being told that the Union troops facing them were black. In fact no black troops in Sherman's army saw any serious fighting in Georgia that year, but the rumor of black brigades in the Union line was persistent, and after any number of engagements Southern prisoners expressed surprise that they had not encountered the black troops they had been told to expect. While the Southerners thought such troops would not put up much of a fight, that was not the only reason they looked forward to meeting them in battle. At the beginning of the campaign a Confederate soldier wrote about the "discovery" the boys had made: "They have ascertained that a Brigade of negroes is in front of them. If the enemy advances tomorrow those negroes will wish they had never left their masters when they face Gibson's brigade of Louisianians." And a little later that month a Northern soldier described how the Confederates charged his unit in its works: "Their officers had told them that they were to charge a *negro brigade*! They charged calling out 'Kill the negro s– of b—s.' "

In the medical departments of both Northern and Southern armies whiskey figured in the materia medica as a stimulant. It was frequently issued to the troops in a four-ounce ration after a strenuous day or when the men had been out in adverse weather. It also had its uses on a day of battle. Even that pious teetotaler General Howard would acknowledge that in the short term it could make the men outdo themselves, though they would pay for it later. There is no question that both armies relied on its stimulative qualities more than once when they sent troops into combat, in the particularly difficult fighting around Dallas and New Hope Church, for example. The practice was certainly not universal in either army; it seems to have been used in one brigade and sternly prohibited in the next. Troops mounting an assault were ideal candidates. Some men said they knew they would be charging works when the whiskey barrels were set out and the soldiers permitted to fill their canteens; others said that when they realized what was in store they themselves asked for the whiskey. Since the Southerners took the offensive in the big July battles, it is not surprising that the testimony on the use of alcohol among them is more abundant, particularly during the Battle of Ezra Church. That day one Union soldier reported them to be "drunk as loons," and others said they saw Rebels wandering about in a daze or leaning against trees, where they were "shot down like dogs." Nothing but an advanced state of inebriation could explain the scene witnessed that day by a Wisconsin diarist:

> Just before the last infantry charge, a full batterie came dashing up to our works and unlimbered within 15 rods from our works. Our men were, so to speak, dumbfounded. They did not believe their eyes seeing a battery running to certain dead and destruction. Not a shot was fired by our men until the batterie's men had unlimbered the guns, when in less than a minute men and horses of that batterie were down.

But in the crisis of combat the men could as often be brought to accomplish the impossible by other means. Sometimes they could be galvanized and their spirits sent soaring by a single dramatic gesture or act. Brigade and division commanders knew this could be done and that they had the power to do it. At New Hope Church, on the afternoon of May 27, it looked as though General Mark Lowrey's brigade was about to be overwhelmed by bluecoats. Lowrey wrote in his autobiography: "I dashed into their midst on old 'Rebel,' my favorite horse, and the position was held." At Jonesboro, on September 1, General Absolom Baird accompanied one of the brigades in his division "nearly to the enemy's works, riding his horse and encouraging his men." At the battle fought the preceding day, there was another example of signal courage: Union General John A. Logan watched in admiration as Confederate General Patton Anderson and his staff "rode fearlessly along his lines in front of the Second Division, and did all that a commander could do to make the assault a success." Logan watched as many of Anderson's staff were shot from their saddles, and ultimately the general himself: "I could not

help but admire his gallantry, though an enemy." Anderson's Confederate colleague, General Manigault, took a more nuanced view: "It certainly was an act of consummate generalship to push forward 7 or 800
men, just defeated, of scattered commands & no other troops to support
them within 500 yards, against I do not know how many thousands."

But the men could be inspired by words as well as by example. More
than once a rousing speech by a brigade commander could send them
scampering over their own works and straight toward those before
them. A call or an appeal from a respected leader could have a remarkable effect. We have a striking example of this in the case of the Eleventh
Michigan in the fighting of August 7, 1864. The men of the Eleventh
were "short-timers," due to be discharged in seventeen days; the end of
three long years of harsh and dangerous living was in sight. To send
them on a bloody assault against the Confederate works now, when they
were so close to the end, seemed "too cruel," one of them recalled. When
the order came they didn't move; a mutiny was in the making. Then
their commander, Lieutenant Colonel Melvin Mudge, climbed up on
their works, drew his sword, and in full view of enemy marksmen called
on them in ringing tones to be true to themselves and do their duty. As
he concluded his appeal a general on horseback came thundering up
with an urgent call for the men to advance. Colonel Mudge then shouted
"Eleventh Michigan—forward—double time—guide center—march!"
One of the soldiers later said: "it was like an electric thrill. With one
impulse every man leaped the works." The Eleventh stormed and took
the Confederate works; in the process more than thirty of them fell.

Then, after what seemed an interminable time, the ferocity of the battle would decline, the fire would slacken, and the exhausted, begrimed
soldiers would begin to hope that they had made their last charge or
repelled their last assault for the day. As the sun sank lower the hope
would become a conviction: The battle was over. Sometimes the official
battle accounts closed with an eloquent turn of phrase, something like:
"Our troops rested confidently on their arms, ready for whatever the
morrow would bring." Closer to the mark was the recollection of a
Union soldier named A. G. Brackett after the hard fighting of July 28:
"Our men talked over the results of the battle in low tones, and prepared
for the morrow as quietly as could be, for at that time the full gravity of
the war was well understood by everyone, and there was little or no
vaporing on either side." Those who had come through the battle
unscathed talked about the boys who had not. One had been seen
headed for the rear, clutching a bloodied arm; another had gone with
them on the last charge but had not returned, and one of those present

Battle   193

thought he had seen him fall but wasn't sure. Many of the missing were by then a few miles away, recovering from the twin traumas of battle and capture, and preparing to spend their first night as prisoners of war. A considerable number of the men taken prisoner had been pinned down in sight of the enemy works; if they were badly exposed, they might make a sign, waving a handkerchief, for example, indicating they wanted to give themselves up. Or sometimes, during a lull in the battle, the officer commanding the defenders might order firing along the works stopped and call out an invitation to those who wanted to surrender to come into the lines. As a man got up and started in, the defenders would call out to him to come to one place, then another: "Each wants the fun of taking him in and would commence hollering 'Come on, Johnny, you shant be hurt.' The fellow would start, when another would yell at him to come there, thus completely bewildering him."

If by chance the assailants made it over the enemy works in sufficiently imposing numbers, their arrival could precipitate the surrender of an entire command; there were several such instances in the Atlanta campaign. The Battle of Atlanta was an unusually confusing engagement for those who fought in it, with assaults coming from unexpected directions and the fortunes of battle changing drastically from one moment to the next. Arkansas troops, pinned down in front of the Sixteenth Iowa's works, came in and surrendered, but before they could be moved to the rear other Confederate troops appeared from that very direction; the Iowans tried to put their prisoners between this new threat and themselves, but the Arkansans became belligerent and began to take up arms again. There was a period of total confusion; in the press an Iowa soldier asked an Arkansan which side was surrendering, and the Rebel answered with a laugh: "I'll be damned if I know." In the end it was the Sixteenth Iowa that went off in captivity.

Only occasionally were there problems with these surrenders on the field of battle. At the Jonesboro battle of September 1, when General Govan's Arkansans were overwhelmed, they were with difficulty brought to lay down their arms; apparently General Govan had to talk them into it. One source describes the Arkansans as crying tears of mortification, while another account describes them as "saucy"; what is clear is that for a time emotions ran very high among both victors and vanquished. Occasionally too, concern for protocol created problems in surrender on the field. Colonel Lankford, who so steadfastly bore the battle flag of the Thirty-eighth Alabama into the Union line, just as steadfastly refused to surrender and give up his arms to anyone of lower rank than himself. In that instance the captors were inclined to be understanding,

but when a Federal colonel, pinned under his dead horse, refused to surrender to the Texas private whose shot had brought horse and rider
down, he was told "to surrender or receive a six-shooter ball. He acted
prudently and acknowledged the gallant youth as his captor."

If the captors were heavily engaged or anticipating another round of
fighting, they might not want to spare men to escort the prisoners to the
rear; in that case they would send the prisoners back on their own recog-
nizance. On their way the captives were frequently subjected to a certain
good-natured raillery by those they encountered, what one veteran
called "a gauntlet of friendly chaff." And they would reply in kind, saying: "they had to fight or give up, for they could not keep out of the
way."

The trickle of prisoners that ran back from the front line was paral-
leled by another stream, this one composed of the wounded. Both
armies had recently taken measures to provide better emergency medical help before the wounded went or were carried to the hospitals, situ-
ated a mile or more to the rear. General Johnston had instituted the
"English" order, requiring that certain physicians remain in attendance
to the front line troops, while Sherman's army had what were essentially
field dressing stations not far behind the line. But those who were hit
during an assault were often marooned on the field with everyone else.
Both armies were using stretcher bearers, but they were of recent introduction and their roles were not well-defined; in any event they did not
venture into the general and indiscriminate fire that swept the area in
front of works.

So the wounded who had not the strength or the opportunity to
regain their lines stayed on the field, waiting for the sun to go down or,
less likely, for a lull or a truce that would bring them succor. They also
speculated on the gravity of their wounds: A wound to the arm or leg,
provided it shattered no bone or joint, was a "good" wound; bullets that
penetrated the chest or the abdomen to any depth were "bad" wounds,
but that could only be determined by the doctor's probe. Feared almost
as much as the mortal wound was one that produced disfiguration. A
Captain Ephraim Hawes attained a kind of grim celebrity in Sherman's
army after he came walking out of the fighting at Resaca with the front
of his uniform covered in blood and much of his lower jaw carried away.
Before horrified onlookers he sat down and calmly wrote in the dirt:
"Good for sixty days' furlough." (Hawes survived the wound and any
number of operations, masked his deformity with a thick beard, and
lived a long, full life.)

J. I. Hall was in the wave of Confederate troops that washed over a section of the Union first line on July 22. He was halfway across the field leading to the enemy's second line of works when a bullet struck him in the left thigh. He went down, but got back on his feet and started back to his lines when a second ball struck him in the right leg and he went down again. He had fallen in a cornfield and in his fall had tumbled into a furrow that gave him some protection. He settled in to wait for dark. Nearby lay another wounded soldier, a young man named Thomas. The two fell to talking. Thomas, who had been hit in the knee, asked Hall where he was wounded. Hall said the legs, but he could move his toes and feet, which he thought was a good sign. Thereupon Thomas said: "If that's any sign, I am all right. See how I can work my leg?" And with that he rolled over on his back, raised his leg, and worked it back and forth without any pain. Dark finally came, and with it help. The two men were carried off in different directions. Shortly afterward Hall made inquiries about his newfound friend; word came back from another field hospital that he had died.

And then there were those who never left the battlefield at all, whose lives were snuffed out in seconds or minutes, or who slowly bled to death waiting for the sun to go down. Just as there were good wounds there were good deaths, and we might think that one that came instantaneously and without warning would be the one a man would choose. But the generation of the 1860s had its own notions about how a soldier's life should end, and if we may read between the lines of the diaries and letters it was the same gentle and moving departure from life one found in the novels of the era: The dying man spoke to his heartbroken comrades clustered about him, his voice fading as life ebbed from him. There were hands to be clasped a final time, messages to be relayed to his family, a photograph and a packet of letters to be returned. As the end came, friends would bend close to catch his last words—for wives and mothers would want to know what they were. Someone would close the dead man's eyes and snip off a lock of his hair to be sent home, and his comrades would see that he was suitably buried and his grave marked, even if it was with boards taken from a cracker box; later his remains would somehow find their way to the family cemetery.

But a man who lost his life on a Georgia battlefield that summer was usually cheated of these last rites. There was a good chance he would die alone and unattended; later the precious letters and photographs he carried would be taken, rummaged through, and then most likely tossed on the ground (descriptions of battlefields the day after often mention papers blowing about among the bodies). The burial party would find him with his pockets turned inside out and perhaps his shoes missing.

And his interment was a final indignity: "The common soldier that fell in battle was thrown into a trench with no winding sheet but his blood-stained garments, and no covering but the cold clods thrown over him by unsympathizing strangers. . . ." After a major battle the number of dead was great and the need to put them in the ground a pressing one. The burial parties—they were often blacks—worked mechanically, with a certain detachment. After the Battle of Ezra Church a Union soldier recalled that the Rebel dead were "laid three or four deep and we covered them like cabbage."

Occasionally the records reveal battle deaths that were exceptions to these grim rules; that of Lieutenant William Ross of the Sixty-sixth Georgia Infantry was one of them. Willie Ross was from Macon; he was nineteen years old in the summer of 1864 and engaged to Miss Emma Jane Kennon of Oxford, Georgia. He was in the thick of the fighting that July: at the Battle of Peachtree Creek he had the tip of his sword shot off; at the Battle of Atlanta two days later a ball cut the strap on his haversack. After the battle he wrote his mother: "It is really strange how I got out alive for I never saw balls come thicker in my life." On August 6 he started a letter to "My own dear Emma," but his position came under such heavy shelling that he broke the letter off in mid-sentence; he never finished it.

The next day his position was overrun; in the fighting he was struck by three bullets, one of them paralyzing his legs. Lying beside him the assailants found one dead Confederate officer and another on the point of expiring. An ambulance took Ross to the hospital of the Second Division, Twenty-third Corps, where physicians saw his case was hopeless and apparently told him as much; a chaplain on duty there remembered him as "a noble looking youth" who "at once commanded the sympathy and respect of all." Major Fitzgibbon, the officer who had taken the young lieutenant prisoner, was similarly impressed and eager to do what he could for his captive. He agreed to get word to Miss Kennon and to keep Ross's sword until some way could be found to return it to his family. The chaplain took charge of some letters that were to be returned and also took steps to see that Ross's body could be located by his relatives. Some time in the night Willie Ross died. Major Fitzgibbon tried to effect a truce the next day, but chose the Georgia Militia, which he said "seem to fear a friendly chat." Not until several days later did he meet a Confederate officer between the lines and pass him a packet for Miss Kennon. The major's letter to her began by explaining briefly the wounding and capture of her fiancé. Then its tone changed:

I assure you I cared for him as tenderly and affectionately as though he were a comrade or a brother. The innocence depicted on his beautiful and manly face—the daring fearlessness he exhibited in the handling of his men, struggling to calm the fears of his fleeing comrades—won my sympathy and my heart. To my care he bestowed a likeness of yours, which I send with this, as also fifty and a half dollars in "Confederate" money which, "Vandal" tho' I am, I also enclose.

He retained his reason to the last moment, but sobbed bitterly as he directed me to take your likeness from his breast pocket. He said that he was betrothed to you, that though it was sad to die, he was prepared to meet his God. . . .

Heartily condoling with you and his family in your bereavement, and from my soul praying that this senseless, wasting war will soon close, bringing peace, union and happiness to our country, I am, sad girl,

> Your very obedient servant
> Thos. C. Fitzgibbon
> Major, 14th Mich. Vet. Vol. Inf.
> U.S.A.

10

◆

A Campaign Ends

In the last week of August General Sherman carried out the intricate maneuver of shifting his troops to the west and south of Atlanta; the Union forces that had so miraculously vanished from the north and east of the beleaguered city, sending the hopes of its inhabitants soaring, had in fact been withdrawn as a part of this delicate and complex movement. There were still two rail lines to cut, and on the 28th Sherman's troops reached one of them, the West Point line; they set about the work of thorough destruction, following their chief's unambiguous if ungrammatical order to "break the road good." Now Atlanta was left with a single lifeline coming from the south, the Macon road, and toward that line the Federal forces drove inexorably. About four o'clock on the afternoon of August 31 a message from General Schofield reached Sherman's headquarters north of Jonesboro: Schofield's troops were astraddle the Macon line and were fortifying and tearing up track. The news spread through the group of officers, sparking a spontaneous celebration. According to an artillery officer who was present and described the scene, Sherman's medical director, Dr. Kittoe, a "grey haired man of over sixty years, jumped out of his chair and kicked so high that his shoe went way up in the air"; as for Sherman, "he jumped up and made a motion with his arm as men do when they cheer."

The bitter fighting at Jonesboro on that day and the next did nothing to alter the current of events now moving strongly in favor of the Northern army. General Hood saw that the campaign for Atlanta was over. On the evening of September 1 his chief of staff, General F. A. Shoup, recorded in his war diary: "At 5 o'clock p.m. our forces commenced the evacuation of Atlanta." It was a day of stifling heat, but by noon word had spread among the inhabitants that Atlanta would be abandoned, precipitating another wave of hasty departures. Amid this mounting confusion General Samuel French tried to carry out an orderly evacuation by the army and the Georgia state troops. At the level of the common soldier there was a good bit of disorder, as classic signs of a withdrawal manifested themselves. The men saw no reason to leave goods on store shelves for the Yankees, and some locals joined in the plundering of shops; French noticed a number of soldiers were drunk. Through the long afternoon and on into the night troops passed endlessly by on their way out the McDonough Road, headed south.

While the garrison and those inhabitants who remained could still get out of Atlanta, there was no way to evacuate the large quantities of war matériel stored about the city. Commissary officers threw open some of their warehouses and invited the citizens to help themselves; among other things the commissary employees gave away a half-million pounds of cornmeal. Ordnance officers set about having cannon spiked and quantities of small arms and ammunition dumped into wells (some of this ordnance was turned up in expressway excavations a century later). General Shoup listed an eighty-one-car ordnance train and five locomotives as "destroyed"; we know something of how this was done from a Georgia militiaman named L. A. Rumph, who was a member of the demolition party. They poured five barrels of tar over and into each locomotive in the hopes it would burn with sufficient heat to ruin mechanisms. The train of munitions was drawn up beside the rolling mill; Rumph and the others in his party set fires here and there and then "ran for their lives." That night a little after midnight tremendous explosions reverberated throughout the area; some people heard them twenty miles away.

As always, a rear guard of cavalry stayed behind, but by early morning the town was essentially empty of troops. An Alabama soldier named John R. Green had been placed as a picket at an important downtown intersection called Five Points. As the night wore on, Green found himself totally alone; he could see no other pickets and began to wonder if they had been withdrawn, while he had been somehow overlooked. "It was," he recalled a half-century later, "the most dismal place I was ever in." Sometime around three or four in the morning he decided he had done his duty; through dark and silent streets he too headed for the McDonough Road. Through the night wagons and pedestrians moved along the roads and byways leading away from the city. Rumph's party had also been given the task of destroying the Confederate army's postal center, which was said to contain a hundred thousand letters. This destruction they carried out in their own way: They rode away from the city in a wagon loaded with mail, tearing open the envelopes to look for money, throwing the letters away. Rumph remembered that "the Covington Road was paved with paper for a distance of ten miles." Late that same night some Confederate soldiers on bivouac not far from Jonesboro were startled when the sound of women singing came to them through the still country air. It was an ambulance filled with evacuees from the city passing by, and the women were singing "Dixie"—the funeral dirge for Confederate Atlanta.

The night had also been an eventful one in the Union camp. The explosions coming from the direction of Atlanta caused a considerable stir; General Sherman roused a local farmer and asked him what he thought they were, while the men of the Second Minnesota were fairly sure they knew, for they had heard the same kinds of detonations just before the Confederate forces pulled out of Corinth, Mississippi. At first light Union columns began to probe the city's defenses. Just which Federal unit had the distinction of entering the city is not clear, though it is quite possible that the first soldiers in were exploring "on their own." (The chaplain of the Twenty-second Wisconsin claimed men of his regiment were the first to enter the city but forgot to bring a flag to raise over it.) We do know that Mayor Calhoun, accompanied by two city councilmen and several other citizens, went out of the city to surrender it and met a column led by Colonel John Coburn, to whom he turned over his city. "The fortune of war has placed Atlanta in your hands," the mayor said, and he went on to ask protection for the citizens and their property. Colonel Coburn answered in kind, according to a sworn statement the mayor later prepared, saying: "we did not come to make war upon non-combatants or on private property." Mayor Calhoun wrote out his statement for Colonel Coburn's superiors, but got no written pledge of protection in return. With these formalities Atlanta passed into the hands of the Union army. The army's entrance into the city was essentially a peaceful one, with only a few shots exchanged with the departing Rebel cavalry. A soldier in one of the New York regiments that came in that morning wrote his wife: "There were some who welcomed us to the city by waving handkerchiefs." In the midst of these events a young Confederate soldier in Atlanta made his withdrawal: Sixteen-year-old J. B. Thornton of the Fifth Georgia Infantry, who had overslept, awoke to find the streets full of blue uniforms. He walked through the streets of Atlanta unchallenged and headed home.

The news of the city's fall spread rapidly through various units of Sherman's armies and was known almost as quickly throughout the country, where it was joyfully received. In South Bend, Indiana, where Ellen Sherman happened to be, crowds came to cheer her and two bands appeared to serenade her. A traveler who left New York by train for Chicago reported: "all night long we traveled with the sound of clanging bells, the shouts of rejoicing multitudes in our ears and the glare of bonfires lighting up our way. The people seemed intoxicated with delight." Those who were politically attuned speculated on how much the fall of Atlanta would enhance Lincoln's chances for reelection, while others simply saw it as a sign the end was finally in sight. "The Dark Days are Over," proclaimed the *Chicago Daily Tribune*, "we can see our way out." Most of those in Sherman's army saw things that way. "Atlanta is ours! Thank God!" a Union soldier exulted, "the Rebs have received the biggest whipping they ever had. We are going to be paid and the army have a rest, then finish fighting and go home." Another wrote his parents: "I tell you rebbledom is going up fast. The news to day is that Hood's armey will all desert before an other week."

The Army of Tennessee was in fact going through something of a crisis of conscience, the culmination of a series of disappointments and disasters, to which must be added the state of exhaustion that an extremely wearing campaign had produced in the soldiers of both armies. All through the summer the Southern soldier had been a tough, resourceful combatant with more than his share of "grit," as his vigorous assaults in the July battles had proved. Indeed Union soldiers sometimes wondered how their opponents could keep going in the face of adversity: "I am afraid that I should feel like giving up if we were driven from the Ohio River," wrote one Yankee veteran, "yet they have fought like demons since crossing the Chattahoochee." But the bloody, indecisive collisions had their effect; that elusive, indefinable essence we might call the spirit of the army began to change, or so a scanning of diaries and letters strongly suggests. There is less of the old braggadocio, and less of the puckish, perverse humor that sustained this "hard-luck" army. Gone is the confident talk about Sherman being drawn southward to his doom, while somber and agonizing assessments of the future become more plentiful. The new mood was certainly visible by the end of July, when the army had fought three particularly punishing battles and gained nothing. A Georgia soldier named Fleming Jordan wrote in his diary on the last day of July: "A part of the army with which I am in contact do not talk right. They say they will charge no more brest works. Their morale is not good." Jordan's own morale was not particularly good. "I have no faith in our ability to hold Atlanta," he wrote, "or any other part of Georgia. The state will be over-run." The fall of Atlanta provoked another wave of despair and bitterness in the regiments. James Madison Brannock, surgeon of the Fifth Tennessee Infantry, had been an optimist throughout the entire campaign—at least in letters to his wife. But even he admitted to a case of "the blues" when Atlanta fell. Another soldier wrote his wife that the fall of the city had strongly affected him: "I cannot think of it without shame and mortification." Many men blamed General Hood and roundly denounced his poor generalship. Daniel P. Smith said Hood's obsession with taking "guns and colors" had decimated the army to no purpose. A Mississippi soldier named Ben Robertson wrote his sister five days after the fall of Atlanta: "I can tell you that Hood is no more a Gen. than is your negro girl & all this disaster is caused by his blunders."

The leaders in turn had their complaints about the men. Straggling of unusual proportions had weakened the Confederate forces in the fighting around Jonesboro. The withdrawal from Atlanta had been attended with so much straggling and plundering that Hood ordered roll calls each time the army stopped to rest on road marches—every fifty minutes. J. B. Sanders, who had seen the march from Atlanta up close, painted it in the darkest colors: "It was one of the worst conducted retreats I ever saw. Every commander was drunk and no one New what to do but take care of themselves."

After the opposing armies separated and the fighting ended, the inactivity of camp life gave the Southern troops time to savor the debacle, and as always with armies, idleness bred more discontent. With the fall of Atlanta the postal service of the Army of Tennessee had been seriously disrupted; naturally the interruption of the mails had a further depressing effect. Some soldiers even suspected the blackout was intentional: "I think they must be afraid for us to let the people know how bad we have been beaten," a Georgia soldier wrote his sister, "and the bad management that is here . . . "

At Lovejoy's Station and Palmetto there were serious problems of discipline. To fill the soldiers' time their commanders ordered daily sessions of drill, but in a Mississippi brigade the men were not having any of it: "Orders came from brigade headquarters for the men to be drilled two hours in the morning and same in the evening, but the privates and non-commissioned officers of the 24th and 27th Mississippi regiments refused and every man went to his tent and lay down. . . ." Other regiments were ordered under arms to quell the mutiny, and after some tense moments the men agreed to drill.

Far more grave were complaints by officers that the men had lost their grit. General Hood said after Jonesboro that the men simply wouldn't fight. Of particular concern was a manifest reluctance to charge breastworks. General Stephen D. Lee, whose corps had failed to take the Union works at Jonesboro on August 31, called the men together one division at a time. A soldier named Dent was present when Lee spoke to his division: "He told them of the poor fighting they did at Jonesboro on the 31st and talked to them very plainly about what they ought to do and how they ought to fight." Dent agreed with what his general said:

The spirit of our troops is very bad and unless they do better I do not see what is to prevent Sherman from going any where he pleases. If we had been successful at Jonesboro we could have held Atlanta now and there is no reason why we should not have been successful. The men did not fight and Hood ought not to be blamed for that. I feel badly over the result of that fight. It is a new thing for our men to refuse to fight or what is the same thing to fight with no spirit.

One finds a striking echo of this charge in the diary entry made by an Illinois major one day after the battle in question: "One cannot help pitying these soldiers. They have been whipped here until they have lost all spirit. They don't fight with any spirit when they are attacked and it's more like butchery than a battle." The malaise was general. The much-traveled Bishop Henry Lay was back with the army in mid-September and detected "some trouble and lack of spirit." So serious was it that General Hardee told Lay he thought he would invite President Davis to visit the army. General Hood embraced the idea and Davis agreed to come. The much-troubled Army of Tennessee waited for the arrival of its commander in chief.

In the meantime the Union army was taking possession of the city and its soldiers were taking possession of what wares the departing Confederate garrison and the populace had left on store shelves. It took about twenty-four hours to set up a military administration for the city, and in that time the men had free rein through the town. A soldier named Nichol wrote his sister on September 4: "The boys had free access to the town and lett me tell you they made use of their liberty, every one was loadened down with plunder." The chief prize was tobacco, and in Atlanta the Union troops seem finally to have put behind them the chronic shortage that had helped make the campaign such a hard one; they found and quickly emptied an entire warehouse of the stuff. But in fact the soldiers would take anything. A sergeant with the Twentieth Connecticut, one of those who came into the town early and on their own initiative, had already taken a ham and a bag of flour when he noticed some soldiers breaking into a jewelry store; he hid his booty between two buildings and joined them, concluding that "it was a good time to get a watch." He found nothing in the store and so went to retrieve his cache, only to find it gone. So he tried his luck again in a store strewn with all sorts of merchandise. He had just noticed that the floor was covered with friction matches and loose gunpowder when a blast blew him into the street, where he landed on all fours. He got to his feet, uninjured but a wiser man: "I returned to camp with only four boxes of matches and a plug of tobacco."

Troops continued to stream into Atlanta throughout the day and into the evening, with some turning their attention to the residential areas. Among the families waiting there was the household of Cora Warren Beck, then the twelve-year-old daughter of a Baptist minister. As night came their street was unusually dark; there were no lights in nearby homes because all their neighbors had fled. The family sat on their back porch, the back gate shut, listening to the sound of men moving up and down the street: "I remember saying to my sister, 'It makes me think of the night when the Angel of Death "passed over" the homes of the children of Israel.'" About ten o'clock they heard a man's voice at the gate, demanding entrance. Cora's father went out to ask what he wanted, and the man replied: "I want your watch"; after some discussion he agreed to settle for a meal. As he lit his pipe they could see he wore the shoulder straps of a Union officer. He was the first of many callers that night.

Sometime that evening the Second Massachusetts Infantry entered Atlanta. Its commander, Colonel William Cogswell, had been designated commandant of the post of Atlanta; he in turn named Lieutenant Colonel Charles Fessenden Morse provost marshal, with two Massachusetts regiments and one Pennsylvania regiment as provost guard; by the next morning order was established in Atlanta and the open pillage stopped. By all accounts Colonel Morse kept strict order. The provost guard picked up and confined some two hundred Confederate stragglers found in the town. Several Union sick and wounded made themselves known; they had slipped out of Confederate hospitals and found hiding places with sympathetic Atlantans. The Union army also fell heir to four Confederate military hospitals with about three hundred patients; a Northerner who visited the wards said the Southern physicians there appeared to be well-trained but "worn out."

On the afternoon of September 3 the first train entered Atlanta under Union auspices—a locomotive and caboose filled with men singing "Hail Columbia" and "Yankee Doodle," among them newspaper reporter J. B. Berry; by then the city was also linked with the North by telegraph. As Sherman's forces moved to their new quarters General Thomas's Army of the Cumberland received Atlanta with its battlements and outskirts, with the Twentieth Corps becoming the city's garrison; the Army of the Ohio moved into Decatur and the Army of the Tennessee settled into quarters around East Point. There was something of a scramble for housing among the army's senior officers, with mansions at a premium. Sherman arrived on the 8th, moving into a large house on the corner of Washington and Mitchell Streets; he found its front porch much to his liking. General Thomas moved into the Herren house on Peachtree Street, while the staff of General Geary picked out the home of Mayor Calhoun. Atlanta's new administrative officers, Colonel Cogswell and Lieutenant Colonel Morse, shared what Morse called "one of the finest houses of the city." Officers of lesser rank moved into houses when they could. One reported to his sister that he had found quarters in a "small but comfortable and clean dwelling" where he was rediscovering the pleasures of civilized life: "I have just risen from a refreshing night's sleep on a real bedstead between cotton sheets. . . . In a few minutes I shall be summoned to breakfast, sit upon a cane seated chair to a fine rosewood table covered with a snow white table spread and eat upon white china plates. . . ." Added to this pleasant existence was the possibility of leaves and furloughs, which were granted with some liberality.

The troops settled in too. The Northern soldiers, like their Southern counterparts, found that with the campaign ended there was less leisure than they had anticipated, with the drills, dress parades, inspections, and other irksome aspects of camp life, which they had not known for four months. Still, there were advantages: clothing was issued to replace their ragged uniforms; their diet improved. On September 10 one diarist recorded: "soft bread for the first time," and another noted that same evening a ration of fish and a full ration of whiskey. Lorenzo Pratt, who had found himself a bunk in a house and had drunk his first glass of milk in several months, wrote his parents: "Golley, it is most like a ferlow."

The men all wanted to see Atlanta, and their commander had no objection to their inspecting the prize they had won. "Sherman means to give us all the enjoyment that he can after so hard a campaign," wrote one visitor, "yesterday when I was in town, a brigade of the 23rd Corps

was marched into town and was turned loose to run like cattle into a
new pasture." One party of five soldiers organized their own tour. They
climbed aboard a train in Marietta, carrying with them all the food they
could, for they planned to stay overnight; in town they "found a boarding hous by us furnishing the grub"; they looked up old friends in the
garrison and saw the sights. The soldiers gaped at the damage done to
the town, particularly the Northern portion, which had taken the most
shells, and the areas around the rail depot and roundhouse, which Sherman's artillerymen had used as aiming points. A Michigan soldier
counted the holes in the various residences and wrote his brother: "It
now looks as if each house was a pigeon coop." The men also went
down to the ruins of the rolling mill and stared at what little was left of
General Hood's ordnance train. The massive iron wheels remained on
the tracks, but the cars had been blown to flinders; the site was heavily
strewn with shell fragments; here and there along the tracks were curious metallic patches where lead had melted and run from the cars to
form shiny frozen pools. Men went to look at the Confederate cemetery.
"Upon a board over a mound was written 'please do not tread on this
grave,'" wrote one visitor. He found inscriptions penciled on other
boards indicating where soldiers from various Southern states were
buried. In one corner of the cemetery were the graves of five Wisconsin
soldiers who had died in the Atlanta hospitals.

In spite of the battering it had taken, the town generally impressed
the visitors; many commented on the gardens, yards, and multitudes of
trees; as one soldier put it, Atlanta was "not compactly built" like most
of the towns they knew, and they found the spaciousness to their liking.
The first, tentative contacts between the soldiers and the city's inhabitants went better than either side expected. Some Atlantans, who had
been bracing themselves for the "vandal hordes," acknowledged that
once the initial looting had been brought under control, the enemy soldiers behaved themselves "pretty well." Each day brought its incidents
and its frictions, but in general good order prevailed. Northern soldiers
reported that Atlantans had told them their arrival had proved less
costly to the citizens' possessions and peace of mind than the departure
of the Confederates. William Dunn, surgeon of a Pennsylvania regiment,
wrote his wife:

The men have behaved themselves the best I saw them either home
or abroad. Every man has seemed to be on his good behavior since
we entered Atlanta. The women have been dressed up waiting for
our men to commence *Raping* but they have waited in vain. There has

not been a single outrage committed in this city, a circumstance that the people say they cannot say for the Rebel Army.

On the other hand a soldier named Cy Titus, who was in Atlanta unloading stores and guarding commissaries, worried about fraternization between the soldiers and certain local women, who would for a little money, "part with their good name, if ever they claimed to have one." A soldier named Rufus Mead was taken with a young widow whom he met, "gentle, pretty and charming," whose age he put at twenty-two or twenty-three; but when he learned she had three children, the oldest thirteen, "it took away the romance considerably."

For better or worse these contacts between the population of Atlanta and its garrison were suddenly disrupted by an order expelling the Atlantans from their city. Back in March Sherman and Grant had talked of holding and fortifying the town once it had been taken, and hardly was Atlanta in his possession than the commander of the Military Division of the Mississippi took steps to incorporate this addition to his vast domain. On the morning of September 3 he ordered supplies at Allatoona and Marietta brought to Atlanta; Orlando Poe was already in the town following Sherman's instructions to plan its fortifications, which would embrace a considerably smaller perimeter than Confederate Atlanta had enjoyed. In this stronghold there would be no place for a civilian population; it could not earn its livelihood because Federal Atlanta would have no commercial activity, and certainly no ties with the Confederacy—and the army could not be expected to feed the city's population when it had all it could do to keep itself supplied.

The expulsion order, dated September 5, was issued over the signature of Colonel Cogswell; it contained three brief, portentous paragraphs:

ALL FAMILIES NOW RESIDING IN THE CITY OF ATLANTA—THE MALE REPRESENTATIVES OF WHICH ARE IN THE SERVICE OF THE CONFEDERATE STATES, OR HAVE GONE SOUTH—WILL LEAVE THE CITY IN FIVE DAYS. THEY WILL BE PASSED THROUGH THE LINES AND WILL GO SOUTH.

ALL CITIZENS FROM THE NORTH, NOT CONNECTED WITH THE ARMY, AND WHO HAVE NOT AUTHORITY FROM MAJOR-GENERAL SHERMAN OR MAJOR-GENERAL THOMAS TO REMAIN IN THE CITY, WILL LEAVE WITHIN THE TIME ABOVE MENTIONED. IF FOUND WITHIN THE CITY AFTER THAT DATE THEY WILL BE ARRESTED.

ALL MALE RESIDENTS OF THIS CITY, WHO DO NOT REGISTER THEIR NAMES WITH THE CITY PROVOST MARSHAL WITHIN FIVE DAYS, AND RECEIVE AUTHORITY TO REMAIN HERE, WILL BE IMPRISONED.

To Mayor Calhoun Sherman delegated the task of designating two citizens to take a message from Sherman to General Hood. In his letter Sherman announced the evacuation and asked Hood's cooperation in receiving the families who wanted to go south. The general then had a flurry of correspondence with both the mayor and the Confederate commander. Mayor Calhoun and two of the councilmen who remained in the city petitioned the general to reconsider his decision because of the immense hardship it would impose, particularly on women and children. In his somewhat rambling reply rejecting their appeal, Sherman used the celebrated phrase "War is cruelty and you cannot refine it." The correspondence with Hood—five letters exchanged in the space of a week—was even more rambling, covering a variety of military, juridical, and humanitarian considerations, and it was more emotionally charged; at one point in his final letter General Hood wrote: "We will fight you to the death!" Yet Hood did agree to a truce at a railway station south of town, Rough and Ready, where the families going south could pass into the Confederate lines.

Colonel William Le Duc, who was in Atlanta as quartermaster of the Twentieth Corps, had known Sherman before the war; when he got a copy of the expulsion order he found Charles Ewing, who was on the general's staff, and asked him to relay a message: "Tell Cump Sherman from me that this order won't read well in history." Sherman sent a message back: "You tell Bill Duc I care not a damn how others read it—I am making history, and the citizens of this rebel town shan't eat the rations I need for my army. Tell him to turn them out." In a letter to General Halleck Sherman had said he expected the people to "howl"; the people of Atlanta did not hide their shock and their anger, and it was recorded by their conquerors, who were generally unsympathetic. "It raises quite a commotion among this community, " wrote Rufus Mead, "some are raving mad of course for they calculated to stay here and live on the government while they could act as spy or smuggler." An army correspondent of the *Louisville Daily Journal* reported: "Many say they do not intend to go either way, but they certainly have not yet become well acquainted with our commander."

Colonel Le Duc enlisted Mayor Calhoun and a committee of citizens to help in the removal and began issuing transportation orders and instructions to people as they showed up in his office. Sherman's directive permitted the evacuees to take "clothing, trunks, reasonable furniture, bedding, etc.," and servants as well, though he stipulated that "no force shall be used toward the blacks, one way or the other." In addition the travelers could not take with them firearms or other "contraband" items. It seems pretty clear that the Federal authorities did little screening of the evacuees, but let people depart in the direction they chose; nor could the five-day rule be enforced; there were people waiting for transport north long afterward.

In the meantime, Major William Clare of Hood's staff and his Federal counterpart, Colonel Warner, met at Rough and Ready on the morning of September 12 and arranged details of a ten-day truce. Sherman's Special Field Order No. 70 had stipulated the suspension of hostilities would cover Rough and Ready and a seven-mile radius, as well as the roads connecting it with Atlanta and with the Confederates' rail head at Lovejoy's Station. The truce would expire at daybreak, September 22.

The evacuation proceeded apace. While Sherman had spoken of using railway cars, the bulk of the travelers seem to have gone to Rough and Ready by wagon. For ten days convoys of about a hundred wagons and ambulances left Atlanta on the twelve-mile trip to the exchange point; about thirty of the vehicles would be ambulances crammed with evacuees, almost all of them women and children, while the wagons were piled high with their possessions. A Union officer named George Nichols rode out to Rough and Ready during the exchange and has left a description of it. He said it "as completely answers to the first part of its name as one could imagine." The exchange point consisted of "two miserable shanties, the respective quarters of the Federal and Rebel guards, separated for a distance of about 200 yards." Here, after brief formalities, the passengers and their possessions were switched to wagons and ambulances of the Confederate army for transportation to Lovejoy's Station and trains carrying them south. Colonel Le Duc had installed an army kitchen "so that no-one need go away hungry, or without a cup of coffee."(The Union army also supplied, for those who asked, five days' rations to see them through their trip.)

There was considerable waiting involved, and Nichols struck up a conversation with a "rebel lady" (he probably singled her out from the rest of the refugees, whom he described as "almost entirely from the lower class"). The woman told him that while she was sorry to leave her home, "We would much rather give up our homes than live near the Yankees." She added that she did not think any other two countries anywhere were so divided by enmity. Nichols told her that he didn't feel any hatred, whereupon she replied: "Well, sir, we hate you." The dialogue turned into an argument, and in Nichols's version he had the last word. He told her the defeat of the South was sure and imminent: "Then you will [have] thoroughly learned what your people have never before the war in the least understood—how to *respect us*." There were other meetings of the two sides at Rough and Ready that were more amicable. A number of officers met and chatted; Captain Poe had an appointment to meet a Confederate artillery officer and ended up making acquaintance with several of General Hood's staff, everyone trying "as hard as possible to forget that a state of war existed. . . ." Each side had sent a small guard detachment to Rough and Ready. Though General Hood had stipulated that "there shall be no familiarity or unnecessary intercourse with the Federal guard," the Northern and Southern soldiers got along so well that they camped together. The hundred-man Northern detachment contained a number of soldiers from the Sixth Iowa, and one of them recalled the experience of camping with the Johnnies as "exciting but pleasant."

The exodus of Atlantans heading north began at the battered rail depot. Captain William L. Patterson of the 111th Pennsylvania presided over the departures, aided by a detail of twenty-two men. Here the wait was even longer, with the families camping at the station for several days and living on U.S. Army rations; those who could not find space within the depot buildings put up quilts and blankets, tent-fly fashion. Many of those heading north were fairly well-off and arrived with considerable baggage, including more than one piano. The family with whom surgeon William Dunn was living were going to Canada, so they made arrangements with him whereby he was to "watch over" the house and purchase for $125 a magnificent piano imported from England at a cost of $1,000. (Dunn never got his piano out of Atlanta.) The hegira to the North involved nearly five hundred families, which took with them on the average a ton of baggage. The diarist Samuel Richards was able to get an entire boxcar for the stock of books from his store (these he later sold in Louisville).

As early as September 17 Sherman wrote President Lincoln that Atlanta was "pretty well cleaned out of the families, so that endless source of trouble is disposed of." This judgment was somewhat premature, since the movement north would continue for another two weeks. Just how many people were expelled from the city cannot be known with any surety. The Federals counted about seventeen hundred who left through Rough and Ready, and the 446 families mentioned as headed north would mean a total number of perhaps thirty-five hundred people; in any event Colonel Le Duc's assertion that he "turned 12,000 people out of their Atlanta homes" seems much inflated. The city was not completely emptied of its inhabitants. Some notables remained, prominent among them Mayor Calhoun, who did not abandon the city much before Sherman did. A sizable number of blacks stayed on in the town, most of them working in some capacity for the Union forces.

There were also some whites who remained as employees of the town's new masters; and in late October Captain Conyngham indicated that a number of Unionists were still living in Atlanta.

The expulsion of the citizens of Atlanta was an act virtually without precedent in the war. Albert Castel cites a parallel of sorts in the 1863 expulsion of the inhabitants of three Missouri counties along the much-inflamed Kansas-Missouri border, but he pronounces the emptying of Atlanta "the harshest measure taken against civilians by Union authorities during the entire Civil War." Yet it accorded quite well with the tough-minded approach to the war that now prevailed in political and military circles in Washington. General Halleck, Lincoln's closest military collaborator, gave his wholehearted approval: "Your mode of conducting war is just the thing we want now."

And the rank and file of Sherman's army approved; virtually all Northern soldiers who wrote about the expulsions defended the action. Captain Poe, who saw the misery and destitution flow by at Rough and Ready, put the best face on it he could: "This seems hard, but it really is an act of humanity. . . . They are permitted to take away with them all their movable property—which makes the hardship much less. . . . Their friends will meet them with wagons, and take them on their way rejoicing." But others saw the deportation of Atlanta's citizens as a grim necessity with a high cost in human suffering. A soldier who visited the train depot on September 13 found the condition of the civilians huddled there "more wretched than soldier life." Many of the women bore "unmistakable evidences of refinement," but now they were trying to cook over small, smoky fires "with crying and fretting children clinging to not overly clean dress skirts." "I could only say, God pity them! and return to my quarters, pondering on the cruelties of war."

Major Clare saw the pitiful aftermath of the exodus through Rough and Ready; he told General Shoup that as the train brought him back after the truce had ended, he saw numbers of the exiles marooned at the various stations along the line. Without any clear destination or haven, they had gotten off the train here and there, and now they were "without any shelter or any one to provide for them." But someone did provide for them, and that was Joe Brown. He had the state's quartermaster general gather them up and transport them at state expense to Dawson, Terrell County, in Southwest Georgia; there they were fed and shelter was built for them. Brown had no appropriation for such purpose, so as he later explained before the legislature, he bent the rules and used his "military" funds. In that body, which contained any number of Brown's mortal enemies, no voice was raised in objection.

As the news of the expulsions spread throughout Georgia, it got worse with the telling. It had been accompanied by the refined cruelties for which the "Vandals" and their leader were increasingly known. Thus in the version that reached most Georgians' ears, those expelled had been allowed to take nothing at all with them save the clothes on their backs. This was the version related by a journalist in the Milledgeville paper, who warned his readers that these cruelties and others could also be visited upon them: "Tongue cannot tell, pen cannot portray the hell of horrors which the people of Georgia will have to endure when Sherman becomes their lord and master."

Rough and Ready was the site of another unusual event, and this was an exchange of prisoners. The Southern commander proposed a general exchange, but Sherman limited the number to two thousand, about the number of prisoners he had immediately available. He also insisted that the Union soldiers presented for exchange be men recently captured, men who would be able to go on campaign immediately. It was agreed that Hood would give up General Stoneman and receive General Govan, who had been taken at Jonesboro. Sherman wrote Grant that Hood "raised the question of humanity but I am not to be moved by such tricks of the enemy."

The Confederate authorities may have had trouble coming up with the number of Union prisoners who met Sherman's requirements or they may have misunderstood those requirements, but there were cases in which Colonel Warner, Sherman's representative, refused to accept Union soldiers. For the men, fresh from Andersonville and standing on the threshold of liberation, the blow was almost unbearable: "The poor, emaciated boys so near to freedom were obliged to turn back towards their prison. Many of them were utterly broke down and wept like children." On one such occasion the prisoners rejected for exchange made a run for the Union line, and the truce came close to ending in gunfire. One of the Northern guards recalled:

> Of course it was our duty to stop them, but our boys were very dilatory about it and some got away. The Johnny officers threatened to have their guards fire on them. Our boys began to get angry and it looked as though we might have serious trouble, but it was quieted down. But some 150 of our boys who had been prisoners got away and I am glad of it.

At the end of September James Dunn wrote his wife: "the excitement of cleaning out the natives has subsided," adding that the town was well on the way to assuming its new guise as a military bastion. The new Atlanta was especially distinguished by the fortifications that were going up under the direction of Captain Poe. "Every day," wrote Dunn, "splendid mansions disappear and an unsightly earthwork with two or three of Uncle Sam's persuaders takes their place." Other houses were vanishing as their timbers were stripped off to construct "shebangs," the huts the soldiers of the Twentieth Corps favored for winter quarters. "We are busy laying out streets, fixing up quarters," wrote a Massachusetts soldier. He was proud of his little cabin; it measured eight feet by ten, had two windows, and contained bunks for him and his roommate. The men considered Sherman had given them carte blanche not only for the wood in abandoned houses, but also title to their furnishings. "I remember of one instance," one soldier wrote, "where a soldier had a costly mirror which almost covered one side of his hut." Military authorities had taken over any number of buildings for the army's use. Large structures around the depot were jammed with rations; part of the depot itself housed cases of hardtack; in other buildings black stevedores moved stocks of bacon, salt, sugar, and coffee. Trinity Methodist Church became a warehouse; the basement of Central Presbyterian Church served as an abbatoir, while horses were stabled in its Sunday-school rooms.

Sherman had announced that occupied Atlanta could not offer a livelihood to a civilian population, but the town's economic life began to pick up as the Union army settled in. Sherman himself had a role in this, first by letting sutlers bring their wares to Atlanta. As early as September 6 the correspondent of the *Louisville Daily Journal* reported that "sutlers, artisans and news-dealers are fast coming in, and receiving permits to occupy houses." Then Sherman's Special Field Order No. 72 authorized the army's quartermaster and commissary to purchase forage, subsistence, stores, and beef cattle locally, paying the market rate. Sherman wanted to encourage plentiful supplies of fresh fruits and other antiscorbutics. On the outskirts of the town open-air markets sprang up where women brought beans, grapes, and other items. The prices were quoted in both Confederate and Federal currency, but the women much preferred Federal greenbacks. The general authorized the Adams Express Company to open an office and made available one railway car per day for its shipments. Shops and foundries reopened, and the army had some of the captured locomotives put in running order. The city's streets and shops were crowded again, but now the shoppers were almost all in uniform. "The Blue Jackets rule the day," a young soldier wrote his mother, "the streets are crowded with them from morn to night . . . , truly it is a Yankee town now."

Barbershops sprang up like mushrooms, were filled with patrons and brought a harvest of fractional currency. A bakery was under full operation. A post office had been established and a news depot was crowded with purchasers. The Sanitary Commission had found quarters for stores intended for distribution and the express office was a point of much interest in boxes and packages received and sent.

"We led a happy life in Atlanta," one of its garrison recalled; he noted that the churches were open on Sunday and "on week nights the Opera House was run by a variety troupe, the principal performers being furnished by the Third Wisc. Regt." Nor did the town lack for music. The band of the Thirty-third Massachusetts was highly regarded and played often in Federal Atlanta. On the evening of September 24 the band gave a benefit concert in the Athenaeum for Mrs. Welch, widow of the late Masonic grand master, this apparently arranged through the intercession of General Sherman. On other occasions Mrs. Welch sang and played the piano. Social mingling and even romance were in evidence in the brief time between the arrival of Northern troops and the expulsion of most of Atlanta's population, though it is difficult to believe the words of one soldier who wrote home on September 15: "There have been more than fifty weddings now since we got in here and how many more there will be is more than I can tell."

In the case of nearby Marietta, which had a large military presence and a resident civilian population, we know something of the opportunities that town afforded thanks to the notes of William Pepper, who had been detailed there as a teamster. On October 5 he wrote: "I went to see some of my Marietta women. I had a very pleasant time with them." On the following day this was his entry:

Sat up with a sick man, replaced by another soldier at 2 a.m. Soldier and widow. I went to bed and slept with one eye open. I can tell you there was some hugging and loving done there for they was in love. . . . The soldier told her he loved her and her children. You may think this was a queer place for sparking to go on. Nevertheless it is so.

Pepper himself was sparking a Mrs. Brown and boarding comfortably at the home of a family named Kirk. But Pepper and his fellow soldiers were eventually ordered away from this pleasant existence, which they left with considerable regret: "The boys that has married here is making long faces because they have to leave there pretty wives." A little farther away, at Adairsville, where the Fifty-sixth Illinois had been in garrison since the early summer, several of the soldiers had married local girls. When the regiment returned by train from an expedition, an observer who was at the depot when the soldiers arrived noticed that "their young wives 'flew to arms' in the most approved style and with as much alacrity as the most devoted brides of the north."

Meanwhile Atlanta's conqueror was content to pass his time as a resident of the city. He could be seen going about town here and there, and people who passed by the big house on the corner of Washington and Mitchell Streets could often see him on the front porch. He went out and looked at the fortifications Captain Poe was having built and had himself and his staff photographed by George Barnard.

He checked on the progress of his cartographers, from whom he had ordered a huge map measuring seven feet by ten to illustrate his campaign. He took time to reply to a letter from a Confederate chaplain, Reverend J. H. Willoughby of the Eighteenth Alabama. The Reverend Willoughby had lost his horse in what he felt was an unjustified seizure by Union troops. The text of Sherman's reply was soon known in the higher circles of both armies, affording considerable amusement to General Hardee and others. Sherman told the hapless chaplain: "I fear I must reduce your claim to one of finance and refer you to the Great Board of Claims in Washington, that may reach your case by the time your Grand Child becomes a Great Grandfather."

Sherman welcomed numerous visitors, several of whom noted the general was wearing carpet slippers. That relentless traveler Bishop Henry Lay took meals with the general twice and sat with him on the front porch, where the bishop found his host unhappy over the way Hood had treated him in their recent correspondence and very sensitive to the charge of "inhumanity." A number of Georgians were guests of Sherman that September, including three prominent loyalists we have already encountered: Joshua Hill of Madison, Judge Augustus R. Wright of Rome, and William King of Marietta. Hill passed through Atlanta on the way to recover the body of his son Legare, who had been killed in a fight near Kingston. Sherman had given permission for the trip and received the Georgia loyalist with great courtesy. Hill later told an acquaintance that he and the general stayed up most of the night, talking about war and politics. Then at the end of the month rumors circulated that Sherman was receiving an unlikely guest, Joe Brown. A soldier wrote from Decatur on the 27th that he had learned that Brown had just passed through toward Atlanta. Another soldier added a postscript to a letter of the 28th reporting Brown had come to see Sherman under a flag of truce, and that men who had seen him said he had "a real smart intelligent look." The purpose of the visit, the rumors agreed, was to arrange Georgia's return to the Union.

Fantastic as the story appeared, it had a certain basis in truth. Sherman did send Brown an invitation to come and see him in Atlanta, but Brown never came. The general was convinced that he could split Georgia from the Confederacy, exploiting Governor Brown's animosity toward the Richmond government and promising that if the governor took Georgia out of the fight he would spare the state further depredation. Sherman wrote Lincoln about such a démarche, and the president was enthusiastic. Both Hill and King went as emissaries to Brown, while Judge Wright went to Washington and conferred with President Lincoln. The judge got the distinct impression from his talks with Lincoln that if the plan came to fruition he could expect to succeed Joe Brown in the governor's mansion. But Brown would have none of it, and eventually gave the story to the newspapers, no doubt sensing like the keen politician he was that the people wouldn't accept it and would abandon him if he embraced it. He reportedly told Joshua Hill that "the feverish condition of the people" would make it impossible. In 1879 Colonel Avery wrote an extensive account of the episode for the *Philadelphia Weekly Times* and solicited letters from all the major figures in it, including both Sherman and Brown, with their recollections. Not surprisingly, the accounts differ on a number of points. If there is anything to be learned from the affair, it was a certain naïveté on Sherman's part when it came to political realities.

Another visitor was Colonel Horace Porter, of General Grant's staff. Grant had told Porter of Sherman's idiosyncrasies. As if to confirm them Sherman received Grant's emissary on his front porch, the shapeless wool hat jammed down on his head and carpet slippers on his feet. As they sat and Sherman launched into a rapid-fire monologue, his feet playing with his carpet slippers, Porter realized that he was in the company of "one of the most dramatic and picturesque characters of the war." But the purpose of Porter's mission was to sound out Sherman on the prospects for future military operations, and on this subject Sherman talked at length. He was by no means finished with Georgia, where there were a number of possibilities for a late fall campaign; but his plans would depend on keeping his rail communications open and also on neutralizing Hood's army at Palmetto. But the Confederates would not be at Palmetto much longer; General Hood would once again seize the initiative—and where he led Sherman would have to follow.

On September 25 President Jefferson Davis arrived at Palmetto to confer with General Hood and to review the Army of Tennessee—and to do what he could to bolster its morale. For the army was still "out of sorts," as someone put it. The review was not without incident. The troops had been told there was to be no cheering or other demonstration, but this did not stop soldiers from raising a clamor for returning command to General Johnston; some shouted that if Davis gave them back "Old Joe" they would whip Sherman yet. As one soldier said: "they knew it would be impossible to court-martial an entire army." Davis gave no sign he heard these outbursts. In the talks with Hood Davis urged a policy of action on Sherman's rear, so as to compel him either to turn back to defend his communications or to strike out for the coast; in the latter case Hood was to harass the Federal columns with his cavalry while rushing his infantry ahead of the invaders and compelling them to attack his troops in their works. Davis departed on the 27th, leaving the soldiers of the Army of Tennessee with the same prediction he had made in several Georgia towns: Sherman had overreached himself; Atlanta would be for him what Moscow had been for Napoleon.

On the evening of September 28 the Army of Tennessee was placed under marching orders for the following morning. By the 30th Sherman knew something was afoot; furloughs were stopped in the Federal regiments and scouts were sent to pinpoint the Southern army's movement. On October 1 Confederate cavalry reached the Western and Atlantic, Sherman's jugular; they had already begun cutting his telegraph lines, interfering with the flow of intelligence to Atlanta. On the morning of October 3 the Federal signal station atop Kennesaw Mountain sent a semaphore message to Atlanta that Confederate columns were moving to the west of Marietta, near Lost Mountain. General Hood was making a final cast of the dice in a campaign that is still surrounded with controversy. Historians have been hard put to follow the thread of reasoning that led Hood toward his objectives, and sometimes the general himself seems to have been the victim of incertitude, for he altered his agenda as his operations proceeded. What is clear is that the enterprise was conducted with an army that might best be called convalescent in both a moral and a physical sense, with numbers that had shrunk by a third since May, and without adequate supplies or even a reliable supply line (both men and horses would be called upon to subsist much of the time on the same fare—hard corn—and sometimes the officers would have to "stand guard over their horses, when fed, to keep the corn from being stolen").

One might suppose that troops called into the field under such circumstances, not a month after terminating a disastrous and humiliating campaign, would have been pushed into open, wholesale mutiny. Yet there is every indication that as the army took to the roads of North Georgia again its malaise faded as if by magic and its general's stock rose higher than ever before. Hood's rash impulsiveness they took for boldness; the road he took—leading north—sent their spirits soaring, particularly if they were from Tennessee or Kentucky. "Ask them what inspires them," a surgeon wrote of the Tennessee troops, "& they will tell you that they would crawl on their hands and knees if necessary to get back once more to their own beloved Tennessee." But all the troops seemed inspired, and with cause. Now it was their general who was calling the tune, tearing up Sherman's railroad and "gobbling" his outposts, while somewhere behind them Sherman himself was lumbering in futile pursuit. Any number of men wrote home announcing the good news with essentially the same words: "Sherman has been *out-generaled for once.*" In the course of this remarkable campaign General Hood would sometimes sit on his horse as his troops went by, calling to each unit in turn, asking them if they would "grate corn," and assuring them that if they would, he would lead them back to Tennessee, Kentucky, and on across the Ohio. And the men would shout their willingness and wave their homemade corn graters in the air. Senior commanders too were affected by the heady atmosphere; Stephen D. Lee wrote a colleague on October 22: "Sherman is completely out generaled. . . . Old officers of this army say they have never seen it in better spirits or exhibit more enthusiasm. The men are confident, bold and valiant. . . . We are very hopeful here."

In its course northward the Army of Tennessee would veer toward the railroad, then away from it, striking some outposts and bypassing others, in movements Sherman found difficult to follow. Colonel Avery, who never lacked for a colorful phrase, described Hood and his army as "coquetting up the state road." The Confederates had their only serious check at Allatoona on October 5; there the garrison under General Corse beat back the assaults of General French's division, while Sherman anxiously followed the action from the top of Kennesaw Mountain. (At Allatoona the famished Rebels did take a vast stock of hardtack, over a million rations, and pilfered it for what they could carry; they intended to burn the remainder, but the party that was to set the fires had no matches. General Cockrell produced three, but none of them would strike, so the mountain of rations was left intact. Tradition has it—wrongly—that these were the rations that sustained Sherman's men on their famous March to the Sea.) Sherman himself reached Allatoona on the 8th; Chesley Mosman, who saw him the next day, wrote: "Sherman has his old round crowned black hat pulled down over one ear, leaving the other out in the cold. Hood cut his haversack strings and he is mad." He was at the very least discommoded, for Hood's initiative had forced him to shelve his own plans for the time being. He had left Atlanta to be guarded by the Twentieth Corps, and on October 2, with the bulk of his forces, he started back up the road he had taken to Atlanta, tracking Hood and trying to limit the damage to his lifeline.

Elsewhere the Confederates were having better success; they took Big Shanty, Acworth, and other posts, reaping a harvest of over a thousand prisoners. Union soldiers taken in those posts remembered the Rebels as jubilant; they tried to talk the prisoners out of their overcoats and blankets, telling them such things would not be needed at Andersonville, while they would be very useful to the Southerners when they got on the other side of the Ohio River (even Southern prisoners taken at this time manifested such an extreme cockiness that Chesley Mosman felt they merited a thrashing, "though of course we can't hurt unarmed men").

When Hood's troops surrounded the Federal post at Dalton on the afternoon of October 13 the atmosphere was heavy with menace. The Southerners learned that the major element in the Dalton garrison was the eight hundred officers and men of the Forty-fourth U.S. Colored Infantry, which had been transferred from Rome during the summer. The black regiment was already vaguely known to many of the Southern soldiers. Wheeler had threatened the post earlier but had not been able to take it; stories spread that after he withdrew some Southern stragglers had been taken and barbarously murdered by black troops. The Arkansans of General Govan's brigade had a special score to settle with the Forty-fourth as a result of an encounter with them a month earlier: Govan's men had been captured at the second Battle of Jonesboro and were en route back from Chattanooga for exchange at Rough and Ready when their train made a stop at Dalton. There the prisoners came in contact with the men of the Forty-fourth, and the mixture quickly became explosive. One of Govan's men recalled that at the station they "had words" with the soldiers of the Forty-fourth, and "if white troops had not come to protect them, there would have been serious trouble." Before the two bodies of men were separated they apparently exchanged threats of "no quarter" if they ever met again.

General Hood sent in a demand for the garrison's surrender to
Colonel Lewis Johnson of the Forty-fourth, who was post commandant.
Hood promised that if Johnson surrendered, all white officers and soldiers would be paroled "within a few days," but if the Confederates had
to take the place by assault no prisoners would be taken. The message
made no mention of the black troops. Johnson turned down the demand,
but after some preliminary skirmishing he sent out some officers under a
flag of truce and agreed to meet with Hood, who told him he would
have to surrender at once, for the Southern general could not long
restrain his troops. Hood was probably not exaggerating very much.
According to Lieutenant Morris Hall of the Forty-fourth, while the parley was going on Hood turned to General Cleburne and asked if his men
could "take those damn niggers out of the fort." Cleburne in turn asked
his men, who responded with a Rebel yell and said they "would not
need more than five minutes." Lieutenant Hall had the impression the
men were exasperated with Hood for wasting time in a parley. While the
negotiations continued the Texas troops that had been chosen to lead the
attack on the fort asked that the Arkansans should have that honor, and
General Cheatham consented. As they waited "the Texans passed the
word down as though it came from General Cheatham 'Kill every dam
one of them.'" As for the men of the Forty-fourth, they too preferred to
fight, despite the grim odds. As the parley continued they asked Lieutenant Hall if they could expect to be treated as prisoners of war. All he
could tell them was that as a white officer commanding black troops he
would probably be treated worse than they.

In the end Colonel Johnson surrendered his command as prisoners of
war, while the Confederates considered the blacks to have been surrendered "as property." Despite their wishes the white officers were separated from the men. The soldiers were stripped of their shoes and put to
work tearing up track. A Southern officer who was there described the
prisoners as "very insolent." A sergeant who refused to work was shot
on the spot; according to Colonel Johnson five others were shot later
because they couldn't keep up with the fast-moving Confederates. A
considerable number of the soldiers managed to escape their captors; of
the approximately 600 who were in the post and made prisoner, some
350 were transported to Mississippi, where the greater part were turned
over to those who presented themselves as their former masters; by the
end of the year 125 were still working on the railroads. A Confederate
chaplain noticed them at a Mississippi train station, "some in the most
distressing condition—evidently dying." Those who escaped eventually
found their way back to Chattanooga, where with new recruits they

reconstituted the regiment. In December the Confederates would encounter the resurrected Forty-fourth Colored Infantry at the Battle of Nashville. Hubbard Pryor, the soldier who had been photographed before and after his enlistment, was one of the men captured at Dalton. Just what happened to him is a mystery, for he still had not rejoined the regiment when it was mustered out of service several months after Appomattox. But he seems to have survived the war, for his widow, then living in Texas, received a pension in 1891.

After taking Dalton Hood swung his army away from the rail line and headed west toward Alabama, driven there partly by short rations. He came to rest at Gaylesville, Alabama, not far from Rome, then moved farther into Alabama. The route edged northward, and one day those in the line of march heard cheering ahead, and as each regiment advanced it too began to cheer, for they passed a sign announcing that they were entering the State of Tennessee. The Tennesseans were ecstatic; their general had kept his promise. Behind them they left Sherman; he had pursued them as far as Gaylesville before turning back toward Atlanta and objectives of his own. Ahead of them lay two places on their route where they would know some of the most savage fighting of the war—Franklin and Nashville.

PART THREE

THE MARCH

11

◆

Atlanta Delenda Est

During Horace Porter's visit to Sherman the general had told him, "I want to strike out for the sea," and in a letter that Porter carried back to Grant the conqueror of Atlanta elaborated on his idea. The fruitless pursuit of Hood through most of October confirmed the notion in his mind, and he returned to it in his telegrams to Grant, presenting it as the logical solution to the dilemma that his victory had brought him. Atlanta was valuable only because holding it deprived the Confederates of it. Yet holding it also immobilized large forces, and keeping those forces supplied required vast resources and constant vigil. But the city could be abandoned to the Rebels if those things that made it valuable to the Confederacy—its industrial capacity and its rail facilities—were destroyed. The garrison, thus liberated, could carry destruction across the rest of the State and "make Georgia howl," as Sherman put it. Once it reached the coast, the army could replenish and refit with the help of the Union navy and be ready for further operations. The chief impediment to the plan was General Hood, but by late October it was clear he was heading for Tennessee, where Sherman had placed ample forces to deal with him under Generals Thomas and Schofield. "I can make Savannah, Charleston, or the mouth of the Chattahoochee (Appalachicola)," he had already wired Grant on the 11th, "answer quick, as I know we will not have the telegraph long."

Grant and Sherman had discussed how the campaign in Georgia might evolve once Atlanta was taken back when they were laying plans for operations in 1864, and they had considered several scenarios. One would be the march south, such as Sherman was proposing. It could be directed either to the Atlantic or the Gulf, depending on developments. Another possibility was to retain Atlanta and open a corridor with a rail link from the coast to the Gate City similar to the one that passed through the District of the Etowah. Though Sherman was now eager to cast off and head for salt water, Hood's army continued to worry General Grant, so that it was not until November 2 that he gave his permission for Sherman to turn his back on the Confederate forces and "go on as you propose."

Sherman had marshaled solid arguments for his scheme. The material damage the army could do as it passed through Georgia would be great, for it would dedicate itself to "smashing things generally," in Sherman's phrase. The Confederacy had already been severed in two at the Mississippi; now it could be cut again along the line Atlanta-Milledgeville-Savannah, separating the upper and lower South, wrecking rail lines so that Lee's army would no longer receive from Southwest Georgia and Florida the corn and beef that sustained it. In Sherman's view there would be a psychological dividend as well, for it would be another occasion to "astonish" the Southern people, shocking them into the realization that if they persisted they were doomed. In the middle of October he confided to a subordinate: "I want to make a raid that will make the South feel the terrible character of our people."

At that time Sherman had still not entirely abandoned his effort to get Georgia out of the war by negotiation, for it was late October when he sent Judge Wright to meet with Lincoln. While there is no documentary evidence that the proposed march was directly linked to his stalled peace initiative, Sherman may well have seen it as a way to give the balky Georgians a jolt that would propel them back into the Union. If the people of Georgia howled loud enough, their rulers might come to terms. Sherman had promised Brown that if Georgia dropped out of the war he would conduct the movements of his army so as to do the least possible damage; the army would be kept on the main roads, while quartermasters and commissaries would precede the troops, buying whatever was needed. Now the troops would be allowed to forage for themselves, with all that implied for the inhabitants on the line of march.

Well before Sherman had obtained Grant's full assent for the new campaign he began making preparations for it. Just as he had exploited a network of spies and informers in North Georgia and in Atlanta, he set about getting information on South and Middle Georgia as soon as he was settled in the Gate City. On September 14 he addressed a letter to Mrs. M. W. Meyer, 135 Felicity Street, New Orleans: "I wish you to go to

Augusta, Georgia and keep me advised of things along the Savannah River and as far out as Milledgeville. I will pay you and your messengers well." By mid-October he was beginning to shift men and resources in anticipation of a move south. On October 19 he gave orders to his quartermaster to hasten repairs on the Western and Atlantic so that what he called "the wounded and worthless" could be sent out of Atlanta; that same day he instructed his commissary, Amos Beckwith, to empty Atlanta of surplus stores, set aside thirty days' rations of food, and "send all trash to the rear at once." Since the army would be moving without a supply line, it would be a lean, picked force that could sustain itself on the forage from what Sherman knew to be a generally rich agricultural region; at the same time the force would be sufficiently mobile to move on as it "ate out" a locality, covering about fifteen miles a day and replenishing its stock of draft animals as it advanced. There were two major risks: While there were no substantial Rebel forces available to meet the invaders, should the Confederates somehow muster some— by bringing them from Virginia, for example—Sherman's force could not haul with it sufficient munitions for extended fighting. The other threat was from the weather; heavy rains or snow could turn Georgia's roads into quagmires, and the army, immobilized by mud, would starve and disintegrate. Of these two threats, Sherman probably worried more about bad weather. "I can subsist my army upon the country as long as I can keep moving," the general explained to Horace Porter. In the first days of November Sherman was looking for rain, desiring "that the fall rains should come all together, early in November, and give us fine weather for some weeks. . . ." This Sherman confided to young Henry Hitchcock, who had recently joined the general's staff as judge advocate, and whose diary is a major source of information for the March to the Sea.

Having received the green light, Sherman accelerated his preparations; at the same time he took measures to mask the move he was planning. The instructions for wrecking the railroads were put in a "secret" field order, so that the enemy would know nothing until after the process of destruction had begun. The army's mail presented a problem for Colonel Absolom Markland, who worked with the postal authorities. After some discussion Sherman ordered the mail to continue on to Nashville and Chattanooga for fifteen days after the army's departure, so that if the enemy learned of it, "they might be misled into supposing that the movement was a feint"; to further confuse the Confederates, after the fifteen days were up, mail addressed to the army was to be rerouted to Baltimore; only on December 3 would the mountain of letters and parcels—some sixteen tons of them—be loaded aboard the steamer *Fulton*, bound for the blockading squadron off Savannah.

By November 10 the roads of North Georgia were filled with blue columns as the units that were to go on the march headed for Atlanta. As the Union army evacuated North Georgia it began a cycle of destruction that would culminate in Atlanta. Oddly enough the first town— Cassville—was given to the flames not as part of the evacuation but as punishment for attacks on Union soldiers. Since its occupation the town and its environs had from time to time harbored Confederate scouts and guerrillas, and especially members of the First Georgia Cavalry. A good many attacks had been made on the railroad nearby; in the words of Cassville's historian, "the town had not behaved very well from the viewpoint of the Northerners." On the night of October 11 guerrillas had attacked Union soldiers camped with a wagon train within the town itself, killing ten men, and to add insult to injury they had thrown nine of the bodies over the fence onto the grounds of the Female College, where Federal troops were quartered. As punishment the Union authorities had the torch applied to both the town's colleges and several houses. Then at the end of the month Colonel Heath of the Fifth Ohio Cavalry received orders for an extensive punitive expedition that was the town's death warrant. Colonel Heath was to have his men burn the houses of certain suspected guerrillas in Cartersville, then pass on to Canton and Cassville; in each place he was to give the inhabitants some time to remove their belongings, and then "burn the town." On November 5 Colonel Heath reached Cassville and executed his orders. A few structures were spared; one account says three churches and one house escaped the flames. The residents of Cassville were given some time to save their possessions, though how much they were able to save is unclear. Confederate Congressman Warren Akin, who was a native of the town, wrote his wife he had heard that "the Yankees gave Mrs. Headden fifteen minutes to move out her things, and as fast as she carried out any thing they wanted they took it and any thing they did not want, they broke it to pieces."

The homeless citizens of Cassville, like a good many other Georgians that calamitous fall, came to believe that General Sherman personally had singled them out for punishment, stipulating that "not a house" should be left standing inside their corporate limits. But Sherman was not the direct author of their misfortunes; he probably didn't even know the town was destroyed, for three days later he raised the possibility of burning it as a reprisal for other acts of the guerrillas.

On November 8 Sherman was at Kingston. That day the Union army had a pause in its normal routine while the soldiers cast their ballots in the presidential election. As for their leader, he had been watching the weather; it had been raining off and on since November 2, enough to convince Sherman that November had had its quota of precipitation. "This is the rain I have been waiting for," he wired the commandants of all posts, "and as soon as it is over we will be off." That same day an incident occurred near Kingston, an attack by guerrillas, that came to his attention. His involvement tells us a good bit about how he reacted to specific acts of provocation against an enemy he had denounced as no more than thieves and assassins.

The affair began early on the morning of November 8, when the Seventy-fourth Indiana Infantry, then camped at Kingston, received orders to send out a forage expedition. The expedition started out, and about seven miles from town a detail of about thirty men was told to look for forage on the plantation of a Major Linn. Soon after, the detail was attacked by two companies of mounted men who were described as "guerilla cavalry." Most of the Union soldiers managed to escape and rejoin the rest of the regiment, but nine others fell into Rebel hands. Though the regiment outnumbered the enemy they decided they could not catch up with cavalry, so they returned to Kingston, feeling "much sympathy and much anxiety" for their comrades, whom they feared would be given short shrift. Shortly thereafter a man named Berry Houk, who lived near the site of the attack, brought in a wounded Union soldier and said a second wounded man was at his home. Houk seems to have been held in Kingston as a possible participant in the attack.

Just when Sherman learned of this affair is not clear, but on the next day, November 9, he had his aide, Captain Dayton, direct the following letter to General Jefferson C. Davis:

Yesterday a small squad of my guard foraging was attacked, one mortally wounded, one slightly, and the remainder captured by some guerillas. The general commanding wishes you to send out a regiment in the vicinity where it occurred, seize some citizens, and send one to inform the enemy he must bring those men and all others captured in the same manner back at once. They must be returned by tomorrow noon, else the Regiment will burn a dozen houses in retaliation. This occurred near a house marked Berry Houk in the sketch I send, sketched as well as the wounded soldier remembers the country.

Sherman's orders were executed, but not precisely as he had specified. That same evening Lieutenant Colonel Morgan, commanding the

Seventy-fourth Indiana, apparently received "written orders, direct from General Sherman," to make an expedition to the locality where the attack had occurred, "and if he could not secure the return of the prisoners to retaliate upon the neighboring citizens who were supposed to be more or less implicated with the guerillas." It was night when the expedition reached its destination; the soldiers began a thorough search of the houses in the vicinity, arresting several men found there. They picked up a man named Wash Henderson, who was taken "lying on the floor, against his door, completely dressed, and ready to move at a moment's notice." Henderson was armed with a cavalry carbine, and this in itself was an offense, since the citizens in that area were not permitted to have firearms. The last house visited was that of Lindsay Hendricks, who was also arrested. A search of the house turned up a prize: a man armed with two revolvers, who acknowledged himself to be Captain James M. Hendricks, Company I, First Georgia Cavalry, leader of the men who had carried out the attack the day before. Colonel Morgan asked Hendricks for the return of the soldiers he had captured on that occasion, but Hendricks said that was impossible. Morgan then gave orders for the burning of three houses, including those of Wash Henderson and Lindsay Hendricks, and the regiment went back to Kingston with its prisoners—not without some nighttime skirmishing with what they took to be men of Captain Hendricks's command, anxious to free their commander. Colonel Morgan and another officer named Stinson went to Sherman's headquarters to report the outcome of their mission to Captain Dayton. To their surprise and pleasure Dayton took them into Sherman's private room and introduced them to the general. "He shook hands with us," Stinson recalled, "and thanked Col. Morgan for the manner in which he had conducted the expedition and complimented him very highly." On Sherman's instructions Captain Dayton sent the prisoners on to General Davis, with the suggestion that Captain Hendricks be put in irons or tied up "in such manner he cannot possibly get away. He is the captain of the guerillas by his own acknowledgement and will use all effort to escape."

On the 11th Dayton wrote Davis again with instructions on winding up the affair, since Kingston was on the point of being evacuated:

> I am instructed by General Sherman to direct you to let the man Berry Houk return home with written instructions that he must take good care of the soldier now at his house, and when he has sufficiently recovered to deliver him to any U.S. military post, for which he shall receive pay for each day's care at the rate of seventy-five (75)

cents in gold. The other men arrested you will send under good guard to Chattanooga to be imprisoned and held as hostages for the return of the wounded soldier at Houk's house and thirty-one (31) of our soldiers whom they admit having unlawfully captured and made prisoners. The man Hendricks to be kept in confinement beyond possibility of escape during the war. Houk brought in [a] wounded Union prisoner who is now at Chatt. hospital. From this man evidence might be had which would implicate some of these prisoners to greater degree than as citizen hostages.

We have only the sketchiest idea of the outcome of this episode. Despite the precautions taken, Captain Hendricks seems to have escaped. He was recaptured shortly thereafter, carrying in his pockets receipts for prisoners. Some and perhaps all of the Union soldiers his unit captured were thus treated as prisoners of war. The names of two of the men of the Seventy-fourth Indiana have come down to us: Lewis Reynolds and Charles H. Redding of Company G. The history of the Seventy-fourth, published in 1913, indicates they were "missing in action" November 8, 1864, were subsequently confined at Andersonville, and survived to return to their homes in Elkhart, Indiana. We can only speculate on the fate of Berry Houk and the wounded soldier in his charge after Union forces pulled out of the area. Warren Akin refers to Houk a few weeks after the affair: "If Benny [sic] Houk is a traitor I hope our scouts will hang him." Perhaps the most curious aspect of the affair is the way it was embroidered and deformed by rumor. Thousands of Union troops were passing through the town, and various versions of the story spread among them, for it appears in many diaries and letters, in some cases almost unrecognizably. Many soldiers thought Hendricks was to be hanged and were disappointed they had to leave and miss the event. The number of his victims increased and their fate became more horrible. A soldier named Joseph Hoffines wrote his wife from Kingston on the 11th that a "Gurilla band" had murdered nine soldiers: "some were shot, some were hung and two had their throats cut." In another version the captured men were found in a grove of trees, "hung up by the heels with their throats cut." In still another version a "Captain Henderson" and his band had murdered their prisoners "by cutting off their secrets." Thus "atrocities" and "outrages" tended to have a life of their own, with the core incident being transformed in various ways; we will encounter this phenomenon again.

Such stories may have had some effect on the men charged with the work of destruction in North Georgia; in any event the soldiers seem to have accepted the idea that the towns should be burned. As early as October Chesley Mosman and those he talked with had agreed Atlanta should be destroyed. A soldier named Inskeep noted in his diary for November 2 that Rome was to be "evacuated and burned," though Sherman did not send General Corse instructions for the work of destruction until two days later. Sherman's order for Rome was precise and detailed: "Destroy in the most effective manner by fire or otherwise all bridges, foundries, shops of all kinds or descriptions, barracks, warehouses and buildings especially adapted to military use, lumber or timber, as also all cars off the track or material that cannot be moved. . . ." When the town was evacuated on November 10 the Fifty-second Illinois Infantry was left behind to carry out the program of destruction, which also included quantities of Union army stores and supplies. Units leaving the city left their camps intact and tents still erected; details then came to collect and burn everything. Later Henry Hitchcock quizzed General Corse about the destruction of the city and was assured that Sherman's order had been faithfully executed: "No private residences were burned nor was any violence done to the people. This was the order and General Corse . . . today answered my express inquiry by the assurance that it was strictly obeyed under his personal supervision." In fact the destruction went beyond what was authorized. A soldier who was there on the evening of November 10 saw homes intentionally set afire by the soldiers and consumed in a conflagration so vast that "the country is light with the burning of Rome. . . . It seemed melancholy to see the property being destroyed. It is against orders—but the soldiers want to see it burn." An officer named Platter made a similar observation: "All is the work of rowdy soldiers." It was a phenomenon that would be repeated many times in North Georgia, for the soldiers were interpreting orders in their own fashion, transforming their notions into policy. Thus Joseph Hoffines witnessed the destruction around him and explained to his wife: "This Government is now Entering upon a new policy. We are ordered to burn Cities and Barns and Houses where Ever we go and lay waste the Entire Country"; another wrote: "We are under command of General Sherman and will destroy all before us."

November 12 was the last day the Western and Atlantic operated under General Sherman's auspices, and the last day it would operate for some time to come. For days the traffic on the line had been intense. "All the trains go down empty and come up full," a soldier observed on the 9th. Andrew Hickenlooper watched the "up" trains rattle by: "Train after train of open cattle and freight cars heavily loaded with the impedimenta of war and surplus ammunition were being rushed northward

with inconceivable recklessness and haste. Human life was a cheap commodity, and the wounded, sick, disabled and returning soldiers were
placed like sardines in every available space." Soldiers were surprised to
see that some trains were packed with women and children, for there
was another exodus of civilians under way.

The last "up" train to leave Atlanta was an immensely long one,
pulled by two or three engines. The cars were heaped to the ceiling with
supplies, and their roofs were crowded with soldiers who would have to
brave the rain and cold that November had brought to North Georgia.
This train carried special cargo: the last letters the soldiers would be able
to send their friends and families for over a month. It also carried a huge
quantity of cash, for the troops had been paid and were sending money
home by way of chaplains, officers, and returning comrades; one surgeon carried over twelve thousand dollars, carefully distributed in
envelopes, each bearing the recipient's name. At each station the passengers would exchange farewells with those along the track: "Good-bye,"
"Good luck," "God bless you."

The train passed through Kingston about two o'clock in the afternoon, with the usual shouts exchanged; then, almost before it was out of
sight, the wrecking crews began dismantling the railway, burning the
ties, giving the rails the "Yankee twist" with their cant hooks, toppling
water towers, burning trestleworks, and wrecking culverts. At the same
time the telegraph lines were taken down, the poles thrown on the fire
with the crossties. This systematic destruction had already begun to the
south and would be followed to the north as soon as the last train had
passed. While some soldiers were destroying the railway and the telegraph, others turned their attention to Kingston. "Set fire to the town,"
was the succinct entry of an army diarist. Another noted that when
Kingston was well ablaze they then took the road south, "burning all
vacant houses." An officer following in their wake recorded "no houses,
no fences, and the roadside strewn with dead mules and broken wagons." On the 13th came the turn of Cartersville: "This morning all that is
burnable is burned. . . . Most of the families have gone either north or
south but a few, from some cause, have failed to get away and now they
are weeping over their burning homes. The sight is grand but almost
heartrending." Next came Acworth and then Big Shanty, where the
troops set fire to the two-story "RR eating house" that gave the place its
name. A diarist following in the wake of the destruction recorded with a
touch of humor that the two places had been "entirely destroyed by fire
which was done by the 'Yankee vandals.'" The rather generalized practice of burning homes may have been an "over-application" of an order

Sherman issued for the destruction of all structures that had been used to store army supplies—a number of houses in each town had been used for this purpose.

The auto-da-fé of Marietta came on Monday, November 14. Once again details were sent to set fire to specific structures that might serve the enemy (Sherman had particularly designated for destruction a large steam mill), but others went up in flames as well. One observer blamed these unauthorized fires on stragglers, who made a specialty of setting fire to empty houses. Mrs. Minerva McClatchey, who lived on the outskirts of the town, asked the Union soldiers who were setting fire to houses if it was something they did because it pleased them. They told her it made no difference whether they liked it or not, they were under orders to do it. Shortly before noon Henry Hitchcock reached the town square, where he saw some soldiers with a fire engine trying to put out a fire in the courthouse. He and other officers watched fires break out elsewhere and were unanimous in condemning such indiscriminate destruction. On inquiry Hitchcock learned that guards set in the town had left with their column and after they departed fires were set *without orders.* At this juncture Sherman appeared, and he and Hitchcock stood watching the courthouse, where flames had broken out again; according to Hitchcock the following dialogue took place:

> HITCHCOCK: "'Twill burn down, Sir."
> SHERMAN: "Yes, can't be stopped."
> HITCHCOCK: "Was it your intention?"
> SHERMAN: "Can't save it—I've seen more of this thing than you."
> HITCHCOCK: "Certainly, Sir."

The two men continued their conversation as they headed for Sherman's headquarters nearby. As they passed some soldiers the general pointed to them and said: "There . . . are the men who do this. Set as many guards as you please, they will slip in and set fire. That court house was put out—no use—dare say the whole town will burn, at least the business part." Sherman continued in the same vein: "I never ordered burning of any dwelling—didn't order this, but can't be helped. I say *Jeff Davis burnt them.*" Hitchcock said he wanted to apologize if he had quizzed the general too closely about the fire; he was just anxious that Sherman not receive blame for things he had not ordered. Sherman replied: "Well, I suppose I'll have to bear it."

As the flames spread, the streets in the center of town filled with smoke, presenting problems for the columns of troops passing through.

When the Seventy-fifth Indiana went by a sergeant recalled that "it was almost suffocating with heat and smoke. Our men would have to break ranks and run out to get their breath while marching." By the time Albert Champlin's unit came through the place was well on the way to becoming a pile of ashes, a fate Champlin did not think was too harsh for "the once beautiful but rebel-breeding villiege of Marietta." A soldier who went up on top of Kennesaw found before him an apocalyptic scene: "All the way to Allatoona & along the line of the RR was a continuous cloud of smoke. . . . Southeast at the foot of the mountain lay Marietta all in flames. All over the country south and east were innumerable columns of smoke showing where buildings were burning." A soldier named Gibson probably saw the survivors of the Marietta fire when he recorded in his diary: "the fields were filled with women and children, half-naked refugees from their burning homes."

On to the south, where Gibson was heading, Atlanta awaited the arrival of the forces that Sherman would lead farther into the state. Its garrison had passed nearly a month in virtual isolation while the bulk of the army pursued Hood. In that period there had been a brief threat from General Iverson's cavalry and some state troops, yet the town's new defenses were never seriously tested. Beyond those defenses guerrilla and irregular bands waited for the unwary: On November 7 a band of guerrillas attacked some army wagons a mile from the Chattahoochee, carrying off twelve mules and two drivers. But the greatest threat to Federal Atlanta had been the severing of its rail connection to the north for most of the month of October. By the middle of the month the officers and men of the Twentieth Corps were becoming seriously concerned. "We are getting pretty hard up for rations," a Michigan soldier wrote his brother. "If the road is not opened soon we will see some hard times. Our horses and mules are dying of starvation every day. . . . We sent out fifty wagons today and I hope they will succeed in getting something."

General Slocum, commander of the Twentieth Corps and ruler of Atlanta, was in fact faced with a difficult problem. In addition to his own corps he had to provide for nearly thirteen thousand sick, wounded, and convalescent soldiers of other commands who had been left in his charge; an even heavier charge was providing for about five thousand horses and mules. His problems were compounded when he had to send part of his forage supplies to Rome, where the garrison was in even worse condition. There was no choice but to reduce rations and try to draw forage from the surrounding countryside. The first expedition went out on October 10, and there were succeeding expeditions

until November 4. These were major sorties conducted as military operations. The forage expedition that departed on October 16 was composed of several hundred wagons, two brigades of infantry, a battery of
artillery, and a small force of cavalry. The expedition moved with strong
advance and rear guard and cavalry protecting its flanks. The commander of the operation had orders not only to fill his wagons with forage of
all kinds but also to "seize and bring with you all serviceable horses,
mules, and all cattle and sheep." The expedition went out about twenty
miles east of the city, returning on October 18. This expedition was the
first of four major efforts, each mobilizing some three thousand men and
upwards of five hundred wagons and staying out two or three days.
General Slocum estimated that in corn alone the forages had brought in
about two million pounds.

For the men engaged in it foraging had the "spice of danger" that
was not unwelcome to garrison troops. Occasional shots were fired at
them, and they never knew what they might encounter as they
approached a house or barn. One of the expeditions went into Gwinnett
County, where at least one forager was killed by two local boys, aged
twelve and fourteen. When a foraging party visited the Lewis Nash
place they found no livestock, for Nash had hidden them in the swamp.
But one of Nash's slaves named Greer told the soldiers where the stock
was hidden and rode off with them when they left. But for some reason
Greer returned to that section of Gwinnett County a few days later and
was taken by a local home defense unit called the Rangers. They "carried him to the East Bank of Yellow River, some distance below the
bridge, and the negro was never heard from again."

Some men who were new to foraging found it unpleasant work.
"This thing of foraging is hard for a bashful young man," wrote a soldier
named Carnahan. "The old women storm, the young women cry, beg,
intreat that you will not take their subsistence, but it must be done and
you have to turn a deaf ear to every plea." Surgeon James Dunn wrote
his wife after going on one of the expeditions: "We took all of the corn in
a neighborhood, and I have no doubt but the majority of the families
from whom we took will starve, for the rebels had taken everything they
could spare of. When we came we took the remainder." General John
Geary, who directed some of the foraging expeditions, said simply: "we
take everything from the people without remorse."

The descents of the foragers must have been the ultimate calamity for
those Georgians inhabiting the countryside around Atlanta, robbing
them of their food supplies just as winter was approaching. In truth it
only put them on a par with those Georgians trying to survive farther to

the north. They too had been plundered, and in addition they had virtually ceased farming. A Southern officer who accompanied a scouting
party northwest of Atlanta passed over the track made by the contend-
ing armies that summer:

> A more desolate country I never saw; not a domestic animal or fowl,
> and scarcely a bird could be seen; the woods where we fed our
> horses shelled corn had grown up in corn more than knee high, and
> there were no animals to crop it down; the fences had all been torn
> down to build barricades, and the crops had been without cultivation
> or protection since the early summer; the corn had made small ears
> and the people were subsisting on corn bread made of grated meal
> and syrup made in the crudest manner.

The tribulations of a family named Perkerson were probably typical
of those who lived in the vicinity of Atlanta that fall. Their home was
ransacked the day after the invaders first appeared, but that was only
the beginning; an ambulance train and wagon train lingered three days,
taking their chickens, robbing their beehives, and even carrying off their
cooking utensils. The visits did not stop. In addition to food and livestock the Perkersons began to lose their outbuildings—not to arsonists
but to soldiers looking for firewood or planks for their shebangs. Toward
the end of the year Elizabeth Perkerson wrote to her brother Angus, who
was a soldier in Virginia: "Ang, it would make you sick to see this
country now. Pa's place has not got two hundred rails on it and not a
building on it except the house and the old kitchen and the smoke
house." The neighbors were faring no better, with some driven to abandon
their homes: "Terry's place looks like it had been swept with a brush
broom. . . . Old man Terry stayed at home until they took everything
they had and then went off and let them ruin his house."

For many who lived in "occupied" Georgia that fall, there must have
come a day—when the bluecoats swarmed over their property for the
tenth or the twentieth time—that they could take no more. From many
sources it is evident that there was a steady stream of such refugees,
heading either north or south. The Howards, who had shown themselves to be survivors earlier in the year, at some point left their home
near Adairsville. Minerva McClatchey clung to her Marietta home—she
said it would take "a personal order from Sherman" to evict her—but
the struggle was never-ending. One detachment of soldiers after another
cut down her trees, tore up her fences, and turned her garden into a
campground. One reason she survived was that somehow she held on to

her cow. Once it disappeared but was found wandering in downtown Marietta and recovered for her by the Federal provost guard—for Mrs. McClatchey sold and traded milk to the soldiers, and in the process became acquainted with them; soon the Yankees came not only to trade but also to visit, and to advise her on how to protect herself from the thieves and sharpers in their own ranks. As the garrison of Marietta began packing up in November, she found that every soldier with whom she had become acquainted wanted to give her something, including enough coffee to supply her needs for the rest of the war. Somehow, almost imperceptibly, the invaders had become "the boys." When the bluecoats pulled out on November 14, Mrs. McClatchey confided to her diary: "I could not suppress my tears."

Beginning about November 1 the news began to spread through Atlanta and the surrounding region that Union forces would be abandoning the region, which would be left a complete wasteland. In the first week of November a stream of refugees arrived in Atlanta seeking passage north on the railway, which apparently the authorities accorded without difficulty. That the exodus was a result of the heavy foraging there is no doubt. A Union soldier in Marietta made this entry in his diary for November 8:

Citizens all around Atlanta, hearing that the Yankees are going to leave the place, are coming in larger numbers to go north. Women leave their homes and all they have, and with their children walk a distance of thirty miles, for the sake of getting to the north. When both armies have been ravaging the country, the people are destitute—haven't anything to eat—and therefore they have to leave their homes.

A number of soldiers saw the refugees at the Atlanta depot, and many were moved by what they saw. Cy Titus was there on November 7: "It was a very pitiable sight," he told a correspondent, "to behold little children almost naked and many women barefooted. I was at the cars where they are loading today and I could not help but feel sorry from the very bottom of my heart to see what destitution this cruel war has brought upon these people." It is clear from the soldiers' descriptions that the great bulk of these refugees were simple country folk, without baggage and without resources, who were going to a strange land where they knew no one—as a matter of sheer survival.

As the refugees were departing, Sherman's army was concentrating on Atlanta. The general himself came into town on the 14th, when plans for the great expedition were virtually complete. In and around the city, waiting for orders to march, were some sixty-two thousand troops, five thousand of them cavalrymen under General Judson Kilpatrick. The force would be divided into two wings, each wing being composed of two corps. It was a force shaped more for movement—an anticipated fifteen miles per day—than for fighting. Each wing was equipped with a pontoon train so that rivers would not slow its progress, and the artillery was composed of only sixty-five cannon, with two hundred rounds for each gun. Each gun, caisson, and forge was drawn by eight horses. The supply wagons were loaded with 1.2 million rations, enough to last the men twenty days, and several thousand beef cattle would accompany the army. The medical service, like the other services, had been pared to the essentials; even so it took six hundred ambulances.

Though Sherman had indicated in his correspondence that he would leave Atlanta "utterly destroyed," the list of structures his engineers prepared for destruction is an unexceptional one: the railroad and all its appurtenances, of course, and then "all storehouses, machine shops, mills, factories, &c., within the lines of the enemy's defenses at Atlanta." Initially Colonel William Cogswell, post commandant, was to have the assignment of destroying the city, or more properly "all buildings and works of any military importance." Cogswell had inspections made, and troops began to undermine walls and chimneys. Powder bags were prepared, and the provost marshal, Lieutenant Colonel Morse, "Tried a perfectly successful experiment on a small house." But on November 6 came an order suspending these preparations; on the 7th General Slocum sent word that the destruction would be directed by Captain Poe, and that Colonel Cogswell need only furnish the manpower. That same day Sherman told Captain Poe to take charge, and on the 12th he told him he could start the work of demolition, but he added an interesting proviso. He didn't want Poe to use fire, which would endanger other buildings than those set apart for destruction. The Michigan and Missouri regiments of engineers and mechanics had special competence for this sort of work, so details from these two units went to work toppling high smokestacks on several plants. The chimney of the gas house was nearly two hundred feet high; a soldier named Lawson watched them undermine it "until it fell with a crash, accompanied by the shouts of thousands of soldiers." The engineers moved on to breaking furnace arches, battering steam machinery to pieces, and knocking holes in boilers. They demolished the rail lines inside the city, tearing up the track, heating it on piles of burning ties—apparently the only exception to the policy of not using fire—and applied the cant hooks. According to Poe

no other fires were set with official sanction until the afternoon of the
15th. Men knocked down stone and brick railway facilities, suspending
a bar of railroad iron as a battering ram. This work also attracted a large
crowd, but the destruction of the great railway bridge over the Chattahoochee was the most spectacular example of this type of demolition:
The engineers cut the braces, took up the track at each end, and then
attached a strong cable to the structure: "A regiment pulled at the cable,
giving the work a swaying motion that increased to a pendulum-like
swing, until at length it began to give way; then huge beams swung
loose in the air, iron rails struck fire as they fell upon the stone piers, and
several spans came crashing down into the turbulent river."

This careful and selective destruction was not the fate many of the
men saw for the city they had fought so hard to conquer. Chaplain John
Hight found in the men "a spirit . . . which said 'Leave not one stone
upon another.'" The men expected the whole city to burn, "but I suppose the wish is father to the thought." In a letter of November 9
Andrew Bush evoked for his wife the image of a city that would be not
only consumed by fire, but also razed and turned into a wilderness:
"Before we leave they will be nothing left but the owls, bats, hawks, buz-
zards and a few wild rabbits to take charge of the uncultivated soil." If
as John Hight said the wish was father to the thought, the thought was
soon father to the deed: On the evening of November 11 fires broke out
in at least one part of Atlanta that were not the work of Poe's men.
Apparently the same thing happened the night of the 12th to the 13th,
for on the 13th General Wheeler wired General Hood from Jonesboro
that his scouts reported for the last two days the enemy had been "burning things in Atlanta," which made Wheeler think the Yankees' departure was imminent.

Inside the city some said the blazes were caused by "rebel incendiaries," but Captain Conyngham claimed the seat of the fire was a block
of wooden buildings on Decatur Street and the fires were set by soldiers.
On the morning of the 13th a group of soldiers were standing around
watching the engineers battering down a stone roundhouse, when someone spotted flames coming from the direction of the Western and
Atlantic tracks. "It was the gas house," said one of the crowd who went
over to see the conflagration. "Some soldiers had thrown in a brand 'to
see how it would burn.'" An officer arrived and offered five hundred
dollars to anyone who could tell him the name of the man who set it
afire—the same sum that had apparently been offered after the fire of the
11th. No one came forward. The witness to this scene concluded that
"Sherman contemplates destroying nothing but the public buildings, but

it is very evident that acts of vandalism by the men will be winked at and there are many who will not be slow to avail themselves of such tacit license."

On the 14th Kilpatrick's cavalry rode out of town carrying eleven days' rations, with the bulk of the infantry scheduled to depart the following day. According to one eyewitness, on the evening of the 14th "numerous officers and privates visited the doomed city for the last time previous to departure, many of them in high glee, having used a liberal quantity of what the indians call 'wild-fire.'" There is other testimony that many of the men were drinking; Chaplain Hight wrote that "drunken men have destroyed whole blocks." By then, and quite possibly before, empty houses were being set afire; sometimes those that were occupied also went up in flames. A soldier named Sawyer wrote his wife that he had known a citizen to offer three thousand dollars to the soldiers to save his home, "but it would burn."

On November 15 Harvey Reid began his diary entry with these words: "Fire! Fire!! Fire!!! in every quarter of the city, but nobody paid any attention to it other than to remark how finely it burns." The regiments were departing now in an atmosphere of smoke, dust, excitement, and confusion. Soldiers who had been sleeping in empty houses now set them afire on departure. When John Hight wrote in the city's last hours: "a notion has possessed the army that Atlanta is to be burned," and when Captain Conyngham wrote: "they wanted a bonfire," their words did not apply only to the army's rank and file. A group of staff officers had planned a farewell breakfast that morning; it started at two A.M. and ended just at dawn. Andrew Hickenlooper, who was one of the revelers, recalled the finale in his memoirs: "The furniture was piled up in the center of the dining room, a match applied and soon that stately mansion, once the shelter of wealth, beauty and refinement, had paid the penalty of its owner's disloyalty."

That day Captain Poe wrote in his diary: "much destruction of private property by unauthorized persons, to the great scandal of our army, and marked detriment to its discipline." Months later, in his official report, he would simply attribute the unauthorized fires to "lawless persons" who were "sneaking around in blind alleys." By then even Poe had authorized the use of fire, and his men lighted the piles of rubbish they had heaped up.

Here and there in the soldiers' accounts we catch glimpses of the few civilians who still remained in Atlanta. Allen Campbell of the Michigan Engineers and Mechanics had been left behind to fire the camp of his departed regiment "and surrounding buildings," some of which were houses: "As I was about to fire one place a little girl about ten years old came to me and said 'Mr. Soldier, you would not burn our house, would you? If you do where are we going to live?' I dropped the torch and walked away." But Campbell noticed that other soldiers were busy setting fires in houses, shouting that they were seeking revenge for the Confederates' burning of Chambersburg, Pennsylvania, back in July. "Most of the people left their houses without saying a word," Campbell wrote, "for they heard the cry *Chambersburg* and they knew it would be useless to contend with the soldiers." As the Thirty-eighth Ohio marched out of the city John Vail noticed "here and there a woman sad and dejected standing by a door or window peering through. . . ." Another man in one of the marching columns described the same scene that had marked the army's departure from Cassville and Rome, from Kingston and Marietta: "Here and there a company of poor people, huddled together in an open lot—They are collecting their scant property from their houses, either now burning or soon expected to burn. Some of the women are crying, some wringing their hands in agony, some praying to the Almighty."

After the sun set the sea of flames continued to light the city. As one of the three regiments forming the city's provost guard the Thirty-third Massachusetts would remain until the following day. That evening its band performed, and those who were still in the city carried away a memory they would keep for a lifetime: Against a background of apocalypse the band struck up "John Brown's Body." By then most of the army was already well away from the city. There were few diarists or correspondents among them who did not try to capture their impressions on paper as they looked back at the city in flames. One compared Atlanta to Babylon, another to Troy, and still another was put in mind of Napoleon's burning of Moscow. One man was moved to pen a line from Shelley, another wrote *Dies irae, Dies irae.* For Reverend Hight it was something straight out of the Old Testament: "In all hues of glory and terribleness, in all forms and fashions conceivable, the flames and smoke surged amongst the burning buildings like ocean waves, and struggled upward like a thousand banners in the sky." Somewhere in the moving columns was the Fifth Ohio Infantry, and in its ranks marched a soldier named Mathias Schwab. He too recorded his impressions of the memorable sight. It did not invoke in him any historical parallels, and no relevant passage from literature came to mind; so as a Cincinnati fireman he simply gave his professional opinion: "The grandest destruction I ever saw."

12

◆

The First Act

Sherman's men have been portrayed as marching out of Atlanta with utter confidence that the new campaign to which their general was committing them would end as victoriously as the last. The confidence was undoubtedly there, but mixed with it was a vague sense of concern. The men did not know what their objective was, or where they would "fetch up," as one of them put it. They would have felt even more uneasy about where they were going if they had known that their leader himself was not entirely sure. Savannah was the objective "of choice," but might not be obtainable for a number of reasons. The commissary and quartermaster departments made plans to have supplies available whether Sherman struck the coast along the Atlantic or somewhere in the Gulf; the Federal navy was keeping an eye out for him from Charleston all the way around to Mobile. Then too, there was a dramatic finality about the way the army left Atlanta. The destruction of the town itself was nothing new, save perhaps in its scope, but the systematic dismantling of the railroad that had been the army's lifeline gave some soldiers pause. To Andrew Hickenlooper it was "like Cortez destroying his ships, that thoughts of retreat might not enter the minds of his men." Another soldier said it was like "going into the hole and pulling the hole in after us," a move that seemed to him "lonesome and foolhardy." The colonel of the Eighty-second Ohio evoked the perspective facing the army that November: "Before us lay a vast stretch of country, containing no organized army, yet thoroughly infested with enemies clear to its natural boundary, the ocean. There was nothing left for us to rely upon but our-

selves, our leader, and the God of battles." Finally, even if the victorious
conclusion of the campaign was unquestioned, every man must have
asked himself if he would be there to see it. "This may be the last letter
you will ever get from me," one soldier mused somberly to his wife.
Captain Poe, writing a final time to his young wife on the eve of the
army's departure, closed by saying: "I durst not trust myself to write
any more or I will go off into a blubber."

The routine of the march was different from what they had known in
North Georgia. While musketry was heard from time to time, the soldiers soon learned that it was only their own foragers shooting the hogs,
sheep, and chickens that would serve as their dinner. And when the men
reached camp, nothing but dinner was on their minds, for the army no
longer threw up field works when it bivouacked for the night. The
columns were also unusual in that the trains were not relegated to the
rear of the column, but were interspersed with bodies of troops. Now
there was no danger that the army would have to deploy rapidly to the
front, while there was a chance that Rebel cavalry might make sudden
dashes on the column's flanks, and with troops and wagons interspersed
it would be easy for the former to come to the rescue of the latter if
Wheeler's men came charging in. This arrangement had another advantage the men would learn when the weather worsened: If the wagons
mired down the soldiers would be nearby to manhandle them out of the
mudholes.

Interspersed with the vehicles and the infantry were men of rather
unusual callings. One of them was George Barnard, the army's photog-
rapher in residence, whose camera has left us some priceless views of
Atlanta and pictures of those who conquered it. (He was to take few pictures on this trip through the heart of Georgia, but would leave some
interesting comments about the campaign.) Somewhat surprisingly,
somewhere in each column were one or more army telegraphers; their
chief function in the coming weeks would be to tap the lines, listen in to
the traffic, and glean information. Occasionally they would also indulge
in the kind of intelligence work the Germans call *Funkspiel*, tapping out
messages themselves, masquerading as Confederate operators and
inquiring how things were in Augusta or if anyone knew Sherman's
whereabouts.

Sherman was often seen on the march with a map in his hand,
reflecting his preoccupation with routes and the state of the roads. The
routes of march for the four columns were not definitively fixed until the
evening before, after topographical engineers and their cavalry escorts
had swept the country ahead. The routes were laid out so that the four

columns would be within supporting distance of one another, yet sufficiently dispersed so that they could all find sufficient forage; they were
to stay in rough alignment, moving in a path that was most often from
thirty to forty miles wide, though the sparse roads occasionally produced problems, as when two corps found themselves crowded together
on the same country lane. During the day the columns kept in touch by
means of messengers who crossed between them, and they could sometimes track one another by the columns of smoke marking their paths.
For communicating at night the Signal Corps had brought a considerable number of rockets and had devised a crude code for signaling; from
time to time in the evenings the soldiers found themselves treated to
pyrotechnical displays, and these added to the festive air that pervaded
much of this remarkable march. Sherman also brought several bands
along. At one encampment, as night was falling over the peaceful countryside, a band struck up "The Blue Juniata." Sherman liked the song and
sent word to play it again, which the band did forthwith. A regiment
nearby began to sing, while other bands joined in as accompaniment:
"The music of 'the Blue Juniata' became for a few minutes the oratorio of
half an army."

Someone had calculated before the army left Atlanta that if all the
forces in Sherman's command were to take the road and form a single
column, it would be some twenty-five miles long; each corps, therefore,
would be five or six miles long. But that was assuming that all the elements were "closed up" and maintaining proper interval; in fact this
was rarely the case over the roads of rural Georgia, and a column could
stretch out to a dozen miles or more; the farther back one was in the column, the more fits and starts and the longer it took to reach camp; there
were cases in a reasonably "normal" day's march when the rear guard
did not make camp until after midnight (fortunately the divisions
rotated positions in the column and so shared the more onerous duty).
To an observer watching the column pass, the first troops to appear were
cavalry or mounted infantry, generally a small detachment with two or
three of their number riding ahead as scouts, carbines at the ready.
Behind them came the lead infantry regiment, though as the campaign
progressed another element took an increasingly important place in the
van, preceding the infantry—the corps of pioneers to clear or repair the
roadway. Sherman's order of November 23 called for the pioneer units
to be expanded in size, and as they grew they changed color, for the
army actively recruited blacks for this work and had no trouble getting
them. If the column encountered any armed resistance, almost always
deployment of the lead brigade sufficed to break the enemy's resistance;

while the musketry crackled up ahead, the men behind dropped down to rest, sitting or stretching out on the roadside. Then eventually the column would start forward again, an endless sequence of vehicles and marching men, the latter swinging along four abreast, not marching in step, but each keeping up with a pace that suited him. The passage of an artillery battery was sometimes an odd sight, since the caissons might be piled so high with forage that they looked like rolling hayricks. The final element was usually composed of herds of driven cattle, the pontoon wagons if the column contained any, and the rear guard.

To the observer watching a column pass, the strongest impression was of sheer mass; Georgians black and white, young and old, would say to each other and sometimes to the invaders themselves that they had no idea there were so many Yankees in the state, or sometimes, in the world. The impression made on the young was one to be remembered for a lifetime. Joel Chandler Harris sat on a fence near Hillsboro and watched the endless succession of men and wagons go by: "There was nothing gay about this vast procession, with its tramping soldiers, its clattering horsemen, and its lumbering wagons, except the temper of the men. They splashed through the mud, cracking their jokes and singing snatches of song." As they came up to the boy sitting on the fence there were endless sallies:

"He's a bushwhacker, boys, if he bats his eyes I'm goin' to dodge."

"Where's the rest of your regiment, Johnnie?"

Gay McKinley was then a boy of six, living near Macon. Three-quarters of a century later he wrote: "I can still feel now the fear in my childish heart as we three boys watched the approach up our road from the main road." Up that road came General John Geary and his staff, followed by a sea of men in blue; the general took quarters in the McKinley home. A wagon train pulled into a hundred-acre field nearby, "and [it] looked to me like a person could have walked all over the field on canvas covered wagon tops without touching the ground."

For some time the number and the location of these vast columns pushing through Middle Georgia were a matter of much conjecture on the part of both Confederate and state authorities, as were the movements that preceded them. To General Joseph Wheeler and his cavalry had fallen the job of locating the enemy and deducing what Sherman was about. The first signs were not easy to read; neither the leveling of Cassville nor the burning of Rome gave any clear indication of Sherman's intentions. But by November 14 Wheeler knew from Northern prisoners and his own scouts that Sherman himself was in Atlanta. Three of his four corps had been identified there, as well as a large force of cavalry under Kilpatrick; extensive fires testified to the destruction of the city and the army's imminent departure. Over the next forty-eight hours Wheeler dispatched a flurry of telegrams to Hood, to General Bragg, now military adviser to the president; to General Beauregard in Tuscumbia, Alabama, to whom Davis had confided general command of the department in which Wheeler and Hood were operating; and to General Hardee, then in Charleston. Wheeler also wired messages to Governor Brown; General Howell Cobb; and General Gustavus W. Smith, commanding the Georgia state troops—the only force other than Wheeler's horsemen that stood between Sherman and the sea. For the most part these messages passed along conjectures about where the Northern forces might be headed: "Augusta and Savannah," "Macon or Mobile," read Wheeler's telegrams of the 14th.

As the Confederates fixed the direction of the invading army's two wings, the two Georgia cities in most immediate danger seemed to be Macon and Augusta. Neither Wheeler nor General Smith was in a position to block the enemy's movement toward the one city or the other, and neither city had much of a garrison. Since the summer's cavalry raids a large number of local defense organizations had been organized, for the most part composed of arthritic old men armed with their own shotguns (Governor Brown supplied powder and lead) and bearing bellicose names such as the Mitchell Thunderbolts and the Paulding County Raid-Repellers; in September the authorities at the Central Laboratory in Macon had formed all white employees capable of bearing arms into a company that drilled on Tuesday and Friday afternoons. Similar units had been organized among workers at the arsenal in Augusta; for additional protection the Augusta authorities had set up a unit of sharpshooters to be posted downstream from the town; they were to pick off the pilots of any Union vessels attempting to come up the Savannah River. Now, as danger approached, both towns were the scene of frantic preparations, and there were days of anxious waiting.

Outside the major towns we can get only the briefest of glimpses of that portion of the state through which the Union columns would pass. The most pressing problems throughout the countryside came up in legislative debates, for the general assembly was meeting in Milledgeville that November. More than anything else, people were alarmed at the epidemic of crime in the countryside, particularly robbery and theft by individuals and bands roaming about. Governor Brown, who as usual had his finger on the pulse of his constituents, urged the legislators to take action against local officials who were not making a serious effort to apprehend stragglers and deserters in their circumscriptions. The solution he urged was a drastic one: He wanted county officers who were not doing their duty to be conscripted; if they were too old for that he proposed calling them into the militia and court-martialing them "for neglect of duty or refusal to obey orders." As for the irregular bands roaming the countryside and plundering its inhabitants, he wanted them declared outlaws, and a blanket authorization given to "any citizen or association of citizens, whom they may attempt to rob, to shoot them down or slaughter them in any other way in their power."

The siege and fall of Atlanta had sent new waves of immigrants southward, and with winter coming on the recent arrivals were hard put to find shelter. For lack of anything better, hundreds of families were living in abandoned railway cars. For a time Mrs. Louise Clack found accommodations there, and though she described it as rough living, she was more fortunate than most: she had three boxcars at her disposal, one for her family, one for "the servants," and one to serve as kitchen. That fall Mrs. Margaret Ketcham Ward and her family took up residence in an abandoned car on a siding near the town of Social Circle; her party consisted of two women, five children, and one man, a slave named Jim. One night they felt a jolt and the car began to move, then came to rest again. Next morning they slid open a door to discover that their car had been pushed out onto a high trestle:

> We awoke and found ourselves suspended in the air with no way of getting water or wood. We had a little bit of a stove that just smoked everything to death, and in order to have ventilation or air and to get rid of this smoke, we had to open the side doors of the car, and you can imagine our state of mind with my four children and one negro child just old enough to tumble out.

Jim went for help, and eventually their car was pulled back off the trestle.

Traveling on the ramshackle rail system offered as many adventures as living in abandoned boxcars, yet great numbers of people seemed to be traveling then. The Reverend Charles Quintard took the train in Columbus on November 9 in an effort to rejoin Hood's army. Quintard was accustomed to comfort and the company of distinguished people, being well-acquainted with most of the generals in the Army of Tennessee. His diary indicates he was shocked by the accommodations he found on the train: The passenger car was in fact a freight car, and he found most of his fellow passengers "of the most disagreeable character." One of them was particularly memorable: "A boy three years old last May was puffing on a full sized cigar with great apparent gusto, and I was not at all surprised later in the day to hear him curse his mother." Mrs. Rebecca Felton and her family caught the train in Macon one evening about the time Sherman's troops were filing out of Atlanta. She had recently lost her young son, who had fallen ill and died in a "terrible refugee shack" near Macon, and now the family was trying to reach Savannah. Their train was a particularly dilapidated one. Their car, normally a "ladies' car," was jammed with people of both sexes, including a number of soldiers. The car had no lamps and some of its windows were broken, letting in blasts of cold air. From time to time they clattered into stations that were lit by burning pine knots. The Feltons had no food, so at one stop Dr. Felton went out to find them something to eat. He came back with "a single handful of fried sweet potatoes, the grease oozing down between his fingers." Somehow, despite all their trials, the passengers kept their spirits up. A soldier took over the task of holding the Feltons' sleeping daughter in his arms. At one point someone in the dark and drafty car began to hum "How Firm a Foundation." Others took it up and soon they were all singing; the mood in the car brightened perceptibly.

Governor Brown had given the militia a month's furlough after the fall of Atlanta, but now they were back under arms and concentrated in the vicinity of Jonesboro. With the departure of these men from their home counties fears rose again about "trouble" with the slaves. As before, the people shared their worries with their governor. Mrs. E. Watkins wrote Brown on October 24 that his recent militia call had taken G. T. Massey, whose departure was a severe loss to their community: "The negroes feared Massey all through these parts, now he gone tha are in no dread"—hence the governor should send him back. Those whose business it was to supervise blacks watched carefully for any change in their behavior. In October the overseer on David Barrow's plantation reported to his employer: "I can tell you that most of the negroes will go to the Yankees if they get half a chance. I can see a wide difference in them & what they were three months ago. It is time for every man to keep his eyes open."

Curiously, as doubts and fears increased about Georgia's blacks, more and more of them were being called into service with the Confederate army. In August General Hood had ordered all soldiers who had been detailed as teamsters, servants, orderlies, cooks, and the like to return to their regiments. The functions they abandoned would be taken up by blacks. That same month the army advertised in Georgia newspapers for two thousand black teamsters, to be given food, shelter, clothing, and medical care (a special instruction went out to set aside separate tents for them in field hospitals). The teamsters would not be allowed to drive ambulances or ordnance wagons. Their masters would be paid for their services at the rate of twenty-five dollars a month and would be compensated if they died in service or went over to the Yankees. While the army advertised for "able bodied and trustworthy negroes," it may have afforded planters a means of sending off those they considered "troublemakers."

There seem to have been fewer complaints about food in the governor's correspondence that fall, though he received a number of letters from refugees from other states who found themselves in difficulty. They could hire out their slaves, with the slaves being fed "on the job," but they themselves were unable to buy food because of government regulations on sales, and at the same time they were not entitled to food distributed to indigent Georgians. The harvest that fall was a bountiful one; Sherman's foragers would find barns and cribs and smokehouses well-filled. James and Nancy Crone of Gordon County wrote their sons in the army that they had the best crop of corn they had ever grown. But they added that they feared Yankee raids. "We don't know how soon we will be broken up."

The fear that the Yankees might advance south from Atlanta was widespread, and many letters dealt with what measures to take. A Confederate soldier near Jonesboro sent a word of warning to his brother shortly after Atlanta fell: "There are now between you and 100,000 Yanks only a skirmish line of cavalry, our battery and the 1st Tenn. battery. . . . Please write soon *immediately* and tell me what preparations you are making for the enemy, whether you intend to remain yourself." He advised his family that they would do well to hide their male slaves and their horses, "all of which will be a dead loss when the Yanks do come."

A number of women made it clear that they did not intend to abandon their homes. A Wilkes County woman named Sallie Bird wrote a relative: "I am of the opinion that we had all better remain. That is the universal opinion and I agree with it." Mrs. E. C. Welbourne of Covington wrote her husband, who was then with the army in Virginia: "I shall risk it at home. I learne that in Marietta the Yankees haven't insulted a lady in no respect." She went on: "if the Yankees come I hardly think they will pester what I have in the house, though they may." Letters such as these certainly reveal an intention to face what came, but later, when the danger was near and their neighbors packed up and joined the refugees streaming south, many people hurriedly changed their minds.

As it turned out, those who were in the area the Federal columns passed through on the first two or three days of the march were taken completely by surprise—this was the case at Covington, for example. Suddenly bluecoats filled the streets, or poured into one's yard, and people could only stare in amazement. The bluecoats were surprised too, to find shops open and people in the streets of towns like Madison and Conyers. "For a long time," one participant in the campaign noticed, "the towns through which we passed have been almost entirely deserted. Our men helped themselves to anything they desired to eat. No effort was made by the officers to stop them." Now, in McDonough, the town was full of "terrified and astonished citizens"; in Social Circle they "all looked alarmed to see the Yankees march through." Some grabbed a few possessions and took flight immediately, only to find they had to share the roads with the invader. "The roads are thronged with refugees going south who cross from one road to another only to meet some portion of our army."

The Union soldiers that the fleeing inhabitants met on country lanes and byways were probably members of the first brigade foraging parties, who were sent out to find sustenance, more often than not without success. Though the locals had clearly been taken by surprise and had had no time to hide their animals or stocks of foodstuffs, yet the foragers those first two days out came back empty-handed most of the time. The explanation was a simple one: The columns were still moving through the zone outside Atlanta that had been visited by the massive foraging parties of the Twentieth Corps in October and early November; they had picked the region clean. Fortunately the men carried three days' rations on them, and these would sustain them until they had put the area behind them. The yield the foragers brought in on the 17th was more promising, and by the next day the men were living in plenty. On November 18, when General Slocum's troops were streaming through Morgan County and its county seat, Madison, they came upon a bonanza: a mountain of freshly harvested sweet potatoes, some three thousand bushels of them, on the plantation of a Mr. Jones. The men helped themselves, and when the last of them had passed, the last sweet potato was gone as well. Nor were sweet potatoes all they took from Mr. Jones, for one of the officers noted that "several of his negroes joined us, concluding they had worked long enough for Mr. Jones."

On the 28th the troops passing through Covington captured a quantity of mail; while the men liked to read the letters for diversion, General Sherman and his staff were more interested in the Georgia newspapers of the 15th and 16th, hoping for news of Generals Thomas and Scofield, who had been left in Tennessee to deal with Hood. They found little on what was happening in Tennessee, but there was further information on Lincoln's reelection; they had known before leaving Atlanta that he had won, but now they learned the details. Among the letters taken was one that created a good deal of interest among Sherman's staff. It was addressed to Governor Brown and was signed by a Miss Izora M. Fair, a refugee from Charleston, South Carolina, who lived in Oxford, just a short distance from Covington. Miss Fair's letter was essentially an intelligence report on Federal-held Atlanta, for she had recently disguised herself as a black by staining her face with the juice from walnut hulls and "frizzing" her hair. To complete her disguise she carried a basket of peanuts to peddle through the town. The young officers on Sherman's staff were captivated with her daring, all the more since they found another letter in the same mail indicating that her "female rebel friends" disapproved of her escapade. Sherman, who didn't like civilians meddling with military matters, decided to have her brought in, telling his staff: "I don't mean to hurt her, but will give her a scare." But Sherman reckoned without Miss Fair; when she saw a detachment of Union cavalry come into the yard she climbed up into the attic of the house in which she was staying, and the cavalrymen did not find her; nor did they find her father, who was in a novel hiding place—he had had himself lowered into a well.

By the time Sherman left Covington, his columns were on the way to solving a serious crisis, one that could have totally derailed his March to the Sea. The horses and mules with which the army left Atlanta had been chosen as the best in Union hands, but they were the best of a very bad lot. The draft animals had suffered heavily from lack of forage, even with the vast sweeps around Atlanta; those with which Sherman left the city were in poor condition and incapable of making a long march. Even though the artillery was "doubleteamed," the artillerymen said they would need "almost an entire new supply of horses." Sherman said little of the problem, but it must have worried him considerably until his foragers began to bring in large numbers of animals from the Georgia countryside to take the place of the poor stock he started with. General Hood had anticipated that Sherman might make the move he did, for on October 27 he sent the following instructions to Wheeler: "Should the enemy advance anywhere you will drive off all the stock in their front and destroy all the wells within ten miles of their line of march, retarding them as much as possible." But to do this Wheeler had to get his horsemen in front of Sherman's columns, and it took him ten days to do this. By then Sherman's mule skinners had replaced their draft animals with fresh stock in excellent condition. An army surgeon who also took an interest in the health of the army's draft stock was categorical: "Had we not been able to capture a large number of mules and horses during the first week it would have been impossible to have brought the train with us."

There remained the danger posed by the weather. It must have been a major preoccupation of Sherman, for Henry Hitchcock notes the general brought it up several times, and before long Hitchcock himself was casting glances at the sky and noting down what he saw. On the 16th he recorded Sherman as saying: "three more days clear and don't care." On the 18th the general remarked as he rode along: "This is the perfection of campaigning . . . such weather and roads such as this." But that same afternoon Hitchcock noticed the sky was "cloudy and threatening." On the morning of the 19th the army woke to rain, and diarists with other columns indicate the rain spread generally across the army's path.

On the 19th diary entries describe the roads as "heavy," "muddy"; by the 20th the combination of steady rain and heavy traffic caused the roads to deteriorate badly. Troops had been marching through fields and woods parallel to the routes, so as to leave the road to wheeled traffic, but now the men could no longer negotiate the saturated fields and returned to the roads, where they spent much of their time trying to move wagons that had sunk to their hubs in mud. "Such roads I've never seen," wrote one soldier, "—and still it rains." The columns only inched along, and those in the rear did not make it into camp until well into the night. One of those in the rear recorded when he finally reached camp: "This night's march many will long recollect, for nearly every man on foot, both officers and men, fell down, some of them dozens of times." On the 21st "the morning dawned dark and lowering, with occasional gusts of rain"; the roads that day were qualified as "perfectly awful." Henry Hitchcock saw ruts eighteen to twenty-four inches deep in "stiff heavy red clay, some half liquified, some like wax, or thickened molasses." That day his column—and Sherman's—made only seven or eight miles; that night Hitchcock wrote in his diary: "no wonder weather is such an element in war."

By now cattle were miring down so deeply their drovers could not free them, so they were shot by the scores and left. Wagons toppled and broke apart and they too were left. Any incline, any bridge or ford, became a bottleneck. A soldier with the Seventeenth Corps encountered one of these: "One six mule team had fallen off a bridge in a narrow and deep gully. The four lead mules had gone down, but two wheelers were hanging by their traces when I came along. The wagon was too large to go down. The two mules hung there until their traces were cut and they fell to their death."

The night of November 21–22 was memorable too. The rain became less frequent but was replaced by a wind that gradually picked up force. At the same time the temperature began to drop markedly (unfortunately none of the army's diarists seems to have had a thermometer with him). For some reason Sherman had set up his headquarters in a field that evening, and it was all his staff could do to keep their tents from being blown away. It became so cold that many men gave up trying to sleep and clustered around roaring fires. By the firelight they could see another change in the weather: occasional flakes of snow flying in the night air. In the morning men found water frozen in their canteens. But the day dawned clear as a cold front swept across Georgia, and the army resumed its march. The sky remained blue and the temperature gradually moderated; by the 27th it was almost balmy, provoking a country woman to exclaim: "The Almighty must be on you'uns' side, for I never seed such weather in this month in thirty years since I have lived here." As for Sherman, the clear skies that appeared on the 22nd were probably all he asked for. His timetable for this first leg of the march—"the first act," as he and his staff dubbed it—called for him to reach Georgia's capital on the seventh day. There a portion of his forces were to come together, and now he knew they would make the rendezvous at Milledgeville.

While Sherman was approaching Milledgeville, on the army's extreme right General Kilpatrick was engaging in running fights with Wheeler's command and menacing Macon, while units of the Fifteenth Corps were wrecking rail lines near the city. General Walcutt's brigade was near the village of Griswoldville; his men had been helping drive Wheeler's cavalry that morning, but at noon they put down some rails for a light defensive line—an ingrained habit—and set about fixing their dinner. They had not finished when muskets began to crack to the front of them and their pickets came running in, shouting: "They're coming. They're coming." For three brigades of Georgia militia were also at Griswoldville, and the stage was set for one of the most appalling "little" battles of the war.

The militia had been on the battlefields around Atlanta, but had not been committed in any of the hard fights; it had yet to be "blooded." The three brigades at Griswoldville were under command of General Pleasant Phillips, since their own commander, General Smith, had been detained at Macon. The militiamen had grown thin-skinned at the jibes they had heard from the soldiers and had apparently resolved that if they ever got into battle, they would prove their worth. Now General

Phillips was going to give them the chance. He had been told by General Smith to avoid an engagement, but he nonetheless ordered an attack (a persistent story says he had been drinking that day). Almost all the accounts of the battle we have are from Union participants, but it appears that about one o'clock the Georgia Militia attacked in three lines, moving across an open field in fine style "with colors flying and loud cheering by the men." Many of the men they were attacking were armed with Spencer rifles, so they went into a storm of fire, pushing to within fifty yards of the Union line before the assault stalled. Most of the militiamen still surviving went into a ravine perhaps a hundred yards in front of the enemy line. They had come onto the field like veterans, and now they stayed like veterans. From their shelter they made three additional sallies, possibly more, each of which withered under the terrific fire (though Walcutt's Brigade had about fifteen hundred men, General Smith estimated his troops had attacked "the larger proportion of one corps"). The fighting went on until dusk, when the militiamen withdrew—those that could—leaving the field to Walcutt's men. Of about two thousand militia engaged, over six hundred remained on the battlefield. Walcutt lost fewer than a hundred men.

Once the firing had stopped Walcutt's men went out to see what remained of their foe. Accustomed as they were to carnage, they were still appalled by what they found: "Old grey-haired and weakly looking men and little boys, not over fifteen years old, lay dead or writhing in pain." In the middle of a heap of dead and dying men they found "a modest looking countryman with gray beard, who exhibited under his coarse shirt a mortal wound in his breast and then making a feeble gesture with his hand, said: 'My neighborhood is ruined, these people are all my neighbors.'" They heard groans coming from another part of the field: "We moved a few bodies and there was a boy with a broken arm and leg—just a boy 14 years old; and beside him, cold in death, lay his father, two brothers, and an uncle." The men carried the boy to the fire and tried to make him comfortable. And other men worked into the night, filling canteens and covering the wounded with blankets taken from the dead, carrying those who could be moved to their surgeons. An Illinois soldier summed up the feeling of many of his comrades that night: "I hope we never have to shoot at such men again."

The fighting at Griswoldville convinced many people in Macon that their city would be attacked by Sherman in great force, but by then he was drawing close to Milledgeville. In Georgia's capital everyone was on the alert, for like most other Georgians, they knew only that Sherman was on the move, and the prudent were leaving or making plans to do so. Governor Brown had been trying to make sense of the telegrams he was receiving from various military authorities. On the 19th he shared with the legislature what he had learned so far. The enemy had burned much of Atlanta and other towns in North Georgia, had destroyed the railroad from Atlanta to Allatoona, including the railroad bridge over the Chattahoochee, "and is now advancing in heavy force in the direction of Macon and probably of this city, laying waste the country and the towns in the line of his march."

If Georgia were to be saved at this grave hour in its history, Brown told the legislators, it would have to save itself, for looking to Richmond was a waste of time. "If the whole manhood of the state will rally to the front," he went on, "we can check his march and capture or destroy his force." To this end Brown wanted the militia obligation generalized to produce a *levée en masse*, mobilization of the entire white male population, exempting only those physically incapable of service. He said there was some excellent raw material in whole categories of men previously exempted from service: "The class of state officers not subject to militia duty, such as Judges, Justices of Inferior Courts, Sheriffs, etc. will amount to a fine regiment." How moved the governor was by the perspective of a universal rush to arms we may judge from another portion of his speech. Once the legislation had been voted for the new general levy, he proposed "that the Governor and Legislature then adjourn to the front to aid in the struggle, till the enemy is repulsed, and to meet again if we should live, at such time and place as the Governor may designate."

Just what inspired this remarkable proposal is impossible to say. The governor may have found it in the course of his readings on military history, for it smacks of the famous *levée en masse* voted by the French Revolutionaries in 1793. The general idea had already been endorsed by newspaper editors, who liked the image of "hireling armies" falling back and dissolving before "the vengeance of an outraged people." Then too, the governor may have been pushed toward this action by an ominous telegram he received two days earlier from Robert Toombs in Macon, saying: "things are very bad here." Toombs concluded: "I believe the Legislative will grant you large and liberal powers. Tell them the country is in danger. Let all of her sons come to the rescue."

That same day the general assembly gave Brown pretty much the legislation he had asked for. The new law made almost all state officers subject to the call, including sheriffs. The lawmakers had a delicate problem with subjecting themselves to service. The Georgia Constitution made the branches of government separate from and independent of one other; if the legislators subjected themselves to the governor's *levée en masse* call, they would be violating the Constitution. In the end they made themselves and the state judiciary morally subject, but not legally so. The legislators also had the foresight to exempt railway personnel and telegraph operators from the call, since their services would be essential for the mass mobilization. Since the law was a radical one, the legislators attached to it a sort of preamble explaining it was necessary because a large body of enemy troops was moving across the state. There was also a reference to Sherman—"a general whose past history is but a recital of every violation of civilized warfare"—that left no doubt he was well on his way to infamy in the eyes of all Georgians.

On November 19 Brown issued his proclamation summoning to the field white male Georgians between the ages of sixteen and fifty-five. The period of service was forty days—the same period of time stipulated in the old feudal levies. The governor was at somewhat of a loss to fix an assembly point in a rapidly evolving crisis, so he ordered the men to report to General Smith at Macon, "or wherever else in Georgia his camp might be" (six days later he designated four instruction camps at Macon, Albany, Newnan, and Athens). Brown's proclamation also told the men subject to call that the railroads within the state would transport them where they needed to go. Should any line refuse, "its President, Superintendent, Agents and Employees will immediately be sent to the front."

November 19 was a day of mounting anxiety in Milledgeville. A woman who was about to head south by carriage wrote a hasty note to a friend saying: "the town has been agitated by a thousand rumors." Dr. R. J. Massey, whose Brown Hospital had come to rest at Milledgeville, recalled it as a day of frantic departures, in which "fabulous prices" were paid for any kind of conveyance. William Gibbs McAdoo Sr. recorded in his diary that two members of the general assembly paid five hundred dollars each for seats in a carriage to the rail depot at Gordon. For the legislature had taken a recess for dinner when Governor Brown received word that Union cavalry were headed straight for the town. The legislators did not return to their deliberations, but joined the swelling exodus. (When Union officers sat in the legislators' places a few days later, they found the desks littered with unfinished business.) Other state officials were departing too. The secretary of state, Nathan C. Barnett, had the presence of mind to remove the Great Seal, which he wrapped up and buried in a hole under his house; his wife concealed the most recent acts of the legislature in a pigpen.

In all this frantic activity one man remained unhurried and unruffled—Joe Brown. While Milledgeville did have fortifications of sorts, there was no one to defend them. There was only a handful of military units anywhere in the vicinity, among them the battalion of cadets of the Georgia Military Institute. The city could not be defended and would fall, Brown knew. At least the losses could be cut with prompt action, and the governor was taking that action. Brown directed the state's adjutant general to move to safety some of the more important archives and furnishings from the mansion (some state papers would be transported as far as Bamburg, South Carolina). The governor assumed Sherman would not burn the State Lunatic Asylum, so other state papers were deposited there. The arsenal would no doubt be burned, and also the stock of pikes and side knives Brown had so carefully accumulated, but there was nothing for it. The penitentiary would probably be given to the flames as well, since parts of it were used for the production of armaments. But Brown felt the prisoners could be salvaged. Sometime in those last hectic days the governor went to the prison and delivered a speech to the assembled inmates. He appealed to their "Southern honor," asked their help to save the state, and offered a pardon to those who would fight the Yankees. They listened politely, and when he was finished all but twenty-five of about two hundred agreed to help Georgia in its hour of need. There were enough volunteers to form a company, so Brown appointed the celebrated burglar Dr. Roberts to serve as their captain. Thus did Roberts's Guards take the field on behalf of the Cause.

On the evening of November 18 William Gibbs McAdoo stopped by the governor's mansion, where he was told that Governor Brown was at table. "Everything in the Executive Mansion was in the wildest uproar. The halls and rooms were filled with convicts [ar]rayed in penitentiary stripes, removing furniture and everything valuable from the Mansion, and Mrs. Brown, pale and hurried, was everywhere in the same instant." McAdoo found Joe Brown having his supper: "The Governor's iron face was unmoved, and he munched his cabbage with as much appetite and composure as we must imagine the imperial cabbage grower Diocletian did in the happy retirement at Spalatio after his abdication." Apparently the governor and his family did not leave until the afternoon of the 20th. They were accompanied by a large, heavily laden wagon. Just as it was pulling out, Brown's mother and a black servant named Aunt Celia put some fresh collard greens on top of the load. It was a banal act, but it would haunt Brown for many years afterward, as his enemies related how he had left valuable state property to be plundered by the Yankees while he fled with a wagonload of his own produce.

After the governmental leaders left the city there was a strange hiatus of perhaps twenty-four hours that was marked by some plundering by people who had stayed in town—the same phenomenon that had been noticed in other towns. The first Union cavalry entered on the evening of the 20th, but the real occupation came on the 22nd, with the arrival of the Twentieth Corps. The entering troops got some cheers from bystanders, but the men noticed that all the smiling faces were black. "We are indeed in a den of enemies," wrote one officer. On their way into the city the first troops noticed the earthworks and halfway expected some opposition; but there were no overt hostile acts—unless one counts the stone a woman threw from a second story window, narrowly missing Private John Cooper, Company I, 104th Illinois Infantry.

The Third Wisconsin Infantry was one of the first regiments to enter the town. It camped in the capitol square, and its commanding officer, Colonel William Hawley, took command of the post of Milledgeville. Colonel Hawley had two regiments, his own and the 107th New York, as provost guard; he left a crisp, meticulous account of his tenure: "My duties mainly consisted of patrolling the streets, ascertaining the amount of public and other property captured and guarding the same, and maintaining—so far as my limited means would allow—good order in the city." A search of the town revealed a considerable quantity of gunpowder and ammunition, most of which was thrown into the Oconee, and about a thousand bales of cotton "which was disposed of by General Sherman." A good bit of miscellaneous military equipment was burned at the arsenal, as were several thousand "lances," Governor Brown's pikes. Colonel Hawley wrote that he also disposed of some fifteen hundred pounds of tobacco by distributing it "among the troops generally."

About the only public institutions still functioning when Sherman's troops entered the city were the two military hospitals; their directors, Dr. Massey of Brown Hospital and Dr. J. R. Bratton of Midway Hospital, went to Colonel Hawley's headquarters for safeguards, and these were furnished. But not long afterward the directors discovered that through some mistake in orders the cavalrymen sent to guard the hospitals had been ordered elsewhere. The two directors had wisely buried their stocks of medicinal whiskey, but their supply of food attracted hordes of bummers, who pushed their way into the establishments and carried off everything edible. Massey had to go back to Union headquarters at the capitol to ask for help; his request was passed on to Sherman himself, who called Massey in to talk to him. The general, "in very pleasant manner," said he would see that food was sent and some medical supplies as well. He also made arrangements for an eight-man provost guard, and thereafter Massey had no more difficulties with Union soldiers.

If the hospitals were now off-limits to the troops, they found other places to visit. They looked the town over generally and were surprised that it was not bigger. They gave widely varying opinions on it. A Minnesota soldier described it as "an ancient, aristocratic place with handsomely shaded trees and dwellings, but it wore an air of quiet decadence and lack of enterprise." A Wisconsin soldier was more succinct: "Milledgeville is a sort of one-horse town." Many soldiers visited the penitentiary, or what was left of it. One officer remembered seeing several women prisoners in confinement whom he described as "pretty hard cases." One of them he later saw on the street wearing a blue uniform; he was told she had "entered our army." The ruins of the arsenal attracted a number of soldiers. One of them wrote: "the arsenal contained some small arms and about four thousand pikes and cutlasses for cutting up Yankees, and now we are here for the sacrifice and the butchers are not at home."

The state capitol building was much visited. In one of the offices were stacks of newly printed Confederate notes, so the soldiers stuffed their pockets with them for future purchases farther south. The state library was also in the building; it saw many soldiers enter and not a few books leave, some of them by the windows. But the legislative chambers were the real center of attraction. Soldiers by the hundreds came to gawk at them and admire the rich furnishings—and one took the inkstand from the speaker's desk as a souvenir to show back in Wisconsin. An Ohio soldier said of the plundering: "Our limited means of transportation was about the only thing that prevented the entire State-House from being carried off."

On the afternoon of the 23rd a mock session of the Georgia legislature took place in the two chambers, with Union officers playing the role of lawmakers. Many diarists and memoir writers mention this episode, but the accounts are mostly brief and contradictory and afford no more than a glimpse of this extraordinary "session." There are several references to drinking and "tipsy" officers, which would account for the general hilarity that reigned in both chambers. Many of the speakers discoursed in what they thought to be Southern "fire-eater" style; some had armed themselves with Governor Brown's side knives, and these they waved for emphasis. A number of bills and resolutions were put forward, including one that brought Georgia back into the Union. At a certain point someone rushed in, shouting "The Yankees are coming!" This produced much "confusion, laughter and mock panic."

So enjoyable was this affair that there seems to have been a second revel organized, a mock funeral service for Governor Brown. Our source here is Dr. Massey, who says that both he and General Howard attended. The ceremony was accompanied by many exaggerated expressions of praise for "His Excellency, Governor Joseph Emerson Brown, departed." The casket borne by the mourners was an empty crate that had once held a hundred of the governor's pikes, and the cortege wound through the streets to the accompaniment of drums, arriving finally at the Baptist church where Brown worshipped. There the casket was placed in front of the pulpit, and a lieutenant colonel delivered the eulogy. "No man from a Southern standpoint," said Dr. Massey, "could have done better."

This affair would have taken place on November 24 and was probably the last memorable event during the army's stay in Milledgeville. Sherman had already departed at ten that morning. Before he left he summoned Dr. Massey, who could not imagine what business the general could have with him. Sherman had a parting gift for the Brown Hospital: ten gallons of rye whiskey that had been carefully buried by the proprietor of the Milledgeville Hotel before the Yankees came and just as carefully unearthed after their arrival. The general also had a favor to ask: He had twenty-eight men too sick to travel and he wanted to leave them in Dr. Massey's care. "If they die, give them a decent burial," Sherman said, "if they live, send them to Andersonville, of course." Dr. Massey may have looked a bit nonplussed at this, for Sherman added: "They are prisoners of war, what else can you do? If I had your men I would send them to prison."

Now the vast columns were moving south again. The weather was fine, the roads drying out. The more observant noticed that the nature of the soil was changing; the treacherous red clay was giving way to a more sandy soil, for at the level of Milledgeville the army had crossed the fall line. The "first act" of the march had ended well, and although the general and his army did not know it, the rest of the drama would play out in even better circumstances. They had put bad weather behind them, and they had fought the first and last real battle of the campaign—the tragic, obscure affair at Griswoldville.

13

◆

The Vandals

As the long columns resumed their movement to the southeast, General Kilpatrick left the infantry behind, and with most of his cavalry struck out on a special mission to a place that was little more than a dot on the army's maps of Georgia—Millen Station. Kilpatrick was going to attempt the same sort of liberation that General Stoneman had tried in his disastrous raid toward Andersonville back in the summer. He was headed for Millen because five miles north of there, along the Central of Georgia Railroad, lay the newest and largest military prison in the Confederacy: Camp Lawton. Confederate authorities had chosen the new site back in July, compelled to do so because of the terrible overcrowding at Andersonville, jammed with more than thirty thousand prisoners, and spurred by a warning from General Johnston that Andersonville might be vulnerable to attack. Construction on the new camp began in August and went on into September, and in the latter month the first prisoners were transferred there from Andersonville. Compared to what they had left, the new camp was an Eden. The stockade enclosed forty-two acres—about fifteen acres more than Andersonville—and was designed for thirty-two thousand prisoners but could take forty thousand. The land was well-drained and the water source was sure and abundant: Magnolia Springs produced some nine million gallons of water each day. Rations were better than at Andersonville, and the first prisoners found inside the enclosure enough leftover wood to build shelters for themselves. Finally the prison commandant, Captain D. W. Vowles, passed for a fair and decent man.

By the time Sherman's columns were approaching Milledgeville
some ten thousand Northern soldiers were confined in Camp Lawton
and they probably had a fair idea that to the north of them something
significant was happening. On Sunday, November 20, a local man came
to the camp with the exhilarating news that Kilpatrick's cavalry was
near Macon. Inside the stockade "three cheers, long and loud, rent the
air." Meanwhile the Confederate authorities decided it was time to move
the prisoners out of Camp Lawton. The prisoners learned about the
move on the evening of November 19; they were roused the next morning at three o'clock and turned out with their meager possessions into a
cold rain (this would have been the same spell of bad weather that
struck Sherman's columns between November 19 and 22). The cars did
not come for an eternity, and the delay led some prisoners to hope that
Kilpatrick might reach them before they could be moved. But about
noon the cars finally appeared. The prisoners at least had the pleasure of
taunting their keepers, calling out to them: "How do you like Sherman's
marching orders?" The train that carried them off toward Savannah
afforded them no shelter, for the cars destined for them were flatcars;
they rode off huddled together against the wind and rain, bound for
other prison camps. Kilpatrick was within a few miles of the camp when
he learned it was empty and had been for several days.

The Northern cavalry leader now had other concerns, for Wheeler
had caught up with the invaders. For the rest of the way to Savannah the
Confederate cavalry put in appearances here and there, with several collisions between Northern and Southern horsemen; this "cavalry war"
was no more than a minor feature of the March to the Sea, being composed essentially of running fights and clashes, with casualties very limited. But if the war was a small affair it was a dirty one. The tendency
toward "feuding" among mounted units has already been noted; on the
road to Savannah it led to a string of atrocities and acts of reprisal. The
origin seems to be in the anger and desire for revenge of the Southern
cavalrymen as they moved in the wake of Sherman's army and saw the
destruction it had left behind. Northern foraging parties most often felt
their anger: When caught in the act of emptying smokehouses or ransacking residences they were frequently shot out of hand. "Many of
them now are filling dishonored graves," one of Wheeler's veterans put
it. Sometimes the bodies were left where they would be found by the
enemy, by way of warning.

Word of these killings of course reached Kilpatrick's men, and since
they were the men most likely to meet the Southern cavalry on even
terms, they undertook to even the score—with the inevitable effect of

provoking Wheeler's men even more. Kilpatrick and Wheeler exchanged notes periodically during the campaign, inquiring after the health of an officer who had been wounded and captured, discussing an exchange of cavalry prisoners, and the like; Wheeler once sent Kilpatrick a hat that had been lost in a skirmish, and that he thought might belong to his Northern counterpart. But the atrocities in the cavalry war crept into their correspondence, filling it with charges and countercharges. Kilpatrick took the matter up with Sherman, citing instances in which he had recovered the bodies of his men with their throats cut, rope burns around their necks, etc. Sherman's response was passed on by his aide de camp, Captain Dayton: "When your men are found, and you are fully convinced the enemy have killed them after surrender in fair battle, or have mutilated their bodies after being killed in fair battle, you may hang and mutilate man for man without regard to rank."

The quarrel became so envenomed that the life of a man taken prisoner in a cavalry fight might hang by a thread. In a clash one foggy morning near Waynesboro one of Wheeler's officers discovered how slender that thread could be:

> In the midst of the battle, with balls whizzing in very direction, I came across a squad of our men who had taken as prisoners four of the enemy. They were threatening to kill them, when I remonstrated and told them to turn them over to the rear guard near by. Just then an officer of higher rank rode up. I appealed to him, telling him that the soldiers proposed killing them. His only reply was "they know what to do with them." As I rode off into the fight, I heard the popping of the pistols, and I could see the prisoners tumbling over the high sage. . . . It would be proper here to say that many most outrageous transactions had been done by the Federals as they passed through Waynesboro, and these were told to the men. It was enough to incite vengeance.

The amount of damage Wheeler's force could inflict on Sherman's columns was minimal. With good roads ahead of them and clear, mild weather persisting, Sherman's army was dedicating itself to two tasks; one was destruction and the other was feeding itself. The general had fixed the guidelines for these two activities with his Special Field Orders Nos. 119 and 120, issued at Kingston on November 8 and 9. He included the texts of both in the section of his memoirs dealing with the march because in his eyes they were "so clear, emphatic, and well-digested, that no account of that historic event is perfect without them." That the two orders are fundamental to understanding the march is incontestable; that they were clear and well-digested is open to question. That the army should destroy all stocks and facilities that could be used in the Rebel war effort seems to have been a given, as a procedure sanctioned by the laws and customs of war. It was understood for example that after the columns had crossed streams they would destroy the bridges behind them. The rail system was not mentioned specifically, though it was Sherman's main target. The route of the march had been chosen in part to destroy long runs of track, and in addition smaller expeditions were sent out to burn bridges and trestles that lay outside the line of march. Sherman said in his memoirs: "I attached much importance to this destruction of the railroad, gave it my own personal attention, and made reiterated orders to others on the subject."

Those things that did not contribute to the Confederacy's warmaking capacity—and the boundary here was a vague one—could nonetheless be destroyed in certain circumstances: "To corps commanders alone is entrusted the power to destroy mills, houses, cotton gins, etc." As long as the army's movement was not hindered, "no destruction of such property should be permitted"; but if guerrillas or bushwhackers appeared, or if bridges had been destroyed and roads obstructed, these acts would be considered signs of "local hostility," and in that case "army commanders should order and enforce a devastation more or less relentless, according to the measure of such hostility." Here we find the principle already applied in North Georgia and elsewhere: If a bridge mysteriously burned, so would the houses of those living near it (the day Sherman drafted this passage he himself ordered the burning of houses outside Kingston in retaliation for the attack on the foragers of the Seventy-fourth Indiana). There is also some obscurity in this text. "Corps commanders alone" had the power to destroy mills and houses, yet "army commanders" (Generals Slocum and Howard) were to "order and enforce" the devastation and presumably fix its severity. If indeed a corps commander had the "power," could he delegate it, and if so, how? This was not a hypothetical question. One brigade commander reported after the campaign was over that he had destroyed no cotton or cotton gins, because he had never received written authorization from his corps commander.

The provisions on foraging are even more worthy of note. They began with a statement that would become celebrated among the troops: "The army will forage liberally on the country during the march." A forage party was to be organized by each brigade commander, who would confide it to "one or more discreet officers." These parties were to bring in enough provisions to keep on hand a ten days' supply of meat, vegetables, meal, etc., and a three-day ration of forage for horses and mules. "Soldiers must not enter the dwellings of the inhabitants, or commit any trespass; but, during a halt or camp, they may be permitted to gather turnips, potatoes, and other vegetables, and to drive in stock in sight of their camp." Do these prohibitions apply only to soldiers marching in the columns? Quite possibly, since it is hard to imagine a foraging party emptying someone's smokehouse over his protest and not being guilty of a "trespass." Moreover the next sentence reads: "To regular foraging parties must be intrusted the gathering of provisions and forage, at any distance from the road." As we will see, few of Sherman's foragers worried about these ambiguities.

It was the general's expressed desire that foraging be done "by the book" and with proper form and decorum; hence the reference to "regular" parties and the injunction that "the parties engaged will refrain from abusive or threatening language, and may, where the officer in command thinks proper, give written certificates of the facts, but no receipts." The instructions also presuppose considerable powers of discrimination on the part of the foragers: "As for horses, mules, wagons, etc. belonging to the inhabitants, the cavalry and artillery may appropriate freely and without limit; discriminating, however, between the rich, who are usually hostile, and the poor and industrious, usually neutral or friendly." Similarly when a foraging party took provisions from a family's larder, the foragers would "endeavor to leave with each family a reasonable portion for their maintenance."

There was nothing that exceptional in Special Field Order No. 120, though later on Sherman was quite unhappy when the text was published in Southern newspapers. Civil War armies had already supported themselves in whole or in part from the resources of a hostile civilian population—Sherman himself was fresh from just such an operation in North Georgia, where his army had foraged closely to supply their needs (an experiment Sherman regarded as a kind of preparation for the March to the Sea). Nor was the practice a violation of the customs and laws of war that had developed in the seventeenth and eighteenth centuries. An army operating in the territory of an enemy could require the local population to furnish it with sustenance; indeed by custom it could also collect the ordinary taxes, impose a special tax of its own, seize all the bells for use as gunmetal, etc. Where there were no local authorities remaining to arrange for subsistence, the army could collect what it needed where it could find it—as Sherman was to point out in a letter to Confederate General Wade Hampton.

While the procedure Sherman laid down for using brigade forage parties was thus not illegal, it was unworkable. It was based on the system used where the army purchased its needs from the local population, with commissaries and quartermasters preceding the army and buying and contracting for what was needed; the supplies were then distributed by those officials at brigade level. But with the men bringing in the forage, distribution at brigade level was unpopular. If men in the foraging party helped bring in a quantity of honey or bacon and then found none in their regiment's evening ration, they would set up a clamor. "The result might have been foreseen," wrote one officer, "there was general dissatisfaction, for there were not enough hams, or chickens, or syrup for all (some got side meat), and under color of the license given by Sherman's orders, every regiment sent out an independent foraging party."

In fact the "official" system was replaced by a variety of expedients, and from comments about foraging in the memoir literature, the variety was very great. Some brigades—in the Fourteenth Corps notably—seem to have followed Sherman's instructions fairly faithfully, with a large brigade party going out every morning under the command of an officer. General Leggett had a foraging party organized for each regiment in his division—one man for every twenty men in the regiment—to be chosen for their physical ability and their bravery, "and for strict obedience to orders." An officer in the 106th Illinois noted that four or five men went out from each company "to roam almost unrestrained through the country," and in the 105th Illinois as well, each company sent out its own foraging party. According to Sergeant Levi Ross in the Eighty-sixth Illinois "the regular detailed foragers do not supply the troops with necessary rations and therefore the soldiers are necessitated to forage for themselves independently of authorities, which is tacitly understood and permitted by the commanding officer." To these parties, large and small, regular and "independent," must be added the cooks and orderlies who went out on behalf of officers, and the foragers of the artillery, the engineers, pioneers, and teamsters. Finally there were men who simply took off "to have a look around" after their units got into camp, and since it was customary for the units at the head of column to march at dawn and reach the next camp in the early afternoon, soldiers in the van could have several hours of free time.

Somewhere in this confused picture we must place the "bummer." As used in the Western Army in the summer of 1864 the term had two related meanings: First it denoted a shirker who avoided work and combat, and generally looked out for himself. By extension "bummer" was used to designate noncombat soldiers by those who had to do the fighting. Several men who were on the March to the Sea tell us how the term was used then, but their definitions vary. To one man the term applied simply to a mounted forager, to another it represented a forager who was independent rather than in a regularly constituted party. In still another use "bummer" meant a forager who worked for himself, not for his comrades; finally, at least by the time the march was over, the word was a colloquial term for "forager" in general. It was destined to evolve further, for the bummer would emerge in the folklore of the war as a flamboyant, picaresque character. Like the term "GI" in a later war, "bummer" moved from a pejorative and restricted meaning to a more general and even flattering one. After the war a veteran of the Georgia campaign might not hesitate to describe himself as one of Sherman's bummers even though he never charmed a chicken from its roost or captured a hive of bees.

It was the usual procedure for the forage parties to depart early in the morning, before the column resumed its march, and return with their spoils later in the day, sometimes waiting at roadside for their comrades to pass, sometimes rejoining them in camp. At first the parties left on foot, but in the course of their travels they soon found horses and began to go mounted, with the formal or tacit approval of their officers. They might return with provisions loaded on a pack mule, but increasingly they used wagons or carriages taken in their foraging. The wagon or cart would not be allowed in the column the following day, but would be burned, the animals that drew it being added to the army's swelling complement of livestock. The arrival of the forager was often a cause for hilarity in the column he rejoined. Some took to returning in outlandish dress they had found: "Once a forager in Continental uniform with cocked hat and plume on a fine horse, strip of carpet for saddle, appeared at the roadside and with mock gravity reviewed the column as it passed." Then too, the foragers sometimes returned in bizarre conveyances: "A wagon loaded with corn and corn fodder, drawn by a thoroughbred horse and a scrawny mule, a silver-mounted family carriage loaded with hams and bacon drawn by a jackass and a cow in rope harness."

The party might depart as a group of fifty or a hundred, but it was common practice for the men to do their foraging in smaller groups, anywhere from two or three to perhaps a score (the lone bummer Scarlett O'Hara had to contend with in *Gone With the Wind* would have been an exception). With groups of this size it would not always be possible to have an officer in command, and discipline might suffer accordingly.

The initial forage parties sent out on the departure from Atlanta were frequently instructed not to venture more than a half-mile from the road being followed by their column, but this restriction seems to have fallen by the wayside, perhaps because there was so little to find in those first days. Those who foraged speak most often of going five or six miles out from the column; ten miles would have been about the maximum if the foragers planned to rejoin the column before night. Parties looking for draft animals tended to be larger and roam farther afield; they would sometimes camp out a night or two before returning.

This "system," if one could call it that, had the disadvantage of being highly inefficient, since at any one time perhaps ten or twenty percent of the army was out obtaining supplies that a handful of commissaries could have brought in under more normal circumstances. The various foraging parties did not divide up the foraging area, nor could they have. All roamed pretty much at large, more times than a few descending on a farm or plantation only to find it had been picked clean. This kind of foraging was also extremely wasteful. When the foragers found hogs they usually shot them on the spot (instead of bayoneting them, as they were told to do to save ammunition). Then, rather than try to get the entire carcass back to the column, they would cut off a choice portion easy to transport, perhaps a ham, and leave the rest. "I have counted one hundred and fifty carcases of slaughtered hogs on one plantation," a soldier recalled, "and have seen dead hogs lying beside the roads that were left nearly whole because everyone in our ranks seemed to have enough." Or the foragers might find a large barrel of molasses and draw off a bucket or two for their use, then pour the rest out on the ground "to keep the Rebs from using it."

Then too, the soldiers' appetites became jaded. At first sweet potatoes were a staple, but before long the men lost their taste for them. As early as November 20 a diarist noted that they were "becoming a drug in camp." Meats came in and out of fashion; toward the end of the march the foragers were going out of their way to find turkeys, because "chicken and pork we are fairly sick of." The wastefulness was compounded by the soldiers' disinclination to settle for leftovers, or to carry food on the march. "Certain I am," wrote the commanding officer of the Seventy-fourth Ohio, "that enough was left in camp almost every day to have subsisted the men during the day, had it been carried along, but the men argued that 'sufficient to the meal was the evil,' and wouldn't carry anything from camp."

The army's seizures of horses and mules were far in excess of what was needed. Those brought in were sorted, and the best replaced weak or broken-down animals; this culling and replacement went on constantly, and the men boasted that their draft animals at the end of the march were far better than those they started with. The animals culled out were shot; a Confederate cavalryman following in the army's wake remembered seeing "time and again, long rows of dead horses, numbering from thirty to a hundred and fifty." The better saddle horses tended to end up as mounts for the officers, their commanding officers giving their permission. Soon the men too were acquiring mounts, their officers either acquiescing or looking the other way. The fad spread from one unit to another. "The 6th Iowa are plumb crazy on the horse question," recorded one soldier.

Cavalry officers had the best chance to acquire fine horseflesh, and some acquired strings of a dozen or more; even Sherman commented that every officer seemed to have five or six mounts. There was endless buying, swapping, and "trading up" to a better horse. Even a young infantry officer named Gibson caught the fever. On November 18 he noted in his diary: "Forage one antiquated quadruped yclept Rosinante." On the 30th he traded Rosinante for Bucephalus, and on December 12, without explanation, he got rid of Bucephalus and started riding a mule. In at least one case the acquisition of a fine horse cost an officer his life. In a swamp near Milledgeville some foragers found a fine pacing mare that had been the property of General Howell Cobb. It was acquired by a young officer who was so captivated with the horse that he rode it constantly and at considerable distance from the column. One day he was found on a country road with his throat cut.

The large numbers of riding horses and even packhorses eventually encumbered the columns so much that Sherman gave orders for the mass of animals to be reduced. The procedure used was a simple one. A guard posted at a bridge simply confiscated the horses and mules from those who had no right to possess them, which was probably most of the army. General Kilpatrick's cavalry, which had lost a sizable number of horses in running fights with Wheeler, got the pick of the confiscated horses.

General Kilpatrick himself had a running grudge against the swarms of foragers who had also taken to riding; with the speed and additional range thus acquired they had become competitors of sorts with Kilpatrick's own horsemen, making it more difficult for them to obtain forage. "If I come to a town or village," Kilpatrick was heard to say, "and stop to obtain forage, I find that the infernal bummers have been there." For in the art of foraging those who sought the virgin territory in front of the army had the best pickings; despite repeated prohibitions, the enter-

prising bummers continued to stay ahead of everyone else. Henry Hitchcock complained that "every place we go to is occupied by scouts and
stragglers ahead of the *advance guard*." Many paid for their adventure-
someness by being picked up by Wheeler's cavalry. Hitchcock estimated
the number lost to be in the hundreds. He raised the matter with Sherman; the general responded: "Serves 'em right—hope they shoot 'em."

Other generals, and some regimental and company officers as well,
saw the overzealous foragers as part of a pattern of disorders and
excesses increasingly visible as the campaign progressed. Most leaders
who saw this disturbing trend worried about what effect it might have
on the army's discipline and cohesion, but some were quite as much
concerned by what they saw happening to the population on which
their own foragers were being unleashed. Most concerned of all was
General O. O. Howard, commander of the Army of the Tennessee, which
constituted Sherman's right wing. An officer close to Howard said that
"the condition of the poor people troubled him greatly, and he often
lamented that the soldiers could not be more effectively restrained." The
deeply pious Howard also confessed that the excesses attendant to the
campaign in which he was playing a major role were troubling his religious life: "For the past year there has seemed to be a cloud between me
and my Savior."

Concern over irregularities in foraging can be read in the orders and
directives on the subject that have been preserved in the *Official Records*.
General Slocum issued several stern reminders to the Army of Georgia,
while corps and division commanders in both armies issued orders of
their own. But General Howard outdid all others in this endeavor. His
Special Field Order No. 167, issued even before the march began,
warned against straggling and called attention to the restrictions
imposed on foragers in General Sherman's orders written at Kingston.
Special Field Order No. 172, issued four days later, reiterated the prohibition on soldiers' entering houses. On November 20 Howard warned
foragers not to go beyond the heads of columns. His General Field Order
No. 26 of November 22 was an emphatic expression of his exasperation
with continuing disorders: It authorized officers to shoot on the spot pillagers whom they could not deal with any other way. The warnings and
prohibitions continued: against burning mills and other facilities without the express approval of the corps commander, and against irregular
foraging. Howard tried to reduce the great number of mounted foragers
and even introduced a system whereby foragers had to have written
authorizations or "tickets."

While General Howard issued a new order every day or two directed at abuses in foraging, the general commanding the expedition issued a single directive on the matter of forage in the month running from the army's departure from Atlanta to its arrival before Savannah. On November 23 Sherman issued Special Field Order No. 127, which called for "more attention" to the matter of foraging, with "none but regular organized foraging parties . . . allowed to depart from the right and left of the road." From time to time Sherman made passing references to foraging in messages to Generals Slocum and Howard, essentially to say it was working to his satisfaction: "Thus far forage has been good and men and animals thrive"; "Troops in fine condition, having fed high on sweet potatoes and poultry." After the March to the Sea was completed he wrote Grant that "liberal and judicious foraging" had kept the army bountifully supplied.

One can't help but wonder just what was happening as the foraging parties spread out across the land day after day. Was Sherman's complacency justified, and were the excesses that concerned Howard really taking place? From what we can glean in the accounts both of the foragers and of the Georgians on whom they descended, there seems to have been a basic scenario, though it was subject to a thousand variations. When experienced foragers approached a homestead they watched for tracks leading in or out and looked to see if there were any saddled horses—such an animal usually meant the house contained a man ready for a fast getaway. One soldier recalled: "in foraging we always went up to the house on the run, so if there were any rebel soldiers in it we could surprise them." If there was anyone at home, she (for almost invariably it was a woman who came to the door) could expect to be closely questioned about food supplies and draft animals; there was a good chance that the house would be entered and searched—ostensibly for Rebel soldiers hidden away. Once inside the soldiers would do some "looking around," and particularly if there were many of them there could be some ransacking, with some things like locked drawers being broken, and some thievery. But the inhabitants would probably come through with their house and the bulk of their possessions intact.

But if there was no one at home, or perhaps only a slave or two left to "look after things," these would be pushed aside and the ransacking would be thorough; considerable damage could be done to the house and its contents. The chances were perhaps two to one that the foragers would find the occupants gone; one man who made the march estimated that they found three out of four Georgians "not at home." When a house was empty, wrote one veteran of the march, "we felt more at liberty to ransack and take away what evidently had been left to us." While some foragers concentrated on the house, others would make a quick survey of the outbuildings and interrogate any blacks they found about where food, livestock, and valuables might be hidden. If there was little to be found, and if the inhabitants insisted "other Yankees" had taken everything, the foragers could usually tell from the tracks about the place or lack of them whether the people were lying. If things had been hidden, they could often find them "by indications they would probably have found hard to describe."

Sherman's injunction to leave some subsistence for the families whose food supplies were taken seems in the main to have been ignored. Wrote one officer: "The question is never asked how much the farmer needs for his subsistence, but all is taken—literally everything." It was much the same with the forbearance to be shown in the case of "the industrious poor." After the march was over an officer in the Seventeenth Corps said that despite Sherman's wishes, the officers' efforts, and five soldiers from the corps sent to the Dry Tortugas for vandalism, they had not been able to control the men, so the "loyal poor" had suffered with everyone else. Another forager acknowledged: "We serve all alike, use partiality to none of them for we take everything." Another who had seen these things and looked back on them felt there was no other way: "Swift and terrible, and not always just, were the strokes of their arms and the works of their hands. Pioneers along a road of desolation, forty miles in width and three hundred in length, their labor was too swift to be discriminating."

It seems unlikely that the men were simply ignorant of the various orders on foraging, for in many instances the orders were read to them, nor was it that they simply ignored what they heard, but some instructions were couched in complicated language, and in talking about the various orders and relating them to others the men interpreted them and distorted them, sometimes making them more draconian than they were. Thus one soldier summed up Sherman's Special Field Order No. 120: "General Sherman orders us to forage liberally but leave one cow and a few necessaries at each house." But another had a different interpretation: "An order was issued by General Sherman to the troops just before leaving Atlanta that we would not leave enough to subsist a flea on the country through which we passed." A cavalryman took Special Field Order No. 120 to mean: "we are to forage as much as we want off the country."

By the same token the men had their own interpretations of the policy of destroying facilities and resources useful to the enemy. Chaplain Hight wrote when the march began that "the impression among officers

and men is that we are to pass through the country burning as we go."
To many soldiers it was simply a continuation of what they had been
doing: "To burn all bublic [public] buildings and any things that would
help the rebs."

Fire was the chief means of destruction available to the army, and we
are in the habit of thinking it was used on a grand scale during the
March to the Sea. Chaplain Bradley of the Twenty-second Wisconsin
said: "no one, without being there, can form a proper idea of the devastation that will be found in our track. Thousands of families will have
their homes laid in ashes, and they themselves will be turned beggars
into the street. We have literally carried fire and sword into this once
proud and defiant land." Other participants in the march spoke of following the progress of other columns by watching the smoke to the left
or right of them. Sherman himself sent this order to General Slocum:
"Dress to the right on the Seventeenth Corps, whose progress you can
rate by the smokes."

Despite the restrictions on burning that figured in Special Field
Order No. 120, a great many officers and men felt themselves entitled to
set certain things ablaze when they found them. One of these was cotton, and another was cotton gins and presses. A captain in a Connecticut
regiment wrote in his journal for November 20: "My impression is that I
have destroyed $150,000 or $200,000 worth of cotton to-day." The men
also felt they had an authorization to touch a match to cotton bales and
to buildings in which they were stored. "Every house containing cotton
is burned by general orders," wrote one soldier, "the boys simply
remarking 'here goes for King Cotton.'" The great clouds and banks of
dark smoke described by diarists on the march were probably made by
stores of burning cotton.

The extent to which fire was used to destroy towns varied considerably. "Public" buildings and warehouses were considered fair game and
were often set ablaze. Where houses went up, they were usually vacant
ones fired by the soldiers, with the flames spreading to other homes
nearby. Before leaving Milledgeville the officers in Sherman's circle had
engaged in considerable discussion about burning the state capitol and
the executive mansion, and Henry Hitchcock implies Sherman ruled
against the step; in any event the two buildings were not fired. A provost
guard seems to have remained in town until the last soldiers had left,
thus preventing "voluntary incendiarism." Louisville was nearly all
burned, apparently on the initiative of the soldiers after a story spread
that a local woman had spat in the face of a soldier; however a soldier
who was in the provost guard there said: "on moveing out we burnt

some of the town just a little to keep our hand in, you no." Sandersville came near to being totally razed because some shots had been fired at Sherman's men from the courthouse, or at least so Sherman and his men believed. According to Henry Hitchcock Sherman relented and ordered Captain Poe to burn the courthouse only (Sherman did not mention this destruction in his memoirs); the men apparently took their own revenge, for one of them recalled: "our boys ransacked and plundered awfully."

There was a "standing order" of sorts that any building from which fire was directed at the troops would be destroyed, and the rule applied to private residences as well. By the same token anyone who impeded the army's progress by burning a bridge would have his house burned if he was identified, and this happened at least once on the march. Less clear was the case of a house near the bridge that had been burned. When Sherman's party encountered a destroyed bridge at Buffalo Creek and waited for the engineers to span the stream, Hitchcock and Colonel Charles Ewing fell to arguing whether they should burn a nearby house in retaliation. Hitchcock opposed, for there was no proof the owner had destroyed the bridge or even had guilty knowledge of it. Sherman listened for a while and then joined in: "In war everything is right which prevents anything. If bridges are burned I have a right to burn all houses near it." Hitchcock persisted, as tactfully as he could, in saying some indication of a man's guilt was necessary. But Sherman had the last word: "Well, let him look to his own people. If they find that their burning bridges only destroys their own citizen's houses, they'll stop it." Sherman had in fact already made it clear in his Special Field Order No. 127 that he would use this kind of reprisal if the Confederates adopted a scorched earth policy: "Should the enemy burn forage and corn on our route houses, barns and cotton gins must also be burned to keep them company." The same order promised to "deal harshly" with the inhabitants nearby if the army encountered "obstructions."

There is a persistent tradition that Sherman's troops burned vast numbers of rural homes—"thousands" was the word used by Chaplain Bradley—and in the decades after the war any chimneys standing alone about the Georgia countryside got the lugubrious name "Sherman's sentinels." But what evidence there is indicates that only a minority of the houses along the army's path were fired by the Northern soldiers—probably a smaller proportion than during the evacuation of North Georgia. That is the impression to be gained from reading the more meticulous diarists; a house in the countryside going up in flames was noted. Henry Hitchcock was constantly on the watch for them but did not note very many. Later studies of the areas the army passed through likewise show that the majority of the houses survived the holocaust of 1864. Using detailed maps prepared by one of Sherman's topographical engineers for the sixty-odd-mile stretch between Covington and Milledgeville, a geographer at the University of Georgia went back over the route in 1955 and discovered that many of the structures had survived not only Sherman's passage, but also accidental fires and termites, and were peacefully succumbing to dry rot. As for Milledgeville and the surrounding area, the author of another study found that "the actual destruction of private dwellings . . . was rare indeed, either in the town or along the route of march."

If the men were not burning houses, they were obviously entering them. Stories circulated of violence to "citizens," both men and women, but the exact place and the circumstances were rarely given, and we will need to examine these charges later. As for assaults on property, the evidence was everywhere, in the outlandish costumes the bummers affected, in the silver cups that now hung from the cavalrymen's saddles, "as common in the command . . . as tin ones used to be," in the bric-a-brac and housewares that arrived in the forager's wagons or on their pack mules, mixed in with trussed chickens and sacks of sweet potatoes. In almost every town the army passed through from Decatur to the gates of Savannah it left spectacular evidence of its destructiveness: streets paved with paper thrown from courthouses and newspaper offices.

Just how serious were such transgressions? After all, similar things had been seen in previous campaigns, in Tennessee, Mississippi, and Alabama. Did the March to the Sea produce a major breakdown in discipline or a new level of violence directed at noncombatants? When Sherman wrote his report to General Halleck at the beginning of 1865 he did not view the behavior of his men as particularly bad: "A little loose in foraging, they 'did some things they ought not to have done,' yet, on the whole, they have supplied the wants of the army with as little violence as could be expected, and as little loss as I calculated." Other observers disagreed, seeing the march as a logical culmination for the whole Georgia campaign, which had marked a new departure from its beginning. Looking back over the campaign many years later, Andrew Hickenlooper wrote: "In the days between May of 1864 and the end of the year, a radical change occurred with respect to the attitude of Federal soldiers toward the property rights of southerners." Already that May a diarist with the Signal Corps noted: "Never before have I witnessed so much wanton destruction as on this march. The soldiers are perfectly abandoned." In August Captain Poe had recorded that the "robbing and plundering" had reduced the population to a state of misery and want "perfectly pitiable to witness . . . and I pray God it may never be my duty to see the like again."

Eloquent as such testimonies are, they do not accord with the picture that has emerged in the preparation of this book. First of all it appears the soldiers behaved no worse in 1864 than in 1862 or 1863; though the evidence is admittedly anecdotal, one does not have the impression— and apparently no one did in 1864—that among the soldier's transgressions the proportion of rapes, homicides, and other serious crimes against persons was on the rise, nor do we hear of the introduction of grave new acts such as the poisoning of wells, maiming of livestock, widespread desecrations, etc. In a word, then, there is precious little here to indicate that the war was degenerating into something more cruel and more frightful. But the March to the Sea did produce a change in one sense; the foraging system increased greatly the incidence of contacts between soldiers of the invading army and the population of the region through which the army passed, and it consequently increased occasions for transgressions to take place. General Alpheus Williams admitted as much when he observed that "the nature of the march was calculated to remove discipline."

We may ask at this point if there were not also something in the nature of Sherman's troops that turned a forage into a scavenger hunt and produced the acts of vandalism and destruction so frequently and graphically described by the men themselves. Some officers believed that such things were done by a small, incorrigibly criminal element in the ranks, a notion that has long been popular among the military. Several regimental and brigade commanders laid all the troubles in their units to these "rotten apples." The commander of a brigade in the Fourteenth Corps said several of his men missing in the course of the campaign would be well-served by a stretch in Andersonville because "they were doubtless in the act of stealing something when captured. I suppose every command has a few such men." At the end of the campaign the colonel of the Thirty-third New Jersey reported some of his missing men as deserters, since they were "all troublesome characters, and, despite repeated remonstrance and punishment and the constant vigil of officers, succeeded in straggling and were captured by the enemy. Their absence being willful, I have marked them as deserters to the enemy, so that after exchange they are to be tried for this heinous offense."

Deservedly or not, whole units got the reputation of ruffians and pillagers. In Sherman's army, for example, the New York regiments were said to be filled with big city criminals and foreigners fresh from the jails of the Old World, while the excesses of the First Alabama Cavalry earned for its commander a letter of rebuke in mid-campaign. Curiously, by the end of the campaign Wheeler's cavalry was regarded by most Georgians who had made its acquaintance as more rapacious and destructive than the Yankees; the outcry was so great that there was a formal inquiry after the campaign was over. The report was severely critical of Wheeler's leadership—indeed damning—but gave the cavalrymen who served under him a clean bill of health. Acknowledging the usual handful of rotten apples, the author of the report affirmed that: "The material of the corps is the same, the very same, as is found in every branch of the Confederate service: it is equally as good as any can be elsewhere." Interestingly historian Stephen Starr probed the composition of one of the more notorious mounted units in Union service and reached essentially the same conclusion: "They were not congenital criminals and ruffians to whom marauding came naturally, but men and boys who had been brought up in decent, God-fearing homes."

We must reach something of the same conclusion here. The swarms of soldiers who swept over the Georgia countryside between Atlanta and Savannah were in the immense majority young men from the farms and villages of the Middle West. They too came from a milieu that was "decent" and "God-fearing," and when the war was over they would reintegrate that milieu easily and naturally. Yet these same young men— by their own testimony—were incontestably the willing and indeed enthusiastic participants in a carnival of pillage and destruction that extended from Atlanta to the sea. We know that the campaign gave them unprecedented opportunities for such behavior, but why did they seize them so readily?

Historian Joseph Glatthaar has argued that these men, motivated partly by a spirit of revenge and partly by a desire to stamp out the rebellion, were "amazingly in tune" with their commander in his strategy of teaching the South the frightfulness of war. This argument has considerable weight, for any number of Sherman's veterans endorsed that very strategy in their diaries and their letters to their families. But motivation can exist at several levels, and the behavior of Sherman's foragers on the March to the Sea—and the behavior of groups of soldiers generally—may spring from impulses more deeply anchored in the psyche than a desire to chastise and humble one's enemies. At this level the historian must ask the assistance of the sociologist and the psychologist.

In the march through Georgia, which is our only concern here, the instances in which acts of violence are clearly engendered by feelings of revenge or very strong antipathy are relatively few. The property and possessions of those who figured prominently in the rebellion were understandably at great hazard. Sherman himself observed this distinction in an episode that occurred just before he reached Milledgeville. He had stopped to warm himself in a slave cabin when he saw on the mantel a box bearing the initials "H.C." He asked the slave whom the plantation belonged to, and the man answered: "Mr. Howell Cobb." Sherman turned and gave the order: "Spare nothing." Virtually everything was burned except the slave cabins. To Henry Hitchcock, who was present, this wholesale destruction seemed eminently justified since Cobb was "one of the *head devils*." With this policy the men heartily agreed. Near Atlanta they had already systematically demolished a house belonging to Governor Brown, and during the march they laid waste to the property of ex-Governor Johnson. Some of the postwar histories would speak of the army's achievements in "laying waste plantations of notorious rebel leaders."

The men reacted strongly to evidence of cruelty to slaves; few whipping posts escaped their ire. "If the negroes on the place told stories of great cruelty they had suffered, or of bitter hostility to the Union, or if there were bloodhounds about, which had been used to run down slaves, the injury was generally avenged by the torch." A man named Stubbs, who lived near Millen, lost everything but his life (and he would probably have lost that had he not been absent when the troops came to his place) because he owned a large pack of hounds reputedly used to track runaway slaves and escaped Union prisoners. The dogs were all shot on the spot, and soon "the house, cotton gin, press, corn ricks, stable, everything that would burn was in flames. . . ." The most violent reaction of the troops was to Camp Lawton. Many recorded their outrage at the time; as one officer put it, "it fevered the blood of our brave boys." Mathias Schwab, the Cincinnati fireman, was still beside himself over a month later when he wrote his brother: "By God, George, after what I have seen at Millen I could just cut every one of [their] throats." Prisoners who fell into the soldiers' hands in the period immediately after their visit to Camp Lawton could expect a rough time of it (American soldiers in a later war reacted similarly toward German prisoners after they had liberated concentration camps). One response to Camp Lawton was to devastate Millen; the men burned "everything . . . that a match would ignite." They also seem to have declared war on any dog that looked as if it might have been used for tracking escaped prisoners and runaway slaves: "Wherever our army has passed," an officer observed, "everything in the shape of a dog has been killed."

Sometimes the soldiers' anger was all too easily provoked; when a group of them had a difference of opinion with an "outsider," a trivial incident could produce a surprising outburst of violence. Captain Conyngham related that he saw "a soldier knock a planter down because a bee stung him." The revenge the soldiers took on the town of Louisville after hearing that a woman had spat in the face of one of their comrades is quite typical. Sergeant Levi Ross related an even more appalling example just before the march. A large group of soldiers were lounging about a railway station when a black man walked past them. One of the soldiers snatched the man's hat, whereupon he tried to take it back. Instantly the nearest soldiers attacked the black man, many others joined in, and by the time officers could intervene the black man had received a fatal beating. In this episode and in many others there is evidence of a drive more basic than a desire to punish Southerners for their transgressions.

There were officers in Sherman's army, and no doubt in all other Civil War armies, who suspected a gradual change was occurring among their soldiers that they usually referred to as "demoralization"; by that word they meant not a decline in morale, but an erosion of moral and ethical values. Some, the least perceptive, felt it was the example of the "rotten apples" that corrupted good soldiers and showed them the road to depravity. Others believed it was the nature of the campaign itself. General Howard said that "the scenes through which we are passing are for a time callousing to our sensibilities," while a lieutenant in the Seventieth Indiana wrote home: "When men are told that they are in an enemy's country and must live off the enemy, it creates a morbid appetite to take things. . . ." Some officers immediately saw difficulties in the forage provisions of Special Field Order No. 120. A captain who was designated for forage duty wrote with a sense of foreboding: "[It] means to take every thing we can find to eat or drink, and I am afraid will be interpreted to mean everything we can carry away." On the second day of foraging he found his worries confirmed: "I find [it] very hard work to keep my men within reasonable bounds."

As for the men, at the inception of the campaign many of them were already looking forward to foraging operations, but not particularly as a means of humbling the Rebels' pride. "Before we started this raid," one soldier wrote his wife, "I had herd the boys tell about going for things when they were out foraging. I thought I wouldn't be much of a hand at such things, but if I remember right I had my share. . . ." For in the Atlanta campaign and earlier the soldiers had sometimes found the occasion to take off and forage on their own, or "Jayhawk," as they called it, and they liked the experience; one soldier who had the chance in North Georgia recalled: "when out on such occasions we really had fun."

From the beginning the soldiers found it hard to distinguish between foraging and what they called "prospecting" for items that, when found, might or might not be contributed to the general larder. The meaning of the term "prospect" we can deduce from the following account: "The boys had a great time last night in Irwinton. The citizens had buried a great many things to keep them from the 'vandals,' and the boys soon found out. Hundreds of them were armed with sharpened sticks probing the earth, 'prospecting.' They found a little of everything. . . ." The narrator of this particular episode relates that immediately thereafter:

> We fell in at retreat, and had general order No 26 read to us for I guess the 20th time. It declares that 'any soldier or army follower who shall be convicted of the crime of arson or robbery, or who shall be caught pillaging, shall be shot,' and gives the officers and non-commissioned ditto the right to shoot pillagers in the act.

When it became clear that even the most rigorous prohibitions had little effect on the men's behavior, company and regimental officers were widely criticized for not using the powers given to them and for not keeping their soldiers well in hand. Captain Orlando Poe, who went so far as to strike pillagers with his fists, lamented: "my attempts to stop this thing are but small and feeble efforts when we regard the great numbers of those who either wink at it, or openly encourage it." But the officers at company and regimental levels would be the first to feel the soldiers' resentment, and even resistance, if they tried to do much. For they knew that many men believed that plundering—they would not call it that—was something they were somehow entitled to do, and at very worst a peccadillo. General Howard, who took the most strenuous measures to restrain the men, saw his efforts come to naught. Though he imposed the death penalty for pillage, and any number of pillagers were apprehended in his command, none was executed. It would have been impolitic at the very least. Even Reverend John Hight was outraged over the nominal imposition of the death penalty: "Just think of shooting American soldiers for the benefit of traitors." General Howard's problems with his men were to continue. In February 1865, while the army was in South Carolina, a man arrested for pillaging was freed by his comrades, who threatened the guards with their rifles. Howard suspected "a regularly organized banditti."

One thing is sure: Each day the march continued, there was less

chance of altering its nature; for the men found in foraging an almost
addictive source of pleasure. Their own comments leave little doubt on
this score: "Went foraging today. Had a good deal of fun"; "In foraging
we find plenty, see much, and in fact enjoy the campaign hugely."
Departing with a foraging party meant first of all liberation from the
tedium of marching with the column. There was the excitement that
comes with any hunt, even if it were only for sweet potatoes or mules,
and the tantalizing possibility of other finds as well, for stories circulated of men finding sacks of gold coins in hollow logs or in hens' nests.
There was the prospect of encounters with the "citizens," about whom
the men were always curious, and the chance of a brush with Wheeler's
cavalrymen to add the zest of danger. To twenty-year-olds, this was a
heady mixture. It would be headier still if the foragers came upon any
alcohol. Some soldiers searched diligently for it, but rarely found much
(in their frustration they would sometimes drink down medicinal bitters
and vegetable dyes). Strong drink and drunkenness rarely figure in
accounts of foraging expeditions.

If the forage party was led by a mature and levelheaded officer or
noncom who dominated his men, there was a good chance that the
party's visit would produce some forage but no violence offered to persons, little or no vandalism, and only minor thefts of personal effects.
Judging from the accounts of those Georgians who received the foragers'
visits, many of the descents seemed to have taken place in a certain confusion, with no person clearly in charge. In the foraging party without a
designated and universally accepted leader, we may suppose that there
was a sort of group dynamic at work. Foraging was not for everyone. We
are told that some men were temperamentally unsuited for it; the timid
and fearful preferred the safety of the column; on the other hand the
adventurous, the curious, and those "brimful of spirit and deviltry" were
likely candidates for the work and no doubt provided de facto leadership, or at least contributed the opinions that prevailed in the group.

One thing the foragers seem never to have done was to have a falling
out or become split into two opposing groups—say over the question of
burning a house. Georgians who were present when their houses were
searched and pillaged sometimes noticed that all the soldiers were not
equally enthusiastic about the plundering. "There were a few," one
woman recalled, "who acted gentlemanly and seemed ashamed of the
way the men generally were acting. They told us to apply for a safeguard. . . ." What they did not do was try to stop the pillage. Levi Ross
was involved in a curious incident that began when a forager-pillager
who went up to a house was shot and wounded (not seriously) by an

elderly "citizen." The forager ran back to bring his comrades, while the women of the house hustled the old man off to safety. When the crowd of foragers arrived the wounded man demanded that the house be burned, and all the others went along with him. Ross, who happened upon the scene, tried to intervene on behalf of the women, but even with the authority a sergeant's stripes nominally gave him, all he could wrest from the crowd by way of concession was a brief delay in firing the house so that the women could remove some personal possessions (the foragers may have gone along with this delay since it gave them time to remove things too).

When the group was faced with a problem or challenge, the most forceful speaker, the most daring proposal, or the most emphatic mode of action would often carry the day, and all the others would follow—a phenomenon known to social psychologists as group polarization. Some soldiers from the 105th Illinois went "foraging" in Milledgeville, making up an "irregular" party simply out to see what they could find to fill their knapsacks. Their attention was drawn to one house displaying a yellow flag, the symbol of quarantine. One of the party pronounced the dread words "small pox," and this gave the others pause (they may have known that there had been several cases of the disease in town). Then a soldier named Strong announced: "I never had the small pox but I am going in to get it." He went up to the door, followed by several others. There they were met by a woman who asked them: "Have you had the disease?" At this point another soldier named Hoffines spoke up: "No, but we want it. We are coming in, and if the patient is bad, we will take him to the hospital." When they got inside they encountered several black servants. According to the soldier named Strong, who related the episode, "the nigs began to grin and roll their eyes, and we were surer than ever that there was no smallpox there." The men trooped in and wandered over the house, taking what they wanted and departing with full knapsacks.

So it probably was with acts of violence and vandalism. If one soldier threw a rope around a planter's neck, or the neck of one of his slaves, and threatened to hang him unless he revealed where the family's valuables were buried, none of the others intervened—or at least there was no mention of protest or intervention when these episodes were described. If the victim, after being strung up for a few seconds, told them where to dig, then they would all run to the spot, whooping and laughing. A few might go with reservations and pangs of conscience, but probably the great majority without an afterthought; having participated in a near-lynching, they rushed off joyously to rob and plunder—all actions they would have found reprehensible and repugnant under other, "normal" circumstances. For not only can the group impose its will on the individual, it can also lure him into participation by absolving him of all personal responsibility for his acts—this by-product of group activity, called deindividuation, has been identified in disturbances in high school cafeterias, in football games, and in rock concerts, and has been an ingredient of lynchings, riots, orgies, and group vandalism. Its effect is apparently enhanced if the subjects are rendered even more anonymous by "indistinct garb," as for example when they all wear blue uniforms.

This deindividuation we can equate with demoralization in the sense we have spoken of earlier: a slackening of the restraints that usually govern men's conduct. The men could indulge themselves in impulsive self-gratification, for example carrying off anything that struck their fancy. While ransacking a house in the Black Creek section of Bryan County the men found an enormous pair of pants. They quizzed the woman of the house about them and said they wanted to see the man who wore such pants. The woman at first said he was away, but eventually agreed to call him if they would promise no harm would come to him. They agreed, she made some sign to the "hideout," and soon a man of gigantic girth came lumbering out of the woods. They kept their word and soon departed—but they took along the pants, to show the "boys." Then they no doubt tossed them along the roadside, where they joined objects like the corpse of a pet monkey that someone had "captured" up the road, the Mexican army shako its wearer had tired of, the milliner's mannequin a soldier carried out of Madison, insisting that she was his "sweetheart," and a thousand other improbable things. There were those who were levelheaded and efficient in their thievery, like the bummer who fell into the hands of Wheeler's men; they searched him, found thirty-odd gold rings in his pockets, and shot him on the spot. But the men took dresses their wives or sweethearts could not wear, books in Latin that they could not read, and musical instruments they could not play; much that was plundered from farms and plantations was probably carried no more than four or five miles. The foragers' wagons that rolled in each evening could apparently contain anything and everything:

> pumpkins, chickens, cabbages, guinea fowls, carrots, turkeys, onions, squashes, a shoat, sorghum, a looking glass, an Italian harp, sweetmeats, a peacock, a rocking chair, a gourd, a bass viol, sweet potatoes, a cradle, dried peaches, honey, a baby carriage, peach brandy

and every other imaginable thing a lot of foot soldiers could take in their heads to bring away.

Much of this plunder would be abandoned at the campsite the next morning—for the army's vehicles and their contents were generally well-policed, and no others were allowed.

Most of the acts of vandalism carried out by the soldiers had something of the same quality as the looting—essentially impulsive and largely done because they simply gave pleasure to the "Vandal," rather than pain to his victim. To be sure there are instances where the obvious purpose was to convey a message, to "rub it in"—that was probably the case of the Union troops who went to the extra trouble of twisting rails so that they resembled the letters "U" and "S" and setting them up along the ruined railway, and that was probably the purpose of the cavalryman who rode his horse back and forth through the pile of books that had been thrown out of the state library in Milledgeville. And yet, inapt though the expression might appear, much of the destruction seems to have been done with the naive abandon of a child. Henry Hitchcock went inside the hotel at Millen, which was already well ablaze, because he thought a mentally deranged woman from the locality might have been inside. Instead he found a number of soldiers wandering around including "one fellow amusing himself knocking off a row of hat hooks fastened to the wall in hall, though sure to be all burned." By and large the vandals did things that did not require great effort and were "fun" to do because they produced a spectacular effect. These appear over and over in the accounts that come down to us: tossing great sheaves of papers from the upper floors of the courthouse, throwing dishes across the kitchen so that they shatter against the wall, one after the other, slashing open featherbeds and sending a blizzard of feathers down a stairwell. And this was being done while "the boys" were laughing and shouting, running about or tossing around the contents of trunks and dressers, and all this to the accompaniment of screaming women, crying children, cackling fowl, and barking dogs. An officer who happened upon such a scene of pandemonium said the men acted as though they were at a frolic. To their minds they were.

The men who did such things—and we're speaking here not of a few "rotten apples" but of a sizable part of the army—spent no great amount of time musing about why they were participating in this carnival of destruction. Some, in their letters and diaries, produced the arguments of their officers and their commander: It was Jeff Davis's fault; or the Southern people had fallen into a dangerous delusion and had to be

shocked out of it. But if somehow, a century and a third after the event,
we could quiz those twenty-year-olds whose fresh and guileless faces
look out at us from the old tintypes, and ask them why they did such
things, most likely a mischievous smile would come to those faces, and
they would tell us it was "fun."

And what of the chief vandal, the "Attila of the West," as H. L.
Mencken would one day call him? Wherein lies his responsibility or his
guilt, if such there was? Those men who saw foraging as a freewheeling
activity probably felt they had at least the tacit support of General Sherman. A story made the rounds in any number of versions that Sherman
met a bummer carrying an outlandish piece of booty. The bummer
greeted his commander with a smile and the words: "forage liberally on
the country." In fact there is testimony that Sherman himself told the
story. General Jefferson C. Davis, talking with Henry Hitchcock about
"straggling, burning, etc.," said: "The belief in the army is that General
S. favors and desires it, and one man when arrested told his officer so."
Hitchcock was developing a great admiration for Sherman; for a time he
preferred to blame junior officers for failing to enforce the terms of Special Field Order No. 120, which were plain enough. But before the March
to Sea was over, he acknowledged a flaw in his idol: "I think Sherman
lacking in enforcing discipline. Brilliant and daring, fertile, rapid, he
does not seem to me *to carry out things* in this respect." Nor did this failure to follow through apply only to matters of discipline; Hitchcock saw
signs that Sherman was giving less attention to destruction of the railroads, and for that reason the job was less thoroughly done than it
should have been. The general needed help in "following up," and perhaps a better staff was the solution.

Albion Tourgee also made the march and reflected on it in the years
following the war. He admitted that his perspective was different, since
he spent the postwar years in the South and learned to see the army's
destructive course through the eyes of the victims. He placed all the
blame for the army's excesses squarely on General Sherman's shoulders:
"By seeming to forbid, and failing to prevent, he left the blame to fall
upon the men, who, without the encouragement of such tacit approval,
would never have dreamed of perpetrating such acts. As a consequence
the opprobrium falls upon the soldiers, instead of resting where it ought,
upon the General." This argument supposes in Sherman a guile that
does not accord well with his character as his biographers have revealed
it or indeed as it has emerged in this study; the man certainly had his
flaws, but deceit was hardly one of them. Then too, both Hitchcock and
Tourgee assume that with the right actions taken by Sherman, the men

would quickly have mended their ways, the provisions of Special Field Orders Nos. 119 and 120 would have been scrupulously observed. This is highly unlikely, given the mindset of this army and its well-established proclivities. In truth, it was the men themselves, sweeping through the Georgia countryside in large groups or small, who really fixed the parameters of desolation—who decided whether a house should be burned or whether a widow with small children should be allowed to keep her cow. And had the saintly O. O. Howard commanded in Sherman's place, they would have done no differently.

It was Sherman who conceived of the march and who argued successfully for it. Since the operation could only be carried out by drawing sustenance from the population, from the moment his project was agreed to, the desolation of some portion of Georgia was assured—and in that sense the general became the author of that desolation. Despite the discrepancy between Sherman's orders and their execution, the pattern of destruction was similar to that occurring elsewhere as Union armies moved through areas with hostile populations and abundant resources—in the Shenandoah Valley, for example, where Grant wanted the inhabitants reduced to such straits that they could give no aid to the rebellion.

Had the Confederates somehow won, had their victory put them in position to bring their chief opponents before some sort of tribunal, they would have found themselves justified (as victors generally do) in stringing up President Lincoln and the entire Union high command for violation of the laws of war, specifically for waging war against noncombatants. The discreetly circulated instruction of April 30, 1864, would have been among the documents the prosecution laid before the tribunal.

By popular demand Sherman would have been the first defendant in the dock. Albert Castel has pointed out that while the general was carrying out a policy his superiors sanctioned and urged on others, his "knack for pithy phraseology"—his pledge to "make Georgia howl," for example—brought him special notoriety. Other generals could conduct campaigns of desolation, but none with the zest and verve of Sherman.

His trial would have been memorable. He would have made a vigorous defense—one can picture him lecturing his accusers, his words coming in torrents. Those words would have served to fix the noose more securely about his neck, for he would have demonstrated that what he did was not only necessary and inevitable, it was also mete and just. All that the Southern people had suffered was but atonement for the original sin of secession.

14

◆

The Victims

As Sherman's troops filed into Milledgeville an old black woman called out to them: "God bless you, yous come at last. We've been waitin' for you all for more'n four years." Northern soldiers were frequently surprised by the knowledge Georgia slaves seemed to have about the war and how it was going. Henry Hitchcock was particularly impressed with a young black woman he met near Stanfordsville, whom he found "smart as a steel trap. She hid and fed three of our men, escaped prisoners: knew about Burnside, McClellan, and Sherman, also the fall of Atlanta, and even the recent unsuccessful rebel attack there." On December 2 General Sherman had a conversation with a black man about fifty years old "who spoke with remarkable clearness and great fluency." He told Sherman he was well-aware of the Emancipation Proclamation, and he also informed him that Andrew Jackson had won the Battle of New Orleans thanks to a black man who had suggested he use cotton bales as breastworks for his men—yet that slave probably had never heard of Frederick Douglass, the most well-known figure of his race in the country.

Nor, closer to home, did the blacks understand at first that their liberators were just passing through and could not take thousands of freed slaves with them: "It was useless to tell them to stay at home, that they would be freed by the war wherever they might be, and that the troops could not feed them. With a blind faith, they persisted in the journey, braving all hardships." For whatever knowledge the slaves of Georgia possessed about what was happening beyond the horizon of the village or plantation where they lived reached them in clandestine, garbled fashion, and was distorted further by a deliberate campaign of disinformation on the part of their masters. After the fall of Atlanta, particularly, whites told their slaves that the Yankees had locked black men in buildings that they then set afire, or they sold the "servants" they captured to a heartless regime of bondage in Cuba. Henry Hitchcock was particularly incensed at these rumors floated among Georgia's slave population, but drew some satisfaction from the assurances of blacks he talked to that they put no stock in such tales.

Yet some doubts remained in their minds, for the image of the black population flying en masse to meet Sherman's columns is not historically accurate. Sherman said as many as seventy thousand joined his columns at one point or another, but this figure is probably far too high. General Williams, who kept a close eye on the Twentieth Corps, estimated that from six thousand to eight thousand joined the column from beginning to end, with only twenty-five hundred or so accompanying it when it went into camp before Savannah. If the other corps had similar numbers of blacks with them, the total quantity with the various columns would not be half of the figure Sherman gave. Since the thirty-odd counties that Sherman's columns passed through between Atlanta and Savannah contained some 150,000 slaves in 1860, it is likely that only a minority succumbed to the temptation to flee to the Yankees. It was just as well that most blacks played a waiting game, for flight to the Northern columns imposed serious hardships on those who undertook it, and most of them did not make it to Savannah: Many were obliged to return to an uncertain welcome on the farms and plantations they had fled. They were thus among the victims of a campaign waged at least partially on their behalf.

That was not the impression held by the rank and file of Sherman's army. They marveled at the way slaves would be waiting for them at country crossroads, and they believed that the blacks had some sort of mysterious intelligence system to spread word of the Yankees' coming, with swift runners coursing through the night. Blacks who joined the column told them that from the moment the Northern troops' coming was known, there was only one question they asked each other when they met: "Is you gwine?" As the appearance of so many blacks along the line of march was a moving sight, so the urge to assume the role of liberator was strong in some officers and soldiers; an officer named Whittle, attached to General Howard's staff, was hurrying on an errand near the village of Scarboro when he saw ahead of him some thirty blacks, gathered at the gate leading to an impressive mansion; nearby stood their mistress, "with pale and frightened visage." As for the slaves, they were following his approach with both excitement and expectation:

> Partaking of the inspiration of the scene, I reined up my horse and stretching out my hand said in an earnest, solemn manner "In the name of Abraham Lincoln I proclaim these colored people henceforth and forever free." The souls of those poor people seemed looking from their eyes as they bent eagerly forward and uttered a broken "Yes, Massa," as I rode on.

On the plantation where Martha Colquitt was then a young girl, she and the other slaves received what must have been a dizzying lesson in freedom and equality from a foraging party:

> Dey busted down de smokehouse door and told her (my mother) she was free now to help herself to anything she wanted, 'cause everything on de plantation was to b'long to de slaves dot had worked dar. Dey took grandma to de kitchen and told me to give her some of de white folkses dinner. Ma said "but de white folks aint et yet." "Go right on," de Yankees said, "and give it to her de best in de pot. . . ."

Yet the foraging parties could give a totally different impression to the blacks on a plantation. Slaves often found their own cabins were ransacked as completely as their master's houses; as one soldier said of the bummers, "color is no protection from these rough-riders." Nor did they hesitate to threaten a slave in order to find where his master's treasure was. One forager explained that it was only necessary to say: " 'Now out with it, or you'll hear a dead nigger fall,' presenting a gun at the same time. It works like a charm, the negro begs and agrees to tell."

The slaves who left their masters and joined the columns got at best a mixed reception. Sherman did not hesitate to tell others of the exalted status he held among the black refugees. "They regard me as a Second Moses or Aaron," he wrote an acquaintance; but at the same time he was exasperated at them for "clogging my roads and eating my subsistence." Officially, able-bodied males were welcome because their labor was needed in the pioneer corps of each column, and in that role they could draw rations. All others were discouraged from following the columns, though the method used varied from one column to another. General Williams said that "the decrepid, the aged, and the feeble were told of the long journey before them, and advised to remain behind," but in no way threatened. General Jefferson C. Davis employed more forcible means: When the column came to a stream that had to be bridged, the army passed over but the pontoons were removed before the mass of blacks following behind could use them (this practice eventually drew much public indignation and invective down on the general's head).

A considerable number of blacks managed to find places within the column itself. Before long the pioneer corps was essentially a black force, and it was their labor that removed obstacles as the army approached the coast—they cleared away trees the Rebels had felled across the roads, or chopped down trees themselves and used their trunks to "corduroy" otherwise impassable routes. Considerable numbers of black men became body servants of officers, for the authorities were very complaisant on this score; others found tenuous status as guides, teamsters, and cooks. Blacks also assumed foraging duties here and there. A soldier noted in his diary on November 21: "Our collored folks are out forgeing. just what sucksess they will have is yet to be seen." In at least one instance a slave took part in skirmishing, though the officer who had taken him into his service told him the men wouldn't like "to see negroes fighting alongside them"; others simply pleaded successfully for permission to stay with the column because they had pressing business in Savannah; their masters or their wives were there. Finally, there are occasional veiled references to black women carried along discreetly in the wagons as "dark houries," the mistresses of officers. Some men were intrigued by the idea of keeping blacks as sources of labor in the future. James Dunn, the Pennsylvania surgeon, wrote his wife he could get her a Negro girl who "can do more work than any hired girl you can get." He told her: "Walter has got a boy about the size of Jim, and intends to take him home with him when he leaves, which will be in another month."

As the soldiers encountered masses of blacks alongside the road, they would often call: "Come on, Sambo," "Come on, Dinah," and the invitation would be accepted joyfully. "Our soldiers urged them to come along with us," an officer lamented, "without stopping to think how they will manage to make their way to freedom." While the blacks who fled to the columns could expect sympathy and kind treatment from many soldiers, others found them objects of curiosity: "They were asked many questions," wrote a soldier named Downing; he himself said he was struck by their "odd remarks." Another soldier noted: "Have been hearing negro talk this evening." To a good many soldiers the blacks were primarily a source of amusement. In the diaries and letters there are references to the army's "sable cloud," its "corps d'Afrique," or "our Nigger Brigade"—the comic relief in a long march. "It was rich," Jacob

Hartness wrote his wife, "to see the negroes flock to the road to see us pass, and richer still to see the boys make them pull off their hats and coats and dance while we were passing."

The images that come down to us of Georgia's blacks in that momentous fall of 1864 were almost all supplied by their white contemporaries, and among those images the childlike innocent and the buffoon predominate. But occasionally whites captured their earnestness and their aspirations. George Pepper had a conversation with a black Georgian who asked only for a life in which he could have the fruits of his own labor: "All I ask is to have my own sweat; and if I could get that, I'd work for my wife and children and never trouble nobody." And Joel Chandler Harris, who has left us the amiable, hat-in-hand figure of Uncle Remus, also had a vivid memory of an old black couple he found in a corner of fence, not far from the road Sherman's army had just passed:

> "Who is that lying there?" asked Joe.
> "It my old man, suh."
> "What is the matter with him?"
> "He dead, suh, But bless God he died free."

The departure of the slaves from their plantations was not totally unexpected by their masters; for some time rumors had come from neighboring states of slaves running away to Union forces operating in the vicinity. Still, when it happened there was a sense of shock, for most left quietly, without elaborate preparations or goodbyes. "It must be excruciatingly painful," wrote one Northern officer, "for the slaveholders to see their property walk off thus, thousands of dollars at a time." Perhaps so, but in his immediate reaction to the news of a slave's departure the owner rarely mentioned the loss in dollars. The mistress of one plantation, Myrta Lockhart Avary, recalled: "We went to sleep one night with a plantation full of negroes, and woke to find not one on the place." Along with the shock, Mrs. Avary felt disappointment: "We had thought there was a strong bond of affection on their side as well as on ours." Joel Chandler Harris wrote that the slaves who most often slipped away were "the younger ones, especially those who by reason of their field work, had not been on familiar terms with their master and mistress." But the more trusted servants, those who spent much of their time in the circle of the master's family, could also go, and in circumstances that were particularly painful or infuriating to their masters and mistresses. Margaret Ketcham Ward believed there was a pattern in such defections: "Those that we depended most upon and trusted and believed they would stay with us through it all were the first to go." Dr. Massey would have agreed. He had a slave named Hercules, whom everyone called "Harkless"; so much faith did Massey put in his servant that when Sherman's troops entered Milledgeville he gave Harkless his watch for safekeeping. But Harkless left with the Union troops, and though he came and told his master, and also told him where the watch was hidden, Massey regarded him as an "ingrate." Massey may have been particularly incensed because one of his acquaintances had a slave who had given spectacular proof of loyalty: The man had confided three thousand dollars in gold to a servant for safekeeping and then had departed Atlanta, leaving the slave to make his own way. His faithful servant found him some months later and turned over the money intact save for a few cents spent to pay a ferryman.

Most slaves who departed left quietly, often under cover of night, but there were occasions when a slave in whom great trust was placed surprised his or her owner with a stunning "betrayal," usually triggered when a Federal foraging party arrived on the plantation. When the Yankees were preparing to leave again, the planter would be astounded to see a trusted servant mounted on one of the plantation horses, ready to ride off with the enemy soldiers. Worse yet, the moment of truth might come when the owner explained to his visitors in his most convincing manner that his draft animals and food stocks had been taken by Wheeler's cavalry, only to have a "boy" he had owned for twenty years step forward and announce that the horses and mules were tied in the creek bottom and the bacon and hams buried under a haystack. A slave who did such a thing was well-advised to leave with the Northern troops, for the owner's anger could know no bounds. An officer of the 103rd Illinois wrote in his diary for December 5, 1864:

A nice yellow girl came to our regiment about an hour after dark. She is the property of Milly Drake, who lives thirty miles back. The girl showed our men where Milly hid her horses and mules, in return for which, after the column passed, gentle Milly took half a rail and like to wore the wench out. Broke her arm and bruised her shamefully.

Captain Horace Tarr of the Twentieth Connecticut long remembered the answer he got when he asked a slave to reveal to him the location of a hidden corral where his master kept his horses. The man refused, saying: "I am too old to go with you's, and I am too young to stay here an' be murdered."

When a slaveholder decided to take family and what possessions he could and move out of the path of the invaders, he usually left a few slaves to "look after" the place, and Northern soldiers noticed that these were usually the old and the infirm. In a household without slaves the family simply closed the door behind them, perhaps locking it and reflecting on the futility of their gesture as they did so. As had been the case in North Georgia, the decision to stay or to flee was often made at the last moment and was influenced by the rumors then current. William Gibbs McAdoo had foreseen the need for a "refuge" a year before, and had selected what seemed to be a remote plantation for that purpose, but when Sherman's forces approached Milledgeville he left his family in their path, fleeing himself with a few especially valuable possessions. Most had no refuge prepared, and some took off with no fixed destination. Such was the case with the Louisiana refugee Louise Clack, whose wanderings had brought her to the vicinity of Milledgeville. Her group was composed of four white women, several children, and several slaves, including the only male in their party, an old man named— almost inevitably—Uncle Sambo.

The women of the Clack household held a "council of war" and decided that since they had already lost their home and most of their possessions, they should try to save what they had left by moving out of Sherman's path; Mrs. Clack's sister Maddie became "commander in chief" and supervised the preparations. They loaded three unsprung country wagons: one with provisions, one with their trunks and the majority of the servants, and one for the family, disposed on seats made of bags and bundles of fodder. They planned to leave at daybreak, but in the night someone brought word that the enemy was expected to arrive in the morning. Scrambling about to complete the last-minute tasks, they rolled off within the hour, and as they passed neighbors' houses they saw lights on in them too, signifying others had gotten the same message. Mrs. Clack remembered the weather as "raw and sleeting," so everyone was huddled under oilcloths. They traveled some forty miles from Milledgeville, probably to the west, where they found a hotel in a small town and rented sleeping space in the parlor, the only room left. They had met many other wagonloads of people in flight on the road, and now they found the hotel jammed with fellow refugees. They bedded down in the hotel parlor for three nights, and then headed back toward Milledgeville, being obliged on their return to pass over the track of Sherman's army. Here they suffered a calamity. A slave named Aunt Hetty had been driving the provisions wagon; when they awoke after camping for the night Aunt Hetty was gone, and so was the wagon (they never learned what had happened either to the servant or to their wagon and team). They were now out of provisions. "At every house or shanty, as we went along, we inquired for food, but the same reply was always given by the inmates—they did not know where they were to get food for themselves." When the houses were empty, Uncle Sambo would forage about, but without luck. The last night out the women took the cornstarch they had been using for facepowder, mixed it with water, and gave it to the children. The adults had an ounce of tea to share, but no pot to make it in; theirs had disappeared with Aunt Hetty, and those whom they asked said Sherman's troops had taken away their cooking vessels as well as their food. Finally Uncle Sambo found a woman with an eight-gallon iron pot she agreed to let them use, "and in this he made our ounce of tea, over a pine fire in the road—the owner of the pot standing by all the time, lest we should run away with her treasure. She had the candor to tell us she would not trust us any more than she would the Federals." They made it back to Milledgeville and found their house intact, though bearing signs of more than one visit by the invaders. Their neighbors had buried provisions before fleeing, and returning to find them undisturbed, they gladly shared with the Clack household. With a roof over their heads again and something to eat, Mrs. Clack and her kin took stock: "Though we were still suffering from the effects of our journey, we were thankful that we had taken it."

For those who chose to stay, as much as for those who fled, there were preparations to be made, and for this purpose people needed to know where the enemy was and if and when he could be expected, but reliable accounts of the enemy's movements were not easy to come by, especially in the first few days of the march. Mrs. Elizabeth Reid, who lived on a Jasper County plantation near the town of Monticello, wrote her brother on November 16 that the confusion and panic over the Federal army's movements were worse than they had been back in the summer when the cavalry raids were under way: "We are in a worse stew, about the Yankees, than we've ever been yet. Yesterday a report came to town that they were advancing, on Macon, in a large body and would, probably, pass through Monticello. I think, however, 'twasn't credited. . . ."

The recipient of this letter, Joseph Addison Turner, lived at Turnwold Plantation in Putnam County, where among other things he operated a hat factory and published a weekly paper known as *The Countryman*. He recorded the state of confusion that reigned there over the next few days:

> During Thursday, and Friday, we continued to hear various rumors, some of which were wild and extravagant, indeed. . . . We were left

completely in the dark, as to whether we ought to undertake to do anything, but just stay, and take it, as it would come—though we really hoped, and believed, it would not come at all.

By Saturday morning Turner had just about convinced himself that his plantation was out of danger when he received a note from a neighbor, who had been talking with a man who passed his place fleeing south; the man said the Yankees were moving in three separate columns, one of which could well pass through their section of Putnam County: "He advised to remove all you could, as they were destroying everything." In the end Turner only sent his mules off to be hidden in the swamp: "For ourself, we determined to remain, knowing that we were a citizen non-combatant, and take things as they came." Later on the inhabitants were better informed; rather quickly they took to sending out "scouts" and sharing what information they could glean with their neighbors; where there were telegraph offices, the operators relayed what news they received. After the first ten days Wheeler's cavalry assumed the task of alerting the population and helping them take the necessary measures.

It was widely expected in various quarters that those measures would include the application of a scorched earth policy and a generalized armed resistance to the invaders. General Grant had warned Sherman that if he made the march he risked being "bushwhacked by all the old men, little boys, and such railroad guards as are still at home," and now Governor Brown sent out a clarion call to arms in his proclamation of the *levée en masse*, while Confederate leaders sent strident appeals that were published in various newspapers. General Beauregard sent a call to arms addressed to "the People of Georgia": "Arise for the defense of your native soil! Rally around your patriotic Governor and gallant soldiers! Obstruct and destroy all roads in Sherman's front, flank and rear, and his army will soon starve in your midst." Georgia's delegation in the Confederate Congress sent a similar message: "Let every man fly to arms! Remove your negroes, horses, cattle, and provisions from Sherman's army, and burn what you cannot carry. Burn all bridges, and block up the roads on his route. Assail the invader in front, flank and rear." Even Robert E. Lee endorsed the idea in a letter to President Davis: "The population must turn out."

But the population of Georgia did not turn out. Most notably they did not rush off to answer Governor Brown's call to arms. Given the spreading confusion throughout the southern part of Georgia and the disruption of communications, many of the men may simply not have known they were called; but probably many others merely declined to leave their homes—with the enemy quite possibly headed in their direction they could not abandon their families. On December 5 Governor Brown sent an officer and six men to Sumter County to arrest all who "shirked," or "ignored" his proclamation; detachments were apparently sent into other counties as well, for Brown's General Order of December 19 speaks of "armed details sent to various counties to arrest and bring up persons refusing to respond. . . ." The *levée en masse* seems to have been a dead letter. As far as is known, no guerrilla bands were formed, nor was there much evidence of bushwhacking, though as a participant in the march pointed out, "it would have been easy and safe to fire into our columns." Foraging parties received fire from concealment from time to time, but whether it was a citizen or one of Wheeler's cavalrymen who fired on them they usually could not tell.

Here and there local men and boys joined in the fight, but first they usually joined Wheeler's cavalry, though the affiliation was an informal one. Berrien McPherson Zettler had been disabled by a wound at the second Battle of Manassas, and was working as a tax collector in South Georgia when the march began; told to shut down his operations, he took his horse and joined the Fourth Tennessee Cavalry. Fifteen-year-old Emory Speer of Macon was sent by his father to take refuge on an uncle's plantation, but on the road he met a cavalryman from Company K, Fifth Kentucky. The trooper was leading a mule and offered the boy a ride on it. They became fast friends, and Speer accepted the invitation to throw in his lot with the Kentuckians, keeping the mule as his mount and picking up a rifle for armament.

Then there was the "gallant old citizen" who went into battle with Wheeler's force one day early in December. His home had been burned the day before, and when General Wheeler asked him to serve as guide, he agreed.

He was not expected to arm himself, but still he voluntarily brought along his double barrel shotgun loaded with buckshot. We boys all laughed at the old man's belligerent intentions, and suggested to each other that we would have no more fighting to do, as the old "Cit" would kill out all of Sherman's army. Well, he was riding along with General Wheeler when the enemy made a charge. . . . The advance guard came rolling back before the enemy, and the old man was a little slow to commence a retreat, and in a moment's time his horse was shot dead under him. By the time he got himself disentangled from the dying animal the guard has passed him, and the

enemy was within a few steps of him. He instantly levelled his shotgun and fired two shots in rapid succession, killing a Yankee at each
shot, and one of them was the officer who led the charge.

The Federal charge immediately lost its impetus, and Wheeler and his
men came galloping back to rescue the old man. "He was very proud of
his feat, and feels that he has taken partial satisfaction for the burning of
his house and turning his family out of shelter."

If it was thus exceptional for the men of a locality on Sherman's route
to take up arms against the invader, it was equally uncommon for them
to do anything to slow the course of the invading army by sabotage. The
reason was a compelling one: The longer the enemy remained among
them the greater damage he would do; the image General Beauregard
conjured up of a Yankee army starving to death in their midst was
scarcely appealing. Thus there are very few cases where civilians are
known to have destroyed bridges in the army's path; in one case where
it was done the citizen was denounced by his neighbors and had his
property burned; in at least one instance when the destruction was by
military authority, local planters protested it would keep the Yankees in
their neighborhood longer.

But the great majority of Georgians who were to encounter Sherman's forces chose to do so at home, and for this encounter they took
what measures they could. In the case of a sizable plantation the preparations were elaborate and time-consuming, usually following the
same general scenario. What supplies were movable were carried off
and hidden. When the master did not feel he could trust his slaves, or
felt they might be frightened into revealing hiding places, he had to do
this work himself, and probably at night. The women decided what to
do with jewelry and household valuables and sometimes put on an
extra dress and clothed their children with a superfluity of garments—
in case the house was burned or garments carried off they would have
a change of clothing. The master or the overseer had the stock driven
off and horses and mules hidden, and then stood ready to depart himself on short notice to a spot where he would camp out until the crisis
was over, taking the able-bodied slaves with him. When there was no
white man on the plantation, the woman would try to carry out these
measures herself.

Most women understood that when the enemy appeared, any hostile
or provocative gesture on their part could cost them heavily—thus a
woman who rushed out and cut her own well rope as thirsty Northern
soldiers came through her gate could well have her house burned by the

furious bluecoats. When a family near Atlanta took in their well bucket and locked their doors the frustrated soldiers called out to them, pounded on the doors, and finally built a fire against one end of the house. The family came running out to put out the fire, claiming that they had been sleeping. Where a house was located on a road one of the columns was using, the soldiers' endless visits to fill their canteens could temporarily make the well run dry. But the visitors also explored the outbuildings and ventured up to the house itself. It was usually not possible for the occupants to keep watch over everything, so they tended to concentrate on keeping pilferers out of the house itself. Outside the house material losses could be massive as ten thousand or fifteen thousand men went by, helping themselves. On November 20 a soldier noted in his diary: "We camped last night on a plantation of 3,000 acres. . . . The fences were just sufficient to cook breakfast for the 17th Corps." An officer and the overseer of a large plantation fell to talking as soldiers loaded wagons with corn from the plantation's cribs. The overseer said he had harvested about thirty-three hundred bushels, worth eight dollars a bushel, but now "there would be nothing left in a few hours." Sherman himself sometimes suggested to people at whose places he stopped to move as much as they could into the house as the best way of holding on to it.

The woman of the house soon learned that if she kept her front door closed and her family inside, soldiers were not timid about coming in; if it was locked they would bang on it, threatening to break it down. When the house was on a road the army was marching on, the best solution seemed to be for the woman to take position on the front porch, to let soldiers know the house was occupied, and thus not theirs to enter as they wished. At the same time she could watch for a general officer, from whom she could sometimes solicit a safeguard to keep men out of the house. Some women were not chary about inviting the general to have some refreshment or even pass the night in the house, for his presence brought a degree of protection. This was the case with Mrs. Bessie Cornwell, who had General Howard to tea, though she was struck by the incongruity of the scene: "While General Howard sat at the table and asked God's blessing, the sky was red from the flames of burning houses." She invited General Howard to stay the night, but he declined, and she saw her protection on the point of vanishing. But Mrs. Cornwell had a piano, and that proved her salvation. The officers accompanying General Howard had formed a chorale of sorts, and they liked piano accompaniment, so they stayed on and sang while Sherman's army tramped by.

There were a number of episodes on the march in which the arrival of the invaders seemed curiously like a reception for out-of-town guests. D. W. Whittle, one of the musically inclined officers on General Howard's staff, wrote that members of the group would knock on doors as soon as they arrived in any locality where they were going to spend the night, looking for a household with a piano, then secure an invitation for the evening. Whittle's accounts describe these as gay evenings, though their hosts, like Mrs. Cornwell, probably regarded their guests as a lesser evil. Nor was it impossible for romantic feelings to be kindled in this environment. An officer named Wimer Bedford spent an evening in the parlor of a Mrs. Hollister, in the town of Gordon, and there he and other Northern officers were completely taken with Miss Mary Folsom, even though she "persists in believing the cause of secession a holy one & fervently prays for our confusion or downfall." The admiring Bedford said of her: "She possesses the refinement and elegant taste to couch her strong feelings in unoffending and polite language." The officers rode south the next morning, all of them regretting that they had to leave "such pleasant society."

Any number of Georgia women must have met an officer named James Edmonds that November. For him the march was a succession of romantic encounters, carefully noted in his diary. Near Lithonia he spotted a pretty girl while setting out pickets and struck up acquaintance. They "had a rattling good conversation for 2 hours, though she smoked a pipe." The next day he spotted a woman with a "pretty foot and ankle" outside Conyers and lingered some time at the plantation of a Mr. Thomas, admiring his daughters, "both good looking and one finely developed bust." A little later he almost lost his heart to a Miss Glen; he encountered some "fine looking women" at Covington, and Sandtown was memorable because of Miss Minerva. But Edmonds's attentions were not always well received. At Shady Dale, at the home of a Mrs. Sparks, something went awry; just what it was Edmonds's diary does not indicate, only that the Sparks ladies "insulted both the Gen'l and myself by language which no well bred ladies would use."

A Miss Harris, who lived in Milledgeville, wrote her brother that during their stay Northern troops had made certain overtures to the young women of the town. Some tried to start a conversation by inquiring if the women were "secesh." According to Miss Harris "some of the miserable wretches went to see some of the girls and asked them to attend a large ball they intended giving. One lady told an officer she did not suppose a white lady would go, that maybe some of the negro wenches would grace the occasion." Miss Harris was not among those invited to attend; she told her brother that while the Yankees were in town she "tried to look as ugly as possible."

While such dalliance could take place where the columns halted in towns and villages, in the outlying countryside, where forage parties showed up at isolated houses, the "rules of engagement" were different. The woman's conduct was affected by her sense of isolation before a group of strange men who were "the enemy." She usually adopted a manner that was polite but formal and distant. The foragers, for their part, were also on the qui vive, especially if they were few in number; they were, after all, in enemy country. One veteran forager said that if the woman or women in the house were cordial and seemed in no hurry for the intruders to leave, it was a pretty good sign that they had sent word to Wheeler's men, and the foraging party had best wrap up its business and move on; if they were attacked, the chances were it would go hard for them. (In one bloody shootout at a house near Milledgeville the Confederate cavalrymen had shot foragers inside a house, including one concealed under a bed; when one Yankee grabbed a woman as a shield, she called on her rescuers to shoot him anyway, and someone managed to get a clear shot at his head, splattering his brains over his hostage.) But one Northern soldier named Marcellus Darling, who was trapped inside a house when the Rebels arrived, came back telling a remarkable tale. He was in the house with a young woman and her mother when there was a flurry of shots outside, the rest of the "boys" took off, and a party of Wheeler's cavalry came thundering up. Darling dived under a bed and watched breathless as Rebels passed where he lay hidden, his face not a foot from their muddy boots. He heard them ask if there were any more Yankees about—and he heard the young woman answer no. After they departed he was obviously in great haste to leave also. But for the rest of his life he remembered the episode: "As stories go I should have married that little southern girl but I didn't. . . . It was the sweetest lie I ever heard, and I still love that little liar."

Though it was uncommon for the occupants of a house to attack foragers who descended on them, it did happen. An old man could become enraged and bring out his shotgun, for example. R. H. Strong claimed that if males succeeded in slipping away from farms and plantations that foragers came to, they would try to get help and return "and creep up on the unsuspecting soldiers. They would kill whole small parties of foragers and bury them in the woods. Not half of the worst side of it have I told, nor will I tell." Georgians who wrote about their experiences when Sherman came through have even less to say about these shootings than Northern sources, since for a period after the war they could lead to charges of murder. There is one curious account of the killing of two of Sherman's bummers when they showed up at a plantation. Those who killed them then had to do something with the bodies, and may have ruled out burial because of the Northern soldiers' propensity for digging into freshly turned earth. They found a solution to their problem in their cotton press, which they used to pack the two bodies inside bales of cotton. A sign was placed on the two bales saying: "not to be sold." Later, through some mix-up, the bales were sold and shipped abroad, where the bodies were found.

Most of the things the foragers sought, for official purposes at least, would be in smokehouses, pens, barns, and cribs, and if these places did not yield much, then they would try to find where the family had hidden them, and more often than not they would be successful. The "citizens" were at something of a disadvantage here, first because the livestock and foodstuffs were not easy to conceal, and secondly because they had little experience in secreting things so they would not be found, while the soldiers had great experience in finding them. When Captain Horace Tarr of the Twentieth Connecticut took a foraging party to a plantation not far from Augusta, he asked the woman of the house if she had anything hidden. Hardly had she said no when Tarr's men came up with several trunks they had pulled up from the bottom of a dry well. The trunks contained only dresses, so Tarr let her keep them. He could not resist teasing her about the episode as he was taking his leave. She replied: "Oh, Captain, these are times to try a Christian's heart." He nodded in agreement, saluted, and rode off to search elsewhere.

Since bulky items could best be hidden underground, the men looked for any sign that earth had recently been turned and often found it. Burying valuables in false "graves" was an old ploy to Sherman's veterans; back in June a party had pulled half a ton of hams from a carefully tended gravesite in North Georgia. The Confederates did similar exploring from time to time. One Georgia soldier wrote in September: "Our boys the night we left Atlanta dug into a newly made grave in the militia camp and found a number of valuables. We are *heavy* on graves." So Sherman's men checked the graveyards on their march, and in freshly dug plots they found any quantity of crates and boxes—and any quantity of cadavers. When they went to former Governor Johnson's plantation, where the pickings were suspiciously thin and there was no evidence of burial about, the foragers forced a slave to reveal the location of the missing possessions—under a carefully tended bed of cabbages. One of the foragers acknowledged that "the ex-Gov had worked it pretty sharp."

When the foragers insisted on coming into her house, a woman could not use her body to bar them from entering, for to do so would be to invite physical contact; for the same reason she could not block their movements once they were inside the house. At best, members of the family could accompany the soldiers as they searched here and there, in hopes that their hovering presence would have some inhibiting effect on the intruders. Some women did not have the self-control to hold their tongues while strangers pawed through and perhaps pocketed their possessions. R. H. Strong, who wrote extensively about his foraging experiences, said of the plantation women he encountered: "Some were rabid rebels and took no pains to conceal it, but all were polite to us except when we were searching their houses." Then he and his men would be called "Lincoln's hirelings, Yankee scum, and bluebellied sons of b-s," and other names Strong said he could not write in his memoirs, probably because they were written for his mother. He remembered one woman threatened to scald them with a kettle as they began to search under her beds, but they told her if she did such a thing they would burn her house. At this threat "she changed her mind." This menace seems to have been made far more often than it was carried out, perhaps because the threat almost invariably produced the desired effect.

The ransacking of the home was for its mistress a particularly outrageous act, a kind of violation. The letters in which women recounted the despoiling of their homes often go into the greatest detail, as though each loss were an injury, a wound. A Mrs. Walton wrote her daughter such a letter after bummers swept through her home in Monroe County:

> The Yankees broke and split up two of my bureau drawers, split up one of my secretary doors, they opened up one of your bundles I don't know what was in it, too[k] the things. They took all my meat, sugar, coffee, flour, knives & forks, spoons all they could get to. . . . They broke up my caster, carried off the pepper box top, stamped the caster & broke it. Tell Mary they took the ambrotype she gave me of Joe's, they took all my corn, hogs, killed the goats, took chickens, broke open every trunk I had in the house. . . . They took my homespun dress & one smarter one, took all my shoes and stockings, my scarf and the silk that was left of my dress. They got my needles, thimble, scissors & thread. . . .

Though the letter was written three months after the event, one senses that the inventory is a complete one, that each item would be remembered as long as Mrs. Walton drew breath. When Mary Jane Crawford reminisced in 1912 about the ransacking of her house almost a half-century earlier she confessed: "my indignation still gets at fever heat when I talk about it." And one senses that for her, as for Mrs. Walton and all the other women of Georgia who suffered that kind of violation, each thimble and ambrotype would be charged in eternity to the personal account of William Tecumseh Sherman.

Was such an experience the worst violation a Georgia woman could expect to endure? Given the preoccupation over "outrage," the euphemism usually employed to signify rape, how was it that the man of the family, if there was one in residence, could leave a wife or daughter to face the "vandal horde" alone? The answers to these two questions are related, and by addressing the second we can arrive at the answer to the first. Despite the impression the Northern troops held that all the men were gone, there were considerable numbers in the Georgia countryside. A sizable quantity were "hideouts," either from the conscription officer or from the provost marshal; others were furloughed, recovering from wounds, or exempted from service for one reason or another, and then there were the "old citizens," in their late fifties and older, many of whom were still vigorous.

Apparently some feared they would be taken up simply because they were of military age. Outside of Milledgeville a loyalist named Vaughn had a long conversation with General Sherman, telling him among other things that "all the men hereabouts are hiding out" because they feared the Yankees "would take them prisoner." But there was a more compelling reason, one that acted on a man named Zettler, who left his daughter to face the Yankees because, as she put it: "Father, hearing of the tortures to which old men were being subjected in order to extort money and valuables from them, had decided to remain out of the way until the army had passed." There were a good many stories current in the Southern press about men being "strung up" to make them talk, and a sufficient number of these quasi-lynchings related in Northern sources, for the concern to have been genuine. Other men were vague about why they acted as they did. A planter named Thomas Maguire wrote his son that he had simply "thought it best" to camp in the woods for two days and one night while Mrs. Maguire stayed at the house: "Gen. S. made his headquarters in the yard, eat in the House, your Mother with his presence was able to keep the Soldiers out of the house." In many other cases the motive for the man's leaving is no clearer than that of Mr. Maguire, but what is clear is a consistent pattern of behavior.

This particular response to the threat Sherman's army posed is plainly not a sign of generalized poltroonery in Georgia's male population, for figures published that year showed Georgia leading all the other Southern states in the number of its sons killed in battle. Moreover it is evident in some cases that the man accepted his role of absentee reluctantly, being pushed into it by other family members; we have already seen the truculence of some "old citizens" and the violence they were capable of if not gotten out of the way before the bluecoats appeared. And they must have been anything but comfortable in their role, if we may judge from the agitation of William McAdoo, as revealed by his diary entries. He left his wife and children in Milledgeville only at what he deemed the last moment, then appears to have changed his mind while on the road and started back, only to revert to his original plan when he met and talked with other men fleeing the town. He did arrange to send a reassuring message to his wife by a slave going to Milledgeville. Then somewhere on the road a horrible realization came to him: "I remembered that I had left some popular anatomical and physiological books illustrated in such a way that I feared if vicious minded Federal soldiers saw the plates their passions would be roused and they might be led to outrage my wife." He thereupon sent his own servant Jim back to Milledgeville with a warning to Mrs. McAdoo—who in any event came through Sherman's passage unscathed.

Though there may not have been a "family council" to decide what measures a household should take when Sherman's men appeared in the vicinity, one has the impression that the man's temporary departure was part of a prearranged plan based on the assumption that if the man stayed there was appreciable risk that some form of violence would be visited on him, and that if the woman received the invaders there was no appreciable risk that she would be subjected to bodily harm. The woman probably counted upon a frail and defenseless appearance to evoke feelings of sympathy among the bluecoats who descended upon her home, for she often heightened the effect by casting herself as a widow when she had no right to that title. To most Union soldiers the large number of widows accorded well with the very small number of men they saw in South Georgia, but at least one bluecoat was suspicious. Cy Titus wrote: "I never saw so many widows in my life. Go up to a house and ask the Lady where her husband is. The reply in nine out of ten would be he was dead." Titus listened politely to the woman's explanations, then mulled them over in his mind and decided in many cases that the woman could not have been telling the truth, for the ages of her children and other details did not fit with her story—but he never pointed this out to her.

In thus meeting the invaders alone, the woman no doubt calculated

that she could preserve her home and also keep her virtue intact, a calculation that appears to have been essentially sound. The number of
rapes that occurred during Sherman's passage through Middle and
South Georgia can never be known. That some occurred is undeniable,
since there is solid evidence in two or three cases. Joseph Glatthaar, who
searched Federal court-martial records, concluded such transgressions
were "rare." One could argue that in an age in which the word "rape"
was rarely pronounced and the act it represented spoken of only in
whispers, these cases preserved in court-martial records could be the
small tip of an immense iceberg. But in fact the question of rape came up
from time to time in soldiers' letters and diaries; two officers, Harvey
Reid and Henry Hitchcock, made frequent inquiries on this subject,
which particularly concerned them; Hitchcock did not hesitate to quiz
corps commanders on the subject. Both were convinced that instances of
rape were rare. D. W. Whittle, who was well-placed to know of such
things in Howard's columns, said he received his first report of rape on
December 3; the perpetrator was unknown but every effort would be
made to "find the scoundrel." Northern soldiers brought the subject up
too, saying that rapes did occur, but almost never providing the circumstances; in some cases what they wrote appear to be the prurient specu-
lations of men who had been too long separated from their wives.

The widespread references to "outrage" in correspondence of the
period can be misleading, for it had several applications; thus when
Mary Gay, a witness to the Federal occupation of Decatur, wrote of "outrages and indignities too revolting to mention," she was not referring to
wholesale sexual assault, but to the way her parlor looked after a ransacking by Garrard's cavalry. The specific matter of rape was occasionally treated in letters Georgians wrote one another, and we must assume
it was the topic of conversation. The only case specifically mentioned in
the period of the march that seems to have been widely known occurred
in the countryside near Milledgeville, when two Northern soldiers raped
Mrs. Kate Nichols, the wife of a captain in the Confederate army. As a
result of the experience she lost her mind and spent the rest of her life in
an asylum; so at least the story comes to us, for there was no legal action,
and the affair seems to have been unknown to Union army authorities at
the time. By the end of the campaign it was mentioned in Southern
newspapers. It may well have been another "core incident," variously
embroidered and distorted as it was recounted until it appeared that
several women had lost their minds after sexual assaults. This seems to
be the case in the article a Texas soldier and war correspondent wrote his

newspaper: "Women, pure and spotless, were violated. Feeling the degradation of their dishonor, reason fled and they were maniacs."

There is another reason to believe that Georgia women felt secure in their persons, and that was their habit of hiding valuables, especially coins, jewelry, and watches in their clothes. Mrs. Clack and her sisters carried gold coins and diamonds, among other things. This custom, like burying things in graveyards, was well-known to old campaigners like the men in Sherman's armies, but while suspicious sepulchers were opened with impunity, only one case was found in which Northern soldiers were accused of stripping a woman and taking her jewelry—they fell into the hands of Wheeler's men, who shot them forthwith. There were close calls and curious episodes. One woman was apparently "frisked." Another was being questioned by foragers when a soldier gave her female servants the order to "close up." They thought he said "clothes up" and lifted their skirts, whereupon their mistress confessed she had some jewelry hidden in her dress. The foragers apparently allowed her to keep it.

Whatever the rumors that circulated in the last weeks of 1864, whatever stories were told afterward, it is significant that widespread rape was not to be among the charges Georgians so often leveled against the men of Sherman's army after the war, though it would have been a telling one, had they been able to justify it. It was not out of a spirit of forbearance that the people of Georgia looked back on their enemies of 1864 as only brutes, ruffians, thieves, incendiaries, and vandals.

15

❖

Aftermath

General Sherman considered the city of Savannah as already taken long before his army drew near it. There was a brief flurry of concern in the Union camp that General Longstreet and his corps had come from Virginia and were planning to attack from Augusta in conjunction with General Hardee's force inside Savannah, but very quickly it became clear that the report was false. Hardee would have to face sixty-two thousand Union troops with what Sherman described as a "mongrel" force, nine thousand men scraped up here and there. On December 13 Sherman watched from the roof of a rice mill as his men stormed and took Fort McAllister; this was in a sense the door to Savannah, since it opened Ossabaw Sound and communications with a Federal fleet; the army again had its "cracker line" back, as well as siege guns and munitions if it needed them. General Hardee received a summons to surrender and a warning that if Sherman was forced to lay siege to the town he would "make little effort" to keep his troops in hand once they took the city. Hardee, who had received instructions not to let his force be taken, slipped his little army out of the town during the night of December 20–21. The Confederates had no pontoon train with which to span the Savannah River, so they rigged one from rice flats and crossed to South Carolina.

The fall of Savannah was in striking contrast to that of Atlanta. Union occupation of the city took place virtually without incident, only minor looting being done by the city's blacks, or its Irish element, or Wheeler's departing horsemen, or the first Union soldiers to enter, depending on which source one reads. The city's population was relieved that its allegiance had been changed with so little damage or loss. Having taken the town intact, the Federals had an interest in keeping it that way, since it would be garrisoned and held. Federal military rule (General Geary was post commandant) proved to be evenhanded and generally beneficent; to add further to their good fortune, Savannah's citizens received a shipload of relief supplies from the North. As for Sherman's soldiers, "their duties were light; they were allowed the fullest liberty consistent with good order, and there was a continual round of sight-seeing and merry-making." To make the victory complete, they and their commander received the news that General Thomas had inflicted a terrible defeat on Hood's forces virtually under the walls of Nashville, Tennessee.

General Sherman was soon engrossed in his "Project for January," getting the army ready for what he called "another swath," this one to be cut across South Carolina by way of its capital, Columbia. The new "leg" of the march began in January. Sherman would later say that the destructiveness he brought to "the Cradle of Secession," when compared to what had been done in Georgia, was as ten is to one. By the time Lee surrendered at Appomattox, Sherman would be in the heart of North Carolina, facing what was left of the Army of Tennessee, and that tattered band would surrender in a matter of days.

While he paused in Savannah, the general was also compiling the record of what his forces had done in Georgia; his report and those of subordinate commanders were subsequently printed in the *Official Records*, where they make impressive reading. The army had wrecked three hundred miles of railway, as well as countless bridges and unnumbered miles of telegraph lines. It had seized five thousand horses, four thousand mules, and thirteen thousand head of cattle, taken for its use nine and a half million pounds of corn and ten and a half million pounds of fodder, destroyed cotton gins and mills without number, and done a total of one hundred million dollars' damage to the state's economy. These figures went into a "statistical summary" that Sherman put in his report for General Halleck, along with many others. Thus we learn that on the entire march Sherman's soldiers fired 1,245,000 cartridges, no more than they would have used during a couple busy weeks in the ditches before Atlanta, almost all of this fire being directed at hogs and chickens. We find that Sherman lost in casualties about one man in a hundred, including a number of "missing," many of whom slept—and still sleep—in obscure graves dug for them by those who shot them down in ambushes and running fights. As a postscript, the medical director of the Army of the Tennessee reported he had left "on the road" two men with broken thighs, "it being deemed impractical to transport them." What became of them is not known.

We have no statistics on losses prepared by Georgia or Confederate authorities with which to compare Sherman's figures. So complete was the confusion that descended upon the state that only in 1868 did Georgia's government begin compiling figures again in any meaningful way; not until the Federal Census of 1870 do we have a good statistical portrait of postbellum Georgia. By then the track of Sherman's army was difficult to follow in statistical terms; while the quantity of draft animals in the Georgia "swath" was catastrophically low as compared to 1860, the figures for other Georgia counties were hardly better. Given the way Sherman's men scattered over the countryside and the casual approach they took to their work of destruction, the figures he gives are open to question. While the length of track destroyed was easy enough to calculate, a good many of the other figures were probably pulled out of the air. Sherman's estimate of a hundred million dollars is similarly suspect, particularly since he was also quoted as saying the army destroyed a million dollars' worth of property per mile, which would add up to three times the sum he put in his final report. If we mark out the lines of march of his four corps, assume all the country between the columns was swept over, and add an additional five miles to each side of this swath for the roamings of foragers and bummers, it appears the area devastated was about 12 percent of Georgia's territory, including some extremely rich areas but also some very unproductive ones. Yet Sherman's figure of one hundred million dollars represents a full third of Georgia's total wealth in 1860, exclusive of slaves.

If we have no reliable statistical accounting of what Sherman's army did, there is no lack of testimony from those who followed its track. The accounts are selective and impressionistic, and uniformly devastating. One of the most compelling is from the pen of Fanny Andrews, who traveled across the state in December in the company of several others, including—incongruously enough—a couple on their honeymoon. They passed through the vicinity of Milledgeville just before Christmas, thus a month after the Federal host. Miss Andrews wrote:

About three miles from Sparta we struck the "Burnt Country," as it is well named by the natives, and then I could better understand the wrath and desperation of these poor people. There was hardly a fence left standing all the way from Sparta to Gordon. The fields were trampled down and the road was lined with the carcasses of horses, hogs, and cattle that the invaders, unable either to consume or to carry away with them, had wantonly shot down to starve out the people and prevent them from making their crops. The stench in some places was unbearable; every few hundred yards we had to hold our noses or stop them up with the cologne Mrs. Elzey had given us. . . . The dwellings that were standing all showed signs of pillage, and on every plantation we saw the charred remains of the gin-house and packing screw, while here and there lone chimney-stacks, "Sherman's Sentinels," told of homes laid in ashes.

Miss Andrews and her traveling companions encountered hundreds of Confederate soldiers along the roads, either traveling on foot or sitting along the roadsides eating what food they had been able to find: raw turnips, meat skins, parched corn, and the like. They met one man wrapped in a white blanket who implored them in "broken Dutch" to take him along; he was a recent recruit into the Union army who had become separated from his unit and from the entire column. The party took him along, deciding that otherwise he would be killed. They stopped at an inn where the proprietress had no food other than pickles, which she kept concealed in the chimney. Here and there they found a train that could be taken a short distance. Thus they were carried within sight of Macon, but the engineer refused to take the train into the city over a weakened trestle; after much argument the passengers got out to cross the span on foot. It was eighty feet high and nearly a half-mile long, but the whole party negotiated it successfully, including several women wearing hoops and a soldier on crutches. Through all these travails Miss Andrews showed neither despair nor fear, but she displayed a considerable anger: "If all the words of hatred in every language were lumped together into one huge epithet of detestation, they could not tell how I hate Yankees."

Somewhat later a Union officer crossed the state under a flag of truce with a Confederate escort, carrying dispatches to Washington concerning the surrender of Southern forces in Macon. He too followed Sherman's track, and he too felt the anger. Though he said little about conditions in the "burnt country" he spoke of the clear danger involved in his passage because of "popular feeling in the track of Sherman's march," and he also noted the "extreme anger" of the home guard units. As for the Confederate troops, the sight of his uniform provoked them to nothing more than lighthearted raillery: "Hello, Yank, come out o' them boots." "Climb down out o' that hat." "What're you dam Yanks doin' hur?" "Say, Yanks, does you'uns b'long to the hoss cavalry?" "Mister, did ye see anything dead up the branch?"

William McAdoo visited the area around Gordon and Macon at the very end of the year and found not anger but apathy and despair; the people were, in his opinion "submissionist." Just how defeatist the people of Georgia had been made by the catastrophe that struck their state is impossible to establish from the scattering of testimony that survives, though there are some poignant letters and petitions in Governor Brown's correspondence. Most likely there was a slow and steady erosion in morale rather than a collapse; that seems to be the pattern with most civilian populations when they are made to feel what Sherman called "the hard hand of war." If the general expected to "astonish" the people of Georgia and generate waves of panic and a universal cry of "Enough!" he was destined to be disappointed. Georgia did not howl.

There was a scapegoat of sorts, General Joseph Wheeler, whose cavalry had been the chief force opposing Sherman's advance. What enraged Georgians above all was that they had been plundered by Wheeler's men long before any Union foragers came into sight; worst of all, the Southern horsemen had taken livestock and destroyed provisions well outside the "swath," though in truth they could not know just where Sherman's columns were headed. The Milledgeville paper reported they had showed up there well after Sherman had departed, and then "loitered about."

The semidisgrace of General Wheeler did not absolve others of blame. Many Georgians, including a number of prominent figures, looked back on what had happened to them as above all else mortifying. The population had fled from Sherman's legions or had passively awaited their arrival, but they had done nothing to arrest the invader's progress. A Georgia soldier wrote home that he had received no letters "since that disgraceful march." "I feel very little inclined to call myself a Georgian any more, and if it were not that you all live in Macon I should disown the state in toto and transfer my allegiance."

When the Georgia legislature reconvened at the beginning of 1865 Governor Brown made a pained reference to the Georgians being "taunted" by the newspapers of neighboring states "because her people did not drive back and destroy the army of the enemy." A Texas soldier wrote home that the people of Georgia had appeared "paralized and set down at home and call upon President Davis to come to their help." He continued:

General Sherman ought to have been totally defeated and ruined, but the sad fact will be handed down to posterity that while Sherman's minions were devastating the country with fire and committing outrages upon defenceless women, the men of Georgia staid at home or at least a large portion of them, trying to save what they had. . . .

An editorialist in the *New York Times* commented on the "extraordinary apathy" of the people, who for the most part did not make "the smallest personal sacrifice in aid of the Confederacy, at the most important juncture in its history." They contrasted this pusillanimous conduct with the spirited resistance offered in the past by peoples such as the Russians and Tyrolese who harassed Napoleon's troops.

Such comments must have stung Georgians, and they must have been hard put to respond to them. Ford McWhorter recalled:

Just above Savannah one night while on picket duty about forty men came from South Carolina to enter service. They asked me what in the hell we meant by letting Sherman march through Georgia. I told them; allright, You will have a chance of it in a few days, for he is sure coming, and you will not be able to stop him either.

It was a good answer, for the people of South Carolina would not rise up against Sherman any more than the Georgians had, or any more than the people of Pennsylvania had opposed General Lee's columns on their way to Gettysburg. No one felt impelled to imitate the Russian peasants or the Tyrolese shepherds—or even the minutemen of Lexington and Concord. Had Sherman's army settled into South Georgia to stay, there is little doubt the area would have become another District of the Etowah; the inhabitants would have recovered from the initial shock, there would have been endless friction between conqueror and conquered, and that friction would have ignited the same guerrilla war that had smoldered from Ringgold to the Chattahoochee. But here it served Sherman's interest to pass through the country rapidly—and it also served the interest of the Georgians along his route to let him pass. Though their leaders sought salvation in stirring appeals and examples from the past, the people chose in that twilight of the Confederacy a path that was unheroic but essentially sound, trying, as the Texas soldier had put it, "to save what they had"—the only course that promised survival and renewal.

As the last bluecoats disappeared to the southeast and people began

to take stock, they took note of the curious quiet that pervaded the countryside: No roosters crowed, no cattle lowed, and there was scarcely a
dog left to bark. The invader also left in his wake a vacuum of power,
which was immediately noticeable in villages and towns. Here the symbols of order soon reappeared. Governor Brown returned to Milledgeville on December 2. He looked at the ruins of the penitentiary and
decided it would not be necessary to rebuild it. Whipping, branding,
and hanging would serve as well, with the noose for robbers, burglars,
and horse thieves. He discovered on his return that between his departure from the capital and Sherman's arrival, a number of inhabitants,
both black and white, had carried off furniture from the mansion as well
as other state property. He let it be known that he would not wait long
for its return before he began searching houses. In Rome the citizens got
together and decided to create a police force composed of every man
between the ages of sixteen and seventy; there were only thirty-eight of
them. They were able to maintain order of a sort inside the town, but a
body of irregular Confederate cavalry arrived to plunder the surrounding countryside.

The handful of Atlantans who remained in their ruined city were
soon joined by hordes of people from the surrounding countryside who
were interested in the contents of abandoned houses; here too the citizens organized a police force to keep order and chose a physician as acting mayor until James Calhoun could return. In addition to pillagers, the
town was plagued by packs of half-wild dogs long since abandoned by
their owners. General W. P. Howard, who entered Atlanta on November
25, reported only four hundred of the city's thirty-six hundred houses
still habitable. A number of fine homes had been taken over by "parties
who six months ago lived in humble style." Mayor Calhoun soon
returned, having covered the last thirty miles of his journey on foot, carrying his overcoat and valise; in January 1865 the Atlanta city council
resumed its meetings. Their town was one of the few where food was
not a constant worry; the Union troops had left sizable quantities of
foodstuffs in the hands of the city's blacks, including such rare com-
modities as cheese. A number of women found a way to provide for
their families by working in what they called the "lead mines," scaveng-
ing minie balls in and around the city that they traded to the Confederate authorities for flour, meal, and meat.

In other towns refugees came back and began picking up pieces of
their former lives. On the last day of December a woman named Donnie
Davis wrote to her brother from Decatur that things were looking up. A
half-frozen pig had wandered up and she had nursed it back to health.

"The exiles are returning to their old homes, the mail goes and comes, the Rail Roads are being built up, and to use a Yankee expression we will soon be living racy again." That same month Mrs. Peggy Berry of McDonough sent word to her children. "You must not be uneasy," she reassured them, "we will live, but not so plentiful as we used to." It's easy to imagine want and desolation coloring everything, but there is evidence that against a backdrop of catastrophe Georgians continued to seek and to find the customary pleasures of life. They celebrated Christmas 1864, and here and there one finds reference to taffy-pullings, living tableaux, and other doings. Well into this century a former trooper in the Second Georgia Cavalry recalled: "I fell in love with my wife at a dance on Christmas leave in 1864. We were married five years later and have lived happily for seventy-one years."

In the country there were signs that farming was being taken up again, and none too soon. In the spring of 1865 a Federal general reported that in the ten counties around Atlanta there were twenty-five thousand to fifty thousand people "destitute of bread or any kind of food." Even in the "burnt country" the land was being worked again. Any number of enterprising individuals had followed in the army's wake, picking up animals that the soldiers had abandoned without bothering to shoot them. A Baldwin County planter named Terrell Barksdale wrote his sister that he had been able to "recruit" more horses and mules than he had lost. Farther to the south, the Yankees left the Zettler family in a grim situation: They had not only stripped their plantation of livestock and provisions, they had used the grounds around the house as an abbatoir, leaving behind the carcasses of countless cows and steers. But the Zettlers were survivors. They set to work, and with the aid of a single slave who had stayed with them they skinned out the carcasses, cured the hides, and rendered the tallow. In January 1865 they took their hides and tallow to Augusta by wagon and train and sold the hides to the Confederate quartermaster for three thousand dollars, with which they bought corn and other things they needed. They traded the tallow to a cotton factory at the rate of one pound of tallow for one yard of cloth, then they repopulated their chicken house by trading a yard of cloth for a hen. So successful were their operations that they permitted themselves a frivolity: a boy's hat for which they paid 150 Confederate dollars.

These were to be sure the brighter spots in a generally somber picture. Fanny Andrews, who had given such a sprightly account of her trip across Sherman's wake, wrote in a different vein at the beginning of May 1865, when the news of Lee's surrender was percolating through the countryside: "The props that held society up are broken. Everything is in a state of disorganization and tumult. We have no currency, no law save the primitive code that might makes right. We are in a transition state from war to subjugation. . . ." Ahead of the state, and the South, lay the Sturm und Drang of Reconstruction. The war was over, but it would not recede quickly and quietly into the past.

Those who had played a prominent role in the fighting in Georgia often found prominent roles in peace. They produced a spate of memoirs and were always in demand for appearances and speeches. General Kilpatrick went on the lecture circuit, where his favorite topic was the March to the Sea; Kilpatrick also coauthored a play about the siege of Allatoona that has been described as historically accurate but "hopelessly dull." A good many former generals were able to translate their popularity with the troops into popularity with the voters. Senator John A. Logan got the Republican party's vice presidential nomination in 1884, and it was said he owed it in part to an indelible impression he had made twenty years before, galloping across the battlefield, black mane flying, to retake an artillery battery lost in the Battle of Atlanta. On Capitol Hill Senator Logan frequently bumped into old comrades and adversaries, among the latter men like Senator Joe Brown of Georgia and Representative Wheeler of Alabama. Whatever their postwar experience, one suspects that for almost all of these men the centerpiece of their lives remained the war. General Cheatham was for a time the head of the Tennessee prison system and ended his days in 1886 as postmaster of Nashville, but in his deathbed delirium he was heard to call out: "Bring me my horse; I'm going to the front."

General Sherman succeeded Grant as commanding general and remained with the army until 1883. He found time to write two volumes of memoirs; published in 1875, they were powerful arguments for the general's skill with the pen as well as with the sword. In 1879 Sherman made a brief visit to Georgia, where he expressed his approval of the new Atlanta. After he left he wrote a letter to the editor of the *Atlanta Constitution*, asserting his appreciation for the hospitality shown him, "though I was regarded as the bete noir of the late war in your region." He also wanted to pass on a suggestion regarding North Georgia: "The present population has not done full justice to this naturally beautiful and most favored region of our country." His solution: "Two or three millions of people could be diverted from the Great West to this region with profit and advantage to all concerned." In 1888, after the death of General Sheridan, he wrote a friend that he had become "the last of the Mohicans." Three years later, full of years and honors, he breathed his last.

Some of those who had fought him minimized his achievements in the war. General French described the March to the Sea as a "mere pleasure excursion," and Colonel T. B. Roy, Hardee's adjutant general, opined that "perhaps the clearer view of history may have more difficulty in discerning the splendor or the lustre of the achievement." Yet Sherman's fame was undiminished. If the war had taught European strategists the word "raid," Sherman's march seemed to them the greatest and most destructive raid of all. Four years after Appomattox the members of the Militärische Gesellschaft in Berlin listened with close attention to a fifty-three-page analysis of the general's campaigns. The speaker, a major named von Meerheimb, concluded: If this frightful way of making war, laying waste to rich countryside, was "reminiscent of the Thirty Years' War," one had to remember that "Sherman used these harshest measures with heavy heart," and only because "they alone would bring a quick and sure peace." In the 1890s the massive series of *Official Records* reached the period of the Atlanta campaign and shed new light on Sherman's generalship; the publication of his letters to his brother (1894) and to his wife (1909) revealed the many facets of his character, though in the editing and selection process for both works some of the more eccentric passages in the general's letters were not retained.

In the 1930s there was a new burst of interest in the general, sparked by a highly flattering biography by a British military analyst, Captain B. H. Liddell Hart. The book made a considerable stir and provoked much commentary. According to Liddell Hart, Sherman had broken new ground in strategy, using what his biographer called "the indirect approach"; the general had exploited the economic and psychological factors in war, attacking the South's "economic and moral rear." Three years before, Liddell Hart had written another book, *Paris, or the Future of War*, which showed the "indirect approach" in twentieth-century terms; it sketched out a scenario in which a nation was defeated through massive air attacks directed at its urban centers, completely disrupting them and sending their maddened populations rushing through the streets. The effect would be enhanced by the use of poison gas, which Captain Liddell Hart thought might prove "the salvation of civilization." "A swift and sudden blow of this nature," argued the captain, "inflicts a total of injury far less than when spread over a number of years." Thus the strategy of the "indirect approach," presumably heralded by the burning of Atlanta, would open the door to the incineration of scores of great cities from Warsaw to Tokyo.

As for those who had been the rank and file of the opposing armies, the war was likewise an episode that would mark the rest of their lives. In the memory of the ex-Confederates the campaign in Georgia was probably less central; they had known better times before that, and they had known far worse times afterward, especially the bloodlettings that the Army of Tennessee endured at the battles of Franklin and Nashville. Yet when they gathered, the old soldiers refought the Atlanta campaign, as the soldiers of defeated armies often do. Had "Old Joe" only kept command of the Army of Tennessee, many of them believed, they would have whipped Sherman, the Yankees would have elected McClellan president, and he would have come to honorable terms with the Confederacy. The sagacity of General Johnston grew steadily in the eyes of his former soldiers: The story was told endlessly of a postwar meeting of Sherman and Johnston in which the Northern general produced a map and asked Johnston: "How in the world did you get away from me here?" And Johnston, without even glancing at the map, told him. Though Sherman and Johnston did meet after the war, this story is the stuff of legend, but the ex-Rebels were not the only ones who would indulge in mythmaking.

As for Sherman's veterans, once they had returned to their midwestern homes they could look back on their year in Georgia as the high point of their military experience. There was first of all the long struggle for that elusive prize, Atlanta, finally crowned with success; then, for the fortunate sixty-odd thousand who struck out south from that city in November, there was the spectacular March to the Sea, the first and most exciting stage in an odyssey taking them to the end of the war five months later. As the years passed and their memories mellowed, a number of the veterans traveled back to Georgia to look at the old battlefields. A former officer named Samuel Pierson went back in 1881; at Pine Knob he found familiar trenchworks. "Above the clay were the head logs still in place," he noted incredulously. In front of the trenches he could still see the sharpened stakes, though trees were now growing on the earthen ramparts.

Other veterans came back because they simply wanted to see Georgia again, and there were those who came back to stay. Of all the places Sherman's men had passed through on the march, none so impressed them as the little town of Madison and the fertile land of Morgan County that surrounded it: "As near a paradise as anything I ever saw," said one of them. That was apparently the judgment of B. H. True, formerly of the 136th New York Infantry, who returned in November 1865, bought some land, and went to farming. His reception, as he later told a congressional committee during the Ku Klux Klan hearings, was friendly. Captain James H. Ainslie could not forget a magnificent grove of trees where he had camped just outside of Madison. He returned in 1867 and bought the grove of trees and four thousand acres besides, at a dollar an acre. In 1870 he moved his family down from Ohio and settled in. When he died forty-three years later the local newspaper said of him: "His record is above reproach and no braver soldier ever drew sword." Farther to the south, in what is today Ben Hill County, the town of Fitzgerald sprang up in the 1890s as a community where old soldiers from both sides could come to warm their bones in the South Georgia sun. The enterprise was a success, perhaps because its planners had a fine sense of equity: they named the streets on the east side of town for Union leaders and those to the west for Confederate personalities. In the center of town sat the Lee-Grant Hotel.

But for every former Yankee soldier who returned to the South, there were ten who relived the war in the meetings of their veterans' organizations, from the Society of the Army of the Tennessee, organized in the spring of 1865 when the army was at Raleigh, North Carolina, to the Grand Army of the Republic, which had General Logan as one of its founders. Understandably the orators in these meetings saw the Federal soldier and his actions in the most favorable light. After the war's end stories had circulated about the excessive and indiscriminate destruction inflicted on helpless populations, and consciously or not, much of the convention oratory was a corrective of sorts. At the Fifth Reunion of the Society of the Army of the Cumberland in 1876, General Manning Force described the soldiers who followed Sherman as "intelligent and energetic men, who became soldiers from the promptings of patriotism." As a consequence "there was less rancor towards the inhabitants of hostile territory, less plunder and pillage, less lawlessness, straggling and crime than is common in armies otherwise constituted." As for the men who made the famous march, the general was emphatic: "That army was not an untrained band of reckless, daring men. It was a disciplined army, as responsive to the word of its leader as a machine to the touch of the engineer."

Yet at the same time the veterans tended to talk about their depredations in general, and those on the march in particular, as though they were all in on some hilarious secret. Thus an old soldier might show someone a watch and say with a wink: "A Southern lady gave me that for saving her house from being burned." Even General Force followed this pattern of behavior: In his speech in 1876 he said: "the first mention of Sherman's march calls up the memory of bummers. Indeed there was some foraging in Carolina." At that point someone in the audience shouted out: "and in Georgia!" Amid general laughter General Force amended his remarks: "Yes, I believe we did find some potatoes in Georgia." Albion Tourgee was struck—and also appalled—by this tendency to speak of the army's foraging and pillaging "as a jest, rather grim and rough, but more comical than otherwise." And in truth the ravaging of Georgia, seen through speeches and a good bit of memoir material as well, appears as one vast prank. Perhaps Sherman's "boys" were trying by this means to trivialize their past actions because that way they would be less burdensome to their own memories and less offensive to others. Or perhaps it really *had* been fun.

Here, certainly, lies a partial explanation for the enormous popularity of the song "Marching Through Georgia." It became the anthem of Sherman's veterans, and no reunion or other patriotic occasion was complete without it. So constantly was it played that the general, whose very appearance was an invitation to the band, developed an almost physical loathing for it. The song had been composed by Henry Clay Work, a Chicago printer and songwriter who put the song together while Sherman and his men were on the road to Savannah. In the first twelve years following its publication it sold an incredible total of five hundred thousand copies. Some have argued that it remained popular after the war because it didn't talk about going into war or battle but "coming triumphantly out." A spritely tune with a rousing chorus, it offered patriotic sentiments interspersed with whimsical references to Georgia turkeys and sweet potatoes, the latter so happy to see the Yankees that they popped up out of the soil—just the musical fare to please conventioneers who had made that jaunt from Atlanta to the sea.

Henry Clay Work's composition was rarely heard in post-Reconstruction Georgia, where in fact for some years it was something of a provocation. When it was played during the appearance of Georgia's General John B. Gordon before a Northern audience the commotion was considerable (and there is a persistent story that on one occasion the tune produced a violent reaction by Margaret Mitchell). For Georgians 1864 was the *année terrible*, and if Sherman's veterans tended to minimize the destructive effects of their passage, a great many people in Georgia were determined to remember everything and forgive nothing. This mindset did not prevail in Atlanta, though that city had been hit hardest of all. Its dynamic, forward-looking spirit reasserted itself very quickly. A British visitor who came a few months after Appomattox could not decide whether he should commiserate with Atlantans over what had happened to their town or congratulate them on its revival; he found hardships enough—the only coffee was made from rye and it had to be drunk black because "Sherman had taken all the cows"—but frontage on Peachtree Street was selling for forty dollars a foot and mounting steadily in price. This resurrection of Atlanta found formal expression in 1887, when the city dropped the locomotive from its seal, replacing it with a phoenix and the motto *Resurgens*. A former Union officer, visiting the city about that time, tried to locate the Howard House, or at least its site, for he had seen Sherman there the day of the Battle of Atlanta. He had no luck, for "the new Atlanta had never heard of it." But if a Union veteran came to settle, he would find a sizable colony of his fellows—and the O. M. Mitchell Post of the Grand Army of the Republic. In the 1890s Northern and Southern veterans met together to talk about offering the city a monument to symbolize reconciliation between North and South; they called it the "duplex" monument because it was to portray in bronze Federal General McPherson and Confederate General Walker in the act of shaking hands; for some reason this project was never carried out.

Atlanta marched to its own drummer, and somewhat out of step with the rest of Georgia, where the memory of the war remained vivid. If Sherman's veterans tended to trivialize the excesses they had committed in the campaign, their sometime victims tended to enhance them, and here again the tendency is most visible in oratory. The speech that Colonel C. C. Jones Jr. delivered before the Sixth Annual Meeting of the Confederate Survivors' Association is an excellent example. The family of Colonel Jones had suffered heavily, but he took a broader, more historical view. He compared Sherman's army unfavorably with the British hirelings General Cornwallis had led through the South eighty years before, and he drew a parallel between Yankee foraging practices and "the passage of the victorious Goths madly plundering an unresisting country." In a finely turned sentence he reminded his listeners that "no less than ten thousand negro slaves were seduced from their allegiance." As for "the insults offered, the outrages perpetrated," no list had been made. "The record exists, however," the colonel added, "and may be authenticated by thousands upon whose homes the shadows of dire calamity descended like the black vapors of hell."

As time passed Georgians increasingly attributed the catastrophe that had struck them to a single man, perhaps because it was easier to focus blame on Sherman than on the faceless mass he led into their state. Here again we enter the world of myth. In North Georgia, for example, it was common knowledge that the general had issued an order (which has not been found) to have a railway car full of prominent citizens or Confederate prisoners placed ahead of the locomotive whenever torpe-

does were suspected on the track ahead. Then there was the letter, sup-
posedly found in Sherman's wake, in which a Union officer reported he
himself had collected about a quart of jewelry on the march; the commanding general's share made him a rich man: "General Sherman has
silver and gold enough to start a bank." In South Georgia the legend lingered that Sherman collected white horses as he came through and eventually had five hundred. (Of this charge too the general seems to have
been innocent. "I could collect plenty of trophies," he wrote Ellen in
March 1865, "but have always refrained and think it best I should.")

And in folklore at least the general took a hand in applying the torch.
In 1875 a Georgia newspaper said he had set fire to a factory in Eatonton; a friend showed the article to Mrs. Sherman, who took up her pen to
deny the charge indignantly. In various communities stories persisted
that a last-minute appeal stayed the general's hand. At Sandersville he
had ordered the burning of the entire town but changed his mind when
a local minister made a Masonic sign to him. At Ringgold he ordered the
destruction of the Catoosa County courthouse. Soldiers had set it afire
but two young girls dashed up with brooms and put out the flames;
Sherman rode up, listened to their impassioned plea, and the courthouse
was saved. The "Attila of the West" revealed a human side in other
places: He spared Madison because he had an old girlfriend there, Covington because it was the residence of a West Point classmate. The general would spend the night in a house and announce to its mistress the
next morning that he was not going to burn it—because she reminded
him of his sister, or because the breakfast she had fixed was the best he
had eaten since he left Chattanooga. The geographer who studied Sherman's march concluded: "if Sherman spent the night in as many places
as is claimed, it would have taken close to a year to make the trip to
Savannah."

As this rich tapestry of legend emerged, those localities that had
escaped the general's visit felt almost slighted. People in Augusta speculated for years on just why Sherman did not make their town a goal on
his march; some argued he had an old sweetheart there, and for her sake
he spared the town. Others said he simply made a strategic blunder in
overlooking a place of such importance. This debate reached the ears of
General Sherman, who wrote a testy letter to the editor of the *Augusta
Chronicle and Sentinel*:

> If the people of Augusta think I slighted them in the winter of 1864–5
> by reasons of personal friendships made in 1844, they are mistaken;
> or if they think I made a mistake in strategy, let them say so, and with

the President's consent I can send a detachment . . . who will finish
the job without costing Uncle Sam a cent.

By the time Sherman died Georgians had sufficiently softened their
opinion to acknowledge that he was a highly competent general, even if
a hard one. The obituary in the *Americus Daily Times* said: "he never
yielded to sentiment but spread fire and devastation on all hands." But
setting aside the rancorous feelings he had engendered, one would have
to concede that "he was the victorious general who really subdued the
Confederacy. By his devastations in Georgia the morale of Lee's army
was so reduced and his ranks so thinned that Grant's success was possible, so that at last Sherman and not Grant was entitled to the credit of
Appomattox."

In 1919 a writer named Stephen Graham followed the route of Sherman's army, talking to the inhabitants as he did so. He found Atlanta a
humming metropolis awash in Ford Runabouts; the people were cordial
enough but clearly busy with other things: "The firing of Atlanta is forgotten," he concluded, "and the pitiful exodus of its humiliated people."
The road south, the one Sherman had taken, was now lined with
"vaudeville sheds, fruit-stalls, and booths of quack doctors and magic
healers"; not until Graham approached Covington did he see some ves-
tige of the Georgia of 1864. The Georgians he accosted were "surprisingly friendly" and struck by the fact that he was not selling anything,
but simply following the route of Sherman's march. "They said they
knew nothing about it themselves, and then took me to the old folk who
remembered." One old Georgian assured Graham that during the war
"the colored people" remained faithful to their masters, while another
told him it was Sherman who set the blacks against the whites. He found
an old black man who remembered "the jubilation" the night the bluecoats appeared, and he found a white Georgian who described in great
detail the ransacking of his parents' home, a scene he had witnessed as a
small boy. The old man grew more and more angry as he recounted the
Yankees' profanations. He told Graham: "I know Sherman is in hell."
But this anger was exceptional; generally Graham found "a surprising
absence of bitterness." Among the old, memories had dimmed and fact
and fable were now sometimes hopelessly mixed, and they said by way
of apology: "it's a long, long time ago now."

Graham's reportage was more about the Georgia of 1919 than the
Georgia of 1864, though he probably didn't intend it that way. It was just
that he found so few traces of that earlier time. The land bore few marks
of the great struggle that had ravaged the state from Ringgold to Savan-

nah, and the generation that had lived through and remembered the year that Sherman came was largely gone. The frail survivors would soon follow; when they went, with them would go the last dim memories of an epic time. So it might have been, had it not been for a young woman named Margaret Mitchell, whom Graham could have met on his visit to Atlanta. She would resurrect that vanishing generation as no historian could, and give them not only life, but a kind of immortality.

Abbreviations

Abbreviations used in notes and bibliography to designate repositories and certain manuscript collections.

AHC	Atlanta History Center, Atlanta, Ga.
AU	Ralph Brown Draughon Library, Auburn University, Auburn, Ala.
CCHS	Mrs. Arthur W. Booth Library, Chemung County Historical Society, Elmira, N.Y.
CFHS	Columbiana-Fairfield Township Historical Society, Columbiana, Ohio.
CHAT	Chattanooga-Hamilton County Bicentennial Library, Chattanooga, Tenn.
CINHS	Cincinnati Historical Society, Cincinnati, Ohio.
CPL	Chicago Public Library, Chicago, Ill.
CRNL	Cornell University Library, Ithaca, N.Y.
CW Misc. Coll.	Civil War Miscellaneous Collection, USAMHI, Carlisle, Pa.
DUKE	William R. Perkins Library, Duke University, Durham, N.C.
ECU	Joyner Library, East Carolina University, Greenville, N.C.
EMORY	Robert W. Woodruff Library, Emory University, Atlanta, Ga.
GCM	Ina Russell Dillard Library, Georgia College, Milledgeville, Ga.
GDAH	Georgia Department of Archives and History, Atlanta, Ga.
GHS	Georgia Historical Society, Savannah, Ga.
HCWR Coll.	Harrisburg Civil War Roundtable Collection, USAMHI, Carlisle, Pa.
HSP	Historical Society of Pennsylvania, Philadelphia, Pa.
HUNT	Huntington Library, San Marino, Cal.
ILHS	Illinois State Historical Society, Springfield, Ill.
INHS	Indiana Historical Society, Indianapolis, Ind.
INSL	Indiana State Library, Indianapolis, Ind.
KENN	Kennesaw Mountain National Battlefield Park, Marietta, Ga.

LC	Library of Congress, Manuscripts Division, Washington, D.C.
MDAH	Mississippi State Department of Archives and History, Jackson, Miss.
MGA	Middle Georgia Archives, Middle Georgia Regional Library, Macon, Ga.
MKNOX	Calvin W. McClung Historical Collection, Knox County Public Library, Knoxville, Tenn.
MSSU	Mitchell Memorial Library, Mississippi State University, State University, Miss.
MSU	Michigan State University Library, East Lansing, Mich.
NA	National Archives, Washington, D.C.
NCSA	North Carolina State Archives, Raleigh, N.C.
ND	University of Notre Dame, South Bend, Ind.
NLM	National Library of Medicine, Bethesda, Md.
NYHS	New-York Historical Society, New York, N.Y.
OHS	Ohio Historical Society, Columbus, Ohio.
OHU	Vernon R. Alden Library, Ohio University, Athens, Ohio.
PHMC	Reference Library, Pennsylvania History and Museum Commission, Harrisburg, Pa.
SEW	University of the South, Sewannee, Tenn.
SHSW	State Historical Society of Wisconsin, Madison, Wisc.
TNSL	Tennessee State Library and Archives, Nashville, Tenn.
TXSL	Texas State Library, Austin, Texas.
UALA	University of Alabama, Tuscaloosa, Ala.
UDC Coll.	Collection assembled by the United Daughters of the Confederacy, Georgia Chapter
UGA	University of Georgia Libraries, Athens, Ga.
UILL	University of Illinois Library, Urbana-Champaign, Ill.
UMAA	Bentley Historical Library, University of Michigan, Ann Arbor, Mich.
UNC	Southern Historical Collection, University of North Carolina Archives, Chapel Hill, N.C.
USC	South Carolina Library, University of South Carolina, Columbia, S.C.
USMA	United States Military Academy, West Point, N.Y.
UTEN	John C. Hodges Library, University of Tennessee, Knoxville, Tenn.
UTEX	E. C. Barker Texas History Center, University of Texas, Austin, Texas.
UVA	Alderman Library, University of Virginia, Charlottesville, Va.
UWVA	University of West Virginia Library, Morgantown, W. Va.
VHS	Virginia Historical Society, Richmond, Va.
W&M	Earl Gregg Swem Library, College of William and Mary, Williamsburg, Va.
WMU	Dwight B. Waldo Library, Western Michigan University, Kalamazoo, Mich.

Notes

1. MISE-EN-SCÈNE

On Saturday, April 30: *The Collected Works of Abraham Lincoln*, ed. Roy P. Basler, 8 vols. (New Brunswick, N.J.: Princeton University Press, 1953), 7: 324.

A hundred miles to: William C. Davis, *Jefferson Davis: The Man and His Hour* (New York: HarperCollins, 1991), 551–53.

It was a somber: *Jefferson Davis, Constitutionalist. His Letters, Papers and Speeches*, ed. Dunbar Rowland, 10 vols. (Jackson: Mississippi Department of Archives and History, 1923), 6: 239–44.

General Grant had hastily: Albert Castel, *Decision in the West: The Atlanta Campaign of 1864* (Lawrence: University Press of Kansas, 1992), 68.

The plan they agreed: Report of General Grant, July 22, 1865, in U.S. War Department, *The War of the Rebellion: A Compilation of the Official Records of the Union and Confederate Armies*, 128 vols. (Washington, D.C.: Government Printing Office, 1880–1901), series 1, vol. 38, pt. 1, 1. This source will be cited hereinafter in the following format: *OR* 1, 38, pt. 1, 1.

If he ranked his: William Tecumseh Sherman (hereinafter WTS) to John Sherman, April 5, 1864, William T. Sherman Papers, LC.

Many of the general's: John F. Marszalek, *Sherman: A Soldier's Passion for Order* (New York: Free Press, 1993), 135–36; WTS to John Sherman, April 5, 1864, Sherman Papers, LC; WTS to Ellen Sherman, July 10, 1860, William T. Sherman Papers, ND; WTS to John Sherman, April 22, 1864, Sherman Papers, LC; WTS to Ellen Sherman, Jan. 25, 1864, Sherman Papers, ND.

Sherman's views in these: WTS to Ellen Sherman, June 26, 1864, Sherman Papers, ND; Marszalek, *Sherman*, 281; WTS to Annie Gilmann Bowen, June 30, 1864, William T. Sherman Letter, USC.

In truth, for Sherman: Orlando Poe Diary, April 20, 1864, Orlando Poe Papers, LC; *The Rough Side of War: The Civil War Journal of Chesley A. Mosman, 1st Lieutenant, Company D, 59th Illinois Volunteer Infantry Regiment*, ed. Arnold Gates (Garden City, N.Y.: Basin Publishing Co., 1987), 158; Lewis W. Day, *Story of the*

One Hundred and First Ohio Infantry (Cleveland: W. M. Bayne Printing Co., 1894), 196.

If driven south, the: James Houston Johnston, comp., *Western and Atlantic Railroad of the State of Georgia* (Atlanta: Georgia Public Service Commission, 1931), 19–21, 38.

The general knew that: WTS to Grant, July 12, 1864, *OR* 1, 38, pt. 5, 123; Mosman, *Journal*, 188.

Beyond Atlanta lay the: David P. Conyngham, *Sherman's March Through the South* (New York: Sheldon & Co., 1865), 30; George N. Barnard, *Photographic Views of Sherman's Campaign*, with a new preface by Beaumont Newhall (New York: Dover Publications, 1977), preface, ix.

This then was the: WTS to Ellen Sherman, March 12, 1864, Sherman Papers, ND.

In January 1864, when he: WTS to Ellen Sherman, Jan. 25, 1864, Sherman Papers, ND; WTS to Ellen Sherman, Jan. 28, 1864, Sherman Papers, ND; WTS to John Sherman, April 11, 1864, Sherman Papers, LC; John Sherman to WTS, April 17, 1864, Sherman Papers, LC.

There is little doubt: WTS to John A. Logan, Dec. 21, 1863, Sherman Papers, LC.

2. JOE BROWN'S GEORGIA

Among the more striking: *OR* 1, 30, pt. 3, 694–700.

Joe Brown—and that: I. W. Avery, *The History of the State of Georgia from 1850 to 1881, Embracing the Three Important Epochs: The Decade Before the War of 1861–5; the War; the Period of Reconstruction, with Portraits of the Leading Public Men of This Era* (New York: Brown & Derby, 1881), 8–10; Eliza Frances Andrews, *The War-Time Journal of a Georgia Girl*, with a foreword by Spencer B. King Jr. (Macon, Ga.: Ardivan Press, 1960), 159.

Brown tried teaching, had: Avery, *History*, 14.

But there was something: Herbert Fielder, *A Sketch of the Life and Times and Speeches of Joseph E. Brown* (Springfield, Mass.: Springfield Printing Co., 1883), 93; Avery, *History*, 12.

Brown's election as governor: Avery, *History*, 68, 88.

Governor-elect Brown announced: Avery, *History*, 62; Horace J. Bass, "Civil War Finance in Georgia," *Georgia Historical Quarterly* 26 (1942): 213.

Brown provided strong leadership: Proclamation to the Mechanics of Georgia, Feb. 20, 1862, *The Confederate Records of the State of Georgia*, comp. Allen D. Candler, 5 vols. (Atlanta: C. P. Byrd, State Printer, 1910–41), 2: 199–201.

While Brown proved a: *Philadelphia Weekly Times*, Nov. 2, 1878.

The Federal census of: Census figures are conveniently grouped in Avery, *History*, 167–69.

There were certain antagonisms: Atlanta City Council Minutes, Jan. 4, 1861, AHC; William Frederick Penneman Reminiscences, UNC, 19.

Georgia's demographic and economic: Avery, *History*, 167.

But in 1861 Georgians: Florence Fleming Corley, *Confederate City: Augusta, Georgia, 1860–1865* (Columbia: University of South Carolina Press, 1960), 360; Lucile Hodges, *A History of Our Locale: Mainly Evans County, Georgia* (Macon, Ga.: Southern Press, 1965), 71.

The first impact of: *Daily Columbus Enquirer*, March 15, 1864; Corley, *Augusta*, 51.

The war seemed to: Lieutenant Colonel Fremantle, *Three Months in the Southern States: April–June, 1863* (New York: J. Bradburn, 1864), 173; Robert Franklin Bunting to the *Houston Telegraph*, Feb. 26, 1864, Robert Franklin Bunting Letters, UTEX; *Macon Telegraph*, Feb. 14, 1860; *Chattanooga Daily Rebel* (published in Griffin, Ga.), Aug. 26, 1864.

More important—and usually: George Washington Rains, *History of the Confederate Powder Works. Address for Memorial Day, April 26, 1882* (Augusta, Ga.: n.p., 1882), 11–21; Corley, *Augusta*, 56.

Macon was selected as: John W. Mallet Memoranda, UVA, 5–8.

As the Confederacy's frontiers: Charles J. Brockman Jr., "The Confederate Armory of Cook & Brother," *Papers of the Athens Historical Society* 2 (1979): 76–78; Thomas Babson Hay, "Lucius B. Northrop, Commissary General of the Confederacy," *Civil War History* 9 (1963): 15; Ovid L. Futch, *History of Andersonville Prison* (Gainesville: University of Florida Press, 1968), 3.

As the war ground: Q. A. Gillmore, "Siege and Capture of Fort Pulaski," in *Battles and Leaders of the Civil War*, ed. Robert U. Johnson and Clarence C. Buel, 4 vols. (New York: Century Co., 1887), 2: 9.

The spring of 1963: *New York Tribune*, June 24, 1863.

But these were only: Susan Cornwall Journal, Feb. 17, 1863, UNC.

Once settled in, they: Unsigned letter to Kate, William H. Watterson Papers, UTEN; Mary Elizabeth Humphrey Howes Diary, April 23, May 1, 1864, Howes-Davis Family Diaries, MGA.

While some refugees, those: Mrs. Irby Morgan, *How It Was: Four Years Among the Rebels* (Nashville: Printed for the author, Publishing House of the M.E. Church South, 1892), 118; Sallie Bird to Elizabeth Harris, July 16, 1864, Edgeworth and Sallie Bird, *Granite Farm Letters: Civil War Correspondence of Edgeworth and Sallie Bird*, ed. John Rozier (Athens: University of Georgia Press, 1988), 172; Andrews, *Journal*, 61.

Governor Brown called upon: Message to the General Assembly, Nov. 5, 1863, Candler, *Records* 2: 506; Unsigned letter to Howard Newman, Howard Newman Correspondence, Hoyt Family Papers, CRNL.

At first the war: Joel Chandler Harris, *On the Plantation. A Story of a Georgia Boy's Adventures During the War* (reprint, with a foreword by Erskine Caldwell, Athens: University of Georgia Press, 1980), 124; Penneman Reminiscences, 112, UNC; Miss Abby (Cyrena Bailey Stone) Diary, Jan. 20, 1864, UGA.

Before long even those: Stephen Elliott, "Letters of the Bishop of Savannah, 1861–1865," ed. Willard E. Wright, *Georgia Historical Quarterly* 32 (1958): 103; George A. Mercer Diary, March 31, 1864, UNC; Louise Clack Reminiscences, Robert Livingston Nicholson Coll., LC; *Atlanta Constitution*, March 20, 1887.

Food was the most: Joseph Paul Johnson, "Southwest Georgia: A Case Study in Confederate Agriculture" (master's thesis, University of Georgia, 1992), 18; Robert A. Jarman History, 14, MDAH.

The Confederate Commissary Department: Dr. Thomas Green to James A. Seddon, May 12, 1864, Letters Received by the Confederate Secretary of War, 1861–65, M0437, NA.

By 1864 people in: Message to the General Assembly, Nov. 5, 1863, Candler, *Records* 2: 504; Kenneth Coleman, *Confederate Athens* (Athens: University of Georgia Press, 1967), 87.

We can get some: Major G. W. Cunningham to Major William B. Cross, Nov. 7, 1864, with enclosures: William Gregg to Major G. W. Cunningham, Oct. 15, 1864, and W. E. Jackson to Major G. W. Cunningham, Oct. 21, 1864, M0437, NA.

One cannot read documents: Avery, *History*, 85; Rev. W. A. Tignor to Brown, Feb. 16, 1864, Joseph Emerson Brown Papers, Telamon Cuyler Coll., UGA.

But in most of the: N. H. Grass to Brown, May 20, 1864, George D. Rice to Brown, Feb. 5, 1864, James N. Smith to Brown, March 20, 1864, Brown Papers, Telamon Cuyler Coll., UGA.

A goodly proportion of: Mary Clemmons to Brown, April 17, 1864, Brown Papers, Telamon Cuyler Coll., UGA; Elizabeth Fields to Brown, Aug. 13, 1864, Brown Papers, Telamon Cuyler Coll., UGA; Samantha J. Adams to Henry C. Wayne, Henry C. Wayne Papers, Telamon Cuyler Coll., UGA.

Most people who turned: Mary Lane to Brown, Feb. 27, 1865, Brown Papers, Telamon Cuyler Coll., UGA.

A succession of crises: Proclamation of Feb. 28, 1862, Candler, *Records* 2: 223–24; Avery, *History*, 91; Brown to Colonel Benjamin May, June 9, 1862, Candler, *Records* 2: 224; A. K. Seago to Brown, June 9, 1864, M0437, NA; G. Locke to Brown, Nov. 25, 1864, Candler, *Records* 2: 553–54.

In its December 1862: Avery, *History*, 251, 315; *Journal of the House of Representatives of the State of Georgia, at the Annual Session of the General Assembly, Begun and Held in Milledgeville, the Seat of the Government, in 1863* (Milledgeville, Ga.: 1863), 25; *Acts of the General Assembly of the State of Georgia Passed in Milledgeville at the Annual Session in November and December, 1863; also, Extra Session of 1864* (Milledgeville, Ga.: 1864), 69.

When the legislature convened: Bass, "Finance," 224; *Acts . . . 1863–64*, 8, 69; *Journal . . . House . . . November 1864*, 25; John B. Beall, *In Barrack and Field: Poems and Sketches of Army Life* (Nashville: Smith and Lamar, Agents, Publishing House of the M.E. Church South, 1906), 397; Judges of Inferior Court, Mount Yonah, Ga., to Brown, Oct. 17, 1864, Brown Papers, Telamon Cuyler Coll., UGA.

By 1864 Governor Brown: Candler, *Records* 2: 191–282; Brown to Jefferson Davis, Jan. 25, 1864, Candler, *Records* 3: 462; Brown to Jefferson Davis, April 1, 1864, Candler, *Records* 3: 501; Brown to Whom It May Concern, April 18, 1863, Candler, *Records* 2: 442.

Brown's rigid defense of: Message to the General Assembly, April 6, 1863, Candler, *Records* 2: 433; General Howell Cobb to Brown, May 23, 1864, Candler, *Records* 3: 566.

While the public followed: Harris, *On the Plantation*, 127; *Augusta Daily Chronicle and Sentinel*, Jan. 25, 1864; *Acts . . . 1863–64*, 123.

The legislature amended the: *Acts . . . 1863–64*, 123; Lucien E. Roberts, "The Political Career of Joshua Hill (1812–1891), Georgia Unionist," *Georgia Historical Quarterly* 21 (1937): 57–62; Frank W. Klingberg, *The Southern Claims Commission* (New York: Octagon Books, 1978), 13–14.

But life was not necessarily easy: Andrews, *Journal*, 16.

In between these extremes: Thomas G. Dyer, "Vermont Yankees in King Cotton's Court: The Case of Cyrena and Amherst Stone," *Vermont History* 60 (1992): 205–29.

Miss Abby visited the: Miss Abby Diary, Feb. 14, 20, March 12, May 21, 28, June 7, and July 21, 1864, UGA.

To Georgia's leaders and: Clarence L. Mohr, *On the Threshold of Freedom: Masters and Slaves in Civil War Georgia* (Athens: University of Georgia Press, 1986), 128.

The menace that the: Harris, *On the Plantation*, 49.

So white Georgians watched: *Columbus Daily Sun*, Dec. 4, 1863; Miss Abby Diary, Jan. 20, 1864; Mohr, *Threshold*, 71; Report of the Provost Marshal General, April 16, 1866, RG 94, Entry 961, 69.

Beginning late in 1863: Colonel R. D. Mussey to Major C. W. Foster, Oct. 10, 1864, RG 94, Entry 306, Letters Received, Colored Troops Division, M-750, NA.

A young officer named: Morris Stuart Hall Reminiscences, Morris Stuart Hall Papers, passim, UMAA.

In that spring of: *Augusta Daily Chronicle and Sentinel*, Jan. 20, 1864.

Perhaps such apocalyptic visions: Harris, *On the Plantation*, 49.

3. THE HOSTS

The census of 1860 put: Craig L. Symonds, *Joseph E. Johnston: A Civil War Biography* (New York: W. W. Norton & Co., 1992), 260.

Union forces had followed: *OR* 1, 38, pt. 1, 89–114.

In its structure: Oliver Otis Howard, *Autobiography of Oliver Otis Howard, Major General, United States Army*, 2 vols. (New York: Baker & Taylor Co., 1907), 1: 509.

The most notable disparity: Samuel G. French, *Two Wars. An Autobiography of Gen. Samuel G. French, an Officer in the Armies of the United States and the Confederate States, a Graduate from the U.S. Military Academy, West Point, 1843* (Nashville: Confederate Veteran, 1901), 25.

A good many of: George Washington Adams, *Doctors in Blue. The Medical History of the Union Army in the Civil War* (New York: Henry Schuman, 1952), 107; Louis C. Duncan, *The Medical Department of the United States Army in the Civil War* (Gaithersburg, Md.: Olde Soldier Books, 1987), 341; Report of Surgeon George F. Cooper, Joseph K. Barnes et al., *The Medical and Surgical History of the War of the Rebellion*, 3 vols. (Washington, D.C.: Government Printing Office, 1875—81), 1, pt. 1, 299; Glenna Ruth Schroeder-Lein, "Waging War Behind the Lines: Samuel Hollings Stout and Confederate Hospital Administration in the Army of Tennessee" (Ph.D. diss., University of Georgia, 1991), 155; F. E. Daniel, *Recollections of a Rebel Surgeon (and Other Sketches), or, In the Doctor's Sappy Days* (Austin, Texas: Von Boeckmann, Schutze & Co., 1899), 215, 19; Fannie A. Beers, *Memories. A Record of Personal Experience and Adventure During Four Years of War* (Philadelphia: J. B. Lippincott, 1888), 156.

While the Northern army: James Miller Wysor to his father, April 12, 1864, James Miller Wysor Letters, VHS; *Daily Columbus Sun*, Dec. 4, 1863.

There was a significant: *History of the Organization, Marches, Campaigns, General Services and Final Muster Out of Battery M, First Regiment Illinois Light Artillery; Together with Detailed Incidents Both Grave and Facetious, Connected Therewith; Compiled from the Official Records and from the Diaries of Different Members* (Princeton, Ill.: n.p., 1892), 174; Major J. C. Thompson to General Alexander P. Stewart, Dec. 8, 1867, Joseph E. Johnston Papers, W&M.

Being armed with inferior: W. W. Gordon to his wife, July 2, 1864, W. W. Gordon Letters, Gordon Family Papers, GHS.

The Southerners suffered from: W. H. Redfield, "Characteristics of the Armies," *Philadelphia Weekly Times*, Feb. 16, 1878.

If they were rural: Henry Clay Reynolds to his wife, Jan. 4, 1865, Henry Clay Reynolds Papers, ADAH.

Tempting as it is: Patrick M. Griffin, "The Famous Tenth Tennessee, or 'Bloody Tenth,'" *Confederate Veteran* (December 1905): 552; Mosman, *Journal*, 248; Larry J. Daniel, *Soldiering in the Army of Tennessee. A Portrait of Life in the Confederate Army* (Chapel Hill: University of North Carolina Press, 1991), 9; *Atlanta Journal*, Nov. 1, 1902.

There were sizable numbers: John W. Storrs, *The "Twentieth Connecticut," A Regimental History* (Ansonia, Conn.: Press of the Naugatuck Valley Sentinel, 1886), 261; James Cooper Nisbet, *Four Years on the Firing Line*, ed. Bell I. Wiley (Jackson, Tenn.: McCowat-Mercer Press, 1963), 202. *Sunny South*, Oct. 5, 1901.

There were also women: Julia Chase, "Mother Bickerdyke," *Transactions of the Kansas State Historical Society* 7 (1901–2): 190; George W. Morris, *Eighty-first Regiment of Indiana Volunteer Infantry in the Great War of the Rebellion 1861–1865* (Louisville: Franklin Printing Co., 1901), 112.

An unknown but probably appreciable number: Joseph Wheeler to Miss E. W. Pick, Feb. 18, 1888, Joseph Wheeler Papers, DUKE; Fremantle, *Southern States*, 173; *Louisville Daily Journal*, Aug. 19, 1864; Report of E. B. Atwood, Oct. 23, 1864, Letters Received, RG 393, pt. 1, Entry 2517, NA.

Women soldiers were also: James Langstaff Dunn to his wife, July 22, 1864, James Langstaff Dunn Correspondence, UVA; Judson L. Austin to his wife, July 21, 1864, Judson L. Austin Letters, Nina L. Ness Papers, UMAA.

In dress and appearance: John J. Hight, *History of the Fifty-eighth Regiment of Indiana Volunteer Infantry* (Princeton, Ind.: Press of the Clarion, 1895), 283; Fenwick Y. Hedley, *Marching Through Georgia. Pen Pictures of Everyday Life in General Sherman's Army from the Beginning of the Atlanta Campaign Until the Close of the War* (Chicago: R. R. Donnelley & Sons, 1887), 63.

The Southern army had its: Fremantle, *Southern States*, 155.

Letters that Southern soldiers: William Harris Bragg, *Joe Brown's Army: The Georgia State Line, 1862–1865* (Macon, Ga.: Mercer University Press, 1987), 51; Andrews, *Journal*, 82.

Though the men of: Marshall P. Thatcher, *A Hundred Battles in the West, Saint Louis to Atlanta, 1861–1865* (Detroit: Author, 1884), 205; [Edmund Randolph Brown], *The Twenty-seventh Indiana Volunteer Infantry in the War of the Rebellion 1861 to 1865; First Division 12th and 20th Corps* (n.p., 1899), 22; W. W. Stribling to his wife, May 1, 1864, W. W. Stribling Letters, Stribling Family Coll., USC.

A visitor to the: *The Tennessee Civil War Veterans' Questionnaires*, 5 vols. paginated as one, comp. Gustavus W. Dyer and John Trotwood Moore, ed. Colleen Morse Elliott and Louise Armstrong Moxley (Easley, S.C.: Southern Historical Press, 1985), 737; Circular of Aug. 5, 1864, RG 109, Entry 86, NA.

We know not only: Andrew Hickenlooper Reminiscences, 257, Hickenlooper Coll., CINHS; B. F. Scribner, *How Soldiers Were Made; or War as I Saw It Under Buell, Rosecrans, Thomas, Grant and Sherman* (New Albany, Ind.: Donohoue & Henneberry, 1887), 257; Brown, *Twenty-seventh*, 469; William Wheeler to his parents, Jan. 5, 1864, *Letters of William Wheeler of the Class of 1855, Y. C.* (Privately printed, 1873), 457.

The Western soldier saw: Mosman, *Journal*, 265; Hickenlooper Reminiscences, 283, Hickenlooper Coll., CINHS.

Extracting a self-portrait of: Edwin Hansford Rennolds Diary, Feb. 11, 1864,

UTEN; Winfield Scott Featherston Memoirs and Official Documents and Reports, CW Misc. Coll., USAMHI.

This particularism of the: James Madison Brannock to his wife, June 8, 1864, James Madison Brannock Letters, VHS; Rennolds Diary, March 8, 1864, UTEN. George Phifer Erwin to his father, April 13, 1864, George Phifer Erwin Papers, UNC.

In sum, large numbers: Benjamin Franklin Jackson to his wife, March 13, 1864, *So Mourns the Dove: Letters of a Confederate Soldier and His Family* (New York: Exposition Press, 1965), 86.

If to these sources: *Mobile Daily Advertiser and Register,* June 14, 1864; James Marsh Morey Diary, May 13, 1864, James Marsh Morey Papers, TNSL.

One of the best: Barnes et al., *Medical* 1, pt. 3, 884–85.

If it's not too: William E. Titze Diary, May 14, 1864, ILHS.

A Northern officer noted: John Vail Narrative, Oct. 18, Nov. 8, 1864, OHS.

For the veterans had: Mosman, *Journal,* 287; M. A. Cameron to his sister, June 3, 1864, Cameron Coll., UALA.

Death seems to have: John K. Duke, *History of the Fifty-third Regiment of Ohio Volunteer Infantry, During the War of the Rebellion, 1861 to 1865* (Portsmouth, Ohio: Blade Printing Co., 1900), 142; Hedley, *Marching,* 294.

Nominally the regiment was: Hedley, *Marching,* 283.

The cohesion, the "oneness": *Tennessee Veterans Questionnaires,* passim.

So strong were the: *Macon Daily Telegraph,* May 20, 1864.

The company and the: Mosman, *Journal,* 285.

The infantrymen, who were: Jacob Adams Reminiscence in *Echoes of Battle,* ed. Larry Strayer and Stephen Baumgartner (Huntington, W.Va.: Blue Acorn Press, 1991), 19.

And the men did: Lloyd Lewis, *Sherman: Fighting Prophet* (New York: Harcourt Brace & Co., 1932), 434; James Madison Brannock to his wife, May 8, 1864, Brannock Letters, VHS.

Sherman's men admired in: Albion W. Tourgee, *Story of a Thousand* (Buffalo: S. McGerald & Son, 1896), 307; Lucius W. Barber, *Army Memoirs of Lucius W. Barber, Company "D" 15th Ill. Vol. Infantry, May 24, 1861 to Sept. 30 1865* (Chicago: J. M. W. Printing Co., 1894), 150.

Sherman inspired confidence in: Charles Wright Wills, *Army Life of an Illinois Soldier, Including a Day by Day Record of Sherman's March to the Sea* (Washington, D.C.: Globe Printing Co., 1906), 239; Conyngham, *Sherman's March,* 49; Joseph H. Strickling Reminiscences, 29, OHS; Hight, *Fifty-eighth,* 406.

Who in Sherman's army: Rudolphe Rey to Lizzie DeVoe, June 19, 1864, Rudolphe Rey Papers, NYHS; Scribner, *Soldiers,* 276.

Western soldiers also liked: John T. Bill, *Tramps and Triumphs of the Second Iowa Infantry, Briefly Sketched* (Omaha: Gibson, Miller, and Richardson, Printers, 1886), 19; Jay Caldwell Butler, *Letters Home,* arranged by his son, Wilson Hubbard Butler (Privately printed, 1930), 137; Mosman, *Journal,* 264.

The senior leaders in: Robert Hale Strong, *A Yankee Private's Civil War,* ed. Ashley Halsey Jr. (Chicago: Henry Regnery Co., 1961), 95.

If sagacity was the: Fremantle, *Southern States,* 159.

From tactical considerations these: T. B. Roy, "Lieutenant General William Hardee," 4, William Joseph Hardee Papers, ADAH; General Alexander P. Stewart to Colonel A. J. Keller, May 31, 1864, Alexander P. Stewart Letter, UGA.

Bravery was also at: Scribner, *Soldiers*, 275; Henry Stone, "The Atlanta Campaign," *Papers of the Military Historical Society of Massachusetts* 7 (1910): 329.

The risks were understood: WTS to Ellen Sherman, July 29, 1864, Sherman Papers, ND; General William Joseph Hardee to his wife, June 25, 1864, Hardee Papers, ADAH.

Both Northern and Southern: Scribner, *Soldiers*, 252.

In both armies the: Thomas Owens, "Penalties for Desertion," *Confederate Veteran* (July 1894): 239; Rennolds Diary, April 18, 1864, UTEN; Clason Miller to his brother, Dec. 16, 1863, Clason Miller Letters, Miller Coll., CINHS; George Little and James R. Maxwell, *A History of Lumsden's Battery, C.S.A.* (Tuscaloosa: R. E. Rhodes Chapter, United Daughters of the Confederacy [1905?]), 33; Rennolds Diary, April 18–20, 23, 1864 UTEN.

If the antagonism between: Strong, *Yankee*, 85; Thomas T. Taylor to his wife, July 28, 1864, Thomas T. Taylor Papers, OHS; *Atlanta Constitution*, April 17, 1887.

With volunteer armies composed: Charles Edwin Cort to friends, April 26, 1864, *"Dear Friends": The Civil War Letters and Diary of Charles Edwin Cort*, comp., ed. with commentaries by Helyn W. Tomlinson (n.p., 1962), 139; WTS to C. B. Richardson, Jan. 18, 1865, Gratz Coll., HSP.

4. FROM DALTON TO THE CHATTAHOOCHEE

Whoever would follow in: Summary of Principal Events, May 1–Sept. 8, 1864, *OR* 1, 38, pt. 1, 54–55.

What struck those who: Mosman, *Journal*, 264.

Then there was continuity: Tourgee, *Story*, 306.

Finally participants noticed a: Luther F. Bradley to Buel, June 19, 1864, Luther F. Bradley Papers, USAMHI.

Yet few imagined that: W. E. Bevens, *Reminiscences of a Private, Company "G," First Arkansas Regiment Infantry* (n.p., n.d.), 49.

A decision General Sherman: General Henry W. Halleck to Grant, Oct. 20, 1863, *OR* 1, 38, pt. 4, 310.

Sherman's General Order No. 6: General Order No. 6, RG 393 Entry 2489, NA; Special Field Order No. 18, June 4, 1864, RG 94, Entry 2504, NA.

Since the transportation of: Samuel Bechtold Diary, July 5, 1864, Bechtold Family Papers, UMAA.

In his memoirs written: William T. Sherman, *Memoirs of Gen. W. T. Sherman*, 4th ed., 2 vols. (New York: Charles Scribner's Sons, 1904), 2: 22; Horace Porter, *Campaigning with Grant* (New York: Century Co., 1897), 207; J. W. Gaskill, *Footprints Through Dixie. Everyday Life of the Man Under a Musket. On the Firing Line and in the Trenches, 1861–1865* (Albany, Ohio: Bradshaw Printing Co., 1919), 103; Wills, *Army Life*, 236; Thomas Doak Edington Diary, June 9, 1864, UTEN.

The effect of short: *History . . . Battery M*, 185; Gaskill, *Footprints*, 100, 103; T. F. Dornblaser, *Sabre Strokes of the Pennsylvania Dragoons in the War of 1861–1865* (Philadelphia: Lutheran Publication Society, 1884), 160.

The Union soldier left: Barnes et al., *Medical* 1, pt. 1, 299–300; Hedley, *Marching*, 129; Ira Blanchard Reminiscences, 122, ILHS; William C. Robinson to Charlie, Aug. 2, 1864, William C. Robinson Papers, ILHS.

The terrain of North Georgia: Morris, *Eighty-first*, 84; Strong, *Yankee*, 218;

William O. Norrell Memorandum Book, 54, 59, AHC; Barnes et al., *Medical* 1, pt. 3, 855.

In the first days: Hickenlooper Reminiscences, 211, Hickenlooper Coll., CINHS; WTS to General George Thomas, June 6, 1864, *OR* 1, 38, pt. 4, 189; WTS to General George Thomas, July 21, 1864, *OR* 1, 38, pt. 5, 213.

Strangely enough many natural: *History . . . Battery M*, 214; Andrew J. Boies, *Record of the Thirty-third Massachusetts Volunteer Infantry, from August 1862 to August 1865* (Fitchburg, Mass.: Sentinel Printing Co., 1880), 71; H. Hampton to Rev. Charles Todd Quintard, June 13, 1864, Charles Todd Quintard Papers, DUKE; *Mobile Daily Register and Advertiser*, June 11, 1864.

Such fortifications had figured: William T. Sherman, "The Grand Strategy of the Last Year of the War," in *Battles and Leaders of the Civil War*, ed. Robert U. Johnson and Clarence C. Buel, 4 vols. (New York: Century Co., 1885), 4: 247.

Traditionally an army in: Nisbet, *Firing Line*, 194; Andrew Jackson Johnson Diary, Aug. 5, 1864, INHS; Edward E. Schweitzer Diary, Aug. 12, 1864, CWTI Coll., USAMHI.

Virtually all the improvements: Caleb H. Carlton Diary, July 11, 1864, Caleb H. Carlton Papers, LC; John H. Marshall to his wife, Aug. 19, 1864, John H. Marshall Letters, MSSU; William Wheeler to his parents, May 30, 1864, *Letters*, 134.

When the Union army: Mosman, *Journal*, 212.

Whether it was the: Peter Hitchcock to Lieutenant Colonel E. M. Owen, July 1, 1864, Peter Hitchcock Family Letters, WRHS.

Those heavy and exceptional: Mosman, *Journal,* 221.

When General Johnston read: Joseph E. Johnston, "The Dalton-Atlanta Operations," *Annals of the Army of Tennessee* 1 (1887): 7; Brown, *Twenty-seventh*, 502.

An even greater burden: John Barfield to his wife, June 4, 1864, Confederate Miscellany, EMORY; Edwin A. Bowen Memorandum, Sept. 8, 1864, HUNT; WTS to Ellen Sherman, Aug. 15, Sherman Papers, ND; Strong, *Yankee*, 95; John Patton Memoir, June 14, 1864, LC.

But Sherman was not: Fourth Corps Diary, May 13, 1864, Wirt-Stanley Papers, USAMHI; WTS to General George Thomas, May 14, 1864, William T. Sherman Papers, USMA; General John M. Palmer to Generals S. G. Johnson and Absalom Baird, May 17, 1864, John M. Palmer Papers, ILHS; James A. Congleton Diary, May 28, 1864, LC; Ogden Greenough to his mother, May 6, 1864, Ogden Greenough Letters, UILL.

The night marches were: Albert A. Champlain Diary, May 25, 1864, Alfred Mewett Papers, WRHS; Levi Ross Diary, May 12, 1864, Levi Ross Papers, ILHS; Morris, *Eighty-first*, 100; John W. Lavender, *The War Memoirs of Captain John W. Lavender, C.S.A. They Never Came Back: The Story of Co. F. Fourth Arks. Infantry, C.S.A., Originally Known as the Montgomery Hunters, as Told by Their Commanding Officer*, ed. Ted R. Worley (Pine Bluff, Ark.: W. M. Hackett and D. R. Perdue, 1956), 92.

Had these nocturnal movements: J. H. Curry, "A History of Company B, 40th Alabama Infantry, C.S.A., from the Diary of J. H. Curry," *Alabama Historical Quarterly* 17 (1955): 210; Carroll Henderson Clark History (unpaginated), CHAT.

Armies that moved by: Thomas E. Smith to his brother, June 22, 1864, Thomas E. Smith Papers, OHS; Brown, *Twenty-seventh*, 510.

The men in some: Cort, *"Dear Friends,"* 138; *Indianapolis Daily Journal*, July 14, 1864; Sergeant E. Tarrant, *The Wild Riders of the First Kentucky Cavalry* (Louisville: Press of R. H. Carothers, 1894), 136.

With the infantry there: John B. Brobst, *"Well, Mary": Civil War Letters of a Wisconsin Volunteer,* ed. Mary Brobst Roth (Madison: University of Wisconsin Press, 1960), 57.

But unless there were: Brobst, *"Well, Mary,"* 79, 107.

Contacts of a reasonably: George W. Pepper, *Personal Recollections of Sherman's Campaign in Georgia and the Carolinas* (Zanesville, Ohio: Hugh Dunne Co., 1866).

But trading wares was: George Drake, *The Mail Goes Through; or, The Civil War Letters of George Drake, 1864–1918; Over Eighty Letters Written from August 9, 1862 to May 29, 1865 by 85th Illinois Vol.,* comp., ed. Julia A. Drake (San Angelo, Texas: Anchor Publishing Co., 1964), 88.

While army commanders sometimes: Division Order Book, in Charles Reynolds Papers, LC.

There was one occasion: Morris, *Eighty-first,* 99; James Miller Wysor to his father, Aug. 7, 1864, Wysor Letters, VHS.

As the movements of: Eleazer B. Doan to Miss Amelia, June 22, 1864, Eleazer B. Doan Correspondence, CWTI Coll., USAMHI.

Documents like this inevitably: James Madison Brannock to his wife, May 15, 1864, Brannock Letters, VHS; General William Joseph Hardee to his wife, June 18, 1864, Hardee Papers, ADAH; *Mobile Daily Register and Advertiser,* June 16, 1864.

But there are other: Henry J. Aten, *History of the Eighty-fifth Regiment, Illinois Volunteer Infantry* (Hiawatha, Kansas: 1901), 85; John G. Parkhurst Diary, May 31, 1864, MSU; Army of the Cumberland, Reports of Operations and Casualties Received, 1863–1865, RG 393, pt. 1, Entry 961, NA, Reports for 1864, passim.

While we think of: *Indianapolis Daily Journal,* June 15, 1864; WTS to John Bell Hood, Sept. 9, 1864, General Sherman's Orders and Letterbooks, vol. 12, RG 94, Entry 159, NA.

There were enough risks: Thomas E. Smith to Maria, July 4, 1864, Smith Papers, OHS.

The most spectacular case: The note is preserved in the Francis Little Papers, W&M. Dorothy Holland Herring, *Company A of the Fortieth Georgia Regiment in Confederate Service* (Privately printed, n.d.), 108.

The deserters generally came: Thomas H. Williams to his father, June 6, 1864, Thomas H. Williams Papers, UMAA.

5. THE DISTRICT OF THE ETOWAH

The war that came: George Gordon Ward, *The Annals of Upper Georgia, Centered in Gilmer County* (Carrolton, Ga.: n.p., 1965), 340; Lloyd G. Marlin, *The History of Cherokee County* (Atlanta: Press of Walter W. Brown Publishing Co., 1932), 86; John D. Lowman to his wife, Aug. 22, 1864, John D. Lowman Letters, INHS.

The region had no: Avery, *History,* 187; Luke C. Tate, *History of Pickens County* (Spartanburg, S.C.: n.p., 1978), 201–4.

Were this not enough: *Augusta Daily Chronicle and Sentinel,* July 2, 1864; M. H. Cofer to Brown, June 5, 1864, Brown Papers, Telamon Cuyler Coll., UGA.

As the storm clouds: Joseph B. Mahan Jr., "A History of Old Cassville, 1833–1864" (master's thesis, University of Georgia, 1950), 97–100; Joseph Aplin Martin to his mother, April 11, 1864, Joseph Aplin Martin Coll., OHU.

People who stayed: Oliver Lyman Spalding Memoirs, Oliver Lyman Spalding Papers, 41, UMAA; *Augusta Daily Chronicle and Sentinel*, July 24, 1864.

Slaves were valuable property: J. P. Cannon, *Inside of Rebeldom. The Daily Life of a Confederate Private* (Washington, D.C.: National Tribune, 1900), 210.

For those who: P. M. West to Henry C. Wayne, April 16, 1864, Wayne Papers, Telamon Cuyler Coll., UGA; Joseph E. Johnston to Brown, June 4, 1864, Candler, *Records* 3: 575.

Then the army itself: Wade Banister Gassman, "A History of Rome and Floyd County, Georgia in the Civil War" (master's thesis, Emory University, 1966), 115; *Mobile Register and Advertiser*, May 28, 1864.

Because they had no: Lyman A. Brewer to his wife, July 6, 1864, Lyman A. Brewer Coll., HUNT; Conyngham, *Sherman's March*, 128.

Then there were those: Frances Thomas Howard, *In and Out of the Lines, An Accurate Account of Incidents During the Occupation of Georgia by Federal Troops in 1864–65* (New York: Neale Publishing Co., 1905), 5–6.

A few days later: Rebecca Hood Memoirs, UDC Coll., GDAH.

In the most fortunate: Lyman Daniel Ames Diary, May 10, 1864, OHS; *Atlanta Journal*, Jan. 3, 1887.

Just south of Adairsville: Morris, *Eighty-first*, 92; Thomas A. Head, *Campaigns and Battles of the Sixteenth Regiment, Tennessee Volunteers, in the War Between the States, with Incidental Sketches of the Part Performed by Other Tennessee Troops in the Same War* (Nashville: Cumberland Presbyterian Publishing House, 1905), 128; *History . . . Battery M*, 176–77.

Occasionally a man would: George H. Cadman to his wife, May 19, 1864, George H. Cadman Papers, UNC.

Many of the towns: Rufus Mead Diary, May 22, 1864, LC; Dornblaser, *Sabre Strokes*, 168; Patton Memoir, vol. 29 (unpaginated), LC; J. E. Brant, *History of the Eighty-fifth Indiana Volunteer Infantry, Its Organization, Campaigns and Battles* (Bloomington, Ind.: Craven Brothers, Printers, 1902), 58.

Most of the plundering: Hood Memoirs, GDAH; Minerva McClatchey Diary, May 1864, McClatchey Family Papers, GDAH.

The Howard family had: Howard, *Account*, 13, 16.

The Howards had in: Howard, *Account*, 22, 33, 143, 145.

Like the Hoods and: Herring, *Company A*, 108–9.

In general terms the: Cort, "*Dear Friends*," 146; Robert Patrick, *Reluctant Rebel: The Secret Diary of Robert Patrick, 1861–1865*, ed. F. Jay Taylor (Baton Rouge: Louisiana State University Press, 1959), 168.

In a region as: Steven Hahn, *The Roots of Southern Populism: Yeoman Farmers and the Transformation of the Georgia Upcountry, 1850–1860* (New York: Oxford University Press, 1983), 60–61.

Given the difficulties of: Wills, *Army Life*, 274.

The official attitude toward foraging: Instructions of April 30, 1864, *OR* 3, 4, 250; Grant to General Henry W. Halleck, April 29, 1864, *The Papers of U.S. Grant*, ed. John Y. Simon (Carbondale: Southern Illinois University Press, 1983), 10: 371.

As for irregular foraging: Manuscript draft of Sherman Memoirs, 41, Sherman Papers, LC.

If the depredations were: *Philadelphia Weekly Times*, Feb. 16, 1878; Stockwell, Elisha, *Private Elisha Stockwell, Jr., Sees the Civil War*, ed. Byron R. Abernethy (Norman: University of Oklahoma Press, 1958), 54; Brobst, "*Well, Mary*," 54.

But the inhabitants soon: Special Field Order No. 22, June 10, 1864, RG 393, pt. 1, Entry 2504.

Steedman set up his: John Bigelow, *The Principles of Strategy* (New York: G. P. Putnam's Sons, 1891), 118.

A "War Democrat" and: General John C. Smith, *Oration at the Unveiling of the Monument Erected in the Memory of Maj. Gen. James B. Steedman at Toledo, Ohio, May 26, 1887* (Toledo, 1887), passim.

An Ohio soldier named: John Wesley Marshall Diary, May 19, 20, 1864, LC.

Though Marshall had no: Report of Captain O. H. Helman, Signal Corps, Sept. 9, 1864, *OR* 1, 38, pt. 3, 188; Barber, *Memoirs*, 153; *Mobile Daily Register and Advertiser*, June 21, 1864; Hedley, *Marching*, 69–71.

These particular episodes were: WTS to John Sherman, April 11, 1864, Sherman Papers, LC.

This frustration can clearly be: The letters are all in RG 393, pt. 1, Entry 2499, NA.

Copies of the letter: General Order No. 2, June 28, 1864, RG 393, pt. 2, Entry 2662, NA.

The applicants for: T. J. Wright, *History of the Eighth Regiment, Kentucky Vol. Inf. During Its Three Years Campaign, Embracing Organization, Marches, and Battles of the Command with Much of the History of the Old Reliable Third Brigade, Commanded by Hon. Stanley Matthews and Containing Many Interesting and Amusing Incidents of Army Life* (St. Joseph, Mo.: Tribune Co.'s Book and Job Printing Office, 1880), 258. The register is in RG 393, pt. 2, Entry 2671, NA; Military Division of the Mississippi, Special Field Order No. 59, Aug. 23, 1864, RG 393, pt. 1, Entry 2504, NA.

Beginning in July there: *Louisville Daily Journal*, Aug. 19 and Sept. 20, 1864.

Not all of the: Howard, *Account*, 67; Hiram Crandall Diary, July 20, 1864, ILHS.

On Tuesday, July 19: Howard, *Account*, 70–77, 80; John Quincy Adams Campbell Diary, July 21, 1864, WRHS.

There were others who: *Atlanta Journal and Constitution*, Oct. 12, 1986; Michael D. Hitt, *Charged with Treason: Ordeal of 400 Mill Workers During Military Operations in Roswell, Georgia, 1864–1865* (Monroe, N.Y.: Library Research Associates, 1992), passim; *Atlanta Journal*, Feb. 28, 1932.

General Steedman appears in: General Order No. 5, Oct. 15, 1864, RG 393, pt. 2, Entry 2662; WTS to General James B. Steedman, July 10, 1864, *OR* 1, 38, pt. 5, 112, WTS to General Webster, July 11, 25; Captain Dayton to General James B. Steedman, Aug. 12; and WTS to General Joseph D. Webster, Aug. 13, 1864—all in RG 94, Entry 159, MS vol. 12.

As it was, General Steedman: General William J. Wofford to Brown, Feb. 8, 1865, Brown Papers, Telamon Cuyler Coll., UGA.

Steedman's troops—and others: Jonathan D. Sarris, "Anatomy of an Atrocity: The Madden Branch Massacre and Guerilla Warfare in North Georgia, 1861–1865," *Georgia Historical Quarterly* 77 (1990): 679–81; Frank W. Tupper Diary, July 3, 1864, Frank W. Tupper Papers, ILHS.

In Resaca General Steedman: James E. Graham Diary, entries for July and August, passim, OHS.

The District of the: Hight, *Fifty-eighth*, 308; Titze Diary, May 26, 1864, ILHS.

In the right setting: Thaddeus C. S. Brown, Samuel J. Murphy, and William J. Putney, *Behind the Guns: The History of Battery I, 2nd Regiment, Illinois Light*

Artillery, ed. with a foreword by Clyde C. Walton, preface by W. G. Putney (Carbondale: Southern Illinois University Press, 1965), 210.

There was one question: Boies, *Record,* 72; James P. Snell Diary, July 26, 1864, ILHS.

To the south, other: Benedict Joseph Semmes to his wife, May 30, 1864, Benedict Joseph Semmes Papers, UNC.

6. THE CITADEL

The Union soldiers who: John M. Carr Diary, July 3, 1864, UNC; Howard, *Autobiography* 1: 293.

And as Sherman's army: Orlando Poe to his wife, July 4, 1864, Poe Papers, LC; Charles D. Inskeep Diary, July 5, 1864, OHS; Thomas T. Taylor to his wife, July 9, 1864, Taylor Papers, OHS; John Geary to his wife, Oct. 1, 1864, John Geary Letters, Geary Family Correspondence, HSP.

While many of Georgia's: A. Hollis Edens, "The Founding of Atlanta," *Atlanta Historical Bulletin* 5 (1940): 77–83.

By the 1850s, with: Ralph Singer, "Confederate Atlanta" (Ph.D. dissertation, University of Georgia, 1973), 19, 66.

Despite its material interest: Singer, "Atlanta," 70–71.

The metalworking capacities of: Singer, "Atlanta," 22, 103; Stephens Mitchell, "Atlanta, the Industrial Heart of the Confederacy," *Atlanta Historical Bulletin* 1 (1939): 20–27.

This new stature was: Franklin M. Garrett, *Atlanta and Environs: A Chronicle of Its People and Events,* 2 vols. (Athens: University of Georgia Press, 1969), 1: 514, 528; Singer, "Atlanta," 117, 230; Earl McGregor Clauss, "The Atlanta Campaign, 18 July–2 September 1864" (Ph.D. dissertation, Emory University, 1965), 29; *Countryman,* Jan. 19, 1863; Ilene Fife, "The Confederate Theater in Georgia," *Georgia Review* 9 (1955): 310.

Atlanta's mayor, a good: Atlanta City Council Minutes, Jan. 1, 1864, AHC.

The city's churches did: Lewis Lawshe Diary, May 29, 1864, Edda Cole Coll., AHC; Medical Director of Hospitals, Circular No. 18, June 5, 1864, RG 109, Ch. 6, Entry 763, NA.

For if armaments plants: R. J. Massey, "Memories of Brown Hospital," *Sunny South,* Oct. 21, 1901.

The hospitals often contained: E. Sledge to Mrs. Cade, Aug. 18, 1864, Miscellaneous Letters, Confederate States of America, DUKE; Beers, *Memories,* 158.

Until the spring of: Mrs. Henry Huntington, "Escape from Atlanta: The Huntington Memoir," ed. Ben Kremenak, *Civil War History* 11 (1965): 160–63; Garrett, *Atlanta* 1: 586; Singer, "Atlanta," 210–11.

But in May the: Garrett, *Atlanta* 1: 589; Samuel P. Richards Diary, May 23, 1864, AHC; Miss Abby Diary, May 22, 24, and 29, 1864, UGA; *Mobile Daily Register and Advertiser,* May 29, 1864.

On June 1 the: Atlanta City Council Minutes, June 1 and 10, 1864, AHC; Clauss, "Atlanta Campaign," 29; Singer, "Atlanta," 253; Andrew Jackson Neal to his mother, July 23, 1864, Andrew Jackson Neal Letters, EMORY.

But July began with: Miss Abby Diary, July 4, 1864; Francis T. Sherman Diary, July 8, 1864, UVA; Richards Diary, July 10, 1864, AHC.

Now it was not: Singer, "Atlanta," 241; Colonel M. H. Wright to Colonel

George Washington Rains, May 25, 1864, RG 109, Chap. 4, Entry 16, NA; J. B. Sanders to his wife, July 13, 1864, J. B. Sanders Papers, MDAH.

On July 6 orders: S. H. Clayton interview, Dyer and Moore, *Tennessee Veterans' Questionnaires*, 513.

When a hospital packed up: Massey, "Memories"; *Chattanooga Daily Rebel*, Aug. 26, 1864; J. B. Sanders to his wife, July 13, 1864, Sanders Papers, MDAH.

In the first days: A. A. Hoehling, *Last Train from Atlanta* (New York and London: Thomas Yoseloff, 1958), 65–66; Richards Diary, July 22, 1864, AHC; Atlanta City Council Minutes, July 11, 15 and 18, 1864, AHC.

Atlanta was now to: Singer, "Atlanta," 256.

The city was now: Morgan, *Four Years*, 101; Richards Diary, July 10, AHC.

Others, with the time: Lawshe Diary, July 9 and 11, 1864, AHC; Singer, "Atlanta," 247; James Miller Wysor to his wife, July 19, 1864, Wysor Letters, VHS; Cannon, *Rebeldom*, 233.

The value of things: Fleming Jordan to his wife, July 9, 1864, Fleming Jordan Letters, UGA; Huntington, "Escape," 163–64.

While the minds of: Henry Champlin Lay Diary, July 10, 1864, and letters to his wife, July 12, 18 and 22, Henry Champlin Lay Papers, UNC.

Sometime in the middle: Adjutant S. H. M. Byers, *What I Saw in Dixie, or Sixteen Months in Rebel Prisons* (Dansville, N.Y.: Robbins & Poore, Printers, 1868), 42–43.

Then there were those: Miss Abby Diary, July 21 and 22, 1864, UGA; William King Diary, July 2 and 3, 1864, William King Papers, UNC.

Most important, the city: Colin Dunlop to his mother, Aug. 17, 1864, Colin Dunlop Letters, AHC; Garrett, *Atlanta* 1: 617; Report of Major Thomas Osborn, Sept. 10, 1864, *OR* 1, 38, pt. 3, 60; Alexander Hamlin Coe, *"Mine Eyes Have Seen the Glory": Combat Diaries of Union Sergeant Hamlin Alexander Coe*, ed. David Coe (Cranbury, N.J.: Fairleigh Dickinson University Press, 1975), 195.

Initially the bombardment drove: Hoehling, *Last Train*, 171; Andrew Jackson Neal to Ella, Aug. 4, 1864, EMORY; Beers, *Memories*, 166.

The town appeared to: Hoehling, *Last Train*, 255–56.

About sundown Arp and: Charles W. Hubner, "Some Recollections of Atlanta During 1864," *Atlanta Historical Bulletin* 1 (1928): 5–7; Rev. Arthur Howard Noll, ed., *Doctor Quintard, Chaplain CSA and Second Bishop of Tennessee, Being His Story of the War* (Sewannee, Tenn.: University Press, 1903), 100; Lyman A. Brewer to his wife, Sept. 10, 1864, Brewer Coll., HUNT.

Then on August 25: Singer, "Atlanta," 251.

7. THE RAIDS

As chief engineer and: WTS to General Henry W. Halleck, July 6, 1964, *OR* 1, 38, pt. 5, 66.

By the 21st Sherman: WTS to General Henry W. Halleck, July 21, 1864, *OR* 1, 38, pt. 5, 211; WTS to Grant, M0504, Roll 304.

At the same time: William B. Sipes, *The Seventh Pennsylvania Veteran Volunteer Cavalry, Its Record, Reminiscences and Roster* (Pottsville, Pa.: Miners' Journal Print., 1905), 108.

Many Georgia farmers and: Joseph J. Printup to his brother, Feb. 14, 1864, Daniel S. Printup Papers, DUKE; Joseph Belknap Smith Diary, June 17, 1864, Joseph Belknap Smith Papers, DUKE.

Northern and Southern cavalry: Steven Z. Starr, *The Union Cavalry in the Civil War*, vol. 3, *The War in the West, 1861–1865* (Baton Rouge: Louisiana State University Press, 1985), 10; Calvin L. Collier, *The War Child's Children. The Story of the Third Regiment, Arkansas Cavalry, Confederate States Army* (n.p., 1965), 120.

As the war continued: Inspection Report of Wheeler's Cavalry Corps, Jan. 22, 1865, 5, Alfred Roman Papers, LC; H. M. Davidson, *Fourteen Months in Southern Prisons* (Milwaukee: Daily Wisconsin Printing House, 1865), 297.

These shortcomings seem to: WTS to Ellen Sherman, Feb. 28, 1864, Sherman Papers, ND; WTS to Grant, Sept. 24, 1864, M0504, Roll 304; WTS to General Washington Elliott, Oct. 7, 1864, RG 393, Entry 2499.

If the Union cavalry: WTS to General Kenner Garrard, July 25, 1864, *OR* 1, 38, pt. 5, 245.

There is an old: WTS to Ellen Sherman, Aug. 9, 1864, Sherman Papers, ND.

The "big raid" was barely: Ford McWhorter Reminiscences (unpaginated), UGA.

General Sherman was undoubtedly: WTS to O. O. Howard, Aug. 4, 1864, *OR* 1, 38, pt. 5, 336; WTS to Ellen Sherman, Aug. 6, 1864, Sherman Papers, ND; Grant to WTS, Aug. 7, 1864, *OR* 1, 38, pt. 5, 407; John M. Schofield to Judson Kilpatrick, Aug. 18, 1864, John M. Schofield Papers, LC.

The fundamental failure of: William David Evans, "McCook's Raid, July 27–August 1, 1864" (master's thesis, University of Georgia, 1976), 201.

When the wreckers were: Herman Haupt, *Reminiscences of General Herman Haupt, Giving Hitherto Unpublished Official Orders, Personal Narratives of Important Military Operations, and Interviews with President Lincoln, Sec. Stanton, General in Chief Halleck, and with Generals McDowell, and McClellan, Meade, Hancock, Burnside, and Others in Command of the Armies in the Field, and His Impressions of These Men* (Milwaukee: Wright & Joy Co., 1900), 131; Special Field Order No. 37, July 1, 1864, RG 393, pt. 1, Entry 2504.

There is evidence that: Army of the Tennessee, Special Field Order No. 170, July 17, 1864, *OR* 1, 38, pt. 5, 168; Evans, "Raid," 73.

The raids had profound: Melvin Grigsby, *The Smoked Yank* (Sioux Falls, S.D.: Bell Publishing Co., 1888), 123–24; Rev. Thomas M. Stevenson, *History of the 78th Regiment O.V.V.I. from Its "Muster-In" to Its "Muster-Out," Comprising Its Organization, Marches, Campaigns, Battles and Skirmishes* (Zanesville, Ohio: H. Dunne, 1865), 295.

For the people of: Julia Pope Stanley to her husband, July 12, 15, and 17, 1864, Stanley Family Papers, UGA.

On July 22 began: Julia Pope Stanley to her husband, Aug. 1, 1864, Stanley Family Papers, UGA.

Into this charged atmosphere: John F. Stegeman, *These Men She Gave: Civil War Diary of Athens, Georgia* (Athens: University of Georgia Press, 1964), 109, 113; Louise Caroline Reese Cornwell Reminiscences, UDC Coll., GDAH, 245; Elizabeth Baldwin (Wiley) Harris Diary, July 23, 1864, Elizabeth Baldwin (Wiley) Harris Papers, Duke; unidentified correspondent to Andrew Jay McBride, July 23, 1864, Andrew Jay McBride Papers, UGA.

The major towns put: John C. Butler, *Historical Record of Macon and Central Georgia, Containing Many Interesting and Valuable Reminiscences Connected with the Whole State, Including Numerous Incidents and Facts Never Before Published and of Great Historical Value* (Macon, Ga.: J. W. Burke & Co., printers, 1879), 261; Arthur E. Boardman to Mrs. Frank Jones, April 28, 1928, Civil War Miscellany, MGA;

Augusta Daily Chronicle and Sentinel, July 23, 1864; Lay Diary, July 12, 1864, Lay Papers, UNC; Isaac Scott Diary, July 31, 1864, MGA.

When the raiders did: Cornwell Reminiscences, 348, UDC Coll., GDAH.

Another affair of this: Kathleen Middlebrooks Heard Reminiscence, 149, UDC Coll., GDAH; Walter A. Clark, *Under the Stars and Bars or, Memories of Four Years' Service With the Oglethorpes of Augusta, Georgia* (Augusta: Chronicle Printing Co., 1900), 149; Dolly Sumner (Lunt) Burge, *Diary,* ed. James I. Robertson Jr. (Athens: University of Georgia Press, 1962), 94.

Covington was a hospital: Mrs. S. E. D. Smith, *The Soldier's Friend; Being a Thrilling Narrative of Grandma Smith's Four Years' Experience and Observation as Matron in the Hospitals of the South, During the Late Disastrous Conflict in America* (Memphis: n.p., 1867); Daniel, *Recollections,* 65; Andrew Jay McBride to Fannie, Aug. 4, 1864, McBride Papers, UGA.

Not many hours later McCook: C. B. Binion to his brother, John R. Binion, Aug. 14, 1864, Frank R. Binion Letters, UGA; Burge, *Diary,* 94–95.

An Illinois trooper named: W. L. Sanford, comp., *History of the Fourteenth Illinois Cavalry and the Brigades to Which It Belonged* (Chicago: R. R. Donnelley & Sons Co., 1898), 214–18.

For many of the: W. R. Carter, *History of the First Regiment of the Tennessee Volunteer Cavalry in the Great War of the Rebellion, with the Armies of the Ohio and Cumberland, Under Generals Morgan, Rosecrans, Thomas, Stanley and Wilson 1862–1865* (Knoxville: Janet-Ogden Co., Printers, 1902), 184; C. Fred Ingram, ed., *Badland to Barrow. A History of Barrow County, Georgia from the Earliest Days to the Present* (Atlanta: n.p., 1978), 54; Report of Horace Capron, 257, M1098, NA; Sanford, *Fourteenth,* 230.

A Yankee trooper's chances: J. W. Blackshear to his wife, Aug. 3, 1864, Baber-Blackshear Papers, UGA; William Gibbs Allen Scrapbook, 63, William Gibbs Allen Papers, CHAT.

At the same time: Robert Franklin Bunting to the *Houston Telegraph,* July 28, 1864, Bunting Letters, UTEX; Beers, *Memories,* 140.

The raids again raised: Julia Pope Stanley to her husband, July 25, 1864, Stanley Family Papers, UGA; Smith, *Soldier's Friend,* 129; Sanford, *Fourteenth,* 194; Report of Horace Capron, 255, M1098, NA.

Immediately after the raids: Governor Brown's Letterbooks, vol. 13, July 1864, passim, Joseph Emerson Brown Papers, GDAH.

Finally, the raids brought: W. E. Canning to his wife, July 28, 1864, 321, W. E. Canning Letters, UDC Coll., GDAH; Hosea Garrett to his wife, Aug. 1, 1864, Hosea Garrett Jr. Letter, AHC; H. T. Howard to his wife, Aug. 11, 1864, 270, H. T. Howard Letters, UDC Coll., GDAH.

A Lieutenant Barringer received: Norma to Lieutenant Barringer, Aug. 19, 1864, Vincent Montgomery Papers, UDC Coll., GDAH.

It is clear that: Julia Pope Stanley to her husband, July 25, 1864, Stanley Family Papers, UGA; M. Baber to Maria, July 28, 1864, Baber-Blackshear Papers, UGA; Varina Howell Davis, *Jefferson Davis, Ex-President of the Confederate States of America: A Memoir by His Wife,* 2 vols. (New York: Belford Co., 1890), 2: 577.

8. IN THE DITCHES

The arrival of the: Brown to Jeffferson Davis, June 29, 1864, Candler, *Records* 2: 462. *Augusta Daily Chronicle and Sentinel,* July 12, 1864.

So it was that: R. T. Wood to his wife, June 29, 1864, R. T. Wood Papers, Rawlings Coll., UGA; B. M. Polhill to Emmie, June 12, 1864, Emily Nisbet Polhill Papers, UNC; Joseph B. Cumming Reminiscences, 64, UNC.

Somewhat later Major Cumming: Cumming Reminiscences, 65, 66, UNC.

The seasoned veterans of: Sam R. Watkins, *"Company Aytch": A Sideshow of the Big Show* (New York: Collier Books, 1962), 189–90; S. B. Barron, *Lone Star Defenders: A Chronicle of the Third Texas Cavalry, Ross' Brigade* (New York and Washington, D.C.: Neale Publishing Co., 1908), 197; Jarman History, 32, MDAH.

Dr. Massey, who treated: Mosman, *Journal*, 259; Butler, *Letters Home*, 141.

Though the Federal offensive: John A. McIntosh to his father, Aug. 9, 1864, John A. McIntosh Letters, WRHS.

It is possible to: S. F. Fleharty, *Our Regiment* (Chicago: Brewster & Hanscom, Printers, 1865), 99; French, *Two Wars*, 221–22.

Most of this lead: Colonel M. H. Wright to Colonel George Washington Rains, July 1, 1864, RG 109, chap. 4, Entry 16; Adin B. Underwood, *The Three Years' Service of the Thirty-third Mass. Infantry Regiment 1862–1865* (Boston: A. Williams & Co., 1881), 219; *Louisville Daily Journal*, Aug. 29, 1864.

This continuous firing produced: Edward Norphlet Brown to his wife, June 26, 1864, Edward Norphlet Brown Letters, ADAH; James O. Breeden, "A Medical History of the Later Stages of the Atlanta Campaign," *Journal of Southern History* 35 (1969): 53–54; Henry H. Wright, *History of the Sixth Iowa Infantry* (Iowa City: Iowa State Historical Society, 1923), 301; Report of Surgeon E. S. Frink, June 11 to Sept. 10, 1864, Barnes et al., *Medical* 1, pt. 1, 318.

The number of Northern: Breeden, "Medical History," 41; *Sunny South*, Oct. 21, 1901.

Yet as a rule: Stanley E. Lathrop to his family, July 9, 1864, Stanley E. Lathrop Papers, SHSW; Wright, *Sixth Iowa*, 315; James R. M. Gaskill to his wife, June 19, 1864, ILHS; Brown, *Twenty-seventh*, 532; Orlando Poe to his wife, June 25, 1864, Poe Papers, LC; Henry Henney Diary, June 6, 1864, Henry Henney Diary and Letters, CWTI Coll., USAMHI.

The men in both: Wills, *Army Life*, 275; Samuel Merrill to Emily, June 27, 1864, Samuel Merrill Papers, INSL.

The soldiers' diaries and letters: Andrew Bush to his wife, June 28, 1864, Andrew Bush Letters, INSL; Hight, *Fifty-eighth*, 415.

Those soldiers who kept: Carr Diary, June 27, 1864, UNC.

Every ploy, every stratagem: *Indianapolis Daily Journal*, July 19, 1864; Arthur S. Fitch to "Friends at home," Arthur S. Fitch Papers, CCHS; Henry Neer Diary, Sept. 30, 1864, UMAA; Andrew Bush to his wife, Oct. 2, 1864, Bush Letters, ILHS.

Reid Mitchell has observed: Reid Mitchell, *Civil War Soldiers* (New York: Oxford University Press, 1988), 56; Charles A. Willison, *Reminiscences of a Boy's Service with the 76th Ohio* (Menasha, Wisc.: George Banta, 1902), 9; Phinehas Hager to his wife, July 14, 1864, Hager Family Papers, UMAA; David T. Grow to his mother, Aug. 8, 1864, David T. Grow Papers, UILL.

Young men who were: Rennolds Diary, April 1, 1864, UTEN; Samuel King Vann Letters, passim, ADAH.

We do not know whether: Rey Papers, 1864 passim, NYHS.

As for the men: W. A. Stokes to his wife, June 19, 1864, Rhind-Stokes-Gardiner Letters, UGA; Ephraim S. Holloway to his wife, May 20, 1864, Ephraim S. Holloway Papers, CFHS; Henry Giese Ankeny, *Kiss Josie for Me!* comp., ed. Florence Marie Ankeny Cox (Santa Ana, Cal.: Friis-Pioneer Press, 1974), 138.

Some men sent their: James Madison Brannock to his wife, March 29, 1864, Brannock Letters, VHS.

Southern soldiers who were: R. T. Wood to his wife, July 6 and 12, 1864, Wood Papers, Rawlings Coll., UGA.

John H. Marshall, on: John H. Marshall to his wife, Sept. 5, 9, and 23, 1864, Marshall Letters, MSSU.

From time to time the: Edward Norphlet Brown to his wife, Feb. 5, 1864, Brown Letters, ADAH; Judson L. Austin to his wife, June 15 and July 25, 1864, Austin Letters, Ness Papers, UMAA.

Reid Mitchell has written: Mitchell, *Civil War Soldiers*, 121; Wayne E. Morris to his wife, June 9, 1864, Wayne E. Morris Papers, UMAA.

But in some situations: Edward Norphlet Brown to his wife, Feb. 12, 1864, Brown Letters, ADAH.

While Vail does not: General Order no. 10, December 24, 1864, RG 393, pt. 2, entry 2662, NA.

It is unlikely that: William Herrick to his wife, Sept. 18, 1864, William Herrick Letter, UGA.

Occasionally soldiers corresponded back: Samuel Yoder Papers, passim, LC; Vail Narrative, Oct. 9 and Nov. 2, 1864, OHS.

The language employed to describe: Loreta Janeta Velazquez, *The Woman in Battle: A Narrative of the Exploits, Adventure and Travels of Madame Loreta Janeta Velazquez, Otherwise Known as Lieutenant Harry Buford, Confederate States Army* (Hartford, Conn.: T. Belknap, 1876), 59; Charles Albertson to his brother, April 23, 1864, Albertson Letters, GMS.

If a man flinched: A. T. Holliday to his wife, July 29, 1864, A. T. Holliday Letters, AHC; Mosman, *Journal* 256; James Garvin Crawford, *"Dear Lizzie": Letters Written by "Jimmy" Garvin Crawford to His Sweetheart Martha Elizabeth "Lizzie" Wilson While He Was in the Federal Army During the War Between the States, 1862–1865*, ed. Elizabeth Ethel Parker Bascom (Ridgewood, N.J.: Bascom, 1978), 277.

It was difficult to: Edward Norphlet Brown to his wife, July 2 and 8, 1864, Brown Papers, ADAH.

Sometimes the men would: John H. Marshall to his wife, Sept. 9, 1864, Marshall Letters, MSSU; Crawford, *"Dear Lizzie,"* 278; Strong, *Yankee*, 70.

Then sometimes in the: Cannon, *Rebeldom*, 240; James Robert Maxwell, *Autobiography of James Robert Maxwell of Tuscaloosa, Alabama* (New York: Greenberg, 1920), 233.

Perhaps the most singular: Patton Memoir, vol. 31 (unpaginated), LC.

On both sides the fascination: Sylvester Noble, "Vett Noble of Ypsilanti: A Clerk for General Sherman," ed. Donald W. Disbrow, *Civil War History* 14 (1968): 24.

A number of "celebrities" appeared: Conyngham, *Sherman's March*, 137; Pepper, *Recollections*, 105.

The Chattahoochee River provided: Congleton Diary, Aug. 19, 1864, LC; Norrell Memorandum Book, May 30, 1864, AHC; Thomas E. Smith to Maria, July 14, 1864, Smith Papers, OHS; Inskeep Diary, Aug. 14, 1864, OHS.

These notions ran counter: General Order No. 15, July 27, 1864, RG 109, Entry 86, NA; French, *Two Wars*, 216; Rennolds Diary, July 15, 1864, UTEN.

Most of the truces: William H. Pittinger Diary, July 8, 1864, OHS; Congleton Diary, July 26, 1864, LC; *Savannah Daily Republican*, Aug. 30, 1864.

When the soldiers did: Strickling Reminiscences, 34, OHS.

Units that opposed each: Wright, *Sixth Iowa*, 315; Brown, *Twenty-seventh*, 515–16.

In August a Wisconsin: Brobst, *"Well, Mary,"* 80.

9. BATTLE

Traditionally the great battle: Thatcher, *Battles*, 400.

We tend to think: Morris, William S., *History of the 31st Regiment Indiana Volunteers, Organized by John A. Logan* (Evansville, Ind.: Keller Printing & Publishing Co., 1902), 264; Wheeler, *Letters*, 43.

The assault Sherman made: Wilbur F. Hinman, *The Story of the Sherman Brigade* (Alliance, Ohio: Press of the Daily Review, 1897), 546; Mosman, *Journal*, 223; Edward G. Whitesides Diary, CWTI Coll., USAMHI, June 26, 1864; Albert Edward Walls Letter, June 28, 1864, CWTI Coll., USAMHI; Wright, *Sixth Iowa*, 288.

On the evening of: Styles Porter Diary, June 27, 1864, OHS; Walter Quintin Gresham to Tillie, June 27, 1864, Walter Quintin Gresham Papers, LC.

How many of the: Ambrose Bierce, "The Crime of Pickett's Mill," in *Ambrose Bierce's Civil War*, ed. and with an introduction by William McCann (Washington, D.C.: Regnery Gateway, Inc., 1988), 42–43.

One veteran of the: Hedley, *Marching*, 260; Strong, *Yankee*, 226.

But more often than: Stockwell, *Private*, 18; Conyngham, *Sherman's March*, 108; Albert Theodore Goodloe, *Some Rebel Relics from the Seat of the War* (Nashville: Printed for the author, 1893), 174.

Did anyone advance into: Wayne E. Morris to his wife, Aug. 6, 1864, Morris Papers, UMAA; James F. Sawyer to his wife, July 21, 1864, James F. Sawyer Letters, SHSW.

At the other extreme: W. W. Gordon to his wife, June 19 and 22, 1864, Gordon Letters, Gordon Family Papers, GHS. Hiram Yerkes to Miss Prevo, Feb. 22, 1864, Hiram Yerkes Papers, UILL; Edwin Hansford Rennolds Autobiography, 23–24, UTEN.

If anyone went into: General Alexander P. Stewart to Colonel A. J. Keller, May 31, 1864, Stewart Letter, UGA; Cumming Reminiscences, 52, UNC.

As for those who: Stephen Pierson, "From Chattanooga to Atlanta in 1864—A Personal Reminiscence," *Proceedings of the New Jersey Historical Society* 16 (1931): 346; Thomas T. Taylor to his wife, July 26, 1864, Taylor Papers, OHS; Charles H. Dickinson Diary, July 20, 1864, SHSW.

General John Geary continued: Report of General John Geary, *OR* 1, 38, pt. 2, 443.

But by this time: Judson L. Austin to his wife, July 21, 1864, Austin Letters, Ness Papers, UMAA; Lorenzo N. Pratt to his mother, Sept. 30, 1864, Lorenzo N. Pratt Letters, CW Misc. Coll., USAMHI; Luther Nutting to his parents, Dec. 2, 1864, Luther Nutting Letters, Mr. & Mrs. Darold Nutting Coll., WMU.

Sergeant Levi Ross of: Ross Diary, Sept. 1, 1864, Ross Papers, ILHS.

Thomas E. Smith, who: Thomas E. Smith to Maria, May 20 and 21, 1864, Smith Papers, CINHS.

Two months later Smith: Thomas E. Smith to his sister, July 11, 1864, Smith Papers, CINHS.

What Smith had discovered: Mark P. Lowrey Autobiography, 6, CW Misc. Coll., USAMHI.

Oddly enough, when one: Thomas E. Smith to Maria, undated, Smith Papers, CINHS; *History . . . Battery M*, 173.

Smith was concerned that: Charles H. Dickinson Diary, June 22, 1864, WSHS.

It would probably have: Bierce, *Civil War*, 39.

But if we put: James H. Goodnow to his wife, May 28, 1864, James H. Goodnow Papers, LC; Ross Diary, Aug. 3, 1864, Ross Papers, ILHS, McWhorter Reminiscences, UGA.

In the heat of: McWhorter Reminiscences, UGA; Elliot McKeever Narrative, 36, WRHS; G. W. Gordon, "The Battle of Kennesaw Mountain," *Annals of the Army of Tennessee* 1 (1878): 108, 113.

Firing discipline was difficult: Eleazer J. Covey to his cousin, Aug. 7, 1864, Eleazer J. Covey Correspondence, Nina L. Ness Papers, UMAA; Rennolds Autobiography, 24, UTEN.

But a preoccupation with: C. C. Briant, *History of the Sixth Regiment, Indiana Volunteer Infantry* (Indianapolis: W. B. Burford, Printer and Binder, 1891), 319.

Certain actions on the: J. W. Kimmel Reminiscences, 33, OHS; Reminiscence of Jim Davis in Ingram, *Barrow*, 233; Cannon, *Rebeldom*, 168.

Sometimes groups of men: Francis R. Baker Memoirs, 35, ILHS.

Then there were moments: Wills, *Army Life*, 263; Report of Brigadier General Mark Lowrey, Sept. 10, 1864, *OR* 1, 38, pt. 3, 727.

Another group response was: Report of Brigadier General Joseph A. J. Lightburn, July 3, 1864, *OR* 1, 38, pt. 3, 179; Earl J. Hess, "Civilians at War: The Georgia Militia in the Atlanta Campaign," *Georgia Historical Quarterly* 66 (1982): 342; Beall, *Sketches*, 408.

Luther Bradley recalled that: Luther Bradley, Recollections (unpaginated), Luther Bradley Papers, USAMHI; James L. Burkhalter Diary, May 31, 1864, James L. Burkhalter Papers, ILHS.

On the other hand: William Frazer True to his brother, May 25, 1864, William Frazer True Letters, HUNT; Scribner, *Soldiers*, 259.

Here we find evidence: H. V. Redfield, "Characteristics of the Armies," *Philadelphia Weekly Times*, Feb. 16, 1878; Bradley, Recollections, USAMHI; French, *Two Wars*, 277.

Flight from the battle: Cort, *"Dear Friends,"* 139; Moses Yoder to his brother, June 9, 1964, Yoder Papers, LC; John W. Hagan, "The Confederate Letters of John W. Hagan," ed. Bell I. Wiley, *Georgia Historical Quarterly* 38 (1954): 277.

Even a good man: Account of Captain Frank Crawford in Brant, *Eighty-fifth*, 56–57.

What caused a man: I. N. Rainey Experiences, 64, Civil War Coll., TNSL.

But a man fought: Howard Michael Madaus, *The Battle Flags of the Confederate Army of Tennessee* (Milwaukee: Military Publications Museum, 1976), 11–13, 18; Strong, *Yankee*, 197; Regimental Circular of Nov. 20, 1863, Hugh D. Gallagher Papers, INSL.

As the most visible: Richard Manning McMurry, "The Atlanta Campaign. December 23, 1863 to July 18, 1864" (Ph.D. dissertation, Emory University, 1967), 166; Claude Lee Hadaway, " 'With Loyalty and Honor as a Patriot': Recollections of a Confederate Soldier," ed. Royce Shingleton, *Alabama Historical Quarterly* 38 (1954): 254; Report of Captain George W. Welch, May 29, 1864, *OR* 1, 38, pt. 3, 840.

The word "charge" usually: Report of Captain N. B. Rouse, Aug. 1, 1864, *OR* 1, 38, pt. 3, 799; Thomas T. Taylor to his wife, June 29, 1864, Taylor Papers, OHS; Henry McIntosh to George McIntosh, Aug. 5, 1864, William H. McIntosh Papers, SHSW.

As the attackers approached: WTS to Grant, July 24, 1864, *OR* 1, 38, pt. 4, 507; Jarman History, 33, MDAH.

But the final and: Pierson, "Personal Reminiscence," 342.

But usually the assailants came: Report of Colonel Bushrod Jones, Sept. 16, 1864, *OR* 1, 38, pt. 3, 835.

Sometimes little groups of: Bierce, *Civil War*, 46–47; George Parsons to his brother, June 30, 1864, UNC; R. B. Meadows, *Experiences and Recollections of R. B. Meadows, a Private in the Confederate Army* (New York: Knickerbocker Press, n.d.), 30; J. R. Kinnear, *History of the Eighty-sixth Regiment Illinois Volunteer Infantry* (Chicago: Tribune Co., 1866), 70.

Occasionally the wave of: Report of Dr. W. Grinstead, July 20, 1864, Barnes et al., *Medical* 1, pt. 1, 309.

In postwar accounts men: Duke, *Fifty-third*, 127; Douglas Cater to Nannie, May 7, 1864, Douglas J. Cater and Rufus W. Cater Papers, LC; William Frazer True to his brother, May 28, 1864 with a P.S. of May 30, True Letters, HUNT.

In the medical departments: Clason Miller to his mother, July 31, 1864, Miller Letters, Miller Coll., CINHS; Pittinger Diary, July 24, 1864, OHS; John Henry Otto Memoirs, 3, pt. 3, 103, John Henry Otto Papers, OHS.

But in the crisis: Lowrey Autobiography, 5, CW Misc. Coll., USAMHI; Report of General William P. Carlin, 277, M1098, NA; Report of General John A. Logan, Sept. 10, 1864, *OR* 1, 38, pt. 3, 109; Arthur M. Manigault, *A Carolinian Goes to War: The Civil War Narrative of Arthur Middleton Manigault, Brigadier General, C.S.A.*, ed. R. Lockwood Tower (Columbia: University of South Carolina Press, 1983), 247.

But the men could: Strong, *Yankee*, 236–37.

Then, after what seemed: Albert G. Brackett, "Operations Before and Fall of Atlanta," *The United Service* (February 1890): 199.

Many of the missing: Hedley, *Marching*, 167; Report of Brigadier General S. R. Mott, Sept. 9, 1864, *OR* 1, 38, pt. 3, 218; Marshall Diary, July 21, 1864, LC.

If by chance the: Report of General D. C. Govan, July 30, 1864, *OR* 1, 38, pt. 3, 738; William Bluffton Miller Diary, Sept. 1, 1864, INHS; William C. Robinson to his father, Sept. 4, 1864, Robinson Papers, ILHS; Brown, *Twenty-seventh*, 475; Robert Franklin Bunting to the *Houston Telegraph*, July 28, 1864, Bunting Letters, UTEX.

If the captors were: *History of the Ninety-sixth Regiment, Illinois Veteran Infantry*, ed. Charles A. Partridge (Chicago: Browne, Pettibone Co., 1887), 642.

The trickle of prisoners: D. V. Cooper Reminiscence, 37, NCSA; Josiah Cotton to his wife, July 18, 1864, Josiah Cotton Papers, LC.

So the wounded: Duke, *Fifty-third*, James Iredell Hall Notes, July 23, 1864, UNC.

But a man who: Dornblaser, *Sabre Strokes*, 164; William Martin, *Out and Forward, or Recollections of the War of 1861–1865*, foreword by Charles M. Sheldon (Privately printed, 1941), 39.

Occasionally the records reveal: William Ross to his mother, July 25, 1864, William Ross Letters, Napier-Blackmon-Ross-Rose Family Coll., MGA.

The next day his: J. E. Chapin to Mary Ann Ross, March 19, 1866, and

Thomas C. Fitzgibbon to Emma Jane Kennon, Aug. 8, 1864, Napier-Blackmon-Ross-Rose Family Coll., MGA.

10. A CAMPAIGN ENDS

In the last week: *OR* 1, 38, pt. 5, 727, 732–33; Eben P. Sturges to his family, Sept. 6, 1864, Eben P. Sturges Diary and Letters, CWTI Coll., USAMHI.

The bitter fighting at: Carrie Berry Diary, Sept. 1, 1864, AHC; French, *Two Wars*, 222; Hoehling, *Last Train*, 401; Little and Maxwell, *Lumsden's Battery*, 50.

While the garrison and: Findings of the Court of Inquiry upon the Loss of the Confederate Stores of Atlanta, March 3, 1865, *OR* 1, 38, pt. 3, 991–92; *Atlanta Journal*, Nov. 2, 1930.

As always, a rear: Dyer and Moore, *Tennessee Veterans' Questionnaires*, 955; *Atlanta Journal*, Nov. 2, 1930; Bevens, *Reminiscences*, 59.

The night had also: Castel, *Atlanta*, 524; Rev. G. S. Bradley, *The Star Corps or, Notes of an Army Chaplain During Sherman's Famous "March to the Sea"* (Milwaukee: Jermain & Brightman, 1865), 49; James Calhoun, Sworn Statement of July 31, 1865, Calhoun Family Coll., AHC; Emory Sweetland to his wife, Sept. 4, 1864, Emory Sweetland Letters, Michael Winey Coll., USAMHI; J. Ben Thornton Memoirs, 12: 40–42, UDC Coll., GDAH.

The news of the: *Louisville Daily Journal*, Sept. 19, 1864; Tourgee, *Story*, 316; Lorenzo N. Pratt to his parents, Sept. 6, 1864, Pratt Letters, CW Misc. Coll., USAMHI.

The Army of Tennessee: Butler, *Letters Home*, 139; Rennolds Diary, Sept. 5, 1864, UTEN; James Madison Braddock to his wife, Sept. 12, 1864, VHS; Stouten Hubert Dent to his wife, Sept. 10, 1864, Stouten Hubert Dent Papers, AUB; Ben Robertson to his sister, Sept. 7, 1864, William and Ben Robertson Papers, MDAH.

The leaders in turn had: J. B. Sanders to his wife, Sept. 6, 1864, Sanders Papers, MDAH; James Watkins to Frankey, Sept. 9, 1864, James W. and Frankey Watkins Papers, Wiley Coll., EMORY.

At Lovejoy's Station and: Jarman History, 35–36, MDAH.

Far more grave were: Stouten Hubert Dent to his wife, Sept. 7, 1864, Dent Papers, AUB.

One finds a striking: Wills, *Army Life*, 297.

In the meantime: David Nichol to his sister, Sept. 4, 1864, David Nichol Papers, HCWR, USAMHI; Storrs, *"Twentieth,"* 262.

Troops continued to stream: Cora Warren Beck Memoir, 12, ECU.

Sometime that evening the: Charles Fessenden Morse, *Letters Written During the Civil War, 1861–1865* (Privately printed, 1898), 188–89; Alonzo H. Quint, *The Record of the Second Massachusetts Infantry 1861–1865* (Boston: J. P. Walker, 1867), 245; J. Hamp Se Cheverell, *Journal History of the Twenty-ninth Ohio Veteran Volunteers, 1861–1865* (Cleveland: n.p., 1883), 123; Josiah Cotton to his wife, Sept. 4, 1864, Cotton Papers, LC.

On the afternoon of: *Louisville Daily Journal*, Sept. 17, 1864; Morse, *Letters*, 188; Harvey Reid to his sisters, Sept. 5, 1864, Harvey Reid Papers, SHSW.

The troops settled in: Mead Diary, Sept. 10, 1864, Rufus Mead Papers, LC; Lorenzo N. Pratt to his parents, Sept. 6, 1864, Pratt Letters, CW Misc. Coll., USAMHI.

The men all wanted: Thomas M. Small Diary, Sept. 5, 1864, INHS; Allen

Campbell to his family, Oct. 16, 1864, Campbell Family Papers, MSU.

In spite of the: Hoehling, *Last Train,* 434; Rufus Mead to his family, Sept. 8, 1864, Rufus Mead Papers, LC; James Langstaff Dunn to his wife, Sept. 19, 1864, Dunn Correspondence, UVA; Cy Titus to Nannie, Sept. 9, 1864, Cy Titus Letters, Blanch Spurlock Bentley Papers, TNSL.

For better or worse: The relevant letters are in Sherman, *Memoirs* 2: 116–28.

Colonel William Le Duc, who: William G. Le Duc, *Recollections of a Civil War Quartermaster. The Autobiography of William G. Le Duc* (St. Paul, Minn.: North Central Publishing Co., 1963), 128–29; Rufus Mead to his family, Sept. 19, 1864, Rufus Mead Papers, LC. *Louisville Daily Journal,* Oct. 6, 1864.

Colonel Le Duc enlisted Mayor: Sherman, *Memoirs* 2: 118; Special Field Order No. 70, Sept. 12, 1864, RG 393, pt. 1, Entry 2504, NA.

The evacuation proceeded apace: Inskeep Diary, Sept. 12, 1864, OHS; George Ward Nichols, *The Story of the Great March, from the Diary of a Staff Officer* (New York: Harper & Brothers, 1865), 20–23; Le Duc, *Recollections,* 129.

There was considerable waiting: Nichols, *Great March,* 21–22; Orlando Poe to his wife, Sept. 18, 1864, Poe Papers, LC; Wright, *Sixth Iowa,* 335.

The exodus of Atlantans: John Richards Boyle, *Soldiers True: The Story of the One Hundred and Eleventh Regiment Pennsylvania Veteran Volunteers, and of Its Campaign in the War for the Union 1861–1865* (New York: Eaton and Mains, 1903), 248–49; Storrs, "*Twentieth,*" 147; James Langstaff Dunn to his wife, Sept. 19, 1864, Dunn Correspondence, UVA.

As early as September: Le Duc, *Recollections,* 11.

The expulsion of the: Castel, *Atlanta,* 549; General Henry W. Halleck to WTS, Sept. 28, 1864, in Sherman, *Memoirs* 2: 128–29.

And the rank and: Poe Diary, Sept. 7, 10, and 13, 1864, Poe Papers, LC; Wright, *Sixth Iowa,* 275–76.

Major Clare saw the: General F. A. Shoup Diary, Sept. 22, RG 109, Entry 122, NA; Avery, *History,* 318.

As the news of: Laura Nisbet Boykin, *Shinplasters and Homespun: The Diary of Laura Nisbet Boykin,* ed. Mary Wright Stock (Rockville, Md.: Printex, 1975), 22; *Confederate Union* (Milledgeville, Ga.), Sept. 20, 1864.

Rough and Ready was: WTS to Grant, Sept. 19, 1864, RG 393, pt. 1, Entry 2499, NA.

The Confederate authorities may: D. W. Whittle Anecdotes and Incidents, 130–32, LC; Theodore Freylinghuysen Upson, *With Sherman to the Sea: The Civil War Letters, Diaries & Reminiscences of Theodore F. Upson,* ed. with an introduction by Oscar Osburn Winther (Baton Rouge: Louisiana State University Press, 1943), 27–28.

At the end of: James Langstaff Dunn to his wife, Sept. 27, 1864, Dunn Correspondence, UVA; Boies, *Record,* 290; Angus L. Waddle, *Three Years with the Armies of the Ohio and the Cumberland* (Chillicothe, Ohio: Scisto Gisette Book and Job Office, 1889), 78.

Sherman had announced that: Marshall Diary, Sept. 10, 1864, LC; *Louisville Daily Journal,* Sept. 16, 1864; David Nichol to his mother, Oct. 26, 1864, Nichol Papers, HCWR, USAMHI.

"We led a happy life": Samuel Toombs, *Reminiscences of the War, Comprising a Detailed Account of the Experiences of the Thirtieth Regiment New Jersey Volunteers in Camp, on the March, and in Battle* (Orange, N.J.: Journal Office, 1878), 172; Underwood, *Thirty-third,* 236; Brobst, "*Well, Mary,*" 84.

In the case of: William A. Pepper Papers, ILHS; Van S. Bennett Diary, Oct. 14, 1864, Van S. Bennett Papers, SHSW.

He checked on the: Charles Prentiss to his wife, Sept. 29, 1864, Charles Prentiss Letters, Archie Nevins Coll., WMU; WTS to J. H. Willoughby, Sept. 16, 1864, RG 393, pt. 1, Entry 2499.

Sherman welcomed numerous visitors: Wayne E. Morris to his wife, Sept. 28, 1864, with a P.S. of Sept. 30, 1864, Morris Papers, UMAA.

Fantastic as the story: J. P. Austin, *The Blue and the Gray. Sketches of a Portion of the Unwritten History of the Great American Civil War* (Atlanta: Franklin Printing and Publishing Co., 1899), 145–46; *Philadelphia Weekly Times*, Dec. 6 and 13, 1879.

Another visitor was Colonel: Horace Porter, *Campaign with Grant* (New York: Century Co., 1897), 207.

On September 25 President: Bevens, *Reminiscences*, 60.

On the evening of: Richard M. McMurry, *John Bell Hood and the War for Southern Independence* (Lexington: University of Kentucky Press, 1982), 158–61; Rennolds Autobiography, 34, UTEN.

One might suppose that: James Madison Brannock to his wife, Oct. 21, 1864, Brannock Letters, VHS; Stephen D. Lee to Patton Anderson, Oct. 22, 1864, Patton Anderson Letters, J. C. Bonner Coll., GCM.

In its course northward: Avery, *History*, 305; French, *Two Wars*, 264; Mosman, *Journal*, 288.

Elsewhere the Confederates were: Barber, *Memoirs*, 162; Mosman, *Journal*, 291.

When Hood's troops surrounded: W. E. Sloan Diary, Aug. 15, 1864, TNSL; Bevens, *Reminiscences*, 59, 60.

General Hood sent in: Report of Colonel Lewis Johnson, Oct. 17, 1864, *OR* 1, 38, pt. 1, 717–21; Hall Reminiscences, 20, Hall Papers, UMAA.

In the end Colonel: J. W. Ward to his sister, Oct. 18, 1864, Ward Family Letters, CSA Records, UTEX; Rennolds Diary, Oct. 13, 1864, UTEN; Charles Todd Quintard Diary, Nov. 15, 1864, SEW; M0594, Compiled Records, 44th U.S. Colored Infantry, NA.

After taking Dalton Hood: Rennolds Autobiography, UTEN.

11. ATLANTA DELENDA EST

During Horace Porter's visit: Sherman, *Memoirs* 2: 164–66; Porter, *Campaigning*, 211.

Sherman had marshaled solid: WTS to Colonel Green B. Raum, Oct. 16, RG 393, pt. 1, Entry 2499.

At that time Sherman: WTS to Lincoln, Oct. 24, 1864, RG 393, pt. 1, 2499.

Well before Sherman had: WTS to Mrs. M. W. Meyer, Sept. 14, 1864, RG 94, Entry 59, General Sherman's Orders and Letters, vol. 12; Sherman, *Memoirs* 2: 159; Henry Hitchcock, *Marching with Sherman: Passages from the Letters and Campaign Diaries of Henry Hitchcock, Major and Asst. Adjutant General of Volunteers, Nov. 1864–May 1865*, ed. M. A. DeWolfe Howe (New Haven, Conn.: Yale University Press, 1927), 42.

Having received the green: Undated memo in the Absalom H. Markland Papers, LC.

By November 10 the roads: Mahan, "Old Cassville," 121–26; Warren Akin to his wife, Dec. 26, 1864, in *Letters of Warren Akin, Confederate Congressman*, ed. Bell Irvin Wiley (Athens: University of Georgia Press: 1959), 300.

Just when Sherman learned: WTS to General Jefferson C. Davis, Nov. 9, RG 393, pt. 1, Entry 2499, NA.

Sherman's orders were executed: Archibald D. Stinson to Charlie, Dec. 17, 1864, Archibald D. Stinson Papers, INHS; Captain Lewis M. Dayton to General Jefferson C. Davis, Nov. 10, 1864, RG 393, pt. 1, Entry 2499.

We have only the: *Chattanooga Gazette*, Nov. 25, 1864; Will F. Peddycord, *History of the Seventy-fourth Regiment, Indiana Volunteer Infantry* (n.p., 1913), 66–67; Akin, *Letters*, 307; Joseph Hoffhines to Nancy, Nov. 11, 1864, Joseph Hoffhines Letters, OHS; C. C. Platter Diary, Nov. 11, 1864, UGA; John Wesley Daniels Diary, Nov. 11, 1864, John Wesley Daniels Papers, UMAA.

Such stories may have: Inskeep Diary, Nov. 2, 1864, OHS; Platter Diary, Nov. 10, 1864, UGA; Hitchcock, *Marching*, 43–44; Joseph Hoffhines to his wife, Nov. 11, 1864, Hoffhines Letters, OHS; E. P. Burton Diary, Nov. 10, 1864, Wiley Coll., EMORY.

November 12 was the: Vail Narrative, Nov. 9, 1864, OHS; Hickenlooper Reminiscences, 261, Hickenlooper Coll., CINHS.

The last "up" train: Strong, *Yankee*, 7; Hedley, *Marching*, 254.

The train passed through: Tourgee, *Story*, 334; Daniels Diary, Nov. 12, 1864, Daniels Papers, UMAA; Platter Diary, Nov. 12, 1864, UGA; Porter Diary, Nov. 13, 1864, OHS; Hedley, *Marching*, 252, 256.

The auto-da-fé of Marietta: Nichols, *Great March*, 37; McClatchey Diary, Nov. 14, 1864, McClatchey Family Papers, GDAH; Hitchcock, *Marching*, 52–53.

As the flames spread: Champlain Diary, Nov. 14, 1864, Mewett Papers, WRHS; Miller Diary, Nov. 14, 1864, INHS; Gibson's diary in Tourgee, *Story*, 334.

On to the south: Whittle Anecdotes and Incidents, Nov. 7, 1864, LC; Allen Campbell to his brother, Oct. 16, 1864, Campbell Family Papers, MSU.

General Slocum, commander of: General Henry W. Slocum to Colonel James Sidney Robinson, Oct. 15, 1864, James Sidney Robinson Papers, OHS; Slocum's Report, Jan. 9, 1865, *OR* 1, 44, 157; Brant, *Eighty-fifth*, 74.

For the men engaged: J. C. Flanigan, *History of Gwinnett County, Georgia, 1810–1943* (Hapeville, Ga.: Tyler & Co., 1943), 229.

Some men who were: James R. Carnahan Diary, Oct. 21, 1864, James R. Carnahan Papers, INHS; James Langstaff Dunn to his wife, Oct. 18, 1864, Dunn Correspondence, UVA; John Geary to his wife, Nov. 1, 1864, Geary Letters, Geary Family Correspondence, HSP.

The descents of the: Barron, *Lone Star*, 231–32.

The tribulations of a: Elizabeth Perkerson, "A Civil War Letter on the Capture of Atlanta," ed. Medora Field Perkerson, *Georgia Historical Quarterly* 28 (1944): 259–60.

For many who lived: Minerva McClatchey Diary, Sept. 1, 19, Oct. 18, Nov. 3, 14, Dec. 1, 1864. McClatchey Papers, GDAH.

Beginning about November 1: Fleharty, *Our Regiment*, 107; Alexander G. Downing, *Downing's Civil War Diary*, ed. Olynthus B. Clark (Des Moines: Historical Department of Iowa, 1916), 312; Cy Titus to Nannie, Nov. 7, 1864, Titus Letters, Bentley Papers, TNSL.

Though Sherman had indicated: Captain Orlando Poe's Report, Dec. 26, 1864, *OR* 1, 44, 56; Quint, *Second Massachusetts*, 247.

That same day Sherman: Captain Orlando Poe's Report of Oct. 8, 1865, *OR*

1, 44, 60; Harvey Reid, *The View from Headquarters: Civil War Letters of Harvey Reid*, ed. Frank L. Byrne (Madison: State Historical Society of Wisconsin, 1965), 200; Fleharty, *Our Regiment*, 110.

This careful and selective: Hight, *Fifty-eighth*, 409; Andrew Bush to his wife, Nov. 9, 1864, Bush Letters, INSL; General Joseph Wheeler to General John Bell Hood, Nov. 13, 1864, Joseph Wheeler Letterbooks, Wheeler Family Papers, ADAH.

Inside the city some: Mead Diary, Nov. 12, 1864, LC; Conyngham, *Sherman's March*, 236; Reid, *Headquarters*, 201–2.

On the 14th Kilpatrick's: James F. Sawyer to his wife, Dec. 18, 1864, Sawyer Letters, SHSW.

On November 15 Harvey Reid: Reid, *Headquarters*, 202; Hight, *Fifty-eighth*, 409; Conyngham, *Sherman's March*, 237; Hickenlooper Reminiscences, 263, Hickenlooper Coll., CINHS.

Here and there: Allen Campbell to his brother, Dec. 18, 1864, Campbell Family Papers, MSU; Vail Narrative, Nov. 15, 1864, OHS; Hight, *Fifty-eighth*, 410.

After the sun set: Hight, *Fifty-eighth*, 410; Mathias Schwab to his mother, Dec. 24, 1864, Mathias Schwab Civil War Letters, CINHS.

12. THE FIRST ACT

Sherman's men have been: Hickenlooper Reminiscences, 263, Hickenlooper Coll., CINHS; Report of Colonel James Sidney Robinson, Dec. 28, 1864, *OR* 1, 44, 253; James Greenalch to his wife, Nov. 5, 1864, "Letters of James Greenalch," ed. with an introduction by Knox Mellon Jr., *Michigan History* 14 (1960): 228; Orlando Poe to his wife, Nov. 11, 1864, Poe Papers, LC.

Interspersed wth the vehicles: Stevenson, *78th Regiment*, 312.

Someone had calculated before: Special Field Order No. 127, Nov. 23, 1864, RG 393, pt. 1, Entry 2504, NA; Hedley, *Marching*, 281.

To the observer watching: Harris, *On the Plantation*, 228; Gay Cummins McKinley Memoirs, J. C. Bonner Coll., GCM.

For some time the: The various Confederate and state dispatches are grouped in Candler, *Records* 2: 669–74.

Outside the major: Brown's address to the legislators is in Candler, *Records* 2: 771–72.

The siege and fall: Louise Clack, *Our Refugee Household* (New York: Blelock & Co., 1866), 66; Margaret Ketcham Ward, "Testimony of Margaret Ketcham Ward on Civil War Times in Georgia," ed. Aaron M. Boom, *Georgia Historical Quarterly* 39 (1955): 386.

Traveling on the ramshackle: Quintard Diary, Nov. 9, 1864, SEW; Rebecca Felton, "A Night in the Confederacy," *Atlanta Journal*, Oct. 4, 1902.

Governor Brown had given: Mrs. E. Watkins to Brown, Oct. 24, 1864, Brown Papers, Telamon Cuyler Coll., UGA; Baker Daniel to David C. Barrow, Oct. 6, 1864, David C. Barrow Papers, UGA.

There seems to have: James and Nancy Crone to their sons, Oct. 6, 1864, James and Nancy Crone Letter, INHS.

The fear that the: Bill to John, Sept. 20, [1864], Bowman-Howard-Domingos Correspondence, MGA.

A number of women: Edgeworth and Sallie Bird, *Granite Farm Letters: Civil*

War Correspondence of Sallie and Edgeworth Bird, ed. John Rozier (Athens: University of Georgia Press, 1988), 46.

As it turned out: Hight, *Fifty-eighth,* 416–17; William C. Meffett Diary, Nov. 17, 1864, SHSW.

The Union soldiers that: Conyngham, *Sherman's March,* 245; Oliver Sanders Narrative, Nov. 18, 1864, WRHS.

On the 18th the: Hitchcock, *Marching,* 72–73; Clark, *Stars and Bars,* 150.

By the time Sherman: Report of Major A. J. Reynolds, Dec. 26, 1864, *OR* 1, 44, 354; Report of Surgeon Harry Z. Gill, Dec. 30, 1864, *OR* 1, 44, 222.

There remained the danger: Hitchcock, *Marching,* 63, 67.

On the 19th diary entries: Pittinger Diary, Nov. 20, 1864, OHS; Mead Diary, Nov. 21, 1864, LC; Hitchcock, *Marching,* 80–81.

By now cattle were: Report of Major Alfred B. Smith, Dec. 24, 1864, *OR* 1, 44, 245.

The militia had been: Morton McInvale, "All That Devils Could Wish For: The Griswoldville Campaign, November, 1864," *Georgia Historical Quarterly* 60 (1976): 127; Hight, *Fifty-eighth,* 365–67.

Once the firing had: Upson, *With Sherman,* 38; Wright, *Sixth Iowa,* 368; Wills, *Army Life,* 324.

The fighting at Griswoldville: Candler, *Records* 2: 790–91.

Just what inspired this: Robert Toombs to Brown, Nov. 17, 1864, *OR* 1, 44, 527; *Augusta Daily Chronicle and Sentinel,* July 21, 1864.

That same day the: *Journal . . . House,* Nov. 1864, 122–23; *Acts . . . 1864,* 19.

On November 19 Brown: Candler, *Records* 2: 799–802.

November 19 was a: *Sunny South,* Nov. 9, 1901; Mary McKinley to Captain Howell Cobb, Nov. 19, 1864, Civil War Correspondence, Ellis Merton Coulter Historical Manuscripts, UGA; Avery, *History,* 307; William Gibbs McAdoo Sr. Diary, Floyd-McAdoo Families Papers, LC; Anna Maria Green Cook, *History of Baldwin County* (Anderson, S.C.: Keys-Hearn Printing Co., 1925), 54.

In all this frantic: Avery, *History,* 307–9.

On the evening of: McAdoo Diary, Nov. 19, 1864, Floyd-McAdoo Families Papers, LC; *Sunny South,* Nov. 30, 1901.

After the governmental leaders: Fleharty, *Our Regiment,* 115; Douglas Hapeman Diary, Nov. 24, 1864, ILHS; Julian Wisner Hinkley Diary, Nov. 22, 1864, SHSW.

About the only public: *Sunny South,* Nov. 30, 1901.

If the hospitals were: Allen Campbell to his mother, Dec. 18, 1864, Campbell Family Papers, MSU; Miller Diary, Nov. 23, 1864, INHS.

The state capitol building: W. C. Johnson, "The March to the Sea," in *The Atlanta Papers,* ed. Sidney Kerksis (Dayton, Ohio: Press of the Morningside Bookshop, 1981), 813.

On the afternoon of: *Sunny South,* Nov. 9, 1901; Boies, *Record,* 102.

This affair would have: *Sunny South,* Nov. 30, 1901.

13. THE VANDALS

By the time Sherman's: Davidson, *Prisons,* 337; John McElroy, *Andersonville: A Story of Rebel Military Prisons; Fifteen Months a Guest of the So-called Southern Confederacy; A Private Soldier's Experience in Richmond, Andersonville, Millen, Blackshear and Florence* (Toledo: 1879), 254–55.

Word of these killings: George B. Guild, *A Brief Narrative of the Fourth Tennessee Cavalry Regiment, Wheeler's Corps, Army of Tennessee* (Nashville: n.p., 1913), 109; Captain L. M. Dayton to General Judson Kilpatrick, Dec. 1, 1864, *OR* 1, 44, 601.

The quarrel became so: Guild, *Narrative,* 108.

The amount of damage: Sherman, *Memoirs* 2: 174–76, 180.

Those things that did: Report of Lieutenant Colonel John S. Pierce, Dec. 31, 1864, *OR* 1, 44, 194.

While the procedure Sherman: Hedley, *Marching*, 291; Frank D. Baldwin Narrative, 162, Frank D. Baldwin Papers, HUNT.

In fact the "official": Fleharty, *Our Regiment*, 117.

Somewhere in this confused: Wright, *Sixth Iowa*, 413; Morse, *Letters*, 187; Charles Carleton Coffin, *Four Years of Fighting: A Volume of Personal Observations with the Army and Navy from the First Battle of Bull Run to the Fall of Richmond* (Boston: Ticknor & Fields, 1866), 398–99; Nichols, *Great March*, 142.

It was the usual: Aten, *Eighty-fifth*, 258–59.

The party might depart: Daniel E. Bruce Diary, Nov. 21, 1864, INSL; Report of General Alpheus Williams, Jan. 9, 1865, *OR* 1, 44, 211; Strong, *Yankee*, 47.

Then too, the soldiers' appetites: Fleharty, *Our Regiment*, 110; John Van Duser, "The John Van Duser Diary of Sherman's March from Atlanta to Hilton Head," ed. Charles J. Brockman Jr., *Georgia Historical Quarterly* 53 (1969): 238. Report of Major R. P. Findley, Dec. 30, 1864, *OR* 1, 44, 178.

The army's seizures of: Guild, *Narrative*, 109; Wills, *Army Life*, 320.

Cavalry officers had the: Tourgee, *Story*, 336–39, 343; Conyngham, *Sherman's March*, 270.

General Kilpatrick himself had: Coffin, *Four Years*, 398; Hitchcock, *Marching*, 109.

Other generals, and some: Whittle Anecdotes and Incidents, 138, LC.

Concern over irregularities in: General Howard's various orders are recorded in the divisional order book in Reynolds Papers, LC.

While General Howard issued: General Field Order No. 127, Nov. 23, 1864, RG 393, 1, Entry 2504, reproduced in *OR* 1, 44, 527; WTS to General Henry W. Slocum, Nov. 20, 1864, *OR* 1, 44, 501; WTS to General O. O. Howard, Nov. 22, 1864, *OR* 1, 44, 519; Sherman, *Memoirs* 2: 206.

One can't help but: Strong, *Yankee*, 52.

But if there was: Pepper, *Recollections*, 246; Willison, *Recollections*, 102; Aten, *Eighty-fifth*, 260.

Sherman's injunction to leave: Bradley, *Star Corps*, 184; James R. Morrow Diary, Dec. 16, 1864, CWTI Coll., USAMHI; Louis Elseffer to his uncle, Jan. 3, 1865, Charles and Louis Elseffer Letters, Harry S. Elseffer Papers, LC; Stevenson, *History*, 311.

It seems unlikely that: Porter Diary, Nov. 16, 1864, OHS; Cort, *"Dear Friends,"* 169.

By the same token: Hight, *Fifty-eighth*, 406; Eden Bloodworth to his mother, July 14, 1864, Civil War Papers, AHC.

Fire was the chief: Bradley, *Star Corps*, 207; WTS to Slocum, Dec. 2, 1864, *OR* 1, 44, 609.

Despite the restrictions on: Storrs, *"Twentieth,"* 148; Bradley, *Star Corps*, 189.

The extent to which: Hitchcock, *Marching*, 86–87; James Essington Diary, Nov. 30, 1864, INSL; Mead Diary, Nov. 25, 1864, LC.

There was a "standing order": Hitchcock, *Marching*, 92–93.

There is a persistent: D. J. De Laubenfels, "Where Sherman Passed," *Geographical Review* 47 (1957): 385; James C. Bonner, "Sherman at Milledgeville in 1864," *Journal of Southern History* 22 (1956): 280.

If the men were: Thomas Jordan to his wife, Dec. 18, 1864, HSP.

Just how serious were: Sherman's Report of Jan. 1, 1865, *OR* 1, 44, 14; Hickenlooper Reminiscences, 261, Hickenlooper Coll., CINHS; Paul M. Cooper Diary, May 21, 1864, HSP; Poe Diary, Aug. 30, 1864, Poe Papers, LC.

Eloquent as such testimonies: Report of General Alpheus Williams, Jan. 9, 1865, *OR* 1, 44, 211.

We may ask: Report of Lieutenant Colonel James W. Langley, Jan. 3, 1865, *OR* 1, 44, 201; Report of Colonel G. W. Mindil, Sept. 7, 1864.

Deservedly or not, whole: Inspection Report on Wheeler's Cavalry Corps, Jan. 22, 1865, Roman Papers, LC; Starr, *Cavalry . . . West*, 15.

Historian Joseph Glatthaar has: Joseph T. Glatthaar, *The March to the Sea and Beyond: Sherman's Troops in the Georgia and South Carolina Campaigns* (New York: New York State University Press, 1985), 135.

In the march through: Avery, *History*, 434; Hitchcock, *Marching*, 84; Samuel P. Bates, *History of Pennsylvania Volunteers, 1861–5*, 5 vols. (Harrisburg, Pa.: B. Singerly, State Printer, 1869–71), 1: 434.

The men reacted strongly: Hedley, *Marching*, 270; Stevenson, *History*, 317; Downing, *Diary*, 234; Nichols, *Great March*, 85.

Sometimes the soldiers' anger: Conyngham, *Sherman's March*, 269; Levi Ross Diary, October 2, 1864, Levi Ross Papers, ILHS.

There were officers in: Whittle Anecdotes and Incidents, 26, LC; Samuel K. Harryman to Maggie, Dec. 8, 1864, Samuel K. Harryman Letters, INSL; Storrs, "*Twentieth*," 149–50.

As for the men: Greenalch, "Letters," 230.

From the beginning: Wills, *Army Life*, 326.

When it became clear: Poe Diary, Aug. 30, 1864, Poe Papers, LC; Hight, *Fifty-eighth*, 419; General O. O. Howard's letter to Brigade Commanders, Feb. 25, 1865, in Reynolds Papers, LC.

One thing is sure: Will H. Judkins Diary, Dec 2, 1864, INSL; Allen Morgan Geer, *The Civil War Diary of Allen Morgan Geer, Twentieth Regt., Ill. Vols*, ed. Mary Ann Anderson (Denver: R. C. Appleman, 1977), 180.

If the forage party: Strong, *Yankee*, 67–68; Hitchcock, *Marching*, 108.

One thing the foragers: Berrien McPherson Zettler, *War Stories and School-Day Incidents for the Children* (New York: Neale Publishing Co., 1912), 159.

When the group was: David G. Myers, *Social Psychology*, 3rd ed. (New York: McGraw-Hill, 1990), 286; Strong, *Yankee*, 68.

So it probably was: Daniels Diary, Nov. 29, 1864, Daniels Papers, UMAA; Myers, *Social Psychology*, 281, 303.

This deindividuation we can: Hodges, *History*, 71; Barron, *Lone Star*, 120; Samuel Merrill to Emily, Dec. 15, 1864, Merrill Papers, INSL.

Most of the acts: Hitchcock, *Marching*, 132.

And what of the: Hitchcock, *Marching*, 86.

Albion Tourgee also made: Tourgee, *Story*, 366.

By popular demand Sherman: Castel, *Atlanta*, 549.

14. THE VICTIMS

As Sherman's troops filed: Samuel Merrill to Emily, Dec. 15, 1864, Merrill Papers, INSL; Hitchcock, *Marching*, 81, 127–28.

Nor, closer to home: Bradley, *Star Corps*, 312.

Yet some doubts remained: Paul D. Escott, "The Context of Freedom: Georgia's Slaves During the Civil War," *Georgia Historical Quarterly* 58 (1974): 81, 88; Report of General Alpheus Williams, Jan. 9, 1865, *OR* 1, 44, 211.

That was not the impression: Fleharty, *Our Regiment*, 116; Whittle Anecdotes and Incidents, 67, LC.

On the plantation where: Interview with Martha Colquitt in *The American Slave: A Composite Autobiography*, 31 vols., ed. George P. Rawick et al. (Westport, Conn.: Greenwood Press, 1972–77), 12, Georgia Narratives Part 1: 247; Pepper, *Recollections*, 276; Kinnear, *Eighty-sixth*, 167.

The slaves who left: WTS to S. P. Chase, Jan. 11, 1865, S. P. Chase Papers, HSP; General Alpheus Williams Report, Jan. 9, 1965, *OR* 1, 44, 211.

A considerable number of blacks: Essington Diary, Nov. 21, 1864, INSL; Conyngham, *Sherman's March*, 277; James Langstaff Dunn to his wife, Dec. 22, 1864, Dunn Correspondence, UVA.

As the soldiers encountered: Samuel Merrill to Dinah, Dec. 15, 1864, Merrill Papers, INSL; Bradley, *Star Corps*, 196; Downing, *Diary*, 232, note 1; Elijah P. Burton, *Diary of E. P. Burton, Surgeon, 77th Regiment Illinois 3rd Brigade, 2nd Division, 16 Army Corps* (Des Moines: Historical Records Survey, 1939), 47; Jacob M. Hartness to his wife, Dec. 18, 1864, Jacob M. Hartness Papers, INHS.

The images that come: Pepper, *Recollections*, 190; Harris, *On the Plantation*, 231.

The departure of the slaves: Harris, *On the Plantation*, 130; Ward, "Testimony," 378; *Sunny South*, Oct. 5, 1901, Feb. 22, 1902.

Most slaves who departed: Wills, *Army Life*, 332; Storrs, *"Twentieth,"* 154.

When a slaveholder: Clack, *Refugee*, 192–206.

They bedded down: Clack, *Refugee*, 207–11.

The recipient of this letter: Lawrence Huff, " 'A Bitter Draft We Have Had to Quaff': Sherman's March Through the Eyes of Joseph Addison Turner," *Georgia Historical Quarterly* 72 (1988): 316–19.

It was widely expected: Sherman, *Memoirs* 2: 189–90; Robert E. Lee to Jefferson Davis, Nov. 19, 1864, *OR* 1, 44, 869.

But the population of Georgia: Brown's Orders of Dec. 5 and 19, 1864, Candler, *Records* 2: 808, 815.

Here and there local men: Zettler, *War Stories*, 117; *Atlanta Journal*, June 1, 1902.

Then there was: Sloan Diary, 85–86, TNSL.

If it was thus exceptional: Hinkley Diary, Nov. 25, 1864, SHSW; Bradley, *Star Corps*, 193.

Most women understood: Strong, *Yankee*, 46; Bradley, *Star Corps*, 202; Hitchcock, *Marching*, 83.

The woman of the house: Cornwell Reminiscences, UDC Coll., GDAH.

There were a number: Wimer Bedford Diary, Nov. 24, 1864, LC.

Any number of Georgia: James E. Edmonds Diary, November 16–20, 1864, James E. Edmonds Papers, USAMHI.

A Miss Harris, who: R. Harris to her brother, December 1, 1864, Iverson L. Harris Papers, DUKE.

While such dalliance: *Sunny South*, Nov. 30, 1901; Marcellus Darling, *Incidents and Comments of My Life* (n.p., n.d.), 128. *Columbus (Ga.) Ledger-Inquirer*, April 16, 1961.

Most of the things: Storrs, *"Twentieth,"* 153.

Since bulky items could: Bill to John, Sept. 20, 1864, Bowman-Howard-Domingos Correspondence, MGA; William F. Saylor Letter, Dec. 15, 1864, SHSW.

When the foragers insisted: Strong, *Yankee*, 62–63.

The ransacking of the home: M. A. E. Walton to her daughter, Feb. 21, 1865, Ward Family Letters, CSA Records, UTEX.

Apparently some feared they: Hitchcock, *Marching*, 83; Zettler, *War Stories*, 134; Thos. Maguire to his son, Dec. 4, 1864, AHC.

This particular response: McAdoo Diary, Nov. 21–23, 1864, Floyd-McAdoo Families Papers, LC.

Though there may not: Cy Titus to Nannie, undated, Titus Letters, Bentley Papers, TNSL.

In thus meeting the invaders: Glatthaar, *March*, 74; Whittle Anecdotes and Incidents, 70, LC; Harvey Reid Narrative, 203, Harvey Reid Papers, SHSW; Hitchcock, *Marching*, 73, 76, 158.

The specific matter of rape: Robert Franklin Bunting to the *Houston Telegraph*, Dec. 7, 1865, Bunting Letters, UTEX.

There is another reason: Strong, *Yankee*, 43.

15. AFTERMATH

General Sherman considered the city: WTS to General William Joseph Hardee, Dec. 17, 1864, *OR* 1, 44, 737.

The fall of Savannah: Aten, *Eighty-fifth*, 266.

While he paused in Savannah: The relevant reports are in *OR* 1, 44, 6–66.

We have no statistics: Avery, *History*, 331.

If we have no: Andrews, *Journal*, 31–32.

Miss Andrews and her: Andrews, *Journal*, 33–49, 57.

Somewhat later a Union officer: L. M. Hosea, "The Last Ditch," *Sketches of War History: Papers of the Ohio Commandery, Military Order of the Loyal Legion of the United States* 3 (1890): 294–96.

William McAdoo visited the area: McAdoo Diary, Dec. 31, 1864, Floyd-McAdoo Families Papers, LC; Resolutions of the Citizens of Wilcox County, Jan. 14, 1865, Brown Papers, Telamon Cuyler Coll., UGA.

There was a scapegoat: P. A. Lawson to Jefferson Davis, Dec. 27, 1864, *OR* 4, 3, 967; *Confederate Union*, Dec. 6, 1864.

The semidisgrace of General Wheeler: G. Dunbar to his cousin, Jan. 14, 1865, Baber-Blackshear Papers, UGA.

When the Georgia legislature: Robert Hill to his sister, Jan. 8, 1865, John W. Hill Papers, UTEX.

Such comments must have: McWhorter Reminiscences, UGA.

As the last bluecoats: Stephen Graham, "Marching Through Georgia. Following Sherman's Footsteps Today," *Harper's Magazine* 140 (1920): 615; J. H.

Parks, *Joseph E. Brown of Georgia.* (Baton Rouge: Louisiana State University Press, 1977), 312, 318; Gassman, "Rome," 122.

The handful of Atlantans: Report of General W. P. Howard, *Macon Telegraph,* Dec. 12, 1864; Noble C. Williams, *Echoes from the Battlefield; or, Southern Life During the War* (Atlanta: Franklin Printing and Publishing Co., 1902), 46; Mary Gay, *Life in Dixie During the War 1861–1862–1863–1864–1865* (Atlanta: C. P. Byrd, 1897), 260–63.

In other towns refugees: Donnie Davis to her brother, Dec. 31, 1864, and Peggy Berry to her children, Dec. 14, 1864, Confederate Miscellany, EMORY; H. W. Mathis Reminiscence, UDC Coll., GDAH.

In the country there were: *New York Times,* June 27, 1865; Zettler, *War Stories,* 139–40.

These were to be: Andrews, *Journal,* 198.

Those who had played: Willard Welsh, "Civil War Theater: The War in Drama," *Civil War History* 2 (1955): 265; Noll, *Quintard,* 2.

General Sherman succeeded Grant: WTS to Clark Howell, Feb. 13, 1879. WTS to John E. Tourtelotte, Aug. 7, 1888, Sherman Papers, LC.

Some of those who: Samuel G. French to Henry W. Fair, Nov. 6, 1897, Samuel G. French Papers, MDAH; T. B. Roy's preface to a sketch of General Hardee's life, Hardee Papers, ADAH; F. von Meerheimb, *Shermans Feldzug in Georgien* (Berlin: Ernst Siegfried Mittler und Sohn, 1869), 53–54.

In the 1930s there was: B. H. Liddell Hart, *Sherman: Soldier, Realist, American* (New York: Dodd, Mead & Co., 1930), preface, vii, 170; *Paris, or the Future of War* (New York: E. P. Dutton & Co., 1925), 24.

As for Sherman's veterans: Pierson, "Personal Reminiscence," 345.

Other veterans came back: Robert H. Russell to his wife, Dec. 26, 1864, Robert H. Russell Papers, OHS; Interview with Andrew Ainslie and papers he furnished for the author's examination; Maud and Isidor Gelders, "Fitzgerald, Georgia: A Soldiers' Colony," *Georgia Review* 7 (1953): 165–73.

But for every former: *Society of the Army of the Cumberland. Fifth Reunion, 1872* (Cincinnati: 1872), 90–93.

Yet at the same time: Graham, "Marching," 817; *Society . . . Fifth Reunion,* 90; Tourgee, *Story,* 355.

Here, certainly, lies: Edwin Tribble, "Marching Through Georgia," *Georgia Review* 21 (1967): 423–29.

Henry Clay Work's composition: *Atlanta Constitution,* Oct. 1, 1887; John H. Kennaway, *On Sherman's Track, or, The South After the War* (London: Deeley, Jackson and Halliday, 1867), 108, 115; Oliver Lyman Spalding Reminiscences, 46, UMAA.

Atlanta marched to its: C. C. Jones Jr., *Address Delivered Before the Confederate Survivors' Association in Augusta, Georgia at its Sixth Annual Meeting, on Memorial Day, April 20, 1864* (Augusta, Ga.: Confederate Survivors' Association, 1884), 16, 18.

As time passed Georgians: *Atlanta Journal,* Aug. 20, 1894; Copy of a Letter Picked up on the Battlefield at Camden, S.C., in 1864, UDC Coll., GDAH; "And More About Sherman's Nags," *Georgia Historical Quarterly* 58 (1974): 117; WTS to Ellen Sherman, March 23, 1865, Sherman Papers, ND; Hedley, *Marching,* 67; Allen Scrapbook, 23, Allen Papers, CHAT.

And in folklore at least: Anna McAllister, *Ellen Ewing, Wife of General Sher-*

man (New York: Benziger Brothers, 1936), 341; *Atlanta Journal,* April 3, 1938; D. J. De Laubenfels, "With Sherman Through Georgia," *Georgia Historical Quarterly* 41 (1957): 295.

As this rich tapestry: *Augusta Chronicle,* Nov. 11, 1990.
By the time Sherman: *Americus Daily Times,* Feb. 15, 1891.
In 1919 a writer: Graham, "Marching," 613–19.

Bibliography

PRIMARY SOURCES

Unpublished Documents

NATIONAL ARCHIVES
Record Group 94, Records of the Adjutant-General's Office
Entry 159, Generals' Papers and Orders, General Sherman's Orders and Letter-books
Entry 306, Letters Received, Colored Troops Division
Entry 961, Reports of the Provost Marshal General
Record Group 109, War Department Collection of Confederate Records
Entry 36, "Ledger" of the Powder Factory, 1861–65
Entry 82, Department of Georgia, Orders and Circulars, 1864–65
Entry 86, General Orders and Circulars, Army and Department of Tennessee
Entry 89, Miscellaneous Records, Army of Tennessee, July 1864–Feb. 1865
Entry 120, General S. G. French Papers, 1861–65
Entry 121, General T. C. Hindman Papers, 1861–64
Entry 122, General J. B. Hood Papers, 1862–64
Entry 134, General C. L. Stevenson Papers, 1863–65
Entry 135, General E. C. Walthall Papers, 1864–65
Entry 136, General Joseph Wheeler Papers, 1863–64
Ch. 2, vol. 19 1/4, Letters sent, Inspector General of the Army of Tennessee, 1864–65
Ch. 2, vol. 27 1/2, Orders and Circulars, General W. H. Jackson's Cavalry Division, Army of Tennessee, June–Sept. 1864
Ch. 2, vol. 265, Records of General P. R. Cleburne's Division, Army of Tennessee
Ch. 2, vol. 272, Orders and Circulars of General W. J. Hardee's Corps, Army of Tennessee, Feb. 1863–March 1865
Ch. 2, vol. 273, Letters Sent and Orders Received by General J. B. Hood's Corps, Army of Tennessee, March 1864–Feb. 1865
Ch. 2, vol. 349, Special Field Orders and Special Orders, Army of Tennessee, 1862–65

Ch. 4, vols. 10, 11, and 16, Letters and Telegrams Sent, Atlanta Arsenal, 1862–64
   Record Group 393, Records of U.S. Army Continental Commands, Part 1
Entry 961, Army of the Cumberland, Reports of Operations and Casualties Received, 1863–65
Entry 2480, Military Division of the Mississippi, Letters Sent, Oct. 1863–Aug. 1866
Entry 2481, Military Division of the Mississippi, Telegrams Received and Sent, March 1864–May 1865
Entry 2489, Military Division of the Mississippi, General Orders, Oct. 1862–Aug. 1866
Entry 2491, Military Division of the Mississippi, Special Orders, Oct. 1863–Aug. 1866
Entry 2498, Military Division of the Mississippi, Letters Sent in the Field, April–May 1864
Entry 2499, Military Division of the Mississippi, Letters Sent in the Field, May 1864–Jan. 1865
Entry 2504, Military Division of the Mississippi, Special Field Orders, May 1864–May 1865
Entry 2517, Military Division of the Mississippi, Letters Sent by the Provost Marshal General, March 1864–Jan. 1865
Entry 2520, Military Division of the Mississippi, Report of Property Seized from Citizens, July–Dec. 1864
   Record Group 393, Part 2
Entry 2651, District of the Etowah, Letters Sent
Entry 2655, District of the Etowah, Register of Letters Received
Entry 2657, District of the Etowah, Letters Received
Entry 2658, District of the Etowah, Reports
Entry 2661, District of the Etowah, Telegrams Received
Entry 2662, District of the Etowah, General Orders
Entry 2665, District of the Etowah, Special Orders
Entry 2671, List of Civilians to Whom Permits Have Been Issued to Live Within Three Miles of the Railroad
Entry 2687, District of the Etowah, General Orders, Special Orders, Special Field Orders, and Circulars Issued by the Provost Marshal
   Microfilm Collections
M0345 Union Provost Marshal's File of Papers Relating to Individual Civilians
M0416 Union Provost Marshal's Files of Papers Relating to Two or More Civilians
M0437 Letters Received by the Confederate Secretary of War, 1861–65
M0504 Telegrams Collected by the Office of the Secretary of War, 1860–70
M0594 Compiled Records Showing Service of Military Units in Volunteer Union Military Organizations: Files on 44th U.S. Colored Infantry
M0621 Reports and Decisions of the Provost Marshal General, 1863–66
M0935 Inspection Reports and Related Records Received by the Inspection Branch in the Confederate Adjutant and Inspector General's Office
M1098 Generals' Reports of Civil War Service, 1864: Reports of Generals:

   Daniel Butterfield
   William P. Carlin
   Horace Capron

Manning F. Force
William B. Hazen
Alvin P. Hovey
Emerson Opdycke
Alpheus S. Williams
GEORGIA DEPARTMENT OF ARCHIVES AND HISTORY
Letterbooks of Governor Joseph E. Brown
ATLANTA HISTORY CENTER
Minutes of Meetings of the Atlanta City Council, 1861–64

Unpublished Diaries, Letters, Memoirs, etc.

Miss Abby (Cyrena Bailey Stone) Diary, UGA
Bristow Adams Family Papers, CRNL
Mary Adams Correspondence, CWTI Collection, USAMHI
R. Q. Adams Recollections, UDC Collection, GDAH
Calvin Ainsworth Diary, UMAA
Akin Family Papers, UGA
Warren Akin Letter, AHC
Albertson Letters, GHS
Manning P. and Pellona David Alexander Letters, UGA
William A. Allen Papers, ILHS
William Gibbs Allen Papers, CHAT
Lyman Daniel Ames Diary, OHS
John Emerson Anderson Memoir, LC
Mrs. Kirby-Smith Anderson Memoir, UDC Collection, GDAH
Patton Anderson Letters, J. C. Bonner Collection, GCM
Patton Anderson Letters, C. W. Misc. Collection, USAMHI
Walter Howell Anderson Reminiscence, UDC Collection, GDAH
George W. Andrews Letters and Diary, HUNT
Robert G. Ardrey Letters, ILHS
Z. J. Armistead Letters, UDC Collection, GDAH
William C. Armor Collection, PSA
William C. Armor Diary, EMORY
Arnold Family Papers, MSU
Lester Arnold Papers, OHS
Israel Atkins Letters, MSU
Merritt B. Atwater Recollections, SHSW
Austin Family Letters, UGA
Mrs. J. T. P. Austin Reminiscences, UDC Collection, GDAH
Judson L. Austin Letters, Nina L. Ness Papers, UMAA
Myrta L. Avary Papers, UVA
Baber-Blackshear Papers, UGA
Samuel Bachtell Letter, AHC
Bailey Diary, Wiley Collection, EMORY
Bailhache-Brayman Letters, ILHS
Francis R. Baker Memoirs, ILHS
Otis T. Baker Papers, MDAH
Frank D. Baldwin Papers, HUNT
Harris Elizabeth Baldwin Diary, DUKE
John William Baldwin Diary, OHS

Charles L. Ballard Papers, SHSW
John Banks Diary, Banks Collection, UGA
George Bargus Diary, CWTI Collection, USAMHI
Abdiel Barker Letters, ILHS
Jennie Meta Barker Collection, AHC
Lorenzo Barker Diary, UMAA
William R. Barksdale Letters, MDAH
Barksdale-Smith Civil War Letters, GCM
Geoffrey Barnsley Manuscripts, UGA
David C. Barrow Papers, UGA
John Batchelor Diary, ILHS
Robert Battey Papers, AHC
William G. Baugh Papers, EMORY
Lionel Baxter Collection, CWTI Collection, USAMHI
Edwin Clifton Beach Papers, OHS
Richard Beard Letter, LC
Samuel Bechtold Diary, Bechtold Family Papers, UMAA
Cora Warren Beck Memoir, ECU
Wimer Bedford Diary and Essay, LC
John Bennett Letters, Calvin and Lucy Millard Papers, WMU
Van S. Bennett Papers, SHSW
Carrie Berry Diary, AHC
Betty Family Papers, TNSL
Mary Ann Ball Bickerdyke Papers, LC
Frank R. Binion Letters, UGA
Frank Bisel Papers, ECU
Hugh Black Letters, AHC
Nellie Peters Black Reminiscences, AHC
James A. Blackshear Diary, EMORY
J. William Blackshear Papers, DUKE
Wylie Blair Papers, INHS
Ira Blanchard Reminiscences, ILHS
Robert Lewis Bliss Papers, ADAH
Charles F. Blood Papers, CRNL
Mrs. Ben Bloodworth Account, UDC Collection, GDAH
Ferdinand F. Boltz Papers, DUKE
Bomar Family Papers, EMORY
Bomar-Killian Family Papers, AHC
Jennette Bonebrake Papers, UNC
Edwin A. Bowen Memorandum, HUNT
Bowman-Howard-Domingos Correspondence, MGA
William H. Bradbury Papers, LC
Luther F. Bradley Papers, USAMHI
Hamilton Branch Letters, Margaret Branch Sexton Collection, UGA
James Madison Brannock Letters, VHS
Bratton Family Papers, USC
Lyman A. Brewer Collection, HUNT
Abbie M. Brooks Papers, AHS
William E. Brooks Collection, LC
Charles S. Brown Papers, DUKE

Brown Family Papers, UGA
Edward Norphlet Brown Letters, ADAH
Joseph Emerson Brown Papers, AHC
Joseph Emerson Brown Papers, EMORY
Joseph Emerson Brown Papers, GDAH
Joseph Emerson Brown Papers, Telamon Cuyler Collection, UGA
Nathan Atkinson Brown Papers, UGA
O. V. Brown Collection, INSL
W. C. Brown Diary, CHAT
William H. Brown Correspondence and Diary, CWTI Collection, USAMHI
R. H. Browne Papers, UNC
Daniel E. Bruce Diary, INSL
Magnus Brucker Papers, INHS
Alfred C. Brundage Letters, HUNT
Chauncey Brunson Welton Papers, UNC
Brush Family Papers, ILHS
Levi D. Bryant Letters, Michael Winey Collection, AMHI
Buck Family Papers, Civil War Miscellany, MGA
Irving A. Buck Papers, UNC
C. W. Buckley Letters, MSSU
Robert Franklin Bunting Letters, UTEX
Newel Burch Diary, USAMHI
Alfred Burdick Diary, SHSW
George Burgess Diary, CWTI Collection, USAMHI
James L. Burkhalter Papers, ILHS
E. P. Burton Diary, Wiley Collection, EMORY
Andrew Bush Letters, INSL
Martin D. Bushnell Letters, USAMHI
Nicholas Buswell Papers, ILHS
Thomas Butt Diary, CWTI Collection, USAMHI
Anson W. Buttles Correspondence, SHSW
George H. Cadman Papers, UNC
Caldwell Family Correspondence, CWTI Collection, USAMHI
Frank Hollis Caldwell Reminiscences, CHAT
Calfee Family Papers, W&M
Calhoun Family Collection, AHC
Morgan Callaway Papers, EMORY
W. A. Callaway Reminiscences, UDC Collection, GDAH
Cameron Collection, UALA
Campbell Family Papers, MSU
John Angus Campbell Letters, J. C. Bonner Collection, GCM
John Quincy Adams Campbell Diary, WRHS
William W. Campbell Reminiscences, SHSW
W. E. Canning Letters, UDC Collection, GDAH
Horace Capron Papers, LC
Elijah Carley Manuscripts, UGA
Caleb H. Carlton Papers, LC
James R. Carnahan Papers, INHS
John M. Carr Diary, UNC
John S. Casement Papers, HUNT

John Peter Casler Narrative, Arthur Miller Collection, WMU
Douglas J. Cater and Rufus W. Cater Papers, LC
Aden Cavins Papers, ILHS
Raymond Cay Reminiscence, UDC Collection, GDAH
Joseph Wright Chamberlain Papers, INHS
Orville T. Chamberlain Letters and Diaries, INHS
Sydney S. Champion Papers, DUKE
Albert A. Champlain Diary, Alfred Mewett Papers, WRHS
Nathaniel P. Charlot Papers, AUB
George W. Chase Papers, UMAA
S. P. Chase Papers, HSP
George L. Childress Diary, ILHS
William Chunn Papers, EMORY
Byron Churchill Letters, Stephen L. Lowen Papers, WMU
Civil War Correspondence, Ellis Merton Coulter Historical Manuscripts, UGA
Civil War Miscellany, MGA
Civil War Papers, AHC
Civil War Soldiers' Letters, ADAH
Louise Clack, Reminiscences, Robert Livingston Nicholson Collection, LC
Carroll Henderson Clark History, CHAT
Joseph H. Clark Diary and Letters, Clark Family Papers, CINHS
Clay Collection, GHS
Henry D. Clayton Papers, UALA
William Clemens Narrative, UILL
Henry Cleveland Letters, UGA
William B. Cliften Letters, Union Miscellany, EMORY
Howell Cobb Papers, UGA
Samuel Coble Civil War Diary, INHS
L. L. Cody Reminiscence, UDC Collection, GDAH
Benjamin Cohee Letters, USAMHI
Edda A. Cole Scrapbook, AHC
D. Coleman Diary, UNC
George K. Collins Correspondence, Collins Family Papers, CRNL
A. M. Colton Letters, UDC Collection, GDAH
Joshua and Merrit Comfort Papers, DUKE
George N. Compton Reminiscences, ILHS
Thomas Jefferson Conely Papers, UMAA
Confederate Microform Miscellany, EMORY
Confederate Miscellany, EMORY
Confederate Soldiers' Letters, Wilbur G. Kurtz Collection, AHC
James A. Congleton Diary, LC
D. V. Cooper Reminiscences, NCSA
Paul M. Cooper Diary, HSP
William Dudley Cooper Diaries, UNC
John Cope Papers, LC
W. B. Corbett Diary, Wiley Collection, EMORY
Caleb Core Letters, Core-Porter Family Papers, OHS
Susan Cornwall Journal, UNC
Louise Caroline Reese Cornwell Reminiscences, UDC Collection, GDAH
Josiah Cotton Papers, LC

J. W. Courtney Letter, AHC
William Cove Reminiscences, GCM
Israel P. Covey Correspondence, Nina L. Ness Papers, UMAA
Eleazer J. Covey Correspondence, Nina L. Ness Papers, UMAA
Charles Harding Cox Papers, EMORY
Jacob Dolson Cox Diary, DUKE
Jacob Dolson Cox Papers, LC
Joseph R. Cox Letters, ILHS
Charles Craig Letters, UMAA
Hiram Crandall Diary, ILHS
James Porter Crane Letters, AHC
Robert Burns Craw Memoirs, CWTI Collection, USAMHI
Mary Jane (Baugh) Crawford Reminiscences, UDC Collection, GDAH
James R. Crew Papers, AHC
John Crittenden Letters, Davenport-Crittenden-Harvey Papers, UTEX
James and Nancy Crone Letter, INHS
W. O. Crouse History, INHS
Richard Robert Crowe Papers, SHSW
James Gardiner Crozer Papers, USMA
Joseph B. Cumming Reminiscences, UNC
Kate Cumming Papers, ADAH
Cunningham Family Letters, UGA
William L. Curry Papers, OHS
Margaret Daily Journal, Confederate Miscellany, EMORY
John Wesley Daniels Papers, UMAA
Sylvester Daniels Diary, Theophilus M. Hagan Collection, HUNT
Davidson-Terry Family Letters, AHC
A. W. Davidson Letters, AHC
Davis Family Papers, MSU
J. M. Davis Letters, Malcolm Papers, UGA
Jefferson C. Davis Papers, INHS
Newton N. Davis Papers, ADAH
Davis-Quillin Family Papers, AHC
Ephraim Cutler Dawes Narrative, CINHS
James Dawson Papers, AHS
Wesley W. De Haven Diary, UDC Collection, GDAH
Alfred Long Dearing Diary, UGA
Denny Confederate Letters, AUB
Stouten Hubert Dent Papers, AUB
Charles H. Dickinson Diary, WSHS
John Sherman Diltz Papers, DUKE
Mumford Dixon Diary, EMORY
Eleazer B. Doan Correspondence, CWTI Collection, USAMHI
Edwin Shelby Dodd Diary, TXSL
J. C. Dodge Reminiscences, UDC Collection, GDAH
Ambrose Doss Letters, KENN
Julius Dowda Papers, GDAH
John William Draper Papers, LC
William A. Drennan Papers, MDAH
John Witherspoon DuBose Papers, ADAH

O. G. Dunkel Papers, MSU
John Dunlap Letter, AHC
Colin Dunlop Letters, AHC
James Langstaff Dunn Correspondence, UVA
Washington Dunn Diary, UDC Collection, GDAH
D. H. Duryea Letters, UNC
Henry O. Dwight Papers, OHS
Richard F. Eddins Correspondence, CWTI Collection, USAMHI
John Theodore Edgar Letters, LC
Andrew Edge Correspondence, EMORY
Thomas Doak Edington Diary, UTEN
James E. Edmonds Papers, USAMHI
Edwards Family Collection, AHC
Isaac Z. Edwards Letter, UMAA
Peter Ege Papers, SHSW
John E. Eicker Memoir, USAMHI
Robert Newell Elder Papers, OHS
Eliza McKay Elliot Scrapbook, Thurmond-Swift-Tutt Collection, UGA
Fergus Elliot Diary and Letters, CWTI Collection, USAMHI
Collins D. Elliott Papers, TNSL
Charles and Louis Elseffer Letters, Harry S. Elseffer Papers, LC
Benjamin Epler Papers, OHS
George Phifer Erwin Papers, UNC
Joseph Espey Letters, Espey Family Papers, UNC
James Essington Diary, INSL
William David Evans Papers, WRHS
J. H. Everett Papers, GHS
Charles Ewing Papers, LC
Faw Family Papers, KENN
Winfield Scott Featherston Memoirs and Official Documents and Reports, CW
    Misc. Collection, USAMHI
Winfield Scott Featherston Narrative, J. F. H. Claiborne Papers, UNC
Rebecca Latimer Felton Papers, UGA
Lewis R. Fenton Diary, LC
John N. Ferguson Diaries, LC
Samuel Wragg Ferguson Autobiography, Heyward-Ferguson Papers, UNC
Samuel W. Ferguson Papers, MDAH
Michael Ferry Diary, AHC
Nathan Finegan Papers, OHS Robert Stuart Finley Papers, UNC
John W. Fisher Diary, Union Miscellany, EMORY
Julia Fisher Diary, UNC
Arthur S. Fitch Papers, CCHS
Michael Hendrick Fitch Papers, SHSW
Fleming Correspondence, UGA
J. H. Fleming Sr. War Record, UDC Collection, GDAH
James Monro Forbes Letters, HUNT
Manning F. Force Papers, LC
Michael Forry Diary, KENN
John Porter Fort Memoirs, CWTI Collection, USAMHI
Tomlinson Fort Papers, CHAT

Louis R. Fortescue Diary, UNC
Nathaniel W. Foster Papers, OHS
George Thornton Fowler Civil War Papers, GDAH
John Fox Papers, USC
Allen D. Frankenberry Diaries, UWVA
Thomas J. Frazee Letters, ILSL
Freeman Family Papers, UGA
Samuel G. French Papers, MDAH
Hugh D. Gallagher Papers, INSL
James Bruton Gambrell Recollections, AUB
Charles D. Gammon Diary, Union Miscellany, EMORY
Hosea Garrett Jr. Letter, AHC
William Garrett Letters, USAMHI
James R. M. Gaskill Papers, ILHS
Joseph W. Gaskill Papers, WRHS
John Geary Letters, Geary Family Correspondence, HSP
Noah L. Gebbart Paper, DUKE
George Gegner Letters, UNC
Andrew Gennett Collection, DUKE
Charles W. George Confederate Letters, AUB
Furniaful George Papers, DUKE
Georgia Portfolio, DUKE
Charlotte Gignilliat Reminiscences, USC
Gillis Family Letters, EMORY
Ephraim Girdner Papers, Wiley Collection, EMORY
Samuel P. Glass Collection, PSA
Mrs. John M. Godown Letters, H. C. (Mary) McLauchlin Papers, INSL
Othniel Gooding Papers, MSU
James H. Goodnow Papers, LC
F. M. Goodwin Letter, UGA
W. W. Gordon Letters, Gordon Family Papers, GHS
Nathaniel Gorgos Letters, OHS
Nathan C. Gould Letters, SHSW
D. C. Govan Letter, UGA
William Sammons Grady Correspondence, Henry Grady Papers, EMORY
James E. Graham Diary, OHS
William Graham Diary, DUKE
Lemuel Pratt Grant Papers, AHC
Gratz Collection, HSP
Graves Family Papers, UNC
Tully Graybill Letters, J. C. Bonner Collection, GCM
Green Family Papers, UVA
Green-Cook Family Papers, UGA
Ogden Greenough Letters, UILL
J. J. Gresham Letters, Wiley Collection, EMORY
Walter Quintin Gresham Papers, LC
Alva C. Griest Diary, Griest Family Papers, HCWR, USAMHI
Daniel F. Griffin Papers, INSL
Eli Griffin Papers, UMAA
Grinnell Family Papers, WRHS

Ole Grinsteedt Reminiscences, SHSW
David T. Grow Papers, UILL
George W. Grubbs Diary, INHS
Hagan-Roberts Family Civil War Letters, GDAH
Hager Family Papers, UMAA
E. W. Hall Papers, LC
James Iredell Hall Notes, UNC
Morris Stuart Hall Papers, UMAA
W. F. Hall Papers, MDAH
Frank Hannaford Reminiscences, ILHS
Roger Hannaford Papers, CINHS
Douglas Hapeman Diary, ILHS
William Joseph Hardee Papers, ADAH
Edward Jenkins Harden Letterbooks, UNC
Lyman Hardman Diary, WRHS
C. M. Hardy Letters, UDC Collection, GDAH
O. P. Hargis Narrative, Confederate Miscellany, EMORY
Francis Harkey Papers, UTEX
George Washington Finley Harper Diary, UNC
Elizabeth Baldwin (Wiley) Harris Papers, DUKE
Iverson Louis Harris Papers, DUKE
Benjamin Harrison Papers, INHS
Samuel K. Harryman Letters, INSL
Albert Gaillard Hart Papers, WRHS
Noah Hart Correspondence and Diary, NLM
Matthias Harter Papers, UMAA
Jacob M. Hartness Papers, INHS
G. M. Harvey Papers, UGA
Oliver C. Haskell Diary, INHS
Sidney Hauxhurst Letters, SHSW
Thomas R. Havens Papers, UTEX
William Hawkins Letters, UDC Collection, GDAH
William B. Hazen Papers, USAMHI
Kathleen Middlebrooks Heard Reminiscence, UDC Collection, GDAH
Charles Wesley Heath Diary, LC
Celathiel Helms Letters, UDC Collection, GDAH
Henry Mortimer Hempstead Diary, UMAA
Henry Henney Diary and Letters, CWTI Collection, USAMHI
William Herrick Letter, UGA
Andrew Hickenlooper Reminiscences, Hickenlooper Collection, CINHS
Borden Hicks Collection, WMU
Charles Davis Higby Letters, Higby Family Papers, OHS
John W. Hill Papers, UTEX
Junius Hillyer Memoirs, AHC
Hiram Hines Papers, INSL
Julian Wisner Hinkley Diary, SHSW
Wilbur F. Hinman Papers, WRHS
Henry Hitchcock Letter, HUNT
Henry Hitchcock Papers, LC
Peter Hitchcock Family Letters, WRHS

Galen Hodges Papers, UTEX
George W. Hodges Papers, WRHS
Hodgson Journal, C. C. Jones Collection, UGA
Joseph Hoffhines Letters, OHS
Stephen Washington Holladay Letters, Civil War Collection, UTEN
A. T. Holliday Letters, AHC
Jonathan E. Hollingsworth Diary, Charles Campbell Papers, OHS
Ephraim S. Holloway Papers, CFHS
William R. Holloway Manuscripts, INSL
Charles Wesley Homsher Memoirs, CWTI Collection, USAMHI
Thomas Corwin Honnell Papers, OHS
Honnoll Collection, MSSU
Honnoll Family Papers, EMORY
Rebecca Hood Memoirs, UDC Collection, GDAH
Zeralda Hood Letters, INSL
Aristide Hopkins Diary, UNC
Charles Milton Hopper Papers, UNC
Daniel D. Hopper Papers, WRHS
Daniel A. Horn Diary, and Letters, HUNT
Saunders Richard Hornbrook Diary, INHS
Z. T. Hoskins Account, UGA
Michael Houk Diary, UTEN
H. T. Howard Letters, UDC Collection, GDAH
Simeon A. Howe Papers, MSU
Evan Park Howell Letters, Howell-Foreman Families Papers, AHC
Mary Elizabeth Humphrey Howes Diary, Howes-Davis Family Diaries, MGA
James Hughes Papers, OHS
James A. Hull Papers, Walter King Hoover Collection, TNSL
John Humphrey Letters, EMORY
William T. Humphrey Diary, CPL
Daniel Robinson Hundley Papers, UNC
Jesse C. Hunt Diary, CW Misc. Collection, USAMHI
William Huntziger Diary, Daniel Waite Howe Papers, INHS
Hurt Family Papers, ADAH
Henry Hurter Diary, CWTI Collection, USAMHI
Hutchinson Family Civil War Letters, GDAH
William D. Hynes Letters, INSL
I. H. Inman Interviews, Arthur Crew Inman Collection, AHC
Charles D. Inskeep Diary, OHS
F. H. Ivy Letters, UDC Collection, GDAH
Evelyn Harden Jackson Diary, Harden-Jackson Carithers Collection, UGA
David G. James Papers, WSHS
Matthew Jansen Reminiscences, ILHS
Robert A. Jarman History, MDAH
James Jennings Memoirs, ILHS
Andrew Jackson Johnson Diary and Letters, INHS
Mrs. E. V. Johnson Reminiscences, UDC Collection, GDAH
George S. Johnson Papers, INHS
Joseph E. Johnston Papers, W&M
Joseph P. Jones Papers, EMORY

Luman Jones Papers, INHS
Newton Jones Papers, SHSW
Tighlman Howard Jones Papers, UILL
Fleming Jordan Letters, UGA
Thomas J. Jordan Civil War Letters, HSP
Will H. Judkins Diary, INSL
Henry S. Keene Diary, SHSW
Peter B. Kellenberger Letters, LC
James H. Kelly Papers, INHS
Thomas F. Kelly Papers, DUKE
William D. Kendall Collection, HUNT
Charles Deal Kerr Diary, HUNT
Harrison M. Key Papers, USAMHI
R. H. Key Letters, UGA
Madison Kilpatrick Papers, AUB
Edwin O. Kimberly Letters, SHSW
J. W. Kimmel Reminiscences, OHS
Frank R. King Letters, ADAH
James W. King Papers, WMU
Lewis King Memoirs, INSL
William King Papers, UNC
William F. King Papers, INHS
Edmund Kirby-Smith Papers, UNC
Moses J. Kirkland Papers, EMORY
John A. Lair Collection, LC
Delos Lake Letters, HUNT
Henry Archer Langdon Letters, CINHS
Stanley E. Lathrop Papers, SHSW
Thomas S. Latimer Collection, NLM
Lewis Lawshe Diary, Edda Cole Collection, AHC
Alexander Robert Lawton Papers, UNC
Henry Champlin Lay Papers, UNC
James Leath Papers, HUNT
John F. Leonard Papers, UNC
John F. Lester Papers, INHS
Joseph Lester Papers, LCMS
William August Lewis Papers, UMAA
Francis Little Papers, W&M
DeWitt Clinton Loudon Papers, OHS
John C. Love Papers, UMAA
Mansfield Lovell Papers, HUNT
Mansfield Lovell Papers, LC
George W. Low Papers, HUNT
William Harrison Lowdermilk Papers, UTEN
William W. Lowes Papers, OHS
John D. Lowman Letters, INHS
Mark P. Lowrey Autobiography, CW Misc. Collection, USAMHI
Stephen L. Lowry Letters, WMU
Jesse B. Luce Diary, AHC
J. D. Lyon Diary, OHS

Benjamin Benn Mabrey Papers, INHS
W. W. Mackall Papers, UNC
George B. MacMillin Diary, SHSW
Robert Major Diary, USAMHI
John W. Mallet Memoranda, UVA
A. H. Markland Letter, ILHS
Absalom H. Markland Papers, LC
Richard Markle Papers, ILHS
James Marrow Diary, CWTI Collection, USAMHI
Steven Marsh Diary, Guy Marsh Papers, WMU
John Marshall Letters, MSU
John H. Marshall Letters, MSSU
John L. Marshall Letters, NYHS
John W. Marshall Papers, OHS
John Wesley Marshall Diary, LC
Charles A. J. Martin Papers, UGA
George Washington Martin Family Papers, GDAH
John D. Martin Diary, INHS
Joseph Aplin Martin Collection, OHU
William Thompson Martin Papers, UTEX
George S. Mason Letters, USAMHI
R. H. Massey Collection, LC
H. W. Mathis Reminiscence, UDC Collection, GDAH
Clark Mattox War Record, UDC Collection, GDAH
Richard E. May Diary, HUNT
William Gibbs McAdoo Sr. Diary, Floyd-McAdoo Families Papers, LC
Andrew Jay McBride Papers, UGA
McClatchey Family Papers, GDAH
James M. McClintock Papers, HUNT
James M. McClintock Papers, LC
Jacob S. McCollough Diary, INSL
A. S. McCollum Reminiscences, UDC Collection, GDAH
M. C. McComb Letter, ADAH
James A. McCord Letters, Civil War Collection, UTEN
McCormick Family Papers, PSA
William A. McCreary Papers, DUKE
William B. McDowell Letters, UDC Collection, GDAH
Andrew J. McGarrah Letters, INHS
B. L. McGaugh War Experiences, UDC Collection, GDAH
Philip McGrath Letters, Wiley Collection, EMORY
John A. McIntosh Letters, WRHS
William H. McIntosh Papers, SHSW
Elliot B. McKeever Narrative, WRHS
Thomas Jefferson McKie Papers, USC
Gay Cummins McKinley Memoirs, J. C. Bonner Collection, GCM
Samuel McKittrick Papers, KENN
John C. McLain Diary, MSU
Anna Blue McLaurin Papers, UNC
Isaac McMillan Papers, WCCWR INSL
James H. McNeil Diary, ILHS

James Birdseye McPherson Papers, LC
Ford McWhorter Reminiscences, UGA
Chauncey Mead Papers, WRHS
Rufus Mead Papers, LC
William C. Meffett Diary, SHSW
George Mercer Diary, UMC
Hugh Mercer Papers, EMORY
John Samuel Meriwether Papers, EMORY
Robert S. Merrill Diary, Merrill Family Papers, ADAH
Samuel Merrill Papers, INSL
George B. Miles Diary, J. C. Bonner Collection, GCM
Military Manuscripts Collection, PSA
Calvin and Lucy Mason Millard Papers, WMU
George Mercer Diary, UNC
Alonzo Miller Diary and Letters, SHSW
Clason Miller Letters, Miller Collection, CINHS
Frank H. Miller Scrapbook, W&M
George Knox Miller Papers, UNC
Marshall M. Miller Collection, LC
Steven A. Miller Papers, INHS
William Bluffton Miller Diary, INHS
Hubbard T. Minor Papers, CW Misc. Collection, USAMHI
Robert H. G. Minty Papers, USAMHI
Miscellaneous Letters, Confederate States of America, DUKE
Mitchell-Fondren Family Civil War Papers, GDAH
Robert G. Mitchell Papers, UGA
George W. Modil Diaries, MDAH
David Monat Reminiscences, 29th Regiment Pennsylvania Infantry Records, HSP
James H. Montgomery Diary, LC
Vincent Montgomery Papers, UDC Collection, GDAH
Martin Moor Papers, INHS
Mrs. J. Threatt Moore Reminiscence, UDC Collection, GDAH
T. V. Moore Diary, UDC Collection, GDAH
William H. Moore Letters, Jeanette Hepburn Parsons Papers, ADAH
James Marsh Morey Papers, TNSL
James R. Morgan Reminiscence, UDC Collection, GDAH
Leila C. Morris Reminiscences, AHC
Wayne E. Morris Papers, UMAA
Thomas Morrison Civil War Letters, SHSW
James E. Morrow Diary, CWTI Collection, USAMHI
Moseley Family Papers, MDAH
Racide Mosher Letters, UMAA
Leonidas Brantley Mosley Collection, MGA
Jacob Muhleman Diary, ILHS
Daniel Musser Collection, PSA
Briggs H. Napier Family Collection, MGA
Napier-Blackmon-Ross-Rose Family Collection, MGA
Francis H. Nash Diary, UGA
Andrew Jackson Neal Letters, EMORY

Henry Neer Diary, UMAA
Isaac C. Nelson Diary, CWTI Collection, USAMHI
John W. Nesbitt Letters, James Nesbitt–Isaac P. C. Raub Papers, MSU
William Henry Newlin Manuscript, LC
Howard Newman Correspondence, Hoyt Family Papers, CRNL
David Nichol Papers, HCWR, USAMHI
Henry G. Noble Papers, UMAA
Mary W. Noble Letters, Noble-Hattaway Papers, UNC
William O. Norrell Memorandum Book, AHC
James Nourse Diary, DUKE
William H. Nugen Papers, DUKE
Nuther Nutting Letters, Mr. & Mrs. Darold Nutting Collection, WMU
Henry Oberlin Diary, UMAA
William C. Olds Letters, INSL
Charles Hart Olmstead Papers, UNC
Emerson Opdyke Papers, OHS
Edwin Osband Diary, MSU
John Henry Otto Papers, OHS
John M. Palmer Papers, ILHS
Pardee-Robinson Papers, USAMHI
Horace Park Letter, UGA
John G. Parkhurst Diary, MSU
John G. Parkhurst Papers, UMAA
Martin Van Buren Parkhurst Papers, Wiley Collection, EMORY
William M. Parkinson Correspondence, OHS
Nathaniel Parmeter Diary, OHS
George Parsons Papers, UNC
John Patton Memoir, LC
Thomas Patton Papers, NCSA
William C. Patton Diary, INHS
George Pease Reminiscences, SHSW
William Frederick Penneman Reminiscences, UNC
William A. Pepper Papers, ILHS
R. M. Perry Letters, SHSW
Horace H. Persons Diary, SHSW
Richard Peters Memoir, Nellie Peters Black Papers, AHC
Elisha A. Peterson Papers, DUKE
Edmund Pettus Papers, ADAH
Thomas E. Pierce Diary, CWTI Collection, USAMHI
Jacob S. Pierson Letters, Emma Harris Papers, OHS
Jacob Pinick Papers, UWVA
William H. Pittinger Diary, OHS
Abi Pittman Reminiscences, UDC Collection, ADAH
Plant Family Reminiscences, UNC
C. C. Platter Diary, UGA
James B. Plessinger Papers, INSL
Orlando Poe Papers, LC
Emily Nisbet Polhill Papers, UNC
Leonidas Lafayette Polk Papers, UNC
Albert Quincy Porter Diary, A. Q. Porter Collection, LC

Styles Porter Diary, OHS
Eugene Powell Memoir, 66th Ohio Infantry Records, OHS
Lorenzo N. Pratt Letters, CW Misc. Collection, USAMHI
Charles Prentiss Letters, Archie Nevins Collection, WMU
Prescott-Jones Families Papers, GDAH
Alfred Prescott Letter, UDC Collection, GDAH
Emma Jane Jacqueline Prescott Reminiscences, UGA
Price Family Letters, ILHS
Daniel S. Printup Papers, DUKE
E. J. Pritchard Letters, Union Miscellany, EMORY
A. Purviance, Jr., Papers, DUKE
Davis Quillen Papers, AHC
Charles Todd Quintard Diary, SEW
Charles Todd Quintard Papers, DUKE
Joseph M. Raab Papers, INHS
I. N. Rainey Experiences, Civil War Collection, TNSL
George Washington Rains Papers, UNC
Lavender R. Ray Letters, and Diary, EMORY
William E. Records Diary, INSL
Horace Lafayette Reed Account, "Our Story of His War Experiences," UTEX
Harvey Reid Papers, SHSW
Samuel Chester Reid Family Papers, LC
James Theodore Reeve Diary, SHSW
Edwin Hansford Rennolds Autobiography, UTEN
Edwin Hansford Rennolds Diary, UTEN
Rudolphe Rey Papers, NYHS
Charles Reynolds Papers, LC
Henry Clay Reynolds Papers, ADAH
Rhind-Stokes-Gardiner Letters, UGA
Nannie Rice Papers, MSSU
Robert Richards Civil War Letters, SHSW
Samuel P. Richards Diary, AHC
John C. Rietti Papers, MDAH
Joshua Rilea Diary, ILHS
J. B. Ritchey Diary, Northcut Family Papers, TNSL
Hezekiah Robb Letters, Michael P. Musick Collection, USAMHI
Cyrus M. Roberts Diary, HCWR Collection, USAMHI
William and Ben Robertson Papers, MDAH
James Culbertson Robinson Papers, ILHS
James Sidney Robinson Papers, OHS
William C. Robinson Papers, ILHS
Alfred Roman Papers, LC
Samuel Roper Collection, HUNT
Anne Roulhac Rose Diary, Hermione Ross Walker Collection, UNC
Isaac Roseberry Papers, EMORY
Lawrence Sullivan Ross Letters, UTEX
Levi Ross Papers, ILHS
William Ross Letters, Napier-Blackmon-Ross-Rose Family Collection, MGA
William Rule Papers, MKNOX
Robert H. Russell Papers, OHS

Marden Sabin Memoirs, INSL
Birdie Varner Sanders Papers, GDAH
J. B. Sanders Papers, MDAH
Oliver Sanders Narrative, WRHS
James F. Sawyer Letters, SHSW
William F. Saylor Letter, SHSW
Frederick E. Schmitt Account, SHSW
John M. Schofield Papers, LC
Mathias Schwab Civil War Letters, CINHS
Edward E. Schweitzer Diary and Correspondence, CWTI Collection, USAMHI
Johann Conrad Schweizer Notes, UNC
Isaac Scott Diary, MGA
Robert Kingston Scott Papers, OHS
Joseph J. Scroggs Diary, CWTI Collection, USAMHI
Ferdinand Sebring Papers, WCCWR, INSL
Benedict Joseph Semmes Papers, UNC
Henry C. Semple Papers, ADAH
Emma Maria Service Papers, UNC
Aaron M. Sewell Letters, EMORY
Charles Thomas Shanner Diary, INHS
Henry Gilman Shedd Diary, CWTI Collection, USAMHI
William E. Shedd Letters, CWTI Collection, USAMHI
Shelton Gift, UGA
Francis T. Sherman Diary, UVA
George Sherman Papers, USAMHI
William T. Sherman Letter, USC
William T. Sherman Papers, HUNT
William T. Sherman Papers, USMA
William T. Sherman Papers (microfilm edition), LC
William T. Sherman Papers (microfilm edition), ND
Steven V. Shipman Diary, SHSW
Jacob Sigmund Collection, PSA
A. S. Skilton Diary, CWTI Collection, USAMHI
Albert L. Slack Letters, OHS
Sligh Family Papers, UMAA
W. E. Sloan Diary, TNSL
Thomas M. Small Diary, INHS
James L. Smart Letters, UGA
Smith Family Papers, MSU
Charles M. Smith Letters, AHC
Daniel Pratt Smith Papers, UVA
George Gilman Smith Autobiography, UNC
Jacob K. Smith Civil War Diary, INSL
James Smith Papers, OHS
Joseph Belknap Smith Papers, DUKE
Joseph T. Smith Letters, INHS
Thomas E. Smith Letters, CINHS
Thomas E. Smith Papers, OHS
James P. Snell Diary, ILHS
W. J. Snelling War Record, UDC Collection, GDAH

John L. Snook Diary, Mr. & Mrs. Lester Mange Collection, WMU
Society Miscellaneous Collection, HSP
Oliver Lyman Spalding Papers, UMAA
Robert Ann Rhodes Speight Memoir, ECU
James Scott Speir Civil War Letters, GDAH
D. H. C. Spence Letters, Walter King Hoover Collection, TNSL
Springs Family Papers, UNC
Edward P. Stanfield Letters, INHS
Stanley Family Papers, UGA
William M. Stanley Letters, Wiley Collection, EMORY
Stephen Z. Starr Collection, CINHS
David Stathem Diary, OHS
Daniel Merrill Stearns Correspondence, HUNT
Peter Stekele Letters, UMAA
John Stevens Narrative, CWTI Collection, USAMHI
Alexander P. Stewart Letter, UGA
Mrs. Walter Stewart Correspondence, UGA
James R. Stilwell Papers, OHS
Archibald D. Stinson Papers, INHS
Mary L. Stoddard Letter, Wiley Collection, EMORY
Marcellus Stovall Papers, UNC
W. W. Stribling Letters, Stribling Family Collection, USC
Oliver V. Strickland Letters, EMORY
Joseph H. Strickling Reminiscences, OHS
William E. Strong Narrative, ILHS
Owen Stuart Papers, ILHS
William Roberts Stuckey Letters, INHS
Eben P. Sturges Diary and Letters, CWTI Collection, USAMHI
Johann Heinrich Sudkamp Diary, CW Misc. Collection, USAMHI
Thomas William Sweeney Collection, HUNT
Emory Sweetland Letters, Michael B. Winey Collection, USAMHI
Spencer Bowen Talley Memoirs, HCWR Collection, USAMHI
William Talley Autobiography, KENN
Thomas T. Taylor Papers, OHS
Ella Gertrude (Clanton) Thomas Journal, DUKE
Henry B. Thomas Diary, CHAT
Isham W. Thomas Letters, MSU
James Thomas Papers, E. Merton Coulter Collection, UGA
Heber S. Thompson Diary, Wilbur G. Kurtz Sr. Collection, AHC
Samuel Thompson Papers, UNC
William N. Thompson Letters, KENN
David C. Thorn Diary, CW Misc. Collection, USAMHI
J. Ben Thornton Memoirs, UDC Collection, GDAH
Thurmond-Swift-Tutt Collection, UGA
Cy Titus Letters, Blanch Spurlock Bentley Papers, TNSL
William E. Titze Diary, ILHS
Vincent F. Trago Diary, UGA
W. L. Trask Diary, KENN
William Frazer True Letters, HUNT
Benjamin C. Trumble Papers, NYHS

Frank W. Tupper Papers, ILHS
Miletus Tuttle Papers, UGA
Isaac Barton Ulmer Papers, UNC
Union Microfilm Miscellany, EMORY
Union Miscellany, EMORY
John Vail Narrative, OHS
Delos Van Deusen Letters, HUNT
Augustus M. Van Dyke Papers, INHS
Maymie Van Landingham Collection, AUB
Samuel King Vann Letters, ADAH
Levi Wagner Memoir, CWTI Collection, USAMHI
C. Irvine Walker History, UNC Albert Milton Walls Letter, CWTI Collection,
    USAMHI
Albert Edward Wall Letter, USAMHI
Ward Family Letters, CSA Records, UTEX
William D. Ward Diary, INHS
Warden Family Papers, MSU
G. W. S. Ware Reminiscences, UDC Collection, GDAH
James W. and Frankey Watkins Papers, Wiley Collection, EMORY
John Watkins Collection, UTEN
Robert Watson Diary, CRNL
W. J. Watson Diary, UNC
William H. Watterson Papers, UTEN
Henry C. Wayne Papers, Telamon Cuyler Collection, UGA
Henry Clay Weaver Papers, LC
Edward A. Webb Papers, WRHS
Peter Weidner Papers, OHS
Benjamin Wells Papers, Professor Carlton F. Wells Collection, WMU
Cauncey Brunson Welton Papers, UNC
Claiborne J. Welton Letter, CWTI Collection, USAMHI
West-Stanley-Wright Family Papers, USAMHI
Martin A. Westcott Diary, Mason Family Papers, UMAA
Joseph Wheeler Letterbooks, Wheeler Family Papers, ADAH
Joseph Wheeler Papers, DUKE
Lysander Wheeler Papers, ILHS
Sam Whigham Collection, ADAH
William D. Whipple Letters, Lewis Leigh Collection, USAMHI
H. L. G. Whitaker Letters, Charles A. J. Martin Papers, UGA
Daniel C. White Diary, HUNT
George D. White Correspondence, NLM
Jessie B. White Papers, INHS
Louisa Kenan White Reminiscences, UDC Collection, GDAH
M. E. Whitehurst Papers, William L. Horner Collection, ECU
Edward G. Whitesides Diary, CWTI Collection, USAMHI
Lewis Whitsel Diary, INSL
D. W. Whittle Anecdotes and Incidents, LC
D. W. Whittle Papers, LC
Lewis Neale Whittle Papers, UNC
John A. Widney Diary, ILHS
Lyman S. Widney Diary, AHC

Elizabeth S. Wiggins Papers, DUKE
Aaron Wilbur Papers, EMORY
Sabin S. Willard Letters, USAMHI
E. D. Willett Diary, ADAH
Josiah D. Williams Diary and Letters, Worthington B. Williams Family Papers, INHS
Matthew J. Williams Diary, Confederate Miscellany, EMORY
R. P. Williams Memoir, UDC Collection, GDAH
Thomas H. Williams Papers, UMAA
Aurelius W. Willoughby Diary, INSL
C. D. Wills Papers, ILHS
Lawrence Wilson Papers, LC
Walter P. Wilson Diary, INHS
J. H. Winder Letter, MGA
Thomas Winston Correspondence and Diary, NLM
Roger L. Winter Civil War Letters, INSL
Wirt-Stanley Papers, USAMHI
W. H. Wiseman Papers, OHS
James Edgar Withrow Diary, UILL
Laurens W. Wolcott Diary, WRHS
R. T. Wood Papers, Rawlings Collection, UGA
Abram Woodward Journal, Don E. Truax Collection, WMU
Edwin Woodworth Letter, Civil War Miscellaneous Papers, AHC
Marcus J. Wright Papers, AHC
Marcus J. Wright Papers, UNC
James Miller Wysor Letters, VHS
Benjamin Cudworth Yancey Papers, UNC
Hiram Yerkes Papers, UILL
Samuel Yoder Papers, LC
Emily Smith York Papers, AUB
Julia Goree Zimmerman Diary, Wiley Collection, EMORY
23rd Alabama Infantry Records, AHC
66th Ohio Infantry Papers, OHS
107th–161st New York Infantry Collection, CCHS

Published Materials

STATE AND NATIONAL DOCUMENTS

U.S. War Department. *The War of the Rebellion: A Compilation of the Official Records of the Union and Confederate Armies*. 128 vols. Washington: Government Printing Office, 1880–1901.

Candler, Allen D., Comp. *The Confederate Records of the State of Georgia*. 5 vols. Atlanta: C. P. Byrd, state printer, 1910–41. Georgia, General Assembly. *Acts of the General Assembly of the State of Georgia Passed in Milledgeville at the Annual Session in November and December, 1863; also, Extra Session of 1864*. Milledgeville: Boughton, Nisbet, Barnes & Moore, state printers, 1864.

———. *Acts of the General Assembly of the State of Georgia Passed in Milledgeville at an Annual Session in November, 1864*. Milledgeville: Boughton, Nisbet, Barnes & Moore, state printers, 1864.

Georgia House of Representatives. *Journal of the House of Representatives of the State of Georgia in the Annual Session of the General Assembly Commenced at Milledgeville, November 3, 1863.* Milledgeville: Boughton, Nisbet, Barnes & Moore, state printers, 1863.

——. *Journal of the House of Representatives of the State of Georgia in the Annual Session of the General Assembly Commenced at Milledgeville, November 3, 1863.* Milledgeville: Boughton, Nisbet, Barnes & Moore, state printers, 1864.

Georgia Senate. *Journal of the Senate of the State of Georgia, at the Annual Session of the General Assembly, Begun and held at Milledgeville, the Seat of Government, in 1863.* Milledgeville: Boughton, Nisbet, Barnes & Moore, state printers, 1863.

——. *Journal of the Senate of the State of Georgia, at the Annual Session of the General Assembly, Begun and Held at Milledgeville, the Seat of Government, in 1864.* Milledgeville: Boughton, Nisbet, Barnes & Moore, 1864.

NEWSPAPERS

Atlanta Constitution
Atlanta Journal
Atlanta Southern Confederacy
Augusta Chronicle
Augusta Daily Chronicle and Sentinel
Chattanooga Daily Rebel
Chicago Daily Tribune
Cincinnati Daily Enquirer
Columbus Daily Sentinel
Columbus Daily Sun
Confederate Union (Milledgeville)
Countryman (Turnwold Plantation, Putnam County, Ga.)
Daily Columbus Enquirer
Daily Intelligencer (Atlanta)
Indianapolis Daily Journal
Louisville Daily Journal
Macon Daily Telegraph
Mobile Daily Advertiser and Register
New York Times
New York Daily Tribune
Philadelphia Weekly Times
Richmond Enquirer
Southern Confederacy (Atlanta)
Southern Recorder (Milledgeville, Ga.)
Southern Watchman (Athens, Ga.)
Sunny South (Atlanta)

MEMOIRS, LETTERS, DIARIES, ETC.: COLLECTIONS AND ANTHOLOGIES

Coleman, Kenneth, ed. *Athens, 1861-1865, as Seen Through Letters in the University of Georgia Libraries.* University of Georgia Libraries Miscellanea Publications, No. 8. Athens: University of Georgia Press, 1969.

Dyer, Gustavus W., and John Trotwood Moore, comps., and Colleen Morse Elliott and Louise Armstrong Moxley, eds. *The Tennessee Civil War Veterans' Questionnaires.* 5 vols. paginated as one. Easley, S.C.: Southern Historical Press, 1985.

Kerksis, Sidney C., comp. *The Atlanta Papers*. Akron, Ohio: Press of Morningside Bookshop, 1980.

Lane, Mills, ed. *"Dear Mother: Don't Grieve About Me. If I Get Killed I'll Only Be Dead." Letters from Georgia Soldiers in the Civil War*. Savannah: Beehive Press, 1977.

Our Women in the War. The Lives They Lived, the Deaths They Died. Charleston, S.C.: News and Courier Book Presses, 1885.

Mathis, Gerald Ray and Douglas Claire Purcell, eds. *In the Land of the Living: Wartime letters by Confederates from the Chattahoochee Valley of Alabama and Georgia*. Troy, Ala.: Troy State University Press, 1981.

Rawick, George et al. Eds. *The American Slave: A Composite Autobiography*. 31 vols. Westport, Conn.: Greenwood Press, 1972–77.

Strayer, Larry, and Stephen Baumgartner, eds. *Echoes of Battle*. Huntington, W.Va.: Blue Acorn Press, 1991.

MEMOIRS, LETTERS, DIARIES, ETC.: INDIVIDUAL WORKS

Adamson, A. P. *Brief History of the Thirtieth Georgia Regiment*. Griffin, Ga.: Mills Printing Co., 1912.

Akin, Warren. *Letters of Warren Akin, Confederate Congressman*. Ed. Bell Irvin Wiley. Athens: University of Georgia Press, 1959.

Ambrose, Daniel Leib. *History of the Seventh Regiment Illinois Volunteer Infantry*. Springfield: Illinois Journal Co., 1868.

Ames, Amos W. "Diary of Prison Life in Southern Prisons," *Annals of Iowa* 40 (1969): 1–19.

Andrews, Eliza Frances. *The War-Time Journal of a Georgia Girl 1864–1865*. Foreword by Spencer B. King, Jr. Macon, Ga.: Ardivan Press, 1960.

Andrews, W. H. *Diary of W. H. Andrews, 1st Sergeant, Company M, 1st Georgia Regulars, from February, 1861 to May 2, 1865*. East Atlanta: 1891.

Ankeny, Henry Giese. *Kiss Josie for Me!* Comp., ed. Florence Marie Ankeny Cox. Santa Ana, Cal.: Friis-Pioneer Press, 1974.

Anonymous. *Ninety-second Illinois Volunteers*. Freeport, Ill.: Journal Steam Publishing House and Bookbindery, 1875.

Ardrey, Robert G. *The Story of Sergeant Robert G. Ardrey, 111th Ill. Infantry, 1862–1865*. Comp., ed. Joseph E. Gisendrath Jr. St. Louis: Genealogical R&P, 1980.

Aten, Henry J. *History of the Eighty-fifth Regiment, Illinois Volunteer Infantry*. Hiawatha, Kansas: 1901.

Austin, J. P. *The Blue and the Gray. Sketches of a Portion of the Unwritten History of the Great American Civil War*. Atlanta: Franklin Printing and Publishing Co., 1899.

Bailey, George W. *A Private Chapter of the War 1861–1865*. St. Louis: G. I. Jones & Co., 1880.

Banks, Robert W. "Civil War Letters of Robert W. Banks: Atlanta Campaign." Ed. George C. Osborn. *Georgia Historical Quarterly* 27 (1943): 208–16.

Barber, Lucius W. *Army Memoirs of Lucius W. Barber, Company "D" 15th Ill. Vol. Infantry, May 24th, 1861 to September 30th, 1865*. Chicago: J. M. W. Jones Stationery and Printing Co., 1894.

Barnard, George N. *Photographic Views of Sherman's Campaign*. Preface by Beaumont Newhall. New York: Dover Publications, 1977.

Barnard, Harry Vollie. *Tattered Volunteers. The Twenty-Seventh Alabama Infantry Regiment, C.S.A.* Northport, Ala.: Hermitage Press, 1965.

Barnes, James A., et al. *The Eighty-sixth Regiment Indiana Volunteer Infantry: A Narrative of Its Services in the Civil War of 1861–1865.* Crawfordsville, Ind.: Journal Co. Printers, 1895.

Barron, S. B. *Lone Star Defenders: A Chronicle of the Third Texas Cavalry, Ross' Brigade.* New York and Washington, D.C.: Neale Publishing Co., 1908.

Bartmess, Jacob W. "Jacob W. Bartmess Civil War Letters." Ed. Donald F. Carmony. *Indiana Magazine of History* 52 (1956): 49–74 (part 1); 52 (1956): 157–186 (part 2).

Batchelor, Benjamin Franklin, and George Quincy Turner. *Batchelor-Turner Letters, 1861–1864. Written by Two of Terry's Texas Rangers.* Annotated by H. J. H. Rugeley. Austin, Texas: 1961.

Bates, David Homer. *Lincoln in the Telegraph Office: Recollections of the United States Military Telegraph Corps During the Civil War.* New York: Century Co., 1907.

Beach, John N. *History of the Fortieth Ohio Volunteer Infantry.* London, Ohio: Shepherd & Craig Printers, 1884.

Beall, John B. *In Barrack and Field: Poems and Sketches of Army Life.* Nashville: Smith and Lamar, Agents, Publishing House of the M.E. Church South, 1906.

Beers, Fannie A. *Memories. A Record of Personal Experience and Adventure During Four Years of War.* Philadelphia: J. B. Lippincott, 1888.

Belknap, William W. *History of the Fifteenth Regiment, Iowa Veteran Volunteer Infantry.* Keokuk, Iowa: R. B. Ogden & Son, 1887.

Bennett, L. G., and William M. Haigh. *History of the 36th Illinois Volunteers.* Aurora, Ill.: Knickerbocker & Hodder Printers, 1876.

Benton, Charles E. *As Seen from the Ranks: A Boy in the Civil War.* New York: G. P. Putnam's Sons, 1902.

Berryhill, William Harvey. *The Gentle Rebel: The Civil War Letters of 1st Lt. William Harvey Berryhill, Co. D, 43rd Regiment, Mississippi Volunteers.* Ed. Mary Miles Jones and Leslie Jones Martin. Yazoo City, Miss.: Sassafras Press, 1982.

Bevens, W. E. *Reminiscences of a Private, Company "G," First Arkansas Regiment Infantry.* N.p., n.d.

Bevier, R. S. *History of the First and Second Missouri Brigades.* Saint Louis: Bryan, Brand & Co., 1879.

Bierce, Ambrose. *Ambrose Bierce's Civil War.* Ed. and with an introduction by William McCann. Washington, D.C.: Regnery Gateway, Inc., 1988.

Bill, John T. *Tramps and Triumphs of the Second Iowa Infantry, Briefly Sketched.* Omaha: n.p., 1886.

Bircher, William. *A Drummer Boy's Diary: Comprising Four Years of Service with the Second Regiment Minnesota Veteran Volunteers, 1861–1865.* St. Paul, Minn.: St. Paul Book and Stationery Co., 1889.

Bird, Edgeworth, and Sallie Bird. *The Granite Farm Letters: Civil War Correspondence of Edgeworth and Sallie Bird.* Ed. John Rozier. Foreword by Theodore Rosengarten. Athens: University of Georgia Press, 1988.

Bird, Hiram Thornton. *Memories of the Civil War.* N.p., n.d.

Blackburn, J. K. P. *Reminiscences of the Terry Texas Ranger.* Austin: University of Texas Press, 1919.

Bogle, Joseph. *Some Recollections of the Civil War.* Dalton, Ga.: n.p., 1991.

Boies, Andrew J. *Record of the Thirty-third Massachusetts Volunteer Infantry, from August 1862 to August 1865.* Fitchburg, Mass.: Sentinel Printing Co., 1880.

Bowman, Samuel Millard, and R. B. Irwin. *Sherman and His Campaigns.* New York: C. B. Richardson, 1865.

Boykin, Laura Nisbet. *Shinplasters and Homespun: The Diary of Laura Nisbet Boykin.* Ed. Mary Wright Stock. Rockville, Md.: Printex, 1975.

Boyle, John Richards. *Soldiers True: The Story of the One Hundred and Eleventh Regiment Pennsylvania Veteran Volunteers, and of Its Campaign in the War for the Union 1861–1865.* New York: Eaton and Mains, 1903.

Boynton, Henry Van Ness. *Sherman's Historical Raid. The Memoirs in Light of the Record.* Cincinnati: Wilstach, Baldwin & Co., 1875.

Brackett, Albert G. "Operations Before and Fall of Atlanta." *The United Service* (February 1890): 194–200.

Bradley, Rev. G. S. *The Star Corps or, Notes of an Army Chaplain During Sherman's Famous "March to the Sea."* Milwaukee: Jermain & Brightman, 1865.

Brainard, Orson. "Orson Brainard: A Soldier in the Ranks." Ed. Wilfred W. Black. *Ohio History* 76 (1967): 54–72.

Brant, J. E. *History of the Eighty-fifth Indiana Volunteer Infantry, Its Organization, Campaigns and Battles.* Bloomington, Ind.: Craven Brothers, Printers, 1902.

Breckenridge, W. C. P. "The Opening of the Atlanta Campaign." In *Battles and Leaders of the Civil War*, ed. Robert U. Johnson and Clarence C. Buel, 4 vols. New York: Century Co., 1887. 4: 277–81.

Briant, C. C. *History of the Sixth Regiment, Indiana Volunteer Infantry.* Indianapolis: W. B. Burford, Printer and Binders, 1891.

Brinton, John H. *Personal Memoirs of John H. Brinton, Major and Surgeon, U.S.V., 1861–1865.* New York: Neale Publishing Co., 1914.

Brobst, John B. *"Well, Mary": Civil War Letters of a Wisconsin Volunteer.* Ed. Mary Brobst Roth. Madison: University of Wisconsin Press, 1960.

[Brown, Edmund Randolph.] *The Twenty-seventh Indiana Volunteer Infantry in the War of the Rebellion 1861–1865; First Division 12th and 20th Corps.* N.p., 1899.

Brown, Thaddeus C. S., Samuel J. Murphy, and William J. Putney. *Behind the Guns: The History of Battery I, 2nd Regiment, Illinois Light Artillery.* Ed. with foreword by Clyde C. Walton, preface by W. G. Putney. Carbondale: Southern Illinois University Press, 1965.

Brown, William H. "Soldier of the 92nd Illinois: Letters of William H. Brown and His Fiancee, Emma Jane Frazey." Ed. Vivian C. Hopkins. *New York City Public Library Bulletin* (February 1969): 114–36.

Bryant, Edwin E. *History of the Third Regiment of Wisconsin Veteran Volunteer Infantry, 1861–1865.* Madison: Democrat Print Co., 1891.

Buck, Irving A. *Cleburne and His Command.* Jackson, Tenn.: McCowat-Mercer Press, 1959.

Buegel, John T. "The Civil War Diary of John T. Buegel, Union Soldier. Part Two." Trans., ed. William G. Bek. *Missouri Historical Review* 40 (1946): 503–40.

Bull, Rice C. *Soldiering: The Civil War Diary of Rice C. Bull, 123rd New York Infantry.* Ed. K. Jack Bauer. San Rafael, Cal.: Presidio Press, 1977.

Burdette, Robert J. *The Drums of the 47th.* Indianapolis: Bobbs-Merrill Co., 1914.

Burge, Dolly Sumner (Lunt). *Diary.* Ed. James I. Robertson Jr. Athens: University of Georgia Press, 1962.

Burson, William P. *A Race for Liberty; or My Capture, Imprisonment, and Escape.* Wellsville, Ohio: W. G. Foster, Printer, 1867.

Burton, Elijah P. *Diary of E. P. Burton, Surgeon, 77th Regiment Illinois 3rd Brigade, 2nd Division, 16 Army Corps.* Des Moines: Historical Records Survey, 1939.

Butler, Jay Caldwell. *Letters Home.* Arranged by his son, Wilson Hubbard Butler. Privately printed, 1930.

Byers, Adjutant S. H. M. *What I Saw in Dixie, or Sixteen Months in Rebel Prisons*. Dansville, N.Y.: Robbins & Poore, Printers, 1868.

Cadenhead, I. B. "Some Confederate Letters of I. B. Cadenhead." *Alabama Historical Quarterly* 18 (1956): 564–71.

Cain, J. I. "The Battle of Atlanta as Described by a Confederate Soldier." *Georgia Historical Quarterly* 42 (1958): 109–11.

Calhoun, W. L. *History of the 42nd Regiment, Georgia Volunteers, Confederate States Army, Infantry*. Atlanta: n.p., 1900.

Calkins, W. W. *The History of the 104th Regt. of Ill. Volunteer Infantry*. Chicago: Donohue & Henneberry Printers, 1895.

Campbell, Henry. "Skirmishing in East Tennessee, the Atlanta, and Nashville Campaigns, the End of War . . . and Home." *Civil War Times Illustrated* (January 1965): 36–39.

Campbell, J. L. P., ed. *John Angus Campbell, PFC, C.S.A*. Atlanta: n.p., n.d.

Candler, Allen Daniel. "Watch on the Chattahoochee: A Civil War Letter." *Georgia Historical Quarterly* 43 (1959): 427–28.

Candler, Myrtie Long. "Reminiscences of Life in Georgia During the 1850s and 1860s." *Georgia Historical Quarterly* 33 (1949): 303–13 (part 4); 34 (1950): 10–18 (part 5).

Cannon, J. P. *Inside of Rebeldom. The Daily Life of a Confederate Private*. Washington, D.C.: National Tribune, 1900.

Cannon, Newton. *The Reminiscences of Sergeant Newton Cannon, from Holograph Material Provided by His Grandson, Samuel M. Fleming, Jr*. Introduction by Stanley F. Horn. Ed. Campbell H. Brown. Franklin, Tenn.: Carter House Association, 1963.

Capron, Thaddeus H. "War Diary of Thaddeus H. Capron, 1861–1865." *Journal of the Illinois Historical Society* 12 (1919): 330–406.

Carpenter, C. C. "A Commissary in the Union Army: Letters of C. C. Carpenter." Ed. Mildred Throne. *Iowa Journal of History* 53 (1955): 59–88.

Carter, W. R. *History of the First Regiment of the Tennessee Volunteer Cavalry in the Great War of the Rebellion, with the Armies of the Ohio and Cumberland, Under Generals Morgan, Rosecrans, Thomas, Stanley and Wilson 1862–1865*. Knoxville: Janet-Ogden Co., Printers, 1902.

Cavins, Aden G. *War Letters of Aden G. Cavins Written to His Wife Matilda Livingston Cavins*. Evansville, Ind.: n.p., n.d.

Chamberlin, William Henry. *History of the Eighty-first Regiment Ohio Volunteers During the War of the Rebellion*. Cincinnati: Gazette Steam-Print House, 1865.

Chambers, Joel Ridings. *War Fever Cured: The Civil War Diary of Private Joel R. Chambers, 1864–1865*. Ed. Cheryl H. Beneke and Carole D. Summer; Phillip C. Neal, assistant editor. Memphis: W. R. Glasgow, Citizens Education Counsel, 1980.

Chambers, William Pitt. "My Journal." *Publications of the Mississippi Historical Society* 5 (1925): 221–335.

Chapman, R. D. *A Georgia Soldier in the Civil War, 1861–1865*. Houston: n.p., 1923.

Chetlain, Augustus L. *Recollections of Seventy Years*. Galena, Kans.: Gazette Publishing Co., 1899.

Clack, Louise. *Our Refugee Household*. New York: Blelock & Co., 1866.

Clark, Charles T. *Opdycke's Tigers*. Columbus, Ohio: Spahr & Glenn, 1895.

Clark, Walter A. *Under the Stars and Bars or, Memories of Four Years Service with the Ogelthorpes of Augusta, Georgia*. Augusta, Ga.: Chronicle Printing Co., 1900.

Cody, Darwin Dianthus. "Civil War Letters of Darwin Cody." Ed. Stanley P. Wasson. *Ohio Historical Quarterly* 68 (1959): 371–407.

Coe, Hamlin Alexander. *Mine Eyes Have Seen the Glory: Combat Diaries of Union Sergeant Hamlin Alexander Coe*. Ed. David Coe. Cranbury, N.J.: Fairleigh Dickinson University Press, 1975.

Coffin, Charles Carleton. *Four Years of Fighting: A Volume of Personal Observations with the Army and Navy from the First Battle of Bull Run to the Fall of Richmond*. Boston: Ticknor & Fields, 1866.

Colton, Mathias Baldwin, and William Francis Colton. *Column South: With the Fifteenth Pennsylvania Cavalry from Antietam to the Capture of Jefferson Davis*. Comp. Suzanne Colton Wilson, ed. J. Ferrell Colton and Antoinette G. Smith. Flagstaff, Ariz.: J. F. Colton, 1960.

Connelly, James Austin. *Three Years in the Army of the Cumberland: The Letters and Diary of Major James A. Connolly*. Ed. Paul M. Angle. Bloomington: Indiana University Press, 1959.

Connelly, Thomas W. *History of the Seventieth Ohio Regiment*. Cincinnati: Peak Bohrs, 1902.

Conner, James. *Letters of General James Conner, C.S.A.* Ed. Mary Conner Moffett. Columbia, S.C.: R. L. Bryan Co., 1950.

Connolly, James Austin. "Diaries and Letters." *Illinois State Historical Society Proceedings* (1928): 215–438 .

Conyngham, David P. *Sherman's March Through the South*. New York: Sheldon & Co., 1865.

Cook, Anna Marie (Green). *The Journal of a Milledgeville Girl, 1861–1867*. Ed. James C. Bonner. Athens: University of Georgia Press, 1964.

Cooke, Chauncy. "A Badger Boy in Blue: The Letters of Chauncey H. Cooke." *Wisconsin Magazine of History* (1934): 75–100 (part 4); (1935): 63–98 (part 5).

Cooke, Samuel Alonza. "The Civil War Memoirs of Samuel Alonza Cooke." Ed. Bill O'Neal. *Southwestern Historical Quarterly* 74 (1971): 535–48.

Cooper, James Litton. "The Civil War Diary of Captain James Litton Cooper, September 30, 1861 to January, 1865." Ed. William T. Alderson. *Tennessee Historical Quarterly* 15 (1956): 141–73.

Cope, Alexis. *The Fifteenth Ohio Volunteers and Its Campaigns*. Columbus: Press of the Edward T. Miller Co., 1865.

Cort, Charles Edwin. *"Dear Friends": The Civil War Letters and Diary of Charles Edwin Cort*. Comp., ed. with commentaries by Helyn W. Tomlinson. N.p.: 1962.

Cotton, John. *Yours 'Til Death: Civil War Letters of John W. Cotton*. Ed. Lucille Griffith. University: University of Alabama Press, 1951.

Cox, Charles Harding. "Gone for a Soldier: The Civil War Letters of Charles Harding Cox." Ed. Lorna Lutes Sylvester. *Indiana Magazine of History* 68 (1972): 182–224.

Cox, James Dolson. *Military Reminiscences of the Civil War*, 2 vols. New York: Charles E. Scribner, 1900.

Crawford, James Garvin. *"Dear Lizzie": Letters Written by James "Jimmy" Garvin Crawford to His Sweetheart Martha Elizabeth "Lizzie" Wilson While He Was in the Federal Army During the War Between the States, 1862–1865*. Ed. Elizabeth Ethel Parker Bascom. Ridgewood, N.J.: Bascom, 1978.

Culver, Joseph Franklin. *"Your Afectionate Husband, J. F. Culver": Letters Written During the Civil War*. Ed. Leslie W. Dunlap, notes by Edwin C. Bearss. Iowa City: Friends of the University of Iowa Libraries, 1978.

Cumming, Kate. *Kate: The Journal of a Confederate Nurse.* Ed. Richard Barksdale Harwell. Baton Rouge: Louisiana State University Press, 1959.

Cumming, Katharine H. *A Northern Daughter and a Southern Wife: The Civil War Reminiscences and Letters Of Katharine H. Cumming, 1860–1865.* Ed. W. Kirk Wood, with a foreword by Joseph B. Cumming. Augusta, Ga.: Richmond County Historical Society, 1976.

Curry, J. H. "A History of Company B, 40th Alabama Infantry, C.S.A., from the Diary of J. H. Curry." *Alabama Historical Quarterly* 17 (1955): 159–222.

Dabney, T. G. "Campaigning in North Georgia." *Confederate Veteran* 14 (1906): 75–76.

Dacus, Robert H. *Reminiscences of Company H, 1st Arkansas Mounted Volunteers.* Dardanelle, Ark.: 1897.

Daniel, F. E. *Recollections of a Rebel Surgeon (and Other Sketches), or, In the Doctor's Sappy Days.* Austin, Texas: Von Boeckmann, Schutze & Co., 1899.

Darling, Marcellus. *Events and Comments of My Life.* n.p., n.d.

Davidson, H. M. *Fourteen Months in Southern Prisons.* Milwaukee: Daily Wisconsin Printing House, 1865.

[Davidson, Henry M.] *History of Battery A, First Regiment of Ohio Vol. Light Artillery.* Milwaukee: Daily Wisconsin Printing House, 1865.

Davidson, John, and Julia Davidson. "A Wartime Story; The Davidson Letters 1862–1865." Ed. Jane Bonner Peacock. *Atlanta Historical Bulletin* 20 (1975): 8–21.

Davis, Jefferson. *Jefferson Davis, Constitutionalist. His Letters, Papers and Speeches.* Ed. Dunbar Rowland. 10 Vols. Jackson: Mississippi Department of Archives and History, 1923.

Davis, Varina Howell. *Jefferson Davis, Ex-President of the Confederate States of America: A Memoir by His Wife,* 2 vols. New York: Belford Co., 1890.

Day, Lewis W. *Story of the One Hundred and First Ohio Infantry.* Cleveland: W. M. Bayne Printing Co., 1894.

Day, W. W. *Fifteen Months in Dixie.* Owatonna, Minn.: People's Press Print, 1899.

De Leon, T. C. *Four Years in Rebel Capitals.* Mobile, Ala.: Gossip Printing Co., 1890.

Develling, Charles T. *History of the Seventeenth [Ohio] Regiment, First Brigade, Third Division, Fourteenth army Corps, Army of the Cumberland, War of the Rebellion, 1861–1865.* Zanesville, Ohio: E. R. Sullivan, 1889.

Dodge, Grenville M. *Personal Recollections of Abraham Lincoln, General Ulysses S. Grant and General William T. Sherman.* Council Bluffs, Iowa: Monarch Printing Co., 1914.

Dodge, William Sumner. *A Waif of the War, or, The History of the Seventy-fifth Illinois Infantry, Embracing the Entire Campaigns of the Army of the Cumberland.* Chicago: Church & Goodman, 1866.

Dornblaser, T. F. *Sabre Strokes of the Pennsylvania Dragoons in the War of 1861–1865.* Philadelphia: Lutheran Publication Society, 1884.

Dougherty, Michael. *Prison Diary of Michael Dougherty, Late Co. B. 13th Pa. Cavalry.* Bristol, Pa.: C. A. Dougherty, Printer, 1908.

Dougherty, William Thompson. "Civil War Diary of an Ohio Volunteer." Ed. Donal J. Coan. *Western Pennsylvania Historical Magazine* 50 (July 1967): 171–86.

Douglas, James P. *Douglas's Texas Battery, C.S.A.* Ed. Lucia Rutherford Douglas. Tyler, Texas: Smith County Historical Society, 1966.

Downing, Alexander G. *Downing's Civil War Diary.* Ed. Olynthus B. Clark. Des Moines: Historical Department of Iowa, 1916.

Dozier, Jesse L. "Marching with Sherman Through Georgia and the Carolinas." Ed. Wilfred W. Black. *Georgia Historical Quarterly* 52 (September 1968): 308–36 (part 1).

Drake, George. *The Mail Goes Through; or, The Civil War Letters of George Drake, 1864–1918; Over Eighty Letters Written from August 9, 1862 to May 29, 1865 by 85th Illinois Vol.* Comp., ed. Julia A. Drake. San Angelo, Texas: Anchor Publishing Co., 1964.

Drake, J. Madison. *Fast and Loose in Dixie.* New York: Authors' Publishing Co., 1880.

Duke, John K. *History of the Fifty-third Regiment Ohio Volunteer Infantry During the War of the Rebellion 1861 to 1865.* Portsmouth, Ohio: Blade Printing Co., 1900.

Dun, R. G. "Letters of R. G. Dun." Ed. James D. Norris. *Ohio History* 71 (1962): 138–47.

Dunbar, Aaron, and Harvey M. Trimble. *The History of the 93rd Regiment, Illinois Volunteer Infantry.* Chicago: Blakely Printing Co., 1898.

Dunham, Albertus A., and Charles Laforrest Dunham. *Through the South with a Union Soldier.* Ed. Arthur H. DeRosier Jr.; foreword by John S. Ezell. Johnson City: East Tennessee State University Research Advisory Council, 1969.

Dwight, Henry Otis. "How We Fought at Atlanta." *Harper's* (December 1864): 128–36.

Dwinnell, Melvin. "Letters of Melvin Dwinnell, Yankee Rebel." Ed. Virginia Griffin Bailey. *Georgia Historical Quarterly* 47 (1963): 193–203.

Dyer, John Will. *Reminiscences; or, Four Years in the Confederate Army.* Evansville, Ind.: Keller Printing and Publishing Co., 1898.

Eckel, Alexander. *History of the Fourth Tennessee Cavalry U.S.A. War of the Rebellion 1861–1865.* N.p., 1929.

Eggleston, Edmund T. "Excerpts from the Civil War Diary of E. T. Eggleston." Ed. Edward Noyes. *Tennessee Historical Quarterly* 17 (1958): 336–58.

Elliott, John G. B. "Civil War Letters of Lieutenant John Elliott." Ed. John Barnwell. *Georgia Historical Quarterly* 65 (1981): 203–39.

Elliott, Stephen. "Letters of the Bishop of Savannah, 1861–1865." Ed. Willard E. Wright. *Georgia Historical Quarterly* 32 (1958): 104–20.

Ewing, Charles. "Sherman's March Through Georgia: Letters from Charles Ewing to His Father Thomas Ewing." Ed. George C. Osborn. *Georgia Historical Quarterly* 42 (1958): 323–27.

Fanning, Thomas W. *The Hairbreadth Escapes and Humorous Adventures of a Volunteer in the Cavalry Service.* Cincinnati: P.C. Browne, Printer, 1865.

Farr, Henry M. "The Career of Henry M. Farr, Civil War Surgeon." Ed. Phillip D. Jordan. *Annals of Iowa* 44 (1978): 191–211.

Fitch, Michael. *Echoes of the Civil War as I Hear Them.* New York: R. F. Fenno & Co., 1905.

Fleharty, S. F. *Our Regiment.* Chicago: Brewster & Hanscom, Printers, 1865.

Fleming, Francis P. "Francis P. Fleming in the War for Southern Independence: Letters from the Front." Ed. Edward C. Williamson. *Florida Historical Quarterly* 28 (1949): 38–210.

Fletcher, W. A. *Rebel Private Front and Rear.* Beaumont, Texas: Press of the Greer Print., 1908.

Foote, Corydon E. *With Sherman to the Sea: A Drummer's Story of the Civil War, as Related by Corydon Edward Foote to Oliver Deane Hormel.* Ed. Olive Deane Hormel. New York, 1960.

Foster, Samuel T. *One of Cleburne's Command. The Civil War Reminiscences and*

Diary of Captain Samuel T. Foster, Granbury's Texas Brigade, C.S.A. Ed. Norman D. Brown. Austin: University of Texas Press, 1980.

Fox, James D. *A True Story of the Reign of Terror in Southern Illinois, a Part of the Campaign in Western Virginia and Fourteen Months of Prison Life at Richmond; Macon, Georgia; Charleston, South Carolina, and Columbia, South Carolina.* Aurora, Ill.: J. D. Fox, 1884.

Francis, Charles Lewis. *Narrative of a Private Soldier in the Volunteer Army of the United States During a Portion of the Period Covered by the Great War of the Rebellion of 1861.* Brooklyn: W. Jenkins & Co., 1879.

Fremantle, Lieutenant Colonel. *Three Months in the Southern States: April–June, 1863.* New York: J. Bradburn, 1864.

French, Samuel G. *Two Wars: An Autobiography of Gen. Samuel G. French, an Officer in the Armies of the United States and the Confederate States, a Graduate from the US Military Academy, West Point, 1843.* Nashville: Confederate Veteran, 1901.

Gage, M. D. *From Vicksburg to Raleigh, or, A Complete History of the Twelfth Regiment Indiana Volunteer Infantry and the Campaign of Grant and Sherman with an Outline of the Great Rebellion.* Chicago: Clarke, 1865.

Gardner, Washington. "Civil War Letters of Washington Gardner." *Michigan History* 1 (1917): 3–18.

Gaskill, J. W. *Footprints Through Dixie. Everyday Life of the Man Under a Musket. On the Firing Line and in the Trenches, 1861–1865.* Albany, Ohio: Bradshaw Printing Co., 1919.

Gause, Isaac. *Four Years with the Armies.* New York and Washington, D.C.: Neale Publishing Co., 1908.

Gay, Mary. *Life in Dixie During the War 1861–1862–1863–1864–1865.* Atlanta: C. P. Byrd, 1897.

Geer, Allen Morgan. *The Civil War Diary of Allen Morgan Geer. Twentieth Regt., Ill. Vols.* Ed. Mary Ann Anderson. Denver: R.20C. Appleman, 1977.

Gibbons, A. R. *The Recollections of an Old Confederate.* Shelbyville, Mo.: Herald Printers, 1913.

Gibson, J. T., Ed. *History of the Seventy-Eighth Pennsylvania Volunteer Infantry.* Pittsburgh: Press of the Pittsburgh Printing Company, 1905.

Goodloe, Albert Theodore. *Some Rebel Relics from the Seat of the War.* Nashville: Printed for the author, 1893.

Gordon, G. W. "The Battle of Kennesaw Mountain." *Annals of the Army of Tennessee* 1 (1878): 106–14.

Goss, Warren Lee. *The Soldier's Story of His Captivity at Andersonville, Belle Isle, and Other Rebel Prisons.* Boston: Lee and Shepard, 1869.

Gray, John Chipman, and John Codman Ropes. *War Letters, 1862–1865.* Boston: Houghton-Mifflin Co., 1927.

Green, John Williams. *Johnny Green of the Orphan Brigade; The Journal of a Confederate Soldier.* Ed. A. D. Kirwan. Lexington: University of Kentucky Press, 1956.

Greenalch, James. "Letters of James Greenalch." Ed. with introduction by Knox Mellon Jr. *Michigan History* 14 (1960): 188–240.

Griffin, Daniel F. "A Hoosier Regiment in Georgia, 1864." Ed. Arville L. Funk. *Georgia Historical Quarterly* 48 (1964): 104–9.

Griffin, Patrick M. "The Famous Tenth Tennessee, or 'Bloody Tenth.'" *Confederate Veteran,* December 1905: 552.

Grigsby, Melvin. *The Smoked Yank.* Sioux Falls, S.D.: Bell Publishing Co., 1888.

Griscom, George L. *Fighting with Ross's Texas Cavalry Brigade, C.S.A. The Diary of George L. Griscom, Adjutant, 9th Texas Cavalry Regiment.* Hillsboro, Texas: Hill Junior College Press, 1976.

Grose, William. *The Story of the Marches, Battles and Incidents of the 36th Regiment, Indiana Volunteer Infantry.* Newcastle, Ind.: Courier Co., Press, 1891.

Guerrissey, Alfred H. "Sherman's Great Raid." *Harper's New Monthly* (October 1865): 571–89.

Guild, George B. *A Brief Narrative of the Fourth Tennessee Cavalry Regiment, Wheeler's Corps, Army of Tennessee.* Nashville: n.p., 1913.

Hadaway, Claude Lee. " 'With Loyalty and Honor as a Patriot': Recollections of a Confederate Soldier." Ed. Royce Shingleton. *Alabama Historical Quarterly* 33 (1971): 240–63.

Hagan, John W. "The Confederate Letters of John W. Hagan." Ed. Bell I. Wiley. *Georgia Historical Quarterly* 38 (1954): 170–200, 268–89.

Hammontree, Alexander. "The Hammontrees Fight the Civil War: Letters from the Fifth East Tennessee Infantry." Comp., ed. Lewis A. Lawson. *Lincoln Herald* 78 (Fall 1976): 117–22.

Hancock, Richard R. *Hancock's Diary: or, A History of the Second Tennessee Confederate Cavalry, with Sketches of First and Second Battalions; also, Portraits and Biographical Sketches.* Nashville: Brandon Printing Co., 1887.

Hannaford, E. *The Story of a Regiment: A History of the Campaigns, and Associations in the Field of the Sixth Regiment, Ohio Volunteer Infantry.* Cincinnati: Author, 1868.

Hardee, William J. "Biographical Sketch of Major-General P. R. Cleburne," in John Francis Maguire, *The Irish in America.* London: Longmans, Green & Co., 1868, 642–53.

Harden, H. O. *History of the 90th Ohio Volunteer Infantry.* Stoutsville, Ohio: Press of Fairfield-Pickaway News, 1902.

Harris, Joel Chandler. *On the Plantation. A Story of a Georgia Boy's Adventures During the War.* Foreword by Erskine Caldwell. Athens: University of Georgia Press, 1980.

Haupt, Herman. *Reminiscences of General Herman Haupt, Giving Hitherto Unpublished Official Orders, Personal Narratives of Important Military Operations, and Interviews with President Lincoln, Sec. Stanton, General in Chief Halleck, and Others in Command of the Armies in the Field, and His Impressions of These Men.* Milwaukee: Wright & Joy Co., 1900.

Hazen, William B. *A Narrative of Military Service.* Boston: Ticknor & Co., 1885.

Head, Thomas A. *Campaigns and Battles of the Sixteenth Regiment, Tennessee Volunteers, in the War Between the States, with Incidental Sketches of the Part Performed by Other Tennessee Troops in the Same War.* Nashville: Cumberland Presbyterian Publishing House, 1905.

Hedley, Fenwick Y. *Marching Through Georgia. Pen Pictures of Everyday Life in General Sherman's Army, from the Beginning of the Atlanta Campaign Until the Close of the War.* Chicago: R. R. Donnelley & Sons, 1887.

Hermann, I. *Memoirs of a Veteran Who Served as a Private in the 60's in the War Between the States.* Atlanta: Byrd Printing Co., 1911.

High, Edwin. *History of the Sixty-eighth Regiment, Indiana Volunteer Infantry 1862–1865.* N.p., 1902.

Hight, John J. *History of the Fifty-eighth Regiment of Indiana Volunteer Infantry.* Princeton, Ind.: Press of the Clarion, 1895.

Hill, Andrew Malone. "Personal Recollections of Andrew Malone Hill." *Alabama Historical Quarterly* 20 (1958): 85–91.

Hinkley, Julian W. *A Narrative of Service with the Third Wisconsin Infantry.* Madison: Wisconsin History Commission, 1912.

Hinman, Wilbur F. *The Story of the Sherman Brigade.* Alliance, Ohio: Press of the Daily Review, 1897.

History of the Organization, Marches, Campaigns, General Services and Final Muster Out of Battery M, First Regiment Illinois Light Artillery; Together with Detailed Incidents Both Brave and Facetious, Connected Therewith; Compiled from the Official Records and from the Diaries of Different Members. Princeton, Ill.,1892.

History of the Sixth Wisconsin Battery with a Roster of Officers and Members. Lancaster, Wisc.: Herald Book and Job Room, 1879.

Hitchcock, Henry. *Marching with Sherman: Passages from the Letters and Campaign Diaries of Henry Hitchcock, Major and Asst. Adjutant General of Volunteers, Nov. 1864–May 1865.* Ed. M. A. DeWolfe Howe. New Haven, Conn.: Yale University Press, 1927.

Holmes, James Taylor. *Fifty-second Ohio Volunteer Infantry: Then and Now,* vol 1. Columbus, Ohio: Berlin Printing Co., 1898.

Hood, John Bell. *Advance and Retreat; Personal Experiences in the United States & Confederate States Armies.* Ed. with an introduction and notes by Richard N. Current. Bloomington: Indiana University Press, 1959.

Hopkins, Charles A. *The March to the Sea.* Providence: Society, 1885.

Hosea, L. M. "The Last Ditch." *Sketches of War History: Papers of the Ohio Commandery, Order of the Loyal Legion of the United States* 3 (1890): 289–98.

Hough, Alfred Lacey. *Soldier in the West; The Civil War Letters of Alfred Lacey Hough.* Ed. Robert G. Athearn, with an introduction by John Newbold Hough. Philadelphia: University of Pennsylvania Press, 1957.

Hovden, George Johnson. *The Civil War Diary of George Johnson Hovden.* Trans. Norma Johnson Jordahl, ed. O. M. Hovden. Decorah, Iowa: Luther College Library, 1971.

Howard, Frances Thomas. *In and Out of the Lines, An Accurate Account of Incidents During the Occupation of Georgia by Federal Troops in 1864–65.* New York: Neale Publishing Co., 1905.

Howard, Oliver Otis. *Autobiography of Oliver Otis Howard, Major General, United States Army,* 2 vols. New York: Baker & Taylor Co., 1907.

Hubert, Charles F. *History of the Fiftieth Regiment Illinois Volunteer Infantry in the War of the Union.* Kansas City, Mo.: Western Veteran Publishing, 1894.

Hubner, Charles W. "Some Recollections of Atlanta during 1864." *Atlanta Historical Bulletin* 1 (1928): 8–16.

Huff, Sarah. *My Eighty Years in Atlanta.* Atlanta: Privately printed, 1937.

Huntington, Mrs. Henry. "Escape from Atlanta: The Huntington Memoir." Ed. Ben Kremenak. *Civil War History* 11 (1965): 160–77.

Huntsinger, William. *History of the 79th Regt. Indiana Volunteer Infantry.* Indianapolis: 1891.

Huntzinger, William. *The Camp Life and Campaigns of William H. Huntzinger and Brothers, a Day-to-Day Record, 1862–1865.* Ed. Floyd B. LaFavre. Tujunga, Cal.: Floyd B. LaFavre, 1971.

Hurst, Samuel H. *Journal-History of the Seventy-third Ohio Volunteer Infantry.* Chillicothe, Ohio: n.p., 1866.

Jackman, John S. *Diary of a Confederate Soldier: John S. Jackman of the Orphan*

Brigade. Ed. William C. Davis. Columbia: University of South Carolina Press, 1990.

Jackson, Benjamin Franklin. *So Mourns the Dove: Letters of a Confederate Infantryman and His Family.* New York: Exposition Press, 1965.

Jackson, Oscar L. *The Colonel's Diary.* Ed. David D. Jackson. Sharon, Pa.: n.p., 1922.

Jamison, Matthew H. *Recollections of Pioneer and Army Life.* Kansas City, Mo.: Hudson Press, 1911.

John, Enoch D. "'With Tears in Their Eyes'; on the Road to the Sea: Shannon's Scouts." Ed. Paul Scott. *Civil War Times Illustrated* 21 (1983): 26–29.

Johnson, Richard W. *A Soldier's Reminiscences in Peace and War.* Philadelphia: J. B. Lippincott & Co., 1886.

Johnston, John. "The Civil War Reminiscences of John Johnston, 1861–1865." Ed. William T. Alderson. *Tennessee Historical Quarterly* 13 (1954): 65–82 (part 1); 14 (1955): 244–76 (part 2); 14 (1955): 329–54 (part 3).

Johnston, Joseph E. "The Dalton-Atlanta Operations." *Annals of the Army of Tennessee* 1 (1887): 7–16.

—. *Narrative of Military Operations.* New York: D. Appleton & Co., 1874.

Jones Family. *The Children of Pride: A True Story of Georgia and the Civil War.* Ed. Robert Manson Myers. New Haven: Yale University Press, 1972.

Jones, Jenkin Lloyd. *An Artilleryman's Diary.* Madison: Wisconsin History Commission, 1914.

Kelly, William Milner. "A History of the Thirteenth Alabama Volunteers (Infantry) Confederate States Army." *Alabama Historical Quarterly* 9 (1947): 115–89.

Kennaway, John H. *On Sherman's Track, or, The South After the War.* London: Deeley, Jackson and Halliday, 1867.

Key, Thomas J. *Two Soldiers: The Campaign Diaries of Thos. J. Key, C.S.A., and Robt. J. Campbell, U.S.A.* Ed. Wirt Armistead Cate. Chapel Hill: University of North Carolina Press, 1938.

Kiene, Francis A. *A Civil War Diary: The Journal of Francis A. Kiene, 1861–1864: A Family History.* Comp. Ralph E. Kiene Jr. Shawnee Mission, Kansas: R. E. Kiene, 1974.

Kimberly, Robert L., and Ephraim S. Holloway. *The Forty-first Ohio Veteran Volunteer Infantry in the War of the Rebellion, 1861–1865.* Cleveland: W. R. Smellie, 1897.

Kinnear, J. R. *History of the Eighty-sixth Regiment Illinois Volunteer Infantry.* Chicago: Tribune Co., 1866.

Ladd, James Royal. "From Atlanta to the Sea." *American Heritage* 30, no. 1 (Dec. 1978): 6–11.

Lavender, John W. *The War Memoirs of Captain John W. Lavender, C.S.A. They Never Came Back: The Story of Co. F. Fourth Arks. Infantry, C.S.A., Originally Known as the Montgomery Hunters, as Told by Their Commanding Officer.* Ed. Ted R. Worley. Pine Bluff, Ark.: W. M. Hackett and D. R. Perdue, 1956.

Law, Sallie Chapman (Gordon). *Reminiscences of the War of the Sixties between North and South.* Memphis: Memphis Printing Company, 1892.

Le Duc, William G. *Recollections of a Civil War Quartermaster. The Autobiography of William G. De Luc.* St. Paul, Minn.: North Central Publishing Co., 1963.

Lewis, George W. *The Campaigns of the 124th Ohio Volunteer Infantry.* Akron, Ohio: Werner Co., 1894.

Lewis, Whitsel. *A Union Soldier's Diary, Written by Lewis Whitsel, 1864.* Ed. David Lewis Osborn. Independence, Mo.: n.p., 1964.

Lincoln, Abraham. *The Collected Works of Abraham Lincoln.* Ed. Roy P. Basler. 8 vols. New Brunswick: Princeton University Press, 1953.

Little, George, and James R. Maxwell. *A History of Lumsden's Battery, C.S.A.* Tuscaloosa: R. E. Rhodes Chapter, United Daughters of the Confederacy [1905?].

Lucas, Daniel B. *History of the 99th Indiana Infantry, Containing a Diary of Marches, Incidents, Biography of Officers and Complete Rolls.* Lafayette, Ind.: Rosser and Spring, Printers, 1865.

Magee, Benjamin F. *History of the 72nd Indiana Volunteer Infantry of the Mounted Lightning Brigade.* Lafayette, Ind.: S. Vater & Co., 1882.

Malcolm, Frank. " 'Such Is War': The Letters of an Orderly in the 7th Iowa Infantry." Ed. James I. Robertson Jr. *Iowa Journal of History* 58 (October 1960): 321–56.

Mallett, John W. "Work of the Ordinance Bureau." *Southern Historical Society Papers* 37 (1909): 112–23.

Manigault, Arthur M. *A Carolinian Goes to War: The Civil War Narrative of Arthur Middleton Manigault, Brigadier General, C.S.A.* Ed. R. Lockwood Tower. Columbia: University of South Carolina Press, 1983.

Marshall, John W. *Civil War Journal of John Wesley Marshall, Recorded on a Daily Basis and Sent, When Practicable, to His Fiancee, Rachael Ann Tanner.* N.p.: 1958.

Martin, William. *Out and Forward, or Recollections of the War of 1861–1865.* Foreword by Charles M. Sheldon. Privately printed, 1941.

Mattox, Henry E. "Chronicle of a Mississippi Soldier: The Civil War Letters of Samuel H. Davis of Kemper County." *Journal of Mississippi History* 52 (1990): 199–214.

Maxwell, James Robert. *Autobiography of James Robert Maxwell of Tuscaloosa, Alabama.* New York: Greenberg, 1920.

Mayfield, Leroy S. "A Hoosier Invades the Confederacy: Letters and Diaries of Leroy S. Mayfield." Ed. John D. Barnhart. *Indiana Magazine of History* 39 (1943): 144–91.

McDermid, Angus. "Letters from a Confederate Soldier." Ed. Benjamin Rountree. *Georgia Review* 18 (1964): 267–97.

McMurray, W. J. *History of the Twentieth Tennessee Regiment Volunteer Infantry C.S.A.* Nashville, 1904.

Meadows, R. B. *Experiences and Recollections of R. B. Meadows, a Private in the Confederate Army.* New York: Knickerbocker Press, n.d.

Merrill, Samuel. *The Seventieth Indiana Volunteer Infantry.* Indianapolis: Bowen-Merrill Co., 1887.

Mills, Anson. *My Story.* Ed. C.H. Claudy. Washington, D.C.: The Author, 1918.

Mims, W. J. "Letters of Major W. J. Mims, C.S.A." *Alabama Historical Quarterly* 3 (1941): 203–31.

Montgomery, Frank A. *Reminiscences of a Mississippian in Peace and War.* Cincinnati: Robert Clarke Co., 1901.

Morgan, Mrs. Irbyg. *How It Was. Four Years Among the Rebels.* Nashville: Printed for the author, Publishing House of the M.E. Church South, 1892.

Morris, George W. *Eighty-first Regiment of Indiana Volunteer Infantry in the Great War of the Rebellion 1861–1865.* Louisville: Franklin Printing Co., 1901.

Morris, William S. *History of the 31st Regiment Illinois Volunteers, Organized by John*

A. Logan. Evansville, Ind.: Keller Printing & Publishing Co., 1902.

Morse, Bliss. *Civil War Diaries.* Comp., ed. Loren J. Morse. Pittsburg, Kansas: Pittcraft, 1964.

Morse, Charles Fessenden. *Letters Written During the Civil War 1861–1865.* Privately printed, 1898.

Morse, John Holbrook. *Civil War: The Letters of John Holbrook Morse, 1861–1865.* Ed. with commentary by Bianca Morse Federico, with the assistance of Berry Louise Wright. Washington, D.C.: Federico, 1975.

Mosman, Chesley A. *The Rough Side of War: The Civil War Journal of Chesley A. Mosman, 1st Lieutenant, Company D, 59th Illinois Volunteer Infantry Regiment.* Ed. Arnold Gates. Garden City, N.Y.: Basin Publishing Co., 1987.

Murphree, Joel. "Autobiography and Civil War Letters of Joel Murphee of Troy, Alabama, 1864–1865." Ed. H. E. Sterkx. *Alabama Historical Quarterly* 19 (1957): 170–208.

Newberry, Thomas Jefferson. "The Civil War Letters of Thomas Jefferson Newberry." Ed. Enoch C. Mitchell. *Journal of Mississippi History* 10 (1948): 44–80.

Newlin, W. H., comp. *A History of the Seventy-third Regiment of Illinois Infantry Volunteers.* Springfield, Ill.: 1890.

Nichols, George Ward. *The Story of the Great March, from the Diary of a Staff Officer.* New York: Harper & Brothers, 1865.

Nisbet, James Cooper. *Four Years on the Firing Line.* Ed. Bell I. Wiley. Jackson, Tenn.: McCowat-Mercer Press, 1963.

Noble, Sylvester. "Vett Noble of Ypsilanti: A Clerk for General Sherman." Ed. Donald W. Disbrow. *Civil War History* 14 (1968): 15–39.

Noll, Rev. Arthur Howard, ed. *Doctor Quintard, Chaplain CSA and Second Bishop of Tennessee, Being His Story of the War.* Sewanee, Tenn.: University Press, 1903.

Norton, Reuben S. "The Diary of Reuben S. Norton Records What Happened in Rome from 1861 to 1865." Ed. Roger Aycock. *Georgia Life* 3 (1977): 18–19, 36.

Nugent, William L. *My Dear Nellie. The Civil War Letters of William L. Nugent to Eleanor Smith Nugent.* Ed. William M. Cash and Lucy Sommerville Howorth. Jackson: University Press of Mississippi, 1977.

Offield, John, Joseph Offield, and William Offield. "Letters from the Offield Brothers, Confederate Soldiers from Upper East Tennessee." Ed. Leona Taylor Aiken. *East Tennessee Historical Society Publications* 46 (1974): 116–25.

O'Leary, Daniel. "The Civil War Letters from Captain Daniel O'Leary, U.S.A." Ed. Jenny O'Leary and Harvey H. Jackson. *Register of the Kentucky Historical Society* 77 (1979): 157–85.

Orendorff, Henry. *We Are Sherman's Men: The Civil War Letters of Henry Orendorff.* Ed. William M. Anderson. Macomb: Western Illinois University, 1986.

Orr Brothers. *Campaigning with Parsons' Texas Cavalry Brigade, CSA: The War Journals and Letters of the Four Orr Brothers, 12th Texas Cavalry Regiment.* Ed. John Q. Anderson. Hillsboro, Texas: Hill Junior College Press, 1967.

Osborn, Thomas Ward. *The Fiery Trail; A Union Officer's Account of Sherman's Last Campaigns.* Ed. with an introduction by Richard Harwell and Philip N. Racine, with a foreword by William S. McFeely. Knoxville: University of Tennessee, 1986.

Owen, Urban G. "Letters of a Confederate Surgeon in the Army of Tennessee to His Wife." Ed. Enoch L. Mitchell. *Tennessee Historical Quarterly* 5 (1946): 142–81.

Owens, Ira S. *Greene County in the War.* Xenia, Ohio: Torchlight Job Rooms, 1872.

Partridge, Charles A., ed. *History of the Ninety-sixth Regiment, Illinois Veteran Infantry*. Chicago: Brown, Pettibone Co., 1887.

Patrick, Robert. *Reluctant Rebel: The Secret Diary of Robert Patrick, 1861–1865*. Ed. F. Jay Taylor. Baton Rouge: Louisiana State University Press, 1959.

Peddycord, Will F. *History of the Seventy-Fourth Regiment Indiana Volunteer Infantry*. Warsaw, Ind.: n.p., 1913.

Peifer, James A. "The Military Experiences of James A. Peifer, 1861–65." Ed. George D. Harmon. *North Carolina Historical Review* 32 (1955): 385–409 (part 1).

Pepper, George W. *Personal Recollections of Sherman's Campaign in Georgia and the Carolinas*. Zanesville, Ohio: Hugh Dunne Co., 1866.

Perkerson, Elizabeth. "A Civil War Letter on the Capture of Atlanta." Ed. Medora Field Perkerson. *Georgia Historical Quarterly* 28 (1944): 251–69.

Phillips, John R. *Story of My Life*. N.p., n.d.

Pierce, Lyman B. *History of the Second Iowa Cavalry*. Burlington, Iowa: Hawk-Eye Printing Establishment, 1865.

Pierson, Stephen. "From Chattanooga to Atlanta in 1864—A Personal Reminiscence." *Proceedings of the New Jersey Historical Society* 16 (1931): 324–56.

Porter, Horace. *Campaigning with Grant*. New York: Century Co., 1897.

Puntenney, George H. *History of the Thirty-seventh Regiment of Indiana Infantry Volunteers*. Rushville, Ind.: Jacksonian Book & Job Department, 1896.

Quint, Alonzo H. *The Record of the Second Massachusetts Infantry 1861–1865*. Boston: J. P. Walker, 1867.

Rainey, Isaac Nelson. *Experiences of I. N. Rainey in the Confederate Army*. Columbia, Tenn.: n.p., 1965.

Rains, George Washington. *History of the Confederate Powder Works. Address for Memorial Day, April 26, 1882*. Augusta, Ga.: n.p., 1882.

Ransom, John L. *Andersonville Diary*. Auburn, N.Y.: n.p., 1881.

Read, Ira. B. "The Campaign from Chattanooga to Atlanta as Seen by a Federal Soldier." Ed. Richard B. Harwell. *Georgia Historical Quarterly* 25 (1941): 262–78.

Reid, Harvey. *The View from Headquarters: Civil War Letters of Harvey Reid*. Ed. Frank L. Byrne. Madison: State Historical Society of Wisconsin, 1965.

Richardson, William A., and George S. Richardson. *"For My Country"; the Richardson Letters*. Comp., ed. Gordon C. Jones. Wendell, N.C.: Broadfoot Publishing Co., 1984.

Ridley, Bromfield L. *Battles and Sketches of the Army of Tennessee, C.S.A.* Mexico, Mo.: Missouri Printing & Publishing Co., 1905.

Rietti, J. C. *History of the Organization, Military Service and a Record of Battles and Marches of the Mississippi Rifles, Companies A and D, Tenth Regiment Mississippi Volunteers*. Jackson, Miss.: n.p., 1865.

Robuck, J. E. *My Own Personal Experience and Observations as a Soldier in the Confederate Army During the Civil War, 1861–1865*. N.p., n.d.

Rose, Victor M. *Ross's Texas Brigade: A Narrative of Events Connected with Its Service in the Late War Between the States*. Louisville: Courier-Journal, 1887.

Roy, T. B. "General Hardee and Military Operations Around Atlanta." *Southern Historical Society Papers* 8 (1880): 335–87.

Rumpel, John W. "Ohiowa Soldier." Ed. H. E. Rosenberger. *Annals of Iowa* 36 (1961): 110–48.

Rusling, James F. *Men and Things I Saw in Civil War Days*. New York: Eaton & Maines, 1899.

Sanders, Lorenzo Jackson. "The Diary of an 'Average' Confederate Soldier." Ed. Lowell H. Harrison. *Tennessee Historical Quarterly* 29 (1970): 256–71.

Sanford, W. L., comp. *History of the Fourteenth Illinois Cavalry and the Brigades to Which It Belonged.* Chicago: R. R. Donnelley & Sons Co., 1898.

Saunier, Joseph A., ed. *A History of the Forty-seventh Regiment Ohio Veteran Volunteer Infantry, Second Brigade, Second Division, Fifteenth Army Corps, Army of Tennessee.* Hillsboro, Ohio: Lyle Printing Co., 1903.

Schofield, John M. *Forty-six Years in the Army.* New York: Century Co., 1897.

Scribner, B. F. *How Soldiers Were Made; or War as I Saw It Under Buell, Rosecrans, Thomas, Grant and Sherman.* New Albany, Ind.: Donohoue & Henneberry, 1887.

Seaton, Benjamin M. *The Bugle Softly Blows: The Confederate Diary of Benjamin M. Seaton.* Ed. Howard B. Simpson. Waco, Texas: Texian Press, 1965.

Se Cheverell, J. Hamp. *Journal History of the Twenty-ninth Ohio Veteran Volunteers, 1861–1865.* Cleveland: n.p., 1883.

Sharland, George. *Knapsack Notes of General Sherman's Grand Campaign Through the Empire State of the South.* Springfield, Ohio: Jackson and Bradford Printers, 1865.

Sherlock, Captain E. J. *Memorabilia of the Marches and Battles in Which the One Hundredth Regiment of Indiana Infantry Volunteers Took an Active Part 1861–1865.* Kansas City, Mo.: Press of Gerard-Woody Printing Co., 1896.

Sherman, William T. "The General Strategy of the War." *Century Magazine* (May 1888), 582–98.

Sherman, William T. *Home Letters of General Sherman.* Ed. M. A. DeWolfe Howe. New York: Charles Scribner's Sons, 1909.

Sherman, William T. *Memoirs of Gen. W. T. Sherman,* 4th ed, 2 vols. New York: Charles L. Webster & Co., 1891.

Sherman, William T. "Old Shady, with a Moral." *North American Review* (October 1888): 361–68.

Sherman, William T. *The Sherman Letters. Correspondence Between General and Senator Sherman from 1837 to 1891.* Ed. Rachel Sherman Thorndike. New York: Charles Scribner's Sons, 1894.

Sherwood, Isaac. *Memoirs of the War.* Toledo: H. J. Chittendon Co., 1923.

Simmons, L. A. *The History of the 84th Regt. Ill. Vols.* Macomb, Ill.: Hampton, 1866.

Sipes, William B. *The Seventh Pennsylvania Veteran Volunteer Cavalry, Its Record, Reminiscences and Roster.* Pottsville, Pa.: Miners' Journal Print., 1905.

Smith, Benjamin T. *Private Smith's Journal; Recollection of the Late War.* Ed. Clyde C. Walton. Chicago: R. R. Donnelley, 1963.

Smith, Daniel P. *Company K, First Alabama Regiment, or Three Years in the Confederate Service.* Prattville, Ala.: Survivors, 1878.

Smith, Gustavus W. *Confederate War Papers.* New York: Atlantic Pub. and Engraving Co., 1884.

Smith, Gustavus W. "The Georgia Militia Around Atlanta," in *Battles and Leaders of the Civil War,* 4 vols. Ed. Robert U. Johnson and Clarence C. Buel. New York: Century Co., 1887, 4: 331–35.

Smith, Mrs. S. E. D. *The Soldier's Friend; Being a Thrilling Narrative of Grandma Smith's Four Years' Experience and Observation, as Matron in the Hospitals of the South, During the Late Disastrous Conflict in America.* Memphis: n.p., 1867.

Speed, Thomas. "The Civil War Memoirs of Captain Thomas Speed." Ed. James R. Bentley. *Filson Club Historical Quarterly* 44 (1970): 235–72.

Stanley, David S. *Personal Memoirs of Major General D. S. Stanley, U.S.A.* Cambridge, Mass.: Harvard University Press, 1917.

Stauffer, Nelson. *Civil War Diary.* Ed. Norman E. Tanis. Northridge: California State University, Northridge Libraries, 1976.

Stearns, Albert. *Reminiscences of the Late War.* Brooklyn, N.Y.: n.p., 1881.

Stevens, William C. "Scouting, Foraging, and Skirmishing: The Federal Occupation of Atlanta as Seen in the Letters of Major William C. Stevens, Ninth Michigan Cavalry." Ed. Albert Castel. *Atlanta Historical Journal* 23 (1979): 73–89.

Stevenson, Rev. Thomas M. *History of the 78th Regiment O.V.V.I. from Its "Muster-In" to Its "Muster-Out," Comprising Its Organization, Marches, Campaigns, Battles and Skirmishes.* Zanesville, Ohio: H. Dunne, 1865.

Stewart, Nixon B. *Dan McCook's Regiment. 52nd O.V.I. A History of the Regiment, Its Campaigns and Battles.* Alliance, Ohio: Review Print, 1900.

Stockwell, Elisha. *Private Elisha Stockwell, Jr., Sees the Civil War.* Ed. Byron R. Abernethy. Norman: University of Oklahoma Press, 1958.

Stone, Henry. "The Atlanta Campaign." *Papers of the Military Historical Society of Massachusetts* 8(1910): 341–492.

Storrs, John W. *The "Twentieth Connecticut," A Regimental History.* Ansonia, Conn.: Press of the Naugatuck Valley Sentinel, 1886.

Strong, Robert Hale. *A Yankee Private's Civil War.* Ed. Ashley Halsey Jr. Chicago: Henry Regnery Co., 1961.

Sykes, E. T. *Walthall's Brigade, Army of Tennessee, C.S.A., 1862–65.* Jackson: Mississippi Historical Society, 1905.

Tarrant, Sergeant E. *The Wild Riders of the First Kentucky Cavalry.* Louisville: Press of R. H. Carothers, 1894.

Taylor, A. Reed, ed. "The War History of Two Soldiers: A Two Sided View of the Civil War." *Alabama Review* (April 1970): 83–109.

Taylor, Richard. *Destruction and Reconstruction: Personal Experiences of the Late War.* New York: D. Appleton & Co., 1879.

Terry, James G. "Record of the Alabama State Artillery from Its Organization in May, 1861 to the Surrender in April, 1865." *Alabama Historical Quarterly* 20 (1958): 141–447.

Thatcher, Marshall P. *A Hundred Battles in the West, Saint Louis to Atlanta, 1861 to 1865.* Detroit: Author, 1884.

Theaker, James G. *Through One Man's Eyes: The Civil War Experiences of a Belmont County Volunteer. Letters of James G. Theaker.* Annotated by Paul E. Rieger. Mount Vernon, Ohio: Printed by Print. Arts Press, 1974.

Thoburn, Thomas Crawford. *My Experiences During the Civil War.* Comp., ed. Lyle Thoburn. Cleveland: n.p., 1963.

Toombs, Samuel. *Reminiscences of the War, Comprising a Detailed Account of the Experiences of the Thirtieth Regiment New Jersey Volunteers in Camp, on the March, and in Battle.* Orange, N.J.: Journal Office, 1878.

Tourgee, Albion. *Story of a Thousand.* Buffalo: S. McGerald & Son, 1896.

Tracie, Theodore C. *Annals of the Nineteenth Ohio Battery; or Lights and Shadows of Army Life.* Cleveland: J. B. Savage, 1878.

Tuttle, John William. *The Union and the Civil War and John W. Tuttle: A Kentucky Captain's Account.* Ed. Hambleton Tapp and James C. Klotter. Frankfort: Kentucky Historical Society, 1980.

Underwood, Adin B. *The Three Years' Service of the Thirty-third Mass. Infantry Regiment 1862–1865.* Boston: A. Williams & Co., 1881.

Upson, Theodore Frelinghuysen. *With Sherman to the Sea: The Civil War Letters, Diaries & Reminiscences of Theodore F. Upson.* Ed. with an introduction by Oscar Osburn Winther. Baton Rouge: Louisiana State University Press, 1943.

Urban, John W. *Battle Field and Prison Pen, or Through the War, and Thrice a Prisoner in Rebel Dungeons.* N.p., 1882.

Vale, Joseph G. *Minty and the Cavalry. A History of Cavalry Campaigns in the Western Armies.* Harrisburg, Pa.: E. K. Meyers, Printer, 1886.

Van Duser, John. "The John Van Duser Diary of Sherman's March from Atlanta to Hilton Head." Ed. Charles J. Brockman Jr. *Georgia Historical Quarterly* 53 (1969): 220–40.

Van Horne, Thomas B. *History of the Army of the Cumberland*, 2 vols. Cincinnati: R. Clarke & Co., 1875.

[Vaughan, A. J.] *Personal Record of the Thirteenth Regiment, Tennessee Infantry by Its Old Commander.* Memphis: Press of S.C. Tool & Co., 1897.

Velazquez, Loreta Janeta. *The Woman in Battle: A Narrative of the Exploits, Adventure and Travels of Madame Loreta Janeta Velazquez, Otherwise Known as Lieutenant Harry T. Buford, Confederate States Army.* Hartford, Conn.: T. Belknap, 1876.

Waddle, Angus L. *Three Years with the Armies of the Ohio and the Cumberland.* Chillicothe, Ohio: Scisto Gisette Book and Job Office, 1889.

Walker, T. J. "Reminiscences of the Civil War." Ed. Russell J. Bailey. *Confederate Chronicles of Tennessee* 1 (1968): 37–74.

Wallace, William. "William Wallace's Civil War Letters: The Atlanta Campaign." Ed. John O. Holzhueter. *Wisconsin Magazine of History* 57 (1973/74): 90–116.

Walton, Claiborne J. "One Continued Scene of Carnage: A Union Surgeon's View of War." *Civil War Times Illustrated* (August 1976): 34–36.

Walton, Clyde C., ed. *Behind the Guns: A History of Battery I, 2nd Regiment, Illinois Light Artillery.* Carbondale: Southern Illinois Press, 1965. (Edited version of book originally published ca. 1897.)

Ward, Margaret Ketcham. "Testimony of Margaret Ketcham Ward on Civil War Times in Georgia." Ed. Aaron M. Boom. *Georgia Historical Quarterly* 39 (1955): 268–93, 375–400.

Watkins, Samuel R. *"Co. Aytch"; A Side Show of the Big Show.* With a new introduction by Roy P. Basler. New York: Collier Books, 1962.

Weaver, Henry Clay. "Georgia Through Kentucky Eyes: Letters Written on Sherman's March to Atlanta." Ed. James M. Merrill and James F. Marshall. *Filson Club Historical Quarterly* 30 (1956): 324–59 (part 1); 32 (1958): 336–49 (part 2).

Weller, Edwin. *A Civil War Courtship: The Letters of Edwin Weller from Antietam to Atlanta.* Ed. William Walton. Garden City, N.Y.: Doubleday, 1980.

Westervelt, William B. *Lights and Shadows of Army Life as Seen by a Private Soldier.* Marlboro, N.Y.: C. H. Cochrane, 1886.

Wheeler, William. *Letters of William Wheeler of the Class of 1855, Y. C.* Privately printed, 1873.

Whitney, Joseph. *Kiss Clara for Me: The Story of Joseph Whitney and His Family, Early Days in the Midwest, and Soldiering in the American Civil War. A Collection of Letters.* Ed. Robert J. Snetsinger. State College, Pa.: Carnation Press, 1969.

Willet, Elbert D. *History of Company B (Originally Pickens' Planters).* Anniston, Ala.: Norwood, 1902.

Williams, Alpheus S. *From the Cannon's Mouth: The Civil War Letters of Gen.*

Alpheus S. Williams. Ed. Milo M. Quaife. Detroit: Wayne State University Press, 1959.

Williams, Hiram Smith. *This War So Horrible: The Civil War Diary of Hiram Smith Williams.* Ed. Lewis N. Wynne and Robert A. Taylor. Tuscaloosa: University of Alabama Press, 1993.

Williams, Noble C. *Echoes from the Battlefield; or, Southern Life During the War.* Atlanta: Franklin Printing and Publishing Co., 1902.

Williamson, John Coffee. "The Civil War Diary of John Coffee Williamson." Ed. J. C. Williamson. *Tennessee Historical Quarterly* 15 (1956): 61–74.

Willison, Charles A. *Reminiscences of a Boy's Service with the 76th Ohio.* Menasha, Wisc.: George Banta, 1902.

Wills, Charles Wright. *Army Life of an Illinois Soldier, Including a Day by Day Record of Sherman's March to the Sea.* Washington, D.C.: Globe Printing Co., 1906.

Wilson, Ephraim A. *Memoirs of the War.* Cleveland: W. M. Bayne, 1893.

Wilson, Thomas B. *Reminiscences of Thomas B. Wilson.* N.p., 1939.

Wood, D. W., comp. *History of the 20th O.V.I. Regiment.* Columbus, Ohio: Paul & Thrall Printers, 1876.

Wood, George L. *The Seventh Regiment: A Record.* New York: James Miller, 1865.

Wood, Wales W. *A History of the Ninety-fifth Regiment Illinois Infantry Volunteers from Its Organization in the Fall of 1862 Until Its Final Discharge from the United States Services, in 1865.* Chicago: Chicago Tribune Company, 1865.

Wright, Charles. *A Corporal's Story.* Philadelphia: James Beal, 1887.

Wright, Henry H. *History of the Sixth Iowa Infantry.* Iowa City: Iowa State Historical Society, 1923.

Wright, T. J. *History of the Eighth Regiment, Kentucky Vol. Inf. During Its Three Years Campaign, Embracing Organization, Marches, and Battles of the Command with Much of the History of the Old Reliable Third Brigade, Commanded by Hon. Stanley Matthews and Containing Many Interesting and Amusing Incidents of Army Life.* St. Joseph, Mo.: Tribune Co.'s Book and Job Printing Office, 1880.

Young, Lot D. *Reminiscences of a Soldier of the Orphan Brigade.* Louisville: Louisville Courier Job Print, 1912.

Zettler, Berrien McPherson. *War Stories and School-Day Incidents for the Children.* New York: Neale Publishing Co., 1912.

SECONDARY SOURCES

Theses and Dissertations

Bohannon, Keith Shaw. " 'Not Alone Trained to Arms but to the Science and Literature of Our Day': The Georgia Military Institute, 1851–1865." Master's Thesis, University of Georgia, 1993.

Clauss, Errol MacGregor. "The Atlanta Campaign, 18 July–2 September, 1864." Ph.D. dissertation, Emory University, 1965.

Evans, William David. "McCook's Raid, July 27–August 1, 1864." Master's thesis, University of Georgia, 1976.

Gassman, Wade Banister. "A History of Rome and Floyd County, Georgia in the Civil War." Master's thesis, Emory University, 1966.

Griffin, James David. "Savannah, Georgia During the Civil War." Ph.D. dissertation, University of Georgia, 1963.

Jamieson, Perry D. "The Development of Civil War Tactics." Ph.D. dissertation, Wayne State University, 1979.

Johnson, Joseph Paul. "Southwest Georgia: A Case Study in Confederate Agriculture." Master's thesis, University of Georgia, 1992.

Mahan, Joseph B. Jr. "A History of Old Cassville, 1833–1864." Master's thesis, University of Georgia, 1950.

McMurry, Richard Manning. "The Atlanta Campaign, December 23, 1863 to July 18, 1864." Ph.D. dissertation, Emory University, 1967.

Peeples, Dale Hardy. "Georgia's Railroads: Civil War and Reconstruction." Master's thesis, University of Georgia, 1961.

Riley, James A. "Desertion and Disloyalty in Georgia During the Civil War." Master's thesis, University of Georgia, 1952.

Schroeder-Lein, Glenna Ruth. "Waging War Behind the Lines: Samuel Hollings Stout and Confederate Hospital Administration in the Army of Tennessee." Ph.D. dissertation, University of Georgia, 1991.

Singer, Ralph. "Confederate Atlanta." Ph.D. dissertation, University of Georgia, 1973.

Books and Articles

Adams, George Washington. *Doctors in Blue. The Medical History of the Union Army in the Civil War*. New York: Henry Schuman, 1952.

Adolphson, Steven J. "An Incident of Valor in the Battle of Peachtree Creek, 1864." *Georgia Historical Quarterly* 57 (1973): 406–20.

Alexander, Adele Logan. *Ambiguous Lives: Free Women of Color in Rural Georgia, 1789–1879*. Fayetteville: University of Arkansas Press, 1991.

"And More About Sherman's Nags." *Georgia Historical Quarterly* 58 (1974): 117.

Anders, Leslie. *The Eighteenth Missouri*. Indianapolis and New York: Bobbs-Merrill, 1968.

Anderson, William M. *They Died to Make Men Free: A History of the 19th Michigan Infantry in the Civil War*. Berrien Springs, Mich.: Hardscrabble Books, 1980.

Avery, I. W. *The History of the State of Georgia from 1850 to 1881, Embracing the Three Important Epochs: The Decade Before the War of 1861–5; the War; the Period of Reconstruction, with Portraits of the Leading Public Men of this Era*. New York: Brown and Derby, 1881.

Baker, Robert S. *Chatooga. The Story of a County and its People*. Roswell, Ga.: n.p., 1988.

Barnard, Harry Vollie. *Tattered Volunteers. The Twenty-seventh Alabama Infantry Regiment, C.S.A.* Northport, Ala.: Heritage Press, 1965.

Barnard, John A. *Portrait of a Hero: The Story of Absalom Baird, His Family and the American Military Tradition*. Philadelphia: Dorrance & Co., 1972.

Barnes, Joseph K., et al. *The Medical and Surgical History of the War of the Rebellion*, 3 vols. Washington, D.C.: Government Printing Office, 1875–81.

Barton, Michael. *Goodmen: The Character of Civil War Soldiers*. University Park: Pennsylvania State University Press, 1981.

Bass, Horace J. "Civil War Finance in Georgia." *Georgia Historical Quarterly* 26 (1942): 213–24.

Bates, Samuel P. *History of Pennsylvania Volunteers, 1861–5*, 5 vols. Harrisburg, Pa.: B. Singerly, State Printer, 1869–71.

Benner, Judith Ann. *Sul Ross, Soldier, Statesman, Educator*. College Station, Texas: Texas A&M Press, 1983.

Bigelow, John. *The Principles of Strategy*. New York: G. P. Putnam's Sons, 1891.

Black, Robert C. "The Railroads of Georgia in the Confederate War Effort." *Journal of Southern History* 13 (1947): 510–34.

Bonner, James C. *Milledgeville: Georgia's Antebellum Capital*. Athens: University of Georgia Press, 1978.

Bonner, James C. "Sherman at Milledgeville in 1864." *Journal of Southern History* 22 (1956): 273–91.

Bowen, Elizabeth A. *The Story of Wilkes County, Georgia*. Marietta, Ga.: Continental Book Co., 1950.

Bowlby, Elizabeth. "The Role of Atlanta During the War Between the States." *Atlanta Historical Bulletin* 2 (1940): 177–96.

Boyd, J. L. R. *John Angus Campbell, P.F.C., C.S.A. 1840–1933*. N.p., n.d.

Bragg, William Harris. *Joe Brown's Army: The Georgia State Line, 1862–1865*. Macon, Ga.: Mercer University Press, 1987.

Brannen, Dorothy. *Life in Old Bulloch. The Story of a Wiregrass County in Georgia*. Gainesville, Ga.: n.p., 1987.

Breeden, James O. "A Medical History of the Later Stages of the Atlanta Campaign." *Journal of Southern History* 35 (1969): 31–59.

Brockman, Charles J. Jr. "The Confederate Armory of Cook and Brother." *Papers of the Athens Historical Society* 2 (1979): 74–79.

Brown, Joseph M. *The Mountain Campaigns in Georgia; or, War Scenes on the W. & A*. 3rd Ed. Buffalo: Art Printing Works of Mathews, Northrup & Co., 1888.

Bryan, T. Conn. *Confederate Georgia*. Athens: University of Georgia Press, 1953.

Buck, Polly Stone. *The Blessed Town: Oxford, Georgia at the Turn of the Century*. Chapel Hill, N.C.: Algonquin Books, 1986.

Burt, Jesse C. "Sherman, Railroad General." *Civil War History* 2 (1956): 45–54.

Butler, John C. *Historical Record of Macon and Central Georgia, Containing Many Interesting and Valuable Reminiscences Connected with the Whole State, Including Numerous Incidents and Facts Never Before Published and of Great Historical Value*. Macon, Ga.: J. W. Burke & Co., 1879.

Butterfield, Julia L., ed. *A Biographical Memorial of General Daniel Butterfield*. New York: Grafton Press, 1903.

Bynum, Hartwell T. "Sherman's Expulsion of the Roswell Women in 1864." *Georgia Historical Quarterly* 54 (1970): 169–82.

Capers, Walter B. *The Soldier Bishop: Ellison Capers*. New York: The Neale Publishing Company, 1912.

Carter, Samuel III. *The Siege of Atlanta*. New York: St. Martin's Press, 1973.

Castel, Albert. *Decision in the West: The Atlanta Campaign of 1864*. Lawrence: University Press of Kansas, 1992.

Chase, Julia. "Mother Bickerdyke." *Transactions of the Kansas State Historical Society* 7 (1901–2): 189–98.

Christian, Rebecca. "Georgia and the Confederate Policy of Impressing Supplies." *Georgia Historical Quarterly* 28 (1944): 1–33.

Clauss, Earl McGregor. "Sherman's Rail Support in the Atlanta Campaign." *Georgia Historical Quarterly* 50 (1966): 413–20.

Cleaves, Freeman. *Rock of Chickamauga: The Life of General George H. Thomas*. Norman: University of Oklahoma Press, 1948.

Cobb, John A. "Civil War Incidents in Macon." *Georgia Historical Quarterly* 7 (1923): 282–84.

Coleman, Kenneth. *Confederate Athens*. Athens: University of Georgia Press, 1967.

Collier, Calvin L. *The War Child's Children. The Story of the Third Regiment, Arkansas Cavalry, Confederate States Army.* N.p., 1965.

Connelly, Thomas L. *Autumn of Glory: The Army of Tennessee, 1862–1865.* Baton Rouge: Louisiana State University Press, 1967.

Cook, Anna Maria Green. *History of Baldwin County.* Anderson, S.C.: Keys-Hearn Printing Co., 1925.

Corley, Florence Fleming. *Confederate City: Augusta, Georgia, 1860–1865.* Columbia: University of South Carolina Press, 1960.

Coulter, E. Merton. "Robert Gould Shaw and the Burning of Darien, Georgia." *Civil War History* (1959): 363–73.

Covington, W. A. *A History of Colquitt County.* Atlanta: Foote & Davies Co., 1937.

Cox, Jacob D. *Atlanta.* New York: Charles Scribner's Sons, 1882.

Cunningham. H. H. *Doctors in Gray. The Confederate Medical Service.* Baton Rouge: Louisiana State University Press, 1958.

Daniel, Larry J. *Cannoneers in Gray: The Field Artillery of the Army of Tennessee, 1861–1865.* University: University of Alabama Press, 1984.

Daniel, Larry J. *Soldiering in the Army of Tennessee. A Portrait of Life in the Confederate Army.* Chapel Hill: University of North Carolina Press, 1991.

Davis, Burke. *Sherman's March.* New York: Random House, 1980.

Davis, William C. *Jefferson Davis: The Man and His Hour.* New York: Harper-Collins, 1991.

Davis, William C. *The Orphan Brigade: The Kentucky Confederates Who Couldn't Go Home.* Baton Rouge: Lousiana State University Press, 1980.

De Vorsey, Louis Jr., and Marion Rice. *The Plantation South: Atlanta to Savannah and Charleston.* New Brunswick, N.J.: Rutgers University Press, 1992.

Donnelly, Ralph W. "Confederate Copper." *Civil War History* 1 (1955): 355–70.

Douglas, Lucia Rutherford. *Douglas's Texas Battery, C.S.A.* Tyler, Texas: Smith County Historical Society, 1966.

Downer, Edward T. "Ohio Troops in the Field." *Civil War History* 3 (1957), 253–86.

De Credico, Mary A. *Patriotism for Profit: Georgia's Urban Entrepreneurs and the Confederate War Effort.* Chapel Hill: University of North Carolina Press, 1988.

De Laubenfels, D. J. "Where Sherman Passed By." *Geographical Review* 47 (1957): 381–95.

De Laubenfels, D. J. "With Sherman Through Georgia." *Georgia Historical Quarterly* 41 (1957): 288–300.

Drago, Edmund L. "How Sherman's March Through Georgia Affected the Slaves." *Georgia Historical Quarterly* 57 (1973): 361–75.

DuBose, John W. *General Joseph Wheeler and the Army of Tennessee.* New York: Neale Publishing Co., 1912.

Duncan, Louis C. *The Medical Department of the United States Army in the Civil War.* Gaithersburg, Md.: Olde Soldier Books, 1987.

Dunkelman, Mark H., and Michael Winey. *The Hardtack Regiment. An Illustrated History of the 154th Regiment, New York Infantry Volunteers.* London: n.p., 1981.

Dyer, John P. *"Fighting Joe" Wheeler.* Baton Rouge: Louisiana State University Press, 1941.

Dyer, John P. "Northern Relief for Savannah During Sherman's Occupation." *Journal of Southern History* 19 (1953): 457–72.

Dyer, Thomas G. "Vermont Yankees in King Cotton's Court: The Case of Cyrena and Amherst Stone." *Vermont History* 60 (1992): 205–29.

Edens, A. Hollis. "The Founding of Atlanta." *Atlanta Historical Bulletin* 4 (1939): 275–90; 5 (1940): 65–85.

Escott, Paul D. "The Context of Freedom: Georgia's Slaves During the Civil War." *Georgia Historical Quarterly* 58 (1974): 79–101.

Fielder, Herbert. *A Sketch of the Life and Times and Speeches of Joseph E. Brown.* Springfield, Mass.: Springfield Printing Co., 1883.

Fife, Ilene. "The Confederate Theater in Georgia." *Georgia Review* 9 (1955): 305–15.

Flanigan, J. C. *History of Gwinnett County, Georgia, 1810–1943.* Hapeville, Ga.: Tyler & Co., 1943.

Fleming, W. P. *Crisp County, Georgia. Historical Sketches.* Cordele, Ga.: Ham Printing Co., 1932.

French, Thomas L., and Edward L. French. *Covered Bridges of Georgia.* Columbus, Ga.: Frenco Co., 1994.

Futch, Ovid L. *History of Andersonville Prison.* Gainesville: University of Florida Press, 1968.

Garrett, Franklin M. *Atlanta and Environs: A Chronicle of Its People and Events,* 2 vols. Athens: University of Georgia Press, 1969.

Gelders, Maud, and Isidor Gelders. "Fitzgerald, Georgia: A Soldiers' Colony." *Georgia Review* 7 (1953): 165–73.

Gibbons, Robert. "Life at the Crossroads of the Confederacy: Atlanta, 1861–1865." *Atlanta Historical Bulletin* 23 (1979): 11–64.

Glatthaar, Joseph T. *The March to the Sea and Beyond: Sherman's Troops in the Georgia and Carolina Campaigns.* New York: New York University Press, 1985.

Govan, Gilbert E., and James W. Livingwood. *A Different Valor: The Story of General Joseph E. Johnston, C.S.A.* Indianapolis and New York: Bobbs-Merrill, 1956.

Graham, Stephen. "Marching Through Georgia. Following Sherman's Footsteps Today." *Harper's Magazine* 140 (1920): 612–20; 813–23.

Graves, Ralph A. "Marching Through Georgia Sixty Years After." *National Geographic* 50 (1926): 259–311.

Griffith, Paddy. *Battle Tactics of the Civil War.* New Haven, Conn.: Yale University Press, 1989.

Hagerman, Edward. *The American Civil War and the Origins of Modern Warfare.* Bloomington: Indiana University Press, 1988.

Hahn, Steven. *The Roots of Southern Populism: Yeoman Farmers and the Transformation of the Georgia Upcountry, 1850–1860.* New York: Oxford University Press, 1983.

Hale, Douglas. *The Third Texas Cavalry.* Norman: University of Oklahoma Press, 1993.

Hammock, John C. *With Honor Untarnished: The Story of the First Arkansas Infantry Regiment, Confederate States Army.* Little Rock: Pioneer Press, 1961.

Harris, Charles S. *Civil War Relics of the Western Campaigns 1861–1865.* Mechanicsville, Va.: n.p., 1987.

Harrison, John M. "John Henry Mecaslin." *Atlanta Historical Bulletin* 3 (1938): 120–39.

Hattaway, Herman. *General Stephen D. Lee.* Jackson: University Press of Mississippi, 1976.

Hay, Thomas Babson. "Lucius B. Northrop, Commissary General of the Confederacy." *Civil War History* 9 (1963): 5–21.

Herring, Dorothy Holland. *Company A of the Fortieth Georgia Regiment in Confederate Service.* Privately printed, n.d.

Hess, Earl J. "Civilians at War: The Georgia Militia in the Atlanta Campaign." *Georgia Historical Quarterly* 66 (1982): 332–45.

Hibbard, James, and Albert Castel. "Kilpatrick's Jonesboro Raid, August 18–22, 1864." *Atlanta Historical Journal* 29 (1985): 31–46.

Hicken, Victor. *Illinois in the Civil War.* Urbana: University of Illinois Press, 1966.

Hitt, Michael D. *Charged with Treason: Ordeal of 400 Mill Workers During Military Operations in Roswell, Georgia, 1864–1865.* Monroe, N.Y.: Library Research Associates, 1992.

Hodges, Lucile. *A History of Our Locale: Mainly Evans County, Georgia.* Macon, Ga.: Southern Press, 1965.

Hoehling, A. A. *Last Train from Atlanta.* New York and London: Thomas Yoseloff, 1958.

Hoole, William Stanley. *A Historical Sketch of the Thirty-sixth Alabama Infantry Regiment, 1862–1865.* University, Ala.: Confederate Publishing Co., n.d.

Hoole, William Stanley, and Hugh Lynn McArthur. *The Battle of Reseca, Georgia, May 14–15, 1864.* University, Ala.: Confederate Publishing Co., 1983.

Horn, Stanley F. *The Army of Tennessee: A Military History.* Indianapolis: Bobbs-Merrill Co., 1941.

Huff, Lawrence. "'A Bitter Draft We Have Had to Quaff': Sherman's March Through the Eyes of Joseph Addison Turner." *Georgia Historical Quarterly* 72 (1988): 306–26.

Hughes, Nathaniel Cheairs Jr. *The Civil War Comes to Dade County, Georgia.* Chattanooga, Tenn.: n.p., 1975.

Hughes, Nathaniel Cheairs Jr. *General William J. Hardee, Old Reliable.* Baton Rouge: Louisiana State University Press, 1965.

Ingersoll, Lurton Dunham. *Iowa and the Rebellion.* Philadelphia: J. B. Lippincott & Co., 1867.

Ingram, C. Fred, ed. *Badland to Barrow. A History of Barrow County, Georgia from the Earliest Days to the Present.* Atlanta: n.p., 1978.

Jeffries, C. C. "The Character of Terry's Texas Rangers." *Southwestern Historical Quarterly* 64 (1960–61): 455–62.

Jimerson, Randall. *The Private Civil War.* Baton Rouge: Louisiana State University Press, 1988.

Johnson, Robert U., and Clarence C. Buel, eds. *Battles and Leaders of the Civil War,* 4 vols. New York: Century Co., 1885.

Johnston, James Houston, comp. *Western and Atlantic Railroad of the State of Georgia.* Atlanta: Georgia Public Servive Commission, 1931.

Jones, C. C. Jr. *Address Delivered Before the Confederate Survivors' Association in Augusta, Georgia at its Sixth Annual Meeting on Memorial Day, April 20, 1884.* Augusta, Ga.: Confederate Survivors' Association, 1884.

Jones, James Pickett. *"Black Jack": John A. Logan and Southern Illinois in the Civil War Era.* Tallahassee: Florida State University Press, 1967.

Julian, Allen Phelps. "Atlanta's Last Days in the Confederacy." *Atlanta Historical Bulletin* 11 (1966): 9–18.

Key, William. *The Battle of Atlanta and the Georgia Campaign.* New York: Twayne, 1958.

King, Spencer B. *The Sound of Drums: Selected Writings of Spencer King from His Civil War Centennial Column Appearing in the Macon (Georgia) Telegraph News, 1960–1965.* Macon, Ga: 1970.

Klingberg, Frank W. *The Southern Claims Commission.* New York: Octagon Books, 1987.

Kurtz, Wilbur G. "A Federal Spy in Atlanta." *Atlanta Historical Bulletin* 10 (1957): 14–19.

Kurtz, Wilbur G. "Persons Sent from Atlanta by General Sherman." *Atlanta Historical Bulletin* 1 (1932): 5–7.

Lack, Paul D. "Law and Disorder in Confederate Atlanta." *Georgia Historical Quarterly* 66 (1982): 171–95.

Lash, Jeffrey N. *Destroyer of the Iron Horse: General Joseph E. Johnston and Confederate Rail Transport, 1861–1865.* Kent, Ohio: Kent State University Press, 1991.

Leeper, Wesley T. *Rebel Valiant: Second Arkansas Mounted Rifles (Dismounted).* Little Rock: Pioneer Press, 1964.

Lewis, Lloyd. *Sherman: Fighting Prophet.* New York: Harcourt Brace & Co., 1932.

Liddell Hart, B. H. *Paris, or the Future of War.* New York: E. P. Dutton & Co., 1925.

Liddell Hart, B. H. *Sherman: Soldier, Realist, American.* New York: Dodd, Mead & Co., 1930..

Linderman, Gerald F. *Embattled Courage: The Experience of Combat in the Civil War.* New York: Free Press, 1987.

Losson, Christopher. *Tennessee's Forgotten Warriors: Frank Cheatham and His Confederate Division.* Knoxville: University of Tennessee Press, 1990.

Madaus, Howard Michael. *The Battle Flags of the Confederate Army of Tennessee.* Milwaukee: Military Publications Museum, 1976.

Major, Duncan K., and Roger S. Fitch. *Supply of Sherman's Army During the Atlanta Campaign.* Fort Leavenworth, Kansas: Army Service School Press, 1911.

Marlin, Lloyd G. *The History of Cherokee County.* Atlanta: Press of Walter W. Brown Publishing Co., 1932.

Marszalek, John F. *Sherman: A Soldier's Passion for Order.* New York: Free Press, 1993.

———. "Sherman Tours the South, 1879." *Georgia Historical Review* 66 (1982): 366–83.

Massey, Mary Elizabeth. *Refugee Life in the Confederacy.* Baton Rouge: Louisiana State University Press, 1964.

Mathews, Byron H. Jr. *The McCook-Stoneman Raid.* Philadelphia: Dorrance & Co., 1976.

McCallister, Anna. *Ellen Ewing: Wife of General Sherman.* New York: Benziger Brothers, 1936.

McConnell, Stuart. *Glorious Contentment: The Grand Army of the Republic, 1865–1900.* Chapel Hill: University of North Carolina Press, 1992.

McGlone, John. "A Trust Preserved: The Odyssey of the Bank of Tennessee and the State Archives During the War Between the States. In Memoriam Stephen Kuzma (1915–1987)." *Confederate Chronicles of Tennessee* 2 (1987): 53–80.

McIntosh, John H. *The Official History of Elbert County, 1790–1935.* Elberton: Stephen Heard Chapter, Daughters of the American Revolution, 1940.

McInvale, Morton. "All That Devils Could Wish For: The Griswoldville Campaign, November, 1864." *Georgia Historical Quarterly* 60 (1976): 117–29.

McInvale, Morton. *The Battle of Pickett's Mill: "Foredoomed to Oblivion."* Atlanta: Georgia Department of Natural Resources, 1972.

McKinney, Francis F. *Education in Violence: The Life of George H. Thomas and the History of the Army of the Cumberland.* Detroit: Wayne State University Press, 1961.

McKinnon, John L. *History of Walton County*. Atlanta: Byrd Printing Co., 1911.

McMurry, Richard M. "Atlanta Campaign of 1864: A New Look." *Civil War History* 22 (1976). 5–15.

McMurry, Richard M. "Confederate Morale in the Atlanta Campaign of 1864." *Georgia Historical Quarterly* 54 (1970): 226–43.

McMurry, Richard M. *John Bell Hood and the War for Southern Independence*. Lexington: University of Kentucky Press, 1982.

McMurry, Richard M. *Two Great Rebel Armies: An Essay in Confederate Military History*. Chapel Hill: University of North Carolina Press, 1989.

McNeill, Willam J. "A Survey of Confederate Soldier Morale During Sherman's Campaign Through Georgia and the Carolinas." *Georgia Historical Quarterly* 45 (1971): 1–25.

Meerheimb, F. von. *Shermans Feldzug in Georgien*. Berlin: Ernst Siegfried Mittler und Sohn, 1869.

Miles, Jim. *Fields of Glory: A History and Guide of the Atlanta Campaign*. Nashville: Rutledge Hill Press, 1989.

Mitchell, Ella. *History of Washington County*. Atlanta: Byrd Printing Co., 1924.

Mitchell, Reid. *Civil War Soldiers*. New York: Oxford University Press, 1988.

Mitchell, Reid. "The Northern Soldier and His Community," in *Toward a Social History of the Civil War: Exploratory Essays*, ed. Maris A. Vinovskis. New York: Cambridge University Press, 1990.

Mitchell, Reid. *The Vacant Chair: The Northern Soldier Leaves Home*. New York: Oxford University Press, 1993.

Mitchell, Stephens. "Atlanta, the Industrial Heart of the Confederacy." *Atlanta Historical Bulletin* 1 (1939): 20–27.

Mize, Julia. *The History of Banks County, Georgia, 1859–1976*. Homer, Ga.: n.p., 1977.

Mohr, Clarence L. *On the Threshold of Freedom: Masters and Slaves in Civil War Georgia*. Athens: University of Georgia Press, 1986.

Monroe, Haskell. "Men Without Law: Federal Raiding in Liberty County, Georgia." *Georgia Historical Quarterly* 44 (1966): 154–71.

Montgomery, Horace. *Howell Cobb's Confederate Career*. Tuscaloosa: Confederate Pub. Co., 1959.

Moore, Albert Burton. *Conscription and Conflict in the Confederacy*. New York: Hillary House Publishers, 1963.

Moore, John Hammond. "Sherman's 'Fifth Column': A Guide to Unionist Activity in Georgia." *Georgia Historical Quarterly* 68 (1984): 382–409.

Mruch, Armin E. "The Role of the Railroads in the Atlanta Campaign." *Civil War History* 7 (1961): 264–71.

Myers, David G. *Social Psychology*, 3rd ed. New York: McGraw-Hill, 1990.

Neale, Diane, and Thomas W. Ketcham. "The King of Revolution Is the Bayonet: General Thomas Hindman's Proposal to Arm the Slaves." *Journal of Confederate History* 7 (1991): 81–96.

Nelson, Christopher, and Brian Pohanka. *Mapping the Civil War*. Washington, D.C.: Starwood Publishing Co., Inc., 1992.

Noll, Arthur H., ed. *Doctor Quintard, Chaplain, C.S.A.* Sewanee, Tenn.: University of the South, 1905.

Nottingham, Carolyn Walker, and Evelyn Hannal. *History of Upson County, Georgia*. Macon, Ga.: Press of J. W. Burke Co., 1930.

Palmer, George T. *A Conscientious Turncoat: The Story of John M. Palmer, 1817–1900*. New Haven, Conn.: Yale University Press, 1941.

Parham, Joseph. "Barnsley Gardens." *Georgia Magazine* (October–November 1959): 11–21.

Parker, David B. *Alias Bill Arp: Charles Henry Smith and the South's Goodly Heritage.* Athens: University of Georgia Press, 1991.

Parks, J. H. *Joseph E. Brown of Georgia.* Baton Rouge: Louisiana State University Press, 1977.

Peake, Peveral H. "Why the South Hates Sherman." *American Mercury* (August 1937): 441–48.

Pitts, Lulie. *History of Gordon County, Georgia.* Calhoun, Ga.: Press of the Calhoun Times, 1933.

Plum, William R. *The Military Telegraph During the Civil War in the United States,* 2 vols. Chicago: Jansen, McClurg & Co., 1882.

Powell, Nettie. *History of Marion County, Georgia.*

Reed, Wallace P., ed. *History of Atlanta, Georgia with Illustrations and Biographical Sketches of Some of Its Prominent Men and Pioneers.* Syracuse, N.Y.: D. Mason & Co., 1889.

Roberts, Lucien E. "The Political Career of Joshua Hill (1812–1891), Georgia Unionist." *Georgia Historical Quarterly* 21 (1937): 50–72.

Robertson, James I. Jr. *Soldiers, Blue and Gray.* Columbia: University of South Carolina Press, 1988.

Robertson, James I. Jr., and Richard McMurry, eds. *Rank and File: Civil War Essays in Honor of Bell Irvin Wiley.* San Rafael, Cal.: Presidio Press, 1976.

Rogers, N. K. *History of Chattahoochee County, Georgia.* Columbus, Ga.: n.p., 1933.

Rogers, R. W. *History of Pike County from 1822 to 1922.* Zebulon, Ga.: n.p., 1927.

Rogers, Robert L. *An Historical Sketch of the Georgia Military Institute, Marietta, Ga.* Atlanta: n.p., 1956.

Roster, Charles. *The Destructive War: William Tecumseh Sherman, Stonewall Jackson and the Americans.* New York: Alfred A. Knopf, 1991.

Rowell, John W. *Yankee Cavalrymen. Through the Civil War with the Ninth Pennsylvania Cavalry.* Knoxville: University of Tennessee Press, 1971.

Sarris, Jonathan D. "Anatomy of an Atrocity: The Madden Branch Massacre and Guerilla Warfare in North Georgia, 1861–1865." *Georgia Historical Quarterly* 77 (1993), 679–710.

Savos, Theodore P. "The Life Blood of the Confederate War Machine: George Washington Rains and the Augusta Powder Works." *Journal of Confederate History* 5 (1990): 87–110.

Shivers, Forrest. *The Land Between. A History of Hancock County, Georgia to 1940.* Spartanburg, S.C.: n.p., 1990.

Sievers, Harry. *Benjamin Harrison: Hoosier Warrior, 1883–1865.* Chicago: Henry Regnery Co., 1952.

Smith, Clifford L. *History of Troup County.* Atlanta: Burke Publishing Co., 1923.

Smith, John. *Oration at the Unveiling of the Monument Erected in Memory of Maj. Gen. James B. Steedman by Gen. John C. Smith, Lieut. Governor of Illinois, at Toledo, Ohio, May 26, 1887.* Toledo: n.p., 1887.

Standard, Diffee William. *Columbus, Georgia in the Confederacy: The Social and Industrial life of the Chattahoochee River Port, 1861–1865.* New York: William-Frederick Press, 1954.

Starr, Stephen Z. *The Union Cavalry in the Civil War,* vol. 3, *The War in the West, 1861–1865.* Baton Rouge: Louisiana State University Press, 1985.

Stegeman, John F. *These Men She Gave: Civil War Diary of Athens, Georgia*. Athens: University of Georgia Press, 1964.

Steiner, Paul E. *Medical-Military Portraits of Union and Confederate Generals*. Philadelphia: Whitmore Publishing Co., 1968.

Symonds, Craig L. *Joseph E. Johnston: A Civil War Biography*. New York: W. W. Norton, 1992.

Tate, Luke C. *History of Pickens County*. Spartanburg, S.C.: W.W. Brown Publishing Co., 1978.

Tatum, Georgia Lee. *Disloyalty in the Confederacy*. Chapel Hill: University of North Carolina Press, 1934.

Telfair, Nancy. *A History of Columbus, Georgia*. Columbus: the Historical Publishing Co., 1929.

Temple, Sarah Blackwell (Gober). *The First Hundred Years. A Short History of Cobb County, in Georgia*. Atlanta: Walter W. Brown Publishing Co., 1935.

Tribble, Edwin. "Marching Through Georgia." *Georgia Review* 21 (1967): 423–29.

Turner, Maxine. *Navy Gray. A Story of the Confederate Navy on the Chattahoochee and Apalachicola Rivers*. Tuscaloosa: University of Alabama Press, 1988.

Van Horne, Thomas B. *History of the Army of the Cumberland*, 2 vols. Cincinnati: Robert Clarke & Co., 1875.

Walters, John Bennett. *Merchant of Terror: General Sherman and the Total War*. New York: Bobbs-Merrill, 1973.

Ward, George Gordon. *The Annals of Upper Georgia, Centered in Gilmer County*. Carrolton, Ga.: n.p., 1965.

Wells, Charles F. *The Battle of Griswoldville: Georgia's Gettysburg, November 21–22, 1864*. Macon, Ga.: R. E. Boyles & Son 1965.

Welsh, Willard. "Civil War Theater: The War in Drama." *Civil War History* 2 (1955): 251–80.

Wheeler, Richard. *Sherman's March*. New York: HarperCollins, 1991.

Wiley, Bell I. *Confederate Women*. Westport, Conn.: Greenwood, 1975.

———. *The Life of Billy Yank: The Common Soldier of the Union*. Indianapolis and New York: Bobbs-Merrill, 1951.

———. *The Life of Johnny Reb: The Common Soldier of the Confederacy*. Indianapolis and New York: Bobbs-Merrill, 1943.

Williams, H. David. " 'On the Fringes of Hell': Billy Yank and Johnny Reb at the Siege of Stone Mountain." *Georgia Historical Quarterly* 70 (1986): 126–38.

Williford, William Bailey. *Americus through the Years*. Privately printed, 1960.

Wright, Ana Louise. *Sketch of My Grandfather, Augustus R. Wright of Georgia*. N.p., 1940.

Yates, B.C. *History of the Georgia Military Institute, Marietta, Georgia, Including the Confederate Military Service of the Cadet Battalion*. Marietta, Ga.: n.p., 1968.

Index

■ HarperCollins*Publishers*

New in Hardcover from Lee Kennett

SHERMAN
A Soldier's Life
ISBN 0-06-017495-1

A major new biography of William Tecumseh Sherman based on considerable
fresh archival material, and focusing, more than any current biography, on
Sherman as soldier and warrior—not just the Civil War years but his eventful
decades as Army officer and leader. Sherman enjoyed a glorious post-Civil War
period of 26 years, during which he ruled over large parts of the Western frontier,
wrote his classic *Memoirs,* was commanding General of the Army, and was even
asked to be a presidential candidate.